W9-CKJ-391

Stags' head fresco at Lascaux.

Overleaf: a reconstruction of a bull-headed lyre found at Ur.

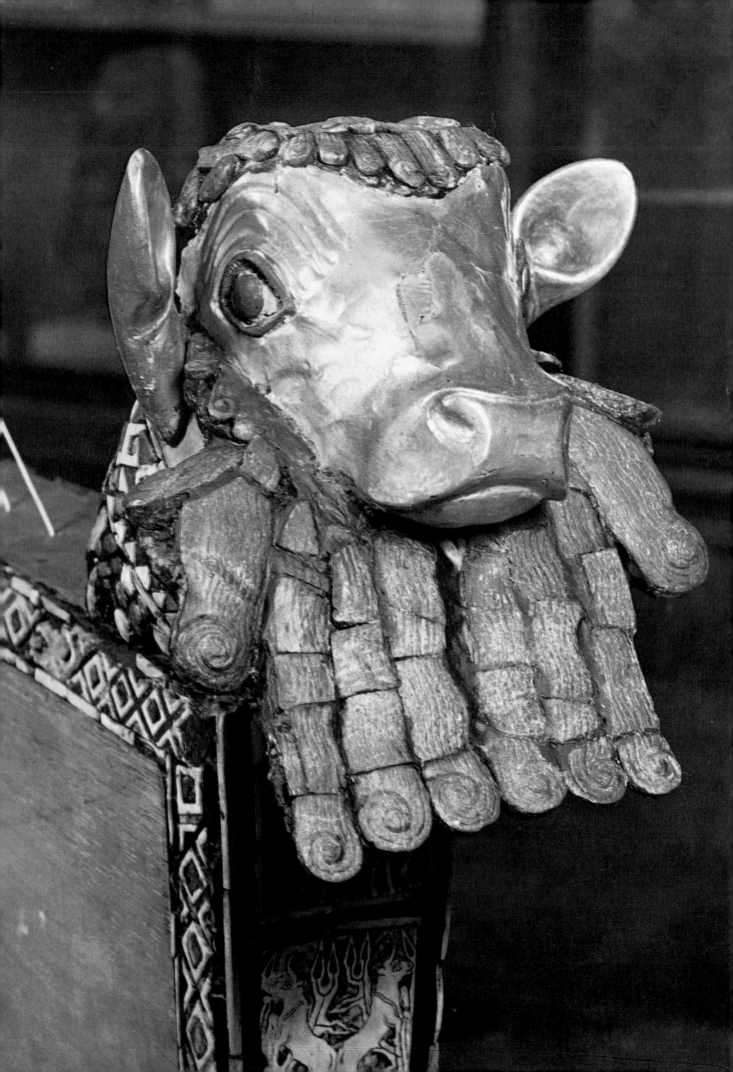

LAROUSSE ENCYCLOPEDIA OF

ANCIENT AND MEDIEVAL HISTORY

GENERAL EDITOR: MARCEL DUNAN
Honorary professor at the Sorbonne

ENGLISH ADVISORY EDITOR: JOHN BOWLE
Foreword by Arnold Toynbee

CROWN PUBLISHERS, INC.
NEW YORK.

Published in the USA by
Crown Publishers, Inc.
419 Park Avenue South
New York, N.Y. 10016

Contributors to this volume:
Jean Piveteau: 'Man before history'
Jean Delorme: 'The ancient world'
Robert Fossier: 'The barbarian invasions' and 'The rise of Europe'
Georges Ruhlmann:'Western Europe and fringe Europe in the thirteenth century';
                'The fourteenth and fifteenth centuries'

Larousse Encyclopedia of Ancient and Medieval History
Translated by Delano Ames and Geoffrey Sainsbury from
Histoire Universelle Larousse
First published in France by
Augé, Gillon, Hollier-Larousse, Moreau et Cie,
Librairie Larousse, Paris

© Copyright 1964 Augé, Gillon, Hollier-Larousse, Moreau et Cie
                Librairie Larousse, Paris
                        &
                The Hamlyn Publishing Group Ltd
                London   New York   Sydney   Toronto
                Hamlyn House
                The Centre, Feltham
                Middlesex, England

Fourth impression 1972
ISBN 0 600 35471 7
Printed in Singapore by Times Printers

MAN BEFORE HISTORY

THE ANCIENT WORLD

EASTERN PEOPLES AND EMPIRES

THE SUPREMACY OF THE EASTERN MEDITERRANEAN

THE GREAT EMPIRES OF ANTIQUITY

THE MIDDLE AGES

THE BARBARIAN INVASIONS

THE RISE OF EUROPE

THE FOURTEENTH
AND FIFTEENTH CENTURIES

COLOUR PLATES

FOREWORD *by* ARNOLD TOYNBEE

In our time, the writing and publication of universal histories is an important public service. We are living in an age in which, for the first time in history, the whole human race, over the whole surface of our planet, is growing together into a single world-society. We have, indeed, to become a single world-family. In the atomic age, this is the only way of banishing the present danger that we may commit mass-suicide. Mankind intends to survive, and therefore we are committed to following the path of unification resolutely to its goal. This is difficult for human beings, because, till now, our paramount loyalty has been given to fractions of mankind, not to mankind as a whole. We have been, first and foremost, adherents of some local nation, civilisation or religion. In future, our paramount loyalty has to be transferred to the whole human race. This means that the different sections of the human race must learn to know each other and, more than that, learn to appreciate and love both each other and each section's particular contributions to the common stock of mankind's cultural heritage. This, in turn, means that we must become familiar with each other's history. If and when the unification of mankind is achieved, the significance and value of our local histories will be seen, in retrospect, to lie in their rôle as preludes to a universal history of mankind as a whole.

For these reasons, the publication of an English edition of the *Larousse Histoire Universelle* is, itself, an historical event. In the French and English languages, this book will be accessible to almost all educated people all over the world.

Our time is the first in which it has been possible to take a literally universal view of human history, because this is the first time in which the whole human race, all round the globe, has come within sight of coalescing into a single society. This situation is new, but it is not without some partial precedents. In the past, a number of empires, and a smaller number of missionary religions, have aimed at universality. None of them, so far, has ever attained to universality in the literal sense. Subjectively, however, the citizens of the would-be world empires, and the adherents of the would-be world religions, have had the experience of feeling themselves to be members of a world-wide society. This past experience is highly relevant to mankind's

present problems, his objectives, and aspirations. It should be given special attention in any universal history that is written for our generation. The editor of the *Larousse Histoire Universelle* has responded to this need of our time.

These previous attempts at unification on a world-wide scale have inspired some of the great historians of the past to look at our history in universal terms. From time to time in the past there have been sudden confrontations of peoples, civilisations and religions that had previously been strangers to each other. This experience, which is also the characteristic experience of our modern age, has frequently stimulated the imagination of people with a sense of history. These perceptive spirits have been aware that the goal of human social endeavours is the unification of the human race which we, in our time, may be on the eve of achieving at last. The tension between our universal common humanity and the piquant local differences in superficial manners and customs has intrigued historical-minded observers who have had the good fortune to have been born in some age in which a large-scale unification has taken place.

For instance the Graeco-Carian historian Herodotus of Halicarnassus was born a subject of the Persian Empire in about the third generation after its founders had united the heart of the Old World politically from the Indus valley to the east to Mount Olympus to the west. He is the earliest historian known to us who has thought and written in universal terms; and evidently the sudden rapprochement between people with different cultural traditions was one of the features of the Persian Empire that excited Herodotus's curiosity. He tells a story (*ben trovato*, even if not true) of a meeting, arranged by the Emperor Darius, between Greek subjects of his, whose custom was to burn their parents' corpses, and Indian subjects of his whose custom was to eat them. When Darius told the Greeks what the Indian custom was, the Greeks held up their hands in horror; but so did the Indians when the Emperor told these, in turn, what the Greek custom was. 'What? Defile the pure and holy element Fire by burning corpses in it? If we hadn't met these fellow-subjects of ours, we could never have dreamed that any human beings could have such a disgusting custom as that. What a contrast to the nice clean way in which we dispose of our own parents' corpses.' This mutual horror reminds one of the present-day feelings of Communists and anti-Communists about each other's respective ideologies.

The manners and customs that cut deepest into the spiritual heart of human life are religious practices and beliefs; and the missionary religions have been still more ambitious than the aggressive empires in their programmes for bringing the whole human race within their fold. The rulers of recently established empires have therefore sometimes been interested in organising debates between spokesmen of different religions to which different sections of their subjects have adhered. The early Mongol emperors, for instance, held together for several generations the largest empire that has yet been built. The Mongol Empire, at its widest, covered the whole Eurasian continent as far west as the Euphrates, Central Anatolia, the Carpathians, and the Baltic, and as far east as the Pacific. India and Western Europe were the only two considerable areas of Eurasia that escaped being conquered and incorporated. The Mongol emperors amused themselves, like Darius, by confronting with each other different sections of their subjects of different religious persuasions: Christians, Muslims, Buddhists, and the rest. And, after the Timurid supplanters of the western Mongols had been driven out of Central Asia and had been pushed into conquering India, the Emperor Akbar, in his turn, used to organise debates between Zoroastrians, Hindus, Muslims, and Jesuit Roman Catholic missionaries.

It is significant that the rise of the Mongol Empire in Eurasia and the rise of the Timurid Empire in India had the same intellectual effect as the earlier rise of the Persian Empire. These later empires, too, produced would-be universal historians who wrote in Herodotus's vein. The Mongol Empire inspired two of the greatest of the Persian historians, Juwaini and Rashid-ad-Din. The Timurid Empire in India likewise produced its crop of broadminded historians.

If these partial unifications of the human race had power to awaken the historical imagination, our present age ought, *a fortiori*, to produce universal historians of even greater stature. It is one of the paradoxes of the present age that the prevalent school of contemporary historians is still working under the spell of parochial nationalism. This is not only paradoxical; it is also unfortunate. For nationalism is a disruptive force; in the Atomic Age, the penalty of disruption would be mass-suicide. Fortunately, a force that is mightier than nationalism is working on the side of unification. Technology is rapidly increasing

the scale of all its major operations to global dimensions, and is thrusting out, beyond the limits of our planet, into outer space. With modern technology's aid, mankind's age-old push towards unification has a fair prospect of prevailing. But the issue between universalism and nationalism is one of life and death for the human race; and the victory of universalism cannot be taken for granted. To ensure it, men and women of good will have to work for it with all their might, and this in all fields of human activity. The incidental work for unification that is being done by our technicians ought to be seconded by conscious and deliberate work done by our historians.

This is why the production of the *Larousse Histoire Universelle*, and its publication in English as well as in French, is an important public service. In this work, Western writers and editors have made a valiant effort to transcend the parochial Western point of view and to present the history of mankind as the sum of all the efforts of all sections of the human race. Perhaps, in our generation, it has not yet become possible for even the most universal-minded scholars to jump completely clear of their own particular local origins and prepossessions. This history is the work of French minds. Non-Western readers will feel that it is the work of Western minds. All the same, the *Larousse Histoire Universelle* has earned the right to its title. It has made a notable new departure in giving the non-Western contributions to mankind's culture a place in the sun. In the splendid illustrations, above all, the non-Western civilisations and religions come into their own.

The illustrations are indeed magnificent. Besides being both delightful and instructive, they give us a warning of what may be in store for us if we fail to break away from our traditional sectionalism now that we have been overtaken by the Atomic Age. These illustrations have been chosen judiciously. They are a fair sample. They reveal what the distribution of human interests has been up to date; and it is horrifying to see the preponderance of our interest in war. In later history, war plays just as prominent a part as it does in earlier histories of the Assyrians, Mongols and Aztecs.

This universal history is a work of scholarship, but it is more than that. It is also a spur to action. We may hope that its readers will not be content just to educate themselves intellectually in the art of seeing human history as a unity. This book will have fulfilled its purpose if it moves its readers to work actively for the consummation of unity. The extreme choice between unity and destruction is that with which history confronts us in our time.

MAN BEFORE HISTORY

Man is the outcome of a long evolutionary development, the end-product of a process which extended over many geological periods; and a succession of manlike creatures marks the stages by which the human form was evolved.

A gradual modification of the lower limb, which later enabled such Hominidae to assume an upright posture and walk on two legs, sets them apart from the other primates. Hands, thus freed, became a means of grasping and manipulating objects. Only in the end, after the slow lapse of long ages, did the brain acquire its present structure. It was not until this was accomplished that mankind can be said to emerge: for the appearance of *Homo* should not be defined simply as the advent of a new zoological genus but, and essentially, as the manifestation of intelligence in the history of life.

The emergence and antiquity of man

The anatomical study of fossilised remains does not tell us the exact moment when man emerged, and we must have recourse to other methods of approaching the question. Bergson's answer to it is often quoted. Man, he said, appeared on earth at the time when weapons and tools were first fashioned. For the palaeontologist, as for the student of prehistory, the phenomenon of man's becoming man is contemporary with the first appearance in history of implements.

For many centuries it was believed that man's appearance on earth was relatively recent. In the sixteenth century, when the Italian Mercati recognised the true nature of chipped flints known as ceraunites, or 'thunderstones', he pictured a bygone age in which metal was unknown, a period which he placed in time between Adam and Tubal-cain. When Jussieu in the eighteenth century showed how these stones resembled the implements then used by primitive tribes (in a sense thus creating the science of comparative ethnography) he too had no idea of their immense age.

It was prehistoric archaeology which first provided conclusive arguments that man was of very great antiquity. As long ago as 1797 an Englishman, John Frere, found in Suffolk a number of hand-axes which he decided must belong to a 'very remote period indeed, even beyond that of the present world'. At the beginning of the last century Tournal and Marcel de Serres brought to light the fact that the bones of certain extinct species showed traces of having been cut by some kind of instrument. In 1833 Schmerling published an important work on fossilised bones in the caverns of the province of Liège in which he described human remains dating, as he put it, from before the Flood.

All of this work made little impression on the scientific public. The new view of man's antiquity became acceptable only after fierce controversy, but when in 1864 Edouard Lartet discovered in the deposits of La Madeleine in the Dordogne an ivory blade on which a mammoth was engraved, it was established beyond doubt that man and mammoth had existed contemporaneously.

At the same time as these researches were being made human palaeontology was gathering its first materials. In 1856, in the gorge of Neanderthal, not far from Düsseldorf in the Rhineland province of Prussia, certain human remains were discovered. Their examination gave rise to lively altercation.

Some anthropologists argued they were the bones of a deformed individual, others those of a primitive man. We now know that the latter view was correct. In any case there could be no doubt that the remains were extremely ancient and contemporary with the mammoth. During the last hundred years discoveries of this sort have been common, so that the twofold evidence — that of fossil remains and that of the products of human industry — have established the great antiquity of man's

A reconstruction of the first identifiable ape-man, the South African hominid *Australopithecus*. Although he had not attained man's structural development, he may have known how to chip stone. British Museum *(Nat. Hist.)*

The mouth of prehistoric man's cave at Font-de-Gaume, Dordogne. *Musée de l'Homme*

13

existence on earth. The greatest pioneer of systematic excavation was an Englishman, General Pitt-Rivers, who collected and classified implements in a way which illustrated their evolution over long periods. By careful classification of finds according to the strata of their distribution, he was able to establish a time sequence. Instead of collecting objects for their curiosity or intrinsic worth, he included everything available, thus giving a comprehensive picture. His collections, begun in 1852, formed the nucleus of the famous Pitt-Rivers Museum in Oxford. This far-ranging vision of human evolution was, of course, greatly reinforced by the influence of Darwin. In the distant background of those periods accessible to history and tradition a new world was revealed — the world of prehistory.

Chronology

The geological classification of Quaternary time is founded basically on climatic phenomena. The Quaternary was marked throughout the northern hemisphere and especially in Europe by a striking development of glaciers. There was not one but several of these glacial encroachments. In the region of the Alps where the phenomenon has been studied with particular care, four individual glacial advances are distinguished. These are separated by phases of returning warmth known as interglacial periods.

Certain countries show no trace of glaciation. Such is the case in the Near East and also in Africa which now furnish prehistory with material of the highest interest. There, too, the time scale has been established by a study of climatic conditions. In these regions during Quaternary times periods of rainfall alternated with periods of dryness, perhaps even of severe drought. It has not been absolutely proved that these periods correspond to the glacial advances of the northern hemisphere.

Such systems of classifying periods of time give us only the order in which physical phenomena took place, and serve as a framework for the great events of human prehistory. They deal with what could be called relative chronology. But efforts have also been made to calculate the duration of the great divisions of prehistory in millennia, in other words to obtain an absolute chronology.

We cannot here go into the details of the various methods which have in turn been employed: astronomical methods, studies in the speed of erosion and sedimentation, and for more recent periods by carbon and potassium isotope tests.

The results obtained are at best approximate and may be radically modified. It is fairly generally agreed that the Günz Period — when true man probably emerged — is at least 600,000 years ago. Man, then, would be at least 600,000 years old. On the historical scale this figure may seem impressive. And yet man's earthly existence has occupied but a brief moment in the total time life itself has taken to evolve. If we take one year as the unit representing all the time that has elapsed since the appearance of life on earth, it would be only on the twentieth hour of the last day of such a year that the Quaternary began — and man arrived.

Primitive man's forms of culture

The first glimpse we have of our beginnings reveals a world in which the development of intelligence has been translated into work in fashioning stone. It was to continue thus for thousands of centuries. This vast period embraces the Palaeolithic or Old Stone Age, and the Neolithic

or New Stone Age. The classification was established by Sir John Lubbock in 1866 and has not been improved on. It covers two phases of the stone industry: Palaeolithic, in which the implements were chipped, and Neolithic in which there was not only chipped stone but many specimens of polished stone implements. It is, however, convenient to insert a short period of transition between the Palaeolithic and Neolithic Ages: namely, the Mesolithic or Middle Stone Age.

The Palaeolithic, Mesolithic and Neolithic Ages constitute the domain of prehistory. After prehistory comes protohistory, comprising the Copper, the Bronze and the Iron Ages. Finally, at dates which vary from region to region, history proper begins.

Obviously the cutting, chipping and polishing of stone was only one of Stone Age men's activities. Their way of life is better described and the social groups that they formed more usefully defined by saying that first they hunted and later they farmed. The Old Stone Age was the age of hunters, the New Stone Age the age of agriculturalists. In Mesolithic times men passed gradually from the former to the latter, impelled by changes in physical environment and by the evolution of civilisation itself.

Our knowledge of prehistory

We have, of course, no written records to help us to understand the life of these ancient men. The prehistorian must, then, attempt to reconstruct the past with the aid of what material he has: fossilised remains, artifacts, manifestations of an artistic nature, such as cave drawings, and indications of certain ritual practices which are often difficult to interpret.

Attempts have been made to supplement this paucity of information by indirect approaches: by an analysis

Above: a megalithic monument in Minorca. *Viollet*
Below: this Magdalenian cave painting confirms that prehistoric man and the mammoth were contemporaneous. *Musée de l'Homme*

of our present psychic nature, a conjectural procedure whose possibilities are quickly exhausted, and by the employment of ethnographic methods which attempt to deduce and interpret the thoughts and beliefs of ancient man by comparing them with those of primitive peoples living today. But the savages of today are not true primitives. They are backward peoples whose development has been arrested: not ancient, merely old. Lethargic and immobile, they are impervious to experience. They develop neither their mentality nor their techniques; their evolutionary potential has, as it were, atrophied. In this sense they are quite distinct from the genuine primitive who carried within him potentialities which grew into the subsequent history of the world.

We cannot, of course, entirely dismiss ethnographic methods, but they must be used with caution. It is essential to maintain direct contact with hard facts of palaeontology and prehistoric archaeology, difficult though these may be to interpret.

The prehistorian, in the manner of the palaeontologist, seeks to retrace the movements of those living creatures who, after they had reached the stage of reasoning, slowly spread over and dominated the earth. To determine the conditions of this expansion, to find out how and why it took place, is the whole object of the study of prehistory and, of course, of all history.

The cradle of humanity

We now approach the prime problem of history: the question of man's first appearance on the globe. Not man of the modern type, *Homo sapiens*, but of the genus *Homo* in the broad sense — that being which crossed the line of demarcation between the manlike creatures, the Hominidae, and true man, a being whose psychic processes were no longer only instinctual but capable also of reflection.

Should we assume the existence of a certain spot on the globe which witnessed the birth of true men, and from which they set forth to take possession of the earth? Or, on the contrary, does it not seem more plausible that the emergence of the human race occurred more or less at the same time in several places?

All the evidence of palaeontology, and everything we know about the origin of various groups of mammals, leads us to conclude that every living creature first appeared in a strictly limited region, and from this 'cradle' gradually spread in all directions where no physical obstacle or biological opposition hampered or arrested its expansion. Hence it would seem that a search for the cradle of humanity is not an unrewarding task.

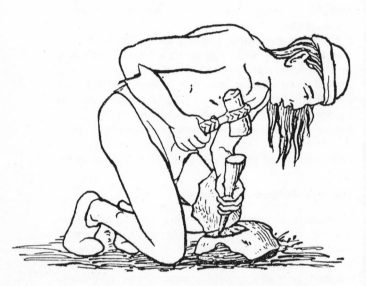

A Stone Age man chipping a flint weapon. An engraving from Holmes's *Handbook of Aboriginal American Antiquities. Musée de l'Homme.*

Specimens of pebble culture from Tihemboka. Pebble industry deposits are often found below Chellean-type tools and must therefore have preceded them.

Colour plate: evidence of Neolithic man in North Africa: a rock painting at Jabarren, in the Tassili Hills. The horse was superimposed at a much later date. *Henri Lhote*

PERIOD	CULTURES	RACES
Lower Palaeolithic	Chellean or Abbevillian Acheulean (flake-tool culture) Clactonian » » » Tayacian	Heidelberg man (Germany) Swanscombe man (England) Fontéchevade man (France)
Middle Palaeolithic	Mousterian (flake-tool culture) Levalloisian (flake-tool culture)	Neanderthal man (Germany)

Upper Palaeolithic	Aurignacian & Perigordian
	    (Bone implements as well stone)
	
	Solutrean (pressure-flaking industry)
	
	Magdalenian
	    (Varied bone implements, fine stone industry)
		Cro-Magnon man (France)
		
		Chancelade man (France)
		
		Grimaldi man (France)

Mesolithic	Azilian (stone industry) Tardenoisian (flint implements) Maglemosian	Ofnet man (Bavaria) Tardenoisian man
Neolithic	Campignian (Flakepoints & pottery) Ertebolle (Scandinavian) Robenhausian (lake dwelling industries)	Various races Increase in brachycephalics

For many years the regions of central Asia were thought to be mankind's place of origin and point of dispersion, though the arguments in favour of this view were never overwhelming. Today palaeontologists and prehistorians are turning their eyes towards Africa. The primitive peoples of America seem to go back only to Neolithic times.

In the course of recent years exploration of the African continent has revealed some very widely scattered evidence of industry in the type of stone artifacts known as Chellean. At first it was supposed that such finds simply indicated that tools similar to those found in Western Europe had spread across the Mediterranean. But the wide distribution of this culture, its richness and variety, suggested the presence of a culture with a long past behind it. If so, there ought to have been signs of its earlier stages and growth — the only way of explaining its exuberance and apparently sudden development.

And, indeed, in several parts of the African continent (in Rhodesia, the Sahara, Morocco, Algeria) exactly such signs have since been found: namely, a very simple stone culture known as *pebble industry*, which reveals an entirely new and extremely primitive level of humanity. Pebble industry deposits are found beneath the Chellean-type tools and must therefore have preceded them. Unfortunately we have no skeletal remains of these people. Recent discoveries, however, suggest that the Australopithecinae — South African hominids who had not reached man's structural development — may have been capable of chipping stone. From this evidence the tentative conclusion has been drawn that the continent of Africa witnessed the appearance of the first men, and the first fossil that can be identified as an ape-man is *Australopithecus*. This primitive hominid had a brain capacity of 700 c.c. It is very probable that he used ready-to-hand tools for hunting but there is no evidence that he used fire. He

Colour plate: a Babylonian seal *(far left)* bearing the inscription of Gudea, Lagash. c. 2050 B.C. *Left*: a Kassite stone relief from the Temple of Ishtar, the great mother-goddess of Babylonia. Uruk. c. 1415 B.C. *Archiv für Kunst und Geschichte*

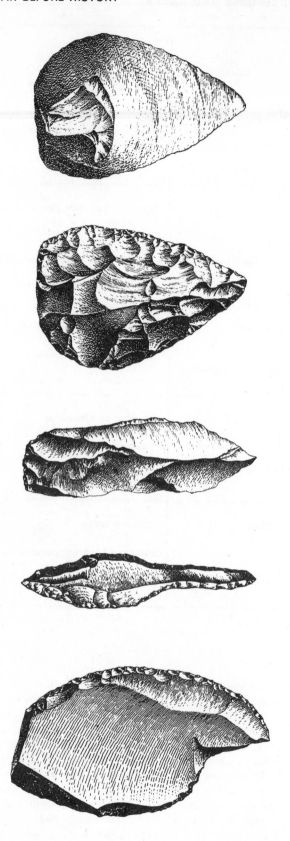

A collection of chipped flints attributed respectively to the following cultures: (A) Acheulean (B) Mousterian (C) Levalloisian (D) Aurignacian and (E) Magdalenian. Perhaps 250,000 years separate the Acheulean stones from the Magdalenian. It is hard to imagine the countless generations and immense effort expended to produce improvements apparently so slight. But they represent the first steps in mankind's ever-developing technical progress. *Musée de l'Homme*, according to Evrard.

dates from the early Pleistocene — making his first appearance perhaps a million years ago.

We are accustomed to think of Europe as an appendage of Asia, a kind of land's end of the greater continent, washed by the waves of humanity and currents of civilisation flowing from the high tablelands of central Asia. Nothing, it is said, originated on the European continent: everything reached it from beyond, more exactly, from the East — and now, it would seem, from Africa. But during the remotest antiquity of mankind Western Europe enjoyed a no less privileged position than Africa.

The plains of the north of France provide one of prehistory's most important theatres. It was research in the valley of the Somme which established the great antiquity of man, and it was in these regions that the abundance of Early Palaeolithic Age industry first gave evidence that ancient man had been very active here. Excavation revealed that a human population was installed here at a much earlier date than had been formerly supposed. On the plains above Montières, a suburb of Amiens, certain flints have recently been found in deposits which are as old as, and perhaps even older than, those in Africa where the pebble industry was discovered. These flints show signs of having been hand fashioned, while some of them, eaten by fire, suggest the existence on this spot of a human hearth. Man had made his appearance on the European continent from the dawn of the Quaternary Era.

From the palaeontological point of view what then remains of the old tradition which supposed Asia to be the centre from which the human race radiated and dispersed? For the moment one fact only may be retained: on certain stag horns found in the deposits of Nihowan in Mongolia — dating back to the very beginning of the Quaternary Era—it is thought that man-made incisions and fire-markings can be recognised.

To sum up: at the beginning of Quaternary times man appears in Africa, in Europe and also, probably, in Asia. This far-flung and apparently sudden expansion is not proof that mankind evolved simultaneously in several parts of the globe, for the erosion of time has effaced the earliest traces of our remote ancestors. We have glimpses of them only after they had attained a certain degree of development. In short, neither palaeontology nor any other historical science can fix the exact moment of man's birth.

The age of the hunters

This obscure period of our origins was followed by one a little less remote: the Palaeolithic, or Early Stone Age — the Age of the Hunters. The Palaeolithic Age alone covers nearly the whole of prehistory. It began, as we have said, several hundreds of thousands of years ago, probably as soon as there were such creatures as men; and it came to an end scarcely ten thousand years before the present era. In so far as man throughout Palaeolithic times lived by hunting, the period presents a certain unity. In other respects there were important changes during the long course of time which elapsed. Distinct cultures followed each other, new opportunities for development arose. From crude artifacts we pass gradually to works of art of great beauty, much as Greek civilisation — in Camille Jullian's phrase — 'began with the shapeless

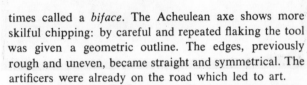

A hunter pursued by a wounded bull. A vigorous painting from La Gazulla, Spain. *Musée de l'Homme*, after Bandi and Maringer.

idols of a primitive religion and ultimately achieved the wonders of art and thought of the Age of Pericles and Plato'.

For this reason Palaeolithic times must be divided into a certain number of sub-periods, or cultures, and a chronology established. Our guide-posts are furnished by the industries of various cultures. It is usual to name the culture from the sites where their remains are most typically found: the table on page 17 outlines the principal European classifications.

Early Palaeolithic cultures

Of the first part of the Age of the Hunters — which is immensely long, roughly covering the duration of the Second and Third Ice Ages (the Mindel and Riss)—little is known except what can be learned from flints left in the places men inhabited. From this period fossilised remains found in Europe are scarce and fragmentary — Heidelberg Man, for instance, is represented by a single jawbone — and we are scarcely able to form a clear picture of what the human type then was.

The typical Chellean tool was the hand-axe, chipped and worked on both its faces and for this reason some-

times called a *biface*. The Acheulean axe shows more skilful chipping: by careful and repeated flaking the tool was given a geometric outline. The edges, previously rough and uneven, became straight and symmetrical. The artificers were already on the road which led to art.

The hand-axe must have served a variety of purposes. As a weapon it could be used for war and for hunting. It is not impossible that the Acheulean *biface* was fitted with a haft. In many deposits the axes are found associated with splinters detached from the core or nucleus of rock. In some sites these flakes predominate and occasionally are found alone. Some prehistorians have concluded from this that Stone Age civilisations followed different and independent paths: one group chipping their implements by percussion and the other flaking them by pressure.

But such an interpretation of the evolution of human history in the Early Palaeolithic period is misleading. There is no fundamental difference between the two types of culture which cannot be explained by a difference in environment.

In some parts of northern France Early Palaeolithic industry is so rich that one might almost speak of hearths and workshops. The essential step in the formation of

A reconstruction of the Mauer mandible, the only known fragment of Heidelberg Man.

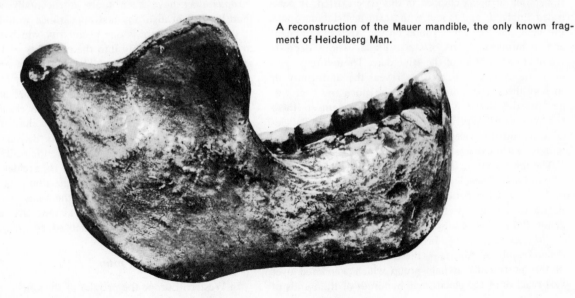

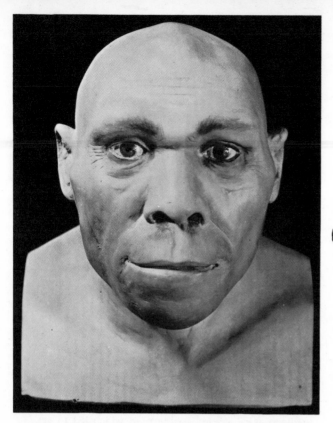
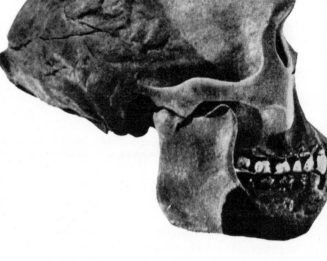

Pithecanthropus, after Weidenreich. Skull *(above rignt)* and head *(above)*. Some traces of industry have been found in association with the remains of this archaic group. *Musée de l'Homme*

human society had already been taken. After all, what is a hearth but a fire round which people gather for warmth, light and comfort? And the workshop is also a gathering place where men share the task of producing objects useful to themselves and others. From such customs the family and then the tribe would be born, and it is possible that here at least they had already come into being.

The stability of Early Palaeolithic cultures

Although the characteristics of Chellean and Acheulean cultures have been described chiefly from findings in French deposits, the area over which this way of life was distributed appears to be very wide. It is found in every part of the ancient world where a raw material susceptible of being chipped in this style existed. It penetrated England, and is met with again in Belgium, Spain, Portugal and Italy; it is found on the African continent and in numerous parts of Asia. These various deposits are obviously not all of the same date. Though they span many thousands of years they reveal the uniformity of such cultures over a large part of the globe and bear witness to the slowness of human development in these remote epochs. With the opening of the Middle Palaeolithic period the pace of time begins to alter: prehistory unfolds with accelerated rhythm.

Though we know so little about the types of humanity who in Early Palaeolithic times inhabited Europe, at more or less the same period in the Far East and in North Africa we find traces of other authentic men, men of the genus *Pithecanthropus*.

Pithecanthropus of Java, *Sinanthropus* of China, *Atlanthropus* of Algeria — these are the representatives of this profoundly archaic group which wandered over vast reaches of the globe some hundreds of thousands of

years ago. A study of them reveals certain aspects of primitive humanity's mentality and manner of life.

No traces of industry have been found in association with the remains of *Pithecanthropus*. On the other hand, the deposits of Ternifine, near Mascara in Algeria, where *Atlanthropus* was discovered, have brought to light a number of chipped flints which resemble the Acheulean axes of northern France. Better still, the site of *Sinanthropus* at Chou-Kou-Tien, near Pekin, has furnished material of the highest interest.

At several levels of the detritus which fills the fissure of Chou-Kou-Tien layers of ash have been discovered, a fact which implies that *Sinanthropus* knew the use of fire. Certain aspects of his stone industry remind us of the relatively developed industries of Europe. So *Sinanthropus* may have been more intellectually advanced than his still brutish physical appearance would lead us to suppose. But there is one peculiarity which allows us to penetrate more deeply into the mentality of this early example of distant humanity. The remains of *Sinanthropus* are found in singular conditions: of their bones, the skulls alone (with unimportant exceptions) are preserved. These are represented sometimes by the cranium and sometimes by the jawbone. Almost all show traces of blows received while still alive, blows delivered either by cutting implements or by rounded stones. The occipital aperture has been enlarged, not by accident but by deliberate intention. The cannibal headhunters of Melanesia still treat their victims in the same way before devouring their brains. We may assume that a similar form of cannibal ritual was practised by *Sinanthropus*.

The dawn of Modern man

In Western Europe the peoples of the Chellean culture

20

Sinanthropus pekinensis, from finds at Chou-Kou-Tien. There is evidence that Sinanthropus knew the use of fire; skull remains suggest that he also practised a form of cannibal ritual. Musée de l'Homme

Mandible of Atlanthropus mauritanicus, from Ternifine, Algeria. Atlanthropus knew how to chip flints, for specimens resembling Acheulean axes have been found.

were succeeded by a highly developed population which in a number of its physical traits seems to foreshadow the modern world. The best examples of these beings have been found in the deposits of Steinheim and Ehringsdorf in Western Germany. However, the mental development of these newcomers does not seem to have kept pace with the improvement in their anatomy. The stone industry found at Ehringsdorf is archaic Mousterian, consisting of small-scale splinters, crude and scarcely retouched.

This type of human being doubtless appeared in the Riss period and vanished from Europe abruptly when the Würm glaciers spread over the lowlands. Some of these people may — by a phenomenon of retrogression allied to geographic isolation — have given birth to Neanderthal men. Others no doubt became Homo sapiens. But of the various phases of this evolution we know practically nothing. We do, however, know, from the grottoes of Palestine, of a Neanderthal type of human creature who could have given birth to modern man.

Mousterian culture and Neanderthal man

The vast stretch of time between the Third or Riss Ice Age and the Riss-Würm interglacial period has left few traces behind for study. But when it came to an end the curtain rose on a new world which, judging from its human inhabitants, seems to have regressed rather than advanced. Within the limits of Western Europe, at least, we now find men who differ from us in their physical aspect even more than those of the previous epoch. An examination of their culture, however, shows us that they are indeed representatives of our race. They have an elongated cranium and a flat, receding forehead; the brow-ridge above the eye socket is massive and promi-

nent, the face slants forward and the chin is still sketchy. They have been classified as a species, or special race, of man, Homo neanderthalensis. The representatives of this new race are relatively numerous. Little by little man was taking possession of the earth.

Neanderthal Man lived in a harsh climate, for he flourished at the beginning of the Fourth Ice Age. He took refuge in caves and other natural shelters. Traces of his presence are generally found on the slopes before the entrance of such caverns, together with the bones of the animals he ate and the products of his industry.

Mousterian stone industry and Neanderthal man

The industry of this period is known as Mousterian and for the archaeologist marks a new form of culture. It differs technically from that of Chellean times. Instead of chipping both faces of a nodule of flint the Mousterian artisan was content to break off a splinter which he afterwards finished by repeated flaking of one face only.

The pointed triangular stones, chipped and reworked on one face, but smooth on the other, are characteristic of Mousterian culture. At first the points were massive, with long flakings; then they became more delicate and slender, some resembling knives and scrapers. Implements included drills and saws with toothed edges: there were also thick circular flakes like discs, while slings made of limestone and flint are common.

Mousterian industry was not entirely uniform: there are variations. Among them we find the typical Mousterian tool worked on one face only; the La Quina-La Ferrassie Mousterian, with its predominance of curved scrapers also flaked on a single face; the Mousterian of Acheulean tradition, in which heart-shaped bifaces are

A reconstruction of the hominid *Australopithecus*. About four feet in height, *Australopithecus* lived in Africa a million years ago. . *British Museum (Nat. Hist.)*

Back to front: reconstructed heads of Java Man, Neanderthal Man and Cro-Magnon Man. From the British Natural History Museum.

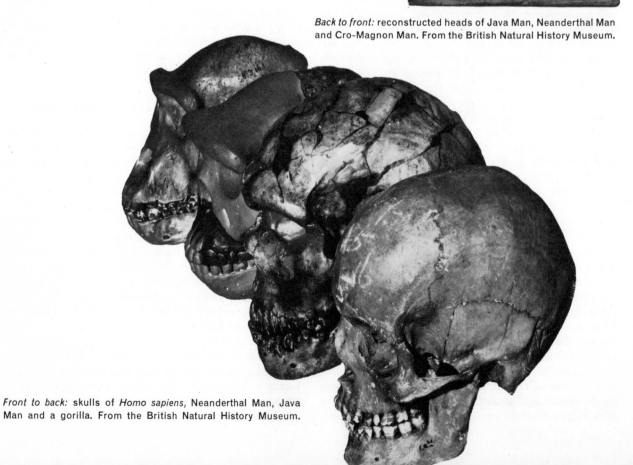

Front to back: skulls of *Homo sapiens*, Neanderthal Man, Java Man and a gorilla. From the British Natural History Museum.

abundant, together with quadrangular knives with edges often chamfered; and the denticulated Mousterian which appears to be a degeneration of Acheulean tradition.

Implements were also made of bone. The lower extremities of the bovine humerus and the humerus and phalange of horses were used as chipping blocks. Others seem to have been used as finishing tools for flaking flint by pressure. Long and sharpened shafts of bone were themselves finished tools. The tines of stags' antlers may have been employed as daggers.

The man called *Homo neanderthalensis* has so far been found only in connection with a single form of Mousterian culture: the La Quina-La Ferrassie type. It is unlikely that the people who created the other types of industry in this period could have been very different from Neanderthal Man, but we know nothing of their physical appearance.

Anatomically, *Homo neanderthalensis* marks a distinct step forward from *Pithecanthropus* and *Sinanthropus*. His skull has a bigger brain capacity, it is higher, less elongated and less cramped behind the eye sockets. He still, however, retains features which recall earlier types of men: low forehead, protuberant brow-ridge and his under-developed chin. His carriage has often been described as brutish. Attempts have been made to reconstruct his facial muscles and discover the expression of his physiognomy. We can only wonder what kind of character existed behind so rude a mask. The fact that he lived in caves is a particularly favourable circumstance, for it has preserved evidence of his behaviour and way of life.

Neanderthal Man was a hunter, and the numerous animal remains which have been found in association with his tools and weapons are simply the refuse of his kitchen. He knew the use of fire, and with it warmed himself, protected himself against marauding beasts, and cooked his food.

Neanderthal funerary practices

With Neanderthal Man we come for the first time in the history of humanity to questions of belief. What thoughts did Neanderthal Man have on the subject of his own nature and the mystery of death? His funerary practices tell us much about him.

For many years the idea of burial rites among Neanderthal Man was dismissed as inconceivable. That such rites had in fact existed was established beyond doubt by the Abbé Bouyssonie and the Abbé Bardon and their celebrated discovery in the Correze of the Man of La Chapelle-aux-Saints. His skeleton had been carefully placed in a shallow grave and certain parts of his body were protected by stones and animal bones. Around the corpse were arranged flints of remarkable workmanship, as well as a bovine hoof which bore evidence that the flesh had still adhered to it when it was put there.

A small cache at the entrance to the grotto contained a bison's horn, various bones of the same animal, and a handsome flint point. A similar grave has been found at La Ferrassie.

The existence of such graves would seem to establish the fact that Neanderthal Man did not believe that death was his ultimate end. Everywhere and without exception, in all stages of culture, the deliberate burial of the corpse implies with little room for doubt a belief in an after-life.

Top: a Cro-Magnon skull from Eyzies, Dordogne. *Centre:* the skull of a young Grimaldi Man. *Bottom:* the skull of Chancelade Man. Together, these three represent the races of *Homo sapiens* distinguishable in Western Europe from Late Palaeolithic times on. Cro-Magnon Man has also been found in North Africa. *Musée de l'Homme*

23

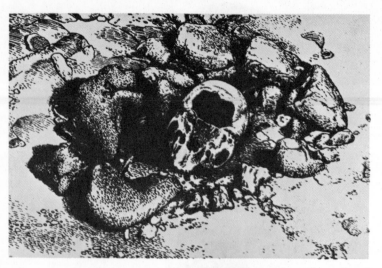

In a cave on Mont Circe, Italy, a Neanderthal skull was found with a greatly enlarged occipital hole. It was surrounded by an ellipse of stones. Here, too, the suggestion is that some cannibal ritual was practised. *Larousse*

found. Such discoveries are so frequent that we cannot attribute the phenomenon to chance and are forced to repeat the question first raised in the case of *Pithecanthropus*: did Neanderthal Man practise the skull cult? An answer may be supplied by examining the grave in the grotto of Mount Circe, south of Rome.

Mount Circe was the legendary abode of the enchantress who turned Ulysses and his companions into swine. From its steep escarpment it dominates the Mediterranean and the Pontine Marshes. It was peopled in very early times. The numerous caves in the hillside sheltered first Neanderthal men and afterwards men of the later Palaeolithic Age. One of them contains human remains which are buried in a very striking fashion. Bones of deer and oxen were scattered about the grotto. A collection of stones was arranged in a sort of ellipse and lying on the floor in the middle of it the skull of a Neanderthal Man was found. The occipital hole had been greatly enlarged and formed an oval more than two and a half inches wide and nearly three and a half inches long. Comparing this with similar mutilations observed in the skulls of the victims of Melanesian headhunters it has been concluded that Neanderthal Man also practised some cannibal ritual.

Homo faber, Homo sapiens

Neanderthal Man has sometimes been called a representative of *Homo faber*, a man capable only of fashioning tools and implements, a forerunner of *Homo sapiens*, who was able to think and reflect as well.

All the research that has been done on Neanderthal Man's methods of chipping his flint implements, however, proves that the process required a series of complex operations. The variety and diversity of his tools show that he was well aware of their meaning and use. It is therefore impossible to maintain the distinction between *Homo faber* and *Homo sapiens*. The two propensities or functions of the human spirit — technical and speculative — have always co-existed. At different epochs one or the other has merely been relatively dominant.

It would be reasonable to assume that the perfected techniques which produced Mousterian implements could not have been handed down by a process of simple imitation. They must have been taught and there must therefore have been language.

Links between Homo neanderthalensis and Homo sapiens

What connections can we discover between vanishing Neanderthal Man and man of the modern type at the beginning of his career? Finds in Palestine at Mount Carmel, Djebel Kafzeh, suggest that there may have been cross-breeding between the two types, while at the other extremity of the Asiatic continent, in the island of Java, Ngandong Man, who is similar to European Neanderthal Man, is sometimes thought to be the ancestor of the Australian Aboriginal.

Classical archaeology teaches that in certain cases one type of culture leads without interruption to another. Perigordian culture, attributed to a very ancient *Homo sapiens*, derived directly from Mousterian industry, which in turn was based on an Acheulean tradition. And since

What form could this future existence take? It seems to have been conceived of as similar to life on earth, since in the tomb exactly those things which men needed in daily life were deposited: weapons, food and so forth.

Moreover, the custom of placing funerary objects in a hiding-place dug near the grave was to be continued by the Egyptians of the later Copper and Bronze Ages — which connects in a striking and unexpected manner two stages of mankind which otherwise differ profoundly and in time are separated from each other by many thousands of years.

It is difficult to be certain that Neanderthal men celebrated funeral rites on their tombs. The Abbés Bouyssonie and Bardon, however, believed that they recognised in the grave at La Chapelle-aux-Saints traces of funeral feasts. The grotto has a very low ceiling and consequently could not, they pointed out, have been used as a dwelling. Within it they discovered reindeer bones belonging to at least twenty-two animals, and the remains of a dozen different bovines. Such a quantity of animals could not have been devoured in a single meal, which suggests that many successive meals were eaten in the shelter, probably festivals celebrated in memory of the dead.

Certain evidence leads us to suppose that Neanderthal Man believed that a corpse had the power to rise from the dead. Both the man of La Chapelle-aux-Saints and the one found at La Ferrassie had their legs bent back in a manner which suggests they were originally trussed up. Were the people who buried the bodies afraid of the dead? Had they bound them so that they could not return to disturb the living? Could this be an ancient form of a belief in ghosts that still persists today? These are questions we cannot answer.

The skull cult

In many caves isolated skulls or jawbones have been

Acheulean culture appears to have been localised in Western Europe it would seem that Western Europe gave birth to the culture which produced so many beautiful examples of Quaternary art. So it is to this part of the globe that we turn, at the beginning of Late Palaeolithic times, to follow man's spiritual evolution.

Late Palaeolithic civilisation and Homo sapiens

We shall for the moment examine only the countries of Western Europe, but it is by no means certain that the course of prehistory was identical throughout the Old World. The passage from Mousterian culture to that of Upper or Late Palaeolithic times took place in a world in which physical and biological conditions were remarkably stable. The cold persisted and even intensified. The animals that Neanderthal Man had known continued to flourish, but the name often given to Late Palaeolithic times, the 'Reindeer Age', is misleading, since reindeer were already very abundant in the Mousterian period.

Rock-shelters and grottoes still served men as places for refuge or ritual; but the newcomers differed profoundly in physical appearance from the Neanderthal men who preceded them. The raised forehead, the reduced brow-ridge, the rounded occipital region and the well developed chin were those of men who completely resemble present-day man. We call them fossils because their bones are mineralised; but nothing else distinguishes them from modern man, who now emerges in all his racial complexities.

This racial differentiation of *Homo sapiens* is demonstrated by all the discoveries that have been made in various parts of the Old World. In Western Europe three races have been distinguished: the Cro-Magnon, the Grimaldi and the Chancelade.

Cro-Magnon Man, so called from the cave in the Dordogne near Eyzies where his remains were found, seems to represent, at least in France, the fundamental type. He was tall — most of the known examples being over six feet — and it has even been suggested that Cro-Magnon Man belonged to a superior caste, ruling over a racially different population. He is found again in North Africa and in numerous variations in Europe. In Oberkassel, near Bonn, two skeletons buried in the same grave (an old man and a young woman) show extraordinary mingling of characteristics. The skulls are of Cro-Magnon type, the facial bones show a marked resemblance to those of Eskimos, while the remainder of the skeletons suggests a Neanderthal-like creature. In Moravia some men of the general Cro-Magnon type have still retained the exaggerated brow-ridge of Neanderthal Man.

The Grimaldi race appears to have had certain negroid affinities; while that of the Chancelade has been found to show Eskimo-like traits.

A very remarkable association has been observed in a deposit situated to the south-west of Pekin, at Chou-Kou-Tien, at the top of the hill where the remains of *Sinanthropus* were discovered. Three skulls have been found, together with fragmentary human remains belonging to a dozen different individuals. One of the skulls, which was that of an old man, still reveals certain Neanderthal traits, while the facial structure suggests the appearance one might expect in a primitive Mongolian. The second skull, a young woman's, is of Melanesian

An Aurignacian ivory statuette: the Venus of Lespugue, a stylised representation of the female body. *Musée de l'Homme*

A rock engraving of bison and horses (probably Magdalenian) from the Trois Frères cave, Ariège. This cave contains some of the finest Palaeolithic engravings. There is also strong evidence that certain parts of the cave were used as sanctuaries for some ritual. *Musée de l'Homme*

A fragment of a Magdalenian bone sling carved in the form of a reindeer's head. Such a weapon increased the accuracy of the hunter's aim and the force of the projectile. *Musée de l'Homme*

Harpoons, arrow-heads and various hunting and fishing weapons were all in use during Magdalenian times. It was at this period that man began to light his cave dwellings with the first oil lamps. The lamp shown comes from the *Musée de l'Homme*

type, while the third, that of a middle-aged woman, resembles the skull of an Eskimo. Thus we find together in Chou-Kou-Tien three racial types which today are very widely dispersed.

If we could see these men of the Late Palaeolithic Age as they lived and worked we should probably distinguish, as we do today, white men, black men and yellow men — or rather, pre-white, pre-black and pre-yellow men.

There was at that time a real upsurge of the human species, accompanied by changes in mentality so great that it marked a new stage in the history of terrestrial life. It would, however, be an exaggeration to claim that mankind's spiritual evolution had taken an entirely new turn. We are still in the Age of the Hunters, and the chief occupation of these men was a constant struggle against their animal rivals for food and for possession of the earth.

Late Palaeolithic industry

From the Aurignacian-Perigordian period onwards we observe an enrichment in the technique of flaking stone which reached its point of perfection with the 'Willow-leaf' work of Solutrean culture. Bone work also shows considerable improvement. In the Aurignacian period this work already achieves the delicacy of the finest work in flint. Towards the end of Solutrean times needles with eyes appear, which allows us to assume that clothes were then worn. Finally, in Magdalenian times, we find harpoons, weapons for hunting and fishing, arrow-heads and the 'sceptres' whose significance is still uncertain. It was at this moment that man first thought of, and created in stone and in bone, a vessel which, like the palm of the hand could retain liquid, but more efficiently; thus the first lamps appeared, which permitted him to illuminate the depths of his caves.

The birth and development of art

The great marvel of this second part of the Age of the Hunters however, the miracle which distinguishes it from previous cultures, was the discovery, or rather the invention, of art.

The problem of the origin of art is full of difficulties. Though we observe no signs of artistic activity in the Mousterian caves, this does not necessarily mean that the harmony and symmetry of certain Early and Middle Palaeolithic tools were not a source of aesthetic pleasure. But it is only from Aurignacian-Perigordian times that sculpture, carving and painting abruptly appear. In earlier periods we are unable to find any indications which might foreshadow this sudden development. The study of such works belongs more properly to the history of art, but it is also of the highest interest to us in our attempt to understand the mentality of these oldest representatives of *Homo sapiens*.

Sculpture developed during the whole of the Late Palaeolithic Age: that of the Aurignacian-Perigordian consists chiefly of statuettes of the female body modelled in the round. They show a striking exaggeration of the hips which shows a striking similarity to the steatopygia, or remarkable accretion of fat around the buttocks, of certain South African bushwomen. Bas-reliefs, which are rare during the Aurignacian-Perigordian period, become relatively numerous in Solutrean and are also found in Magdalenian times. The Solutrean examples depict pregnant women and scenes of horses coupling. It is believed that these figures were connected with some kind of fertility cult.

In the darkest parts of the caves, painted or carved on walls or ceiling, we find pictures of animals, rarely those of human beings. The caves of Altamira in Spain, of Font-de-Gaume at Combarelles and, above all, of Lascaux in the Dordogne contain superb works of Quaternary art.

What meaning can we attach to these works of art? What impulse led men to depict the animals they saw? Was it simply to satisfy an artistic craving? Salomon Reinach, one of the first to offer an answer, considered Quaternary art forms to be essentially magic. 'When we speak nowadays of the *magic* of art', he wrote, 'we do not realise how accurate the word is.' By drawing pictures on the walls of his caves of the animals he ate, and by carving their images on bone or in stone, the Late Palaeolithic hunter hoped to capture them more easily.

Beliefs of this sort doubtless took on a social character and gave rise to ritual practices. Outdoor sanctuaries can be observed in many places. The images of the cult were carved in the rock and formed majestic bas-reliefs, representing animals, often composite, or human figures. There were also more mysterious sanctuaries which were doubtless reserved for the initiated. These are the caves in which the works of art are almost always found in the most inaccessible depths.

The diffusion of Late Palaeolithic culture

The female statuettes of Late Palaeolithic times have sometimes been compared with the ceramic statuettes of ancient Egypt. Steatopygous figurines, comparable to the Quaternary statuettes, are widely distributed in the later Neolithic or New Stone Age. They have been dug up in Egypt, Malta, Yugoslavia and Rumania. But this Upper Palaeolithic culture derived from Acheulean via Mousterian culture, and must have arisen in Western Europe. It is here, too, that the two most advanced cultures of the period are found: Solutrean and Magdalenian.

We can form some idea, at least in the case of Western Europe, of the ties which existed between the peoples of Late Palaeolithic times. The uniformity of their tools and weapons cannot be explained other than by assuming a close contact between them. No less significant in this respect is a study of the shells found in caverns in Belgium, France, Italy and Switzerland. The deposits at Chaleux in Belgium contain the remains of molluscs which came from the region of Versailles. Sand which has been identified as Tertiary sand from Touraine has been found at Laugerie-Basse, near Eyzies in the Dordogne. In the Grimaldi Grottoes on the shores of the Mediterranean species of shellfish were collected that live exclusively in the Atlantic Ocean. Fossils from the region of Vienne have been discovered at Thayngen in Switzerland. Thus we begin to discern the vague outlines of what might almost be called the 'trade routes' between the peoples of the Late Palaeolithic Age.

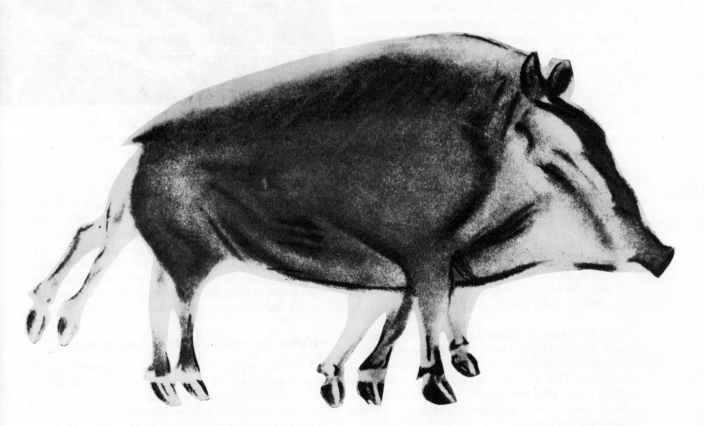

A Quaternary painting of a wild boar. From the caves of Altamira, Spain. In the darkest, remotest parts of his caves, prehistoric man painted and carved animals: mammoths, reindeer, wild boars, bulls and horses. Art for him was often a medium of magic; by representing, say, a boar pierced by an arrow he hoped to induce success in the hunt.

The habitat of Late Palaeolithic man

It seems improbable that *Homo sapiens* in Late Palaeolithic times used caves as his normal dwelling-place. Like Neanderthal Man he must have spent most of his time at the entrance to such caverns. Here he chipped his flint tools and prepared his food.

Though such clues give us only a vague notion of the daily life of these men, discoveries made in Russia and Siberia have thrown some light on their social organisation. At Timonov-Ka in the basin of the Dnieper, for instance, a site inhabited by Aurignacian hunters has been found. They had permanent dwellings, rectangular in shape, which are not dissimilar to those in which certain Siberian tribesmen on the shores of Lake Baikal live today. On other sites, circular in form, temporary tents were undoubtedly erected.

The French prehistorian Peyrony has also called attention to traces of habitations in the shelter at Fourneau du Diable in the Dordogne and at Laugerie-Haute, near Eyzies.

Such agglomerations suggest social organisation, and we can imagine people gathered together in families and even larger groups and, as we shall see, congregating around burial places.

Funerary practices

Late Palaeolithic Man had a cult of the dead which was very similar to that practised by Neanderthal Man. Because Late Palaeolithic times are not so remote as Mousterian the examples of burial are more common.

In the *Grotte des Enfants* at Grimaldi an old woman and a young man were buried in Aurignacian times. They were adorned with a sort of crown and bracelets of nassa shells, and their legs were sharply bent back in the manner of Peruvian mummies. This double interment is sometimes advanced as evidence of a ritual practice — the sacrifice of a living being on the tomb of the dead — a practice which is believed to be found again in the Neolithic period, and which in some countries persisted until recent times.

Not far from Grimaldi, the Grotto della Arena Candide — or White Sands — contains a burial place which is also Aurignacian. In it a young boy was buried, with his head pointing to the north. Large stones covered the hands and feet, and a portion of the jawbone had been removed and replaced by a pile of yellow ochre. Arranged at his side were adornments of shells and stags' teeth and four of those enigmatic works of Late Palaeolithic craftsmanship known to archaeologists as 'sceptres'.

The corpse found at Chancelade in the Dordogne had been so tightly folded and bound that the feet were drawn up to the pelvis and the knees were in contact with the dental arch. Thus the skeleton occupies a space some eighteen inches wide and only twenty-six inches long.

In all these tombs a large quantity of ochre had been spread over the corpse.

As in the case of Neanderthal Man there seems to be no doubt that the care expended in burying these bodies indicates a belief in some form of survival, and that this after-life was thought to be similar to life on earth.

With these Late Palaeolithic men we again encounter

Skeletons found in the *Grotte des Enfants* at Grimaldi. The double interment is sometimes advanced as evidence of a ritual in which a living being was sacrificed on the tomb of the dead. *Larousse*

the skull cult. The most typical example is furnished by the deposit at Placard in the Charente of France. Human skulls had been arranged on flat stones and adorned with shells and other objects. Some of the brain-pans had been fashioned into cups and set upright side by side. They were flanked by bones — a humerus and a femur; and one of them had contained red ochre. The probable explanation is that this was a sacred depository such as we still find among certain primitive tribes.

Painting the body, clothes and adornment

The discovery in many deposits of pigments and of bone implements with which such colour could be applied to the skin makes it probable that Late Palaeolithic man was in the habit of painting his body.

Painting the body is one method of adornment. There are, of course, others; and the men of the second part of the Reindeer Age—like the Aborigines of Australia—wore necklaces and chains made of shells. In addition to shells they used the teeth of animals, especially the canine teeth of carnivorous beasts and of deer. These teeth were perforated for stringing and were often embellished by carving. The ornaments worn by men seem to have been richer than those worn by women. As Grosse points out, among primitive people personal adornment follows the same pattern as among the higher animals. In both cases this is because the male pays court to the female. There are, as he says, no spinsters among primitive peoples or animals. The female is sure to be mated while the male must often make great efforts to find a companion.

We have scant information about the garments worn during these times: a loin-cloth from the statuette of Lespugue in the Haute-Garonne, the skins worn by the dancers of the Mège shelter in the Dordogne, the skin in which the Man of Angles-sur-l'Anglin in Vienne is clothed. The presence in several deposits of bone buttons, needles provided with eyes and tools for preparing skins suggests that clothes were fashioned and sewn with thread made from reindeer tendons or horsehair.

Hunting

It is not easy to imagine the material conditions in which the people of the Late Palaeolithic Age lived. They subsisted by gathering wild fruits and berries, by fishing and, above all, by hunting.

They employed a fairly large variety of weapons. They had the lasso, for a horse carved in the grotto of Combarelles has a running knot around its neck. Stones, both thrown and slung, should be mentioned at least as accessories to hunting: they have been found in many Aurignacian deposits and they were known as far back as Mousterian times. A sling with a reindeer horn handle some twelve inches long would increase both the accuracy of the aim and the force of the projectile. Such weapons date only from Magdalenian times, but it is possible that they existed in wood as early as the Aurignacian period.

To draw up a list of the game that Palaeolithic Man hunted would be simply an enumeration of most of the mammals which existed in Quaternary times. But he seems to have had his preferences. The reindeer must have been his favourite quarry, in view of the abundance of reindeer bones found in various deposits. The mammoth also appears to have played an important role. The horse was certainly much hunted, and we may add to this list the aurochs and the bison. Carnivorous animals, with the exception of the bear, seem to have been more or less neglected.

Methods of hunting are illustrated by the drawings and carvings found in caves. One such scene, which comes from Laugerie-Basse and is carved on reindeer horn, shows a human being enveloped in the skin of an animal creeping up on an aurochs with the intention of casting his spear at close range, a method that was employed by the Amerindians as recently as the nineteenth century.

There were also organised animal hunts, which meant a certain degree of co-operation. The game was driven towards a spot where it could be captured more easily or into corrals made of palisades — as in the drawing in the grotto of Marsoulas, or forced over the edge of a precipice — as depicted on the rock at Solutre.

In the Dordogne and in Germany traces have been

Honey-gatherers from a Palaeolithic rock drawing. Man had already learned to rely on the resources of nature for certain items in his diet. *Historia Photo*

found of pit-traps. Late Palaeolithic Man also drew diagrams of which the best known examples are geometrical designs in the form of triangular huts. The triangles frequently enclose an animal. They have therefore been interpreted as representing traps, but it has been pointed out that the trapped animals do not belong to the same layer of painting as the triangular signs.

As game, birds played a minor role in the Palaeolithic hunter's life. They seem not to have been hunted in either the early or middle periods of the age. And the rare later Palaeolithic representations of birds give us no indication of how they were caught. In the deposit of Meiendorf, however, the pelvis of a ptarmigan-like bird has been found, and the sternum of a crane which was wounded by arrows shot from a bow or from some similar weapon.

Fishing

Fishing was perhaps of less importance to Late Palaeolithic man, though harpoons and fish-hooks made of bone or stag horn were sometimes used.

Marine molluscs must have furnished a large part of   29

In Mesolithic times the human form as well as animals was often represented in paintings. From Teruel, in Spain, this hunter clad in trousers suggests that the skins of captured prey were put to good use. Thread was probably made from horsehair or animal tendons.

Azilian bone harpoons from Laugerie-Basse and Mas d'Azil, France. Finely chipped flints, harpoons and pebbles are characteristic of Azilian culture.

the food eaten by those peoples who lived near the coast. All along the western shores of Portugal piles of shells of such molluscs (*concheiros*) have been found and can be identified as belonging to the Middle and Late Palaeolithic Ages. There are also mussel shells, oyster shells and numerous salt-water snails, or periwinkles.

The Mesolithic or Middle Stone Age

The Age of the Hunters did not pass directly to the Age of the Agriculturists, that is, from the Palaeolithic to the Neolithic. Between the two there was a period of transition during which some Palaeolithic tendencies persisted while others, Neolithic in character, gradually emerged. In the north the new era began about 8000 years B.C.

The climate had become milder, and in Western Europe the glaciers had withdrawn to more or less the position they occupy today. The reindeer had emigrated to the north and the stag had replaced it.

The peoples of Europe displayed a certain diversity. For the most part they were long-headed men (dolichocephalous); but we note the appearance — for instance in the deposit of Ofnet in Bavaria — of the first brachycephalous, or round-headed, men. They were all small of stature, but they were not pygmies, as it has sometimes been claimed. Neither does the fact that they were prognathous connect them with the black races. Genetically they appear to be more closely related to Chancelade Man who was a Late Palaeolithic type.

Archaeology recognises several kinds of stone industry during this period. The Azilian — named from Mas-d'Azil in the Ariège — is characterised by fine-chipped flint, flat harpoons and coloured pebbles. Tardenoisian — from Fère-en-Tardenois — was also a culture of fine-chipped flint and geometric shapes: triangles, lozenges, and segments of circles. Sauveterrian — from Sauveterre-la-Lémance in the Lot-et-Garonne — is noted for a spearhead of a special type. Maglemosian must have begun in Denmark and afterwards spread over the Scandinavian and Baltic regions. Men of the Maglemosian culture worked in wood as well as in stone.

In general, art becomes inferior and more formalised and, on the coloured pebbles of Mas-d'Azil, animals are no longer represented except by symbols. Elsewhere, for example in the grotto of Romanelli in southern Italy, drawings that resemble a comb represent herds or flocks.

The rock drawings of eastern Spain are exceptions. Actually the age of these drawings is disputed: according to some prehistorians they go back to the Late Palaeolithic Age, according to others they belong to Mesolithic or even Neolithic times. Probably this eastern Spanish rupestrian art is largely contemporary with the Franco-Cantabrian art of the end of the Palaeolithic Age, and simply continued into Mesolithic times.

This rock drawing art introduces a deeply original note into man's artistic activities. The human form is frequently represented and almost always in groups. Men and women wear garments, and the men carry bows and arrows. They are therefore undoubtedly a hunting people.

In Mesolithic times we again find funerary rites, the same rites as in the preceding age. The corpses are covered with red ochre and the legs deliberately bent; the funerary furnishings include all that could be of use

A line of menhirs at Lagajär, Brittany. *Lala Aufsberg Foto*

to the dead man in his future existence. There are individual tombs, skeletons buried in little groups and collective tombs. Prehistorians have described an odd ritual in the deposit of Téviec, a small island off the coast of Brittany: burial under stag horns. It is believed that in this strange rite lie the origins of the myth that the nature of the stag is somehow sacred, a myth encountered in Gallic mythology and again in the Christian legends of the Middle Ages and even in our own day — for instance, in the legends of Saint Hubert, Saint Guensel and Saint Nennoch.

The skull cult, too, continued. In the grotto of Ofnet some twenty skulls were arranged concentrically, their faces turned towards the setting sun. Some of them wore ornaments made of shells and the canine teeth of stags. Many of them showed signs of physical violence. This grotto probably formed a ritual depository.

From what we can reconstruct of these people's existence, life was precarious and difficult. In Brittany Mesolithic man kept himself alive on the products of the sea, especially those which were easy to gather, like molluscs and crustaceans. Indeed, all along the coast from Denmark to Portugal we find, dating from this period, little hillocks which contain the remains of innumerable shellfish. These deposits are known by Danish archaeologists as *kjökkemmodinger* ('kitchen refuse').

Mesolithic people lived in groups, in villages; the foundations of such villages have been discovered in Portugal and in Palestine.

They domesticated the dog, who thus became man's first pet; and it has been thought that, in the Near East at any rate, they learned how to cultivate grain. In the deposit at Mugharet el-Ouad in Palestine their sickles made of bone have been found, which leads to the conclusion that there was at least a harvest. This does not, of course, prove that the harvest was planted, for there are certain reasons for believing that wheat, as well as barley and rye, could have grown in Palestine spontaneously. But even if Mesolithic men did not sow grain they reaped it. They also ground it, for millstones too have been found in the El-Ouad deposit.

Thus the domestication of animals was begun, though   31

limited to a single species. We are also approaching the moment when man was to cultivate the soil. These two events announced the great transformation of the prehistoric world, the dawning of a new age which, in turn, leads to historic times. The new age was the Neolithic.

The Neolithic metamorphosis

The study of the Neolithic or New Stone Age has presented particular difficulties. The historian scarcely dares to stray into territory which offers him no written texts, while the physical anthropologist feels lost in a world where evolution is so rapid that he is unable to apply his normal methods of investigation.

The period is nonetheless of capital importance because of the revolutionary changes it witnessed, changes which were of the greatest consequence to humanity and may, without exaggeration, be called a metamorphosis. For the Neolithic Age is characterised by the more or less simultaneous appearance in widely scattered parts of the world of polished stone, of pottery, of agriculture and of the domestication of animals.

It is not simple to define its exact duration. Its beginnings are, generally speaking, easy enough to determine.

Pottery from pre-dynastic Egypt. c. 4000 B.C. The Neolithic Age was one of revolutionary change in which polished stone, pottery, agriculture and the domestication of animals made an almost simultaneous appearance in widely scattered parts of the world. *Victoria and Albert Museum*

A prehistoric pot from India

Certain kinds of stone industry, geometric flints for example, suggest an insensible passage from Mesolithic to Neolithic; but the arrival of polished stone and pottery indicates a definite stage at which the Neolithic Age began. But naturally they did not arrive everywhere at the same time. In Northern Europe the time can be approximately fixed by a study of variations in the salt content of the Baltic, and by a critical examination of the peat bogs. There the new age began between five and six thousand years ago. In Egypt it goes back perhaps ten thousand years.

For several reasons it is almost impossible to put a date to the end of the Neolithic Age. Even today certain primitive tribes exist who, judged from their tools, are still in a Neolithic stage of culture. In other regions of the world contemporary social organisation seems little different from what it was in the identical region in Neolithic times. There is a final complication: in Europe itself polished Neolithic stones can be found together with objects made of metal. Basically, there is hardly such a thing as Neolithic culture in its unadulterated state, and Teilhard could state without paradox that in the Mediterranean world the last five millennia represent merely the zenith of the Neolithic Age and its slow transition to an industrial era which we are only now beginning to approach. In this broad but true sense the Neolithic period has hardly ended. But it is the convention to say that the Neolithic Age came to a close when metal first appeared, that is, about 5000 B.C. in Egypt and Chaldea, and towards 500 B.C. in the regions around the Baltic.

There are two theories of how Neolithic culture began:

The first is that throughout the entire Old World a single cultural metamorphosis took place which caused man to pass from the Age of Hunting to the Age of Agriculture. The Neolithic cultures of Europe, of Egypt and of China were simply three parallel offshoots which sprang up simultaneously from the same root.

Neolithic culture would thus appear to be one phase in the evolution of the human species. Between the Palaeolithic Age of flaked stone and the protohistoric, or modern age, which employs metal came the Neolithic — a necessary stage in the organic evolution of the race which was passed through, often slowly and irregularly but in one general advance, by the whole of humanity in the course of its development. Such is the so-called 'hologenetic' theory.

In the second or 'monogenetic' theory emphasis was laid on the unity of Neolithic culture as a whole and its clearly defined characteristics where so many variations might have been expected. For it to crop up independently and without connection in various parts of the world seems incredible. There must, therefore, have been a centre of dispersion from which its waves spread out to cover the earth.

The monogenetic theory is now generally accepted. It is agreed that Neolithic culture was born in the zone which extends from Egypt to Iran and embraces Palestine. From this centre a series of currents spread the new order in all directions. The indigenous populations with whom it came in contact naturally modified it, thus imparting a local character to the culture of different regions. France remained outside the main stream of this new movement. After having seen brilliant artistic achievement in Late Palaeolithic times, she was now to receive only the faint glow of more distant fires.

We cannot attempt to retrace the actual paths by which the use of polished stone was spread: they are still uncertain and complicated by conflicting evidence. We shall attempt therefore to study the significance of these new contributions to man's life purely from the biological angle.

New techniques

The appearance of the new polished-stone industry does not seem to reveal a new or special kind of mentality; and chipped flints are still common in Neolithic deposits. Nevertheless man had invented new implements: a knife for cutting the branches of trees, a hatchet for the thicker tree trunks, a pickaxe for breaking the soil. It is possible that the art of mining had been discovered, which would mean that it pre-dated metallurgy. At Spiennes in Belgium Neolithic attempts to dig a mine have been observed, and also in the Aveyron where the rockface was attacked with stag-horn picks. At Grimes Graves in Suffolk, England, deep and long-worked flint mines have been discovered.

A knowledge of ceramics provided man with material more supple than stone, so that his fingers could at will fashion the most varied objects. Such pottery he decorated, and the ornaments themselves modified the shape and usage of the product. Thus the discovery of pottery

marks a new and richer phase of that toolmaking activity which we defined as contemporary with the emergence of man proper. It marks a further stage in the conquest of the earth.

The domestication of animals and agriculture

Man had domesticated the dog in Mesolithic times; he now began to exploit other animals. The facts are obscure, but it seems probable that the animals he domesticated were simply modifications of the wild animals he found in the neighbourhood.

In sites studied in Switzerland six domestic animals have been identified: the dog, the pig, the horse, the goat, the sheep and the cow. Hence, in order to feed himself Neolithic man no longer needed to rely on hunting. He had not by any means given it up; the deer would seem to have been his favourite game, but he also chased and fought the wild boar, the bear and the wolf.

But the most decisive aspect of the Neolithic revolution was man's new and close relationship with the earth: the discovery of agriculture.

Most of our information about the plants then cultivated comes from the finds made in the Swiss 'palafittes', or lake dwellings, built on piles. Cereal culture was already developed. The inhabitants of the lake villages, according to Sir John Lubbock, cultivated three varieties of wheat. They also possessed two kinds of barley and two kinds of millet. The oldest and most important of these crops were the six-eared barley and the small-

Stonehenge, Wiltshire, built during the Neolithic and Bronze Ages to serve some ritual purpose. It is doubtful whether popular associations with druidical rites have any foundation.

A reconstruction of prehistoric lake dwellings. By Evrard after A. de Mortillet. *Musée de l'Homme*

eared wheat. Millstones provided a means of grinding the grain into flour, and in the waters of the Swiss lakes certain specimens of bread made in this way have been found. They had various kinds of fruit: apples, pears, strawberries, sloes and hazel nuts. The vine was also known, though we do not know if Neolithic Man practised the art of making wine.

The dwelling and the village

In Neolithic times we observe the rudiments of our urban life in its humble beginnings — the village. Some of these villages were built not far from a river. For example, in France, on the plateau of Hautes-Bruyères near Villejuif, commanding a bend in the river Bièvre, the remains of inhabited huts containing tools and utensils have been found, and nearby hearths or kitchens with cinders, charcoal and calcined bones. Scattered through the mountainous parts of France many enclosures have been found, some of which go back to Neolithic times. Their ramparts are sometimes built of earth and sometimes of rough stone.

There is another type of habitation whose purpose has provoked much discussion. During the winter of 1853-54 the level of Lake Zurich fell and so revealed numerous posts driven into the bed of the lake. These were considered as evidence that villages were built on piles, and that local Neolithic men must have erected their dwellings in the lake itself. Recent studies have questioned this view. The so-called lacustrian villages were, it seems, actually built by the shores of the lakes during the course of a period of drought and the piles simply formed part of the wall-structure of the houses. The

rainy climate which prevailed in Western Europe at the close of the Neolithic Age caused the lake waters to rise and forced the inhabitants to abandon their houses, which were left embedded in the lake.

The construction of permanent dwellings brought about a regular intercourse between peoples, at first by land but also by river transport and possibly by sea.

Neolithic art and burial practices

Art was inferior at this period. The naturalistic art of the Late Palaeolithic Age had disappeared and given way to a more formalised style which was no doubt a reflection of new beliefs, and which seems to have quickly evolved into a kind of sign-writing.

The cult of the dead took on new forms. Trepanning was frequently practised — at times on living subjects — and also decapitation. Tombs are extremely varied, which indicates a development in the cult of the dead: real dwelling-places were built for the deceased. But Neolithic peoples sometimes also cremated their dead. Here, as with several peoples in historic times — the Etruscans, the Greeks and the Latins, for instance — we find two forms of funerary practice.

Another custom practised by Neolithic peoples was that of stripping the flesh from the dead before burial: the body, exposed to the air, rotted away and only the skeleton was placed in the tomb. In fact this funerary rite seems to have been performed even in earlier Palaeolithic times, and still persists among some modern primitive peoples. Very frequently the corpses were trussed up and the legs forcibly bent back.

Finally, it seems that Neolithic Man believed in a

The remains of piles that once supported prehistoric dwellings, near Neuchâtel, Switzerland. *Musée de l'Homme*

higher and more refined form of survival than his Palaeolithic predecessors. The dead are no longer provided with weapons and familiar objects, but only with ritual furnishings.

The emergence of man, with which prehistory begins, is the supreme manifestation of that major tendency of life to acquire through evolution an ever higher mental and physical development. When, after countless millennia, the human level was reached, man himself was to continue the movement. Historically there was a global genesis of the human race.

In considering this progress in man's development we seldom realise the importance of prehistoric times, or give true value to all that we owe to these remote ages. Yet the forward strides then made were immense. The discovery of fire and the invention of tools took place in the age of *Pithecanthropus*. A form of religious sentiment already stirred in the days of Neanderthal Man. Art was born during the latter part of the Old Stone Age. Finally, and perhaps most important of all, a stage of rudimentary society was reached, and savage hunters gradually became men who were able to live together and perform the collective tasks required by an agricultural way of life.

Submitted for so long to the harsh laws of an incessant struggle for existence, man had succeeded in freeing himself a little from the daily and precarious job of keeping alive. This enabled him at last to pause and reflect, to use his brain — the possible consequences were incalculable. We see Neolithic Man try first this, then that; and in the effort he sketched out the shape of the future. Our own history begins with his.

Below: an example of Neolithic spiral culture.

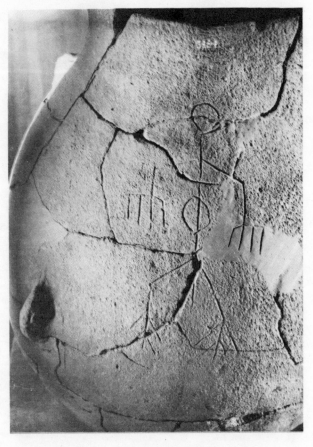

35

Above: a skeleton of a prehistoric woman dating from c. 3000 B.C. found buried in sand. The coffin in which it has now been placed is a reconstruction. *British Museum*

Below: a rock carving from Bohuslan, Sweden. *Claes Claesson*

Above: a prehistoric figurine carved in limestone. Senorbi. Musée de Cagliari. *Yan*

Left: a Neolithic baked clay figurine from Moravia. The many prehistoric statuettes of the female figure are interpreted as symbols of fertility cults.

Below: the Venus de Laussel, an Aurignacian rock carving found in an open dwelling. This figure was probably associated with a fertility cult. *Musée de l'Homme*

THE ANCIENT WORLD

Many hundreds of thousands of years were needed for prehistoric man to gain a firm foothold on the earth and acquire the material means to leave his still latent animal nature behind him. History opens at the moment when man found a means of transmitting to his neighbours or his descendants the fruit of his thought and labour — it begins with writing. With this discovery the rate of man's progress accelerates and true civilisation is born. It is the prime factor in the four millennia that comprise the period we call Ancient History. Everywhere, on every continent and especially in the Far East and central Asia, in the Near East and around the Mediterranean, civilisations and empires are born, confront each other, and perish. But in spite of these often bloody clashes — in which unbridled passions seem to sweep away all the first

conquests of reason — knowledge is exchanged, social contacts take place, different cultures mingle, and our own heritage is slowly forged. The horde becomes the clan, the clan the kingdom, or at other times the city. The beautiful, the good, the useful are discovered, sought after and promised. Out of the cringing animal terror of creatures challenged by forces of nature that they had not begun to understand the ancients arrive at the conception of a divine and unique Being.

Alexandrian Hellenism and the Roman Empire open the way to Christendom. But the journey was to be hazardous and the wrench so cruel that the Ancient World would founder and sink between the fourth and seventh centuries of our era. It was, however, from the events and philosophies of these early civilisations that the medieval world was fashioned. From their heterogeneous contributions evolved the drama of mankind that is still being played out in our own age.

EASTERN PEOPLES AND EMPIRES

It is not easy to determine the exact moment when history may be said to begin, that is, history in the sense of a catalogue of events, dated with some degree of accuracy and based on written records. The transition period between prehistory and history proper varies in length according to the peoples it deals with, and belongs to the realm of protohistory. Protohistory, drawing upon material furnished by archaeology, together with the study of legends and tradition, gives us a first glimpse of the manner in which the early peoples lived. The protohistory of different nations, of even the most celebrated nations, begins of course at different times. For example, at the opening of the second millennium before our era Twelfth Dynasty Egypt could already retrace many centuries of a civilised past, while continental Greece was still in the Neolithic Age. The curtain of history, then, rises on a night sky in which here and there a rare star feebly twinkles. Until the second millennium B.C. such stars were few. The first to shine with any brilliance was Egypt, followed, though very much later, by Mesopotamia. A few rather vague facts about China can be established towards the end of the third millennium. The rest of the world was still sunk in the Stygian gloom of prehistory from which it was slowly to emerge and burn bright.

CHAPTER ONE

THE FIRST
HISTORICAL PEOPLES

THIRD MILLENNIUM-1900 B.C.

The formation of Egyptian unity

In the course of Egyptian protohistory, which is known as pre-dynastic, it is believed that a constant tendency towards unity was at work. The nomes — primitive local communities — became federated into kingdoms which grew bigger and bigger. The kingdoms finally constituted two powerful and opposing forces: the valleys to the south and to the north the Delta. At last the South conquered the North. The only records we have to help us reconstruct this process are simple pictographs, and they do not tell us whether there were not periods when the process was arrested or even temporarily reversed. Possibly the communal civilisation which extended throughout the country in the fifth millennium is evidence of a political unification effected by the Northern Delta (Lower Egypt); but nothing is less certain.

On the other hand, the conquest of the Delta by the Valley kings of the South is an historical fact. The illustrated records which enable us to reconstruct this episode reveal that the struggle must have been long. The name of the first sovereign who was finally able to assume the double crown (the white crown of the Valley and the red crown of the Delta) was Narmer — and not Menes, whom the historian Manetho, writing the chronicles of the thirty Egyptian dynasties in about 280 B.C., listed as the first pharaoh. The date of this important event cannot be definitely fixed. Contrary to the view which was still recently accepted, the Egyptians could not at that time have known enough about astronomy to establish a calendar sufficiently accurate to place Narmer's assumption of the double crown in about 3064 B.C. The date can only be estimated by means of rare parallels with events in the neighbouring civilisations — which bring it forward to about 2850 B.C., a date still highly debatable, as are those of most early historical events.

The Thinite monarchy

Very little is known about the history of the first two dynasties, called Thinite after the city of This and believed to have been the capital of the first pharaohs. Even a list of the kings and the duration of their reigns is not agreed upon. Nevertheless we can be sure that from this time onwards Egypt had to defend herself against her neighbours, and that reciprocally she endeavoured to extend her own natural frontiers for reasons which were partly commercial and partly political. Towards the south Nubia was a natural field of expansion. In the west the incursions of Libyan nomads had frequently to be repelled. In the east especially other nomads were a constant menace to the Delta. In this direction the pharaohs were obliged to undertake numerous

Early pictographs are the only records that help to unravel the history of the first civilisations that sprang up in the Middle East. This tablet, a cast of one of the earliest, probably records some sort of accounts. Fourth millennium. *British Museum*

41

Top: gathering lilies. A Saite bas-relief. *Larousse*

expeditions which, from the reign of Smerkhet about 2690 B.C., brought them to the mines of the Sinai peninsula. We have practically no information of the internal history of this time: we do not know under what conditions the First Dynasty was replaced by the Second. The existence of the Second Dynasty was doubtless brief — from 2650 to 2585 B.C. approximately. It was troubled by political and religious disturbances which for a time brought the eclipse of the god Horus, the recognised protector of the monarchy, and the ascendancy of Set, a Delta divinity. This period may have followed a revolt among the Delta inhabitants and was short-lived.

More is known of the institutions of this period. The Thinite pharaohs were absolute sovereigns whose power derived from their divine nature. They were identified with the chief god of the country, Horus. But even a god had to take political realities into consideration: the union was still too recent to allow the Southern conquerors to ignore the susceptibilities of the defeated Delta. Everything connected with the administration and with the person of the king recalled the fundamental

The Delta's victory over the Valley brought the introduction of the double crown, or *pschent*, of Egypt, symbolising the unity of the two kingdoms. It is worn here centuries later by an androsphinx found at Camiros, Rhodes. *British Museum*

The pyramids of Cheops, the largest in the Giza group. Standing 480 feet high and made of more than two and a half million blocks of stone averaging two and a half tons each, its construction occupied 100,000 slaves for ten years. *Shell*

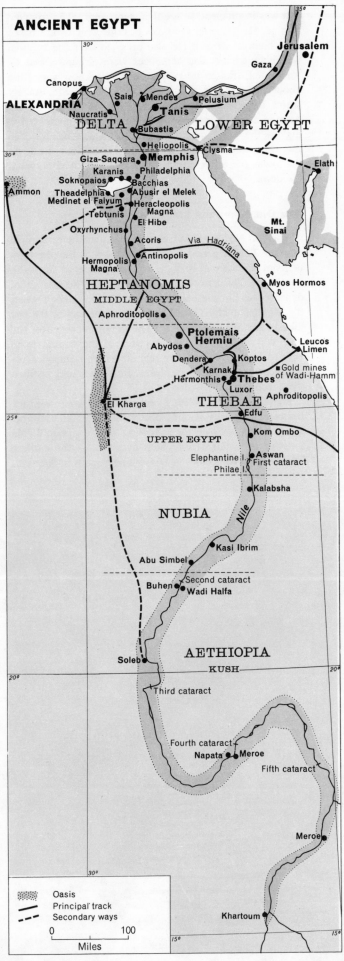

duality of the kingdom. Two goddesses, one from the North, one from the South, protected the monarchy and by a complex protocol were associated in each of the pharaoh's titles. During his coronation the king assumed the double crown. An essential element in the façade of the royal palace was the symbolic double-door.

Similarly, in the administration of the country, which the king personally directed at this period, each ministry — or 'house' — was divided into two sections. We know that there was a chancellery, a treasury and a record office. Doubtless there were other services, such as a war ministry, of which we know nothing. Administrative duties were already complex and must have required a body of functionaries and scribes who doubtless laid down the principles and rules of hieroglyphic writing. The unit of local government was still the traditional *nome*. Its chief, the nomarch, bore a revealing title: he was the *adj-mer*, the 'superintendent of canals'. His role was to see that the irrigating waters of the Nile were properly controlled and agricultural prosperity maintained. It was his duty to observe the level of the river and, if it was insufficient, to see that steps were taken to avoid famine. He gathered the taxes at rates which were based on a biennial census. He also presided over the tribunal whose judgments and sentences were circumscribed by traditional, though uncodified, law. We know very little about the customs which regulated family life; society seems to have been matriarchal. We can guess almost nothing about its organisation. Possibly the peasants living on the great domains, most of which belonged to the king, were reduced to a kind of serfdom, while in the towns the artisans and shopkeepers enjoyed personal freedom.

The Old Memphite kingdom

The Old Memphite kingdom is not much better known than the Thinite period which preceded it. It lasted roughly from 2585 to 2140 B.C., and according to Manetho covers the Third to the Sixth Dynasties. The change of dynasty was not the outcome of revolution, since Djoser, the founder of the Third Dynasty was the son of the last king of the Second Dynasty. The important event of the time was undoubtedly the transfer of the capital from This to Memphis. The new regime marks a considerable advance in every way over preceding times and justified the chronological division.

Djoser, the king, is less famous than his great minister Imhotep, who was at once doctor, architect and author. To Imhotep we owe the invention of the pyramid. He constructed a terraced or step pyramid — the earliest form of such edifices — in Djoser's necropolis at Saqqara.

The palette of Narmer, the first king to rule united Egypt. It commemorates the final unification of the two kingdoms.

The head of the Sphinx at Giza. Constructed during the reign of Chephren, it wears the uraeus, or cobra emblem, of the Pharaoh. The sphinx is a mythical animal with a lion's body and human head and is thought to represent the rising sun. *Shell*

Right: The scarab of Imhotep, the famous minister of Djoser.

Left: Imhotep, Djoser's talented minister and patron of medicine. It was Imhotep who built the first pyramid.

The Pyramid of Chephren at Giza seen from the Pyramid of Cheops, two famous monuments that immortalise the otherwise unrecorded history of two Fourth Dynasty pharaohs. *Viollet*

Below: the Step Pyramid at Saqqara. Designed by Imhotep to house the remains of Djoser, it was the first of many similar structures built by succeeding pharaohs. *Shell*

A wooden statue of a Memphite official and his wife. The old capital of This had been transferred to Memphis and the new regime was proving progressive in every way. It was a period of foreign conquest and commercial expansion. *Chevojon*

And that is all that we can say with certainty about the reign of Djoser. Nothing is known of his successors, and the dynasty itself could not have lasted more than half a century.

The Fourth Dynasty was founded by Sneferu in about 2530 B.C. Again we do not know what caused the change, but the personality of Sneferu is more clearly defined. We catch a glimpse of him as a mighty warrior, subduing Nubia in revolt, fighting the Libyans, chasing the Asiatics from the route which led to the Sinai peninsula. He was a great builder too; to him we owe the first perfected pyramid, that of Dahshur. It was certainly Sneferu who initiated the important artistic movement which flourished during the reigns of his successors, Cheops, Chephren and Mycerinos, who constructed the great pyramids of Giza. These celebrated monuments may with justice be said to have immortalised their builders, but that is all we know about them. The last kings of the Fourth Dynasty did not leave even pyramids behind them.

When, perhaps a little after 2400 B.C., the Fifth Dynasty replaced the Fourth we seem for the first time to perceive something of the cause of the dynastic change. According to legend the first three kings of the Fifth Dynasty were sons of Re, one having been high-priest to that god at his accession to the throne. They added to their royal names the title 'Son of Re'. There seems to be little doubt that the priests of Heliopolis — which was the centre of the cult of Re — had played an important part in the accession of the new dynasty which, in token of gratitude, was obliged to relinquish some of its absolute power, both material and moral. But, to judge from their monuments, these pharaohs were very pious and maintained harmonious relations with the priests. From the little we know about it, their foreign policy appears to have been enterprising.

The greatest pharaoh of the Sixth Dynasty — which was founded in about 2255 by Teti — was Phiops I, builder and conqueror. His general, Uni, re-opened the route to Sinai where the nomads, profiting from the long absence of the Egyptians, had installed themselves. It required no fewer than five military campaigns to dislodge them. Commercial relations with Phoenicia and Crete were strengthened. In this exchange Byblos and Ugarit were the chief trading centres. In the south, Phiops I and his sons finally succeeded in conquering the whole of Nubia. Also in the south, commerce was developed, taking the Red Sea route to the land of Punt — today, the coast of Somalia — where ivory and gold were procured.

The first intermediary period

These successes were to be the last triumphs of the Old Kingdom. By the end of the long reign of Phiops II — somewhere between 2202 and 2140 — complete decadence had set in. To understand the rapidity of this degeneration we must study the evolution of Egyptian institutions since the Third Dynasty.

Authority was still based on a belief in the king's divinity. This had been reinforced by the total unification of the administration. But the administration was no longer entirely in the hands of the pharaoh, because a sort of Grand Vizir had been created — the *tati* — who was the chief of all the ministries. The bureaucracy had grown

A brewer. Fifth Dynasty tomb statue. c. 2400 B.C. *Archiv für Kunst und Geschichte*

A Sumerian cylinder seal of the protohistoric period. Pre-3000
B.C. Soapstone. Uruk. *British Museum*

and was becoming all-encroaching. The scribes who composed it formed a select group in their 'House of Life' or
palace school. They were personages of importance, jealous of their functions and avid of titles and honours.
In the provinces the Nomarch — originally a simple magistrate who could be replaced at will — now held his office
for life, and finally became an hereditary governor. First
in practice and then in law, he formed a local ruling
family. In this way a true feudal system evolved, following a pattern similar in some respects to that seen during
the Middle Ages with the disintegration of Charlemagne's
Empire. The first family line of these hereditary magnates is known to have flourished from about 2240. By
the beginning of the twenty-second century the phenomenon was general.

This state of affairs was not dangerous as long as the
pharaoh was, without question, venerated as a god —
and so long as he remained richer than the greatest of
the new magnates. But during this same period religious
thought was developing in a manner which cast doubt
on the king's divine pre-eminence and finally brought
about a social revolution. The aid given to the usurping
pharaohs of the Fifth Dynasty by the priests of Heliopolis had to be paid for by a constant parade of piety,
by increasingly valuable gifts in land which impoverished
the treasury, and by privileges which diminished the absolute power of the monarchy. Again, in the primitive
beliefs of the Egyptians, only the king was destined to
become immortal. But the idea that the after-life in every
way resembled life on earth led the king to give a place
in his tomb to his servants. This place was at first a subordinate one, but it implied that domestic followers also
shared his paradise, where they continued to serve him

as they had done on earth. This charming privilege, originally reserved to the pharaoh, was soon usurped by the
feudal nobility; and, while the royal cemeteries grew less
sumptuous, the underground tombs of the great provincial nobles multiplied. These hypogeums were rich
with works of art and commemorative inscriptions, and
it is from them that we know more about the decadence
of the Old Kingdom than about the days of its splendour.

The Sixth Dynasty was thus divested of its authority
over the Nomarchs, of a large part of its landed property
and of its religious prestige. It was in addition paralysed
by the old age of Phiops II and fell into a state of anarchy.
The minor pharaohs of the Eighth Memphite Dynasty
(after a very short Seventh) were unable to restore order
and unity to the kingdom. In the South, the Nomarchs
of Koptos usurped the pharaoh's authority but were
unable to impose their own over all the Upper Valley,
where the loyalty of the princes of Thebes, among others,
was more than doubtful. It was a time of universal insecurity: the rich were sometimes driven from their estates
by the poor and terror reigned. The evils of lawlessness
and disorder were aggravated by foreign invasion, and
the nomads seized the opportunity afforded by relaxing
vigilance on the Eastern frontier and overran the Delta.

The restoration of unity

These excesses eventually brought their own cure,
but recovery was not immediate; the re-establishment

Colour plate: a winged goddess from the second gold shrine of
Tutankhamun. *Roger Wood*

48

of order came only very gradually. From about the year 2100 B.C. the active and energetic Theban family of the Antef supplanted the feeble rulers of Koptos and extended their power northwards down the Nile as far as Abydos. Towards the end of the century they were the undisputed masters of Upper Egypt. At about the same time the Nomarchs of Heracleopolis founded the Tenth Dynasty, restored the unity of the Middle Valley and succeeded in gaining control over the Asiatic nomads of the Delta. For a long time these tasks delayed further conflict between the two states. But as each began to feel more firmly established internally it became inevitable that one should attempt to put an end to the partition of Egypt and dominate the other. Fighting began again in 2000 B.C. and was for many years inconclusive. It took a more decisive turn with the advent of Mentuhotep of Thebes. Between 1960 and 1951 B.C. he pushed down the Nile in a vigorous military offensive from Abydos to Asyut and Hermopolis. The capture of Memphis brought about the downfall of the kings of Heracleopolis. A few years later Mentuhotep was master of the Delta and had reestablished the unity of the country. Egypt's second era of greatness had begun: the Middle Kingdom.

The first city-states of Mesopotamia

In Mesopotamia history was even slower to emerge from the shadows of prehistory than it had been in Egypt; nor can its arrival be marked by an arbitrary date such as the reign of Menes-Narmer. Whereas Egypt, surrounded by trackless desert, formed an almost closed community where unifying factors prevailed, Mesopotamia was composed of more diverse elements and had no natural frontiers. Its history, then, is more troubled, and its periods of unity rare. In such conditions it is not surprising that weak, geographically limited and ephemeral states have left us but few and scattered traces of their existence.

The first cities of Mesopotamia are found in the extreme south of the country, on land which had recently been won from the Persian Gulf by the silting-up of the Tigris and the Euphrates. There, in the shelter of the marshes and winding river banks several centres of population had sprung up. They formed little independent states, each with its own ruling dynasty. Chronological knowledge of these dynasties is uncertain. Excavations at Ur have revealed the only royal necropolis yet discovered and brought to light the oldest sovereign whose existence does not rely solely upon traditional lore: King Meskalamdug. They give us an idea of the civilisation of these remote times — some 2600 years before the birth of Christ. The series of records discovered at Lagash (Telloh) is richer, longer and more continuous.

In these city-states the true sovereign was the god. The temporal chief was only his representative, his lieutenant — his *patesi* or *ishshak*. Nothing was done without first consulting the god. Everything that happened was the result of his will. He was worshipped above all for his creative power. Hence he was always associated with a female companion — a prototype of the Semitic Ishtars. The divine couple saw to it that human beings, flocks and fields were fertile; or rather they brought about fertility by their own action. The duty of the faithful was first and foremost to be submissive, to know the divine will by means of divination and to conform to it by ritual

Pottery jars found at Byblos, believed to be the world's oldest city. Buried below the floors of dwellings, the jars contained the bodies of the dead who, according to ancient beliefs, were thus enabled to participate in family life. *Peter Fenwick*

Colour plate: The Bull of Minos, Cnossus. *Viollet*

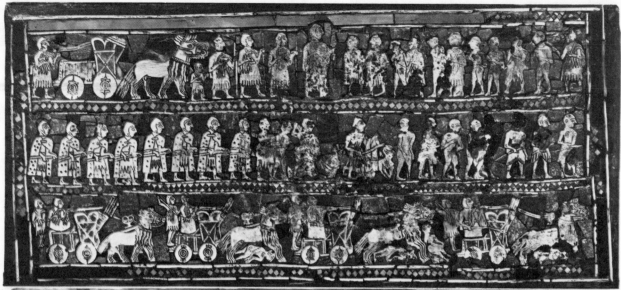

The Standard of Ur, a double-sided panel with inlaid mother-of-pearl figures set in a lapis lazuli mosaic background. On one side (*above*) horizontal registers show Sumerian battle scenes and the king inspecting captives; on the other (*below*) the king celebrates a victory with a parade of subject peoples. *Mansell*

exercise. In this way the goods of this world were obtained, for belief in a life beyond the grave where moral judgment played a part does not yet seem to have occurred to them. The practice of such a religion connotes the existence of a numerous clergy, and the temple was always the chief building in the city, the centre of a powerful organisation, enriched by sacrifices on which it levied a tithe, by pious bequests and by a share of the booty after victorious war. It played a part of the first importance in the government and economic life of the state.

The patesi owed his power in the first place to his position as chief of the priesthood. He governed with the support of an oriental court in which public functions were closely mingled with private service. He was also chief of the army, a vitally important role at a time when warfare was endemic. Fighting took place on foot and in four-wheeled chariots drawn by donkeys; the weapons were the axe and the javelin. The bow, was — curiously — still unknown. These facts are known to us from the panels discovered by the joint expedition of the British Museum and the University of Pennsylvania under Sir

Leonard Woolley. Known as the 'Standard of Ur' the panels provide us with an idea of what the men who made this civilisation were like. We call them Sumerians and they may have come from the Caucasus. They spoke a language of the agglutinative type, a system of word formation in which significant words or roots are added to each other, preserving something of the original meaning, yet together expressing something more. The Sumerians' cuneiform inscription is the earliest known form of record, at first chiselled in stone and later drawn on wet clay tablets.

From the scattering of isolated facts revealed by the rare records in our possession it is difficult to draw the broad outlines of a continuous history but it would seem that the main stream of events was composed of warfare in which cities fought each other for local hegemony. The victor imposed on the vanquished an ephemeral bondage which was never accepted and was continually menaced by the ambitions of others. It seems that the most powerful of these many rivals was the city of Ur. Ur had emerged from prehistory by about 2600 B.C. and the

The Stele of the Vultures, from Telloh (Lagash), records an agreement between victor and vanquished. One side depicts the god Ningirsu with Eannatum's enemies securely entangled in a net, while the other (*above*) shows the king at the head of his troops marching over their conquered foes. *Giraudon*

treasures found in the tombs of its rulers show that a civilisation of considerable wealth and brilliance had already been achieved. After the Flood — or rather the floods, for several inundations devastated different parts of the land of Sumer at different dates — it was Ur again which furnished the first of the historic dynasties — founded in about 2472 B.C. by Mesannipadda. At more or less the same time other royal lines were coming into existence, of which the best known is the ruling house of Lagash. Ur-nanshe ruled Lagash in about 2450 B.C. and was in turn succeeded by ten more patesi. The most renowned of these was the third, Enannatum, who at the beginning of the twenty-fourth century led several victorious expeditions against Ur, where he overthrew the First Dynasty. He also conquered Umma and celebrated the event by having the famous 'Stele of the Vultures' sculpted. After Enannatum the history of Lagash seems to have been much troubled by social conflict. Three high priests in succession seized power, oppressed the poorer townsmen and pillaged the temple treasury. The neighbouring Elamites took advantage of the confusion to make raids on Lagash territory. A reaction against priestly abuses came with Urukagina, a small official who towards 2250 B.C. seized power with the support of the people, deprived the priests of their inordinate privileges, and recognised the rights of the common people to own property.

But this social revolution, if it can be thus described, weakened the city which, it would seem, had already fallen under the control of Kish. Urukagina threw off the yoke of Kish only to clash with another external enemy. Lugalzaggisi, the patesi of Umma, Lagash's old rival, stormed the city and overthrew Urukagina. He destroyed Lagash, then seized Uruk and, in a series of successful campaigns, extended his power from the Persian Gulf to the Mediterranean, thus founding the first of the great Mesopotamian empires. Hardly had these conquests been concluded, towards 2225 B.C., than a new people entered the scene of history: the Semitic Akkadians. Under their king, Sargon, they defeated Lugalzaggisi and put an end to the first Sumerian kingdom.

A Sumerian limestone plaque showing tributes being offered to the king and (*bottom register*) sacrifices in the temple.

The ziggurat of Ur, with the ruins of the city in the foreground. Excavations gave historians a written record that could be dated as far back as 2600 B.C. The treasures found in the royal tombs suggest an early civilisation of wealth and brilliance.

The Stele of King Naram-sin found at Susa. An Akkadian trophy of victory over the Elamites. Above the king, who leads the attack, can be seen the emblems of his protecting divinities. Louvre.

The Empire of Sargon

The origin of the Semites is hypothetical. We cannot say for certain whether they came from Arabia Felix, from the Negeb or from the land of the Amorites in Upper Syria. At the dawn of history we find them installed in Upper Syria from which they spread southwards into Palestine. In the age of Sargon they were already firmly established in Babylonia. Sargon soon became a legendary figure, but our actual knowledge of him is slight. It seems that he originally came from Kish where he rose to power in about 2236 B.C. He then made the city of Akkad — the site of which is still unknown — his capital. His first exploit was the overthrow of Lugalzaggisi and the seizure of Uruk. Sargon then pushed towards the south and occupied all of Sumer as far as the Persian Gulf. He swung east towards Elam and took Susa, where he erected a monument to commemorate his victories. Further campaigns assured his mastery over the land of the Amorites and the shores of the Mediterranean. His power was felt as far north as Cappadocia where he protected the Semitic merchants who were established there from this time on.

This not inconsiderable empire was divided into smaller districts, so that the authority of the 'Son of the Palace', appointed by the king, might be constantly felt. The subject peoples had, however, not accepted submission passively. At the end of his reign Sargon had to put down a general insurrection and at one stage was actually besieged in his own capital. His successors exerted all their strength in efforts to maintain their contested authority. The first, Rimush (2180-2172?), and more especially the second, Naram-sin (2156-2120 B.C.), were eminently successful and 'continued to implant Semitic culture and influence in Sumer and Elam.

The Gutians

After the reign of Naram-sin, however, the Empire was endangered not only by instability within but by threats from beyond the border. Asiatic tribesmen, the Lullubians and the Gutians, raided the plains from highland strongholds in the Zagros mountains and Armenia. Naram-sin's successor, Shar-kali-sharri (2119-2095?) struggled without respite against enemies, both internal and external. Then total anarchy ensued, during which the Sumerian cities regained a precarious independence. Meanwhile the savage Gutians overran the Empire, founded a kingdom in the north of Assyria around Arapkha, ravaged Mesopotamia, pillaged towns and destroyed temples. Thus, in a brief hundred years, civilisation was put back by centuries.

Devastating as the Gutians' depredations were, they did not destroy the entire country. They were settled in the extreme north of Mesopotamia and their raids seldom penetrated as far south as Sumer. Towards the end of this period certain Sumerian cities regained their prosperity with some degree of independence. Such was the case of Lagash in the reign of Gudea and his son Urningirsu, about 2050 B.C. Gudea especially seems to have been a rich and powerful sovereign and a patron of the arts, which during his reign attained their classic perfection. Other cities also rose from their ruins and made preparations to throw off Gutian tyranny. In this struggle victory went finally to Uruk under its king, Utu-hegal. The last Gutian king, Terigan, was defeated in 2023 B.C. and taken prisoner. Thus the ill-fated deeds of his ancestors resulted only in the ruin of Akkad and the end of Semitic ascendancy. The way was prepared for a new and final phase of Sumerian power.

The Third Dynasty of Ur

The glorious reign of Utu-hegal was brief (2025-2019?) and Uruk did not profit from its newly won freedom. The fruits of victory fell to the ancient city of Ur where in 2038 B.C. Urnammu had founded a new dynasty, the Third. Leaving the task of destroying the last of the Gutians to the city of Uruk, Urnammu established an empire over Sumer and Elam which his son Shulgi (c. 2020-1973 B.C.) rounded off by seizing Uruk itself. Shulgi perfected the administrative system which his father had begun.

In order to ensure the unity of the wide territory over which their authority extended the kings of Ur built roads and canals, created a large police force to maintain public order, and sent out couriers and inspectors in every direction to make certain that their commands were obeyed. This administration involved considerable expense which was met by the temple treasury at Nippur, which also paid for the upkeep of the cult and of the court. The treasury received gifts from the king and from private individuals, and also collected the contributions that each city was forced to make over a period of years according

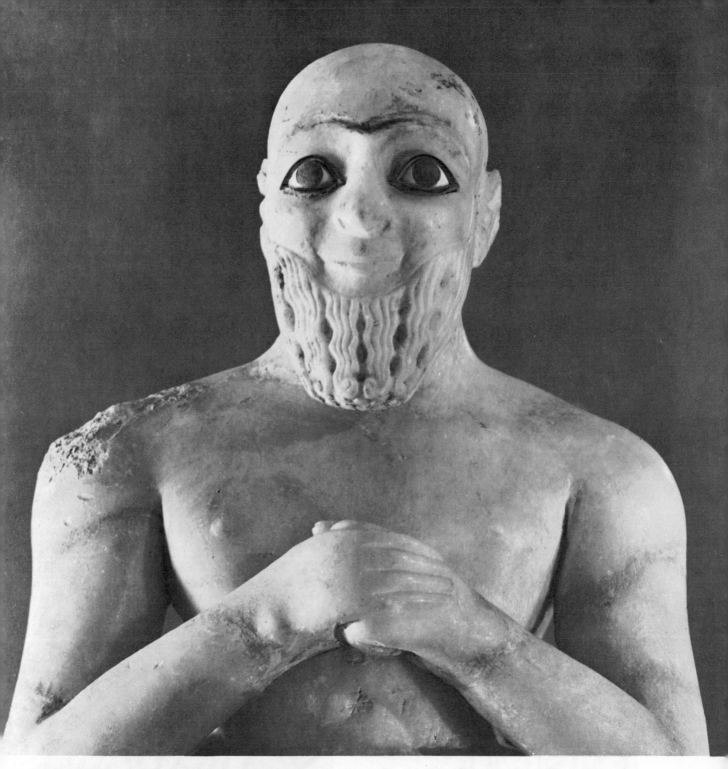

Ebih-il, governor of Mari. Sumerian. Third millennium. *Larousse*

Part of a Sumerian cylinder seal showing a worshipper led by a goddess (possibly a deified king of Ur). Ur III. c. 2050 B.C.

to its importance. Finally it made money loans at interest to groups and to individuals, and loans of cattle and seed. An organisation as complex as this could not function without an accurate system of book-keeping. Numerous accounts of such transactions have been excavated, all drafted on baked clay tablets by an army of scribes, and carefully verified by innumerable supervisors.

Nevertheless Ur could have known little peace either at home or abroad. In the days of Urnammu the semitisation of Sumer was far advanced and the process continued. The Sumerian ruling class, resembling an oligarchy, was supported with increasing resentment. Moreover, barbarian pressure on the frontiers did not relax. Though the Gutians had been decimated, their cousins the Lullubians and the Simurrians had constantly to be driven back into the Zagros mountains. In the west, the Amorites were equally restive. Against them Shulgi's grandson, Gimil-sin, constructed a kind of Great Wall which was no more effective there than such walls have been elsewhere.

It is therefore not surprising that the decline of Ur was rapid. After two short reigns in which an appearance of security was maintained, Ibi-sin struggled for twenty-five years against the inevitable. Abroad, he lost control over Elam, and the Amorites overran the Great Wall. At home anarchy broke out and the cities regained their freedom. Independent dynasties were founded at Larsa and Isin. In 1931 B.C. catastrophe was total: the Amorites and the Elamites invaded the country simultaneously and the Elamites reached Ur itself. Ibi-sin was led captive to Elam; the last Sumerian Empire had vanished.

During the period which we have just considered — broadly speaking, the third millennium before Christ— only Egypt and Mesopotamia have come on to the stage of history. For the rest of the world we still have no written records to enable us to describe, even briefly, the course of events. This does not, however, mean that no civilisation worthy of the name existed in other parts of the world. On the contrary, India, China and the Aegean world already offer remarkable evidence of such civilisations. Only the science of archaeology, however, can tell us anything about them.

The India of Harappa and of Mohenjo-daro

The first part of India to develop was that region of the lower Indus which is today a semi-desert. There, a civilisation seems to have been born which is related to that of Jamdat-Nasr in Mesopotamia. It is characterised by its polychrome pottery, the most numerous examples of which have been found on the site of Amri. Great strides were made in the period which followed: the chief centres of this progress were Harappa and Mohenjo-daro. The discovery in Mesopotamia of objects belonging to this civilisation means that it must have dated from the Second Dynasty of Ur and the Dynasty of Akkad, in other words, towards 2300 B.C. In this epoch the people of Harappa and Mohenjo-daro made use of copper and bronze, wove cotton, made pottery with a potter's wheel and built large commercial cities. They had a system of writing which has not yet been deciphered. This civilisation which, with variations, extended over the entire basin of the Indus and as far as Baluchistan, disappeared at the beginning of the second millennium, destroyed either by the invasion of a new people or by lack of water as the climate altered. But it laid the foundations of subsequent Hindu India.

Primitive China

What we know of China in the third millennium is derived from legends which were later perpetuated in writing. According to the tradition thus preserved, the first

Cylinder seals from Mohenjo-daro; 2400-2000 B.C. Although more than 1200 of these have been found, certain stock themes recur, the commonest being the owner's name and the symbol of a god whose favour he hoped for. The elephant, tiger and rhinoceros are found, as well as the bull and unicorn. All are animals that figure in later Hindu mythology. *British Museum*

imperial dynasty, the Hia dynasty, was founded in 2205 or — and this is more likely — in 1989 B.C. The period before this is filled with tales of mythical heroes: the Three Kings and after them the Five Emperors, the last of whom was Yu the Great, founder of the Hia dynasty. To them was attributed the invention of hieroglyphic writing, the discovery of cereals, the drainage of the Hwang-ho valley and the dykes which controlled the river's flow. These stories must be interpreted with great caution. During all this period the Chinese people, who still occupied only the regions of the north-east between Loyang and Kaifong, remained in the Neolithic Age.

The first civilisations of the Eastern Mediterranean

At the other extremity of the then civilised world, in the eastern basin of the Mediterranean, human life was already assuming a new aspect; though here, too, the period of history proper was yet to come. As in China, all we have are legends handed down from very remote times, and archaeology is our sole source of reliable information. The geographical conditions prevailing in this part of the world, with its myriad islands and sharply indented coastline, are unknown, a circumstance which helps to explain the complexity and diversity of the facts available. These regions seem to have been peopled at a fairly late date: no certain traces of Palaeolithic culture have been discovered. At the beginning of the third millennium there were two active centres of Neolithic culture: in the north, Thessaly and its southern dependencies; in the south, Cyprus and Crete. Between these centres the Cyclades and the Asiatic coast appear to have been inactive. Shortly after 3000 B.C. these backward zones become more animated. In the Cyclades, the islands of Syros and Melos especially produced ceramics of originality, decorated with motifs inspired by daily life, and also marble statuary. A striking aspect of this work is the emphasis given to commercial and seafaring activities. On such activities the fortunes of Troy were later founded. Troy, though it had no port, was favoured in its situation near the Hellespont: it commanded the straits. Thracian tribes undoubtedly colonised the site in about 2500 B.C. By 2300 it was a rich and powerful fortified city, and its civilising influence was felt as far as the river Sangarius and in Pisidia. Its temporary ruin was probably caused by the initial wave of Indo-Europeans as they poured into Asia Minor.

These developments could not have been without effect on the neighbouring regions, though Thessaly and Cyprus remained obstinately faithful to their Neolithic traditions. In the south of the Hellenic peninsula, however, in Boeotia, in the Peloponnesus and especially in Crete the new influences made themselves felt. In Crete metal appeared in about 2500 B.C. and at once gave rise to artistic productions of great beauty which were inspired by the islands' and Eastern influences and were an original synthesis of both. The chief characteristics of this charming art are found in the red and black *flammée* pottery of Vassiliki in Thessaly and in the intaglios which were used for seals; they reveal a taste for colour, an exuberance of design and an insistence on perfection of detail. These qualities are already the hallmark of Minoan civilisation at its greatest. But before reaching that point the peoples of the Eastern Mediterranean were to meet with many setbacks.

The hero Gilgamesh, holding a lion. Said to have been an early king of Erech, his adventures finally took the form of a narrative drawing on diverse and complex sources. *Bulloz*

CHAPTER TWO

THE EARLY CIVILISATIONS

OF THE EAST

1900-1200 B.C.

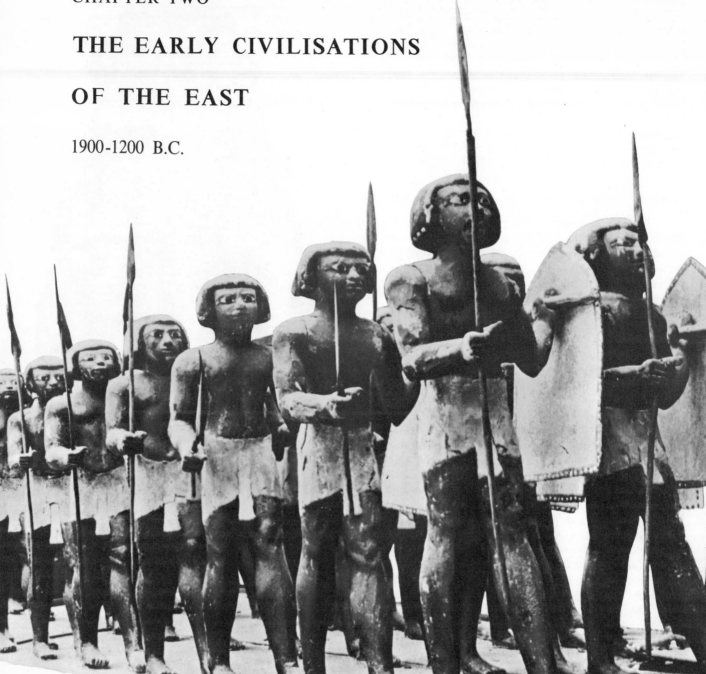

Spearmen of Asyut. *Boucher*

The Indo-Europeans before the invasions

In the history of the ancient East the turn of the third to the second millennium is marked by the invasion of a new group of peoples who were destined to continue to dominate the history of the world until our own days: the Indo-Europeans. Before their actual appearance on the stage of history almost everything about them is obscure and enigmatic. The only fact that is certain is that they spoke languages which were derived from a single parent tongue of which no trace now remains. We cannot say whether they descended from a common racial stock; it seems, in fact, more probable that they did not. Nor do we know where they came from; the theories that have been advanced fluctuate between Scandinavia and the steppes of Asia. Certain linguistic peculiarities lead us to believe that before their dispersion they were nomadic pastoral folk who travelled in horse-drawn wagons and from time to time settled long enough to sow and reap an occasional harvest. Some scholars have believed that there is evidence of a class system among the early Indo-Europeans which divided them into three social castes: priests, warriors and peasants. A pantheon of their gods has been reconstructed and even a common mythology. But positive proof of such hypotheses is still lacking. The nature of the civilisation is unknown.

56

Uncertainty is equally great in all that concerns the itinerary, the chronology and the causes of their migrations. Their itinerary obviously depends on their supposed origin. The date of their departure cannot be fixed, neither can we say at what moment they make their first appearance, for the nature of certain peoples who may have been their advance-guard is disputed. Such are the Louwites of central Anatolia and the Dimini who founded a civilisation in Thessaly. If it is agreed that these tribes formed the first wave of Indo-European peoples, then their appearance may be said to date from the middle of the third millennium. Certainly by the end of the millennium Indo-Europeans were firmly established in Asia Minor, in the great bend of the river Halys and on the Iranian plateau. In Europe they had penetrated the Balkan peninsula as far as Boeotia, reached the plains of southern Russia and pushed up the Danube valley perhaps as far as Bavaria. This considerable expansion was due in part to the speed and mobility given them by the horse, for they were the first to domesticate it. Also, they possessed a formidable weapon: a war-axe which their skill in metallurgy, inherited perhaps from Asiatic peoples, enabled them to cast in bronze. And in addition, their organisation aided them: a society dominated by a nomad aristocracy which ruled a subjugated and chiefly pastoral population. In contrast to these characteristics common to them all there were marked cultural differences between one group of these Indo-Europeans and another, a result of the varying influence of the different peoples they had come in contact with in the course of their long migrations.

Middle Kingdom Egypt

The effect of the Indo-European invasion on the civilised Near East was felt only in successive stages. Egypt, farthest from their centre of dispersion, was the last to be affected. The history of the Middle Kingdom is uninfluenced by the Indo-European invasions save in its final days. Towards 1950 B.C. Mentuhotep II had succeeded in reuniting the country. The last years of his reign, and the reigns of his two obscure successors, were occupied with warfare on the eastern frontiers of the Delta with the object of repelling or keeping in check the nomad tribes which had been attracted by prospects of pillage during the troubles which beset the 'First Intermediary Period'. But this indispensable work did not earn the dynasty permanent ascendancy. Towards 1890 B.C. it was overthrown and another dynasty assumed power. This was the Twelfth, founded by Ammenemes I, who was also of Theban origin. Peace·had been sufficiently restored in the north for Ammenemes to make his headquarters at Ittaouy, so that the capital city was again at the junction of the two parts of the country.

The restoration of unity did not efface all traces of past disorder. It is true that the pharaohs of the Twelfth Dynasty revived the traditions of the Old Kingdom and again set up a vast centralised and specialised administration. At its head a Prime Minister was in charge of foreign affairs, of the police and of the administration of justice. Other ministers, of whom the principal was the minister of finance, regulated the country's business and employed an army of civil servants.

Affairs of outstanding importance were dealt with by

Khertihotep, one of the vast hierarchy of zealous and able servants who ensured the sound administration of the pharaohs. Middle Kingdom. *Larousse*

A superintendent of public granaries. Mural in tempera from Thebes. c. 1500-1400 B.C.

57

the thirty 'Grandees of the South' who were at the same time judges of the Supreme Court and inspectors-general of local administration, which continued to be entrusted to the nomarchs.

The nature of the royal power, however, still bore the marks of the 'social revolution' which had disturbed the last years of the Old Kingdom. It proved politically impossible to suppress the hereditary rights of the nomarchs, who had quite possibly helped Ammenemes I to gain the throne. But at all events the nomarch, before he succeeded to his title, had to receive his investiture from the royal hand. He had to pay into the royal treasury the taxes he gathered and, in case of war, raise the contingents which the law prescribed. He also commanded such troops, but he commanded them in the king's name. But it is certain that the pharaohs did not rest until they had suppressed these dangerous feudal practices, and it would seem that they finally succeeded in doing so in the reign of Sesostris III, about 1778-1740 B.C.

Though the pharaohs thus gradually eliminated one of the chief evils which had contributed to the decay of the Old Kingdom, their endeavours to regain power were less successful in the field of religion. They were never able to recover the awe-inspiring prestige of their predecessors. Probably there was no insurmountable difficulty in imposing the cult of the Theban god Amun on the entire country, especially since Amun was merged and

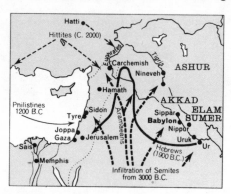

The Middle East in the third and second millennia B.C.

identified with the ancient dynastic divinity Re, but the exclusively royal privilege of immortality had vanished. From now on every Egyptian was assured of his own personal survival after death, and his faith was justified by the religion of Osiris, which, during the Middle Kingdom, captured the imagination of all Egypt and was accepted by the kings themselves.

This religious revolution had its social consequences as well. Equality in the after-life upset the class barriers of life on earth. Class distinctions certainly continued to exist, but they were only a transitory phase of material possessions. As far as the law was concerned, every Egyptian enjoyed equality. All forms of employment were open to him. The peasant was no longer a serf and had become the proprietor of his land. The artisan had always been free, but the old corporate regulations governing working conditions had been forgotten. He followed the trade of his choice and the trade secrets of former days were no longer kept. Even foreigners seem to have been protected by legal statute from arbitrary mistreatment.

In spite of these profound changes, the pharaohs of the Twelfth Dynasty still commanded the means to rival their

Harpocrates, a form of Horus the sun god, and usually depicted finger in mouth, as a symbol of childhood. He was later adopted by the Greeks and Romans who, mistaking the gesture, made him god of silence. *Archiv für Kunst und Geschichte*

The identification of Amun with the ancient dynastic divinity Re allowed the cult of the new god to be imposed rapidly throughout the Middle Kingdom. Here, a painting from Abd-el-Qurna shows the building of a temple dedicated to him.

predecessors both in the arts of warfare and in those of civilisation. Under the Twelfth Dynasty military and commercial expansion took on a new lease of life. It was backed by the creation of a permanent army. The weight of this force was thrown mainly against Nubia, which was penetrated by Sesostris I and finally annexed by Sesostris III. Nubia was controlled by powerful fortresses, colonised by commercial interests and taught the religion of Egypt. It served as a base for merchant ventures into the Sudan and Ethiopia from which the Egyptian trader brought back ivory, gold and black slaves. To the east of the Delta the policy of the pharaohs was

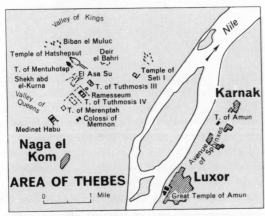

primarily defensive. In about 1865 B.C. Ammenemes I had had the 'Wall of the Prince' erected against the Asiatic nomads. But it was sometimes necessary to pursue these turbulent marauders to their lair, and the expeditions to Canaan of Sesostris I and of Sesostris II seem to have been punitive rather than for the purpose of conquest. In any case they assured — as did the presence of an Egyptian fleet in the eastern Mediterranean — the continuance of Egyptian commercial relations with Byblos, Crete, Cilicia and Cyprus. Escorted caravans regularly set out for the Sinai peninsula and returned with the gold and precious stones extracted there by the colonies of Egyptian miners.

The Twelfth Dynasty was a period of great brilliance. The sculpture which has been preserved from this time is executed with admirable vigour; the painting — such as that at Beni Hasan — is particularly celebrated for its realism and clear, vivid drawing. Perhaps the outstandingly original contribution of the period was the appearance of a literature which in prose as well as in verse achieved classical perfection. The story or the tale, as we might expect in an Eastern people, was the most popular form; but certain religious poems are not inferior to the greatest and most profound that oriental literature has produced.

Mesopotamia at the time of Hammurabi

At much the same period another brilliant civilisation was flourishing in Mesopotamia. The rulers of Isin and of Larsa, who were responsible for the downfall of the Third Dynasty of Ur, had at once begun to quarrel between themselves after their victory. Their fruitless rivalry encouraged the infiltration of Semitic elements who came from the land of the Amorites in the west of Mesopotamia. The new-comers founded Babylon. They soon established their own independence and were not long in making a bid for supremacy. Towards 1813 B.C. Sumuabum founded the first Babylonian dynasty, which is known as the Amorite dynasty, and immediately made

Bast (Ubasti), one of the many feline goddesses of ancient Egypt; she is sometimes represented as lion-headed and sometimes as a cat-headed woman. *Archiv für Kunst und Geschlichte*

Apis, the image of the soul of Osiris. *Archiv für Kunst und Geschichte*

Though Egyptian in form, the Hyksos sphinx at Tanis is a reminder of Asiatic invaders who dominated Egypt for a century.
Audrain-Samivel

war on his neighbours. The struggle was long and resistance stubborn, and the Babylonians imposed their will only after a complicated series of alliances broken as soon as made. The credit of gathering together the entire Land of the Two Rivers under a single sceptre finally fell to the most illustrious of the Babylonian sovereigns, Hammurabi (1711-1669 B.C.), though not without a lengthy struggle with his last rival, Rim-sin of Larsa, who was driven from his capital only in 1683.

The fame of Hammurabi rests on the establishment of an efficient government at Babylon. From this point on until the Christian era it was to be the political and intellectual centre of western Asia. Hammurabi's accomplishments in the fields of legislation and administration are well known to us not only from his famous Code but also from the correspondence which he maintained with his provincial governors. Many of the letters he wrote — incised with a stylus on baked clay tablets — have been found in the archives of the cities he conquered, Larsa and Mari among others. The nature of the royal power had evidently evolved since the days of the Sumerian kings. Though Hammurabi still considered that he derived his power from the god, he believed he participated in their divinity. Oaths were sworn in his name. He was the 'God of Kings'. His theocratic power was justified, moreover, by the service he rendered: he saw to it that justice prevailed, he protected the weak and 'made men's flesh content' by assuring the country's economic prosperity.

In order that this programme could be properly carried out a large body of functionaries was divided between the palace, where the specialised branches of the administration were centred, and the provinces, where the governors were obliged to give frequent account of their activities and were supervised by inspectors. The towns administered themselves through a council of notables who elected a *rabianum*, a kind of mayor. State officials, and in particular the army, were supported by grants of land. These grants were inalienable and for life, and they often became hereditary. Expenses, necessarily great, were met partly by the revenues of the royal domain, the lands of which were sub-let to small-holders or supported state-controlled flocks, and partly by taxes gathered in kind or in silver by an army of tax-collectors.

We see, in examining the Code of Hammurabi, that his authority extended over a very highly organised society. Social relationships were minutely regulated by laws in which there was a curious mingling of ancient taboo and traditional custom — such as trial by ordeal — and of modern practices like written contracts and loans at interest. For, though life was essentially agricultural, capital and its needs were beginning to appear. Commerce by water and by caravan prospered. Merchants formed themselves into companies and established 'branch offices'. Banking itself was not unknown and loans with security at high rates of interest were in current usage.

The development of letters was no less remarkable. The frequent employment of written contracts implies a reasonably widespread knowledge of writing. Scribes appear to have been numerous and it was they who gave form to the liturgy of the period and wrote down what was known to their contemporaries of mathematics. Some of their works, inspired by mythology, attained an epic quality, such as the tale of the adventures of Gilgamesh. But, poets though they were, they did not forget their legal background, and they were eager to conserve the greatest possible number of ancient records. These, carefully indexed and classified, form the first libraries — which Hammurabi, himself a poet and man of letters, seems to have supported and encouraged. Compared with the splendours achieved in literature, the plastic arts were

60

A bearded god before a sacred tree. Assyrian.

Winged genius with eagle's head. From the Palace of Sargon II, Khorsabad.

undistinguished. Dominated by Sumerian traditions, no national school of art arose in an otherwise notable age.

Primitive Assyria

In the north of Mesopotamia at this time, though in rather obscure circumstances, an empire was born which was destined to play an important part in history: Assyria. The Assyrians were of Semitic origin, and their oldest capital was Assur which seems to have achieved its complete independence relatively late. In the days of the Third Dynasty of Ur Sumerian prefects governed the country. But even then Assyrian expansion was foreshadowed by the existence of a very active colony of its merchants in Cappadocia. After the fall of Ur, Assur took advantage of the ensuing anarchy to throw off Sumerian domination, and Ilu-shuma, a contemporary of Sumu-abum, prided himself on having imposed his authority on Akkad. Towards 1775 B.C. one of his successors, Sargon I, ruled over the colony of Cappadocia. It was with Shamsi-Adad I (1726-1694 B.C.) that this first Assyrian empire acquired its greatest extension, reaching westwards to the Mediterranean. But it did not recover from the onslaught of Hammurabi, and it seems that after Hammurabi took Mari in 1679 B.C. the whole of Assyria was reduced to a state of vassalage — which would explain the dynastic troubles of 1650 B.C. in which the last descendant of Shamsi-Adad fell.

Crete of the first palaces

Crete at this time was making remarkable and original contributions to civilisation. The immediate cause was doubtless a concentration of political power in certain centres, notably Cnossus, Mallia and — perhaps a little

The Code of Hammurabi. Inscribed with the famous codification of the law, the stele also shows the god of justice, Shamash, dictating his laws to Hammurabi. Black diorite. Taken from Babylon to Susa by Elamite invaders.

A relief from the Temple of Ramesses at Medinet Habu showing the Pharaoh hunting. New Empire. *Audrain-Samivel*

A detail from Queen Hatshepsut's obelisk. Sister and queen of Tuthmosis II, she usurped power on his death and ruled in place of Tuthmosis III — the nominal Pharaoh. Her policy of deliberate pacifism weakened Egypt's power in Asia. *Viollet*

later — Phaestus. The rulers of these towns displayed their recently acquired fortunes by erecting palaces — singular constructions in which the most striking feature was a lack of unity in their conception. They were, rather, a capricious grouping of halls and chambers around a huge central court. In them we find private chapels, great cellars with their jars for provisions, and rooms where the archives were kept. These records consist of tablets covered with a hieroglyphic script which scholars have so far been unable to decipher. The royal builders of these palaces ruled over a seafaring population which was so confident in the protective power of its fleet that fortifications were considered unnecessary. Crete was famous for the work of its goldsmiths and its engravers, and it excelled in the production of ceramics. Its exports went everywhere, but especially to Cyprus, Ugarit and Byblos, from which centres of trade Cretan products were re-exported and ultimately reached Egypt.

The Indo-European invasions

During the course of the eighteenth and seventeenth centuries B.C. the brilliant civilisations of the Aegean world were menaced by incursions of restless peoples pushing in from the East. Most of the newcomers belonged to peoples which had long been settled in the East. But all of them had felt the rude impulsion of the most recent invaders, the Indo-Europeans. We have seen the Indo-Europeans first arrive at the beginning of the second millennium. At this time the civilisation known as Minyan arose in Boeotia and in the Peloponnesus. There was a noticeable lowering in the standard of culture, which linguistic considerations lead us to attribute to an invasion of the first branch of the Greek peoples, presumably the Ionians. These barbarians were incapable of appreciating the subtleties of Cretan products and, at least at first, contact between the island of Crete and the Greek mainland was almost entirely broken off. Little by little it was renewed in the nineteenth century through the intermediacy of Argolis, but towards 1700 B.C. the arrival of a fresh wave of Greek barbarians, the Achaeans, drove both the newly settled and the older populations southwards. One of these retreating bands took possession of Crete and utterly destroyed the first palaces. The disaster was, as we shall see, only temporary. East of Crete the site of Troy also bears marks of the invaders.

The destruction of the second town of Troy in about 2150 B.C. came perhaps with the arrival of the Ionians, and that of the third town, two hundred years later, was a result of Achaean aggression.

It was in Asia that the coming of the Indo-Europeans had the gravest repercussions. In about 2000 B.C. it seems that the first bands made their appearance in Anatolia and in Persia. We do not know whether their arrival took the form of a violent invasion or a slow infiltration. In Cappadocia the colony of Assyrian merchants prospered until the beginning of the eighteenth century. They disappeared towards 1760 B.C. and the region was submitted to the rule of a new people, the Hittites. The Hittites, as the structure of their language demonstrates, were indisputably Indo-Europeans, but their vocabulary seems to have been borrowed from the indigenous population. This fact, in conjunction with other evidence, suggests that the true Hittites, who alone were Indo-Europeans,

formed a ruling class which subjugated the native population and partially imposed upon it their own language and religion. At this period there was probably nothing which could be described as a unified kingdom, but rather a loose confederation of principalities grouped around the most powerful, Khattusha or Boghazkoy. A similar state of affairs seems to have existed in the mountains of Zagros on the Persian border, where the Kassites were installed. The first known Kassite king, Gandash, reigned from about 1661 to 1646 B.C., but he was not the first of his line.

These new peoples were a danger to the Babylonian Empire from the time of Hammurabi's death. During the reign of Hammurabi's successor, Samsuiluna (1668-1631 B.C.), an initial Kassite invasion was repelled, but it incited the people who were subject to Babylon to revolt. A certain Rim-sin proclaimed himself king of Larsa and twenty-six other princes are said to have followed his insurrectionary example. Samsuiluna overcame them, as

The cartouche of the Pharaoh Amenhotep III (1411-1375 B.C.) from his temple at Thebes. *Shell*

he had the Kassites, at the battle of Kish in 1655 B.C. But he was unable to put down the Sumerians, who rose under the leadership of Ilima-ilum, founder of a second Babylonian dynasty, which took its name from the swamp lands of Lower Chaldea that had provided the rebels with an impenetrable stronghold.

Ilima-ilum's successors were unable to prevent the Kassite king Agum I (1645-1624 B.C.) from establishing himself in the plain. But it was the Hittites who eventually dealt Babylon the fatal blow. Since the days of the princes Pitnanash and Anittash, who had completed the subjugation of Cappadocia, the Hittites had extended their territory towards Pontus, Armenia and Cilicia and disputed upper Syria with another Indo-European power, the kingdom of Mitanni which was founded around 1600. Towards 1550 B.C. the Hittites under Khattushilish I had seized upper Syria and afterwards lost it. The exploits of their new king, Murshilish 1 (1540?-1500?), were more glorious. Towards 1515 B.C., in a sudden and furious assault, he led them against Mesopotamia, seized Babylon, which he sacked, and dethroned the last of Hammurabi's successors. Very likely the purpose of the expedition was simply plunder, for he withdrew immediately and the real beneficiaries of his victory were the Kassites, who forthwith took possession of the city and founded a Third Dynasty which was to endure for centuries.

63

The end of the Middle Kingdom: the Hyksos

Egypt, too, at last felt the impact of the Indo-European migrations. The ground had already been well softened and prepared for invasion by the internal decadence of the Twelfth Dynasty. The successors of Sesostris III seem to have been weak sovereigns. Again the feudal nobility had emancipated itself and from 1721 B.C. a local dynasty had assumed the royal title at Avaris. The disintegration spread rapidly. The Twelfth Dynasty disappeared ingloriously in about 1690 B.C. and gave way to two Theban dynasties, the Thirteenth and Fourteenth, which were successful in maintaining the unity of the country only for short intervals. To add to the general confusion the Asiatic nomads, though their efforts to penetrate the Delta in force had been vigorously repelled, had been permitted to enter Egypt when they arrived in small, peaceful groups. It was during one of these infiltrations, possibly between 1900 and 1800 B.C., that Abraham visited Egypt, as the Bible relates. Thus the Delta contained foreign enclaves which were only partially assimilated.

Hittite gods. *Above:* Early Bronze Age, from Alaca Huyuk c. 3000 B.C. *Below:* a double idol made of gold. Middle Bronze Age c. 2000 B.C. *Right:* a disc-shaped idol of the third millennium, with arm stumps and stem neck. *Salchow*

An impressive statue of Ramesses II (1290-1224 B.C.) one of the most powerful rulers of the Nineteenth Dynasty. *Roger Wood*

A painted intaglio relief on limestone showing prisoners taken by Ramesses II during an uprising. From the Temple of Ptah, Memphis. Egypt. Nineteenth Dynasty. *Roger Wood*

The sun chariot of Trundholm, Denmark. c. 1000 B.C. *Danish National Museum*

These groups were easily kept under control as long as the central government was firm; if it faltered they were more than willing to welcome invaders of their own race. At the beginning of the seventeenth century B.C. Syria and Canaan were in a state of effervescence. The installation of the Hittites in Cappadocia and the spread of their empire towards upper Syria sent bands of natives — or of Semites mixed with Indo-Europeans and Aegeans — scurrying southwards. These fugitive bands were hemmed in between the sea and the desert, and overflowed into the Delta. They crossed the frontier en masse towards 1650 B.C.

These invaders were the Hyksos, and Egypt was left with bitter memories of them. It seems, however, that their conquest of the country took place without their striking a blow. Their chiefs made every effort to adopt the culture they found in Egypt; yet they remained outsiders and were accused of all manner of crimes. In the north-east of the Delta, in the neighbourhood of Avaris, the Hyksos were particularly numerous, though some of their rulers, such as Apophis, who protected the Hebrew Joseph, managed towards 1630 to extend Hyksos sovereignty southwards up the Nile valley. But the Hyksos were unable to prevent Thebes from once again leading the national movement of resistance. Towards 1625 B.C. a Theban prince founded the Seventeenth Dynasty. For many years the struggle for liberation was fruitless, but in 1565 B.C. Kamose (1566-1555) seized Hermopolis, a grave setback for the Hyksos intruders. Five years later the co-regent, Amosis, delivered the decisive blow by taking Avaris. Now the sole king, Amosis founded the Eighteenth Dynasty in 1555 B.C.

Egyptian conquests in Asia under the New Empire

With the accession of Amosis a complete change in foreign policy took place. Until then Egypt's chief preoccupation had been to protect herself against invasion; she now became imperialist. It is true that the object was primarily defensive: to create a buffer zone beyond the frontiers of the Delta. But conquest breeds conquest and since two warlike states existed in Asia — the Mitanni and the Hittite kingdoms — the fifteenth century was to witness the opening of a long phase of warfare. For the first time in history we perceive that the contacts between nations have ceased to be sporadic and become continuous; international relations have been created. Not only do armies face each other in battle, but diplomacy develops, diplomacy employing skill and finesse, and thinking in terms of the future. More, we find increasing peaceful exchanges in economic and spiritual fields.

In order to understand the complexity of Egyptian foreign affairs we must briefly sketch the political situation in the Middle East towards the end of the sixteenth century. On the eastern frontier of the Delta, Palestine and Syria were nominally ruled by Babylon. In fact the Hyksos, driven from Egypt, had thrown the Babylonians into such a state of confusion that the central government was incapable of making its authority respected in the provinces. Until its downfall in 1158 B.C. the Kassite dynasty played an ineffectual role. Admittedly, in about 1430 B.C. it had subdued Sumer. But Assyria remained independent of Babylon, even though the new dynasty which arose in Assyria after the troubles of 1648 B.C. never succeeded in restoring the brilliance achieved by Shamsi-Adad I, and indeed foundered during the new convulsions of 1429 B.C. or thereabouts.

The two most important contemporary powers were the Mitanni and the Hittite kingdoms. The Hittite state had not yet attained complete stability, and its power was displayed in fits and starts. The successors of Murshilish I, who was undoubtedly assassinated, lost the territory he had conquered, and for half a century they are enveloped in obscurity. In about 1460 B.C. a new dynasty took over and Hittite power again began to expand, chiefly at the expense of Mitanni. Mitanni, straddling the upper Euphrates and northern Syria, had long since achieved maturity. Its sovereigns were important figures. Shaushshatar (c. 1450-1420 B.C.) was able to repulse the Hittite incursions, to impose his will on Assyria, and at the same time prove himself a worthy adversary of the great Pharaoh Tuthmosis III.

The struggle with Mitanni

Mitanni was the first obstruction imperialist Egypt was to come up against. Though Amosis, towards the end of his reign, had led an expedition as far as the Dead Sea, his chief ambition seems to have been to bring Nubia back into the Egyptian orbit. After him, Amenhotep I (c. 1542-1526 B.C.) then Tuthmosis I (c. 1525-1512 B.C.) undertook several campaigns in Palestine, in Syria, and as far as the Euphrates without, however, gaining permanent control of the invaded territory. As soon as the Egyptian armies returned to their bases revolts would immediately break out, revolts chiefly fomented by the Mitanni. Even the partial success which Amenhotep and Tuthmosis attained was gravely compromised by the voluntarily pacifist policy of Queen Hatshepsut (1490-1475 B.C.). The real founder of the Empire was Tuthmosis III (c. 1475-1435 B.C.) who installed permanent garrisons in the conquered towns, saw that the local governors were supervised by Egyptian officers, and fortified strategic positions. In spite of these precautionary measures he required the full force of his strategical genius to achieve his ends. Though on his accession to the throne he had defeated a coalition formed by the prince of Kadesh, it took him ten years, from 1467 to 1457 B.C., to subdue and pacify Palestine and Syria. Again in 1457 B.C. a general uprising almost destroyed all that he had done, and after his death, during the reign of Amenhotep II (1435-1414 B.C.), Shaushshatar succeeded in regaining part of Syria.

This Mitanni counter-offensive was arrested by the Hittite menace. The Hittite king Khattushilish II took Aleppo from the Mitanni Artatama I (1420-1400?), a setback which decided Artatama to change allies. The Hittite peril seemed to him greater than the threat of Egyptian expansion, which had been dormant since the death of Tuthmosis III. In about 1408 B.C. he therefore concluded a treaty of peace and alliance with Tuthmosis IV and gave him his daughter's hand in marriage. He had, however, merely exchanged one danger for another, this time nearer home. One party of the aristocracy refused to accept this radical change of policy, and thenceforth Mitanni was split into two camps which intrigued for power and, incited and encouraged by the Hittites, promoted palace revolutions.

The hierocephalic god Horus protecting the Pharaoh Tutankhamun (1352-1343 B.C.). Under Tutankhamun the cult of Aten introduced by his predecessor Amenhotep (Akhenaten) gave way once more to the older worship of Horus. Louvre.

Cartouche of Ramesses II (1290-1224 B.C.). His energetic reign brought temporary postponement of the final decline of the New Empire. *Archiv für Kunst und Deschichte*

Suppiluliumash, the Great Hittite

Mitanni could not survive this internal strife. The real power of the country passed into the hands of the Hittites under their greatest ruler, Suppiluliumash (1380-1347 B.C.). Suppiluliumash, profiting by the discord in Mitanni, imposed on it a king of his own choice. At this same time Egypt was in the throes of a complicated internal crisis and had totally neglected the defence of her empire. Undermined by Hittite plots and intrigues, Egypt's empire began to crumble during the reigns of Amenhotep IV (1370-1352 B.C.) and his successors; and the might of Suppiluliumash was felt as far as Jerusalem. His power also reached towards the west, and all of Anatolia as far as the Aegean seems to have been subject to him. To the east Suppiluliumash's sway extended to Armenia and the frontiers of Assyria. At the end of the fourteenth century the 'Great Hittite' was the arbiter of the East.

The widow of a pharaoh — Amenhotep IV or Tutankhamun — actually implored him to send her one of his sons as a husband to help her govern Egypt.

The decline of Egypt which this incident illustrates was transitory. The reins of government were again firmly grasped by a new dynasty, the Nineteenth, founded in about 1314 B.C. by Ramesses I. The two pharaohs who succeeded him, Seti I (1312-1290 B.C.), and more especially Ramesses II (1290-1224 B.C.) were as outstanding as their greatest predecessors. Seti I, on coming to the throne, at once restored order in Palestine, Syria and Phoenicia. Two years later a Hittite counter-offensive was repelled. These victories alone were not, however, sufficient to re-establish the Egyptian Empire on a firm footing, The Hittite king, Muwattali (1311-1282 B.C.), was patiently preparing his revenge. In 1285 B.C. Ramesses II found himself faced by a vast coalition which imperilled northern Syria. The battle of Kadesh was nearly an Egyptian disaster, and only the pharaoh's personal bravery compensated for his lack of foresight. His success, however, fell far short of the total triumph which his *Annals* suggest, for the war dragged on for another five years.

A change in Hittite policy rather than his own military achievements allowed Ramesses II finally to bring his campaign to a successful conclusion. On the death of Muwattali internal strife had broken out among the Hittites. Muwattali's son and heir, Hurri-Teshub, was dethroned and exiled in 1275 B.C. by his uncle, the usurper Khattushilish III. Then, too, the Hittite Empire was at this time threatened in the east by a revival of Assyrian power. The feebleness of the Kassite dynasty had allowed Assyria to wrest from Babylon its northern provinces. In Mitanni too an energetic king had arisen, Shalmaneser I (1271-1242 B.C.). It was thus to the interest of the Hittites and the pharaoh to put an end to their rivalry.

Lengthy negotiations resulted in the treaty of 1269, and the actual text of this document still exists, written in the two languages. In it the two sovereigns undertake to respect existing frontiers, conclude a pact of mutual assistance against internal and external dangers, and promise not to suborn each other's allies. In addition,

The mask from the coffin of Seti I (1312-1290 B.C.)

Queen Nefertari, wife of Ramesses II. A statue at Abu Simbel.

Ramesses II in 1256 B.C. married one of Khattushilish's daughters, and Khattushilish himself came to Egypt in great pomp for the wedding.

The invasion of the 'Sea Peoples'

Peace, however, was at once disturbed by a new and devastating invasion which owed its impetus, as preceding ethnic irruptions had done, to Indo-European pressure: the invasion of the 'Sea Peoples', as the Egyptian inscriptions call them. The first to feel the thrust was the Hittite Empire. At the death of Khattushilish III in about 1250 B.C. it suffered the savage onslaught of the Mushki of Phrygia and collapsed almost at once. Practically nothing is known of Khattushilish's successors, Tuthaliya IV and Arnuwanda — not even if they had any descendants. This abrupt collapse had allowed the Assyrian king, Tukulti-Enurta, to seize Babylon in about 1235 B.C. But the Mushki then attacked Tukulti-Enurta and slew him, while Babylon, thus liberated, invaded Assyria. Babylon's triumph was short-lived, for the Elamites threw themselves on the city in 1163 B.C. and before retiring sacked it. They carried off booty of inestimable value: the stelae of the first Sargon and of Naram-sin, the Code of Hammurabi and so forth — which modern archaeologists have in part recovered in the excavations at Susa. The Kassite dynasty was finally exhausted and in 1158 B.C. disappeared.

Syria had not escaped the consequences of the new upheaval. Strangers had thronged into the country in masses, Semites, Indo-Europeans, Arameans, Hebrews and Philistines. Merneptah (1224-1204 B.C.), the son of Ramesses II, was obliged to exert all his energy to put down a general uprising. The Delta itself was menaced by the Libyans and their pirate allies who arrived by sea, some of whom were related to the Achaeans of Greece and the islands. Merneptah managed to defeat them, but his death was followed by twenty-five years of anarchy. Order was restored by the new dynasty, the Twentieth, which was founded by Set-Nekht in 1179 B.C. The Twentieth Dynasty had the good fortune to produce another great ruler, Ramesses III (1170-1139 B.C.). Ramesses III not only succeeded in twice throwing back from the Delta a massive invasion of the Sea Peoples, which in 1163 B.C. coincided with a Libyan attack, but himself invaded Asia where, for the last time, the armies of Egypt appeared on the banks of the Orontes. After his death the Egyptian Empire came to an end. The last pharaohs of Ramesses' line were paralysed by domestic difficulties and renounced further foreign adventure. Syria and Palestine were entirely lost, and from then onwards the peoples whom the great invasions of the thirteenth and twelfth centuries had left there followed their own independent course, no longer politically influenced by Egypt.

Egyptian civilisation in the New Empire

Persistent warfare had not prevented the flowering of brilliant civilisations during the troubled course of this period. Again it is the culture of Egypt which is best known, for at this point, Egyptian civilisation reached its full splendour. Historically, the most important aspect of Egyptian life is the religious development which took place. The first rank among the gods was now occupied

Osiris, one of the most important Egyptian gods. Among other things he was god of the Nile and Judge of the Dead. Luxor.

A New Kingdom satirical drawing depicting animals in traditional poses of gods and pharaohs. *British Museum*

by Amun of Thebes, to whose aid the victory over the Hyksos had been attributed. As the Empire expanded, so had the prestige of Amun: the victorious pharaohs enriched his shrines with part of their booty and with tribute exacted from subject peoples. In actual fact it was the priests who profited, and their worldly domain became a state within the state. The High Priest of Amun rose to a political position which made him the equal of the Prime Minister.

The rising power of the priesthood could have imperilled the monarchy had not the first pharaohs of the Eighteenth Dynasty been strong rulers. Their policy was to continue and uphold the traditions of their predecessors. Thus we find no great change in the central administration: a Prime Minister still directed it, though finances — an important exception — tended more and more to escape from his control. Finance was a heavy responsibility which Tuthmosis II lightened by dividing the Empire into two territorial provinces. Or perhaps his motive was to discourage some possible usurper. For similar reasons positions of state were not allowed to become hereditary. Local ruling families still existed in the nomes, but they were stripped of all real power. The chief towns were ruled by military governors who obeyed only the king, and local administrators took their orders from the king's minister. This is not to say that no crisis ever disturbed the dynasty. The right of succession does not seem to have been perfectly established: we have one indisputable example of usurpation, that of Queen Hatshepsut, the sister-wife of Tuthmosis III, who kept the legitimate sovereign in obscurity for fifteen years while she herself governed Egypt.

These palace revolutions were of small consequence, for they simply brought to the throne energetic leaders whose military prestige was of value to the country. But when Tuthmosis III had for a time ensured the safety of the Empire and put an end to further conquest, internal problems became of prevailing importance. The power acquired by the priests of Amun was now seen to be dangerous. It was, perhaps, chiefly to undermine their influence that Amenhotep IV (1370-1352 B.C.) crossed swords with them and attempted an extraordinary and radical reform which was to affect all aspects of Egyptian civilisation.

Thebes, which was the city of the god Amun, was abandoned as the political capital, and all the administrative services were transferred to a town specially built on the site of Amarna. War was declared on Amun and his cult may even have been forbidden. Amenhotep changed his name to Akhenaten and called his new capital Akhetaten in honour of the new god, Aten, whom he hoped to impose upon his subjects and whose high priest he himself became. The new religion was a solar cult, familiar to Egypt but taking as its material symbol the winged disc of the sun which was worshipped as the creator of the world and the source of all life. The theology of the new religion is known to us by the hymns to the sun which the king was the first to sing and may himself have composed. Though Akhenaten's religious reform served certain political ends, we must not dismiss the possibility of more far-reaching aims: he may have sought to unite by moral bonds all the inhabitants of his wide Empire in the worship of a divinity acceptable to everyone. The influence of the revolution which took place at Amarna can be felt in all aspects of contemporary Egyptian life and gives to the art of the period a special tone of naturalism, sometimes approaching caricature, a feeling for the inner life and a love for nature and humanity.

Amenhotep IV (Akhenaten) did not live long enough, nor were his descendants sufficiently forceful, to ensure the survival of his revolution. It challenged too many

70

firmly established beliefs and interests. It roused the anger of the priests of Amun and offended the religiously conservative; it humiliated the people of Thebes and perhaps wounded national pride, for in the religion of Aten no single race or nation occupied a privileged position. On the death of Amenhotep IV, Tutankhamun (1352-1343 B.C.) was forced to restore the national god Amun to his supreme place of honour, return with the government to Thebes and publicly condemn the new religion. The dynasty, discredited by this humiliating surrender and by the collapse of its Asiatic empire, could not survive. Horemheb, a general, seized power and restored internal order (1340-1314 B.C.). On his death one of his companions in arms, Ramesses I (1314-1312 B.C.), founded the Nineteenth Dynasty.

The Decline of Egypt

With the Nineteenth Dynasty, under Seti I (1312-1290) and Ramesses II (1290-1224 B.C.), Egypt again reverted to her old traditions. But the period was also the beginning of a long decline. It is true that these two sovereigns restored much of her brillance both abroad and at home, where they were great builders, the heirs of a long artistic tradition which continued to produce masterpieces. But with the Pharaoh Merneptah the assault of the Sea Peoples battered the frontiers of Egypt. After Merneptah's death in 1204 B.C. twenty-five years of anarchy finally destroyed the power of the country. The restoration of monarchical authority by Set-Nekht who founded the Twentieth Dynasty in 1179 B.C. and the reign of Ramesses III (1170-1139 B.C.) were only the last spasms of a country in the throes of political decline. The feeble successors of Ramesses III allowed their power to slip away and the priests of Amun to take control.

The pharaohs of the Nineteenth Dynasty had indeed taken care to distribute their bounty among different gods. The god Set, especially, seems to have enjoyed a position of favour under both the Nineteenth and Twentieth Dynasties. It is also true that the pharaohs had built themselves a new capital at Tanis in the Delta, which was strategically better placed than Thebes. But once the royal authority weakened or wavered, the might of Amun proved irresistible. For more than half a century the real power of Egypt was wielded by Amun's high priests. Finally, on the death of Ramesses XI in 1056 B.C., one of them, Her-Hor, threw off his priestly mask and proclaimed himself king. Meanwhile, at Tanis, a kinsman of the fallen dynasty called Smendes maintained a pretence of legitimate sovereignty.

Hittite and Mitanni civilisations

The Asiatic civilisations of Mitanni and of the Hittites are less well known, and the study of their languages is still incomplete. It is impossible to draw even a broad historical outline of their empires, and for the most part we are ignorant of their institutions. But the spirit which animated their religion and their art seems to be the same for both countries. Doubtless the influence of the indigenous peoples who constituted the basis of the population was predominant. Although their gods bear Indo-European names they were inherited from the Sumerians. The pantheon was headed by a divine couple: a god of

A relief of Queen Akmet, mother of Hatshepsut, from Hatshepsut's temple at Deir-el-Bahri. *Viollet*

Ramesses II receiving bound Libyan captives. Fresco from the tombs at Thebes. *Mansell*

Less renowned than Nefertiti, queen of Amenhotep IV, this unidentified queen's beauty has clearly broken through the strict formalism of 'official' Egyptian style. Louvre. *Giraudon*

A colonnade in the temple of Luxor. Eighteenth Dynasty. *Audrain-Samivel*

the sky and a mother-goddess who may be identified with Cybele. From their union was born a young god who was both son and lover of the goddess: a prototype of Adonis. This triad is frequently represented in sculpture that is always forceful and animated, but less concerned with detail than with general effect. All we know about the architecture of the Hittites we know from the ruins of their ancient capital, Hattusas, and from a few other cities. The immensity of the ruins, the might of their fortifications, the crude and grandiose sculptures which adorn their gates fit well with the picture one forms of these vigorous, warlike people who perhaps vanished before they had achieved full spiritual maturity.

Crete and King Minos

The Aegean World, though on the fringe of the battle for continental domination, was none the less affected by the displacement of the Indo-European speaking peoples. In Crete the first palaces were quickly replaced, and the splendour of the second palaces soon made the memory of their predecessors fade. They were rebuilt on a larger scale and, though they retained the same architectural features, they show an advanced technical skill and introduce a new art-form: the mural fresco. Surrounding the palaces there were groups of large houses, less imposing but also luxurious, which prove the existence of a rich and powerful aristocracy. One city, Cnos-

sus, little by little gained pre-eminence over the others. From 1500 B.C. onwards Cnossus alone continued to prosper while the others declined — perhaps an indication that one royal line, that of the legendary King Minos, had succeeded in extending its authority over the whole island.

It was at this time that Cretan, or Minoan, civilisation reached its peak. Until Minoan records have been more thoroughly deciphered we cannot be certain how the island was governed or how society was organised. Nor do we know how far Crete's maritime empire extended — probably not much farther than the southern Cyclades. On the other hand, artistic remains are innumerable and their wide distribution seems to reveal intense commercial activity. In the preceding epoch trade had been carried on chiefly with Egypt and Syria; now the principal markets were the Greek mainland and the coast of Asia Minor as far as Troy. The character of Minoan artistic production remained basically unaltered, with the love of colour emphasised. The fresco painters indulged in such an orgy of colour that it finished by triumphing over the keen powers of observation and fidelity to nature which were typical of this people. From the frescoes we can draw some conclusions about the religion and the society which produced them. In both a capital role was played by women. A goddess of fertility was the central figure of their pantheon and in her temple she was served by priestesses.

The Valley of the Kings. Here, close to Thebes, the pharaohs of the New Empire carved out their monumental underground tombs from the heart of the rock. All his life the Pharaoh was engaged in preparing a fitting and richly furnished burial place for himself. *Audrain-Samivel*

Above right: a seal impression of the labyrinth of the Minotaur, the monster kept by Minos, semi-legendary king of Crete.

Above left: a seal-stone with a bull design from Cnossus. Candia.

Like the bull, the snake goddess is an important figure in Minoan culture. A symbol of fertility, she can be identified in other primitive cultures. *Candia Museum*

Mycenae and the Achaean Empire

Cretan civilisation had a particular influence on Argolis. It was from the plain of Argos that the invasion was launched which had once nearly destroyed Crete. The region of Argolis, favoured by agriculture and commerce, had since then become the centre of Achaean power. Achaean civilisation remained essentially warlike, as we can see by the great fortresses at Mycenae and Tiryns, and the large number of weapons discovered in the tombs. Certain other characteristics of Achaean culture also distinguished it from its Cretan model: for example, the plan of the *megaron* — the great central hall of the Mycenaean house — and in art a taste for depicting scenes of warfare, and a respect for logical composition. But inspiration derived from Cretan originals soon became so deceptive that it is often impossible to distinguish whether certain objects of this period are of Cretan or Mycenaean origin. Those which undoubtedly come from Argolis reveal the cultural level which the Achaeans had attained in the fifteenth century B.C. Proof of their great wealth was discovered in the tombs at Mycenae. Their skill in building is demonstrated by huge tombs with cupolas, like the Treasury of Atreus which remains one of the largest domed buildings known; their artistic sense is illustrated by objects such as the golden goblets of Vaphio.

It was not long before the strength of this vigorous

73

A rhyton in the form of a man's head. From Asine, Peloponnesus. Nauplia Museum. *Mansell*

young power was felt beyond its borders. The first blows it struck were against the land which had influenced its civilisation most. Towards 1400 B.C. Crete was invaded, as it had been three centuries previously. But this time the island did not recover from the assault; the invaders remained as settlers and introduced their own customs and culture. Many Cretan artists, on the other hand, were forced to emigrate. They dispersed throughout the East, and we find traces of them in Greece, in Asia Minor, and even in the Egypt of Amenhotep IV. It is possible that it was not only the artists who fled from the Achaean invaders, for, according to the Bible, the Philistines came from Crete.

Achaean expansion did not stop with Crete. Many indications lead us to believe that the Achaean Empire extended not only to the archipelago and to Crete, to Boeotia and possibly farther north, but to Rhodes and Cyprus. It is still an open question whether the Ach-chi-ya-wa mentioned in the Hittite archives were or were not Achaeans; but it could well be so. It seems that these scattered territories never formed a unified empire. But, if we may rely on the traditions and folklore which the Homeric epics preserve, it is possible that the Achaean states formed a loose federation which in times of war rallied under the leadership of the princes of Mycenae.

We can see how this could occur on one celebrated occasion: the Trojan War. It must, however, be confessed that this celebrated episode — apart from the bare fact that it certainly took place — belongs less to history than

Two sides of a bronze and gold dagger from the Treasury of Atreus at Mycenae, showing a royal lion hunt. Homer's King Agamemnon, the leader of the Greeks in the Trojan War, was head of the 'House of Atreus' of Mycenae. His story is told in Aeschylus' trilogy the *Oresteia*. *Mansell*

to legend. Even its date remains in dispute. According to those who place it at the beginning of the fourteenth century B.C. it was connected with the first wave of Achaean expansion of which the occupation of Crete was the opening move. To those who believe it occurred some two hundred years later, during the twelfth century, it was an episode in the great migrations of the Sea Peoples, of which the new Dorian invasion formed a part. For the second school of thought the Trojan War would be the last great feat of arms performed by the Achaean Empire, under pressure from new enemies.

The Aryans in India

The waves of invading Indo-Europeans also broke against India, but their arrival there remains enveloped in mists of uncertainty. The civilisation of Harappa and Mohenjo-daro declined by the early second millennium and was followed by another, the principal centres of which were Djhoukar and Tchanhou-daro, also situated in the region of the lower Indus. The new civilisation was noticeably less advanced, and the date and cause of its disappearance are uncertain. Perhaps it was connected with the coming of the Aryans. It is thought that the Aryans, descending from the steppes of southern Russia, first established themselves in north-west Persia and then split into two groups, one continuing towards Asia Minor and the other penetrating India by way of Afghanistan. The Rig-Veda, the oldest of India's sacred poems, which is believed to have been orally composed between 1500 and 1000 B.C., described the Aryans as settled in the Punjab, from which they may have driven out the Dasyus who had perhaps inherited the civilisation of Djhoukar. According to the same poem, the Aryans had also penetrated into the basin of the Ganges. But no precise conclusions can be drawn from such legendary material. These invasions swamped but did not destroy the native culture. The Harappa people had, for example, established a massive urban life, comparable to that of Ancient Egypt and Mesopotamia, while the Aryan pastoralists were relatively primitive. The religion of the original inhabitants, moreover, survived. The cult of the mother goddess, and of a deity who was the prototype of the Hindu Shiva, is already apparent; these indigenous cults developed directly into later Hinduism, which is the oldest of all the great religions, going back to times contemporary with the archaic cultures of the Near East, where continuity has been broken.

The art of the pre-Aryan peoples is already recognisably similar to that of later Hindu India: the sacred bull, the pipal tree, the elephant and the buffalo are depicted and figures are extant of ascetics in postures familiar in historic times. The seals represent various domestic and jungle animals, and it is plain that a considerable agriculture, including the cultivation of cotton, was already in being. The foundation of subsequent Indian civilisations thus go back to pre-Aryan times, and the strong religious bias characteristic of India is already manifest.

But the Aryan invaders probably wrecked the irrigation system on which the cultures of Harappa, Mohenjo-daro and their successors depended, so that the conquerors tended to push eastwards into areas of better rainfall, first between the great rivers of the Punjab, and later into the basin of the Ganges itself. As they did so,

Drawing of a fragment of a silver rhyton from Shaft Grave IV, Mycenae. It shows Mycenaean soldiers storming a town.

A detail from a Minoan rhyton, or drinking vessel. *Viollet*

they became less exclusively a pastoral people, and began to practise agriculture and develop conquered cities.

China during the Shang Dynasty

The immense mountain barriers of central Asia sheltered China from the Indo-European migrations. Until the Shang Dynasty came to power in about 1558 B.C. the territory properly described as Chinese was still limited to the middle reaches of the Hwang-ho valley. Under the new dynasty two important developments took place: the discovery of bronze and the beginning of colonisation. Nothing very certain is known about the Shang Dynasty itself, but the discovery of the An-yang tombs reveals that remarkable advances in civilisation had already been made. Indeed Chinese art never again created anything more vigorous than the bronze vases of this epoch. The An-yang excavations display a literate civilisation already characteristically Chinese: the oracle bones and bronze vessels used in ritual already have inscriptions in characters ancestral to later Chinese script. Thus

Chinese culture, though its origins cannot be directly traced as far back as those of Egypt or Mesopotamia, has a direct continuity like that of Hindu India, unbroken since the middle of the second millennium. The Shang Dynasty, which, unlike Harappa and Mohenjo-daro, survived in legend, created a vague tradition of political unity which the subsequent period of feudal warfare never destroyed. We also know that pioneer Chinese colonists were swarming in all directions. They reached and perhaps passed the Hwai-ho in the south, and in the east settled in the region of Shantung. In the west they pushed up the banks of the Wei, though not without meeting stiff resistance from native tribesmen. In this manner principalities were created whose total independence was an embarrassment and an offence to the Shang emperors. Rivalry among these quarrelsome states brought about their downfall. Their moral decadence made them unpopular and in about 1050 B.C. they were overthrown by Wu-Wang, Lord of Chou in the west. Wu-Wang fought and slew the last of the Shang Dynasty and assumed the imperial title himself.

Achaemenian gold rhyton in the form of a winged lion. The Achaemenians were highly skilled metal workers. Teheran Museum. *Josephine Powell*

A Shang bronze owl. c. 1300 B.C. Two events of major importance marked the Shang Dynasty: the discovery of bronze and the first efforts at colonisation.

A bust from Mohenjo-daro. Karachi Museum. *Josephine Powell*

CHAPTER THREE

THE BIRTH OF NEW NATIONS

1000-600 B.C.

The East after the invasion of the Sea Peoples

In the Levant, the invasion of the Sea Peoples had far greater political consequences than the earlier Indo-European migrations. It destroyed empires which had endured for thousands of years, and sometimes it annihilated the very peoples who had formed the empires. It was a long time before new powers were again to flourish on the ruins of these ancient civilisations. A scattering of tiny nations, of whom we often know practically nothing but the names, shared the territories devastated by the invaders. But by the vastness of its geographical units Asia has produced empires with world-wide ambitions, and so at the end of the period we see conquering peoples reappear, not only in the Near East, but in India and China. However, at least in the west, the smaller nations conserved a lively sentiment of their past independence, and Assyrian domination, despite the military might which backed it, was never accepted. Assyria herself was destined to perish brutally when faced by the union of down-trodden but unsubmissive peoples.

The disappearance of the Hittite Empire and the decadence of Egypt left Syria and Palestine to be broken up into the small units which their geography tends to encourage. From the eleventh to the ninth century they were a patchwork of small states whose territory was sometimes enclosed within the walls of a single city. But their insignificant size is often no measure of their historical importance. Nor in this apparent confusion is it impossible to introduce a certain order and to arrange the various groups according to their racial origin. The narrow strip of plain, bordered on one side by the sea and on the other by hills which rise higher towards the north, is divided into two parts by Mount Carmel. The Philistines had settled in the south, the Phoenicians in the north. The interior had been occupied by the Arameans who were established at the crossroads of the caravan routes connecting Egypt with Asia Minor and the Mediterranean with the Euphrates. Finally the Hebrews and their related tribes had set their hearts on the land of Canaan and the neighbouring deserts.

The Philistines

The Philistines are the only one of these peoples who were not of Semitic origin. According to Biblical tradition they arrived from Crete, and it seems, in fact, that they did come from the Greek archipelago. Among them there must have been a certain number of Indo-Europeans. They formed a confederation of five cities: Ashdod, Ascalon, Ekron, Gath and Gaza. They established themselves in strongholds from which they resisted the assaults of the Hebrews. The resistance of the Philistines was so stubborn that the land of Canaan subsequently became known as Palestine. All we know of their history and their culture is what we learn from the Bible. From this it would appear that the Philistines were a warlike and seafaring people. They had a monopoly in the manufacture of iron, and they were also industrious. From their predecessors they had adopted the agrarian cult of the god Dagon (or Baal).

The Phoenicians

To the north of Mount Carmel commercial traditions were much more vigorous. As far back as the third millennium ports like Byblos and Ugarit had, as a result of their relations with Egypt, been prosperous. Amanus (Mount Taurus) and Lebanon furnished them with wood for their fleets and precious money in exchange for goods. From Mesopotamia too came caravans laden with products for export. In these early days it appears that the local population was Semitic, but many foreign conquerors left traces of their dominion on Phoenician civilisation. When Phoenicia achieved independence we find her divided into maritime cities, governed by local ruling houses and split by local rivalries which came to a head in the struggle for ascendancy between Tyre and Sidon. In the ninth century Tyre was victorious and her kings reigned also over Sidon, but when the Assyrian conquest dealt Tyre the fatal blow in 667 B.C. Sidon profited.

Marble boundary stone of Evil-Merodach, King of Babylonia, 721-711 B.C.

Hardy seamen and sagacious traders, the Phoenicians soon became the carriers of the eastern world, the link between nations, and gained an almost complete monopoly of international commerce. On the Asian continent they concluded treaties with neighbouring states which brought caravans bearing merchandise to Phoenician ports. Their maritime policy was even more striking. The shores of the Mediterranean were dotted with trading posts and warehouses crammed with local products which the fleets of Phoenicia carried to the East. From the tenth century we find the Phoenicians established in Cyprus, in the ninth century in Sicily, in Sardinia, in Spain and, above all, in Africa. The foundation of Carthage in 814 B.C. was the first time a Phoenician colony acquired considerable territory. The historical consequences were to be great.

The Phoenicians' contributions to civilisation are less notable. They were imitators rather than innovators, and even in the realms of religion they adopted the agrarian cults of the neighbouring peoples. But we do owe to them one immensely important invention, which partly explains their commercial success: that of an alphabet which was to become the basis of that used in Europe. This alphabet certainly dates from the thirteenth century B.C. and may go back much farther.

The Arameans

As a centre of communications Syria occupied a privileged geographical position; but the Phoenicians held the coast and Syria's commercial opportunities lay rather in the direction of the continental hinterland. The Arameans, who had come from the north of Mesopotamia to install themselves astride this busy crossroad of trade after the disintegration of the Hittite Empire, were,

The god Baal (the 'Lord') worshipped by the Phoenicians and Canaanites. It was for Baal that some Hebrews deserted Jehovah after reaching the Promised Land. *Louvre*

A Phoenician ship of c. 800 B.C. From an Assyrian relief. Skilled seamen and shrewd traders helped to make Tyre and Sidon, Phoenicia's rival cities, the most important trading centres in the ancient world from the third millennium onwards. They were first to establish commercial relations with the East.

in a sense, the complement of the Phoenicians. The Phoenicians were masters of navigation; the Arameans were landsmen, skilled in caravan traffic. They were divided into minute kingdoms of which the most important in the tenth century was that of Damascus. Their little colonies were scattered all over the Near East and drained the commerce of the countryside into their chief cities, especially Damascus. Their contributions to civilisation were slight; but their language, written in characters derived from the Phoenician alphabet, spread everywhere and became, and remained until the days of Christ, an international tongue.

The Hebrews before the Exodus

The land of Canaan was less favoured by nature. The zone of the high hills between the Jordan and the coastal plain was dry and unfertile. Many waves of peoples had, however, succeeded each other here. The hazards and uncertainties of growing crops explain why nomadism always prevailed in Canaan. Among these wandering shepherds were the ancestors of the Jews. According to the Book of Genesis they came originally from Chaldea; towards 1900 B.C., in the days of Abraham, they reached Harran, on the great bend of the Euphrates, and at an unknown date penetrated Canaan. From there, always accompanied by other closely related tribes, a certain number of Jews filtered into Egypt at the same time as the Hyksos, or possibly even before the end of the Twelfth Dynasty, towards 1700 B.C. They must have prospered in Egypt — as the story of Joseph illustrates —

Neo-Babylonian goddess of fertility. Ivory. Subject and style are borrowed from Crete; the flounced skirt is common in Minoan work. Archaeological finds at Ugarit have included Minoan pottery, proving that there was contact from 1000 B.C. *Giraudon*

Above: cartouches of prisoners, each representing a conquered country. Karnak. *Viollet*

Below: a Roman merchant ship carved on a rock sarcophagus at Sidon. *Archives Photographiques, Paris*

A fresco from a tomb at Beni Hasan, *c.* 1900 B.C., showing Semitic nomads trading in Egypt. *Larousse*

until the restoration of Egyptian unity. The Exodus, however, is not contemporary with the expulsion of the Hyksos. The Book of Genesis makes much of the persecutions which the Jews were said to have suffered under the pharaohs — which can only be understood if the pharaohs were the powerful sovereigns of the Eighteenth Dynasty. Thus the Exodus must be placed at the time of the Egyptian Empire's greatest splendour. The crossing of the Jordan, forty years later, would then be contemporary with the troubled period when Amenhotep IV (Akhenaten) attempted his unsuccessful religious reforms. In any case the Pharaoh Merneptah listed the Israelites among the number of his enemies. It can therefore be concluded that they were installed in Canaan before the end of the thirteenth century.

The Hebrews in the Promised Land

The Exodus was an event of capital importance in the history of the Jewish people. It was then that their feeling of national solidarity was born. It was then that the final form was given to the Law, and the Jews received their first social and political organisation. The name of Moses is indissolubly linked with these profound innovations. His role as religious and military leader was decisive. It was Moses who maintained the unity and the faith of his people during their tribulations in the desert. But he did not preside over their entrance into the Promised Land. The infiltration into Canaan took place under the leadership of the Judges, whose functions were at once political, military and religious. There was no general plan of campaign and Canaan was penetrated by small Jewish groups, while other tribes, refusing to continue the bitter struggle, remained beyond the Jordan. The majority of the Canaanites were hostile and the territory which the Jews conquered was under constant threat of attack and reprisal from its former occupants.

The fiercest resistance to the invasion came from the Philistines, who more than once inflicted severe defeats on the Jews, as the story of Samson reminds us. The need for co-operation and leadership which war demanded, as well as the example of the neighbouring peoples, brought a basic alteration in Jewish organisation: the establishment of a royal house. Kings were not accepted without opposition from the priestly class from whom

King David. From the ninth-century Golden Psalter. During his reign Israel established her capital at Jerusalem, made an alliance with Hiram of Tyre against the Philistines and repelled the Arameans.

The ruins of Babylon, the city where the Amorites settled and where Hammurabi was to lay the foundations of the first empire of Babylonia.

Left: from the summit of Mount Nebo Moses was able to look into the Promised Land, separated from it by the River Jordan's meandering course through the surrounding desert. *Popper, Atlas-Photo*

83

the Judges were themselves recruited. The first experience of a royal house, in which Saul (c. 1020 B.C.) came to the throne, was disappointing. After some successes against the Philistines and the Ammonites, Saul was faced with the revolt of his son-in-law, David, in alliance with his own son Jonathan. Weakened, he was defeated and slain by the Philistines at Gilboa. After a series of plots, bloodshed and scheming, David assumed the throne without further contest.

David and Solomon

During the reign of David (1010-970 B.C.) Israel became a full-fledged nation. In about 1003 B.C. David captured Jerusalem, which he made his capital; he repelled the Arameans of Damascus and made an alliance with Hiram of Tyre against the Philistines. These successes raised his reputation and served to mask palace intrigues which, with Absalom, became open rebellion, rendered easier by the fretful independence of the tribes. Even so, David succeeded in organising a central government, in imposing the authority of his governors in the provinces and in raising forced labour. His son Solomon (970-930 B.C.) perfected this organisation and enriched the country by developing its trade with Phoenicia. He strove to centralise the cult at Jerusalem where he expended large sums of money in building the Temple. The unity of the state, however, did not survive him. His son, Rehoboam, was stripped of the major part of the kingdom by Jeroboam who was supported by Egypt. From then on the Jewish nation was split into two enemy kingdoms, Israel and Judah. The days of its greatness were past.

The religion of Israel

Israel's contributions to civilisation were limited, with one superlatively important exception: her religion, the oldest religion of the western world. Surrounded by peoples who worshipped many gods, her belief in one god only, her absolute monotheism, was a striking proof of originality. Not that the Jews were not often tempted to fall into idolatry: their kings, even Solomon himself in his last years, 'turned away his heart after other gods and went not fully after the Lord'. But a reformer would always arise, a prophet raise his voice to recall those who had strayed to the worship of the one true God. The foundation of Israel's monotheism had been laid in the revelations made at Mount Sinai which were written down in the books of the Law and completed by a collection of subsequent prophecies and religious writings attributed in particular to David or Solomon.

The importance of the Pentateuch, the first five books of the old Testament, is the second distinguishing feature of the religion of Israel. It contained not only religious dogmas but also the basis of a system of morality and law, drawn, it is true, from older documents such as the Code of Hammurabi, and dating from various preceding periods. But the laws are not presented as the codification of common law; instead they appear to stem from moral principles of universal validity. Since the Book contained all that was indispensable to the life of a nation it is not surprising that the government always had a theocratic tendency. At first the priests saw to it that religion and politics were intimately mingled. Later, when the secular power had itself assumed the priestly role, inspired leaders of the people arose spontaneously: the Prophets, who respected no power on earth save the reign of the Law. These distinctive qualities, which ensured the individuality and often the very survival of the Jewish people, were in themselves remarkable enough, but leaving their imprint, as they later did, on Christianity, they became part of the world's inheritance. The influence they have had is what gives the Hebrews such an exceptional place in universal history.

Two steles in the Nahr-el-Kelb (Dog River) valley recall that a succession of early peoples passed this way in search of new lands to conquer. Carved in the rock are records of their passage. Here an Egyptian stele of Ramesses II stands alongside that noting the passage of the Assyrian Esarhaddon. *Peter French*

Above: a Middle Assyrian seal. 1000-539 B.C. A winged bull kneels before a sacred tree. *British Museum*

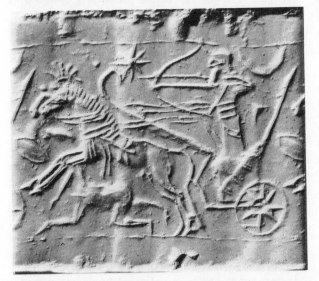

Above: a bowman shooting from a two-wheeled chariot. A pointed tool was used to achieve the linear effect of this seal. Assyrian linear. 1000-539 B.C. *British Museum*

Portion of a bronze band from the gate of Shalmaneser III, King of Assyria. 859-824 B.C. British Museum. *Mansell*

The ravages of the Sea Peoples also extended to Asia Minor, but the tribes that settled there and formed new states are not known to us through any records they themselves left. What we know about them comes from the archives of their enemies, in particular the Assyrians. Most of the new states were of necessity confined within the limits of the natural frontiers which geography imposes in this mountainous region. Some of them must have become dangerously strong, since they were able to worry the Assyrian kings at the height of their power. Such were the Armenians of Urartu (or Ararat) and the Mushki under king Mitas, who has been identified with the Phrygian Midas, son of Gordius. In addition, there were the tribes who inhabited the mountainous eastern borders of Mesopotamia, the Elamites especially, who were concentrated in the south around their citadel of Susa. The Elamites were, of course, of older origin, and we have already noticed their appearance in the history of the East.

It was over these peoples that Assyrian domination was first extended. Assyria had once been powerful under Tukulti-Enurta I, but the kingdom was unable to survive the disastrous invasions that took place during the twelfth century. For half a century we hear nothing of Assyria. Then, under another great sovereign, Tiglath-Pileser I (1112-1074 B.C.), expansion began again — and was to continue for five centuries. It would be unprofitable to enumerate all the campaigns and battles that were fought during this long period, and we shall confine ourselves to examining the direction, nature and stages of Assyrian conquest.

The nature of Assyrian conquest

The armies of Assyria fought with practically all the peoples who then inhabited the Near and Middle East, though sometimes the wars they waged seem to have

An Assyrian baked clay brick bearing the name and title of Shalmaneser III. It commemorates his restoration of the ziggurat at Nimrud. British Museum. *Popper*

The stages of Assyrian conquest

By the end of the twelfth century B.C. and the beginning of the eleventh, Assyria's career of expansion had begun. Under Tiglath-Pileser I the Assyrians conquered Cappadocia in 1112-1108 B.C., reached the Mediterranean in 1106 B.C., and in 1097 B.C. pillaged Babylon. But Tiglath-Pileser's obscure successors were unable to follow his example and for two centuries no further progress was made. The forward march was resumed under Ashur-nasir-pal II (883-859 B.C.) and Shalmaneser III (858-824 B.C.). Their campaigns were waged, in particular, in Syria and Palestine where the kings of Israel rallied the spirit of resistance. During the reigns of Shamsi-Adad V (823-811 B.C.), of Adad-Nirari III (810-783 B.C.) — in whose name the Queen Mother, Semiramis, ruled as regent for five years — and of his three sons, Assyria was on the defensive, facing threats from the Urartians and the Babylonians, and the end of the period was disturbed by grave internal problems.

Assyria recovered from her difficulties under Tiglath-Pileser III who reigned from 745 to 727 B.C. He made his authority absolute in Syria and assumed the kingship of Babylon. When Sargon II (722-705 B.C.) came to the throne Babylon revolted and was not again humbled until 710 B.C. Meanwhile Sargon had pushed the frontiers forward as far as Egypt, driven the Urartians back into their mountains, conquered Israel and deported her inhabitants. The reign of Sennacherib (705-681 B.C.) was largely spent in a struggle with Elam which was aiding and abetting a fresh revolt in Babylon. Not until 688 B.C. was Sennacherib finally triumphant.

Sennacherib was assassinated and succeeded by his son Esarhaddon, whose one aim and object seems to have been the conquest of Egypt. For some years now Egypt had continually intrigued against Assyria in Palestine and Syria, and could be considered a potential danger. Egypt had been enfeebled by a century and a half of mis-government, during which the real power was in the hands of the high priests of Thebes. It was shaken by religious crises and torn by strife between the priests and the Twenty-first Tanite Dynasty. The Libyans, who had infiltrated from the west into the Delta, set up a Twenty-second Dynasty with Shashanq I (935-914 B.C.) who for a time played the part of a mighty pharaoh, leading his soldiers into Palestine. But, when faced by the feudal magnates, whom the confusion of the times had allowed to regain power, his dynasty quickly foundered. Once more, for two centuries, anarchy reigned. A Twenty-third Dynasty, also Libyan, set up rival kings to those of Shashanq's successors, but neither dynasty was able to wield authority. Meanwhile Nubia, under the leadership of fugitive Egyptian priests whom Shashanq I had possibly driven from Thebes, had become independent and was waiting only for an opportunity to invade Egypt itself. The occasion arose when, towards 720 B.C., a petty king of the Delta, Tefnakhte, made a bid to restore the unity of the country in his own interest. The Thebans, who resisted his pretensions to the throne, appealed for help to Piankhi, the Nubian of Napata, who overthrew Tefnakhte. Piankhi's grandson Shabaka completed the work in 705 B.C. by slaying Tefnakhte's son, Bocchoris, who had attempted to reverse the situation caused by his father's defeat. Thus the unity of Egypt was restored.

been defensive rather than aggressive. Their object in these cases was simply to protect the kingdom from those who endangered its conquests or its existence. Thus they took counter-measures against the peoples of the north and the north-west, the Armenians of Urartu and the Kashshu of the Zagros region, descendants of the Kassites who had taken refuge in the ancient mountain retreats of their forefathers. The intermittent campaigns undertaken against these peoples indicate that definite conquest was not intended. To the south and the west, on the other hand, the Assyrians fought tenaciously to carve out a territorial empire. Here they came up against the various Semitic populations of Syria and Palestine, primarily the Arameans who put up a long and desperate resistance. They also encountered the old Babylonian empire which still retained sufficient pride and strength to refuse to accept foreign domination.

The most striking aspect of the Assyrian conquest is its precarious nature. In the extremely detailed annals which the Assyrian kings have left, the same peoples and the same cities constantly appear and reappear among the number of their vanquished foes. In other words, the vanquished never recognised Assyrian supremacy unless under the constraint of force, and shook off the yoke of foreign oppression the moment the Assyrian army left the neighbourhood. This was made possible by the Assyrian method of governing the territories they conquered, for they were content to impose on the local ruling houses a tribute and a treaty of vassalage, while leaving the administration of the country in their hands. Another factor in the continual revolts was certainly the sense of solidarity which these peoples had acquired during the period of their independence. Such uprisings the Assyrians crushed with a ruthless brutality which only fanned the spirit of resistance. The destruction and burning of cities, tortures and massacres, and the deportation of entire populations, roused a universal hatred of the oppressor which broke out from the moment of the first Assyrian reverse, and helps to explain the rapidity with which an apparently invincible empire collapsed.

A genius worshipping a sacred tree. Relief from the Palace of Nimrud. *Giraudon*

Above: a battle between Ashurbanipal and Ieummen, King of Susa. *Mansell*

Right: a well-ordered file of Assyrian archers. Louvre. *Giraudon*
Far right: King Ashurbanipal. During his reign Assyrian civilisation reached its cultural and military zenith. *Giraudon*
Below: Ashurnasirpal hunting lion in his chariot. 668 B.C. British Museum. *Viollet*

Esarhaddon, before undertaking his projected conquest of Egypt, had other problems to solve: to put an end to the palace revolution which had cost his father his life, to face an invasion of the Cimmerians in 678 B.C., and again, two years later, to repel a much more dangerous irruption of the Scythians. He had also to deal with revolts in Sidon and in Phoenicia (677-671 B.C.). These tasks held up the great expedition to Egypt until 671 B.C. Preceded by two military reconnaissances which had thrust forward as far as the Egyptian frontier in 675 and 673 B.C., the final assault was overwhelming. In four months Esarhaddon conquered the entire Delta, seized Memphis and forced the Pharaoh Tirhakah to withdraw up the Valley. Esarhaddon was unable to pursue his triumphant course; he fell ill during the campaign and died less than two years later.

The work he had begun was finished by his son Ashurbanipal (669-626 B.C.). Even before the death of Esarhaddon the Pharaoh Tirhakah had retaken Memphis (669 B.C.) and was rousing the Delta to revolt. Ashurbanipal in 666 B.C. drove him back beyond Thebes. In 663 B.C. Tirhakha's son Tanutamon made a last attempt to repulse the invader which merely brought the victorious Assyrian army up to Thebes. The subjugation of Egypt was complete.

In the east, meanwhile, threats to the Assyrian Empire were still very real. In 661 B.C. the Elamites again attempted to invade Babylonia. A few years later, in 652 B.C., Elamite hostility was made more dangerous by the defection of Ashurbanipal's brother, Shamash-shum-ukin, whom their father had placed on the throne of Babylon. Shamash-shum-ukin had become attached to his adopted country and wished to restore its independence. It required four successive campaigns to defeat him. After Ashurbanipal's ultimate victory in 648 B.C. he made his full authority felt by turning on Elam which he ravaged and destroyed systematically, even sowing the land with salt in order to render it infertile. This deadly work was completed in about 640 B.C. by the sacking and burning of Susa, the Elamite capital. At that moment Ashurbanipal appeared indeed to be Lord of the Earth.

Assyria in the age of Ashurbanipal

During the reign of Ashurbanipal Assyria reached the highest point of its civilisation and at the same time its greatest territorial extension. We can reconstruct a fairly accurate picture of the times from the astonishingly realistic sculptures which decorate the numerous and monumental palaces and temples which the kings of Assyria erected to their own glory. In this, Ashurbanipal was among the foremost. He was also passionately interested in archaeology and collected an immense library which by chance has been preserved. The civilisation revealed by means of these sources owes much to Babylon; but also it is indebted to the other conquered peoples, a fact which is explained by the exchange of goods and the traffic of different races which took place within so vast a unified empire. Though in this way Assyrian culture lost some of its original local character it gained a cosmopolitan quality.

In this nation of warriors the army and the king played the essential role. The sovereign was the source of all authority. As the representative of the gods he was above mere mortals and in his palace lived apart from them, isolated in his majesty. It was the desire of every Assyrian king to erect his own palace, if not to build an entirely new capital city: thus Sargon II founded Dur-Sarrukin (Khorsabad). The king's primary function was to command the army. The army was composed of mercenary troops commanded by Assyrian officers, and its effectiveness in battle it owed to its chariots. It was, however, no less invincible in the art of the siege, and its corps of engineers was furnished with a variety of siege equipment.

The civil administration is less well documented and

89

appears to have been less skilfully organised. The public services seem to have been merged with the personal service of the king. Nevertheless the administration continued to expand, above all in the provinces, where the system of ruling through a protectorate was more and more replaced by direct central control. During the reign of Ashurbanipal authority was almost everywhere in the hands of governors, assisted by scribes whose frequent and detailed reports kept the king informed of all subversive movements which might disturb the security of his empire.

The downfall of the Assyrian Empire

This powerful and mighty empire collapsed in the brief course of a few years. Ashurbanipal's successors are shadowy figures, simply, it may be, because their authority was unquestioned. But it would seem that there were troubles within the palace. The Babylonians took advantage of this state of affairs to reassert their independence, and in 626 B.C. Nabopolassar founded a new Chaldean dynasty in Babylonia. Ten years later he went to war, and all lower Mesopotamia rallied to his cause. The Assyrians were beaten at Arapkha. Suddenly the situation seemed so grave that Egypt, fearing in Babylonia a possible future enemy, sent reinforcements to the Assyrians, but in vain. At the same time the Medes attacked in the region of the upper Tigris. In 614 B.C., under the command of Cyaxares, they fell upon Ashur, the oldest capital of the empire, and sacked it. A year later, it is true, Nabopolassar encountered such stiff Assyrian resistance that he was forced to fall back on Babylon. But by the following year, 612 B.C., the Chaldeans and the Medes, this time acting in unison, marched against Nineveh, which succumbed after a heroic struggle. The last Assyrian king, Ashur-uballit II, still held out at

An unidentified god from the Palace of Ashurbanipal at Kalach c. 800 B.C. *Archiv für Kunst und Geschichte*

Harran. In 610 B.C. the coalition seized Harran. Meanwhile Necho II had marched from Egypt with his relieving army. It was met at Megiddo by Josiah, King of Judah, and there on the bloody field of Armageddon Josiah perished. Necho's victory was hollow, for he was a year too late to save his ally. The Assyrian Empire had vanished.

The Dorian invasions

The invasion of the Sea Peoples was only one aspect of a great ethnic movement which also had its repercussions in the Balkan peninsula. Here it took the form of a fresh wave of Greek peoples in search of new territory: the Dorians. The region which they invaded was not again to experience such an upheaval for more than a thousand years. The date and the duration of the Dorian invasions can only be approximately determined as having taken place between the twelfth and the ninth centuries. On the other hand, the origin of the new tribes appears to be certain: they came from the valley of the Danube whence they reached Thessaly via the Morava-Vardar gap and the valley of the Haliacmon in Macedonia. From there one group of the invaders made westwards across the Pindus mountains and, proceeding by way of Epirus and Acarnania, crossed the gulf of Corinth and reached Elis where they settled. The other group did not cross the Pindus range but continued southwards as far as Boeotia. From there they sailed round Attica and reached Argolis.

This migration left deep furrows in its wake. In Greece itself the invaders did not traverse lands already populated and civilised without adopting many local customs or without bringing in their train some of the uprooted people whose homes they had burnt and left in ruins. The result must have been a vast melting-pot of peoples on the move, an exchange of habits and a mingling of populations. This, of course, destroys the legend of the racial purity of the Dorians, and makes it impossible to attribute to them all the innovations which appeared in Greece at this time. Beyond the Greek mainland the consequences of the Dorian invasion were also far reaching. The inhabitants, fleeing before the invader, emigrated to the islands and the coastal regions of the Aegean Sea, with the result that these too became settlements of the Greek race. This colonial movement was especially important in the coastal regions of Asia Minor, though it is impossible for us to follow the stages by which it took place.

The formation of the 'Polis'

Both on the mainland and in the new Aegean colonies the Greeks tended to split into small autonomous groups. This was due not only to geographical factors, but to a political and social phenomenon: the formation of the *polis* or city-state. Even centuries later, under the Roman Empire, the *polis* remained the normal centre of Greek life; it was much more than a geographical unit formed by the city and the countryside around it. The *polis* had a life and individuality of its own, though the institutions it developed were similar in form in nearly all the Greek cities. It was an attitude of mind, an intellectual conception, the one form in which the Greeks could conceive the

Fragment of a musicians' procession from a relief at Ashur-banipal's palace at Nineveh. 650 B.C. *Archiv für Kunst und Geschichte*

political framework of their civilisation. Wherever they settled or formed colonies they gathered together in cities.

This pattern was to develop self-contained political units, with each city-state having its own code of laws. The city-state was small (only Athens could count 20,000 citizens). In a democracy of this size a representative system was unnecessary. The individual citizen participated in administrative and judicial affairs. The assembly was an assembly of all citizens, with equal rights of vote and speech. Essentially, citizenship — usually granted through descent from a citizen family — conferred certain privileges, among them the right to vote in the assembly, the right to own property, to hold public office, to be paid for attendance in the assembly and for court service, and a right to enter into a marriage contract with another citizen.

The idea of the city-state was born and developed during the shadowy and ill-documented period before the seventh century B.C., and it is therefore almost impossible to trace the first phases of its growth. To be sure the topography of Greece, with its many islands and indented coastlines, encouraged its development, but that was only a contributory factor. There were others of greater importance. In that troubled epoch the military situation must certainly have been a major element in creating and forming the *polis*. Isolated groups of people whose very existence was constantly menaced were forced to live in a permanent state of mobilisation, and the rank which a man held in the army tended to become the rank he held in civic life. Religion must also have influenced the growth of the *polis*; for we notice that the most primitive groupments — the tribe, the phratry and the *genos* — are essentially of a religious nature. Nor can we neglect the part played by economic factors. Finally, we cannot determine what influences giving rise to this form of organisation the Greeks may have inherited from their predecessors, in particular the Mycenaeans, or for that matter from their own prehistoric traditions: both must have been considerable.

The age of the kings

Thanks to the poems of Homer and Hesiod, as well as to survivals into historical times of earlier institutions, we are in a slightly better position to retrace the early evolution of the Greek *polis*. But it is important to emphasise that deductions drawn from these various sources must be accepted with caution; and, since the examples at our disposal are few and far between, there is the additional risk that what was an exception may be mistaken for the rule. It would seem, nevertheless, that in the beginning Greek political and social life was dominated by the *genos*, or clan. Claiming noble ancestry — often descent from a god — the *genos* owed its solidarity to blood-relationship and religion, and its strength to a monopoly of the only form of wealth known at that epoch: fields and flocks. Those who did not belong to a *genos* — such as country labourers, artisans and tradesmen — were defenceless and without consequence. Doubtless there were very few of them. The chief of the most important *genos* was the king, but the title carried little weight. His powers were not great. He commanded the army, but in those days when a battle was merely the sum of individual combats, valour and glory did not pertain to

91

him alone. He rendered justice, but it was not he who punished crime: the criminal was dealt with by the kinsmen of the offended party, in other words by vendetta. The king, in fact, was only the arbiter. In religious matters he had more power, but even in the exercise of his least contested authority he was constantly attended and closely watched by a council of the chiefs of the other clans. The lesser nobles were sometimes convoked in an assembly of the people, but only in a consultative capacity. In spite of its very modest powers the monarchy eventually disappeared. At first hereditary, it became elective; finally its authority was divided among several magistrates who were usually elected annually.

Social unrest during the age of the nobles

This clan system bore in itself the germs of its own destruction. Those who did not belong to the *genos*, or who had been banished from it, had no legal rights and very often no means of gaining a livelihood. Moreover, the system made it a simple matter for the great nobles to acquire exclusive possession of the land. By taste, tradition and military necessity, the nobles were raisers of cattle, above all of horses. The defenceless countryman was deprived of his land and, since it was required for pasturage, was often unable to remain even as a tenant farmer. He became part of a dispossessed proletariat which, with the banished members of the noble class, was ready for any adventure.

At the same time other forces were at work to undermine the status quo. In the course of the seventh century changes in military tactics and armament had begun to give to the *hoplite*, or heavily armed foot-soldier, a distinct advantage over the mounted soldier. But the hoplites were effective only when employed in a solid yet flexible mass, the phalanx. The outcome of battles ceased to depend on single-handed encounters between 'heroes'. Victory went to the big battalions. Every city was obliged to extend its military recruitment. The nobles, who until then had been the sole fighting class, were no longer able to furnish enough combatants. The new classes to be conscripted into the military service of the city resented their political and social inferiority even more fiercely now that they were called upon to assume heavier responsibilities. The time was approaching when the oligarchy would be forced to consider their demands.

At the same time industry and commerce, though badly hit by the Dorian invasions, were by no means at a standstill. Especially in the Greek cities of Asia Minor commercial activity was powerfully stimulated by neighbouring peoples who were rich and highly civilised. In other parts of the Greek world, too, trade continued on a reduced scale. Certain technical progress contributed to its revival. Ceramics, the chief Greek industry, continually improved both its methods of manufacture and the beauty of its products: more and more people demanded Greek pottery. The invention of new kinds of ships which made navigation safer and quicker created busier shipyards. Above all, at the beginning of the seventh century, the invention of money — the final step in a series of improvements in methods of exchange — gave fresh impetus to economic life. In all these ways new social classes came into being, and their numbers and wealth increased. The new commercial classes did not as a rule fit into the

A Cypriot statue. The frontal style of archaic sculpture owed much to Egyptian influence. *Giraudon*

An archaic relief of a Greek soldier. Athens. *Schneider-Lengyel*

old tribal system based on the *genos*; and it was natural that they should attempt to overthrow the old order and gain a position in the state they felt they deserved.

The result of these complex changes was twofold: on the one hand grave internal disturbances gradually modified the social and political organisation of the Hellenic world; on the other, many of the victims of the changes felt that the only solution to their problems was to emigrate. In consequence, between the eighth and the sixth centuries, numerous Greek colonies sprang up all round the shores of the Mediterranean, spreading the language and civilisation of Greece everywhere. These two results hastened the process of evolution: a fresh crisis in the city would drive a fresh wave of emigrants abroad, while subsequent trade with the new colony thus formed would increase the influence of the commercial classes and the complexity of social problems at home.

These recurrent disturbances often went as far as civil war, with its train of implacable hatreds and bloody revenge; and the cities attempted various methods of solving the problem. First we see the 'new-rich' acquiring political equality with the nobles with the introduction of a timocracy: those whose fortune in money was as great as the nobles' fortune in landed property were given equal access to public office. This did nothing to satisfy the great masses of the agricultural and urban proletariat, who continued to clamour for the abolition of debts, the sharing out of lands and constitutional reform.

The Law Givers

Appeal was often made to some outstanding citizen who commanded general respect and confidence. Such men were granted full powers to arbitrate, and their chief task was to draw up a code of laws — hence the generic name which history has given them: the Law Givers. Previously the nobles had administered the law, which was handed down by oral tradition, a system which was open to frequent abuse. It was felt that an end to civil strife could be made by written laws which clearly fixed the rights and duties of all citizens. The earliest of the legislators, Zaleucus of Locris, dates from the beginning of the seventh century. The last of them, including Solon of Athens, the most illustrious of all, belong to the following century. We know little of their personalities or their careers, but the service they rendered the public was of capital importance: on the ruins of the juridical privileges of the nobles they erected the authority of the state in criminal affairs, and thereby further contributed to the dissolution of the *genos*.

The tyrants

Though the establishment of a written code of law was a step in the right direction, it did not automatically solve the social problem; nor had all the cities yet taken even this step. More than peaceful persuasion was needed to break the power of the nobles; strong men, able to exert force, were required. This explains the appearance, also towards the beginning of the seventh century, of autocratic governments in many cities. The autocrats or the tyrants — a word which in its original sense had no pejorative significance — had a long career of success, longer than the Law Givers. The last of the tyrants was not overthrown until 460 B.C. Nevertheless the period in which this unconstitutional form of government was most widespread covers only a century, from about 650 to 550 B.C.

We know little about ancient Greek tyranny, which naturally varied according to the place, the time and the

Canino, a 'parasite', a common stock figure in early comedy. British Museum. *Schneider-Lengyel*

93

The fixed smile was a characteristic feature of early Greek sculpture. Later, when more was known of anatomy, it gave place to less rigid stylisation.

character of the tyrant himself. But in every case it was social unrest and strife which brought the tyrant to power, and the policy of every tyrant presents many characteristics common to them all. The tyrants were in the main of noble blood, yet each presented himself as a leader of the popular party and an avowed enemy of the aristocracy. They would normally seize power by a coup d'état which consisted in occupying the citadel and installing in it a mercenary garrison.

Once in power the tyrant would conduct himself in the most 'untyrannical' manner possible. He would make every effort to respect at least the outward forms of constitutional government and to shed as little blood as possible. Instead of massacring his enemies the tyrant preferred their more or less voluntary exile, though he did not eschew private assassination when this seemed necessary. His most powerful weapons were the city's prestige and economic prosperity. His foreign policy was enterprising and took a colonial rather than a military form, for defeat in battle would have been disastrous to his position. His domestic policy was to undertake vast public works that gave employment to the workless, embellished the city and flattered the masses. Such a policy was costly, but the growth of public and private revenue allowed the expenses to be met. Protests against the financial exactions of the tyrants were rare. Above all they worked without respite to raise the standard of living of the lower

strata of society at the expense of the nobles. Few radically revolutionary measures were taken, but the development of commerce and industry improved the lot of the urban proletariat, while in the country the peasants received the lands of the exiled aristocracy.

Farmers were given loans which permitted them to establish their economic independence on a solid foundation. Tyranny, wherever it was instituted, solved the agrarian problem by destroying the former monopoly of land by the *genos*.

Greek colonisation

Colonisation was another solution which the Greeks hit upon to remedy the evils of oligarchical domination. Most of the emigrants who from the beginning of the eighth century left their native soil were country people in search of land to cultivate. It is important, however, to notice that not every emigrating Greek became a colonist. Many of the more adventurous hired themselves to eastern sovereigns as mercenary soldiers. Nevertheless Greek colonisation was of the greatest historical significance since it resulted in the formation of a 'New World' which was Hellenic. At first a hunger for land was the prime motive which sent the Greek countryman across the seas. But as commerce began to assume a place of greater and greater importance in the life of Greece, other preoccupations arose: a search for new export markets, the seizure of strategic positions in order to protect trade from competitors. But it was not until the seventh century that these things became matters of deliberate policy.

The colonial movement was at first haphazard and unplanned: the colonists formed groups at will and settled wherever they found a suitable place. But unoccupied land was rare and the natives often unfriendly. To install themselves in such places required force, and warlike preparations had to be made in advance. Not all Greek cities were populous, and it was sometimes difficult to find a sufficient number of emigrants to form a colony. The venture had then to be made in conjunction with neighbouring cities. In the end colonisation became so important for economic and imperialist reasons that the state took over its direction. The city government would appoint a leader. In charge of the group of intending colonists, he was the *oikistes*, or founder. He was given his destination and provided with a staff of soothsayers and surveyors. When the colony was established it adopted the religion and the laws of the city which founded it. The Greek colonies were usually politically and economically independent from their very beginnings, though in a few instances the mother-city interfered either to protect the colony or if she disapproved of the new city's foreign policies. Corinth tried to maintain a strict control over her colonies, and this policy resulted in violent conflicts with the more powerful of them (notably Corcyra) when they claimed the right to determine their own fate.

No attempt is made here to enumerate the colonies which the Greeks planted, and we shall limit ourselves to indicating the general directions in which Hellenic civilisation spread. The way to the East was barred by the presence of powerful and civilised states. Egypt, however, received many expatriated Greeks as mercenary troops,

One of the lions of Delos, an island in the Cyclades. Made from
Naxian marble and presented by the people of Naxos to form
an avenue at the sanctuary of Apollo. The treasury of the Delian
Confederacy was housed here. *Viollet*

though the xenophobia of the native Egyptian forced the pharaohs to confine these foreigners to the Delta city of Naucratis, the only trading settlement in Egypt open to the Greeks. In the north Greek colonisation crept along the coasts of Macedonia and Thrace, reached the Propontis and, after the foundation of Byzantium by Megara and Argos in about 660 B.C., spread round the shores of the Black Sea. These settlements were made chiefly by the Ionian city of Miletus. But the most numerous and prosperous of the new Greek colonies were those in Sicily and southern Italy. By 750 B.C. there were settlements as far up the Italian peninsula as the Bay of Naples, at Cumae, beyond which they never penetrated; and by the end of the seventh century the majority of their larger cities had already been founded. These cities, whose basis was agriculture, gradually created a network of trade round the shores of the Mediterranean. In central Italy the Greeks encountered the Etruscans and farther to the west they came up against the Phoenicians. Their only really successful colony in this part of the Mediterranean was Massilia, or Marseilles, founded by the Phocaeans in about 600 B.C.

More or less all the peoples of Greece contributed to this wide expansion. In the beginning the colonists came from every part of the Greek world: for instance, the eighth-century settlements on the Italian peninsula were made not only by large cities with thriving and prosperous industries, but also by smaller towns whose economy was still in a purely agricultural phase. Little by little, however, certain cities took the lead in colonial enterprise — namely, the cities which were commercially the most highly developed: on the Isthmus, Corinth and Megara; in Euboea, Eretria and Chalcis; and pre-eminently in the Greek cities of Asia Minor, the chief of which was Miletus. Some of them even succeeded in establishing a monopoly over certain territories, as Miletus did in the Black Sea. On the border of Macedonia the name Chalcidice still preserves the memory of the colonial predominance of Chalcis.

The colonial movement had begun before the middle of the eighth century and reached its greatest activity during the seventh. Towards the middle of the sixth century it died down and, for a variety of reasons, ceased. In the first place, its object — that is, to cure the congestion of crowded and land-hungry Greek cities — had been almost achieved. In the second place, Greek expansion had run into ever-increasing resistance. Indigenous populations did not often passively accept being dispossessed of their lands and on more than one occasion they fought ferociously against the new-comers. Then other imperial powers contested territory which seemed vital to them: thus the Phoenicians considered Spain and North Africa to be their spheres of interest. Finally, the Greek metropolis was exhausted, no less than the colonies themselves by internecine warfare; and, looming black on the Eastern horizon, there was the Persian menace which turned the thoughts and energies of Greece in a new direction.

Archaic Greece

To form a complete and balanced idea of the Hellenic world at this time a picture of its infinite regional diversity would have to be drawn. This is impossible; for to reconstruct the archaic epoch we have little more than

folklore and legend to rely on. We possess a few details of very dubious accuracy about the more important cities, which at least indicate that the political and social developments, which have already been discussed in general terms, occurred in different ways in different localities. In one community the growth of the *polis* had scarcely begun, in another it took shape only after a long delay, in still others local conditions altered its evolution or halted it entirely. On the whole, the process began earlier and took place more rapidly in cities where commerce was most active, in other words, especially in the seaports of the Aegean, while agricultural communities remained relatively unaffected.

This was the case among the peoples of the north and centre of the Greek mainland, and of the Peloponnesus — with the exception of Sparta, which followed a course of its own. In Sparta a kind of feudal system prevailed. Here an ostentatious and warlike aristocracy ruled over an enslaved peasantry. The city in the sense of the *polis* hardly existed. Sparta still remained not far removed from the tribal system which had existed in the days of the invasions. Among Greek cities of this time religious confederations (amphictyones) were formed, the most celebrated of these being the league of Delphi; but the bonds which drew them together were weak and internal rivalry often made such confederations a pretext for quarrel rather than a factor of union. On the shores of the Aegean, however, communities arose whose future was to be brilliant. Some of them, to be sure, sprang up and withered quickly, like Chalcis and Eretria in Euboea which towards 700 B.C. fought a long and mutually exhausting war for possession of the rich lands of the Lelantus plain, and divided early Greece into two hostile camps. Corinth, on the other hand, never ceased to prosper, first as an oligarchy ruled by the Bacchiadae, and then, from 657 B.C., under the tyrant Cypselus and his successors. Corinth's ceramic, metallurgic and textile industries stimulated commerce which in its turn demanded constant improvements in shipbuilding. It was in Corinth in 704 (?) that Amenocles was said to have invented the trireme. Corinth was among the foremost in planting colonies; she became the head of a veritable colonial empire whose destruction led to the downfall of her tyrants in 582 B.C.

Ionia and Lydia

But no city on the Greek mainland, or on the islands, was as advanced as the Greek settlements in Asia Minor. Not all of these, of course, developed with equal rapidity: Aeolis, except for its offshore island of Lesbos, remained in the agricultural phase of civilisation, while Doris was more advanced. Ionia, however, was at this time the heart of the Greek world. Of its dozen towns three were unrivalled in the rest of Greece. Miletus had been immensely enriched by trade with the colonies she had founded in the Black Sea, although she did not neglect other markets. Ephesus was more oriental, as her famous temple to Artemis demonstrates, for the Diana of Ephesus was in fact a version of the eastern Great Mother Goddess. Ephesus traded by caravan with Sardis.

Colour plate: the Royal Tombs at Mycenae. *A.F. Kersting*

Finally Samos, in spite of her aristocratic administration, looked for her livelihood towards the sea.

Ionia, comprising as it did the coastal fringe of Asia Minor, could have been submerged by the great continental empires. But she was fortunate, in her early days, to have neighbouring states which were unambitious: the Phrygia of Midas, and then the kingdom of the Sardonidae in Lydia. But towards 685 B.C. the Sardonidae were overthrown by Gyges who made Sardis his capital. Half by force and half by diplomatic skill he succeeded in making Ionia a Lydian protectorate. Gyges was an admirer of Hellenic civilisation, which lightened the burden. Then, some thirty years later, the Cimmerians, breaking from their homelands in the Caucasus and the steppes of the Caspian Sea, invaded Lydia and in 652 B.C. killed Gyges. Ionia too was ravaged. The storm, however, quickly passed. Ardys, Gyges' son, resumed his father's policy and after eleven years of war concluded a treaty of alliance with Miletus.

The Mermnadae dynasty of Lydia, which Gyges had founded, realised that tolerance was more profitable than coercion. The Lydian sovereigns opened the kingdom to Greek maritime traders and, by improving the caravan routes, encouraged their own subjects to trade with the hinterland. The tolls they collected, the golden sands of Pactolus and a thriving agricultural production made the kings of Lydia proverbially rich, and the Greeks shared largely in their prosperity. Sardis became an almost half-Greek city. Exchange between the two peoples was not limited to merchandise. Although Ionia partly Hellenised Lydia, Lydia in turn gave Ionia technical skills, artistic themes, religious beliefs and customs which were oriental in origin.

The commercial and industrial activity of Ionia doubtless encouraged a precocious political and social development, but the details of the process are imperfectly known. As early as 600 B.C. Chios seems to have possessed democratic institutions. At Ephesus, on the contrary, the government was in the hands of the Basilidae, an oligarchical family allied by numerous marriages with the Lydian sovereigns, the Mermnadae. Ephemeral tyrants were unsuccessful in getting rid of them. In Samos government by tyrants did not appear before the sixth century. Miletus, on the other hand, was governed by tyrants a century earlier. The best known of these was Thrasybulus who made the treaty of alliance with Ardys. But the tyrants of Miletus were unable to solve the social problem which was no longer purely agrarian.

Sparta and Athens

Sparta and Athens must be treated apart, in view of the roles they played in subsequent Greek history. Their early days are also better documented, though the records are not always reliable, especially those of Sparta who, in the classic epoch, loved to veil her past in mystery. Sparta described herself as Dorian, and her history was no doubt more influenced by the Dorian invasions than that of other Greek cities. The valley of the Eurotas, which the future Lacedaemonians occupied towards the end of the tenth century, was already inhabited by a

rich and civilised people whom it took the invaders more than a century to subdue, and with whom they had, at times, to come to terms. Then, without further pause, they attacked the neighbouring territories. They drove the Argives from the Aegean coast beyond the Parnon range, and wrested from the Arcadians certain mountainous districts of their southern highlands. A twenty years' war (c. 735-716 B.C.) made them masters of Messenia. In the seventh century their enemies reacted with violence. Under Phidon in 670 B.C. Argos recaptured her lost provinces and the Messenians rose in revolt. It took thirty years, from 640 to 610 B.C., to crush them.

This troubled history goes far to explain the military character of Spartan civilisation and institutions. The Spartan citizen was first and foremost a soldier. From infancy he received a collective education directed by the state, and until the age of thirty lived a communal life with his fellow soldiers. In order that he might give his whole attention to a military career each Spartan was provided with a piece of land which was cultivated by state-owned serfs: the *helots*. Spartan institutions were in advance of the times. Two kings ruled jointly and both commanded the army. They were assisted by a council of elders, the *gerusia*, and supervised by five *ephors*. The *apella* — or assembly of the people — still played an active role.

At this time Sparta was not yet the closed city she later became. She took part in the colonial movement and welcomed outside influences, from Ionia, for example. Sparta, in those days, appeared to be a friendly and wide-awake community.

The development of Athens was much slower. Attica was spared the Dorian invasions and, geographically broken up into small parcels of land, it was long before she achieved unity. In after days the honour of uniting Attica was attributed to Theseus, but it is probable that the local ruling families were always closely connected with the master of the Athenian Acropolis. Though such a connection did not prevent the persistence of local customs and differences, it tended in the end to concentrate political power in Athens. For generations the absence of contact with the outside world encouraged a government of the aristocratic type. The clans who owned the richest lands formed the nobility — the Eupatridae. The Eupatridae furnished the three archons who in 683-682 B.C. replaced the kings, as well as certain auxiliary magistrates. Power was in fact wielded by the council which assembled on the hill of Ares — the Areopagus — while the assembly of the people had little voice in the matter. In all essentials this form of government remained unchanged until the end of the seventh century.

Greek civilisation in the Archaic Period

With all their divisions and their incurable passion for self-government we find the Greeks, as they emerge from the shadows of their formative period, in possession of a common civilisation which gave them a lively sentiment of their own individuality and difference from other peoples. This does not mean that their civilisation at the end of the seventh century had not assimilated foreign elements or become rigidly fixed. On the contrary, it continued to develop its own distinctive character.

The chief factor which contributed to the unity of

Colour plate: detail of a terracotta panel depicting Phrygian soldiers; from Pazarli. c. 800 B.C. *Josephine Powell*

Greek civilisation was, in spite of its numerous dialects, the Greek language. The Greeks had adopted and adapted the Phoenician alphabet perhaps as early as the tenth century, and had not been long in putting their traditional oral literature into writing. The first and outstanding work of this literature was the verse attributed to Homer. Everything about the Homeric poems is subject to debate: their date, the origin of the legends they contain, the identity of the author or authors. What is certain is that the Greeks knew them by heart. From Homer they learned of the glorious exploits of their ancestors; he reflected their sentiments and stirred their imagination; he even supplied them with political arguments. If we make an exception of Hesiod's *Works and Days*, which is a countryman's poem full of high moral precepts, the aristocratic tone of Homer's poems is found again in the works which followed. The lyric poets echo the preoccupations of the times; and the ineradicable hatreds fanned by the political and social strife already described lend a note of violence to many of these verses.

This violence, however, is not apparent in the art of the period, in which an oriental inspiration predominates. The principal art form was ceramics. After the geometric period, illustrated by the great funerary amphoras of the Dipylon at Athens, the oriental style in pottery became general. The vases of Rhodes and of Corinth show the results of the new influences and techniques: a rich polychrome surface which imitates the texture of fine material, a taste for decoration drawn from plant-life, representations of animals and monsters, scenes in which man only later begins to take a place — a still subordinate place.

Religion, such as it appears to us in Homer, was already a mixture of elements. The gods were of varying origin, often borrowed from neighbouring states, or sometimes imported from distant lands through which Greeks had migrated. But all the gods were united in a single pantheon and the poets had already woven the great legends into a popular mythology. Olympus continued to welcome foreign divinities, especially those who came from the East. The religious unity of the Greeks, however, was based less on Mount Olympus than on religious rites which were similar all over the Greek world. These rites were especially associated with certain fixed places or sanctuaries. In this epoch the sanctuary assumed its essential elements: the sacred enclosure, the altar, and finally the temple. The temple would soon provide a location for artistic originality and beauty.

Some of these sanctuaries became of more than local importance: during the festivals celebrated in honour of the god, neighbouring cities would send delegations to compete for the prizes awarded for music or athletic games. Certain festivals soon attained an international reputation, such as the games at Olympus which were held for the first time in the year 776 B.C. A general truce was declared during these celebrations so that the safety of pilgrims to the Olympic games was respected. During the contests a high level of sportsmanship and fair play were scrupulously maintained, though it may be doubtful whether Olympus or Delphi or any other pan-hellenic sanctuary could have suppressed local patriotism entirely.

Hermes and a Charite. At this period the gods were portrayed wearing the clothes of contemporary society. *Giraudon*

In any event participation in common rites and festivals, and a respect for the same ideals, was a further contribution to the growth of Greek national sentiment.

Primitive Italy and the origins of Rome

The end of the second millennium and the following five centuries saw the beginnings of civilisation in Italy. The basic population, composed of Neolithic tribes of unknown origin, was overrun by a succession of invaders arriving from various directions. The *terramare* came before 1200 B.C. from eastern Europe and brought with them bronze; they dotted the plains of the Po valley with their villages built on piles. Towards the year 1000 B.C. the Villanovians of Hungary penetrated as far as the Tiber and brought iron into general use. The Illyrians took possession of the eastern Adriatic coast of the peninsula and penetrated into the central Apennines. The Phoenicians and the Greeks introduced oriental influences, especially from the beginning of the eighth century.

From this moment it is the region of the western slopes of the Apennines that is of greatest historical interest. In the section of Italy which is now Tuscany the Etruscan people became powerful. The origin of the Etruscans is still disputed: they may have been indigenous, or invaders from the North, or emigrants from Asia Minor who arrived at a date set somewhere between the thirteenth and the eighth century, according to whether they were Peoples of the Sea or victims of the Cimmerian invasions. Whatever their origin, they colonised the country by following the rivers inland from the coast, and their principal towns were built in the interior of the peninsula. Though they were primarily an agricultural people they had a thriving metal industry. They lived in cities which were rather loosely organised into confederations. Etruscan kings were soon replaced by an oligarchy composed of the great landed proprietors. The native population had been reduced to serfdom and was often on the point of revolt. Etruscan civilisation was in many respects related to that of the East, notably in its religion in which divination played an important part. But from the seventh century it was largely influenced by Greek culture: Corinthian at first, and then Attic. Attic pottery became an essential feature in Etruscan burial rites.

Farther to the south, Latium, between the inhospitable coast and the volcanic barrier at the foot of the Apennines, formed a region which had sufficient pasturage to support herds and flocks. Its population of lawless shepherds was scattered in numerous villages perched on the many hills which dominated the marshy lowlands. They were grouped in religious leagues, the most important of which had its centre at Alba Longa. Across the Tiber, which formed the frontier with Etruria, there was a ford where the road from Campagna crossed the trail by which the salt from the marshes was carried inland to the mountains, and here an active trading centre arose. On the group of hills dominating this ford Rome was founded, according to legend in the year 753 B.C. Romulus, the founder, was said to have come from Alba. The quarrel in which he murdered his brother Remus is perhaps a legendary account of a fight between the new-comers who had installed themselves on the Palatine Hill and those who already occupied the Aventine Hill nearby. Similarly, the rape of the Sabines would illustrate

the struggle with the Sabine occupants of the Capitoline Hill. What is certain is that until the end of the seventh century Rome was not a single town but a group of villages. The institutions which were formed as the villages confederated retained traces of the original Latin-Sabine dualism: the kings were alternatively, or perhaps even simultaneously, Latins and/or Sabines. The former ruled as warrior-kings and the latter, assuming that their functions were divided, as priest-kings. There is little doubt that in the beginning there were two tribes, the Ramnes and the Taties. There were double colleges of priests. The only event which distinguishes the early history of the sprawling village was the capture — and destruction — of Alba, illustrated by the episode of the Horatii and the Curiatii which resulted in Rome's joining the confederation of Latin cities. Such were the obscure beginnings of the future mistress of the Mediterranean World.

The Aryan kingdoms of India

The history of India until the sixth century B.C. is the history of Aryan expansion in the great Indus-Ganges plain, and very little is known about it. The conquering invaders spread towards the east, the natural direction for their expansion. They did not form a unified empire but dissolved into a series of feudal principalities which were constantly at war with each other.

During the course of the centuries the more eastern states tended to be more powerful. Thus as the time of the last Vedic collections, that is, between 1000 and 800 B.C., the chief state was the kingdom of Kuru,

established in the Doab. It was here that traditional Brahmanism is said to have taken form.

In the eighth and seventh centuries the leading clans were those of northern Behar who formed the kingdom of Videha. But in the age of Buddha (563-483 B.C.) the centre of gravity moved westwards to Benares in Oudh, and the kingdom of Kosala rose to importance.

Feudal China and the Chou Dynasty

The Chou epoch in China was a period of feudal principalities and civil wars. Responsibility for this disorder lay with the founder of the new dynasty, Wu-wang, who was more interested in his own principality than in the empire. Wu-wang shared the former Shang domains between members of his own family, who were not slow to assert their independence. The process was facilitated by the wars which the Chou emperors were obliged to wage against the barbarians of the north-west and the Man tribesmen, who were culturally half Chinese, of the Yangtze valley. These wars left the emperors progressively enfeebled until at last, in 771 B.C., the enemy destroyed their capital city of Hao. The emperors then took refuge in Honan, near Lo-yang, from which new capital the dynasty reigned for the next five hundred years — until 249 B.C. Meanwhile independent feudal principalities continued to fight among themselves; one after another gained a brief hegemony, but never succeeded in establishing a central authority. In the resulting confusion the barbarians of the Yangtze were powerful enough to spread Chinese civilisation into many new regions.

An early Attic kylix depicting Jason, prince of Iolcus, in Thessaly, and leader of the Argonauts. According to legend, it was with his help that Medea captured the Golden Fleece. Early fifth century B.C. *Anderson*

Left: ruins of the Palaestra at Olympia where pan-hellenic games were celebrated every four years in honour of Zeus. Symbolic of an ideal, the Games imposed a period of truce so that contestants and spectators of every city and tribe might attend without fear of being molested by traditional enemies. The Games took place regularly until A.D. 394 when Theodosius forbade them.

CHAPTER FOUR

CONFLICT BETWEEN EAST AND WEST

500-400 B.C.

The dissolution of the Assyrian Empire did not restore freedom to the subject peoples. New empires succeeded it, and to the west of these a new power, a civilisation of an entirely different kind, grew to maturity, a civilisation which was first to arrest the expansion of Oriental empires, then to dispute their ascendancy in Asia itself, and finally, in the age of Alexander the Great, to subjugate them. In the period between the defeat of Assuruballit II and the Persian wars historical interest lies in the ever-growing hostility between Asia and Europe, between the theocratic and absolutist imperialism of the East and Greek patriotism, inspired and sustained by the love of liberty.

The Neo-Babylonian empire

It was the Babylonians who apparently reaped the greatest immediate profit from the defeat which they and the Medes had inflicted on the Assyrians. Nebuchadrezzar (605-562 B.C.), the son and successor of Nabopolassar, ably began his reign by repulsing the Pharaoh Necho who had marched to the relief of his Assyrian ally. Pursuing the defeated pharaoh, Nebuchadrezzar met with and broke the resistance of the king whom Necho had imposed on Judah after his victory at Megiddo in 609 B.C. Jerusalem was taken and, with its king, a part of the population was led captive to Babylon in 597 B.C. The king's successor failed to take warning from this lesson, rebelled, and was in his turn crushed ten years later. Jerusalem was razed to the ground and the country annexed. At the price of Judah's downfall Necho had at least avoided a Babylonian invasion of Egypt.

From then on peace reigned in the kingdom of Babylon, and the dynastic troubles which brought the downfall of Nebuchadrezzar's son, Evil-Merodach (Amel-Marduk), who was overthrown by Neriglissar (560-556 B.C.), then the accession of Nabonidus (556-539 B.C.), did little to disturb it. All of these sovereigns, Nabonidus especially, were devout. They were enthusiastic constructors of sacred buildings and their many edifices gave magnificence and splendour not only to Babylon but to all the cities of the Chaldean empire.

The Medes and the Persians

The future, however, did not belong to the Chaldeans but to their allies, the Medes, and to the Persians, a people closely related to the Medes. The history of these two peoples is not well known until the point at which they rose to dominate the eastern world. During the course of the second millennium the Medes were an obscure group of Indo-European tribes who lived beyond

An early terracotta figure from Tanagra, Boeotia. It is probably Gaea, the earth goddess. Usually represented as a gigantic woman, Gaea was a divinity of the primitive Greeks and was supposed to have given birth to the gods and then to the first mortals.

the Zagros mountains, and it is not until the ninth century that they are referred to in Assyrian texts. Like the Persians, who did not settle until much later in their historic homeland along the Persian Gulf, the Medes were still marauding nomads. They remained partially nomadic even in the epoch of their greatness, for theirs was poor agricultural land. Nomadic society does not encourage the concentration of authority in a single hand, and in spite of frequent conflict with the Assyrians — who never really subdued them — the Medes' first supreme sovereign was Cyaxares, the conqueror of Nineveh. The development of the Persians was still slower. It was not until the time of Cyrus that they achieved unity — and the circumstances are not known.

Cyaxares' victory over the Assyrians had given him Urartu and part of upper Mesopotamia. Profiting from the absence of contention between the Medes and the Chaldeans, the Median king, after a five-year war (590-585 B.C.) with Alyattes, king of Lydia, extended his territory as far as the river Halys. It is also possible that he bequeathed to his son, Astyages, nominal suzerainty over the still divided Persians. There was a Persian prince, Teispes, king of Anshan, whose family – the Achaemenidae — may have established itself in this part of northern Elam after the kingdom of Elam had been devastated by Ashurbanipal. It is unlikely that Teispes was even the chief among the petty Persian royalty. But his son, Cyrus the Great, who succeeded him in 557 B.C., was destined for the highest pinnacles of fame.

Cyrus the Great

The birth and youth of Cyrus are shrouded in legend. The first solid fact we know about him is that sometime before 549 B.C. he revolted against Astyages, defeated him, made him prisoner, seized his capital and imposed his own authority over both Medes and Persians. From this time onwards Cyrus went from victory to victory. Renewing the policy of Cyaxares, he chose Lydia as his first adversary. Croesus, who reigned in Lydia between 560 and 546 B.C., had raised the kingdom to its greatest strength: he had made Ephesus a protectorate and conciliated Greek opinion by his fabulous generosity towards their sanctuaries and his admiration for their institutions.

Tradition attributes the initiative of the war to Croesus, but it is hard to see why he should have been tempted to open hostilities. Cyrus had prepared his campaign with diplomatic skill, having made alliances with Nabonidus of Babylonia, with Amasia of Egypt, and even with Sparta. Croesus underestimated his enemy. He was defeated in Cappadocia and again before the walls of Sardis, his capital. He withdrew into the citadel of Sardis which was then taken by surprise. It was the end of Lydia. Revolt against Cyrus the following winter, supported by the Greek cities of Ionia, only resulted in the final submission of Ionia itself. At the same time the Persians subdued the neighbouring peoples and after the year 540 B.C. the whole of Asia Minor recognised the sovereignty of Cyrus.

During this period we know nothing of the personal activities of the Great King himself. He appears again in 539 B.C. in conflict with Babylon, and again he is overwhelmingly victorious. Ill-defended, perhaps by Balthazar, son of Nabonidus, who appears to have done

Many classical sculptures were inspired by sport, for the Greek ideal embraced the cult of physical as well as mental fitness. The gymnasium and the palaestra were found in every city.

An Elamite goddess. *Arc. Photo.*

Bronze warrior figure of the sixth century B.C.

An Ionic column at Delphi. Less ponderous than the Doric column, it was topped with a capital of graceful volutes.

An Etruscan bronze frieze of the seventh century B.C. showing an army on the march. Originating in Asia Minor, the Etruscans settled in Italy in the seventh or eighth century B.C. Their skill in metalwork can be seen in the many surviving examples. A bellicose people, their art is frequently decorated with scenes of warfare and warriors. *Giraudon*

nothing, Babylon held out only for a few days. With his habitual clemency, Cyrus demanded no more than that the old king be held his prisoner; and, by showing his respect for local customs and beliefs, he received the submission of the entire Chaldean empire without striking a further blow. The end of his reign, until 530 B.C., was occupied by campaigns of which little is known. They seem to have been hard-fought and were waged mainly in the east to safeguard the frontiers of the young empire and to keep open the markets with which Persia traded in the steppes of central Asia.

Egypt before the Persian conquest

On his death Cyrus was succeeded by his oldest son, Cambyses. Little is known about the first years of Cambyses' reign: possibly he was obliged to dispose of his brother Smerdis, to whom Cyrus had entrusted the eastern provinces. Five years later, when Cambyses invaded Egypt, his history becomes less vague. Since the Assyrian conquest Egypt had been governed by the Twenty-sixth Saite Dynasty. The founder of the dynasty, Necho I, had won the confidence of Ashurbanipal only to betray it. His son, Psammetichus (663-609 B.C.) had re-unified Egypt with the aid of Greek and Carian mercenaries. He dealt firmly with the priests of Amun and limited the power of the feudal magnates.

This wise policy permitted his successors to give Egypt, internally, the appearance of being once more a great power. But the pharaohs were less successful abroad. We have seen how Necho II (609-594 B.C.) failed in his attempt to save the Assyrian empire. Psammetichus II (594-588 B.C.) and Apries (588-568 B.C.) were forced to watch impotently while Judah was conquered by Nebuchadrezzar. But within Egypt itself prosperity returned. The commerce of Arabia flowed through the canal which Necho had dug between the Nile and the Red Sea. In art, notably in sculpture, there was a brilliant renaissance. Amasis, who was raised to the throne by the revolt of Apries' Egyptian troops, was obliged to assume the

outward appearance of a xenophobe although he continued the pro-Hellenic policy of his predecessors. It was during his reign that Naucratis was founded and relations between Egypt and the Greek world were closest.

Cambyses in Egypt

Amasis (568-525 B.C.) had anticipated the Persian attack and, to counter it, had formed alliances which at the decisive moment failed him. He had constructed a fleet which proved useless, since the attack came by land. He did not witness the failure of his precautions, as he died in 525 B.C. at the moment when Cambyses went into action. The Persian invasion had been carefully prepared, both militarily and diplomatically. The nomads not only allowed the Persians to march unchallenged across the desert of Syria, but supplied them with water. The mercenary troops of Psammetichus III were overwhelmed by sheer numbers at Pelusium. The Pharaoh was besieged at Memphis where he was forced to capitulate, and the rest of the country was occupied without further resistance.

Darius I

Cambyses had remained in Egypt for three years when his throne was usurped by a Mede of the tribe of the Magi, a certain Gaumata, who claimed to be one of his brothers. Cambyses at once returned to Persia to fight him, but in 522 B.C. he was accidentally killed. Gaumata was unable to hold the position he had seized. The Persian nobles rose against him for reasons which are as uncertain as those which originally brought him to power, and he was executed by the conspirators almost immediately after Cambyses' death. Cambyses had left no direct descendant and it was the chief of the conspirators, a distant relative, Darius I, who was proclaimed king.

These dynastic disorders very nearly destroyed the empire. Revolts on a national scale broke out every-

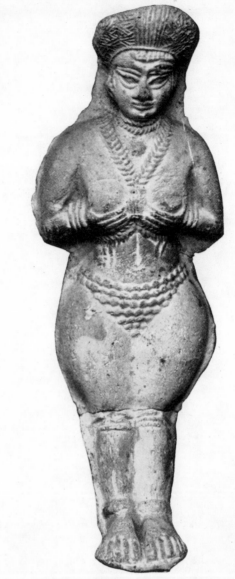

A Neo-Babylonian goddess. *Archives Photographiques, Paris*

A cylinder seal impression. Darius, King of Persia, hunting lion, with the winged disc of the god Ahuramazda above. The two palms are the conventional way of depicting the southern Meso-potamian landscape. There is a trilingual inscription 'Darius the Great King' in Old Persian, Elamite and Babylonian cunei-form. *British Museum*

where, and the satraps (the governors of the provinces), taking advantage of the Great King's embarrassment, attempted to set up independent principalities. The energy of Darius succeeded in restoring order, though the task took many years. He suppressed the leaders of the revolt with merciless ferocity, in some cases inflicting them with brutal torture, though the people themselves were not severely maltreated. The satraps who had shown too much independence were also punished. Darius celebr-ated his final victory in about 517 B.C. by inscribing the rocky mountainside of Behistun with his exploits. Though these famous inscriptions are in three languages the order of events is often unclear.

Darius restored peace not only by military action but also by reorganising the administration of his empire. Although his sovereignty was absolute he was obliged to respect the traditional privileges of the Persian nob-ility who occupied a predominant position in the state.

He was not too proud to summon the chief nobles in council where each could speak his mind freely, but final decisions were made by Darius alone. A chancellery then drew up his orders and transmitted them to the satrapies. The formation of these provincial governments certainly dates from the time of Cyrus, but it was Darius who made them universal and fixed their number at twenty. The satrap was, in fact, a viceroy, always independent and often tempted to make a bid for the royal succession. He wielded every power except command over the army, which was reserved to officers who depended directly on the king. Darius also sent inspectors into the pro-vinces who were known as 'the eyes and the ears of the king'. Local administration was left in the hands of the natives themselves and followed traditional forms. The authority of the Great King did not rest on military might alone — though he was able to mobilise millions of men from the Mediterranean to the Indus; the tribute paid into his treasury by each satrap also made him immensely rich.

Having restored peace to his great empire Darius undertook to expand it. His first enterprise was, it seems, directed towards India sometime before 512 B.C. It is possible that the expedition was undertaken to reaffirm a domination already established by Cyrus. It was pre-ceded by a nautical reconnaissance of the lower reaches of the Indus, of which the Greek Scylax of Caryanda has left us an account in his *Periplus*. Darius seems to have annexed, or re-annexed, what is now the province of Sind. When he had thus made sure of his eastern frontiers he turned towards the north. On the steppes of southern Russia the Scythians had formed a kingdom which prospered on its trade with the Black Sea colonies of Miletus. Since the Caucasus mountains were impas-sable, Darius attempted to attack the Scythians from the

A daric of the Great King. The use of money in Persia was prob-ably copied from neighbouring Greece and Lydia. *Giraudon*

107

Left: a glazed brick relief of archers from the Palace at Susa.

west. He passed over the Bosphorus on a bridge of boats, conquered Thrace and, marching northwards, crossed the Danube. But the Scythians still evaded him, and for fear that his army might run short of food and supplies he was forced to turn back. This check, however, left Darius master of the Straits and of Thrace, the conquest of which was completed as far as the river Strymon on the Macedonian border by his general Megabyzus. The next phase of Persian expansion should reasonably have led to the conquest of Greece. But Darius does not seem to have considered this a normal consequence of a systematic plan for universal domination. It was the Greeks themselves who incited him to invade their country.

Greece in the sixth century

The Greeks seem to have been unaware of the Persian danger, so absorbed were they in their own problems. The sixth century followed the course which had been laid in the preceding period. There was little change in those regions which were still ruled by oligarchies. But in the more advanced cities tyranny had given way to systems of government in which new classes of society, created by economic development, were called upon to play a part. Naturally the tyrants had attempted to keep the reins of government in the hands of their own families. Cases where they succeeded in bequeathing their power to their sons are not rare, but there is no example of third-generation tyrants preserving their heritage. The downfall of a tyrant did not always benefit those who expected to reap the profit. In Megara, for instance, the townsmen were obliged to defend themselves against an attempt by the nobles to regain power. In Miletus they had to crush an uprising of the proletariat. Although tyranny had not been able to establish a durable social structure, it had once and for all destroyed the exclusive domination of the landed aristocracy.

Athens: the laws of Draco and Solon

The power of the tyrants had not entirely disappeared at the beginning of the sixth century. Economically, Greek cities were not all equally advanced and in those that lagged behind tyranny still had its mission to fulfil. This was so in Athens whose importance in the Greek world, previously modest; began and continued to grow. Much of her progress she owed to her tyrants. In the second half of the seventh century the Athenian oligarchy had seemed to be in serious danger. An impoverished peasantry which had fallen deeper and deeper into debt to the nobles formed a revolutionary proletariat while the new bourgeois class, which had grown rich as mercantile activity developed, now seemed capable of demanding a share in the government; in other words, of setting up a timocracy, a society in which political rights were given according to a property qualification. But the attempt in 632 B.C. of a young noble, Cylon, to seize power and make himself a tyrant proved premature.

Social unrest, aggravated by a war against Megara, then plunged the city into a state of turmoil. To quell the disorder a law-maker was appealed to — Draco (621 B.C.). The details of his work and the character of Draco himself are vague. Even before Cylon's attempt to seize power the task of codifying the law had been entrusted

Babylon, too, had its brick reliefs. The unicorn is one of the mythical beasts from the Ishtar Gate c. 570 B.C. The technique employed was curious: the whole figure was modelled in the wet material, cut into bricks while still soft and then glazed. Finally, the bricks were pieced together again jig-saw fashion.

An immense double-headed bull capital now fallen to the ground. From Persepolis. The Xerxes Gate is seen in the background.

A coin struck by Peisistratus. The owl is the symbol of the city-state of Athens and of Athene, the city's goddess.

to six 'thesmothetes' who acted as judges and law-givers, but nothing had come of it. Draco was more successful, and it would seem from the little we know of his laws that his work was of capital importance. Until this time, the crime of murder was avenged by the clansmen of the murdered man. Draco put an end to this barbarous custom by obliging the relatives of the dead man to appeal to the public magistrates. Thus the *genos*, or clan, lost one of its chief reasons for solidarity.

Although the loss of the right to enforce the law privately was a blow to the nobles, its effect was not felt immediately. They still retained the power which the possession of land gave them, and this was the basic cause of trouble. The number of peasants reduced to slavery by debt continued to increase. Those who were overshadowed by the same fate clamoured for the abolition of debts and the distribution of land. Once more appeal was made to a law-giver: Solon.

Solon was himself a noble, but he had travelled widely and his *Elegies*, poems in which he demanded from everyone equal sacrifices, had gained him a reputation for impartiality. In 594-593 B.C. (or possibly 592-591) he was elected archon (chief magistrate) and given full powers. The details of his immense and important legal reforms are imperfectly known, but the results are clear enough. His first measure, the *seisachtheia*, which cancelled all debts and abolished the slavery which debt had previously entailed, ended the agrarian crisis. Though Solon refused to redistribute the land, it is seen that from his time onwards there was a distinct increase in smallholdings, though exactly how this significant change came about is uncertain. Other provisions he made protected property, made idleness illegal and encouraged the growth of crops destined for export, especially the olive. He further stimulated trade by reforming the system of weights and measures and by improvements in the coinage.

In the field of law he went farther than Draco in attacking the solidarity of the *genos*, while the constitution he drew up reduced the political privileges of the nobles. It recognised four classes, graded according to their wealth. Rights and freedom to hold office were in proportion to income, but even the poorest had access to the assembly of the people and to the new popular tribunal of the Heliaia, a popular assembly organised as a court. A council of four hundred members was instituted which limited the authority of the Areopagus, the highest judicial body in Athens and made up of about 220 ex-archons. In these ways the foundations of the future democracy were laid. But there was a long road to travel before Athens achieved the government under which she became the glory of Greece.

The tyranny of Peisistratus

Solon's laws satisfied no one, since he had tried to maintain a fair and equal balance between contending parties. As soon as he resigned from office the struggle between the nobles and the reformers began again. Their rivalry permitted an Athenian tyrant, Peisistratus, to assume power. Peisistratus was an astute man who was also a popular and victorious general in the war against Megara. He formed a party among the malcontents and was provided by the people with a bodyguard with which

Solon, one of the early law-givers, did much towards establishing a democratic state. His reforms granted the lower orders greater privileges and also stimulated trade. When he gave up office the social strife began again for, aiming at being fair to all, his reforms succeeded in pleasing no one. *Giraudon*

he seized the Acropolis in 561-560 B.C. His adversaries twice forced him into exile, and twice he regained power, and from 542 B.C. held it without further trouble. In spite of early difficulties Peisistratus accomplished a remarkable amount of good work. He was supported by the people, respected constitutional form and limited his financial demands to a land tax of five per cent. The more turbulent of the nobles were forced into exile, which allowed Peisistratus to improve the peasants' position by allotting to them the exiles' lands. He encouraged commerce and industry by exploiting the silver mines of Laurium and by increasing Athenian trade with the rest of the Greek world. He built a fleet, seized the mouth of the Hellespont and thus laid the foundations of the future Athenian maritime empire. Finally, his devotion to the cult of Athene, his own good taste, and the public improvements he carried out gave to the city of Athens monuments of beauty and made her an early leader in the field of intellectual and artistic creation.

On his death in 527 B.C. the accession to power of his two sons, Hippias and Hipparchus, took place without difficulty and brought no change in the system of government. In appraising the accomplishments of these tyrants it is not always easy to determine how much is owed to the father and how much to the two sons. But all was suddenly changed by the assassination of Hipparchus, who seems to have been the victim of private vengeance. Hippias, who had escaped a like fate by chance, now distrusted everything and everybody. His reign became tyrannical in the literal sense. Meanwhile the international horizon grew darker: the Persians had over-run the territory Peisistratus had acquired, his old allies, Lygdamis

Head of an archer from the Temple of Aphaia, Aegina c. 480 B.C. *Schneider Lengyel*

of Naxos and Polycrates of Samos had disappeared; and Athenian alliance with Plataea in 519 B.C., which caused Plataea to withdraw from the Boeotian confederacy that Thebes was striving to form, also caused bitter enmity between Athens and Thebes. The hand of Sparta often appears in this deterioration in the Athenian situation. Sparta, though jealous of Athenian expansion, hesitated to intervene directly and decided to act only after the repeated advice of the oracle at Delphi, bribed by Athenian exiles. After an ineffective effort in 511 B.C. Sparta succeeded in forcing Hippias into exile the following year.

Sparta in the sixth century

To be able thus to interfere in the internal affairs of another city meant that Sparta had become the most powerful state in Greece. She owed her position to military superiority and to a political and social organisation which had reached the height of its efficiency.

The Spartan constitution had assumed its definitive form: the *apella*, or popular assembly, had been restricted in its functions to a simple vote of yes or no by acclamation, which left the real direction of civil affairs to the *gerusia*, or council of elders.

Military authority remained the joint province of the two kings, but balancing their authority was that of the five ephors whose task it was to make certain that neither king attempted to seize absolute power. Elected annually by the people, ever suspicious, always watchful, the ephors became the chief magistrates of Sparta. All citizens were eligible for election to the post.

The Doric Temple of Aphaia, Aegina. *Viollet*

The body of free citizens was still numerous and among them equality continued to exist. The Perioeci — or old Achaean inhabitants — who occupied the frontier provinces held a monopoly of economic life and their cities enjoyed a certain amount of local autonomy. They were not yet burdened by military charges and their loyalty was unquestionable. Even the helots (a class of serfs) showed no signs of restiveness. This state of affairs seemed so satisfactory that towards the middle of the sixth century it was decided to make it permanent and forbid all further change. This curious resistance to new influences is clearly reflected in Spartan civilisation. Roughly before 550 B.C. Sparta was an active city exporting ceramics of high quality. It was an intellectual and artistic centre where choral lyricism was highly valued. It was open to foreign influences, Ionian in particular. But after 550 B.C. it closed down: nothing further was produced for export, no more temples were built or statues sculpted, no new songs were composed. Foreigners were expelled and the Lacedaemonians were forced to remain at home. For a time, this haughty turning in upon itself exalted Sparta's sense of her own uniqueness and doubtless kindled patriotism. In the long run it was the death sentence of Spartan greatness.

For, at the same time, the situation beyond the frontiers was developing in a way which was to make the Spartan attitude untenable. At the beginning of the sixth century, while Sparta was still conquering the Peloponnesus, she had called a halt to further territorial expansion. From then on she was satisfied to impose treaties of alliance on neighbouring cities. But certain of these cities, notably Corinth, had extensive commercial and political relations with the rest of the Greek world from which Sparta could not hold herself aloof. And then her reputation was such that it attracted requests for help from outside, flattering appeals from such powers as Lydia and Egypt. Torn between her desire to resist further change and her will to have power, Sparta's foreign policy was often incoherent. She did not respond, for instance, to the Ionian call for help against the Persians, but took part in the struggle against Lygdamis and made war on Polycrates, tyrant of Samos. She was hostile to tyrants and friendly to oligarchies, as these two examples — and the case of Hippias in Athens — demonstrate; but that scarcely constituted a foreign policy.

The first conflict between Sparta and Athens

Sparta's policy of isolation, if it could be called a policy, was to be violated in the Athenian affair itself. The expulsion of Hippias left two opposing factions in Athens, one led by Isagoras which was oligarchical, the other democratic and headed by Cleisthenes. The oligarchical party seemed at first to have the upper hand, but Cleisthenes undermined its influence by causing the assembly of the people to make laws which broke the power of the nobles. These measures were so effective that Isagoras, although he was archon, was obliged to call on Sparta for aid in 508-507 B.C. The Spartan king, Cleomenes, perhaps on his own responsibility, responded and took possession of Athens. A popular uprising drove him out. In the following year, 506 B.C., Sparta formed a powerful coalition against Athens which, however, disintegrated before a single blow had been struck. Finally in 505 B.C.,

Sixth-century statue of Athene. Aegina. *Viollet*

Left: spices being weighed in the presence of Arcesilaus of Cyrene. From a sixth-century Spartan kylix. *Historia Photo*

Right: Poseidon attacking Polybutes with his trident gives us an idea of a Greek warrior in action. Greek kylix. *Giraudon*

Chariot racing. A detail from a fifth-century amphora.

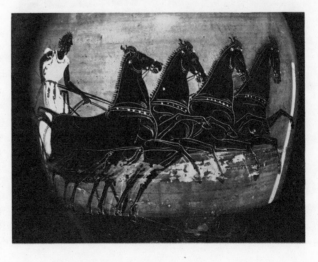

An archaic figure found near the Parthenon. *Alinari*

The Treasury of the Athenians at Delphi.

thinking perhaps to unite the partisans of oligarchy and tyranny against Athenian democracy, Sparta was reconciled with Hippias. But her allies refused to support this unnatural combination.

Cleisthenes and Athenian democracy

These Spartan setbacks gave Cleisthenes full scope for carrying out the reforms which he had already started. By breaking all connections between the old social clans and political power, they completed the work which Solon had begun. The basis of the new system was the *deme*, or local community, which with its assembly, its magistrates and its administrative capacity played an important part in the city's political life. There were 168 demes, divided among ten new tribes based not on blood relationship but on purely territorial divisions. The decimal system from now on was common through all the political machinery of Athens: there were five hundred members of the Council, ten magistrates to each college, and ten prytanes (members of the Council) shared the presidency for a tenth of the year instead of the twelve monthly intervals of the religious year. In this new organisation there was no place for the great noble families. Their members were now distributed among the demes and tribes, and their lands divided between the new territorial districts. Nevertheless Cleisthenes considered these measures inadequate and sought to protect his work by the institution of ostracism, by which once a year the people had the right to impose a sentence of ten years' banishment on any prominent citizen whose presence in Athens might seem dangerous to the State.

Greek civilisation in the sixth century

On the eve of the Persian Wars — the ordeal in which Greece was to achieve maturity — Hellenic civilisation had begun to fulfil the promise it had shown in the archaic period. From this time onwards man himself was the measure of all things. First, the human body became of predominant importance as an object of artistic study and representation. Towards the end of the seventh century, the first statues had already been sculpted, possibly in Crete. In ceramics oriental influences were on the decline, and in the pottery made at Athens — which by the year 550 B.C. had supplanted all rivals, even Corinth, in the export markets — the scenes so admirably depicted are all drawn from life or from mythology. Then, man dominated art by his will to impose on matter a form conceived by the mind and obeying laws of composition, an aspiration far beyond that of simple craftsmanship. All artistic activities of the period show a concern for logic hitherto unknown. The tendency appears most plainly in the formation of the architectural orders, above all the Doric order, a form of geometry in stone. It can also be discerned in works of literature, in which moral and philosophical interests replaced the narrative charm of earlier poetry. This does not mean that Greece had rejected all foreign influence: the orient still retained its prestige and there was even a revival of popular interest in eastern mystery cults. It was still in Asia Minor, of course, where this influence was most strongly felt. Ionia preferred the grace of its elegantly adorned statues of Persephone, or *korai*, to the austere Doric art of Greece

A tribute-bearer, from a bas-relief at Persepolis (521-486 B.C.)
Roger Wood

Etruscan dancers from the Tomb of the Lionesses, Tarquinia,
c. 520 B.C. *Scala*

proper. Divergence of taste stemmed from a fundamental duality in attitudes of mind. Athens made the first attempt to synthesise the two opposing tendencies. Her success was dazzling, and the days of the first tyrant Peisistratus were her first golden age. The Acropolis was crowned with temples dedicated to protective divinities, while the splendour of Athenian religious and popular festivals gave birth to a new literary form with a prodigious future: the theatre.

The Ionian revolt against Darius I

Ionia had not been destroyed when Cyrus conquered it. Indeed, the Persian yoke was no heavier to bear than the Lydian protectorate before it. Miletus and Ephesus were still the intermediaries between the Aegean world and Asia, and prospered accordingly. The revolt of the Ionian Greeks is therefore hard to understand. Possibly they were made uneasy by the Persian annexation of Samos after the downfall of the tyrant Polycrates. After the splendour and enterprise of Polycrates (c. 532-522 B.C.) the Samians may have feared the arrival of a harsher master. Or perhaps Phoenician competition, which had become increasingly dangerous under Persian benevolence, had brought about an economic crisis. The revolt was instigated by Aristagoras, tyrant of Miletus, who feared that he had incurred the wrath of the Great King. Towards the end of the year 499 B.C. Aristagoras called on the cities of Ionia to proclaim their independence. The Ionians obtained some help from Athens and from Eretria, then, taking advantage of the slowness of Persian mobilisation, they took the offensive in the following spring. A number of coastal cities from Cyprus to the Straits rallied to their cause. The Persian counter-attack took place in 497 B.C. Its success might have been long delayed had not dissension broken out in the ranks of the rebels. Many, and among them some of the most important, deserted. In 494 B.C. a Phoenician fleet blockaded Miletus. The city's defeat was hastened by more last-minute defections but, even so, it held out for two years. In 492 B.C. it was taken by assault and razed to the ground. The inhabitants were deported and all Ionia was severely repressed.

The First Persian War. Marathon

The Ionians had not received much help from the Greek mainland. The aid which Athens and Eretria had sent was therefore all the more noticeable, and Darius felt a lively resentment towards the two cities. In the year in which Miletus was destroyed he prepared his revenge. As a first step he ordered his son-in-law Mardonius to reconquer Thrace and impose a Persian protectorate on Macedonia, an operation which Mardonius carried out with some difficulty. But the expedition which was intended to be decisive did not take place until 490 B.C., two years later, and it was confided to the fleet. Datis, its commander, first occupied the Cyclades and destroyed Eretria. Then, sailing towards Athens, he landed his troops in the bay of Marathon. He seems to have relied upon the treachery of Athenian sympathisers with tyranny. Hippias, now grown old and an exile at Sigeum, had become a vassal of Darius. In Athens his party was still strong: Hipparchus, its leader, had been archon in

The 'Aristion' marble funerary stele discovered in an Attic burial mound. One of the best preserved archaic reliefs, probably that of a nobleman.

Work in a Greek clay pit. An amphora hangs in a sling overhead.
Sixth or seventh century B.C. *Archiv für Kunst und Geschichte*

Already sculpture was beginning to display more movement. The
static frontal approach had been succeeded by energetic groups
like these warriors in combat with two Amazons. A fragment
from a mausoleum frieze. British Museum. *Mansell*

496-495 B.C. But in 490 B.C. the most influential man in Athens was Miltiades. This nobleman, whose family had fled from the tyrants and founded a colony in the Thracian Chersonesus from which the Persian advance had driven them, embodied the spirit of resistance. Miltiades persuaded the Athenians not to wait for the Persians but to take the offensive. Surprised on the plain of Marathon by the Athenian foot-soldiers, Datis was forced, after heavy losses, to re-embark. He then sailed towards the Athenian harbour of Phalerum with the intention of seizing the city while its troops were still at Marathon. Miltiades countered this manoeuvre by a forced march, and Datis again found the Athenian army facing him. He sailed away without risking another landing, and Athens acquired the glory of having single-handed repulsed the first assault of the barbarians.

The Second Persian War. Salamis and Plataea

There can be no doubt that Darius wished to avenge this defeat at once, but in the same year a serious revolt broke out in Egypt. While he was striving to crush it he died — in 486 B.C. His son and successor, Xerxes, was obliged to wage war for two more years before he could restore peace. Then Babylon revolted. But in 481 B.C. Xerxes was able to give full attention to his father's Greek project. With an immense army he crossed the Hellespont. Supported by a fleet which hugged the coast, the Persian host advanced until it reached the borders of Thessaly.

It was not until this moment that the Greeks were roused. Until then, and in spite of the obvious peril, they had returned to their internal bickering. As long ago as 489 B.C. Miltiades had tried to drive the Persians out of the Aegean but, failing to capture Paros, he was compelled to return to Athens where he was impeached and condemned. Then in 487-486 B.C. Athens had attempted to impose her will on her old rival Aegina, but suffered a humiliating setback. Meanwhile Sparta, pursuing her old policy of hegemony in the Peloponnesus, was to all appearances the first power in Greece. It is not then surprising that it should be Sparta who presided over the Isthmian congress which met in the autumn of 481 B.C. to consider the menace which could no longer be ignored. Even Athens, in spite of her naval superiority, recognised Sparta's right to leadership. Athenian naval superiority had been made possible by the discovery of new silver deposits at Laurium, which allowed her to construct a fleet of two hundred triremes. The moving spirit in this enterprise was Themistocles, a far-seeing statesman who had grasped — and made his fellow Athenians grasp — that the city's future depended on the sea.

The assembled Greeks, in spite of numerous backsliders, were able to muster 20,000 men and 300 triremes. It was decided to defend the pass of Thermopylae which gave access to central Greece, the army meanwhile being supported by the fleet off the coast of Artemisium.

The opposing armies met in the south of Thessaly in the spring of 480 B.C. At Thermopylae the Greeks took up a very strong defensive position which commanded the gateway to Boeotia. But a Greek traitor led the Persians in a flanking movement through a mountain pass, so that the Greek position was turned. The main body of the Greek army was forced to retreat to the south while Leonidas and three hundred disciplined Spartans fought and died to a man in order to cover the main withdrawal. There was no alternative but for the Greeks to defend the Peloponnesus at the narrow Isthmus of Corinth. Central Greece and Attica were over-run and Athens, abandoned by its inhabitants on the advice of Themistocles, was devastated. All that remained to the city were its ships, anchored in the Bay of Salamis where they barred the Persian armada's approach to the Saronic gulf and Peloponnesus. Against the advice of the Peloponnesians, whose chief concern was to protect their own peninsula, Themistocles decided to give battle then and there. In the narrow waters between the Isle of Salamis and the coast the Persians could not take advantage of their numerical superiority. The skilful Greek captains outmanoeuvred the vast Asiatic fleet which fell into confusion and was almost annihilated. It was September 480 B.C., and too late in the season for Xerxes to make another attempt. He withdrew to Thessaly, unhampered by the Greeks, and turned over the command of his forces to Mardonius.

In the following spring Mardonius renewed the offensive and again invaded Attica. In order to drive him out the Greek army, commanded by Pausanias, regent of Sparta, marched into Boeotia and in August 479 B.C. faced Mardonius and the Persian host before Plataea. Harassed by the Persian cavalry, the Greeks attempted to fall back on their base in an ill-co-ordinated movement which might have proved fatal. But the solidity of the Greek phalanx proved too strong for the lightly armed Persians and, as at Marathon, the spear was invincible against the bow. Meanwhile revolt had broken out in Ionia. To support it the Greek fleet had occupied Samos and at Mycale won a victory over the Persian fleet which liberated the Greeks of Asia Minor.

Western Hellenism in the sixth century

These victories, which saved Hellenism in the Aegean, had their counterpart in the West, where at the same time the Greek world found itself in peril. Little is known about the history of the Greek colonies in Sicily and in Magna Graecia during the sixth century, but it must have been very troubled. Most of the city-states were governed by tyrants, and local rivalry gave rise to ferocious struggles between them in which certain towns completely disappeared. Thus Siris was obliterated by Sybaris which in turn was destroyed by Croton in 510 B.C. Western Hellenism was on the wane at the moment when, under the direction of Carthage, the Phoenician colonies were enjoying a new lease of life. Greek colonisation had come to a halt, and the last attempt, that of the Spartan Dorieus, had met with disaster first in Libya and then, sometime before 511 B.C., in Sicily itself. The natives of Sicily not only resisted the arrival of new Greek colonists but were only waiting for a chance to expel those that were already there. The occasion seemed to be provided by an outburst of hostility between two opposing pairs of tyrants: Gelon of Syracuse and Theron of Agrigentum on the one hand, and on the other Anaxilas of Rhegium and Terillos of Himera. When Theron drove Terillos from Himera, Terillos called upon the Carthaginians for help. A Carthaginian fleet commanded by Hamilcar then blockaded Theron in Himera. Gelon of Syracuse came to the aid of his ally and in 480 B.C.

Greek terracotta figures with plough and oxen. *Larousse*

An early Etruscan bronze archer. Of Asiatic descent, the Etruscans were the most civilised of the peoples living in Italy. Their architecture was Mycenean in character and they had a flourishing and skilled metal industry. *Mansell*

crushed Hamilcar. The Carthaginian menace was thus dismissed until the end of the century.

The Etruscan Empire

Shortly after this, Syracuse was to save the cause of the Western Greeks from a fresh peril. Since the seventh century the Etruscan Empire had extended its boundaries remarkably. From the middle of the century the Etruscans had begun to dominate Latium and in 616 B.C. Etruscan tyrants from Caere, the Tarquins, replaced the native kings of Rome. Then the Etruscans penetrated farther south into Campagna where they founded Capua and Nola. Contact with the Greeks soon degenerated into conflict. The Etruscans allied themselves with the Carthaginians. First, in 535 B.C., they repulsed the Massaliotes of Corsica from the Italian coast in a naval engagement at Alalia, and then attacked Cumae. Here in 474 B.C. they were routed by Hieron of Syracuse who had succeeded Gelon. This Etruscan defeat put an end to their southerly expansion, already threatened by a revolt of the Latins and the loss of Rome. Towards the north, however, their occupation of the Po valley after the capture of Bologna in 525 B.C. was to endure until the middle of the fourth century B.C.

The early kings of Rome

It was her kings who laid the foundations of Rome's greatness. Tarquinius Priscus established Roman hegemony over the Latins. After his reign Rome was ruled by Servius Tullius to whom reforms are attributed which in fact were made much later: division of the people into centuries according to their property, the introduction of coinage and the construction of vast fortified city walls. The last of the Roman kings, Tarquinius Superbus, was the typical tyrant, surrounded by a bodyguard, courting the favour of the lower classes, and an assiduous builder of public monuments. Dissensions within his own family brought about his downfall in 509 B.C. and an oligarchical form of government was installed.

The institutions of Rome under her kings were based on a division into three tribes, the last of which, the Luceres, is undoubtedly less ancient than the Ramnes and the Taties. Each furnished ten *curias*, who voted in the Assembly, and ten (later twenty) 'centuries', or companies of one hundred men, to the army. Each tribe was composed of a number of clans, the *gentes*, whose chiefs formed the Senate, or King's Council. A patriarchal system was rigorously enforced and the *pater familias* enjoyed unlimited authority over his household. Justice was still a strictly family matter, though, after the expulsion of the kings, the assembly of the people was called upon to pronounce on cases of treason, patricide and the murder of any freeman — a first limitation of the power of the *gentes*.

The India of Buddha

Indian history in the sixth century is important less for its political events than for the contributions which India then made to civilisation. The facts at our disposal are uncertain, but at the beginning of the period the predominant power was the kingdom of Kosala — to-day the province of Oudh. By the end of the century, however, its ascendancy had been destroyed by a new empire, that of Magadha, or southern Behar. Magadha had long been considered a semi-barbarous frontier province; it owed its rise in the world to its king, Bimbisara (c. 543-491 B.C.) who was the protector of the Buddha. He annexed Bengal and prepared the way for the greatness of his son, Adjatasatru.

At this time Indian society had long since hardened into its rigid caste-system. In this system the highest rank was held by the priests or brahmins, followed by the warrior-nobles and cultivators of the soil, while the conquered peoples were relegated to the caste of the sudras — or slaves. In this way the racial purity of the conquering Aryans was to some extent preserved at first but warlike alliances between Aryan and indigenous rulers, and inter-marriage, and the infiltration of Hindu cults in the original Aryan religion in time greatly diminished the racial content of caste. This social organisation was based on original philosophical and religious ideas which were found in the *Brahmanas* and the *Upanishads*, which were written and collected between 800 and 500 B.C. Brahmanism was of pantheistic inspiration: the divine principle, immanent in all things, identifies itself with the individual soul; and salvation is obtained by discovering one's divine origin in oneself by means of the ascetic practices of yoga. The pure form of this religion was limited to a small élite, and in order to retain its hold over the masses, it compromised with popular Hindu beliefs. It was forced to accept the innumerable gods which the people worshipped and, above all, to admit as a fundamental dogma a belief in the transmigration of souls. To liberate the soul and escape from the cycle of this transmigration — or metempsychosis — became the essential aim of religion.

Two reformers rose to purify this debased form of Brahmanism: Mahavira (c. 540-468 B.C.) and the Buddha Sakyamuni (c. 563-483 B.C.). The aim of both was the liberation of the soul from metempsychosis, but while Mahavira, the founder of Jainism, relied on the practice of asceticism alone, Buddha conceived a whole moral and metaphysical system to achieve the desired result. In the beginning he devoted himself to yoga, but understood the vanity of this practice when the Light revealed to him the True Path whereby the soul could attain *moksha*, or liberation. The only method of escaping the cycle of transmigration was through *nirvana* — or the extinction of the individual soul. Now the vital principle of the human being is desire, which leads to suffering; therefore desire must be renounced, and all passions subdued. The Buddhist must sacrifice himself to others. This doctrine of charity, gentleness and abstinence spread the principle of non-violence which is to this day a basic element in Indian ethics. The followers of the new religion formed a monastic church which, during Buddha's own lifetime, converted the kingdoms of Magadha and Oudh.

The China of Confucius

The history of feudal China during the course of the sixth century is little more than a continuation of the confused civil wars between divided principalities which had characterised the preceding period. The principal

Confucius, Chinese sage, c. 551-479 B.C. The altruism which was a fundamental of his teaching has remained the basis of Chinese philosophy until modern times.

Buddha attended by a group of followers. The sixth and fifth centuries B.C. saw the rise of sages, philosophers and religious reformers throughout the world: Buddha, Confucius, Zarathustra, Solon, Daniel and Ezekiel. *Larousse*

political event seems to have been the formation of a kingdom to the south of the mouth of the Yangtze. This new state, the kingdom of Wu, though barbarian, had learned much from Chinese culture and added a new province to the area of Chinese civilisation. But its irruption into the scene in about 584 B.C. only increased the general anarchy by partially destroying the work of the kingdom of Chou.

Nonetheless, the age was one of expanding colonisation and agricultural development. As the Chinese pushed south, they came to rice-lands which could support a larger population, and they infiltrated further into what was to be Indo-China. Their agriculture was laborious and elaborate, making the most of the limited area suitable for cultivation; they grew melons, pears and mulberries and in the time of the Shang, a then unique silk industry was already established — based on a secret unknown to Europe until the sixth century A.D. The Chinese already had a currency of cowries and stamped leather, though not yet one of metal. As population and wealth increased, the administration became more elaborate. A bureaucracy grew up in the various states, and treasurers, local magistrates and scribes became powerful. It was from this official class that Confucius was to come and he defined a code of public morality possible only in a highly organised civilisation. All was consolidated by the cult of the family, the worship of ancestral spirits and intense loyalty to the family's past and continuance which was to mark Chinese society into modern times. There did not grow up a separate or celibate priestly class: the practice of religion was essentially social.

In spite of the political convulsions which shook the country Chinese philosophy attained its highest development in this epoch. Reflecting an essentially agricultural society it was deeply imbued with a sense of the solidarity which unites man with nature. The principal object of religion was to maintain the harmony between the cosmic world and everyday life by the strict observance of detailed rites, the practice of which was in itself a public and private virtue. The search for the underlying unity beneath the apparently contradictory and the reconciliation of opposing principles were the basic concern of Chinese thinkers. The most complete expression of Chinese thought is found in the works of Kung-Fûtsze (c. 551-479 B.C.) who is better known as Confucius. His teachings were above all ethical, and he emphasised the collaboration of man with nature for the attainment of social harmony. Ritual observance was both a condition and a symbol of this attainment. But the individual contribution of this greatest of Chinese philosophers was his insistence on the truth of this world, that is, of the just relationship between man and man, rather than the truth of the Unseen. The altruism which arose from such doctrines led to fraternity and was to remain the ideal of Chinese morality. In spite of the feudal wars of the time, the idea of kingship remained sacrosanct, for rulers were to maintain harmony; and when the Chou rulers called themselves 'Sons of Heaven', they claimed a universal moral authority, to be revived and exploited by the first great Chinese unitary state — the Han empire. Already the civilisation of China was the dominant cultural factor of the entire Far East.

Two horsemen carrying spears. Detail from a Greek hydria.

Etruscan warrior. Bronze.

An archaic bronze statuette of Apollo. Seventh century B.C. *Museum of Fine Arts, Boston*

Chinese bronze figure of a man with a bear on a stick. Chou dynasty. Late sixth or fifth century B.C.

THE SUPREMACY OF THE EASTERN MEDITERRANEAN

500-300 B.C.

The Persian wars and the defeat of the Carthaginians were not simple episodes without consequence. The victory of the Greeks moved the centre of gravity of civilisation towards the West. The will of the East to expand seemed to have atrophied and henceforward it is the peoples of the Mediterranean who possess the power to create and look towards the future. By some curious paradox these peoples who had fought oriental expansion themselves finish by becoming expansionist, and their conquests are achieved only by a renunciation of those very principles which had in the earlier periods of their history made them unconquerable.

The Propylaea of Mnesicles, on the Acropolis at Athens. Every city-state of ancient Greece had its acropolis, or citadel, but none surpassed that of Athens, with its magnificent temples erected to the city's gods. *Mansell*

CHAPTER FIVE

THE AGE OF PERICLES

480-432 B.C.

The foundation and development of the Athenian Empire

The naval victory of Mycale in 479 B.C. was almost immediately followed by the dissolution of the coalition. The Spartans decided that the campaign was finished and that it was in their best interests to return to Sparta. On the contrary, the Athenians, followed by the Island and Ionian Greeks, set sail for the Hellespont and laid siege to Sestus, thus making clear their intention to establish a base for offensive action against the Persian Empire. It was nevertheless the Spartan Pausanias who in the following year took command of the fleet and made his headquarters in Byzantium. But the Ionians rose in protest against his brutal arrogance and the year 477 B.C. saw the definite break-up of the coalition.

Whereas Pausanias was retired from his command by Sparta and remained in Byzantium only as a private adventurer, Athens succeeded in persuading the Ionians and the Islanders to offer her the direction of operations against Persia. The upkeep of the fleet, which was the principal weapon of assault, was the common responsibility of all the allies, but each had the choice between providing a naval contingent of its own or paying for its replacement. Many of the smaller cities chose the latter course, and the Athenian Aristides was charged with the task of apportioning the tribute among members of the confederation. The seat of the confederation was at Delos, where the treasury was administered by Athenian *hellenotames* and where the allies held their assemblies.

They soon took the offensive and under an enterprising and energetic commander, Cimon, the son of Miltiades, cleared the coasts of Thrace of its last Persian garrisons, drove Pausanias from Byzantium in 471-470 B.C., and moved on into Asia where they wrested the coastal regions from the Great King. A resounding victory at the mouth of the Eurymedon in 468 B.C. rallied all the cities of Lycia to the allied cause. The allies, however, were already growing restive under Athen's leadership: Naxos in 470-469 B.C., then Thasos in 465-463 B.C. attempted to withdraw from the confederation. Both were harshly brought to heel.

Sparta and Athens at the time of Cimon

These Athenian successes not unnaturally made Sparta uneasy, though she does not appear to have taken any positive action. It is unlikely, however, that her inertia remained unchallenged by certain Spartans who urged that steps be taken to avoid the danger. Pausanias was one of these and, in an attempt to check the growth of Athenian ambitions, he appealed to the Persian king. The reactionary party in Sparta, which distrusted both kings

One of the caryatids supporting the Erechtheum. Over the years the term caryatid has come to be applied to any draped figure acting as a supporting column. *Viollet*

and foreign commitments, succeeded in having Pausanias recalled and accused of treason. Their caution was justified by the disturbances which at that moment broke out nearer home in the Peloponnesus itself. Elis was uniting and conquering Triphylia; Argos had formed a democratic government and between 472 and 470 B.C. destroyed its rivals Mycenae and Tiryns.

Under the government of Cimon, moreover, Athens hoped to maintain friendly relations with Sparta. Generous, covered with glory, eloquent and affable, the son of Miltiades not only enjoyed the support of the people but also the favour of the aristocratic families whose influence in the country districts was still great. Cimon was anxious to strengthen the Athenian empire but he did not believe that this need involve a rupture with Sparta. He also felt that the Spartan alliance would put a brake on the spread of democratic ideas. On this point Themistocles opposed him. He believed Sparta to be a future threat to Athens and advocated war before the threat could become a real danger. The result of their political struggle was the ostracism of Themistocles in 472-471 B.C.

In spite of Cimon's success, his position was not impregnable. In 464 B.C. charges were brought against him after the massacre of an Athenian expedition in Thrace, but his authority was still intact the following year when the Spartans came to beg for Athenian help in quelling a general revolt of the Messenians and the helots. The rebels had been beaten in open country, but had then taken refuge in the fortress on Mount Ithome from which the Spartans were unable to dislodge them. The Athenian army was famous for its skill in siege-craft and the Spartans asked for assistance. In spite of bitter opposition in the Assembly, Cimon went to Messenia with four thousand hoplites.

Ephialtes

Cimon's departure led to his downfall. His troops obviously included many of his own partisans and their absence weakened his position in the Assembly. The democrats, led by a relatively unknown politician, Ephialtes, took advantage of the situation to attack Cimon's chief prop, the Areopagus. The ill-defined powers of this supreme tribunal, its antiquity and its patriotism during the Persian wars had earned it immense prestige, and its

political influence behind the scenes was considerable. Its members were drawn from the aristocracy and were naturally hostile to the democrats. Some of them were not, however, above reproach and this gave Ephialtes an opportunity to attack their integrity. They were impeached and the Areopagus itself was stripped of all except its judicial functions. There was full democracy, with powers of the Areopagus in the hands of the popular courts, the democratic courts and the Assembly. Meanwhile Cimon had not gained the military success he had expected and in 462 the Spartans brusquely dismissed him and his troops. The insult reflected on Athens, and Cimon, who was held responsible for it, not only failed to defeat the reforms of Ephialtes in the Assembly but was ostracised. Sparta's alliance with Athens was broken off.

The First Peloponnesian War

Athens then launched upon a reckless series of enterprises which in the end proved to be beyond her strength. She joined with Argos to form a network of alliances which blockaded the Gulf of Corinth. She sent aid to Inaros, the Egyptian pharaoh who towards 460 B.C. had risen against Persian domination. Finally in 458 B.C. she attacked her ancient rival Aegina. This audacious foreign policy was at first attended by success. With Athenian assistance Inaros captured Memphis. A Peloponnesian fleet was beaten in the waters of Aegina and the Corinthians defeated before Megara. But at last Sparta moved. She sent a large force into Boeotia which enabled Thebes to unify the country. An Athenian army which was sent to avert this danger was crushed in 457 B.C. at Tanagra.

Energetic Athenian action restored the situation: two months after Tanagra the Thebans were disastrously routed and Athens was again the controlling power of central Greece, and in the following year finally took possession of Aegina.

The next year the Athenian fleet burned Gythium, the port of Sparta. Events in Egypt, however, put an end to the Athenian offensive. In 456 B.C. the Athenians and their allies were beaten by the Persian army, driven from Memphis and encircled on an island in the Nile. There they were besieged for a year and in 454 B.C. massacred. Meanwhile the fleet which had been sent to relieve them was annihilated. The danger seemed so great that the treasury at Delos was removed to the Acropolis.

A Greek metrological relief. From the sixth century B.C. onwards man himself had become the measure of all things and the human body took on predominant importance as an object of artistic study and of sensitive representation.

The finest monument on the Acropolis: the Parthenon, a Doric temple dedicated to Athena Parthenos and designed by Ictinus and Callicrates in place of the earlier temple destroyed by the Persians in 479 B.C. The new temple, erected under the direction of Phidias, was originally brightly painted, as were his sculptures with which it was decorated.

It was fortunate for Athens that Sparta did not choose that moment to attack her in force; the war dragged on for the next few years with minor operations in the Gulf of Corinth and in Thessaly. In 451 B.C. the two cities concluded a five-year truce, and Athens again took up the struggle against the Persians, a course of action advocated by Cimon who had returned from exile. In 449 B.C. a fleet under his command set sail for Cyprus while another was sent to Egypt to support Amyrtaeus, a prince of the Delta, whom the Persians had been unable to subdue. Both operations were disappointing. The enemy fleet was duly destroyed off the east coast of Cyprus in 450 B.C., but Cimon died and the victory was not exploited; Amyrtaeus also died and his son recognised the suzerainty of the Great King. These setbacks inclined the Athenians to make peace: a treaty was negotiated by Cimon's brother-in-law, Callias. By its terms Persian ships were forbidden to sail beyond Phaselis on the coast of Lycia and the Great King recognised the Confederation of Delos.

The time was ripe to put an end to this series of wars with Persia, for the situation had become grave on Attica's own frontiers. Athenian control had not brought peace to the cities of central Greece. It was the Athenian custom to support the local democratic parties, less from systematic policy than because she had not discovered dependable allies among the oligarchies who turned to Sparta for support. In 448 B.C. Sparta took the part of the Delphians against the Phocians. Athens at once sent an army which restored the situation as it had been before Spartan intervention. In Boeotia in the following year Athens attempted to overthrow the oligarchs of Chaeronea and Orchomenus. The force she sent was insufficient and was decimated at Coronea.

The Athenian defeat was the signal for a general uprising, and in June 446 B.C. all of Euboea revolted. At the moment when Pericles landed on the island with a powerful army, a large anti-Athenian coalition was formed to support Megara which had withdrawn from the confederation. The coalition's first action was to ravage the plain of Eleusis. Pericles was recalled and with diplomatic skill, and possibly with bribes to the Spartan king, he broke up the coalition and returned at once to Euboea. There, too, he chose negotiation rather than force: treaties were concluded which defined the rights of the cities and their obligations to Athens, 123 and colonists — *cleruchs* — were planted at Chalcis and Oreus in order to ensure the island's obedience.

To go to war again with Sparta was considered too hazardous. Athens therefore resigned herself to the loss of Megara and to relinquishing the protectorate of Boeotia where Thebes regained her former hegemony. In 446 B.C. she signed a thirty-year peace treaty with Sparta in which each city recognised the other's empire and undertook to refrain from tampering with the other's subject cities. Only those cities which were still independent could be annexed. Under this agreement, precarious though it was, Athens, governed by Pericles, reached the high tide of her civilisation.

Pericles

Pericles, the most illustrious statesman of antiquity, is one we know little about. Unfortunately he had no biographer among his contemporaries and his personality soon became legendary or was distorted by political partisanship. Towards 445 B.C. he was about fifty years old and at the full maturity of his genius. His parents were of the highest nobility, but they also inherited the traditions of Cleisthenes and belonged to the democratic party. It was as a supporter of democracy that Pericles first appeared on the political scene under the aegis of Ephialtes. After the death of Ephialtes, Pericles took over the leadership of the party and gained experience in public affairs as *strategos* — or general — diplomatist and orator. A brilliant politician, his influence over the Assembly soon became uncontested, though there was nothing of the demagogue in his oratory. On the contrary, his style was haughty, reserved and aristocratic. The natural profundity of his mind was enriched by culture of an extraordinary breadth, gained from his teachers, Damon, the gifted sophist, and the philosopher Anaxagoras. His experience in affairs of state was wide, he was far-sighted, his integrity was unimpeachable and his government enlightened. It was under Pericles that so much that was good flowered in Greek art and literature. It was also during his reign that the policy leading to the downfall of Athens and, later, of Greece began.

Greek colonisation and Phoenician expansion from the eighth to the fifth centuries B.C.

The social programme of Pericles

Pericles' aim was to make democracy not only a theory of government but a working reality. The State must not remain in its juridical aspect the province of the rich aristocrat. The influence of the Areopagus was therefore further reduced, and the office of archon was opened to a broader section of the public. In 457-456 B.C. fees were paid to the *heliastes* — or members of the high court — and to the *bouleutes* — or elected senators. It was not yet proposed to pay citizens for attending the Assembly, but at least their material independence could be assured by providing them with work. Hence a programme of public building was inaugurated which stimulated trade and encouraged general employment. These measures were costly and it was the Athenian Empire which had to pay for them. The treasury of the Confederation defrayed expenses which were purely Athenian, and members of the Confederation were obliged to furnish land to the city's surplus population. This system of the *cleruchy* in which the Athenian colonist was granted land abroad but retained his Athenian citizenship was eventually to rouse vehement protest and make the metropolis thoroughly hated in the empire. In the meanwhile it had three advantages: it got rid of the excess population without losing its loyalty, it opened up new markets, and it distributed Athenians at strategic points where they could keep an eye on dubious allies. Finally it was decided to limit the number who enjoyed the privilege of Athenian citizenship, and a law was passed denying citizenship except to those of Athenian parentage.

Athenian imperialism

To fulfil this programme it was essential to keep the empire firmly in hand. During his entire tenure of office Pericles worked ceaselessly for the pre-eminence of Athens and to strengthen her hold over the empire. In the political field the support given to democratic regimes became systematic, and the institutions which were sometimes imposed on cities by force and ensured by military garrisons were modelled on those of the metropolis. City

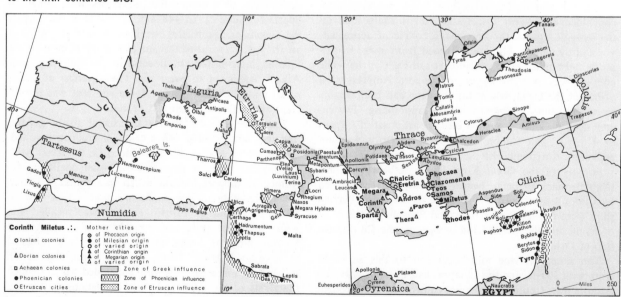

Pericles, the Athenian leader whose ambition was to make the theory of democratic government a reality. Under his enlightened rule all that was best in Athenian culture flourished. At this period the city bubbled with new ideas and seethed with political rivalries. Intellectual life could not fail to quicken under such a stimulus.

magistrates, moreover, were made to take an oath of fidelity. In the judicial field it was insisted that the more important cases, especially political cases, should be tried in Athens, and judged by the court of the Heliaea. The Heliaea was above all interested in military and financial questions, often closely connected. Some of the more powerful members of the Confederation furnished and paid for their own military contingents, but the majority preferred to be free of such responsibilities by paying a tribute. With the proceeds Athens supported an army and, more important, a fleet, which became more and more Athenian and increasingly less Confederate. The allies thus lost their independent power, and with it their voice in fixing the sum of the tribute they paid and control over how it was spent. The Assembly decided on the total budget required and the Senate apportioned the contributions demanded of each member. Those who refused to pay received a visit from the collectors, accompanied if necessary by troops or warships. To defray the expenses of guarding the treasury Athens charged a commission of a sixtieth part.

The oppression suffered by the member cities who attempted to withdraw from the Confederation and were coerced into submission must not be exaggerated. The political hegemony of Athens often succeeded in maintaining internal peace. The justice dispensed by the Heliaea was not inferior to that obtained from local tribunals and it had to a certain extent the advantage of unifying the law, just as the tribute and the economic pre-eminence of Athens spread a unified currency and system of weights and measures. Moreover, the tribute was not excessive. Its rate was revised every four years and was more frequently lowered than raised. Then, as the number of contributors grew, the burden that each had to bear became lighter. Though Athens diverted a part of the treasury to her own use, her power, on the other hand, ensured the safety of the seas and freed commerce from piracy.

It was nonetheless true that in many ways her domination was vexatious and tyrannical. The democracy which Athens imposed on her subject allies seemed, even to local democrats, to be government by the foreigner. National sentiment and political hostility towards the outsider crystallised around the oligarchs who played the part of uncompromising patriots. The Heliaea was not always impartial, far from it. Its judgments were more often inspired by political and social considerations than by strict equity, and to bring a case before it meant a costly stay in Athens, lawyers' fees and, no doubt, an occasional bribe. Discontent was brought to a head by the fiscal and military obligations. It would seem that the payment of the tribute did not always dispense with the obligation to furnish troops, and the increasingly private use to which Athens put such conscripts obscured the real services she supplied. Finally, and above all, the unconquerable passion of all Greeks to rule themselves could not but render odious a domination which could be seen on all sides in the presence of garrisons, *cleruchies*, tax-gatherers, naval vessels.

Pericles and his adversaries

There had been restiveness within the Athenian Empire before the days of Pericles. Cimon had been obliged to

Athene, goddess of wisdom and of war, and protective deity of the city-state of Athens. The owl, helmet and spear are three of Athene's attributes. The owl is often found on Athenian coinage. Greek kylix.

The charioteer of Delphi. Attributed to Pythagoras of Rhegium, the statue was erected in 478 B.C. by the tyrants Gelon and Polyzelus. The intentionally exaggerated legs were hidden by the chariot in which the figure once stood. *Alinari*

stamp out several revolts and by force to impose the dogma that any attempt at secession was an act of rebellion. But with the restoration of peace the burden of Athenian leadership seemed more onerous. The complaints of the Confederates found support in the capital itself and were voiced by the chief of the reactionary party, Cimon's son-in-law Thucydides, son of Melesias. Thucydides pointed out that spending Confederation funds on public works was fraudulent. Pericles replied that Athens was free to dispose of the money because she assumed the defence of the Empire. Debate in the Assembly was acrimonious until in 443 B.C. Thucydides was ostracised. The defeated party had no other recourse but to attack the friends of Pericles: his mistress Aspasia and his teacher Anaxagoras were accused of impiety, and his friend the sculptor Phidias was charged with embezzlement. But Pericles' own position was not shaken and from the year 444 B.C. to his death in 429 he was unfailingly re-elected strategos.

The revolt of Samos

The revolt of Samos turned out to be more dangerous than all previous attempts to secede from the Athenian Empire. The island of Samos was a powerful ally and enjoyed considerable freedom of action. In the beginning of 440 B.C. Samos fought Miletus for possession of Priene. Miletus was beaten and brought the case to Athens for arbitration. Samos refused to accept Athenian arbitration and Pericles had the island occupied and its oligarchical government overthrown. The defeated oligarchs then solicited the aid of the Satrap of Sardis, and with his help regained power, drove out the democrats and turned over the Athenian garrison in Samos to the Persians. At the same time Byzantium declared her independence and the Peloponnesian League had assembled to consider the Samians' appeal for assistance.

The situation was very serious, even though Corinth was opposed to any intervention. Pericles had sailed towards Samos with a large fleet, defeated the rebels at sea and blockaded the city. Under a threat from a Phoenician fleet the siege lasted until 439 B.C. When Samos capitulated the conditions imposed on her were severe: to surrender her fleet, tear down her walls and pay all the expenses of the war. The democracy was then, of course, reinstated.

By these means the Athenian Empire was not again imperilled, and under Pericles it reached its greatest territorial expansion. In Thrace most of the coastal towns were included in the Confederation, and the foundation of Amphipolis in 436 B.C. on the river Strymon protected the gateway to the hinterland, rich in forests and mines. About the same time Pericles extended Athenian influence into the region of the Black Sea by leading an expedition along the coasts of Scythia and Pontus, where he installed *cleruchs* at Sinope and Amisus. He had already been active in the west and in 443, in response to an appeal from the surviving Sybarites, he had organised the founding of a pan-hellenic colony at Thurii.

Greek civilisation in the first half of the fifth century

At Athens itself in the meantime the social programme which Pericles had inaugurated was achieving results.

Greek vase painting drew heavily on myth and legend for its subject matter. This detail from an Attic amphora depicts Hector, son of Priam of Troy and one of the principal figures in the Trojan War. Departure for battle was a commonplace for fifth-century warriors. It is small wonder that the feats of legendary heroes had wide appeal. *Mansell*

The great public works which it included, together with the economic prosperity of the city, was to earn Athens the undisputed intellectual and artistic leadership which remains her chief title to glory. To understand the character and scope of this development we must go back and examine the progress made by Greek thought since the end of the sixth century. The ordeal of the Persian invasions had strengthened that reaction against Ionian grace and facility which had begun even before the war. The patriotic fervour which the war aroused, the heightened sense of crisis and the ensuing self-exaltation at having met and mastered the peril, lends to the art of this period an accent of masculine dignity and justifiable pride, of confidence also in the valour of man and of gratitude to the national gods whose cult was never more sincere.

These qualities are found in all branches of creative activity. Two names dominate the literary scene of the period: Pindar and Aeschylus. Both are deeply religious, and their long, firmly constructed compositions are written in language which is stately and sonorous. The choral lyricism of Pindar was clearly addressed to an aristocratic society in decline, while Aeschylus was the first great writer of tragedies in which the thoughts and actions of Athenian democracy are mirrored. This democracy was, of course, based on a large slave population, which did

128

not vote. It is unlikely that the entire population of Athenian citizens in the time of Plato exceeded 12,000, and of these only a minority were well-to-do. Their relatively primitive way of life was sustained by slavery, though this was not organised, as in Rome, on any great scale. It was 'household' rather than 'plantation' slavery, and the relationship of master and slave was often intimate. Many citizens — and citizenship went by tribal descent — were, like Socrates, quite poor. There was also a large class of resident foreign traders whose part in politics could only have been indirect. The term 'democracy' cannot be equated with modern concepts of universal suffrage.

At the same time, the limited number of citizens and their relative poverty did not prevent them being highly intelligent, so that the poets and dramatists had a quick-witted and critical audience often able to appreciate the profundity of their inspiration. This was closely related to the spirit of the architects who created severely elegant buildings in the Doric style, discreetly enlivened by decorative sculpture which extolled the legends of Greece. An admirable example of this art was the temple of Olympus which owed practically nothing to ancient traditions. Original, too, was the work of the great sculptors in bronze, Pythagoras of Rhegium and Myron of Eleutherae, who concentrated on man in the fullness of his vigour, and the vases of the ceramists of the 'severe style', pupils of the great painter Polygnotus of Thasos.

The age of Pericles

During this period Athens certainly occupied an important position, but her cultural leadership was by no means uncontested. From the moment that peace was restored, however, and Pericles, with the revenues of the Empire at his disposal, could devote his genius to the embellishment of the capital, Athenian supremacy could no longer be challenged. It was Pericles who assumed the direction of the great public works, and in Phidias he found a collaborator worthy of himself. The scope of his projects was considerable and we still do not know its full extent. Since 479 B.C., when the Persians destroyed Athens, the Acropolis had remained in ruins. First, then, a temple was dedicated to Athene, the protective deity of the city: the famous Parthenon (dedicated in 438 B.C.) whose architect was Ictinus. The severity of the building, a marvel of the Doric style, was lightened by a profusion of sculptures executed from clay models by Phidias. The masterpiece of the Parthenon was the virgin goddess — the *Parthenos* — in ivory and gold, which was placed in the sanctuary. It is now lost but the majority of the architectural decoration has been preserved, the most celebrated part of this being the frieze of the *Panathenaea*. Soon after the Parthenon was completed, Mnesicles built the Propylaea (437-432 B.C.), the grace of which is only equalled by its majesty. Buildings for cultural and civic use were also constructed in the city and its port, Piraeus. From this intense activity the Athenian craftsmen gained a skill and mastery which drew foreigners to their workshops, while the works they produced spread throughout the civilised world of the Mediterranean and the Middle

Right: Faithful representations of early Greek ships are rare. Structure, rig and even the number of oars are still subjects of discussion. Greek vase painting offers one of the few contemporary sources of information. This detail is from a fifth-century amphora. *British Museum*

A bronze warrior figure (possibly from Sparta) c. 550 B.C.

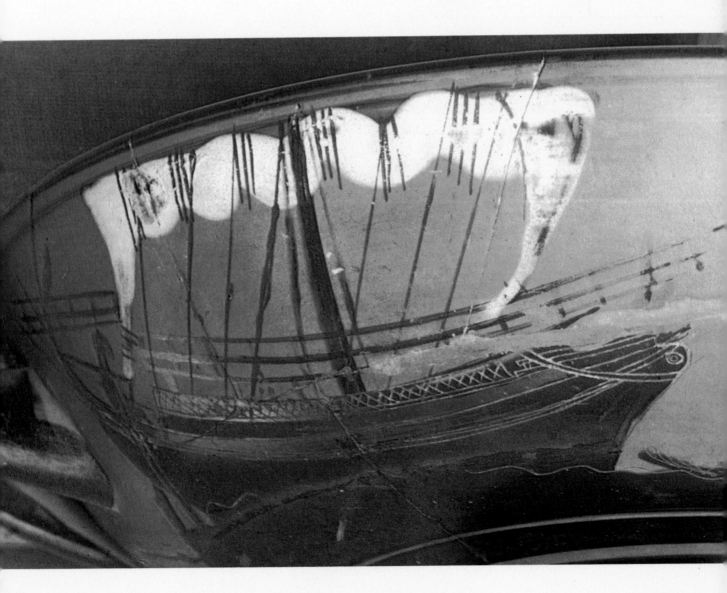

East. Polycletus of Argos paid a long visit to Athens which softened the austerity of his style, as a comparison of his Diadumenos and his Doryphorus demonstrates. For the temple of Olympus Phidias sculpted a colossal chryselephantine Zeus. The beauty of Phidias' style was further popularised by the ceramics it inspired, works of simplicity and purity of line, of nobility and serenity of thought, of perfection in execution.

In a city bubbling with new ideas and seething with political rivalries intellectual life could not fail to quicken with a similar vitality. Philosophy and literature were, in fact, as lively as art itself. In a democracy the gift of words is of primary importance. Athens in the age of Pericles produced brilliant orators, the most brilliant of whom was Pericles himself. Of their actual words only echoes remain, quotations and résumés; but the importance of eloquence in the life of the city was such that schools sprang up to teach this essential art. From these schools arose a philosophical movement which produced the 'Sophists'. The Sophists abandoned as sterile the metaphysical speculations of the Ionian philosophers who had preceded them; their object was less to discover what was true than to determine what was useful. One outcome of this attitude was the study and development of applied science, astronomy, biology and medicine, in which the names of Anaxagoras, Meton and Hippocrates of Cos are still renowned. A second result of the Sophist movement was a study of how society could most effectively be run. This was the chief preoccupation of Protagoras, Gorgias, Prodicus and others, all foreigners who taught at Athens. Their worldliness and pragmatism often made them despicable charlatans, and Socrates (469-399 B.C.) was the spokesman of a reaction. While Socrates preserved their concern with morality, he strove to encourage his own disciples to seek for the Good which each bore within himself. His method was that of friendly conversation in which he exercised his talent for mental 'midwifery' which served merely to bring forth into clear consciousness what was already vaguely in mind — the *maieutic*. His uncompromising search for truth led him from the beaten paths of accepted doctrine, and he roused feverish enmity which resulted in his condemnation and death.

This intellectual ferment spread through all other branches of literature. It is true that for Herodotus history is still mainly an uncritical collection of legends and tales, though told with verve and charm and full of anthropological interest. But with Sophocles and even more with Euripides, whose career overlaps with the succeeding period, tragedy attains perfection. Sophocles, with his pyschological insight coupled with a profoundly religious temperament, with the nobility of his inspiration and the brilliance of his style 'sweetened by human tenderness' is the true contemporary of Pericles. But in Euripides a questioning of traditional beliefs, statements which are more audacious than they at first appear, the analysis of sentiments, even of ignoble sentiments, betray the influence of the Sophists and the approach of an era when the individual will count for more than the group.

Colour plate: a bronze finial (probably from a chariot) in the form of a horse's head. Greece. Fifth century B.C. *British Museum*

Hellenism in the West

Though the pre-eminence of Athens became more and more marked during the course of the fifth century, the rest of Greece had by no means ceased to produce works of vitality. The western Greek world, far from the blinding light of Athens which eclipsed all her neighbours, was the scene of rich and original intellectual activity. The victory of Gelon at Himera in 480 B.C. earned Syracuse a renown which his brother, Hieron, who in 478 B.C. succeeded him, raised to even greater heights when he defeated the Etruscan fleet at Cumae in 474 B.C. Hieron furthered his triumph by extending his rule over the major part of Sicily and making his influence felt in Magna Graecia. But the Syracusian tyranny did not survive his death in 466 B.C. Strife within his own family gave rise to a democratic movement to which his brother and successor, Thrasybulus, was forced to capitulate.

The cities which had been subdued regained their independence and at once quarrelled with Syracuse. Meanwhile, in the contesting cities themselves, the partisans of tyranny had not been disarmed and civil warfare broke out. This state of anarchy encouraged the attempt of Ducetius, chief of the Siculi, an indigenous tribe which the Greeks had subjugated, to set up a native Sicilian kingdom. In 459 B.C. Ducetius succeeded in concentrating his compatriots around the base of Mount Etna where he made his headquarters. He then attacked the neighbouring city of Acragas. This fresh danger made the Greeks forget their dissensions and in 450 B.C., after a hard struggle, the chief of the Siculi was forced to give himself up. He was exiled to Corinth, but escaped and tried again. His efforts were terminated in 439 B.C. by his death. Syracuse had seized the largest share of his kingdom and from then onwards dominated Sicily without rivals.

The disturbances of this period did not affect the prosperity of the country. In addition to agriculture there was a remarkable development in commerce and industry, to which the magnificent coinage of Gelon bears witness. The opulence of the cities was demonstrated in grandiose public monuments with an ostentation which may have reflected the taste of Ionian refugees, numerous since the Persian conquests. The riches of Syracuse attracted poets from mainland Greece, but the literature which was produced was native. The great names were those of the learned philosopher Empedocles and of the comic poet Epicharmus, whose work was not without influence even on the Athenian theatre.

Italy and the early Roman republic

Greek civilisation had shone brightly on the peoples of Italy during the sixth century; in the first half of the fifth its influence was felt much less. This was certainly in part because Sicily at this time was rent by civil wars, but to explain it fully the history of the Italian peoples themselves must be considered. The period was distinguished by the descent of the inhabitants of the Apennines to the coastal plains. Towards the middle of the century they had spread through Campagna: Cumae and Capua were occupied by the Samnites who founded the Oscan state. The Sabines and the Aequi filtered into Latium itself. Farther to the south the Iapygians inflicted on Rhegium and its ally Tarentum a defeat so overwhelming that it imperilled the very existence of the Greek cities of Magna Graecia.

The resulting breakdown in communications between Italy and the Greek world helps to explain the obscurity which surrounds the beginnings of the Roman republic. The expulsion of the Etruscan tyrants marked the opening of a difficult period. In Rome itself the patricians repressed and controlled the plebeians who until then had been well treated. The origin of these two orders, patrician and plebeian, is uncertain: the primitive difference between them may have been racial; or their opposition may have been economic, between patrician herdsmen and plebeian cultivators of the soil; or again, the result of religious rivalry between the worshippers of Jupiter and the worshippers of Ceres; or finally, of all these elements combined. What is certain is that the patricians were the sole masters of the city and alone furnished its magistrates. They composed the senate, bore arms and formed the assembly. The plebeians, excluded from the enjoyment of all rights, were reduced to serfdom.

Thus Roman history in the fifth century is the history of the struggle between plebeian and patrician.

Following the expulsion of the Tarquins the new government of Rome was led by the patricians, who decreed that only their own order might hold office as magistrates and priests, and that the popular assembly alone had no power to make a binding law. These were measures that were naturally resented by the plebeians. With the end of the regal period prosperity had waned: trade abroad declined, large-scale building projects were fewer and Rome had had to renounce a rich hegemony over the Volscians and the towns of central Latium. The result was

Hippocrates, the patron of medicine and regarded as one of the founders of medical science. Spectacular progress was made in all fields of learning during the Periclean age.

A relief from Tarentum showing the twelve Olympians: Hestia, Hephaistus, Aphrodite, Ares, Demeter, Hermes, Hera, Poseidon, Athene, Zeus, Artemis and Apollo. All were to be taken into the Roman pantheon at a later date under different names.

widespread poverty and unemployment. Under existing laws the plebeians could be committed to prison and even to enslavement for non-payment of debts. This fanned the flame of discontent and by 493 B.C. plebeians were threatening to withdraw from the city and found a community of their own on Mons Sacer, a hill three miles away. The patricians were obliged to let them elect in their own special assemblies — based on the territorial tribe — first two, then five *tribuni*. The tribunes were sacrosanct and could by means of the *intercessio* — or intervention — forbid the application of laws. By the *auxilium* — or aid — they could protect any plebeian from the arbitrary action of the magistrates. The *comitia tributa* made decisions — or *plebiscita* — which were binding on the plebeians.

This first plebeian victory was not, however, sufficient; for the law being unwritten, it left the administration of justice in the hands of the religious authorities, who were patrician. In 451 the patricians were forced to agree to a written legal code being drawn up by two successive

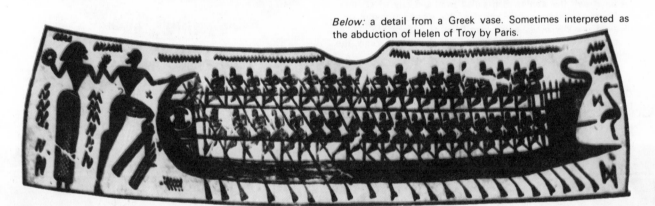

Below: a detail from a Greek vase. Sometimes interpreted as the abduction of Helen of Troy by Paris.

Oedipus and the sphinx. Self-exiled from the city of Corinth, Oedipus rid neighbouring Thebes of the winged monster who plagued the city by killing all who failed to answer her riddle. According to Homer, when his hero gave the correct reply, the sphinx took her own life in chagrin. *Viollet*

A footrace from a panathenaic amphora. The cult of physical perfection is reflected in the many representations of competitive athletic sports and in the many superb sculptures of the human form. *British Museum*

commissions of eleven members. The law of the Twelve Tables which resulted from their work included certain points of constitutional and public law, but was chiefly concerned with the rules of private law in which Greek influence was evident. The chief improvement in the status of the plebeians took place some years later with the institution of the *census*. The rising value of the foot-soldier must have had much the same consequences in Rome as it had had in Greece. Peasants capable of bearing arms at their own expense insisted on having a share in political affairs. In order to draw up a list of those citizens whose fortune allowed them to take part in public life a college of two *censores* was established in about 435 B.C. This important innovation explains the discrepancies found in the consular records: in certain years the election of consuls did not take place, and consuls were replaced by military tribunes. No doubt the reason for this was the patrician desire to avoid having a plebeian occupy the highest office in the city. But the vital step had been taken: henceforth social status was fixed no longer by birth but by wealth.

In foreign affairs the expulsion of the Tarquins had put Rome in a delicate position. Deprived of Etruscan support, she lost her pre-eminence in Latium and even ceased to form a part of the Latin confederation. Tradition has it that at the very beginning of the republic, Rome in 499 B.C. crushed the revolt of the Latins at Lake Regillus and concluded a perpetual alliance with them, the *foedus Cassianum* of 493 B.C. These events are certainly of much later date. Meanwhile Rome had to repulse further Etruscan attempts to regain the city, for instance, during the war with Porsenna, king of Clusium, who is said to have taken Rome in 504 B.C. Certainly the Roman state in these precarious days was a power of little significance. It was only towards 430 B.C., when the mountain folk of the Apennines poured down on to the plain, that the Latins and the Romans forgot their quarrels and united to face the common danger.

The Far East

In India the chief political event of the first half of the fifth century was the reign of Adjatasatru in Magadha (c. 491-459 B.C.). Having assassinated his father Bimbisara, he attacked the king of Kosala with the object of seizing Benares. He was not at once successful, and marched instead to the north of the Ganges where he seems to have conquered the whole of Videha before resuming the war against Kosala. The total conquest of Kosala may have been the work of his descendants. Adjatasatru was at first hostile to Buddhism, but then, like his father, he became converted. His own son, Udayibadhra, founded Pataliputra, which for a thousand years remained the metropolis of Gangetic India. Of his other descendants no record remains.

China during the fifth century continued to be plunged in feudal warfare, and yet the spread of Chinese civilisation did not cease. It reached southwards where a new power, barbarian but imbued with Chinese culture, the kingdom of Yue (Kao-Tsu-Kiang) began to play a part in political affairs. In 473 B.C. it destroyed its predecessor, the kingdom of Wu, but no clear picture emerges from this confused scene of discord in which half a dozen principalities fought for a brief and insecure hegemony.

Boy chasing a hare. Decoration on an Attic kylix. c.500 B.C.

A Greek soldier wearing armour decorated with the head of Medusa, one of the attributes of the goddess Athene.

CHAPTER SIX

THE AGE OF DISCORD

431-362 B.C.

Athene standing between Achilles and Agamemnon; a terra-cotta statue from Tanagra. In legend the goddess of war favoured the Greeks against the Trojans, and helped to reconcile the Greeks among themselves. This group seems to foretell the Peloponnesian War, when Athens acted as the conciliator between the Peloponnesian League (here symbolised by Agamemnon and Thessaly (symbolised by Achilles). *Giraudon*

Under the leadership of Pericles, Athens seemed to be soundly placed to forge the unity of Greece. But her predominance threatened too many interests and could only be imposed by force. Force gave rise to conflict which gradually involved the entire Greek world. This struggle, the Peloponnesian War, was long and pitiless, and in the end it brought about the downfall of Athenian hegemony. Sparta, however, was unable to assume her defeated rival's place, and her victory roused fierce enmities which again plunged Greece into confusion. While the city-states squabbled among themselves, a new power arose to take advantage of the discord, Macedonia, who put an end to the autonomy of the warring cities. The principle of independence for which Athens had first fought and vanquished thus brought the very antithesis of her long-defended ideals.

THE AGE OF DISCORD

Causes of the Peloponnesian War

The Athenian Empire caused resentment and bitterness not only among its own subject members: independent states, too, felt that it menaced their existence. This was especially true of commercial cities which feared that further extension of Athenian economic imperialism would entail ruinous competition. The chief of these was Corinth. Her markets, almost all in the west, were a constant temptation to the insatiable ambition of Athens. The Gulf of Corinth could be blockaded by Athenian allies, the Messenians of Naupactus, while Pericles' foundation of Thurii constituted a further threat in Magna Graecia. Nevertheless, during the Samos incident, Corinth had still been unwilling to intervene militarily. But when towards 437 B.C. Athens herself intervened in a conflict between the Acarnanians and Ambracia, a Corinthian colony, it became evident that Corinth could no longer defend her economic existence without resort to arms.

Athenian provocation increased. The Athenians responded to an appeal from Corcyra, an unruly Corinthian colony which had once revolted and now feared the coalition which Corinth had formed to bring her to heel. Corcyra was defeated but the arrival of an Athenian fleet prevented the Corinthians taking the island by assault. In the west Athens made new alliances with Zacynthus, Rhegium and Leontini. In the east Corinth had a colony at Potidaea in the Macedonian peninsula of Chalcidice whose magistrates were Corinthian while at the same time the city belonged to the Athenian Empire. Athens, disturbed by possible Macedonian intentions, ordered Potidaea to tear down her city walls. Potidaea refused and Corinth secretly supplied her with men and arms to resist the Athenian siege which began in

June 432 B.C. But the spark which set off the general conflict was struck in another city which was equally threatened: Megara. Athens had never forgiven Megara's defection from the Confederation in 446 B.C. and had since tried to keep her from the Bosphorus and the Black Sea. Finally in 432 B.C. an Athenian decree forbade Megaran commerce the use of all ports in the Empire.

The beginning of the war

Megara and Corinth at once appealed to their ally Sparta, who found herself in an embarrassing position. The governing party wished for peace, but further inaction would result in the break-up of the Peloponnesian League, of which she was chief. The first Peloponnesian Congress, which met in the summer of 432 B.C., decided that Athens had violated her treaties. A second Congress met in September; those Spartans who demanded action carried the day and voted for war. The winter of 432-431 B.C. was spent in vain attempts to settle

A wounded warrior from the pediment of the Temple of Aphaia, Aegina, c. 490 B.C. The island of Aegina, just south of Athens, was a member of the Peloponnesian League and a constant thorn in the flesh of Athens. *Giraudon*

the dispute by negotiation. In the spring Thebes attacked Athens' ally Plataea, and the threatened outbreak of war became a reality.

From the very beginning it looked as though the war would go on for ever. The Athenians, aware of their inferiority on land, followed Pericles' advice and, abandoning Attica to the ravages of the enemy, took shelter behind their impregnable Long Walls which connected the city with Piraeus, the harbour. They calculated that their financial strength was such that they could afford to wait until their fleet, vastly superior to the enemy's, had reduced the Peloponnesians to bankruptcy and famine. This coldly logical calculation was very soon upset. The city was packed with refugees, and in the summer of 430 B.C. plague broke out which wrought havoc, killing probably a third of the population. Pericles was blamed for the disaster and condemned to pay an enormous fine. Thanks to certain successes, such as the capitulation of Potidaea, he regained his popularity in the following year, but almost immediately died of the plague himself.

Cleon's war

With the death of Pericles old internal party struggles began again, but no leader of comparable stature emerged.

The Zeus of Artemisium, a bronze statue attributed to Calamis (c. 460 B.C.). The Greeks imagined their gods in human form, and their artists strove to represent the human body perfectly.

135

Athenian strategy was, moreover, half paralysed by the rivalry of Cleon, chief of the democratic imperialists, and Nicias, leader of the conservative peace party. Cleon, often described as a venal, incapable and bloodthirsty demagogue, was certainly not without diplomatic skill and military courage. Impulsive, unimaginative and narrow in outlook, his talents were, however, unequal to his patriotism. Nicias, who was immensely rich and very devout, had no military capacity. Cleon at first carried the assembly with him and by his energy he succeeded in crushing the revolt of Mytilene in 427 B.C., which compensated for the fall of Plataea. But this Athenian victory was tarnished by the execution of the prisoners. In the same way, savage massacres marked the victory of the democrats in Corcyra over their adversaries who had wished to repudiate the Athenian alliance. By these brutal measures the Empire at least remained intact and was able to resume the offensive.

The war was waged on three fronts. In Sicily, where Syracuse was sending supplies to the Peloponnesus and was at the same time attempting to extend her own domination over the whole island, Athens came to the aid of her ally Leontini and in 427 B.C. occupied Messina. The operations dragged on until, three years later, the congress of Gela restored peace. In north-west Greece the Athenian general Demosthenes, marching from Naupactus, tried to cut off Boeotia by way of Aetolia. The

attempt was frustrated by a severe defeat, but he was able to assist the Acarnanians to impose their authority on Ambracia (426 B.C.). Finally in the Peloponnesus the same Demosthenes seized Pylos, from which base he planned to ravage the interior of the peninsula. He was besieged in Pylos by the Spartans, installed in the neighbouring island of Sphacteria. Sphacteria in its turn was blockaded by an Athenian fleet coming to the rescue. Fearing the threat to her own safety, Sparta now asked for peace. Cleon persuaded his countrymen to refuse the offer, arguing that total victory would reduce the enemy to sue for mercy. When victory was delayed Cleon took command of the Athenian forces himself and in 425 B.C., putting Demosthenes' plans into operation, he finally forced the enemy to capitulate. Other successful actions at Cythera and at Nicaea, the port of Megara, raised Cleon to the height of his popularity. He made use of his influence by having the tribute paid by the allies increased.

The Peace of Nicias

Cleon was preparing to further the war effort by crushing Boeotia with the aid of the local democrats when unforeseen difficulties arose in Thrace. Sparta had sent one of her best generals, Brasidas, to Thrace with the mission of stopping the shipment of the indispensable wood

Greece and her allies at the time of Pericles

which Athens needed for the construction of new ships. Then, in the autumn of 424 B.C. several Athenian subject allies deserted. At the same time the offensive in Boeotia was brought to a halt by defeat at Delium. At home the peace party regained the ascendancy, and, since the Spartans wished to free the prisoners on the island of Sphacteria, a truce was concluded towards the end of 424 B.C. But Brasidas continued to undermine the loyalty of Athens' allies in Thrace, and Cleon went there in 422 B.C. and attempted to recapture Amphipolis. The death of Cleon and of Brasidas, the two chief adversaries of peace, allowed a treaty to be concluded in April of the following year. The peace of Nicias, however, applied only to Athens and Sparta. Sparta's allies continued the struggle, which from the beginning made the chances of a lasting settlement extremely unlikely.

The indirect war

The territorial clauses of the peace treaty were not honoured. Each of the two states, in addition, engaged in a policy of forming alliances with the other's enemies. Thus Sparta in 420 B.C. became the ally of Thebes and Athens retaliated by making an agreement with Argos, Elis and Mantinea. The struggle between the two adversaries was resumed through the intermediacy of their respective allies, and ultimately they found themselves face to face again when in 418 B.C. Sparta resolved to put an end to the activities of Argos. She was encouraged to take this step by party strife in Athens where Nicias was now opposed by Alcibiades, a nephew of Pericles, who had become the idol of the populace if not of the democratic leaders. On the Pnyx, Nicias temporarily carried the assembly with him; but he was able neither to restore peace nor to support the Athenian allies who were beaten at Mantinea. The few hoplites who had been sent to reinforce them were of no assistance and the disgrace of the defeat reflected on Athens.

The Sicilian expedition

It was elsewhere, however, that events were taking place which were again to plunge the Greek world into warfare. In Sicily the peace of Gela had been of short duration. Syracuse still nursed ambitions to dominate the island and again attacked Leontini. Then, in 416 B.C., she took Segesta who called on Athens for help. After long and serious debates on the Pnyx it was finally decided to send an expedition to Sicily. Nicias had been against the project and tried to point out its dangers and difficulties. The only result was that he was himself made joint commander of the expedition with Alcibiades. At the moment when the fleet was on the point of sailing it was discovered that all the statues of Hermes in the Agora had been mutilated. The sacrilege sent a shudder of superstitious horror through Athens. Alcibiades was accused of being the perpetrator. He sought an immediate trial, but in order not to delay the departure of the fleet, it was adjourned until his return.

As soon as the expedition sailed disagreement broke out between the two commanders. Alcibiades argued in favour of arranging a coalition of Sicilian cities against Syracuse. His arguments made little impression and while he was trying to further these plans he was suddenly

A bust of Zeus, showing the classical (fourth century B.C.) representation of his features. *Viollet*

A Persian standard-bearer, fallen at the feet of a Greek hoplite. With the battle of Plataea in 479 B.C. the Persian invasions of Greece were halted.

The theatre at Syracuse in Sicily (Greek, built upon by the Romans). In 416 B.C. Syracuse seized Segesta, an ally of Athens. Athens came to her aid and besieged Syracuse in 414 B.C.; the Athenian fleet was nevertheless disastrously routed. *Alinari*

recalled to Athens, accused of sacrilege. Fearing that he would be found guilty, he deserted, and escaped to Sparta where he traitorously fanned the ardour of the war party by denouncing Athenian ambitions of conquest.

Meanwhile Nicias, now the sole commander of the expedition, had decided to lay siege to Syracuse in the beginning of 414 B.C. He entrenched his troops but pushed operations forward so sluggishly that he gave the Spartans time to send a general, Gylippus, who rallied the courage of Syracuse. The Athenian blockade was broken and further reinforcements were on their way from the Peloponnesus. Nicias in terror appealed for help. By the beginning of the following year, 413 B.C., Nicias himself was nearly besieged. His efforts to assure at least the food supply of his troops against a blockading Corinthian fleet were fruitless. In two naval engagements the Athenian ships were destroyed. When Demosthenes arrived with a fresh fleet and more Athenian troops the situation was desperate. A night attack against the Syracusian defences almost succeeded, but was finally repulsed with heavy losses. There was no alternative but immediate retreat, but Nicias delayed — due, it was said, to an eclipse of the moon. When he decided to withdraw it was too late: all his forces, land and sea, were blockaded. For seven days, from the eleventh to the eighteenth of September 413 B.C., the trapped Athenian army suffered heavily, attempting in vain to break out and escape, harassed on all sides, abandoning dead and wounded, dying of thirst, only to be slaughtered at last on the banks of the Assinaros. The losses were overwhelming: forty thousand men and one hundred and sixty ships. It seemed that Athens could never recover.

The Decelean War

Athens did, however, resist for nine years more and at times gave the impression that she could never be beaten. In 413 B.C. her situation appeared hopeless. Agis, king of Sparta, had occupied the village of Decelea, almost within sight of Athens, from where he ravaged all Attica and stopped further mining activity at Laurium, which added to Athenian financial embarrassment. In the Empire, rebellion smouldered, and Sparta was negotiating for Persian aid among the satraps of Asia Minor. The storm broke in 412 B.C. Alcibiades stirred Chios and several Ionian cities to revolt against Athens. At Miletus Sparta concluded an alliance with Tissaphernes, satrap of Sardis. But Athens, by a series of energetic administrative and financial measures, succeeded in rebuilding her fleet. With its aid the democrats of Samos massacred their opponents. Lesbos and some of the Ionian towns were reduced to obedience, and Chios was devastated.

The Revolt of the Four Hundred

Athenian recovery was compromised by a revolution. The war was by no means universally popular. The rich, burdened by high taxes, wanted peace and played into the hands of the determined enemies of the democracy, grouped in secret political clubs, *hetaeries*, who were waiting only for an opportunity to take an active part in affairs. The opportunity was supplied by Alcibiades who had quarrelled with the Spartans and taken refuge with

the satrap of Sardis, hoping one day to return to Athens as a saviour. Alcibiades promised the Athenian oligarchs peace and Persian gold on condition that they overthrew the democrats. The hetaeries rose and attacked their enemies. Although at the crucial moment the satrap withheld his support, the oligarchs had gone too far to draw back. In the ensuing reign of terror the Assembly voted for the abolition of most of the constitution and resigned all political authority to a body of five thousand citizens (the Five Thousand) which the Four Hundred (council of four hundred oligarchs) were instructed to form in June 411 B.C.

These events brought about new Athenian reverses: the revolt of Rhodes towards the end of 411 B.C., then of Byzantium, Chalcedon and Cyzicus — which cut off Athens from the wheat supplies of the Black Sea. This seriously shook the new government. The moderate oligarchs, whose leader was Theramenes, demanded that the Five Thousand should be convened. The Four Hundred could flourish only by treasonable means: they called in the Spartans. Such treacherous behaviour roused general fury and the false rumour that Euboea had left the Empire led to a popular uprising which in September 412 B.C. overthrew the Four Hundred and brought the Five Thousand to power. The Five Thousand were no more successful in maintaining authority. Meanwhile the fleet at Samos

A battle between the gods and the giants, from a Greek red-figured amphora (middle fourth century B.C.). A mythical event which was regarded as symbolic of the triumph of Greece over the barbarians, it appears in many works of art from the time of the Persian Wars onwards.

refused to recognise the oligarchical government and had elected democratic leaders, Thrasyllus and Thrasybulus. Alcibiades immediately got in touch with them and, again promising Persian support, managed to get himself elected strategos. The two Athenian parties, each claiming to be patriotic, felt obliged to renew war operations with vigour. The fleet at Samos destroyed the Peloponnesian fleet at Cynossema and then at Abydos, while Theramenes reduced the islands to Athenian obedience. As Athens regained command of the sea, her forces were naturally inclined to collaborate and, united, they were resoundingly victorious in 410 B.C. off the coast of Cyzicus. Sparta, alarmed, now proposed peace on the basis of the status quo. Athens felt that she was in a strong enough position to do better than this, and refused. During the next two years it seemed as though her decision had been wise: she took Byzantium and Chalcedon, and thereby regained control of the Bosphorus. Then Thasos capitulated, which gave her command of Thrace. These successes, in which the popular party had taken a leading part, facilitated the restoration of the constitution, and in 407 B.C. Alcibiades, whose skill was largely responsible for the victories, returned in triumph to Athens.

Lysander's War

The triumph of Alcibiades' return was short-lived, for him and for Athens. Sparta, foreseeing an attack on her Ionian positions, had sent a naval commander of genius to take charge of the Peloponnesian fleet. Lysander was an able strategist, a skilled diplomatist, energetic and unscrupulous. At the same time the Great King was also worried by Athenian success and had confided the general command of Ionia to his son Cyrus the Younger. Lysander and Cyrus were in complete accord. Liberally provided with Persian money, Lysander raised the pay of his sailors and suborned the Athenian oarsmen. At Colophon towards the beginning of 406 B.C. he inflicted a defeat on Alcibiades, whom the Athenians then relieved of his command. But Lysander's character and his suspected ambitions caused uneasiness in Sparta and he too was replaced. The Athenians at once regained the upper hand. Callicratidas, who had relieved Lysander as admiral of the Peloponnesian fleet, was defeated and killed off the little islands of Arginusae in the summer of 406 B.C. After the battle the victorious Athenian commanders had been unable to save the drowning sailors of the Athenian ships which were sunk, a circumstance which roused a violent outburst in Athens. The eight commanders were accused before the Assembly of criminal neglect. Two fled and the remaining six were condemned to death. They had been Athens' best officers. Meanwhile Sparta reinstated Lysander and put him in command of a new fleet of considerable importance. In August 405 B.C. he surprised the last of the Athenian fleet, ill guarded, at the mouth of the Aegos-Potamos on the Hellespont and destroyed every ship. Those allies which Athens still retained deserted her. In November Lysander laid siege to Athens itself. In April 404 B.C., reduced by famine, the city capitulated. Lysander's terms were fairly moderate: the Long Walls and the fortifications at Piraeus were torn down, the remnant of Athenian shipping handed over, and Athens reluctantly was forced to join the Spartan League.

A Corinthian capital. Leaves and flowers, such as the acanthus leaves of this column, were often used as ornamentation in Hellenistic art of the fourth century B.C. *Viollet*

Part of the theatre at Epidaurus in the Peloponnese, fourth century B.C. In such theatres as this the plays of Euripides, Sophocles, and Aristophanes were performed. *Viollet*

The Temple of Apollo at Corinth, late sixth century B.C. Corinth, a member of the Peloponnesian League, possessed a large fleet, a powerful weapon against Athens. *Viollet*

Part of a bas-relief from the theatre at Corinth (fifth century B.C.). Corinth first became powerful in the eighth century B.C., and was a prosperous and important centre of Greek civilisation in the fifth century. *Viollet*

The Thirty in Athens

The Spartan triumph was complete, allowing Lysander everywhere to impose governments acceptable to Sparta. These were the *decarchies*, a kind of collective tyranny supported by troops under the command of Spartan *harmosts* — governors. In Athens the Assembly, under duress and cowed by the enemy fleet, returned to power thirty oligarchs—known as the Thirty Tyrants. The Thirty inaugurated a reign of terror in which the democratic leaders were slaughtered or forced to flee, while their goods and property were confiscated. A Spartan garrison on the Acropolis prevented physical resistance, but it could not silence complaints. Though the democrats were muzzled, the moderates, still led by Theramenes, called for an end to the bloody tyranny and the establishment of a legally elected government. The Thirty answered by fresh acts of brutality which towards the end of 404 B.C. cost Theramenes his life.

Restoration of the democracy

In the meanwhile the exiled Athenian leaders of democracy were regrouping. They found certain outside support, especially in Thebes which was perhaps beginning to feel uneasy about Spartan ascendancy. Thrasybulus was a refugee in Thebes, and in the winter of 404-403 B.C. he and a band of other exiled Athenians, with Theban blessing, set out for their native land. By spring they had captured Piraeus, and The Thirty did not survive the blow. The Thirty were replaced by The Ten, who were obliged to appeal to Sparta when Thrasybulus besieged Athens. Lysander arrived and blockaded Piraeus. Thrasybulus appeared to be lost when events in Sparta itself reversed the situation. In Sparta Lysander's ambitions were still strongly suspect and he was suddenly replaced by Pausanias. Pausanias, who may have feared Boeotian intervention, undertook to re-establish peace between the two Athenian parties. In the autumn

of 403 B.C. he reconciled them under his aegis and proclaimed a general amnesty from which only The Thirty, the Ten and a few of their confederates were excluded. Even they could be accepted in the community if they made amends for their past. Any Athenian who felt that his life was in danger was permitted to emigrate to Eleusis, which became independent.

The restraint and wisdom of the two political leaders, Thrasybulus and Anytus, brought peace at last to Athens. Anytus strove to reduce the number of applicants for emigration to Eleusis, which was re-annexed two or three years later, and opposed a constitutional measure which would have deprived the democrats of most of their armed forces. On the other hand, he quashed a decree of his adversary which proposed to give Athenian citizenship to all *metics* — aliens who had lived in Athens, often for generations — who had served the city. Thrasybulus, for his part, did not pursue oppressive measures against the oligarchs, who were even allowed to retain the goods they had stolen from the exiles. He also agreed that the war debts of both parties should be the responsibility of the State. By common agreement the constitution was revised under the archontate of Euclides (403-402 B.C.). But moderation was stained by a judicial murder: in 399 B.C. Anytus himself accused Socrates of atheism and of the corruption of Athenian youth. The great philosopher's frankness of speech and his contempt for vulgar prejudice had gained him too many enemies: the restored democracy saw him as the inspiration of oligarchic reaction and condemned him to death.

The leadership of Sparta

The fall of the oligarchy in Athens was not a blow to Sparta: she herself had supervised it, and her old enemy was much too feeble to seem in any way formidable. Athens, too, was well aware of this, and faithfully fulfilled all the clauses of the peace treaty. Thus Sparta, in spite of the hostility of some of her former allies, could

Acrocorinth, the great rock which from earliest times was a citadel. Corinth was the maritime and commercial centre of Greece with colonies all round the Mediterranean. An ally of Sparta, she was the principal enemy of Athens in the Peloponnesian War. *Viollet*

proceed without hesitation to the enlargement of her empire. In the Peloponnesus, Elis, who had maintained her independence during the war, was forced in about 400 B.C. to enter the Peloponnesian League. But Sparta's chief aim was to take the place of Athens in the Near East and become the dominant power in Asia Minor. This ambition was no doubt inspired by Lysander who counted on the help of Cyrus the Younger. Sparta persuaded Cyrus to revolt against his brother Artaxerxes II, the Persian king. She encouraged him to recruit a large force of mercenaries and furnished him with a general and reinforcements. In 401 B.C. he invaded Babylonia, but in his very first engagement at Cunaxa he was killed. His native troops at once disbanded, and the Greeks, left to their own devices, escaped only after an arduous retreat across Armenia. Cyrus' successor in Ionia, Tissaphernes, not unnaturally adopted an unfriendly attitude. Basing his claims on stipulations in the treaty of Miletus, he attempted to levy tribute on the Greek cities of the Near East. These appealed to Sparta who, in 400 B.C., sent an army to protect them. For the next two years military operations were pursued without vigour,

until in 398 B.C. a Persian fleet, commanded by the Athenian Conon, attacked the Spartans and caused the defection of Rhodes. The situation was now so disquieting that in 396 B.C. the Spartan king Agesilaus was sent to Asia to deal with it.

In the following year Tissaphernes was defeated near Sardis and the plains of Phrygia were laid in ruins.

The Corinthian war

This successful campaign was interrupted by an event which had long been foreseen: war between Sparta and Thebes. A trivial frontier incident was the pretext for hostilities, but the jealousy aroused by the Spartan Empire in Thebes, in Corinth and in Argos, Athenian longing for revenge, plus Persian gold, had made war inevitable. The Spartans hoped to encircle their adversaries by advancing simultaneously from the Peloponnesus and from Thessaly. The Thebans, greatly disturbed by this manoeuvre, effected an alliance with Athens. The immediate danger, however, was averted by the defeat and death of Lysander in 395 B.C. at Haliartus in Boeotia.

A large part of Thessaly at once rallied to the victors, and in order to repair the defeat Sparta recalled Agesilaus from Asia. Agesilaus returned by the northern route and forced his way across Boeotia to Coronea. In 394 B.C. he reached the Isthmus at Nemea. But he had done little to weaken the coalition, while the Persian fleet commanded by Conon annihilated the Spartan fleet under Pisander off Cnidus, reunited Ionia and the islands, and even planted a garrison at Cythera.

The 'King's Peace'

These reverses by no means brought Sparta to her knees. She had her revenge in 393 B.C. before Corinth, cutting the city off from her port of Lechaeum. At the same time she hurried Antalcidas, her most skilled diplomatist, to the court of the satrap of Sardis, where he was successful in causing Conon to fall from grace. This turn of events disposed the Athenians to suggest peace, and in 391 B.C. envoys were sent to Sparta. The terms of settlement they proposed were refused however.

freed from their Greek alliances. This last clause ruined the Boeotian confederation, the union of Corinth and Argos, and the embryonic empire which Athens had reconstituted. Athens, however, retained Lemnos, Imbros and Scyros, to which she hastened to send *cleruchs* to prepare for the future.

This Spartan victory, diplomatic rather than military, once more gave her a free hand to impose her authority on Greece. In 385 B.C. Mantinea was destroyed. In Chalcidice Olynthus had formed a prosperous league which she attempted to force Acanthus and Apollonia to join. In 382 B.C. Sparta responded to their appeal for help and, on the way, the Spartan army seized the acropolis of Thebes — the Cadmea — which was delivered into her hands by the Theban oligarchs. Olynthus held out stubbornly against the Spartans, but her resistance was eventually broken and in 379 B.C. the Chalcidian League was forcibly dissolved. In the meanwhile Athens was encouraging the spirit of resistance. By discreet diplomacy and under cover of agreements with native kings she had recovered her influence in Thrace. She won the alliance

A trireme carved in rock at the entrance to the acropolis at Lindos, Rhodes. Following the disaster inflicted upon the Athenians at Syracuse in 413 B.C. the Spartans seized Rhodes, making a further inroad into the Athenian Empire and possessing themselves of valuable ships and men. *Viollet.*

Those members of the coalition who were opposed to peace appeared, in view of what followed, to have been justified. An Athenian general, Iphicrates, trying out new military tactics, inflicted a serious defeat on the Spartans at Lechaeum and in 390 B.C. raised the siege of Corinth. A naval squadron commanded by Thrasybulus restored Athenian influence at Byzantium, at Lesbos and in Asia Minor. In 388 B.C. these new allies consented to contribute to the cost of the war and the Athenian Empire appeared to be on the point of revival. But in the following year the Spartans, installed at Aegina, delivered a disastrous blow by seizing Piraeus and, worst of all, Antalcidas succeeded in renewing the Persian alliance. In order to do this he simply accepted the conditions dictated at Sardis and known as the 'King's Peace': Asia Minor was returned to Persia and all the Greek cities therein were

of Chios. She gave refuge to all exiles who fled from cities whose government was pro-Spartan. It was from Athens that the band of Theban conspirators, led by Pelopidas, set out one night towards the end of 379 B.C. The conspiracy had been well planned and Pelopidas succeeded in slaughtering the Theban oligarchs. The Spartan garrison on the Cadmea was trapped and forced to surrender.

The Second Athenian Maritime Confederation

Though Athens had helped the Theban Pelopidas, she had no intention of abandoning her neutrality. It was Sparta who forced her to do so. Or rather it was the Spartan governor of Thespiae in Boeotia, Sphodrias, who in 378 B.C. on his own initiative attempted to seize Piraeus and failed. Sparta acquitted the author of this felony and Athens broke off relations with her. She allied herself with Thebes and a brilliant team of admirals and diplomatists set sail from Athens. Thanks to their skill, Athens won new allies who, added to those recently acquired, formed a second maritime confederation which in 377 B.C. was formally organised as the Second Athenian League. Great care was taken not to repeat the errors which had been fatal to the first confederation. The independence of the confederates was guaranteed; there was no more tribute, but only freely offered contributions. Decisions were to be taken by the assembled allies in accordance with the popular assembly, or Ecclesia. A mixed court judged violations of the pact. To face these new obligations Athens herself, under the guidance of Callistratus who was her most influential leader at this time, proceeded to reorganise her institutions, particularly her financial institutions, and imposed a capital levy. Once more in possession of military potential, she soon regained mastery of the seas. At Naxos in 376 B.C. the Athenian commander Chabrias swept the last Spartan fleet from the Aegean. A year later Timotheus, son of Conon, set sail towards the west, rallied Corcyra and Acarnania and sank another enemy squadron at Alyzia. But the war proved expensive and Thebes was beginning to become a danger. Led by men of energy like Pelopidas and, more especially, Epaminondas, she had by 376 B.C. already re-organised the Boeotian confederation, and two years later the Spartans were completely driven from Boeotia. Weary and uneasy, Athens came to an arrangement with Sparta on the basis of the status quo.

Peace was ephemeral: Sparta broke it immediately by blockading Corcyra. Though Athens wished to come to the aid of her ally, financial difficulties in 373 B.C. prevented her from doing so. When, in the following year, Callistratus and Iphicrates arrived, the island had liberated itself without assistance. Iphicrates would willingly have taken advantage of his strength to further Athenian influence in this region, but Callistratus was in favour of peace. The attitude of Thebes, moreover, had now become openly hostile. She had seized Plataea, traditionally allied to Athens, and in 373 B.C. was claiming Oropus in Attica itself. Callistratus returned to Athens and sent envoys to Sparta, where the Thebans, too, appeared. In 371 B.C. agreement was easily reached between Athens and Sparta, based on a common respect for the right of self-government and a theoretic division of supremacy: to Athens the sea, to Sparta the continent. But when Epaminondas claimed to sign the treaty in the name of all Boeotia he met with general opposition and Thebes refused to take part in the agreement.

The downfall of Sparta

The conflict could only be resolved by force. A Spartan army had been stationed in Phocis to protect the country against its neighbours. This army received orders to march on Thebes. The battle took place in 371 B.C. at Leuctra. Epaminondas, using tactics of an entirely new kind, won a crushing victory. At Leuctra the military might of Sparta was lost for ever. The invincibility of Spartan arms had, in fact, for long been more legendary than real, a façade which concealed the ruin caused by constant warfare and by the vices inherent in the

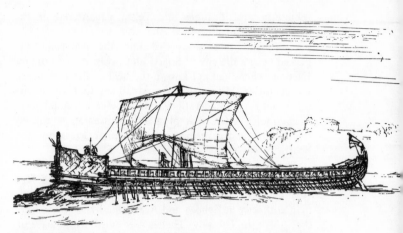

A Greek galley at the time of the Battle of Salamis (480 B.C.), when a united Greek fleet defeated the Persians.

Spartan system. The Ancients themselves attributed the downfall of Sparta to oliganthropy, or lack of man-power. It is of course true that to sustain her imperialist pretensions Sparta had only a few thousand citizens, which was hardly enough to provide the skeleton units of her armed forces. But her ultimate failure was the result of deeper causes, social and political. For many years the famed economic equality of Spartan citizens had been an illusion. Though the land provided by the State to each Spartiate — or member of the dominant race — was inalienable, this was not the case with land belonging to the free but politically unprivileged Perioeci. By buying such land with the proceeds of war booty, to which Spartiate military leaders were avidly addicted, certain families had acquired huge estates. Less fortunate Spartiates tried to limit their families to a single son who lived with difficulty on his hereditary plot of land, slave-driving his helots whose discontent and bitterness smouldered and grew. If he was unable to live off his allotment he was forced to borrow, and, crushed by debt, he sank into the 'inferior' class of those who had forfeited their political rights. At the end of the Peloponnesian War a law authorising gifts and legacies led to a further concentration of land in the hands of the rich. In this way the number of full citizens diminished and the number of those who had lost their rights increased. Their chief preoccupation was of course to regain their former privileges, while the oligarchs themselves, torn between partisans of the royalty and partisans of the ephors, corrupted by war profits and the exercise of totalitarian power, obstinately defended their own position. An atmosphere of jealousy and hate poisoned the city and the old spirit of Sparta was dead. In 399 B.C. the crisis had nearly come to a head: Cinadon, a young man who had sunk into the 'inferior' class, planned, in an effort to mobilise all the discontented, to rouse not only the Perioeci but even the helots to rebel. His plans were discovered before they could be put into action, but the victory of the aristocrats led in the end to their death sentence. Thebes was destined to be the instrument of their execution.

Theban leadership

Scarcely had the defeat of Leuctra become known than the wind of revolt swept the Peloponnesus. Mantinea rebuilt her fortifications and Tegea slaughtered or exiled all Spartan adherents. The year after Leuctra, 370 B.C., Epaminondas descended into the peninsula, appeared before the city of Sparta and ravaged surrounding Laconia which had not known the heel of the conqueror for centuries. He assisted the Arcadians to form themselves into a confederation and to build a capital city, Megalopolis. Then, marching into Messenia, he roused the country and gave them, too, a capital, Messene. For Sparta it was a mortal blow.

Thebes also extended her sway towards the north of Greece. After the battle of Leuctra Epaminondas had subjugated Phocis and the Locrians, and replaced Athenian authority in Euboea and Acarnania by his own. Farther north, in Thessaly, Thebes was allied with Jason of Pherae who, since 374 B.C., had succeeded in extending his dominion over all Thessaly. Thebes was fortunate that this tyrant, whose power was growing dangerously, was assassinated in 370 B.C. In 369 B.C. Pelopidas arrived in Thessaly to impose a Theban protectorate over those cities which hoped to escape the authority of Jason's successor, Alexander. Finally Thebes was successful in gaining the goodwill of the Great King who, at her request, issued a decree confirming Theban hegemony and summoning Athens to keep her fleets in port and to renounce Amphipolis, theoretically recognised in the treaty of 371 B.C. as an Athenian possession.

This anti-Athenian measure, aggravated in 366 by the Thebans' recovery of Oropus, made hostilities inevitable. They had, in fact, already begun indirectly. The news of Leuctra had been coldly received at Athens, and to obstruct the next strategical move which Thebes plainly meant to make Athens attempted, though without success, to rally the Peloponnesian cities to her own banner. In 370 B.C. she sent Iphicrates to the Isthmus of Corinth in an attempt to cut off the route of Epaminondas' returning forces. The following year she concluded a formal alliance with Sparta. In the north, Iphicrates, under the pretext of reconquering Amphipolis, made an alliance with Alexander of Pherae and succeeded in winning Macedonia from Theban influence.

In view of the Great King's decree, however, more energetic measures than these were needed. By land Athens had small success, neither in Arcadia — though the Arcadians themselves displayed little subservience to Thebes — nor in Thessaly where Alexander of Pherae was obliged to recognise Theban suzerainty after being defeated in 364 B.C. at Cynoscephalae, where Pelopidas was killed. By sea, on the other hand, the Athenian commander Timotheus rallied Samos. But the dispatch of Athenian *cleruchs* disturbed certain allies who were threatening to withdraw from the confederation when, in 364 B.C., Thebes attempted to challenge Athenian naval power. A rising in Chios was promptly put down, and Timotheus who had occupied Sestus the year previously firmly suppressed Byzantium's inclination to secede and acquired new strongholds on the coast of Macedonia and Thrace.

The end of the Greek city-states

The last round, however, had not yet been fought. Its scene was the Peloponnesus where, since 366 B.C., confused fighting had continued between Spartans, Elians,

Arcadians and Messenians. In 363 B.C. they finally reached an agreement. But this did not suit Thebes at all, whose garrison at Tegea put the supporters of peace under arrest. Fighting again broke out and Thebes, determined once and for all to impose her own authority, sent Epaminondas into Arcadia with a powerful army. Athens at once came to the aid of Sparta. The subsequent encounter at Mantinea in 362 B.C. was a disaster for both sides. Sparta and Athens were crushed, while Athens was deserted by her principal allies, and the great Epaminondas was killed. He had been the sole Theban capable of guiding and maintaining his country on the difficult path of leadership. As he died, Epaminondas counselled peace, and peace was at once concluded. But it came too late. Greece, torn and exhausted by long and fruitless civil war, could no longer reap the benefit. No city, not Athens, not Sparta, not Thebes, had succeeded in gaining hegemony which would have allowed peace and order to be enforced. None was now capable of saving Greece from an alien domination which was soon to put an end to that jealously defended autonomy which had led to her downfall.

Dionysius of Syracuse

Western Hellenism, in spite of internal dissensions no less violent than in Greece itself, preserved its independence for over a century more, though the dangers it had to face were grave. Hardly had the Sicilians been saved from the threat of Athenian imperialism in Syracuse than they returned to their own domestic quarrels. The moment seemed propitious for the Carthaginians to avenge the disaster of Himera. In answer to the appeal of Segesta, which was threatened by Selinus, the Carthaginians sent a large invading force to the island which in 409 B.C., captured Selinus and afterwards Himera. Then, in 406 B.C., they occupied Acragas. Syracuse had been unable to prevent these reverses, which gave an opportunity to a young Syracusian general of common birth to take over the government. At first Dionysius, the new tyrant, scarcely justified his seizure of power. The Syracusians lost more ground and the city itself would in 405 B.C. have been attacked had not a violent epidemic broken out among the Carthaginians which obliged them to make terms. Dionysius profited by this respite to prepare his revenge. He began by subduing the neighbouring cities (403-400 B.C.). During the next four years he attacked the Carthaginian conquests, recovered them one by one, and finally seized the enemy's military encampment. But the Carthaginians did not consider themselves beaten, and until Dionysius' death in 367 B.C. hostilities were only interrupted by brief periods of truce. Details of the fighting are often lacking, but the war seems to have gone badly more often than well for Syracuse, and in the end her enemies still remained in possession of the west of Sicily.

These failures had, however, been largely compensated for by successes in Italy. In 387 B.C. Dionysius had seized Rhegium and forced the principal cities of Magna Graecia to become his allies. Then, farther afield, he undertook the foundation of colonies in the Adriatic (385 B.C.) and as far away as Corsica. But the reign of Dionysius the Elder had aroused violent hatred among the aristocrats and the regime did not long survive him. His son,

The Theatre of Dionysus, Athens. *A. F. Kersting*

Sassanian rock carving showing the investiture of Ardashir I (Artaxerxes). A.D. 224-241. *Roger Wood*

Dionysius the Younger, was not endowed with his qualities. To maintain his authority in the year 366 B.C. he banished his relative, Dion, who a few years later returned from exile and himself seized power. In 354 B.C. Dion was assassinated.

Greek civilisation

The convulsions which shook the Hellenic world between the beginning of the Peloponnesian War and the rise of Macedonia did not dry up the springs of Greek genius either in the arts or in the field of learning. This is vividly illustrated by the fact that in the darkest moments of her history Athens adorned the Acropolis with two masterpieces: the exquisite Ionic temple of Athene Nike and the graceful Erechtheum. The troubled times did, however, affect the course of social development. In an epoch when the demands of war and its attendant miseries played havoc with the framework of class distinctions, and sent thousands of exiles, fleeing from the smouldering ruins of their homes, to wander the roads of Greece, it was natural that the individual should begin to question traditional beliefs and institutions and to seek a remedy for his insecurity elsewhere. This situation gave rise to two tendencies, apparently contradictory but in fact complementary, which are encountered in all fields of Greek activity. The first tendency was a desire to dominate events, to take an active part in the contemporary struggle. The second arose from a kind of disgust with the wretchedness and baseness of the times, from a longing to find peace within oneself, to abandon a world doomed to annihilation, and seek for truth and beauty in the realms of an ideal world.

The tendency to take an active part in events inspired that form of literature which we may call polemic. In this context the orators come to mind, and there were many of stature: Andocides, Lysias, Isaeus, who were experts in legal matters. There were also eloquent political voices: those of Cleon and, later, of Callistratus. Isocrates was in a class by himself. Essentially a scholar, his discourses were composed to be read, and he never ceased in his efforts to guide the destiny of his country. The art of the pamphleteer, usually anonymous, must also be mentioned. This art was brought on to the stage in the plays of the great traditionalist and patriot Aristophanes, whose truculent verve, sometimes trivial, often ferocious, was joined to a fanciful and poetic imagination which made him a redoubtable enemy of demagogues. History, too, belongs to the same literary movement, especially as written by Thucydides whose apparent coolness, lucidity, impartiality and careful documentation conceal a deep-rooted rancour against the authors of his political disgrace. The activist tendency is perhaps less marked in the case of Xenophon, a man of little originality but honest and curious about everything, whose works range from personal reminiscences of his campaigns — the *Anabasis* — and of conversations with Socrates — the *Memorabilia*, a continuation of Thucydides' history of the Peloponnesian War, treatises on economy and horsemanship, to an historical romance, the *Cyropaedia*. The plastic arts were naturally less influenced by the need for participation and action, though in the allegory of Peace bearing the Infant Plutus, sculpted in about 371 by Cephisodotes the Elder, a desire to comment on events may

be discerned. But the artist who best interpreted the anguish and aspirations of the contemporary soul was undoubtedly Scopas of Paros, of whom it was said that he could 'give a soul to marble'. His passionate, tortured, often dramatic genius reflected the very character of his war-racked and unsettled age.

The desire to renounce the world and evade its miseries found its chief outlet in philosophy. Socrates had refuted the pragmatism of the sophists, but he believed that the formation of citizens as well as of individuals was important. Few of his disciples supported him in this respect and, abandoning all pretensions of taking an active part in affairs, they took refuge in theoretical speculation. Whether the problems concerned pure morality, as with the Cynics and the Cyrenaics, or, as with Plato (428–347 B.C.), interest centred on vast concepts dealing with the nature of the world, the soul and the ideal principles of politics, all the philosophers condemned the society of their times, discouraged their pupils from taking part in it and concentrated their attention on the problems of the individual.

Until the death of Socrates in 399 B.C. Plato had been a supporter of the city-state of Athens, and proud of her traditions and achievements. When Socrates met his death at the hands of the recently restored democracy, which saw in him the potential danger of oligarchic reaction, Plato turned away in disgust and disillusionment. Living in the midst of social disorder that followed the war, he sought a solution to the Athenian misery in philosophy, determining what was the essential good and what the ultimate end of the human soul. His philosophy was the pursuit of wisdom, for only through this could a perfect society be organised. The synthesis of philosophy and statesmanship, the doctrine of the Philosopher King, was the bridge by which Plato hoped to close the wide gap which had opened up between the Athenian man of action and the man of thought. The Academy which he founded to promote his doctrine was a school of philosophic statesmen drawn from all states. Here Plato taught his belief in a world beyond the material world and in the existence of a soul outside the body. Reduced to political terms, Plato's main thesis was that so long as knowledge was seen only as a road to power and wealth, the State would always be led by the ambitious. Ideal government could come only through the rigid training and discipline of the mind.

Aristotle (384–322 B.C.), though stemming from the same school of thought, occupies a special position. Belonging to a generation younger than Plato, he was all his life devoured by a thirst for universal knowledge, and left behind him encyclopaedic works of an amazing variety, based on material gathered by his numerous pupils. His particular field of enquiry was the natural sciences and logic. But the result of his vast researches had little more direct influence on the history of his times than had the metaphysical speculation of his rivals.

Art, too, derived its spirit largely from the same desire to escape the brutal realities of the day. Its chief concern was the achievement of beauty for its own sake, the expression of grace and phantasy, the creation of ideal forms. This was the mainspring of Praxiteles' inspiration. His Aphrodite of Thespiae and his Aphrodite of Cnidus are a homage to feminine beauty which has never been surpassed. The languid grace of his Hermes bearing the   145

A general view of the Acropolis at Athens. During the Thirty Years Peace (445-431), Athens felt secure of a splendid and profitable Empire, and under Pericles she began building the Parthenon. Adorned with the sculpture of Phidias, this was to be the glory of the democratic state of Attica. However, with the Battle of Mantinea (362 B.C.) against Thebes, Athens and Sparta were crushed and no city-state was left which could save Greece from alien domination.

infant Dionysus, of his Apollo Sauroctonos and many others, are in sharp contrast with the energy and virility of the ephebi of the preceding epoch. It is the same desire to give pleasure which guided the brush of painters, like Meidias who was the chief representative of the florid style in ceramics.

With this new art in which individuality triumphed, the days of undisputed Attic pre-eminence had passed. Though Athens still produced men of the calibre of Plato, Aristophanes and Praxiteles, many others, like Aristotle and Scopas, were foreigners, even though they sometimes lived in the city. The great triumphs of architecture were no longer staged in Attica. The chief temples were now constructed in Delphi, Epidaurus, Ephesus, Bassae, Tegea. In Athens itself only the Erechtheum and the sanctuary of Athene Nike were built and they were merely the continuation of Pericles' building programme. Even in ceramics, which had been an Athenian monopoly, there were signs of decadence, of less careful finish, and to escape unemployment after the Peloponnesian War a certain number of the master potters emigrated and set up their workshops abroad, in particular in southern Italy. In this manner Greek art resumed its universal character and prepared for fresh conquests.

Italy

The history of Italy between, roughly, 430 and 360 B.C. was also troubled. About twenty years before this period the Sabellians had begun to descend from the Apennines. This new danger brought about a reconciliation between the Romans and the Latins against the menace of the Aequi and the Volsci. The Roman-Latin alliance did not remain purely defensive, however, and soon undertook the conquest of southern Etruria. Between 406 and 396 B.C. ten hard years of warfare against the Etruscan frontier town of Veii finally opened the way, but the campaign was arrested by a new peril. Since the beginning of the fifth century bands of Gauls had been filtering into the Po valley, there threatening Etruscan ascendancy. Tradition says that the Insubres, a Gallic people, occupied Milan in 396 B.C. In 390 B.C. a horde of Senones, another Gallic tribe, crossed Etruria, crushed the Roman army on the banks of the Alia, captured Rome and burned it. This adventurous barbarian incursion had no lasting consequences: only three years later Rome had recovered sufficiently from the raid to incorporate within her own territory a part of southern Etruria. Danger from the Gauls, however, was still great: their pressure brought about the downfall of the Etruscan empire which, with the capture of Bologna, was complete towards 350 B.C. This obliged the Romans and the Latins to tighten the bonds of their alliance in 358 B.C., thus foreshadowing the ultimate submission of the latter to the former. In Rome itself the first Gallic crisis had, in fact, one result: tradition has it that at this time Manlius and Spurius Cassius attempted to make themselves tyrants. The rivalry between patricians and plebeians attained such a degree of bitterness that the State remained for several years without magistrates. In the end the patricians had to yield to some of the measures the plebeians demanded. In 367 B.C. the Licinian Laws gave the plebeians access to the office of consul, reduced debts, and regulated the distribution of the *ager publicus* — public lands acquired by conquest — which the war in Etruria had greatly increased.

The reign of Artaxerxes II

While Greece, by its civil dissensions, was preparing the way for the Macedonian conquest, the Persian Empire also revealed its weakness in the disorders which marked the reign of Artaxerxes II, surnamed Mnenon (404-358 B.C.). His throne had been consolidated by the death of Cyrus the Younger, but the Persian Empire had not itself been thereby strengthened. Revolts continued to break out, and the ability of the Great King to intrude in the domestic affairs of Greece arose not from his own power but from his cunning in exploiting Greek rivalries. During all this period the huge Persian Empire was, in fact, in danger of falling to pieces. Towards 405 B.C. Egypt, led by Amyrtaeus, regained her independence. A successor of Amyrtaeus, Achoris (393-360 B.C.), gave support to Evagoras, king of Salamis in Cyprus, who for a while unified the island under his leadership. It took ten years to bring him to heel and even then, in 381 B.C., the Persians were forced to leave him in possession of Salamis. This modest Persian success was offset in 365 B.C. by a general revolt of the satraps of Asia Minor, some of whom, moreover, were already quite independent. The undistinguished reign of Artaxerxes ended in a palace tragedy. One of his sons unsuccessfully attempted to assassinate him and was executed: a second committed suicide, and a third was murdered. Grief undermined the health of the Great King, already aged, and he died in 358 B.C.

India and the Far East

In India the history of Magadha after the death of Adjatasatru again becomes vague and uncertain. It was a time in which the Hindu religion became much more elaborate, and Buddhism became more widespread. Towards 375 B.C. the throne passed to the Nanda dynasty, celebrated for its detestation of the warrior caste, but few precise details of the period are available. As for China, though economically and demographically formidable, she remained plunged in the confusion of feudal discord. But in this epoch lived the philosopher who codified Taoism: Chuang-Tsze (c. 380-320 B.C.). The founder of Taoism was a half-legendary personage named Lao-Tsze who was said to have been a contemporary of Confucius. The philosophy derived its name from the universal principle which achieved the reconciliation of opposites and maintained cosmic harmony: the *tao*, or the 'Way'. The aim of the adept of Taoism was to make himself one with this principle beyond the confines of the changing world, beyond the limits even of his own being, and by identifying himself with the *tao* to dominate the universe. The meditations of Chuang-Tsze are of great beauty and profundity. Unfortunately the mysticism which he advocated to attain this union was mingled with magic, which sometimes reduced followers of Taoism to the level of charlatans.

Hermes with the infant Dionysus, by Praxiteles (fourth century B.C.). Praxiteles' art seems to reflect the taste of Athens at the period: the search for grace and beauty, the love of pleasure, peace and luxury. *Alinari-Mansell*

The great winged bulls, which guard the gate built by Xerxes
(486-465 B.C.) at Persepolis, still stand amidst the ruins of the
ancient capital of the Persian Empire. When Alexander crossed
into Asia in 334 B.C. the Persian Empire was a formidable power,
in possession of Asia Minor, Cyprus and Egypt; huge treasuries
paid for its armies of Greek mercenaries, and its Phoenician and
Cypriot fleets. Alexander defeated Darius III (336-330 B.C.) at
Issus in 333 B.C. and at Arbela in Mesopotamia in 331 B.C.
He now called himself 'King of Kings' as the successor of
Darius; he seized the fabulous treasure of the Empire, but during
148   his celebrations he allowed Persepolis to be sacked and burned.

CHAPTER SEVEN

THE MACEDONIAN EPIC

361-323 B.C.

Alexander the Great (336-323 B.C.). On the death of his father, Philip II, Alexander completed the subjugation of Greece and was elected general of the League of Corinth. A united Greece was now ready to avenge the Persian invasion of 480 B.C. Alexander's conquests carried Greek civilisation to the frontiers of India. *Historia Photo*

In the course of less than forty years a new power was to transform the face of the East. In Greece Philip of Macedon overthrew the self-governing city-states and imposed his own undivided authority on the whole country. His achievement, however, was small in comparison with that of his son, Alexander, who conquered the Persian Empire and opened a vast field of expansion to Hellenism. Though the characteristics of Greek civilisation were, of course, modified by new contacts, its ultimate diffusion was to extend from Spain to India; for it was Hellenism that the Roman conquerors, still uncouth, would inherit and spread throughout their own empire. At the time when the Orient fell under Macedonian domination no one could have foretold this eventuality, but in Italy Rome was already taking the first tentative steps on her road to imperialism.

Macedonia at the accession of Philip II

When, in 359 B.C., Philip II came to the throne of Macedonia his country was still barbarous in the eyes of the Greeks. Hellenism had, however, already penetrated Macedonia. Her kings at least were themselves much affected by Greek culture and had attracted Greek poets and artists to the Macedonian court. Commercial relations had been formed, particularly with Athens, and Hellenic colonies dotted the coastline. But inland Macedonia, with its broad plains and many rivers, remained very different from Greece itself. It was inhabited by a hardy, agricultural people, dominated by an aristocracy of horse breeders over whom, little by little, the kings had gained an ascendancy by developing the administration of finance, a road system and a military organisation. The last provided Philip with a powerful and stubborn infantry and a large and aggressive cavalry to which he added a corps of engineers well equipped with siege engines.

Philip and Demosthenes

All that Macedonia had previously lacked in order to make herself felt in the affairs of Greece was a leader like Philip. In his military ability and his aristocratic temperament Philip was typically Macedonian. But in diplomatic talent and education he far surpassed his compatriots. Firm in resolution, cunning and unscrupulous in his choice of means, weighing up his opponents with psychological penetration, Philip was also endowed with the supreme art of allowing his plans to mature and waiting patiently for the right moment — when he would act with lightning speed. Since the days of antiquity it has been the habit to reduce these last years of Greek

freedom to a personal duel between Philip and the Athenian orator Demosthenes. This is to forget that Athens was only one of Philip's adversaries, and that Athens alone did not carry the burden of Greece's destiny. It is, however, true that the great orator was the most courageous and far-sighted of Philip's enemies, and when the difference in their positions is considered it is astonishing that fortune held the balance between them for so long. In other words, Demosthenes was a worthy opponent of the victorious king.

Demosthenes was born in 384 B.C., the son of a rich industrialist. He was orphaned at an early age and then stripped of his fortune by dishonest tutors. To save the little that remained he studied law and rhetoric. Faced nonetheless with poverty, he made a living by composing speeches and pleas for other lawyers, and finally launched upon a political career. His education had given him a solid grounding in legal and economic affairs. His quick and penetrating intelligence raised him far above party politics where the interests of his country were concerned: the grandeur of Athens inspired him with a profound and selfless patriotism from which he never swerved. In the service of these qualities he commanded an oratorical genius which was unequalled in ancient times; his arguments, reinforced by logic, were expressed in close-knit, vibrant phrases, without trace of bombast or verbal inflation. And it was his burning words which for twenty years held in check the most powerful army Greece had ever seen. The duel between Demosthenes and Philip, with its clash of political principles, is stirring even now.

Conflict between Philip and Athens

When Philip II ascended to the throne his first care was to secure his northern and eastern frontiers against the pressure of the barbarians. The task took him no less than two years to accomplish. Having thus made certain that he would not be attacked from the rear, he began towards 357 B.C. to put the first part of his programme into effect: the conquest of the regions bordering his own kingdom. Among them were many allies of Athens, and the chief independent city was Olynthus. Athens, already embarrassed by the attacks on her allies, ignored an offer of alliance with Olynthus. Philip proceeded to attach Olynthus to his own cause by presenting her with Potidaea which he had wrenched from the Athenians. This enabled him to advance into Thrace where he took possession of the rich mines in the Pangaea mountains. Athens attempted to halt his progress by forming a barbarian coalition against him. Philip struck swiftly and in 356 B.C. the threatened coalition was defeated before it could even assemble.

This Athenian reverse was accompanied by one of a much graver nature. For many years Byzantium had proved an unruly ally and Mausolus was making trouble among the principal islands of the Sporades. In 357 B.C. Rhodes, Cos and Chios allied themselves with Byzantium and proclaimed their independence. Twice Athens was defeated before Chios. Her underpaid mercenaries dispersed, and at home the supporters of the politician Eubulus put an end to a war which was unpopular among the well-to-do classes by granting independence to the rebels.

The Third Sacred War

These losses seriously weakened Athens and made it easier for Macedonia to interfere in the domestic affairs of Greece. She found an occasion to do so during the so-called Third Sacred War which began when, at the instigation of the Thebans, the Delphic Amphictyons ('league of neighbours') imposed a fine on the inveterate enemies of Thebes, the Phocians. Amid all the interstate rivalry there were some factors leading towards Hellenic unity. One such factor lay in common religious

grounds and certain shrines maintained not by one city-state but by leagues (Amphictyonies) formed by several states. Part of the leagues' function was to protect such shrines (there was that of Apollo at Delos and at Delphi), to ensure the safe passage of pilgrims to and fro, and to impose certain restraining measures to reduce the fear of war between league members. These, basically, were the terms of reference of the Delphic Amphictyons. Phocia, however, refused to pay and in 357 B.C. her lands were declared forfeit to the god at Delphi. The Phocians, supported by Sparta and Athens, thereupon seized the sanctuary and looted its treasures for the purpose of carrying on the inevitable war against Thebes. In 355 B.C. they invaded eastern Locris and were at first defeated. But in the following year they succeeded in occupying a part of Boeotia and threatening Thebes. Indeed Thebes was saved only by the Phocians' fear of being taken in the rear by Philip of Macedon who, at the same time, had marched into Thessaly under pretext of answering an appeal from certain cities which were menaced by the tyrant of Pherae. Philip was repulsed, but in 355 B.C. he attacked again, and this time he crushed the Phocians to the north of Thermopylae. He was unable to seize this key to central Greece, which the Athenians occupied just in time, but henceforth he was the master of Thessaly with its important resources of grain and horses.

Philip could now have continued his offensive towards the south where the anarchy caused by the Sacred War had worsened, while Sparta added to the confusion by attempting to regain her pre-eminence in the Peloponnesus. He chose, however, to turn towards Thrace where he met with an unexpected check. The princelings of Thrace had again espoused the cause of Athens, and Athenians in 352 B.C. had occupied the Chersonesus. A later offensive was halted by Philip's serious illness, the news of which ruined the effect of Demosthenes' First

Alexander's route across Asia Minor, showing his victories, the limits of his Empire and the new cities (numerous ' Alexandrias ') he founded. At his death the conquered lands were broken up among his commanders, and became a source of endless strife.

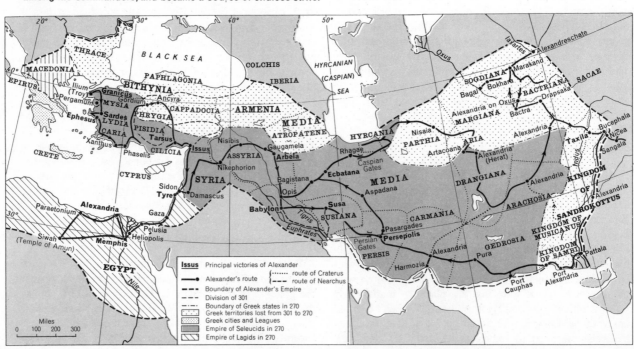

Philippic (c. 351 B.C.) in which the great orator pointed out the peril of Macedonian expansion and the necessity of making preparations to combat it. The apathy with which Demosthenes' warning was received only precipitated the catastrophe. In 349 B.C. Philip invaded Chalcidice and besieged Olynthus. In three passionate speeches, known as the Olynthiac Orations, Demosthenes strove to awaken Greece to the danger and raise forces to send to the relief of the beleaguered city. He was successful in arousing only a half-hearted effort, and in 348 B.C. Olynthus fell and her inhabitants were deported. The Athenians were left with no alternative but to conclude peace. Philip delayed the treaty until the moment when his victory at Olynthus had borne its fruits and given him complete command of Thrace. Having nothing further to concede, the Athenian envoys, led by Philocrates, were unable even to include Phocis in the arrangements and had to be content with Philip's vague promises in 346 B.C. of benevolence towards that country.

Philip II of Macedonia (395-335 B.C.). An able general and a skilled diplomat, Philip created an effective army with which he secured the Macedonian frontiers and made himself master of Greece, thus laying the foundations for Alexander's success.

Athens after the Peace of Philocrates

The promises were not kept. Philip at once occupied Phocis which did not defend itself. He then forced the Amphictyonic Council to decree that the fortifications of every Phocian city should be demolished, an enormous tribute of sixty talents a year paid to him, and that Phocis' two seats in the council should be forfeited to Macedonia. With Phocis no longer a danger, Thebes could at leisure impose her hegemony on Boeotia. These events furnished grim material to those Athenian patriots who followed Demosthenes, and they argued passionately against the party in Athens which advocated resignation or wished to come to terms with Macedonia, of whom the spokesman was a vain but eloquent orator named Aeschines. The patriots lost no opportunity to summon such Macedonian collaborators before the courts, and to prepare for action against the enemy. They repelled Philip's overtures of friendship with a scorn which lacked neither audacity nor dignity. They did all they could to thwart his attempts to occupy the remaining Athenian possessions in Thrace, and strove to acquire new allies. In 342 B.C. when Philip was threatening Cardia, a city on the Thracian Chersonesus, they sent an expedition to defend the town, while a diplomatic campaign in the Peloponnesus rallied Argos, Messene and Arcadia. A year later they won over Euboea, Megara and Achaia to the Athenian cause, and in Athens itself efforts were made to raise money and build ships.

A bronze ornament from Luristan. The Cossaeans of Luristan were one of the tribes Alexander had to subdue to ensure his army's passage from Babylon to Ecbatana. *Giraudon*

Reverse of a Philip II four-drachma coin, showing a horseman and the word 'Philip'. The Macedonian Cavalry was a swift and powerful weapon used to advantage by both Philip and his even more successful son, Alexander. *Hachette*

Philip's final victory

These skirmishes could only lead to a further outbreak of war. Philip himself provoked it when in 340 B.C. he laid siege to Byzantium and Perinthus on the Propontis, thus endangering Athens' very life line, the route by which wheat to feed the city came from the Black Sea. When Philip seized her merchant ships, Athens replied in the spring of 339 B.C. by dispatching a war fleet which obliged him to set them free. Though in this encounter Philip was the loser, he soon found occasion to force another. A new quarrel had arisen over a judgment pronounced by the Delphic councillors, this time against the Locrians, who were allied to Thebes. The councillors

called upon Philip to protect them. The Thebans, in order to forestall his intervention, seized the pass of Thermopylae. This obstacle which Philip was unable to surmount by arms he succeeded in overcoming by diplomacy — and in a most unexpected manner. For it was the Phocians, who had suffered most cruelly at his hands, who came to his assistance. Accepting his offer to reduce the tribute they paid to him, they handed over their capital Elatea, which gave Philip easy access to Locris, Boeotia and even Attica.

The 'surprise of Elatea' left all Athens dumbfounded. Only Demosthenes rose to the event. From the shocked Assembly he obtained a total reversal of policy, which displayed his realism and his courage: an alliance with the erstwhile enemy, Thebes. Demosthenes at once led the Athenian mission to Boeotia, where he was able to dissuade the Thebans from accepting Philip's proposal which had offered them a free hand to pillage Attica. At the end of 339 B.C. Athens and Thebes concluded an alliance. After an intense diplomatic campaign a number of Peloponnesian states joined them. But all was in vain: on the first of September 338 B.C., at Chaeronea, Philip met and annihilated the military might of his enemies, and on that day free Greece perished. Thebes was given a government and a garrison under Philip's orders, and her leadership of Boeotia was taken over by Macedonia. Athens was more leniently treated and allowed to retain the islands which still belonged to her. But the loss of her grain route to the Black Sea put her no less at the mercy of the conqueror than was Thebes. Philip, undisputed master of Greece, organised his empire at the Congress

of Corinth which he summoned to meet in 338 B.C., and from which Sparta alone dared to hold herself aloof. At the congress, a league of all the Hellenic states was formed: each state sent a number of delegates proportional to its importance to an assembly which met at regular intervals at Corinth. The decisions of this assembly were binding and any contraventions were punished by fines. Macedonia herself remained outside the league, but concluded an alliance with it which, in case of war, gave command of all its forces to the Macedonian king.

The beginning of Alexander's reign

Philip did not long enjoy his triumph. In the summer of 336 B.C. he was assassinated, leaving his throne to his son, Alexander, who was hardly twenty years old. Greece at once repudiated the obligations she had contracted to fulfil at Corinth. The new king's reaction was swift and vigorous: he reconquered Thessaly, Thebes and Athens were forced to submit, and a new congress met to renew the treaty which had been signed with Philip. In the following year there was a much more serious uprising, at a time when Alexander was engaged in difficult operations against the Balkan barbarians. It was rumoured that he had been killed and the Great King, worried by the growth of Macedonian power, called upon the Greeks to revolt, promising them a subsidy. Athens and Sparta agreed to his proposition, and Demosthenes armed the banished Thebans who laid siege to the Macedonian garrison that occupied the Theban acropolis, the Cadmea. With the same rapidity that he had shown the year

The theatre and the Temple of Apollo, Delphi. Sacred to the whole Greek world, Delphi was maintained by a league (amphictyon) of several states. In 337 B.C. Phocia refused to contribute to this; supported by Athens and Sparta, she seized and looted the sanctuary. The resulting ' Third Sacred War ' (355 B.C.) gave Philip II of Macedon a chance to intervene; he defeated the Phocians, took Thessaly, and advanced on Thrace.

The Athenian orator Demosthenes (384-322 B.C.). Philip's attacks on the allies of Athens seriously hampered her trade routes and his seizure of Thessaly threatened her frontiers. Demosthenes was the impassioned spokesman of the patriotic party in Athens, who opposed capitulation to Philip.

before, Alexander appeared before Thebes, took the city by assault, destroyed every building in it with the exception of the house of Pindar, and reduced its inhabitants to slavery. This terrible punishment cured the Greeks of a taste for further revolt. Alexander, secure of Greece, could turn his full attention to his great design.

Alexander and the war against Persia

Alexander's ambition was to lead all Greece in an assault on the Persian Empire and thus avenge the insult and injuries suffered a century and a half earlier, during the invasion of Darius and Xerxes. Alexander was not the first to dream of this project. The memory of Marathon and Salamis had never been obliterated. Throughout the fifth and fourth centuries more than one voice had called upon Greece to unite against the barbarian, the eternal enemy. Isocrates, in the fourth century, had eloquently championed the cause of revenge, and his words had found echoes in the opinion of those always ready to suspect the Great King of sinister intentions. More important was the fact that Alexander had inherited the idea of invading Persia from his father. Philip, to be sure, was too much of a realist to be moved by the simple appeal to racial prejudice with which Isocrates inflamed his listeners but he possibly saw in a united expedition against Persia, with its attendant comradeship of arms and possibilities of loot, a means of consolidating the rather unstable alliance he had imposed on the League of Corinth. In any case, soon after the Peace of Philocrates, Philip had come to an understanding with the rebellious satraps of Asia Minor and in 337 B.C. — the year after Chaeronea — he had assumed the direction of a war against Persia, sending into Hellespontine Phrygia a military force under the command of the Macedonian general Parmenion.

The moment to attack the Great King seemed to be well chosen. Ochus, who came to the throne as Artaxerxes III (359-338 B.C.) had just been assassinated, and with him disappeared the last Persian sovereign worthy of the Achaemenian traditions. At his accession Asia Minor had broken away from the Empire and been carved up into independent principalities by rebellious satraps. In eight years Artaxerxes III had reduced them to obedience. A setback by the king of Egypt, Nectanebo II (359-341 B.C.) was followed by an uprising in Cyprus and in Phoenicia, but the treachery of the king of Sidon and of Nectanebus' Greek mercenary leader enabled Artaxerxes to get the better of his enemies. He then victoriously restored Persian authority in Egypt (343-341 B.C.). During his last years he became increasingly disturbed by the expansion of Macedonian power, and gave assistance to Perinthus and Byzantium when they were besieged. But in 338 B.C. he was poisoned by his all-powerful minister Bagoas. Bagoas himself disposed of the throne, giving it first to Arses, then in 336 B.C. to Codomanus (Darius III) who at once disposed of Bagoas. These palace scandals succeeded in undoing most of the good work which had been accomplished during the reign of Artaxerxes III.

The Persian Empire was nevertheless a formidable power. The incalculable treasures stored at Susa enabled the Great King to recruit all the Greek mercenaries he wanted, and they made up the chief strength of his army.

Darius III, King of Persia from 336 to 330 B.C. Artaxerxes III (359-338 B.C.) had succeeded in reducing the rebellious satraps of the Empire, but after his death palace intrigues undid much of his work. As a result, Darius III came to the throne at a time when the Empire was at its weakest; Alexander seized this opportunity to invade the realms of the 'King of Kings'. *Collection Stoclet*

The tholos in the sanctuary of Athena Pronaia, Delphi. Each city state maintained a treasury (tholos) at Delphi containing offerings to Apollo, so that the pronouncements of his oracle would be favourable. The priests of Apollo had immense power; their advice was sought before important decisions were made.

The Phoenician and Cypriot fleet was powerful. In contrast, the forces at Alexander's disposal seemed derisory. Though the Macedonian army was an incomparable fighting machine, it did not exceed 40,000 men. The contingents from the League of Corinth added a further 7,000 troops of dubious fidelity. Alexander's fleet was less than half the size of the Persians': it was composed entirely of allied vessels and he could not depend on its loyalty. Being short of money he soon disbanded it. Furthermore, he was well aware that he left behind him a restive Greece, resentful of his rule, and that, apart from the Hellenic cities of Asia whose enthusiastic support he might expect, he would encounter during his advance only indifference or hostility.

The prospect then was fraught with uncertainties and dangers: Alexander's own genius overcame them all. He cannot be judged according to ordinary standards, so far did he tower above his contemporaries. Indeed, he himself ended by believing in his own divine nature. Philip had possessed many excellent qualities which, in his son, were developed to the highest degree. Alexander, like his father, was endowed with amazing military talent; he was at once an inspired leader of men and a warrior of unlimited personal courage. But in spite of his clear-sightedness in dealing with men he possessed neither prudence nor patience. In the fire and eagerness of his youth he was carried away by an audacity which was at first restrained by his willingness to listen to the advice of more moderate counsellors; his sure grasp of long-range problems was remarkable. Then gradually, intoxicated by power and success, he allowed himself more and

A mosaic from Pompeii showing Darius routed by Alexander's army at Issus (333 B.C.). Here in Syria Alexander met the major force of the Persian army for the first time. Darius was defeated; he could not manoeuvre his huge force to advantage on the rough ground. This victory gave Alexander a clear route through Syria and Phoenicia to Egypt, where he founded his first new city, Alexandria. *Anderson-Giraudon*

Phalanx formation, developed first by Philip II and used successfully by Alexander, in which heavy infantry fought very close together, with shields interlocking and protected by light cavalry on the flanks. Here it waits to close in on enemy cavalry.

more to indulge in the excesses of an undisciplined temperament. The cruelty which on his coming to the throne had led him to assassinate possible competitors in the royal family, later led him either in cold blood or in an access of frenetic rage, to commit unspeakable crimes. His unshakable confidence in his own destiny drove him into the rashest enterprises, while the ardour with which he pursued every pleasure undermined his health. But whatever the excesses of his temperament he transformed the ancient world and spread Greek civilisation through regions until then unknown.

The conquest of Asia Minor

When in the spring of 334 B.C. Alexander crossed into Asia, the Macedonian army of Parmenion had been driven back on to the shores of the Hellespont by Memnon of Rhodes, commander of the Great King's mercenaries. The bridgeheads which Parmenion held enabled Alexander to cross the Straits without interference from the Persian fleet. Memnon's plan was to lay waste the country before him and thus provoke a revolt in Greece, but the satraps refused to follow him. Instead they lay in wait at the river Granicus to challenge Alexander's passage. At Granicus, his first crucial battle, Alexander scattered the enemy in an epic charge, and marched rapidly southward where he captured Sardis, while the Greek cities of Ionia and Aeolis rose in his support. He continued his advance along the coast in order to deprive the Persian fleet of its bases, and took Miletus and Halicarnassus by assault. After he had crossed Lycia, Pamphylia and Pisidia, he swung back towards central Phrygia, where in the ancient capital of Gordium he is supposed to have cut with his sword the Gordian knot which promised him who could loosen it the empire of the world.

In the following spring, 333 B.C., Memnon renewed the offensive by sea, seized Chios and blockaded Mytilene. Memnon's death removed Alexander's most clear-sighted opponent, and enabled him to continue his march into Cilicia. Syria now lay before him, but barring his advance lay the main army of Persia, brought through the narrow mountain defiles of the Amanus by Darius III himself. The two armies met near the gulf of Issus. In this rough terrain the Persian army was unable to deploy its numerical superiority to advantage, and it was decisively crushed. Darius' camp and family fell into the hands of the victor who did not even reply to the offers of peace which the Persian hastened to make.

The conquest of Phoenicia and Egypt

The victory of Issus opened all Syria and Phoenicia to Alexander, and in the course of the winter of 333-332 B.C. he occupied them. The Persian fleet, largely composed of Phoenician vessels, was consequently broken up, in spite of the courageous resistance of Tyre, which Alexander took no less than seven months—January to August 332 B.C. – to reduce. He did not forgive Tyre: the city was destroyed and its inhabitants sold into slavery. Tyre had delayed his advance into Egypt until the end of 332 B.C. He went no farther than Memphis, and the beginning of the year 331 B.C. was occupied by the famous expedition into the desert where at the oasis of Amun

A Greek silver coin of Alexander the Great, c. 300 B.C. Alexander's conquest of Persia put into circulation the huge gold reserve of the Empire and stimulated trade. Persian coinage was standardised with Macedonian, and a silver stater was struck so as not to compete with the gold coinage of the Greek states. This was intended to be standard throughout the Hellenistic world. *Archiv für Kunst und Geschichte*

the priest saluted him as the son of the god. In the western delta he also founded the city of Alexandria whose future was to be as brilliant as the man who gave it his name.

The conquest of Mesopotamia and Persia

Darius, however, was not resigned to defeat, and once more he was determined to meet his enemy on the battlefield. This time in Mesopotamia, near Arbela, he had prepared a field which would give every advantage to the charge of his chariots which were now his principal weapon, since he could no longer recruit Greek mercenaries. Alexander left Egypt in the spring of 331 B.C. and at the beginning of autumn advanced into Mesopotamia. He accepted the challenge to combat on ground of the enemy's own choice, and in October 331 B.C., employing the Macedonian oblique battle front, Alexander utterly destroyed the last great Persian army. Darius had been able to escape, but the heartland of his great empire was now open to the conqueror who successively occupied Babylon, Susa and Persepolis, where he seized the fabulous treasures of the Achaemenian kings. At the beginning of 330 B.C. he marched on Ecbatana where Darius was attempting to gather together yet another army. Alexander surprised him before his preparations were completed and the Great King was obliged to flee towards the Caspian Sea. By now Darius had lost all authority. Bessus, the satrap of Bactria, imprisoned him, usurped his crown and murdered him at the moment when Alexander was coming to his rescue. Alexander buried the mortal remains of the Great King with royal honours and, at the same time, disbanded his allied contingents with rich gifts. Alexander symbolised in these two acts the fact that he now repudiated the fiction of a Greek national war against the barbarians. Henceforth the career he pursued was personal, and its object was none other than the restoration of the Achaemenian Empire, to which he declared himself to be the legitimate successor.

An armed footrace from a Greek amphora (a two-handled wine jar), c. 333 B.C., the year of the Battle of Issus. Athletic contests were often held in honour of the gods at Greek festivals, such as that of Olympia in the Peloponnese. Alexander held games in some of the Persian cities he captured and induced the Persian nobles to join in. *British Museum*

Alexander in India

Though Alexander had firmly established himself in the centre of this vast Empire, mounting problems awaited him in its distant regions, some mountainous, others desert, where the population continued to show hostility. Here, in difficult and unfamiliar terrain, he suffered sharp reverses on several occasions. It took him almost a year to capture Bessus whom in 329 B.C. he executed as a regicide, then a further two years — 329-327 B.C. — to occupy the eastern satrapies: Aria (to-day Khorassan), Bactria and Sogdiana (Russian Turkestan) and Arachosia (Afghanistan). In order to subdue these regions he crushed without pity those who resisted his authority and those who, after feigned submission, rose in revolt behind him. As he advanced he also planted military colonies, some of which were so well situated that they afterwards grew into important cities: such were Alexandria in Arachosia (now Kandahar) and Alexandria in Sogdiana (Khojend).

This arduous campaign was only the preface to another project which Alexander had conceived: the conquest of India. He was drawn to India by the fact that the Achaemenian kings once dominated it and also, no doubt, by the fantastic legends which were told of it. The valley of the Indus, when Alexander approached it, was rent by anarchy and local rivalries in which certain states, more powerful than their neighbours, fought for leadership. Thus Taxila, between the Indus and the Hydaspes, was a rival of Porus, between the river Hydaspes and the Akesines. Through jealousy of Porus, Omphis, the rajah of Taxila, offered to welcome the Macedonian army. In the summer of 327 B.C. the Macedonians moved forward in two bodies, one proceeding by way of the valley of the Kabul, while the other, led by Alexander himself, advanced by way of the foothills of the Hindu Kush.

In 326 B.C. Alexander reached Taxila and attacked Porus whose kingdom was vanquished in spite of its elephants. The rajah was captured but, in recompense for his bravery, he was released and his lands restored to him. In his company Alexander then pushed eastwards and subdued the Kathaioi, beyond the Hydraotes. He was possibly contemplating an attack on Gandhara which commanded the plain of the Ganges when, on the Hyphasis, his troops, weary of an expedition which seemed to be unending, refused to advance any farther. Reluctantly Alexander was obliged to give in. He began the return journey by descending the river by boat, following it until he reached the Indian Ocean. On several occasions his passage was disputed by tribesmen incited by religious leaders. At the mouth of the Indus he divided his army into three corps: one embarked and sailed up the coast of the Persian Gulf, the second returned by way of Arachosia, and the third, commanded by Alexander himself, crossed the desert of Gadrosia (Baluchistan) and on the way suffered considerable losses.

By the spring of 324 B.C. Alexander was back in Susa and was contemplating a new expedition — perhaps to the Western Mediterranean — when on the thirteenth of June, 323 B.C. he died of a fever.

The government of Alexander

Alexander's sudden death at the age of thirty-three left unfinished the vast designs he had conceived. Probably he had dreamed of new conquests. Certainly he had it

157

in mind to give his empire an administrative, economic and social structure, though at his death detailed plans had not been worked out. Some of the principles which would have guided him are, however, apparent from the fragmentary measures which he had already decreed. It is clear that he had discarded the popular, military rule of his Macedonian forefathers and that his monarchy would have been theocratic and absolute. Alexander believed that he was inspired by the gods, and we have seen him crossing the deserts of Egypt to hear himself hailed and acknowledged as the son of Amun. In 328 B.C., five years before his death, he had demanded that all his subjects should in sign of adoration prostrate themselves before him, and four years later he imposed the cult of Alexander, the god, on all the cities of Greece. Such pretensions, together with other autocratic measures, roused bitter discontent among his followers and the inevitable plots against his life were ruthlessly suppressed. In the first of these conspiracies Philotas, son of the great Macedonian general Parmenion, was implicated, and in 330 B.C. both son and father were put to death. Two years later, in the course of a drinking party one of his most intimate companions, Cleitus, who had saved his life at Granicus, told him how thoroughly he was detested, and in a fit of ungovernable rage Alexander killed him with his own hand. The following year Callisthenes, nephew of Alexander's tutor Aristotle and official historian of the Asian expedition, preached insubordination to the king's Macedonian pages, and paid for the liberty with his life. In 324 B.C. even Alexander's veterans revolted.

Although there is no doubt about the nature of the Oriental despotism Alexander intended to set up, the organs of government to enforce it were not established. He had, indeed, appointed a chancellor, a treasurer and, towards the end of his reign, a Prime Minister, but their authority and duties were not fixed, while a bureaucracy which the administration of such an immense empire required did not exist even in embryo. The provinces were administered in much the same sketchy spirit of improvisation. During his early conquests Alexander seems to have been satisfied merely to replace Persian satraps with Macedonians. Later the Persian satraps were themselves allowed to retain their positions. To avoid miscalculations in accountancy, he tried to separate financial, civil and military functions, but no general rule was ever applied and at his death local government remained in a state of total confusion.

His economic policy

Whether Alexander had considered coordinating the varied systems of economy which existed in the many lands he had annexed is impossible to determine. It is unlikely that he did, although his expeditions were accompanied by topographers and men of learning. The actual economic results of his conquests were, nevertheless, very considerable. He had for the first time united under a single rule regions of extreme variety which until then had been separated by traditional hostility. The paths of conquest soon became trade routes, some of which had never previously been dreamed of — such as the link between the Persian Gulf and the Indus. Above all, the flow of money had been affected by the downfall of the old Persian empire, for the immense treasures lying idle in the palaces of the Great Kings were suddenly thrown into circulation. This prodigious influx of gold and silver transformed the conditions of life and commerce throughout the Orient. Not all the consequences were happy, particularly the attendant rise in prices which brought misery to the uprooted classes of society. Trade and commerce were, however, greatly stimulated.

A horse from the Mausoleum at Halicarnassus (353 B.C.), the tomb of Mausolus, Persian satrap of Caria. It reflects Greek influence in Asia Minor in the fourth century B.C. *Schneider-Lengyel.*

A statue of Mars, the god of war, found at Todi (Etruscan, fourth century B.C.). Rome was by this time beginning to assume importance and had subdued her opponents in Italy, including the Etruscans. *Mansell*

Social policy

It was in his social policy that Alexander seems to have had the clearest conceptions, and these he pursued with great tenacity. A variety of reasons must have led him to encourage the racial fusion of the different peoples he had conquered — first of all, the very needs of the conquest itself. To carry it out he required larger and larger armies both for military operations and for permanent garrisons to hold the territory which had been won. From Greece itself he had never been able, or even wished, to draw large military contingents, and he had almost exhausted Macedonia's man power. He was thus obliged to recruit soldiers from among his new subjects. Again, in lands little known or understood by the Greeks, the collaboration of the natives was indispensable for purposes of administration. Finally, by assuming the role of the legitimate heir of the Persian kings, he gradually shed his purely Macedonian loyalties in order that his old and new subjects should be treated with equal favour, a tendency that was increased by the theocratic nature of his authority, which led him to consider all those over whom he reigned as equals in their submission to him. Hence it became his policy to permit those satraps who supported his cause to retain their offices; then he admitted certain Persian nobles to the circle of his intimates, and had thirty thousand young natives — the *epigoni* — instructed in the Greek language and trained in Macedonian military tactics; finally, the phalanx itself was composed of a mixture of Macedonian and Asiatic troops. The seventy colonies he founded were not only strategic in intention, but also an example of the same policy, their population often being made up of native elements leavened with a sprinkling of Greeks and Macedonians.

A final episode — perhaps the most significant — was the 'Marriage of Susa', when in the winter of 325-324 B.C. ten thousand of his soldiers took ten thousand Asiatic brides, while Alexander himself — after having married a Bactrian princess, the famous Roxana — married the daughter of the late king Darius as well. But, as it happened, it was this policy which Alexander pursued so enthusiastically that bore least fruit: many of the colonies he planted were jeopardised by the racial antagonism they were intended to overcome. Many of the conspiracies he was obliged to deal with arose from the resistance his projects encountered within the circle of his own personal entourage. Nor did the Persians themselves show any great eagerness to adopt the customs of the conquerors. Racial fusion did, in fact, take place, but at a much later date and on a much more limited scale than Alexander had desired.

Hellenistic Italy under Timoleon

While triumphant Macedonia was spreading Hellenic civilisation through the East, the Western Greeks seemed to be reverting to their old civil dissensions: the assassination of Dion had plunged Sicily into anarchy. From 354 to 346 B.C. Syracuse had five different masters while her empire disintegrated. In the confusion Dionysius the Younger attempted to regain power, but never succeeded in occupying more than part of the city. Order was restored by the metropolis, Corinth, which in response to the entreaty of numerous private citizens, sent Syracuse one of her most eminent men: Timoleon. Scarcely had Timoleon disembarked in 344 B.C. when he received the submission of Dionysius. The Carthaginians, who were kept informed of what took place in Syracuse, at once dispatched a squadron to challenge the new-comer's authority. Timoleon was able to force the Carthaginians to retire. He then appealed to all Greece for colonists to repeople the island, while the remaining cities of Sicily expelled their tyrants and came to his support. A second effort by Carthage to interrupt Greek resurgence resulted in a disastrous Carthaginian defeat on the banks of the River Crimisus. The peace treaty signed in 339 B.C. limited Carthaginian occupation to the western extremity of the island. Two years later, after having regained Acragas and Gela, Timoleon resigned his command and until his death he was honoured and consulted as an oracle. In Italy his work was completed by the expedition of Archidamus of Sparta who helped Tarentum to repulse the onslaught of the Lucanians (342-338 B.C.). For a few years longer Magna Graecia and Sicily again enjoyed peace and prosperity.

Rome: mistress of central Italy

Meanwhile, to the north, Rome had forged the arms which were to render her mistress of all Italy. The alliance which she had in 358 B.C. reaffirmed with the Latins had warded off the new Gallic danger, and in order to guard against future threats from the same source she had again advanced into Etruria. She was, however, unable to capture Caere and Tarquinii, and had to be satisfied with an alliance with these two cities, the first in 353 B.C., the second two years later. These hard-fought campaigns did not prevent her from watching carefully over her interests in southern Italy and even, it would seem, from shortly afterwards concluding a treaty with Carthage in 348 B.C. After she had repulsed a fresh assault from the Gauls towards 343 B.C., Rome embarked resolutely on a career of conquest. In response to an appeal from Capua, threatened by the Samnites, she led her Latin allies to the relief of the city. But when the allied forces entered Capua, Rome claimed that the inhabitants had delivered over the city to her alone. The Latins, deprived of the benefits of the expedition, rose in revolt. It took the Romans three years, from 340 to 338 B.C., to subdue their allies; and when the task was finished Rome annexed all Latium while the Latin cities became Roman *municipia*. Thanks to the protectorate she had established over the Campagna, Rome was henceforth the chief state in the Italian peninsula, though her domination did not remain undisputed. The Samnite mountain people in particular did not renounce their ambitions to settle in the rich plains of the Campagna. In 326 B.C. they attacked Fregellae and cut off the town's communications with Rome. To turn the Samnite position, the Romans made an alliance with Lucera in Apulia. In 321 B.C., when they attempted to send troops to Lucera, they were ambushed and forced to surrender in the Caudine Forks, narrow passes in the mountains near Caudium. The Roman army was made to march under the yoke, a humiliation Rome never forgot. The defeat did not, however, mark the end of the Second Samnite War, but only its prolongation. Meanwhile in Rome itself social conditions seemed more settled, and the lot of the plebeians continued to improve. From 356 B.C. the office of dictator could be filled by a plebeian, and in 351 B.C. that of censor. From 348 B.C. it was agreed that one of the two consuls should always be a plebeian. Finally in 338 B.C. the *Publiae Philonis* laws obliged the senate automatically to ratify all measures which were voted by the comitia, and gave the force of law to plebiscites. In point of fact these advances in plebeian privileges were of less actual benefit to the lower classes of Rome than to certain great families of the recently annexed territories. Some of the great names of the period are not of purely Roman origin. Publius Philo was himself of Volscian descent.

The 'Warring States' in China

Although China remained culturally and economically predominant in the Far East at the time when Philip and Alexander were forging the unity of the Mediterranean Orient, the anarchic feudal states of China were beginning to regroup in a manner which was the prelude to a restoration of unity. For the time being, however, the situation merely worsened; for until now all the warring principalities which fought for preponderance recognised, in theory at least, the suzerainty of the Chou Dynasty whose kingdom had been reduced to the small domain of Lo-yi. But in 335 B.C. the ruler of one of the principalities assumed the title of king and repudiated even nominal vassalage to the Chou Dynasty. Before the end

of the century his action had been imitated by all his rivals. This was the epoch of the 'Warring States' which was to last for a century longer. Two of these kingdoms already revealed a marked superiority over their rivals. In the south, the kingdom of Chou, in the reign of king Wei (339-329 B.C.), conquered the kingdom of Yu and extended its authority from the mouth of the Yangtze to the mouth of the Hwai-ho. In the north-west, Tsin, a warrior kingdom hardened by stubborn fighting against the nomads of the steppe-lands, in 330 B.C. wrenched the north-east part of Chen-si from Wei, thus initiating a series of conquests which in the long run unified the country under the leadership of Tsin. But China had much to suffer before that result was finally achieved.

It was an age of militarism, superimposed on the massive Chinese economic routine which sustained it. Warlords fought one another over immense territories, and cavalry superseded chariots. The Chinese were expert in shooting from the saddle, an art learnt from the nomad barbarians of the steppe, and armies were better organised. The collapse of what central authority remained was recorded with bitter irony by political philosophers. There was much disillusionment with political action and distrust of political speculation, which was thought to be dangerous. When the Tsin ruler, Shi Hwang Ti, at last re-established centralised government, he ordered a notorious 'burning of the books' to diminish the influence of intellectuals — a policy reversed under the Han empire, which was to sponsor a neo-Confucian revival.

Detail of a chalcedony cylinder seal showing the king grasping a lion by its foot and a bearded man about to flail a bull (Persian 590-330 B.C.). *British Museum*

A chalcedony cylinder seal with a horseman pursuing a rider on a fleeing camel (neo-Babylonian, 612-539 B.C.). In Asia Minor at this period, cylinder seals were used as a method of stamping possessions and as early forms of trade marks. Alexander's brief reign over the Persian Empire introduced the Greek language and Greek methods of record-keeping. *British Museum*

A detail of the 'Alexander' sarcophagus at Constantinople, made for a Sidonian prince during the fourth century B.C. Alexander is shown killing a lion — a feat of which he was more than proud. *Alinari*

CHAPTER EIGHT

THE HELLENISTIC MONARCHIES

THIRD CENTURY B.C.

Alexander had made no provision for a successor. Of his family there remained only Philip's imbecile bastard, Arrhidaeus. His generals persuaded the army to accept a compromise which would respect the nominal integrity of the empire while giving them a share in the spoils: Arrhidaeus and the unborn son of Alexander which Roxana was expecting would be kings, with Perdiccas acting as regent. The satrapies they divided among themselves: to Ptolemy, Egypt; to Antigonus, Lycia and Phrygia; to Lysimachus, Thrace; while Antipater retained Macedonia, which he had previously governed during the conquest with some measure of success.

Greek resistance

The new arrangements were accepted without protest except in Greece. Since 335 B.C. Antipater had been obliged to repress only one attempt by Agis, king of Sparta, to reconquer Arcadia; and Agis, in 331 B.C., had been defeated and killed at Megalopolis. But everywhere the Greeks were waiting only for an opportunity to throw off Macedonian domination. Athens in particular, under the government of Lycurgus, supported by Demosthenes, had staged a remarkable recovery: the body of young citizens — the ephebi — had been reorganised and were now called up for two years' military service. Athenian finances, well managed, allowed for a larger fleet and re-stocked arsenals. The results of this new self-reliance had already been apparent in certain incidents: in 330 B.C., for instance, at the trial of the Crown, when the famous oration on that occasion had been a triumph for Macedonia's arch-enemy, Demosthenes. In 324 B.C. Athens refused to apply a decree of Alexander's ordering the recall of the banished. Unfortunately in the same year the Harpalus affair split Athens into two camps. Harpalus, an absconding superintendent of Alexander's royal treasury, had fled to Athens with an enormous sum of embezzled money. Part of the money, though seques-tered, disappeared: the extremists accused Demosthenes of having received it and he was forced into exile.

The struggles of the Diadochi

Scarcely had the news of Alexander's death in the summer of 323 B.C. reached Athens, than she raised the standard of revolt. The Athenian army besieged Anti-pater in Lamia, Thessaly, but the Athenian fleet, twice beaten in 322 B.C., was unable to prevent reinforcements from Asia reaching Antipater. Athens and her allies were defeated at Crannon; she was forced to accept a Mace-donian garrison and surrender her leading patriots. De-mosthenes preferred to commit suicide. In the meanwhile Perdiccas, the regent, claimed authority over the other generals, or Diadochi, who at once united against him. In 321 B.C. Perdiccas marched on the most powerful of them, Ptolemy. Perdiccas was defeated and slain by his own troops. His rivals met at Triparadisus in Syria and decided on a new division of power, confiding the regency to Antipater, who died shortly afterwards (319 B.C.). War at once broke out between Antipater's son Cassander and Polysperchon whom Antipater had appointed to suc-ceed him as regent. Polysperchon was defeated and was obliged to take refuge in the Peloponnesus. His ally, Eumenes of Cardia, who had carved out a principality for himself in Persia, was handed over by his mutinous troops to his adversaries Antigonus and Seleucus (317-316 B.C.).

When Antigonus laid claim to the possessions of Eu-menes, however, Seleucus made an alliance against him with Ptolemy, Cassander and Lysimachus. In this way began a long struggle in which Antigonus attempted to restore Alexander's empire under his own leadership. Be-tween 315 and 312 B.C. he conquered Syria, the Cyclades and Greece. But his son Demetrius lost Syria again, and Seleucus recaptured Babylonia. By 311 B.C. Antigonus was ready to divide up the empire once more. In the arrangements agreed upon, no central authority was pro-vided for: the fiction of a united empire was dead. Hos-tilities were renewed in 309 B.C. Ptolemy wished to fore-stall the danger to Egypt which Antigonus' command of the islands threatened. After a certain degree of success Ptolemy's fleet was destroyed off Salamis in Cyprus in 306 B.C. He succeeded, however, in repulsing Antigonus' attempt to take Egypt. Finally in 301 B.C. a concentrated attack by his enemies led to his defeat and death at Ipsus. In a new distribution of the spoils Lysimachus received Cistauric Asia, while Syria went to Seleucus. Demetrius had not, however, been eliminated and was still master of part of Greece. He profited by dissension

Ptolemy I Soter, King of Egypt (311-285 B.C.). Ptolemy was one of Alexander's trusted generals; on Alexander's death he be-came satrap of Egypt and, in 311, king. In spite of repeated wars between the Macedonian chiefs, he left Egypt intact and the Egyptians conciliated; he was a patron of letters and science and founded the famous library and museum at Alexandria where great advances were made in mathematics and geography in particular, and later in medicine.

between his enemies and also by the death of Cassander in 297 B.C. to seize Macedonia (294 B.C.). Six years later he was driven from Macedonia by Lysimachus and Pyr-rhus of Epirus. The Greeks rose against him. In a desper-ate attempt to regain power he marched into Asia in 286 B.C. where he was taken prisoner and not long after-wards died.

To his son Antigonus Gonatas he left only a handful of Greek cities which were threatened by both Pyrrhus and Lysimachus. Pyrrhus and Lysimachus, however, dis-trusted each other, which enabled Antigonus Gonatas in 285 B.C. to drive Pyrrhus back into Epirus, while war broke out between Lysimachus and Seleucus. One after the other, Lysimachus was defeated and killed at Coru-pedion, and Seleucus assassinated by Ptolemy Ceraunus, who then, in 281 B.C., had himself proclaimed king of Macedonia by the army of his murdered rival and im-mediately launched upon the conquest of the kingdom of Gonatas. He would, no doubt, have succeeded had not bands of Celtic marauders, the Galatians, who for many years had been advancing through the Balkans, suddenly irrupted into Macedonia in 279 B.C. Ptolemy Ceraunus was killed in an effort to repulse them. The Galatians then invaded Greece, but were driven back by the Aetolians before Delphi and withdrew into Thrace. Gonatas, who was engaged in operations against An-tiochus I — the successor of Seleucus — disembarked his army in 277 B.C. at Lysimachia in Thrace and massacred his enemy. He exploited his victory without delay and invaded Macedonia which he subjugated in a few weeks. **163**

The Hellenistic monarchies

From these complex struggles for power emerged the stable Hellenistic kingdoms. From then on the East was split into three great territorial domains. Greece and Macedonia fell to the successors of Antigonus, Asia to the Seleucids, and Egypt to the Ptolemies. Peace, however, did not follow from the division; for one thing, the authority of these monarchies was often challenged; for another, though no one now dreamed of a world empire, there remained much territory to dispute. In the chaotic conflicts which ensued it was Egypt that most frequently stirred up trouble. Her riches enabled her to finance rebellion among her rivals and she could summon up a national sentiment which was unknown to the others. Egypt, then, was chiefly responsible for the continual strife which ultimately exhausted the Hellenistic kingdoms and hastened their downfall.

The early reign of Antigonus Gonatas

Of the three states into which Alexander's empire was divided that of Antigonus and his successors was, because of its limited resources and the constant hostility of the Greeks, the weakest. Antigonus had hardly established himself in Macedonia and in Greece when he was attacked by Pyrrhus who, subsidised by Egypt, occupied Macedonia in 275 B.C., while Greece rose in revolt. At Pyrrhus' death in 272 B.C. Gonatas restored the situation, installed garrisons at strategic points and governments devoted to his cause in all the cities. Fresh Egyptian intrigues in 266 B.C. resulted in the rebellion of Athens and Sparta. The subsequent Chremonidean war was brought to an end by the death of the Spartan king Areus II. It seems that Gonatas then succeeded in arranging a coalition with Rhodes and Antiochus II against Ptolemy and, in the battle of Cos, gained control of the sea, Miletus and Ephesus having been taken in 259 B.C. by the Seleucids. But when Egypt made peace with his allies a few years later, Gonatas again found himself alone.

The Seleucid Empire under Antiochus I

At the death of Seleucus I surnamed Nicator (the 'conqueror') his descendants, Antiochus I (280-261 B.C.) surnamed Soter (the 'saviour') and Antiochus II (261-246 B.C.) surnamed Theos (the 'god') succeeded him without difficulty. Under them the centre of the Seleucid monarchy was definitely fixed in northern Syria where in 300 B.C. Seleucus I had founded his capital, Antioch, on the banks of the Orontes. Military colonisation attempted to turn the country racially into a kind of second Macedonia. In consequence the oriental satrapies were neglected and tempted to secede. Another difficulty was the nearness of Egypt, and an endless struggle arose between the Seleucids and the Ptolemies for the possession of lower Syria and the coasts of Asia Minor. At the accession of Antiochus I disorder was rife in Anatolia. Though Seleucus had just conquered the region he had been unable to pacify it. Numerous petty rulers, often native, made themselves independent — such as Philetaerus who governed Pergamum. Chaos was increased in 279 B.C. by the invasion of the Galatians. Ptolemy took advantage of the disorder to extend his supremacy over the coastal regions and the islands. In the first Syrian war, between 276 and 272 B.C., Antiochus attempted to halt Egyptian expansion, but only succeeded in losing the coast of Cilicia and several important towns including Miletus and Halicarnassus. In the second Syrian war, which lasted roughly from 260 to 255 B.C., he reduced Ptolemy's gains to Lycia and Caria; but in doing so he had helped Philetaerus' heir, Eumenes I (263-241 B.C.), to add Mysia and part of Lydia to the possessions of Pergamum.

Ptolemaic Egypt

The prosperity of Egypt stood out in contrast to the difficulties which beset the two states which had fallen to the descendants of Antigonus and Seleucus. The prudent policy of Ptolemy I Soter was continued by his son Ptolemy II Philadelphus (285-246 B.C.). But in 270 B.C.,

The Punic Wars

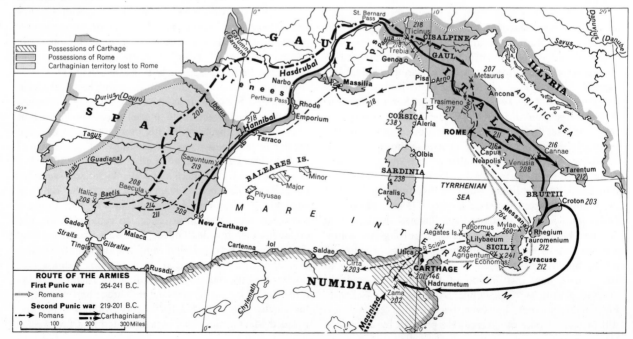

ROUTE OF THE ARMIES
First Punic war 264-241 B.C.
Romans
Second Punic war 219-201 B.C.
Romans Carthaginians
0 100 200 300 Miles

Possessions of Carthage
Possessions of Rome
Carthaginian territory lost to Rome

An archaic Greek statue of Athene, goddess of war. The Romans also adopted Athene as their goddess of war, but called her Minerva.

monopolies, while private workshops had only one supplier and one customer: the king.

In order to meet the requirements of a vast bureaucracy and a large army the Ptolemies gave every encouragement to immigration, although they did not found cities. During the Ptolemaic period there were only three cities of consequence in Egypt, the most important of which was Alexandria. The growth of Alexandria was prodigious: all the commerce of Egypt flowed through its harbour and a large part of Egyptian industry was concentrated in the city. As the Ptolemies' capital, it was embellished with sumptuous monuments and magnificent public buildings, the most renowned of which was the lighthouse, one of the seven wonders of the ancient world, constructed in about 280 B.C. Alexandria became one of the chief centres of Hellenistic culture, though political life was almost non-existent. Her heterogeneous population was divided into racial *politeumata*. The Greeks composed the principal ethnic group, living in the finest quarter of the city, which contained the royal palaces; but the Jewish communities were also numerous and important.

The problems of Macedonia and Syria

Before the end of the third century the foreign policy of the Ptolemies very nearly brought about the ruin of Macedonia and Syria. In their opposition to Antigonus Gonatas of Macedonia, Ptolemy Philadelphus and, more especially, his successor Euergetes (246-221 B.C.), made common cause with two new powers which had appeared in Greece towards the beginning of the century: the Aetolian and Achaean Leagues. The Aetolian League owed its success to its victory over the Galatians in 278 B.C. by which it gained mastery over Phocis and Doris. The Achaean League played a more modest part until 251-250 B.C. when Aratus freed Sicyon from its tyrant and brought the city into the League, which was thereby greatly strengthened. Aratus was elected strategos of the League in 245 B.C. and formed an alliance with Egypt for the purpose of wresting the Peloponnesus from Macedonian domination. In 243 B.C. he captured the citadel of Corinth in a surprise attack, and Antigonus was unable to dislodge him in spite of an alliance with the Aetolians. Antigonus Gonatas' son and successor, Demetrius II (239-229 B.C.) spent his reign defending his kingdom with difficulty against his enemies: the Aetolians whom Aratus had won over to the Achaean side, and Epirus which towards 235 B.C. had become an ally of Aetolia. Demetrius called upon the Illyrian pirates for help, but only succeeded in attracting the Romans to Greece. Finally, the Balkan barbarians invaded Macedonia, and Demetrius perished fighting them.

The Seleucid Empire also seemed to be on the verge of collapse. On the death of Antiochus II in 246 B.C., his first wife, Laodice, had his second wife, who was a sister of Ptolemy Euergetes, murdered. Euergetes at once invaded Syria. The subsequent war was disastrous for Antiochus' heir, Seleucus II, whose kingdom was completely over-run. Though Seleucus was successful in regaining northern Syria and Antioch, all the coast still remained in Egyptian hands when, in 241 B.C., a truce was made. In addition, his brother Antiochus Hierax rebelled against him and seized Anatolia. This fratricidal

after the death of Arsinoë, his sister-bride, Ptolemy Philadelphus' prudence degenerated into cowardice, although until 250 B.C. the Ptolemaic empire remained unshaken. Besides its possessions in the eastern Mediterranean it embraced Nubia and exercised a kind of protectorate over Ethiopia. To the west Cyrene maintained her independence but tended to gravitate into the Egyptian orbit. The power of the Ptolemies, however, was derived less from the territory they ruled than from their great riches. Following the example of the ancient pharaohs, they considered themselves the sole proprietors of the entire country's wealth — and they organised its exploitation with a rigour unknown until their day. Most of the land was leased to native farmers at a rent which in normal times was supportable. In times of drought, however, such tenants were obliged to borrow from the royal treasury, fell into debt and were unable to free themselves. In addition, forced labour was required for the upkeep of the dykes and roads, and for the cultivation of poor lands which the State had not been able to lease. The remaining land of the kingdom was granted either to personages of importance or to *cleruchies*, military colonists who furnished a regular and abundant supply of recruits for the armed forces. Industry was no longer independent. The more profitable industries had been turned into

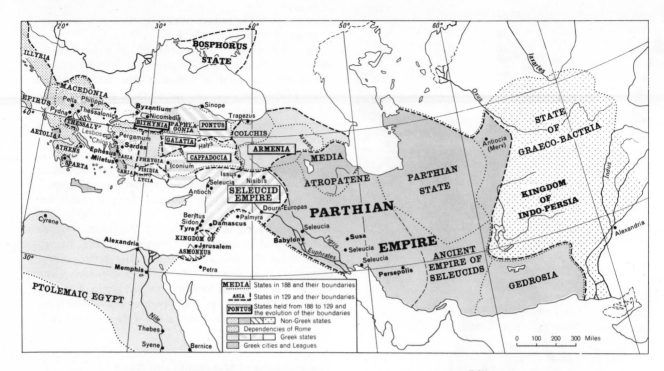

war in 230-228 B.C. allowed Attalus I, who had succeeded Eumenes in 241 B.C., to extend the territory of the kingdom of Pergamum considerably. Seleucus III (226-223 B.C.) could do nothing to recover his losses. The chief gainer seemed to be Euergetes, but already certain indications of weakening had become apparent. Absorbed in his struggle with the Seleucids, he let the command of the Cyclades slip from his hands — and into those of Antigonus. He did not intervene in the 'fratricidal war', and signs of restiveness in Egypt itself foreshadowed the great popular uprisings of the end of the century.

Antigonus Doson and Philip V

The downfall of Macedonia was retarded by two energetic sovereigns. Antigonus Doson, who succeeded Demetrius II, repulsed the Balkan barbarians, while in the Peloponnesus events were taking place which prepared the way for his re-establishment in Greece. A traditional enmity existed between the Achaeans and Sparta, who had not forgotten her past glory. Sparta was, however, paralysed by the faults in her social system. Then in 237 B.C. a king mounted the throne who was determined to introduce revolutionary reforms: Cleomenes. He annulled the constitution, redistributed the land and created a mass of new citizens. His army, thus reinforced, inflicted defeat after defeat on the Achaeans. The Achaean general, Aratus, had no other choice than to turn to Antigonus Doson, to whom in 224 B.C. he returned the citadel of Corinth, the Acrocorinth. In the following year Cleomenes was driven from Arcadia. In 222 B.C. he was overwhelmed by Antigonus at Sellasia and Sparta was occupied.

This alliance between the Achaean League and Macedonia had made the Aetolians very uneasy, and when Philip V, still young, succeeded Doson, the Aetolians attacked him. They were defeated and in 217 B.C. were forced to accept the treaty of Naupactus, which strengthened Macedonia's position. But another and graver danger loomed on the horizon: Roman intervention.

Above and *centre:* obverse and reverse of a coin of Seleucus I of Syria (312-281 B.C.). *Below:* obverse of a coin of Demetrius I Poliorcetes of Macedonia (294-283 B.C.), showing Poseidon.

When Demetrius II unleashed the Adriatic pirates of Agron of Illyria — and later of Agron's widow, Teuta — on the coasts of Greece, the Greek cities of that region, in 229 B.C., begged aid from Rome. Teuta was obliged to abandon the Ionian islands to her former ally, Demetrius of Pharos, who in 228 B.C. betrayed her. Realising that the Second Punic War was imminent and Rome's attention would be elsewhere, Demetrius of Pharos resumed piratical activities in 219 B.C. Rome, however, intervened and forced him to take refuge at Pella in Macedonia.

He called on Philip for help. Philip was absorbed in his first war against the Aetolians and for the moment ignored the appeal. But after the peace of Naupactus, Philip, seeing that Rome was deeply engaged with Hannibal, decided to risk adventure in the Adriatic. On two occasions, once in 216 B.C. and again in 214 B.C., a Roman fleet forced him to raise the siege of Apollonia. It was not until 211 B.C. when Hannibal was immobilised that Rome was able to undertake active measures against Macedonia. She formed a large coalition of states which were worried by Philip's ambitions. Encircled and without a fleet, Philip had to withdraw and with difficulty to defend himself. But Philopoemen, who had replaced Aratus as head of the Achaean League, removed Philip's enemy Machanidas, tyrant of Sparta, who was defeated at Mantinea in 207 B.C. Another enemy, Attalus of Pergamum, was neutralised by Prusias of Bithynia, while in the same year Philip himself ravaged Aetolia and forced her to sue for peace. Rome then made a last effort but, cautiously reserving her strength for the final struggle with Carthage, decided to come to an agreement. The peace treaty, signed in 205 B.C., left Philip in possession of the major part of his conquests. More important, it left him with his prestige intact — which soon incited him to further adventures.

Antiochus the Great

The accomplishments of Philip V were far excelled by those of the Seleucid Antiochus III (223-187 B.C.), known as Antiochus the Great. The beginning of his reign was unpromising, for Egypt occupied his Mediterranean coastline, Attalus held Anatolia, and the eastern provinces had broken away from the empire. Achaeus, the king's cousin, succeeded in driving Attalus back into his former domain but in 220 B.C., at the instigation of Egypt, revolted. Antiochus first attacked Egypt, but was defeated in 217 B.C. at Raphia. Only Egyptian inertia saved him and allowed him to undertake military action against the rebel Achaeus. Having purchased the support of Attalus, Antiochus reconquered Anatolia in 213 B.C. and put Achaeus to death.

His authority being thus reaffirmed in the west, Antiochus now turned his attention to the provinces of the east. The satrapies which Alexander had created in India had not survived his death. They were annexed after 317 B.C. by an Indian prince, Chandragupta, who had overthrown the Nanda dynasty of Magadha and founded the Maurya kingdom. An attempt by Seleucus towards 305 to reconquer the Indian provinces ended in an alliance in which Chandragupta received the additional provinces of Arachosia and the Paropamisadae mountain range. Chandragupta's son, Bindusara (c. 297-274 B.C.), and

Antiochus III, the Great (223-187 B.C.). By recovering Anatolia, Parthia, Media, Armenia and Coele-Syria, by forming an alliance with the Rajah of the Punjab, in order to protect his eastern frontier, and by signing a peace treaty with Egypt in 195 B.C., Antiochus restored the power of the Seleucid Empire. *Giraudon*

The Pharos of Alexandria, the first lighthouse, and one of the Seven Wonders of the World. Built by Sostratus of Cnidus in Ptolemy II's reign, it was destroyed by earthquakes.

more especially his grandson, Asoka (c. 274-236 B.C.), had extended their supremacy as far as the Deccan. Though Asoka was a great conqueror, he is even more illustrious as the apostle of Buddhism which he embraced in about 260 B.C. In his religious enthusiasm he did not, however, neglect his duties as a ruler; for he developed the economy of his kingdom and replaced feudal chaos with a sound administrative system. Chandragupta's court was described by the Greek Megasthenes, an envoy of Seleucus; it was elaborate and well organised, and his vizir, Kautilya, wrote a well known treatise on politics, the *Athasastra*. The Maurya kingdom depended on large armies, which were reinforced with war elephants and based upon well planned camps and wooden fortifications. Economic development was encouraged, reservoirs built and kept in repair, roads and bridges cared for.

This great kingdom was the background to the rule of Asoka. the most famous ruler in Indian history, whose influence extended over most of the sub-continent, and whose prestige is still commemorated in modern India. He was the first monarch in world history to administer a great empire on the principle of non-violence, and his reign is of cardinal importance in Indian history.

The prosperity of the Maurya empire was attended by the first flowering of Indian art, and the style which it then evolved persisted until the beginning of our own era. The sculptured reliefs, inspired by the universal love preached by Buddhism, are especially rich in subjects drawn from the animal world, depicted with exuberant naturalism. The spread of the new religion, however, led to a schism between the *Hinâyâna* and the *Mahâyâna*. The Hinâyâna, nearer to the original doctrine of Buddhism, was most active in Ceylon which had been evangelised in the days of Asoka and was to spread to Burma and Siam. The Mahâyâna, imbued with mysticism, offered to the popular imagination the worship of future Buddhas — the *bodhisattvas* — whose prestige tended to supplant that of the true Buddha: it was to become the dominant form of Buddhism in Nepal, Tibet, China, Korea and Japan.

Much more serious for the Seleucids than Indian resurgence had been the loss of Eastern Persia. Towards 250 B.C. Arsaces, the chief of a nomad Parthian tribe, had made himself independent, while his brother and successor, Tiridates (248-214 B.C.), had occupied Hyrcania and in 247 B.C. overwhelmed Antiochus II. Bactria and Sogdiana thus found themselves separated from the rest of the empire, and their governor, Diodotus, became for all practical purposes independent. His son, Diodotus II (c. 245-225 B.C.) proclaimed himself king and made an alliance with the Parthians. Finally the revolt spread to Media, whose satrap seized Seleucia on the Tigris. In 220 B.C. Antiochus III defeated and killed him, but it was not until eight years later that he was able to undertake the reconquest of the eastern satrapies. The campaign, which lasted for seven years, earned Antiochus a great reputation. First he occupied Armenia, then he drove the new king of the Parthians, Artabanus, from Ecbatana and compelled him to acknowledge his suzerainty. In Bactria he consented — in exchange for a tribute — to leave Diodotus' successor, Euthydemus, in office. In the Punjab he concluded an alliance with the rajah Sophagasenus, and from there returned in 205 B.C. to Persia. The moment seemed ripe to renew the war

A Roman boy wearing the *toga praetexta*, bordered with crimson, and a gold *bulla*, or amulet; these were discarded at the age of seventeen, when the young man would be eligible to wear the *toga virilis*, the symbol of manhood. *Giraudon*

with Egypt. Antiochus attacked in 204 B.C., crushed the Egyptians at Panion in 200 B.C., and finally occupied Coele-Syria. By the peace treaty signed in 195 B.C. the grandeur of the Seleucid Empire was restored.

Decadence of the Ptolemies

The peace treaty also marked the violent downfall of Egypt. The chief cause of the collapse was the wave of rebellion which, paradoxically enough, followed the Egyptian victory at Raphia. In order to deal with the uprising Ptolemy Philopator (221-203 B.C.) was obliged to add 20,000 native troops to his army. Hence the loyalty of the army, the chief support of the regime, was no longer to be relied on. Mutinies broke out at once, and continued to do so for years. They might have been less widespread had it not been for the degeneration of the dynasty. In habits and outlook the Ptolemies had become more and more oriental. To gain the confidence of their subjects it had become their policy to forget — and make their subjects forget — their foreign origin. In particular they showed an ostentatious devotion to the Egyptian gods, from which the priestly caste profited by demanding and obtaining exorbitant privileges. Furthermore, the Greeks of Egypt had followed the example of their sovereigns and gradually blended with and became part of the native masses who played an ever increasingly important role in the administration and the army. This policy at least enabled the Ptolemaic dynasty to prolong its existence for another two centuries.

Hellenistic civilisation

The territorial extension of the Greek monarchies profoundly modified the history of civilisation. Traditional cultural frontiers were broken down. In the domain of politics the city, as an institution, was decaying, although cities were acquiring new territories and — except in Egypt — colonisation was in full swing. But the system itself was degenerating. On the Greek mainland emigration weakened the towns, which grew poorer as centres of trade shifted. A city proletariat soon emerged which was reduced to penury by the rise in prices. In contrast, a rich class had arisen which monopolised public offices. Political strife cloaked what in fact was social conflict. Most important of all, the city had ceased to be, as it were, the centre of the world: the great powers which dominated it left only municipal affairs to its management. And then the city was usually so needy that it was obliged ignominiously to beg financial assistance from the court of the monarchs. The new colonies were, it is true, given institutions characteristic of the metropolis; but the populations were very mixed and lacked the civic spirit indispensable to an active political life.

Power from now on was wielded by much larger political units. In Greece a federal system flourished, in which the cities preserved their internal autonomy while participating by means of deputies in assemblies where a common policy was formulated. That the system, by which it was hoped to reconcile the perennial spirit of localism with the necessity to concentrate force, did not achieve great results was due to the general political decadence of Greece itself. The most vital form of government was the monarchy. Monarchy, except in Macedonia where it had its roots in national tradition, depended on force. The monarch was first and foremost a victorious general. In the beginning even the idea of fixed territorial possessions was foreign to him. Only the hazards of battle determined the boundaries of his hereditary domain. Success, which alone made his power legitimate, soon took on a religious complexion. The sovereign was protected by the gods. All the Hellenistic monarchs were very careful to cultivate this aspect of their authority, and the cult of the ruling dynasty thus became the common bond which held together otherwise very dissimilar peoples. Such absolute and theocratic power demanded a rigid system of centralisation. Everything emanated from the person of the king: ministers and governors were merely his delegates, and their appointments could be made or revoked at his whim. His will was made known through the intermediacy of a large and specialised body of bureaucrats. All the wealth of the kingdom was his personal property, and he exploited it to augment his power.

The exploitation of the kingdom's natural resources brought about profound economic changes. The opening up of the Achaemenian Empire by Alexander must in itself have displaced the former trade routes to the Orient; but the Hellenistic sovereigns hastened the process in their own interests. The improvement of roads and port facilities increased the revenue collected by the royal customs officials. Industry was organised into monopolies. In agriculture, progress in the rotation of crops, greater care in the selection of seed, and the acclimatising of new plants all contributed to the profits of the sovereign. But in the long run an oppressive system naturally killed individual initiative.

At the beginning, however, it produced the effects its promoters hoped for: a rich and powerful state, and an influx of immigrants lured by the promise of opportunities in distant lands.

Cosmopolitanism in thought and art

The outlook of the Hellenistic Greeks, swamped as they were by indigenous populations, was of necessity very different from that of the citizens of the small Greek cities at home. If they were not to be totally submerged they had to forget their traditional individuality. Thus Hellenistic culture tended to become cosmopolitan. Communication between those who spoke different dialects was simplified by the development of a common Greek language, known as *koine*. The tendency towards a unified society was also noticeable in religious practice. Cut off from their ancestral beliefs the Greeks of the emigration turned towards universal deities who could offer individual salvation without the co-operation of the old social group. Hence the revived popularity of those gods who were less attached than others to a special locality: Zeus, Asclepius and Dionysus — whose names in Latin became Jupiter, Aesculapius and Bacchus — and the cult of abstract powers such as Tyche (Fortune). A similar influence explains the evolution of philosophic thought where the emphasis was placed on a search for moral values which could furnish a rule of life for the uprooted individual. This was the chief appeal of the two philosophies which were most in vogue during the epoch: epicureanism and stoicism.

The intellectual climate also encouraged the development of the exact sciences, a movement which was spurred on by contact with new and strange lands and peoples. The movement was warmly supported by the sovereigns, eager not only to heighten their reputation as civilisers but also to increase and take more careful stock of the resources of their empires. The Ptolemies, by creating the museum and library of Alexandria, showed the way, and all their rivals followed their example, notably the kings of Pergamum. Daring voyages of exploration hastened the progress of geography and astronomy, while great strides in the study of mathematics contributed to their understanding. Nor did medicine lag behind. The Ptolemies authorised the practice of dissection, and important discoveries were made in anatomy and physiology. A preoccupation with encyclopaedic knowledge affected even literature and led to the great collections of books at Alexandria and Pergamum with their army of scribes, copying volumes on papyrus or on parchment. In this way literary history and textual criticism were born.

169

The Apoxyomenos (fourth century B.C.), a statue by Alexander's official artist, Lysippus of Sicyon; Lysippus' art showed a grace and refinement suited to the educated bourgeois audience of the Hellenistic period. The young athlete is scraping the oil from his limbs after contest. *Archiv für Kunst und Geschichte*

One of the most striking features of Hellenistic literature may be thus explained: erudition, for a great many of these literary critics were also poets. Their work appealed to the taste of a new public, no longer popular but bourgeois, educated and refined but superficial, a public that appreciated perfection of style, graceful and studied imagery, and was pleased and flattered by recognising learning and cultured allusions. The literature of the period, severed from those profound sentiments which had stirred the citizens during the classic epoch, such literature of self-conscious artistry, lost contact with the common people. The same absence of vitality is found in the other arts. The public buildings of Alexander and his successors gave architects vast scope for display, but the very vastness of their projects was a detriment to formal perfection. Sculpture continued to live on the classical repertory. Lysippus, Alexander's official artist, must be mentioned among the outstanding sculptors: he was a past master in the art of revealing the individual personality depicted as an ideal type. The great paintings of the period are lost, but their inspiration is reflected in the frescoes and mosaics of Pompeii, in which a taste for movement and the portrayal of the individual triumph.

Agathocles of Syracuse

The party strife which had broken out in Sicily on the retirement from public life of Timoleon provided the occasion for an extraordinary bid for power which, had it been successful, might have been a minor counterpart of the exploits of Alexander in the East. Supported by the Carthaginians, Agathocles, leader of the democratic party, was able to seize the government of Syracuse, bring about a complete social revolution and, in the years between 319 B.C. and 313 B.C., extend his authority over the neighbouring cities. Two years later, however, when he attacked the possessions of his Carthaginian allies, they withdrew their support. Hamilcar overwhelmed him at Ecnomus and blockaded him in Syracuse. With astonishing boldness Agathocles outwitted his besiegers and carried the war into Africa itself, where for two years he ravaged Carthaginian territory, though he was unable to occupy Carthage itself. His ill-timed return to Sicily, where the revolt of certain cities demanded his presence, led to the loss of his African conquests. He returned to Africa in haste but was unable to recoup his losses. Carthage was saved but exhausted, and in 360 B.C. sued for peace. Agathocles then turned his attention to Italy where Tarentum was holding out with difficulty against native tribes and had appealed for help to Greek mercenary captains. But Tarentum quarrelled with every such captain she engaged, and as the last of them abandoned her she had no choice but to give command to the ruler of Syracuse. For several years Agathocles' efforts were crowned with success, but he died in 289 B.C. and his will restored liberty to his country. Mutiny then broke out among his mercenary troops — the Mamertini — who were stationed at Messina. They seized the town and their subsequent careers as brigands soon provoked the intervention of Rome.

Rome at the beginning of the third century

Rome had promptly repaired the disaster suffered by her army at the Caudine Forks by completing the conquest of the Pontine plains in 318 B.C., which enabled her to stamp out revolt in the Campagna. The capture of Fregellae in 313 B.C. preceded by one year the final subjection of the country. Then, one by one, the Sabellian mountain tribes were subdued and compelled to accept Roman rule. During the four years between 308 and 304 B.C. Samnium was ravaged; when its capital Bovianum fell it was obliged to sue for peace. Rome's power was now so formidable that Carthage concluded a treaty with her (c. 306 B.C.) which divided their respective spheres of interest, Italy being left to Rome, Sicily reserved for Carthage. A few years later, towards 303 B.C., Rome concluded a similar treaty with Tarentum. A fresh invasion of the Gauls in 299 B.C. upset these arrangements, and all Rome's enemies formed a coalition against her. At the crucial battle of Sentinum in 295 B.C. the Roman army was triumphant. Rome now had access to Lucania and Apulia. Her expansion then spread to the Adriatic where she wrested Picenum from the Gallic Senones. In 283 B.C. the founding of Sena Gallica ensured Roman command of this part of Italy, while the Boi, in alliance with the Etruscans, were overwhelmed at Lake Vadimonis.

A relief found at Thyrea, showing Asclepius (Latin: Aesculapius), god of healing, with his wife and children receiving the sick. Asclepius' sanctuaries were found all over the Hellenistic world, and people made long pilgrimages to visit them. After receiving advice at the shrine, the patient would show his gratitude with an ex-voto offering such as the one above. *Giraudon*

Meanwhile the political progress of the plebs continued unchecked. In 312 B.C. the censor Appius Claudius Caecus introduced a measure by which a man's personal estate was taken into consideration in establishing his census status. The patricians lost their last privileges of a religious nature when the aedile Cn. Flavius made the calendar public, and the *lex Ogulnia* (c. 300 B.C.) admitted the plebs into the sacerdotal colleges. A final plebeian revolt, provoked by the problem of debts, led the dictator Hortensius to pass a law which made it simpler for the peasantry to obtain justice. The peasants received further satisfaction by the agrarian law of 297 B.C. which limited the extent of the state-owned lands known as *ager publicus* which private citizens had the right to occupy.

The war of Pyrrhus

Until the opening of the third century the relations between Rome and Magna Graecia had been few but satisfactory. Indeed the Greek cities looked on Rome as an ally who could attack from the rear the savage tribes which threatened them. Certain Greek cities, such as Thurii, Locri and Rhegium, even asked for Roman garrisons. This disturbed Tarentum, and in spite of the treaty of 303 B.C. she drove the Roman garrisons out. As a reprisal Rome in 281 B.C. invaded the territory of Tarentum, who, as was her habit, called upon a Greek general for help. In 280 B.C. Pyrrhus, king of Epirus, invaded Italy with cavalry troops and — an innovation in Italian warfare — his elephants. At Heraclea he won a costly victory. Again, in 279 B.C. he was the victor at Asculum, but Rome formed an alliance with Carthage against him, whereupon Pyrrhus decided to change his objective. He turned towards Sicily where local rivalries invited intervention, and by 277 B.C. he had conquered all the island except the Carthaginian fringe in the west. As a result of the usual dissensions among the Greeks he lost it a year later and returned to Italy. He suffered a serious check at Beneventum in 275 B.C., and the following year withdrew from the peninsula. The Romans were then able to finish the conquest of Grecian Italy which, after the capitulation of Tarentum in 272 B.C. and of Rhegium two years later, was rounded off in 268 B.C. by the founding of a Latin colony at Beneventum. The long and arduous war with Pyrrhus had not prevented Rome from continuing military operations in Etruria: Caere had been taken in 273 B.C., Volsinii in 265 B.C. She also completed the defeat of Picenum by the capture of Asculum and the founding of Ariminum (Rimini) in 268.

The First Punic War

It was not long before this Roman territorial expansion met with the resistance of more formidable enemies. Rome did not respect the treaty she had made in 306 B.C. with Carthage, and from Rhegium she cast predatory eyes on Messina across the straits. Messina, which was held by the Mamertini, was also coveted by the new king of Syracuse, Hiero. Shortly after his accession in 269 he attacked Messina, but the Carthaginians captured it first. The Mamertini begged for help from Rome, who out of jealousy and fear of Carthage responded to the appeal and expelled the Carthaginian garrison. Hiero, disturbed by this turn of events, allied himself to Carthage and attacked the city for the second time. He was defeated, forced to surrender and, in 263 B.C., acknowledge himself a tributary of Rome, whom he served faithfully until his death. Carthage, in spite of the defection of her ally, continued the war. She was preparing to land an army in Italy when her fleet was destroyed in 260 B.C. at Mylae. This was the first Roman sea victory. Even worse, Africa itself was invaded: following a fresh naval victory at Ecnomus the Roman general Regulus laid siege to Carthage. But with an insufficiently supported army Regulus was defeated in 255 B.C. and Rome's luck seemed to change: two Roman fleets were annihilated, one in 254 B.C. off the coast of Lucania, the other in 249 B.C. before Drepanum. In 251 B.C. they captured Palermo and defeated a vast Carthaginian army. The conquest of Sicily, however, slowly proceeded, though the Romans were held up before the last Carthaginian positions for nearly ten years by the skill and energy of Hamilcar Barca. Roman victory in the Aegates Islands in 241 B.C. finally obliged Carthage to ask for terms. By them she paid a war imdemnity of 3,200 talents and the larger part of Sicily became the first Roman province.

For Carthage defeat entailed an almost fatal crisis: her mercenaries — who had not been paid — in alliance with the rebellious natives nearly succeeded in destroying her. Roman neutrality, however, allowed her in 237 B.C. to overcome the danger, but only at the price of Corsica and Sicily and an increased debt — a humiliation Carthage did not forget.

Rome in the middle of the third century

By the middle of the third century Rome had attained its final territorial extension, and Roman institutions achieved their traditional form. Society was still chiefly agricultural. The great landowners constituted a ruling class from which the magistrates were drawn. This *nobilitas* consisted of both the patrician *gentes* and the great plebeian families. Wealth had replaced birth. The large estates had not, however, swallowed up the smaller holdings. The mass of the Roman people consisted of peasants who cultivated their own family possessions with the aid of their children and a slave or two. Their situation, though modest, was still solid and no trace of a rural exodus is found during this period. But in economic life differences were beginning to develop. Trade had been stimulated by contact with the Greek cities of southern Italy and of the eastern Mediterranean. A sign of the changed economic climate was the introduction of money: from the year 268 B.C. silver was minted in Rome. The legitimate children of citizens were also citizens, as were the children of freedmen, still few in the middle of the third century. Since 241 B.C. citizens had been divided into thirty-five local tribes, covering the total area of Roman Italy which extended over some nine or ten thousand square miles, from Picenum to the Campagna. These tribes provided the framework of the plebeian assemblies, the *concilium plebis tributum*, which had gradually merged with the *comitia tributa populi*, presided over by curule magistrates. All the inhabitants of the tribal territories were citizens, but not all of them had the right to vote. Local communities had little autonomy and lawsuits especially were judged by prefects delegated by the magistrates of Rome. Finally, the citizens were divided according to their property into five classes, the composition of which was revised every five years by the censors. Each of these classes was divided into *centuries*, each having one vote in the *comitia centuriata* which elected the magistrates. At the summit of the hierarchy were the eighteen equestrian *centuries* — or *equites* — from which in theory the cavalry of the legions was recruited. Little by little, however, the title 'equestrian' was extended to include everyone whom the census classified as upper class. They thus constituted a social group which was distinct from the senators and the rest of the population.

Only the popular assemblies had the right to declare war or make peace, to vote for the laws, and to elect magistrates. Continuity of government was assured by the senate, which in actual fact wielded the real power. The senate consisted of 300 members, chosen by the censors from among former magistrates. It met only when called together by a magistrate. Its decisions — known as *senatus consulta* — did not have the force of law; and the senate was obliged to accord its *auctoritas* in advance to all measures decided upon by the people. But the treasury was at its free disposal, all diplomacy was conducted by it, it determined the functions of the magistrates and, by means of the *prorogatio*, it could retain officers in power under senatorial direction if the military situation seemed to demand it.

Most important of all, the senate was drawn almost exclusively from the ranks of a close-knit social class bound together by mutual interests. For although the people elected their leaders freely, in practice they always chose members of the same great families. The nomination of an outsider — or *homo novus* — was the exception. Even the tribunes of the plebs were recruited from among the *nobilitas*. The office of tribune, revolutionary in its origin, had become accepted and normal, and was now arrived at by a series of steps — the *cursus honorum* — which the candidate climbed successively. The first step in a political career was to be elected one of the eight *quaestors*, who were treasury officials. Next, there was the choice of the college of the *aediles*, four in number, who were responsible for the police, public works and morality, or the college of ten tribunes whose role was above all judiciary. Then came the curule magistrates, the praetors, the consuls, the censors and the dictator. There was at first only one praetor, but towards 242 B.C. a second, *praetor peregrinus*, was appointed to deal with lawsuits between Romans and foreigners. In 227 B.C. two more praetors were created to govern the two new provinces of Sicily and Corsica-Sardinia. The praetor was thus not only a judge but also an administrative officer. The consulate was the supreme magistrature and its function was chiefly military. The college of censors was elected only at five yearly intervals; it took the census, drew up the *album* — or senatorial list — and assessed the amount of tax each citizen paid. Finally, in cases of exceptional danger to the State, a dictator was

Elephants being transported across a river during the Second Punic War (218-201 B.C.). Elephants in combat had first been met with in Alexander's campaigns in India; it was a clumsy method of warfare as the animals were slow to turn in battle and needed much space to manoeuvre. When terrified they trampled down friend and foe alike; when charging they could easily be outflanked by swifter cavalry mounted on horses.

appointed for a limited period and given absolute authority.

The rest of Italy was divided into communities which were allied to Rome. Their constitutional status varied according to the treaties of alliance which had been imposed upon them. In general they enjoyed a reasonable amount of internal self-government. The cities of the *jus latinium* — the former Latin League — possessed exceptional privileges: their inhabitants could marry Romans and vote in Roman elections. But they were deprived of this right of marriage — *connubium* — in 268 B.C. and their votes were confined to a single century drawn by lot. Finally, beyond the Italian peninsula, the territories acquired by Rome constituted the provinces. In the provinces Rome, by virtue of the right of conquest, 173

Marche d'Annibal dans les Alpes, depuis Vizille
jusqu'à la plaine du Piemont ou gaule Cisalpine.
1. Grenoble. 2. Vizille. 3. Bourg d'Oisans. 4 Le Mont de Lens.
5. Le Lautaret. 6. Briançon. 7. Le Mont Genèvre.
8. Sezanne. 9. Le Mont Sestriers 10. Suze 11. Col de
la fenestre. 12. Pignerol. —— —— Campement.

A map of Hannibal's route across the Alps. The Carthaginians undertook an immense journey during the Second Punic War: from Spain, they crossed the Pyrenees into Gaul, and then over the Alps to assemble finally in Italy on the banks of the Po. Hannibal arrived with 20,000 foot-soldiers and 6,000 cavalry, including elephants, after an arduous march of six months.

exercised an absolute authority except in the case of allied cities. She was represented by a governor who was responsible for raising the money and the men she demanded, who commanded the troops and rendered justice either in person or by delegating his power to do so to local authorities.

The extension of Roman imperialism

These new possessions gave Rome command of important financial and military resources. The military force at her disposal ran to hundreds of thousands of men, citizens or allies, all of robust peasant stock. In the course of incessant warfare the Roman armies, adopting the most effective of their enemies' weapons, had developed an organisation and a tactical skill which, when well commanded, rendered them in all forms of combat almost invincible. Thanks to these highly trained armies the end of the First Punic War did not mark even a pause in Roman conquest. From 238 to 225 B.C. Corsica and Sardinia were pacified — not without difficulty. From 238 to 230 B.C. Fabius Maximus campaigned in Liguria. When in 232 B.C. the *lex Flaminia* authorised the colonisation of the land occupied by the Senones the Cisalpine Gauls rose in protest and invaded Italy. They penetrated as far as Clusium, but in 225 B.C. were massacred at Cape Telamon. Then Flaminius himself marched north into the Po valley and, by his victory at Clastidium, obliged the Gallic Boii and the Insubres to accept Roman sovereignty (223-222 B.C.). On the north-east coast of central Italy the conquest of Picenum had given Rome harbours on the Adriatic, and hence a contact with the Greek world. Preoccupation with security rather than imperial ambitions had compelled her to take action in the Adriatic, first in order to suppress Illyrian piracy and then, as we have already seen, to counter the seemingly dangerous political and military intrigues of Philip V of Macedonia in search of new Adriatic territory.

The Second Punic War

Rome's principal cause for anxiety, however, was the mounting evidence of Carthage's desire for revenge. For the merchant princes who governed Carthage command of the western Mediterranean was a matter of vital importance. The ruling class in Carthage actually formed only a minority of the population and their authority depended on military power based on mercenary troops. To pay for such troops commercial success was essential, and essential to commercial success was mastery of the sea. Again, in a city where trade had produced a large and restive proletariat, colonisation furnished an outlet for the surplus population. Thus Carthage had planted a chain of trading settlements which stretched from Syrtis as far down the African coast as Senegal and perhaps even to the Cameroons. Therefore the loss of Sicily, Corsica and Sardinia after the First Punic War was a grave threat not only to her prosperity but to her strategic position. To compensate for these losses, and to prepare a base for future revenge, Carthage in 237 B.C. entrusted Hamilcar Barca with the conquest of Spain. The mission was accomplished with skill and energy, and Carthage gained thereby an important accretion of territory and possession of the richest silver mines in the ancient world.

Hannibal's War

The conquest, however, aroused anxiety in the Spanish colonies of Marseilles which was allied to Rome. Rome, at the instigation of Marseilles, made the Ebro Treaty in 226 B.C. with the Carthaginian commander Hasdrubal, who had succeeded Hamilcar Barca. Hasdrubal agreed to remain south of the river Ebro. Five years later Hannibal took command of the Carthaginian forces and laid siege to Saguntum. Though Saguntum was actually situated south of the Ebro it was allied to Rome, and Rome decided that Hannibal had violated the treaty. Hannibal ignored Roman protests, Saguntum fell in 219 B.C., and Rome declared war: the Second Punic War. The Roman plan was to fight the war in Spain itself, but Hannibal was too quick for them. In the spring of 218 B.C. he passed over the Pyrenees with a small army and pushed towards the Rhône valley. Then, turning northwards to avoid the Romans, he crossed the high Alps, an astonishing feat of daring and endurance which brought the Carthaginian army into the Po valley in September. With

very little effort Hannibal was able to incite the Cisalpine Gauls to rise in revolt against the Romans. In the depths of winter he met and defeated the Romans at the Trebia, then again at Lake Trasimenus in the spring of 217. B.C. Shortly afterwards he arrived at the gates of Rome which he did not, however, venture to attack. In 216 B.C. a new Roman army was annihilated at Cannae, and a large part of southern Italy, notably Capua, defected. In 215 B.C. the death of Hiero was the signal for revolt in Syracuse and in consequence Rome lost Sicily. Finally in 213 B.C. Hannibal took Tarentum. In Spain, meanwhile, a Roman army which had been sent out in 218 B.C. under the command of the Scipios took advantage of the revolt in Africa of Syphax, a Numidian king, against Carthage to penetrate as deep into Spain as Andalusia. But when Syphax submitted to Carthage in 211 B.C. the Scipios were defeated and slain.

The triumph of Rome

Since the year 215 B.C. the compaign of the war in Italy had been confided to Fabius Maximus whose tactics won him the sobriquet of Cunctator, the 'laggard'. They consisted in avoiding a head-on encounter with Hannibal and, instead, wearing him down in a series of minor engagements. In this way Fabius was able to reconquer Samnium. In 212 B.C. Rome carried the war into Sicily and regained Syracuse. Then, refusing to be distracted by a raid by Hannibal on Rome itself, Fabius between 211 and 209 B.C. succeeded in recapturing Capua, Brundisium and Tarentum. Hannibal thus found himself encircled in Bruttium and Lucania. To free him from this trap Carthage gave command of an army to Hasdrubal, who marched from Spain by the road which his brother had followed ten years earlier but in 207 B.C. Hasdrubal was crushed and slain on the banks of the Metaurus. An attempt by a third brother, Mago, in Liguria met with a

Hannibal (247-183 B.C.) the great Carthaginian general, son of Hamilcar Barca. In spite of his excellent strategy, the Second Punic War resulted in victory for Rome.

A Roman bireme. The curved stem of the ship was used in ramming enemy ships; the soldiers would then board the enemy and fight hand to hand. *Anderson*

A Graeco-Roman mosaic showing Dionysus, the god of wine. His numerous cults had spread across Greece and the Roman world by the third century. He was known to the Romans as Bacchus, and is often depicted with a panther and crowned with vine leaves and grapes.

Scipio Africanus (236-184 B.C.), so named in honour of his victories against the Carthaginians in Spain and in Africa at the battle of Zama (202 B.C.), which ended the Second Punic War.

similar fate. In Spain the scattered remnants of the Scipios' defeated army had been rallied by the future Scipio 'Africanus'. He was put in command, and between 209 and 206 B.C. he seized Carthago Nova, Baecula and Gades.

Scipio was elected consul in 205. B.C. He crossed into Sicily at once and prepared an invasion of Africa, first making an alliance with the Numidian king Masinissa against Syphax whom he had at first hoped to detach from Carthage. In 204 B.C. Scipio crossed the Mediterranean and the following year, with the aid of Masinissa, inflicted a decisive defeat on Syphax. Carthage then decided to recall Hannibal and Mago. Hannibal, who felt the whole situation had reached a deadlock, offered a truce and began negotiations for a peace treaty. Then the Carthaginians made the fatal mistake of resuming hostilities. They were disastrously defeated in 202 B.C. at Zama. By the terms of the Treaty of Tunis, Carthage lost Spain and her military might was destroyed. She was forced to pay an enormous war indemnity, and a powerful Numidian kingdom was created on her frontiers.

The China of Chi Hwang-ti

The history of China in the third century B.C. is the history of the re-establishment of unity. By about 325 B.C. two principalities, Tsin and Chou, had out-distanced all their rivals. By 311 B.C. war had broken out between them, and in it Chou lost the upper valley of the Han. But before the decisive round, the two opponents had first to subdue certain states of secondary importance. Tsin went about this task with the greatest energy: under the reign of Chao-Siang (306-251 B.C.) Tsin conquered the northern banks of the Hwang-ho and destroyed the principality which occupied Shantung. Meanwhile Chou had seized the entire lower basin of the Yang-tze, and in 283 overran the Hwai-ho valley. In 249 B.C. Chou occupied a part of Shantung. But Tsin had already begun the counter offensive, seizing Chou's capital and driving the enemy back to the Hwai-ho. The final clash was, however, still deferred, since the kings of Tsin chose first to ensure their supremacy over the Northern States.

A decision between the two powers was also delayed by the youth of the new king of Tsin, Chung (246-210 B.C.) who was only thirteen years old. But when he launched upon his career of conquest he acted with lightning speed. During the four years between 230 and 226 B.C. he annexed Honan, Shansi and Hopeh. In 224-223 B.C. the remains of the kingdom of Chou succumbed. Finally in 221 B.C. Shantung surrendered without offering resistance — Chung thereupon assumed the title of Tsin Chi Hwang-ti — the 'First Autocratic Emperor', the name by which he is known to history. The restoration of unity did not arrest his military activities. In 214 B.C. he conquered the region of Canton which he proceeded to colonise. In the north, to protect his empire from the incursion of the Huns, he caused the ramparts which the feudal principalities had constructed without plan, in about 300 B.C. against nomad raiders, to be connected methodically in a single over-all system. This was the Great Wall of China which extended from the sources of the Wei to the gulf of Liaotung. As an administrator the achievements of Chi Hwang-ti were even more remarkable. In order to do away with the feudal system he divided China into thirty-six provinces governed by

Part of the Great Wall of China, built by the Emperor Tsin Chi Hwang-ti in 228 B.C. Tsin had by this time united the Empire and the Wall was necessary protection from the Huns. It ran 1,400 miles along the northern and north-western frontiers.

his own officials. To uproot the political danger of local patriotism he resorted to massive displacements of population, and his reforms in the Chinese script gave the country a common means of written communication. Finally his interdiction of the 'Books' in 213 B.C. put an end to the opposition which traditionalist scholars had offered to his reforms giving expression to the prejudice against learning and discussion already described which had grown up during the time of the Warring States. When such ideas had been thought subversive, he decreed that all books except those on medicine, agriculture and divination should be burnt by the magistrates. Chinese literature was thus impoverished.

The dynasty of Chi Hwang-ti did not survive his death. The chiefs of the army quarrelled over the provinces. The struggle rapidly became a duel between two of their number: Hiang-Yu, a brutal giant, and Liu Pang, a subtle politician. Hiang-Yu, who at first had the upper hand, seized the capital in 206 B.C. and turned it over to his soldiers to pillage. Then, little by little, Liu Pang, who had meanwhile taken refuge in Chensi, drove him back towards the sea. In the beginning of 202 B.C. he crushed him at Kai-hia in Ngan-hui and compelled him to commit suicide. Liu Pang, now the sole master of China,

founded the Han Dynasty, which was to reign for four centuries and which was to be the first truly centralised and adequately administered Chinese Empire, playing a part in Far Eastern history comparable to the Roman Empire in Europe. The age of aristocratic feudalism and warring kingdoms was now past; the Han empire, originally founded by Liu Pang, a peasant adventurer, was to create the political framework of Chinese civilisation which, though disrupted by periods of confusion and alien rule, was never destroyed, so that there is a continuity of development from the Han empire to modern times.

The Han rulers, unlike Hwang-ti, collaborated with the 'Scholar-Sentry', encouraged neo-Confucianism, and reinstated what was left of the ancient books. The first major Chinese historian, Ssu-Ma-Chien, wrote at this time, and the bureaucracy was now organised, centralised, extended. The beginnings of the famous Chinese method of recruitment by examination are discernible under the Han, though it was not fully elaborated until the time of the Tang empire, after which it was to last until the early twentieth century. The Han empire was of vast extent, expanding its boundaries far into central Asia and the south: its importance is cardinal for the history of the Far East.

The Roman eagle, the emblem of the Empire, which was carried by the standard bearer in the forefront of every battle. From Britain to Palestine it was the recognised and often hated symbol of Roman overlordship. *Giraudon*

THE GREAT EMPIRES OF ANTIQUITY

A curious parallel, which is too often overlooked by those for whom history is limited to Europe and neighbouring countries, existed for nearly seven centuries at the two extremities of the ancient world.

While Rome was gaining supremacy in the Mediterranean basin the China of Tsin (whence the name), and then of the Han dynasty, conquered or subdued the Far East. After the civil wars of the first century B.C. the Roman Empire for more than two centuries imposed the *pax romana* on the West, while the later Han emperors, repairing the ruins left by the strife of earlier years, maintained a similar *pax sinica*.

In both empires the centuries which followed were periods of crisis, when power was usurped in Europe and China was split into the 'Three Kingdoms'.

Finally the same torrent swept away both the Roman and the Chinese empires as indeed it destroyed the more recent Indian empire of the Guptas: the furious onslaught of the Hunnish hordes which drove other barbarian peoples before them and, from one end of the ancient world to the other, was a prelude to centuries of upheaval and disruption.

This was neither the first, nor was it to be the last time that the dynamic vitality of central Asia upset the precious but precarious balance of security which the civilisations surrounding it had slowly achieved.

CHAPTER NINE

THE BIRTH OF IMPERIALISM

202-82 B.C.

Of even greater importance at this period than the conquests of Cisalpine Gaul and Spain was the intervention of Rome in the Hellenistic East. The reasons for her intervention are still discussed. From the end of the third century Rome had been involved in Greek affairs, but her wish — it would seem — was to withdraw from the scene as rapidly as possible. In the following century, on the contrary, she took an active part. Whether a deliberate plan of imperial expansion had been conceived or whether the chance turn of events was responsible is not certain. Though the senate as a body may not methodically have organised such intervention, it seems obvious that certain individual senators were not averse from the idea of new and profitable annexations. Again, twenty years of constant war had uprooted a great many Roman peasants and left them with no other resources than the profession of arms. Finally the alliances which Rome had formed during the war with Philip V of Macedonia also drew her towards the East.

Early Roman imperialism in the East

Just before the year 200 B.C. two of Rome's chief eastern allies, Rhodes and Pergamum, realised that their position was precarious. Rhodes had taken the place of Athens as a commercial centre, and through trade had achieved remarkable prosperity which depended on the freedom of the seas. Now, between 202 and 200 B.C. Philip V of Macedonia determined to occupy the Hellespont. This threatened not only Rhodes but Pergamum, which was already very uneasy about a project to partition Egypt between Macedonia and Syria. Rhodes and Pergamum came to an agreement and appealed to Rome for support. In 200 B.C. Rome declared war on Philip. Three years later Philip was beaten by the Roman consul Flaminius at Cynoscephalae and obliged to turn over his fleet, pay a huge indemnity and withdraw from Thessaly and Greece, whose independence Flaminius proclaimed at the Isthmian Games of 196 B.C.

By defeating Macedonia Rome had played into the hands of Antiochus III of Syria who made no secret of his ambition to unite the Hellenistic world under his own leadership. To begin with, he attacked the Hellespont in 197 B.C., together with various cities in Asia. At the request of Eumenes of Pergamum, a Roman committee of investigation was dispatched to report on these acts of aggression. Antiochus was convinced of Rome's hostile intentions and therefore took the offensive in Greece, where Flaminius had become unpopular. In 192 B.C. the Aetolians called on Antiochus for help, though the rest of the Greeks gave him no support. The advance of a Roman army drove Antiochus back to the pass of Thermopylae, and when he was forced to abandon this position he re-embarked. A year later the Romans destroyed his fleet and themselves landed in Asia where in 189 B.C.

at Mount Sipylus near Magnesia they defeated him. Antiochus had no alternative but to accept the treaty of Apamea in 188 B.C. which deprived him of all Asia this side of the Taurus Mountains, which was then divided between Pergamum and Rhodes. His Aetolian allies were reduced to vassalage and, in order to satisfy Eumenes, the consul Manlius Vulso crushed the Galatians. Manlius Vulso returned to Rome from this campaign with a rich haul of booty which, according to tradition, was the beginning of Roman luxury.

Meanwhile in the west the Romans continued to make conquests of capital importance. In northern Italy they subdued the Insubres of Milan in 197 B.C., the Boii of

Minerva, the Roman goddess of war. Her ancestor was the Greek Athene and she still wears the aegis with the Gorgon's head. This is a Roman statue in the Greek archaic style (first century B.C.). *Giraudon*

FARNACIS MAGISTER

ARASCANTUS

ISISGIMINIANA

RES

FEL

A Roman merchant vessel being loaded with grain. The demand for grain increased as Rome prospered, and imports became essential. In order that the trade might proceed peacefully Rome had to have command of the Mediterranean. *Anderson*

Bologna in 192 B.C. and in 187 B.C. the Cenomani. The founding of Aquileia at the top of the Adriatic in 181 B.C. gave them command over Venetia. Spain in 197 B.C. was divided into two provinces, and two more praetors were created to govern them.

Conquests in the Aegean

The Roman victories had not allayed the discontent in Greece. Philip V, in particular, remained suspect to Rome although he had lent his aid in the defeat of Antiochus. He was, in fact, renewing his treasury and rebuilding his army in preparation for revenge against Rome. After his death in 179 B.C. his son Perseus, by his intrigues in Illyria, Aetolia and Thessaly, and more especially by the support he gave to the revolutionary elements, precipitated the conflict. It ended with the destruction of his own army at Pydna in 168 B.C. Macedonia was divided into four republics and finally reduced in 148 B.C. to a Roman province. This war had distracted Rome's attention from the affairs of Asia. Seleucus IV Philopator (187-175 B.C.) had found it almost impossible to pay the indemnity which had been imposed on his father, and the oppressive taxes to which he was obliged to resort had roused violent opposition. But his brother and successor, Antiochus IV Epiphanes (175-164 B.C.), freed from this burden, was able to invade Egypt — which Rome forbade him to annex. In the west the pacification of northern Italy continued with the difficult task of subduing Liguria (185-170 B.C.). In Spain Roman expansion met with the resistance of the Iberian Celts, whom Sempronius Gracchus in 181-179 B.C. finally succeeded in pacifying by his humane behaviour. During the period of peace which followed colonisation progressed and prosperity, based on the exploitation of the Spanish silver mines, increased.

The fall of Macedonia left the Achaean League the principal power in Greece. In spite of its alliance with Rome relations between the two were strained. The cause of the contention was the fate of Sparta, and also the social policy of the League which, unlike Rome who supported established governments, had become revolutionary. Conflict broke out when in 147 B.C. Rome took Sparta from the League and also occupied other important strategic points. The Achaeans at once decided to reoccupy them. The disproportion between the two forces was too great, and in 146 B.C. the Achaeans were overwhelmed. Revolution then broke out in Corinth and the Roman consul Mummius razed the city to the ground. All enemies of Rome were slaughtered and Greece was reduced to a province. To impose her will on the remainder of the east, Rome had almost no need to intervene. Syria was torn by civil strife: when in 168 B.C. Antiochus Epiphanes attempted to introduce the cult of Zeus at Jerusalem and plunder the treasury of the Temple the Jews rose in revolt under the leadership of the Maccabees. Antiochus was incapable of suppressing the uprising and, with the support of Rome, Simon Maccabaeus obtained the recognition of Jewish independence in 141 B.C. His success was largely due to internal dissension within the Seleucid family. The fourth Antiochus had in fact usurped the throne, and after his death the constant struggles for power between his descendants and the descendants of Seleucus IV reduced the monarchy to impotence.

Formation of the province of Asia

There remained Rhodes and Pergamum to deal with. Rhodes had little to be pleased with in the attitude of Rome after the treaty of Apamea. Hence she had been

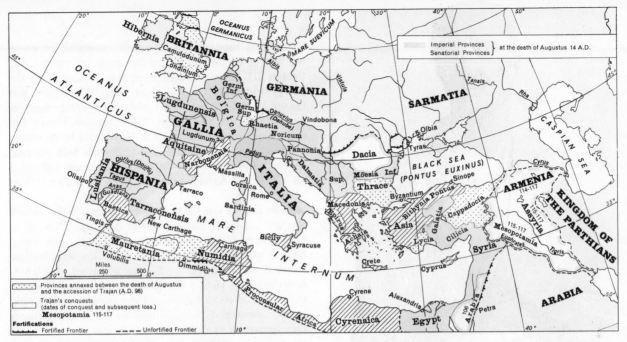

The Roman Empire under the Caesars

reluctant to lend aid to Rome during the war against Perseus. Her aloofness was now punished by the loss of her Asiatic empire, and even more severely in 168 B.C. by the transformation of Delos into a free port, which ruined her trade. The enfeeblement of her fleet gave free rein to Cretan piracy. Eumenes II (197-160 B.C.) of Pergamum had also shown little enthusiasm for the Roman cause, and was treated with suspicion. He was at least able to perfect the administration of his country, work for its prosperity and embellish its capital. Relations between Pergamum and Rome became less strained under Attalus II (160-139 B.C.). The outstanding act of his successor, Attalus III, who reigned between 139 and 133 B.C., was his last will and testament in which he bequeathed to Rome his domains and his treasures, and restored freedom to the Greek cities of his kingdom. At his death Aristonicus, a natural son of Eumenes II, roused the masses to revolt. It took the Romans two years (131-129 B.C.) to deal with the uprising and to organise the new province of Asia.

Having subdued the Po valley and Liguria, Rome advanced into the Alps, pushed eastwards towards Dalmatia in 157 B.C., and westwards towards Marseilles in 154 B.C. Finally, in the arduous campaigns of 143-140 B.C., she forged northwards and seized the gold mines of the Salassi. In Spain peace was broken in 154 B.C. by a renewal of hostilities against the Iberian Celts and the conquest of Lusitania, where resistance was led by the guerilla chief Viriathus (147-139 B.C.). In the course of these battles the Roman troops commanded by incapable generals were frequently routed, and operations had to be put under the command of Scipio Aemilianus. In 133 B.C. he captured the city of Numantia, and native resistance finally ceased.

The Third Punic War

By the Treaty of Tunis, Carthage had been forbidden to wage war without the permission of Rome. Though her trade had been ruined, Carthage had compensated for its loss by scientifically exploiting her agricultural riches and regained much of her former prosperity. But the king of Numidia, Masinissa continually encroached on her territory, which was tolerated by Rome though less well supported by Carthage. By 150 B.C. her patience was exhausted and she decided to fight. Masinissa defied her and demanded a tribute. Rome became uneasy at the growing power of her Numidian protégé and landed an army in Africa. Treacherously the commander first demanded that both sides lay down their arms, then ordered the Carthaginians to withdraw within their own frontiers. A wave of patriotic emotion swept through Carthage at the sight of her traditional enemy, and she defended herself heroically though without hope during a siege which lasted three years. In 146 B.C. Scipio Aemilianus carried the city by assault, utterly destroyed it, sold its population into slavery and laid a solemn curse on the very ground it was built on. The remaining Carthaginian territory was turned into a Roman province.

The decline of the Senate

The senate's skill, courage and success in the conduct of the Second Punic War had earned it incomparable prestige, and in gratitude the people of Rome had left the full direction of the government in its hands. They had allowed the senate to strengthen its position by encroaching on the prerogatives of the *comitia*, while at the same time it protected itself against the personal ambitions of its own members. The institution of commissions of inquiry, and then of *quaestiones perpetuae* — permanent juries composed of senators — limited the jurisdiction of the popular assemblies. Towards 149 B.C. the people's tribunes received the right to enter the senate. The position of the magistrates was weakened: the *lex Villia annalis* of 180 B.C. had regulated the *cursus honorum* in a manner calculated to frustrate the ambitions of young aristocrats, while in 151 B.C. a consul was by law forbidden to serve more than one term of office. The dictatorship had, since 202 B.C., practically disappeared. Though united in a desire to increase their privileges, the nobles were split into rival coteries. Scipio Africanus, who affected the airs of a ruling sovereign, clashed with Cato, a farmer-soldier who defended the traditional virtues.

Marius (156-86 B.C.), a Roman consul and leader of the popular party. Under his guidance the army was opened to the poor; it therefore became a popular army, unswervingly loyal to its general and a formidable political and military weapon. *Giraudon*

Cato finally brought about his rival's downfall by accusing him of corruption during the campaign against Antiochus III. Scipio refused to appear in answer to the charge and in 183 B.C. died in exile. When Cato was censor in 184-183 B.C., he introduced spiteful measures against the rich, and enforced laws against luxury and corruption. But the adherents of Scipio were by no means exterminated. His party regained influence with the censor Gracchus, a son-in-law of Scipio Africanus, and above all with Scipio Aemilianus whose career was a succession of illegal acts.

More serious was the upheaval in Roman society which war and conquest had brought in their train. The peasantry was rapidly falling into decay, while the urban proletariat was swelled by oriental freedmen who had no attachments or loyalty to Roman traditions. The enormous spoils of victory corrupted the senators, who gave themselves over to luxury and debauchery and systematically plundered the provinces to repair the fortunes they constantly ran through. On many occasions the senate was obliged to summon up the courage to condemn provincial governors who had been guilty of extortion and misappropriation. The moneyed class, the knights enriched by war plunder and the exploitation of conquered lands, became more and more influential. Towards the end of the third century they were powerful enough to save one of their own members from the course of justice. In 158 B.C. they compelled the senate to reopen the mines of Pangaea closed since the battle of Pydna.

On the intellectual plane Hellenistic ideas spread throughout the Roman world. The monuments which began to spring up everywhere in Rome followed her contact with the Orient. The first masterpieces of her literature were produced in imitation of Greek models. Such were the comedies of Plautus and Terence, and the epic poems of Ennius; Cato's prose style, too, deserves mention. The influence of Hellenistic law made Roman judicial procedure more flexible, and by introducing the concept of equity helped to humanise jurisprudence. But the adoption of oriental religious and philosophic conceptions by minds unprepared to digest them tended to destroy traditional morality. Irreverence undermined the foundations of the national religion, and charlatanism took its place. How widespread the decadence had become was revealed in 186 B.C. by the scandal of the Bacchanalia, orgies in which members of the best society were compromised. The imposition of stricter laws had not the least effect and the evil continued to worsen, giving free rein to the ambitions of the powerful and the lowest appetites of the depraved.

This dangerous development led finally to the downfall of the regime. The first crisis was provoked by the agrarian question. Altered social and economic conditions had made it impossible for the peasant class to make a living off the land. The cultivation of grain was endangered by the importation of foreign wheat, which was much cheaper. In order to survive the farmer was obliged to concentrate on grazing or the cultivation of fruit; but for this purpose capital and workmen were required, which only the rich possessed. The rich, by the payment of modest rentals, had meanwhile cornered the land belonging to the State which they worked with gangs of slaves, while at the same time they put pressure on the small proprietor in order to evict him.

In addition, colonial expansion had been stopped since 177 B.C., which further aggravated the peasant crisis.

The Gracchi

Certain members of the nobility were well aware of the danger. Even a close friend of Scipio Aemilianus, Laelius, had proposed to present an agrarian measure to curtail the right of the rich to occupy the public lands. But the first to take action was Tiberius Gracchus. Elected tribune for the year 133 B.C., he proposed a bill limiting the extent of public land — *ager publicus* — which one man could occupy to roughly three hundred acres, with additional land for every son. The land thus freed was to revert to the State and be allotted in smaller parcels to citizens without resources. Tiberius Gracchus, who was descended from an illustrious family, at first found some support in the senate. But his self-will and determination, fostered by his stoic philosophy, soon roused enmity and led him to overcome opposition by violence and unlawful acts. He had his fellow tribune, who had vetoed his bill, deposed. He had his father-in-law and his brother elected to the triumvirate in charge of the recovery of the public lands. He defied the growing opposition by illegally seeking re-election for the following term. He was beaten and, during a riot which the nobles had stirred up against him, murdered.

His policy, however, did not die with him, and ten years later his brother Caius was elected tribune. In Caius the senate was to encounter a more dangerous adversary. Here the burning passion of Tiberius was tempered by a much more subtle grasp of political reality. He realised that to fight the enemies of his brother's agrarian laws he must form a coalition with all the other elements in the city, and he set about winning their support by a remarkable series of reforms. To the equestrian order, the knights, he gave greater judicial powers, and the right to collect the taxes in Asia. To the urban worker he supplied bread at a lower price, by means of laws regulating the price of wheat. The Italians had been excluded from the benefits of Tiberius' law and would even have suffered by it, since many of them occupied public lands. Caius proposed to give full Roman citizenship to the Latins and the privileges of the *latinium* to the other allies. Finally the rural population was promised not only the allotments offered by the original bill but the renewal of colonisation.

The senate was at first dumbfounded by these proposals. Then, to impair Caius' popularity, they countered by an even more exaggeratedly popular programme. They fanned the people's outraged egotism at the thought of granting citizenship to the Italians, and at last accused Caius of having violated the solemn curse which weighed upon the territory of Carthage by planting a colony there. Again, an opportune riot allowed the senatorial party to massacre Caius in 121 B.C., together with some thousands of his supporters.

Marius and the popular party

The victory of the reactionary party was, however, soon to be nullified by events abroad. Senatorial diplomacy was at first sufficiently successful. The Balearic Isles were occupied in 123 B.C., and in response to an appeal from Marseilles, which was threatened by the Salyes, a powerful Ligurian tribe, the conquest of Mediterranean Gaul was undertaken. Within three years — 125 to 122 B.C. — the Salyes were subjugated and the event was marked by the founding of Aix-en-Provence. The hostility of the independent Celts, notably of the Arverni, was overcome and Languedoc up to the Pyrenees was annexed (122-118 B.C.). Narbonne, the first Roman colony outside the Italian peninsula, became the capital of the new province.

But the situation in Africa had worsened. In 118 B.C. on the death of Micipsa, son and successor of Masinissa, the kingdom of Numidia was seized by Jugurtha, who massacred the Roman community at Cirta. After a semblance of punitive operations on the part of Rome, Jugurtha obtained peace in 111 B.C. by bribing Roman senators. When this scandal was known the senate was forced to send out an energetic general, Metellus, who in two years — 109 to 107 B.C. — succeeded in forcing Jugurtha to take refuge with the king of Mauretania. But the people of Rome found the progress of the war too slow, and in 108 B.C. the popular assembly had one of their own officers, Marius, elected consul. Hoping to corrupt him the senate gave Marius authority to raise men and money. Marius avoided the pitfall by enrolling the poor, who in theory were excluded from the army. The importance of this innovation cannot be over-estimated, for its consequence was that the Roman army became a professional army, devoted solely to its chief, willing to execute all his orders and capable, as it will soon appear, of fighting against Rome herself. For the moment, however, Rome was justified in the hopes she placed in Marius: in 105 B.C. he brought the war to a speedy conclusion and returned to Rome with Jugurtha in chains.

Other external events contributed to the downfall of the senate's prestige. Since the middle of the second century central Europe had been agitated by vast migratory movements of barbarian tribes. A Celtic tribe, the Scordisci, had invaded Thrace in 135 B.C. and sacked Delphi in 114 B.C. It required four years of campaigning (112-108 B.C.) to drive them out of Greece. Farther west the Cimbri and the Teutoni, Germanic tribes, invaded Noricum and in 113 B.C. inflicted a disastrous defeat on the Romans. Then in 109 B.C. they crossed the Rhine and marched on Aquitania. Servilius Caepio, chief of the senatorial party, had been sent out to punish the Volcae

A Roman legionary in combat with a barbarian. The Roman is distinguishable by the finely worked helmet. The legions included light cavalry and heavy infantry, the latter made up of Roman citizens and forming the backbone of the army.

Tectosages who were besieging Toulouse. He defeated them in 106 B.C., in the process appropriating enormous booty, but in the following year was overwhelmed at Orange by the Germanic invasion of Italy. Marius and his army were recalled in haste from Africa, and Marius held the consulship uninterruptedly from 104 to 100 B.C. His election was a violation of the law, but it seemed justified by his success against the barbarians who committed the imprudence of dividing their forces: the Teutoni were crushed in 102 B.C. at Aix-en-Provence, and the Cimbri were slaughtered in 101 B.C. at Vercellae.

Under the leadership of Marius the popular party was all-powerful in Rome. But Marius was no politician. He allowed himself to be led by two demagogues, Saturninus and Glaucia, who forced through by violence a series of laws to destroy the authority of the senate: agrarian laws rewarding the veterans of Marius' army, a corn law doling out bread to the populace, a law which turned the tribunals over to the knights, a law of lese-majesté aimed to protect the demagogues themselves and enable them to strike down their enemies on the slightest provocation. But as matters went from bad to worse, the senate summoned the consuls to repress the demagogues. Marius, complying with the summons, permitted his former allies to be slain and in the year 100 B.C. retired in disgrace.

The Social War

The victorious party did not remain united. The Roman world at this period was sharply class-divided. The equestrian order broke away from the senators and the senators were unable to support the tribune Livius Drusus. Though himself an aristocrat, Livius Drusus was a demagogue whose tactics were to offer Roman citizenship to the allied Italian cities — the *socii*. The assassination of Drusus in 91 turned popular discontent to savage war, the Social War — between Rome and her allies in Italy. Local loyalties were strong and active, especially among the backward peoples of the Apennines. Two tribes, the Marsi in the north and the Samnites in the south, rallied the other *socii* against Rome. In the year 90 B.C. the city itself was encircled and appeared to be at the mercy of the insurgents. The gravity of the situation was overcome only by Rome's tardy concession of political rights: in 90 B.C. the *lex Julia* offered Roman citizenship to those allies who were willing to lay down their arms. In the following year the *lex Plautia Papiria* granted similar rights to all individuals who applied for them. Social tension was eased by these concessions but only temporarily. Within a year skilful manoeuvring of the *comitia tributa* was cheating the new electorate of its full power.

The Colossus of Rhodes, an enormous bronze statue of the Roman sun-god Helios, by the sculptor Chares of Lindus, a disciple of Lysippus. It was one of the Seven Wonders of the World and was destroyed by earthquake in 224 B.C. In the sixteenth century it was believed that the statue had straddled the entrance to the harbour, as in this engraving.

184

Mithridates, King of Pontus

These internal crises had increased the dangers which threatened Rome in the East. The kingdom of Pontus, to the south of the Black Sea, one of the native principalities which had arisen in the beginning of the third century during the struggles between the heirs of Alexander, had become a power to be reckoned with under Mithridates Eupator. Mithridates had in 107 B.C. annexed the Greek cities of the Cimmerian Bosphorus — which unites the sea of Azov with the Black Sea — and firmly organised his conquests. His ambitions then turned towards Anatolia where, about seven years later, he fought the Bithynians for possession of Cappadocia. Rome, however, protected the independence of Cappadocia. Mithridates then made an alliance with Tigranes, king of Armenia, and resumed his career of conquest. Sulla, governor of Cilicia which had been annexed by Rome between 102 and 100 B.C. in order to stamp out piracy, repulsed Mithridates in 92 B.C. Mithridates realised that he could not carry out his plans without first expelling Rome from Asia. He seized the opportunity given him by the crisis which occurred in Bithynia on the death of Nicomedes II. In 90 B.C. Mithridates intervened on behalf of his own claimant to the throne, and in 88 B.C. slaughtered all the Italians in Asia as well as those on Delos. He thus assumed the role of liberator of the Greeks and leader of the social revolution.

The choice of a general to conduct the subsequent war was the cause of new upheavals in Rome. Marius succeeded in having the command given to himself, but it was also coveted by his former lieutenant, Sulla, whose brilliant success during the Social War had resulted in his being elected consul. Sulla, at the head of his army, marched on Rome, entered the city and, when he had put Marius to flight, forced the terrorised population to give him command of the campaign. His departure for Asia left the field free to his enemies: Marius, who died almost immediately afterwards in 86 B.C., and Cinna. Cinna butchered all Sulla's partisans in the senate, distributed their property and assumed the consulship. Meanwhile Sulla had captured and sacked Athens, which had been allied to Mithridates, and twice defeated the enemy. But he was threatened by forces which the popular party in Rome had itself sent to the East. He therefore hastened to make peace with Mithridates which, in 85 B.C., left him free to deal with the situation at home. Having first extorted an indemnity of twenty thousand talents from the Greek cities of Asia, he re-embarked for Italy in the spring of 83 B.C. He was joined by the leading Roman nobles, but he had to fight his way back to Rome. It was only at the end of 82 B.C. that he entered the city as a conqueror. In the rest of Italy the rebellion continued for another year. Africa too had risen and was not reconquered by Pompey until 80 B.C. Spain, rising in revolt under Sertorius, resisted until 72 B.C.

Decadence of the Hellenistic monarchies

In the meanwhile what was left of the two last Hellenistic monarchies had fallen into complete decay. In Egypt the degeneration of the Ptolemaic dynasty had produced sovereigns who were depraved, incapable and criminal. By their palace intrigues the queens of Egypt only aggra-

Mithridates Eupator (120-63 B.C.), King of Pontus. At a time when Rome itself was torn by rival parties under Sulla, Marius and Cinna, Mithridates threatened the eastern Empire by seizing the Greek cities of the Cimmerian Bosphorus and posing as the liberator of Greeks in Anatolia. Sulla defeated him, but was forced to make peace and return home to quell an uprising.

vated disorders born of quarrels between rival pretenders to the throne, while the seditious population of Alexandria rose in frequent revolt against their infamous rulers and, on occasion, massacred them. Egypt nonetheless attempted to meddle in the convulsions which shook the Seleucid kingdom which was also rapidly sinking into anarchy as the two branches of the royal family fought for ascendancy. The Seleucids still produced a few energetic sovereigns, but their efforts were fruitless: Egypt encouraged and supported usurpers of the throne and even directly attacked Coele-Syria. The Jewish kingdom became constantly stronger, in spite of the opposition of the Hellenised ruling family and of the Pharisees. Native principalities, such as Commagene and Osroene, gained their independence.

Central Asia in the second century

The paralysis of the Seleucid empire facilitated the expansion of the Parthians. Antiochus III had once driven them back, but under their king Mithridates I (174-136 B.C.) the Parthians resumed their conquests. Mithridates conquered Media and Persia, and in 145 B.C. seized

Soldiers attacking a fort in *testudo* (tortoise) formation. The attackers would lock their shields together and thus protected from missiles hurled by the besieged would mount each others' shoulders and scale the wall. The Romans used the *testudo* with great success. *Mansell*

Seleucia on the Tigris, which he made his capital. Parthian power, however, suffered an eclipse during the migratory movements which at this time disturbed the peace of central Asia. They rose again to importance under Mithridates II (123-86 B.C. approximately) who imposed his protectorate on Armenia and in 88 B.C. invaded Syria.

He was forced to withdraw, however, at Sulla's ultimatum, and his death was followed by some years of anarchy.

The eastern satrapies of the Seleucid empire regained their independence by the inevitable force of circumstance, though details of how this came about are lacking. The last of the Maurya sovereigns was assassinated by one of his officers who towards 184 B.C. founded the Sunga dynasty. His authority scarcely extended beyond Magadha, and the rest of India was divided between local princes. Demetrius of Bactria, successor of Euthydemus, profited by Indian disunity to extend his dominion to Gandhara and the Punjab. At the same period two other Greek conquerors, Menander and Apollodotus, who were perhaps lieutenants of Demetrius, were active in India. Menander is thought to have led his troops as far as Magadha, while Apollodotus penetrated beyond the lower Indus. Towards 168 B.C. Demetrius was menaced by the attack of another Greek leader, Eucratidas, who took east-

ern Persia from him, while Menander made himself independent in the Punjab but lost Magadha.

The existence of these Graeco-Indian kingdoms was brief. Towards 160 B.C. the Parthians deprived Eucratidas of his western possessions. But the chief cause of their disappearance was the upheaval in central Asia and the racial chaos which resulted from the overflow of migratory peoples. Driven from Mongolia by the Huns, the Yueh-chi towards 175 B.C. crossed Turkestan and occupied Sogdiana and Bactria towards 130 B.C. Other tribes accompanied them, among whom the Sacae, Scythian nomads, imperilled the very existence of the kingdom of Parthia. They settled in the region of Seistan, in eastern Persia and south-west Afghanistan, where Mithridates II finally brought them under Parthian authority.

The China of Wu Ti

The reign of Liu Pang, who attained power in 221 B.C. and took the imperial name of Kao Ti (202-195 B.C.), and the reigns of his first successors though so decisive in Chinese history were beset with difficulties. Though he established the centralised Han empire, Liu Pang had been obliged to allow a partial revival of feudalism in order to reward military chieftains who had helped him

to gain power. He was forced to recognise the virtual
independence of Canton and the region it occupied.
Above all, the Huns were beginning to become extremely
dangerous. They had already invaded Shansi in 201 B.C.
After they had driven the Yueh-chi from Mongolia towards the west their raids on China became more frequent. But some decades later they came up against the
great emperor Wu Ti (140-87 B.C.). Wu Ti began his
reign by reducing the feudal nobility to functions of a
purely honorary nature, while, like Liu Pang, he reconciled the learned class to the regime by confiding the
administration to its members. He then attempted to encircle the Huns by forming an alliance with the Yueh-
chi. When this move proved unsuccessful he attacked
them head on, entrusting the armies of China to a group
of able generals. Over and over again the Chinese forces
penetrated into Mongolia, slaughtered large numbers of
the barbarians, and even pushed as far as the Ferghana
range, while military encampments were established along
the frontiers to maintain security. A certain number of
humiliating setbacks during the early years of the first
century did little to arrest this progress. Wu Ti completed his successful work by extending imperial authority towards the south: in 138 B.C. the king of Tunghai
(in Chou-kiang) became his vassal; three years later the
king of Min-yu in Fukien submitted to his overlordship.
Canton was taken in 111 B.C. and all the kingdom of
Nan-yu, which included Tonkin, was annexed.

A young Negro slave in a Roman household. Slavery was an
integral part of the social structure of Imperial Rome; it was of
a domestic not 'plantation' kind. *British Museum*

A statue of Roman origin showing Greek influence. *British
Museum*.

A bronze head of Caesar (100-44 B.C.), from Egypt. In spite of
numerous foreign campaigns and struggles against his rival,
Pompey, Caesar found time to overhaul Roman government,
redistribute land, and found colonies. *Archiv für Kunst und
Geschichte*

187

Part of the 'Ludovisi' sarcophagus, showing a battle between the Romans and the Gauls. Julius Caesar had gradually extended his control of Gaul and by 57 B.C. had reached Belgium. In 53 B.C. however, Vercingetorix, a young Arverni chieftain, rallied the Gauls and defeated Caesar near Clermont-Ferrand, but his success ended when the Romans trapped him in the town of Alesia; his fate was to be led as a prisoner in Caesar's triumphal procession in Rome. Gallic resistance was finally crushed in the years 51-50 B.C. *Mansell*

CHAPTER TEN

THE AGE OF CAESAR

81-31 B.C.

The triumph of Sulla was a vital moment in the decay of the Roman republic. For the first time the traditional constitution was not only violated but legally abolished, and a mandate to reconstruct the State was given to a single man with absolute power. The attempt did not succeed, but it inspired others and in the end led to the Empire. From the beginning of the first century the future government of Rome was an open question.

Sulla's dictatorship

At the end of the year 82 B.C. Sulla was master of Rome. By a law forced through the terrorised assemblies he had himself made dictator for life with discretionary powers. These he first employed to dispose of all his enemies: official lists were drawn up which made them outlaws. They could be killed without trial and their murderers were given a reward. The principal victims of these hideous proscriptions were equestrians, and the slaughter continued for nearly a year. Sulla in the meanwhile redrafted the constitution. He doubled the number of senators and increased both their legislative and judicial powers. So that a sufficient supply of senators would be automatically available he raised the number of praetors to eight and of the quaestors to twenty. The people's tribunes were silenced. The government of the provinces was reorganised. Since the number of curule magistrates was henceforth equal to the number of provinces, consuls and praetors had to serve one year's term of office at home and the year following administer a province. Local government in Italy, which had not been regularised since the Social War, was based on autonomy accorded to the municipia. A criminal code was drawn up and specialised permanent tribunals were instituted. Finally Sulla attempted to introduce religious and moral reforms, though without great success.

His authority, which he surrounded with monarchical splendour and sought to dignify with the aura of religious prestige, appeared to be unshakable. He was further strengthened by the veterans of his army who were provided for on the senatorial domains of the Campagna, and by the support of 10,000 former slaves of his liquidated opponents to whom he had granted freedom. But Sulla had not won over the lesser nobility to his cause. And then the scandal caused by the fact that certain of his close friends had personally profited by the proscriptions reflected on himself, Placed by the senate in the dilemma of obeying his own laws or of breaking resistance to his will by force, in 79 B.C. he chose to abdicate. This strange character, cynical, violent and pleasure loving, but at the same time a brilliant soldier, a subtle politician and a sound legislator, has remained an enigma to this day. It may be that Sulla's

189

ambition was to make himself king of Rome. In any case when, after a brief period of dictatorship, he retired to private life he restored power to the senatorial oligarchy.

Restoration of the Senate

The authority of the senate was, however, precarious. Scarcely a year later Lepidus, one of the consuls, attempted to retain his power by a revolution, and when this failed he raised the standard of insurrection in 77 B.C. in Etruria. He was defeated and fled to Spain which, since the year 80 B.C. had been held by Sertorius, a partisan of Marius. Sertorius was a curious individual who seems to have dreamed of erecting the grandeur of Italy on the ruins of Rome. In 76 B.C. he had succeeded in driving an army which Sulla had sent against him out of Spain. Four years later, however, Pompey came to Spain and finally reconquered it. Meanwhile the senate was occupied in quelling a savage uprising of slaves who ravaged southern Italy and Sicily. To suppress it Crassus (73-71 B.C.) required no fewer than ten Roman legions, who put an end to the rebellion by brutal and wholesale massacres.

But the senate encountered its gravest difficulties in the East. In spite of the conquest of Pamphylia between 78 and 75 B.C., piracy was still rampant in the eastern Mediterranean. Then the question of Bithynia, bequeathed to the people of Rome but seized by Mithridates in 74 B.C., led to a renewal of war. In a series of brilliant engagements the consul Lucullus defeated Mithridates and drove him back into Pontus. Then in three years, 74 to 71 B.C., Lucullus conquered Pontus and attacked Armenia, where Mithridates' son-in-law, Tigranes, had, at the expense of the Parthians, carved out a powerful state extending to Media and northern Mesopotamia. But the harshness of Lucullus and the hostility of the equestrian order, whose opportunities for enrichment he attempted to limit, led in 68 B.C. to the revolt of his army and the loss of his conquests.

Pompey and the First Triumvirate

This setback, together with the failure of Marcus Antonius against the pirates of Crete in 71 B.C., and the scandal of the action against Verres, the corrupt praetor of Sicily, hastened the downfall of senatorial government. The tribunes regained their former powers and the knights resumed their place in the tribunals. In the year 70 B.C. Pompey and Crassus were elected consuls in defiance of the senate. The dangerous situation in the East again called for military action. To stamp out the continuing menace of piracy the *lex Gabinia* in 67 B.C. conferred on Pompey exceptional powers of command; it was said that he took only 40 days to fulfil his task. Another law was at once passed, the *lex Manilia*, which in 66 B.C. gave him command of the war against Mithridates. He employed his forces in a general conquest of the Orient. He crushed Tigranes and in 65 B.C. advanced to the Caucasus. He then marched into Syria, dethroned the Seleucids in 64 B.C. and annexed their kingdom. In 63 B.C. he imposed a Roman protectorate over the Jews and invaded the Arab kingdom of Petra.

When in 62 B.C. he returned to Italy the Republic was in the throes of the bitterest party strife. Caesar, who had

Augustus, originally called Gaius Octavius (63 B.C.-A.D. 14), the first of the Roman Emperors. While Antony was occupied with the eastern half of the Empire, Augustus strengthened his hold on the west and made the frontiers safe. He defeated Antony at Actium in 31 B.C., and was given the title 'Augustus' in recognition of his services to Rome. *Archiv für Kunst und Geschichte*

been elected aedile in 65 B.C., had reorganised the popular party. Catiline, a renegade patrician, had rallied all the dissatisfied and undesirable elements of society in preparation for revolution. His conspiracy was foiled by Cicero, who was consul in 63 B.C., but Cicero was unable to remedy the social evils. The senate, instead of gratefully welcoming the return of the victorious Pompey, who would doubtless have put his services at its disposal, refused to approve his arrangements in Asia Minor and rebuffed his request for a grant of land for his troops. Pompey therefore came to an understanding in 60 B.C. with two other ambitious men, Crassus and Julius Caesar, and the three — the first triumvirate — planned to share the empire among themselves. As a result of their co-operation Caesar was elected consul for the year 59 B.C. He ratified Pompey's arrangements in Asia, passed measures to the financial advantage of revenue collectors, of whom Crassus was the chief, and himself received the governorship of Illyricum and of both Gauls, Cisalpine and Transalpine, for five years. Before he left Rome he took the precaution of having Clodius elected tribune. Clodius was a rabble-rouser whose acts of violence paralysed the senate. Clodius, forgetting that he owed his position to the triumvirate, fell foul of Pompey who met Caesar at Luca in 56 B.C., where the triumvirate was reaffirmed. Caesar obtained a five-year prolongation of his command, while Pompey was given Spain, and Crassus Syria. This agreement allowed Caesar to accomplish the conquest of Gaul, and at the same time determined the future destiny of Rome and the Republic.

Gaul before the Roman conquest

The territory of Gaul extended in the east to the banks of the Rhine and supported a population of perhaps fifteen million people of very diverse racial stock. The aboriginal tribes were doubtless related to the Ligurians and the Iberians. They were overrun during the course of the first millennium by a large influx of Celts coming from the south of Germany who finally constituted the dominant element. The Celts had arrived in several distinct waves, the first appearing perhaps before the year 1000 B.C. After that date they pushed as far southwards as the borders of Provence and Aquitania, which regions they had conquered in a final advance towards the sixth century. The lands which they had left vacant in the north were then filled by a new wave of barbarians, the Belgae, whose coming was contemporary with the great migratory movements which between the fifth and third centuries brought other Celtic tribes into Asia Minor. Already fresh invaders, Germanic peoples, threatened to follow. By 113 B.C. the Cimbri and the Teutoni had penetrated Gaul and spread terror and ruin throughout the country, until in 102 B.C. Marius annihilated them near Aix. From that year the Mediterranean region lost its independence; for Rome, anxious to ensure her overland line of communications with Spain, had between 125 B.C. and 118 B.C. annexed and organised it into a new province. Rome had taken under her protection the Greek maritime colonies which Marseilles, since her own foundation at the beginning of the sixth century, had scattered from the Pyrenees to the Alps. The civilising influence of these colonies was out of all proportion to their modest numerical importance.

These circumstances and the physical nature of the new province explained its lack of unity. Provence was far from being Romanised, and its climate, Greek background, and its maritime commercial activity gave it a character of its own. In the south-west, between the Garonne and the Pyrenees, Celtic settlement was sparser, and the affinity between the population and the neighbouring peoples of Spain was close. In the north-east, as far down as the Seine, the new-comers, the Belgae, differed from the other Celts in certain physical traits and in their lesser degree of civilisation. The land of the Gauls was pre-eminently the centre of France. Here political division was the rule, and independent peoples abounded. Most of them, however, tended to gravitate towards certain more powerful tribes which fought interminably among themselves for leadership, or made war against each other in unstable alliances. Social conditions were no less troubled. Power was in the hands of an aristocracy with a strong sense of family solidarity, but the various leading families were themselves in a state of constant rivalry. They united only in order to destroy ambitious members of their ranks who attempted to seize absolute power. They were supported by a large personal following and imposed their authority on a plebeian class whose position was not far from servitude.

The civilisation of the Gauls themselves, if not yet in full flower, was rich in promise. Founded on an agriculture which was sufficiently prosperous to feed a population of a density exceptional in antiquity, the Gauls revealed rare technical aptitudes from which the Romans later profited. They were skilled in metal work and taught

A statue of Mars, the god of war, wearing the helmet and cuirass of the Roman soldier. Many Greek gods found their way into Roman mythology, and Mars has an ancestor in the Greek Ares. He was the most important of the Roman gods, firstly because he was believed to be the father of Romulus, founder of Rome, and secondly because he was the god of war, and therefore a symbol of the ambition and soldierly duty of every Roman.

their conquerors the use of a great many iron implements. They used the wheeled plough and the reaper. They were also masters in the art of carpentry and waggon building. They introduced and spread the fashion of trousers or breeches, of the cape and the hood. Their cobblers fashioned the galosh (*gallica*) or wooden clog. Their art, too, bears witness to qualities which Mediterranean influence could have ripened and disciplined, had it had the time to reach maturity. In the religion of the Gauls we find the profusion of divinities common to all agrarian cults, but it was distinguished by the existence of a clergy, the druids, drawn from the nobility, whose political and social influence was profound at the time of Caesar.

Caesar's conquest of Gaul

When Caesar left Rome after his consulship he had planned to go to Illyricum, but the Germanic threat drew him towards the west. The tribe of the Suevi had crossed the Rhine at the invitation of one group of little peoples then fighting for hegemony in Gaul. The Arverni and the Sequani, whose hostility had been fired by social strife and the problem of relations with Rome, had had the imprudence to call in the aid of Ariovistus, the Suevian chief, in their war against the Aedui who were allies of Rome. Ariovistus installed himself in Alsace and planned to seize the territory of the Helvetii, who asked for Roman authorisation to proceed to Provence. Caesar refused their request and drove them back into their own country. Next, in 58 B.C., in response to the appeal of the Aedui he attacked Ariovistus and drove him back into Germany. Then, ignoring the pretext which had brought him to Gaul, Caesar began step by step to extend his authority: in 57 B.C. he reached Belgium, in 56 B.C. he held the Atlantic coastline. His reconnaissance forces next penetrated into Britain, and Germany, and the Gauls began to feel increasingly uneasy. Several revolts broke out in Belgium. In 52 B.C., encouraged perhaps by Caesar's enemies in Rome, the entire country rallied to the standard of a redoubtable young Arverni chieftain, Vercingetorix, who succeeded in uniting all the tribes under his command. Caesar was defeated at Gergovia near Clermont-Ferrand, and might quite possibly have been compelled to evacuate the territory he had won had he not succeeded in trapping Vercingetorix in Alesia. Caesar besieged the town so effectively that no relieving forces were able to get through to Vercingetorix. After the fall of Alesia, Caesar, in the two years of 51 to 50 B.C., brought all further Gallic resistance to an end.

The break-up of the Triumvirate

At the other extremity of the Mediterranean world Crassus, who like Caesar was in search of glory and profit, suffered a very different fate. After the death of their king, Mithridates II, the Parthians again sank to secondary importance while Tigranes of Armenia reaped the benefit. The Parthians therefore made an alliance with Pompey against Tigranes and were thus enabled to reoccupy Mesopotamia. But a dynastic quarrel broke out among them which the Romans sought to use in order to weaken the kingdom. Against the royal claimant Orodes, the Romans supported Mithridates III. Crassus, on arrival in Syria, organised a vast expedition to conquer Mesopotamia. He very rashly engaged the Parthians in the steppes of Osroene and his army was decimated by the enemy's elusive cavalry. In 53 B.C. at Carrhae (Haran) his troops were overwhelmed and Crassus himself was assassinated while negotiating a treaty.

The death of Crassus left Caesar and Pompey in direct and open opposition. Good feeling between the two men had until this time been maintained by the circumstance that Julia, Caesar's daughter, was Pompey's wife. Her death, and the death of Crassus, together with troubles in Rome arising from the gang murder of Clodius by Milo, disrupted their friendship. To suppress the riots in Rome the senate had in 52 B.C. been obliged to name Pompey sole consul with powers which went to his head. The pretext of the definite rupture between Pompey and Caesar was the question of Caesar's recall. Caesar claimed the right to retain his proconsular powers and his army until the moment when he could run again for election as consul, ten years after he had first held that office. By removing him from his command before its legal term had expired the senate virtually delivered Caesar to the mercy of Pompey, who still retained the government and army of Spain. During the year 50 B.C. Caesar negotiated with his senatorial opponents. He obtained nothing by this means, and with his army in the beginning of 49 B.C. he crossed the Rubicon, which marked the frontier between his province and Italy itself. The act was tantamount to a declaration of war against the Republic.

Caesar's struggle for power

Pompey and many of the senators abandoned Italy to Caesar and embarked for the East. Before pursuing them Caesar turned towards Spain where at Ilerda he destroyed the army loyal to Pompey. He then returned to Italy in 49 B.C., but on the way subdued Marseilles which had declared its neutrality. The following year he crossed the Adriatic. Although Pompey was master of the sea he failed to make use of his advantage and Caesar met him at Pharsalus. There Pompey was overwhelmingly defeated and fled for refuge to Egypt. Caesar followed him but when he reached Egypt Pompey had just been murdered by the Egyptians. Caesar attempted to punish the authors of this crime, but the Alexandrians rose in revolt and blockaded him in the royal palace where, in danger of his life, he was a prisoner until the spring of 47 B.C. In the meanwhile Pharnaces, son of Mithridates, had reoccupied Pontus. Caesar, marching from Egypt, inflicted a shattering defeat on Pharnaces, briefly conveying the results of his campaign in the celebrated despatch sent to the Senate: *Veni, vidi, vici* (I came, I saw, I conquered).

Italy and Rome were in the throes of the gravest social disturbances. The burning question of debts had been cunningly exploited by agitators like Caelius in 48 B.C. and Dolabella in 47 B.C. to rouse the population to a frenzy of rebellious fury. The senate, dominated by the members Caesar had nominated in 49 B.C., met the situation by now creating him dictator, with Mark Antony as commander of the cavalry. The insurgents were

The Colosseum, Rome. Once the stage for impressive gladiatorial displays, it became a fortress in the sixth century. *Cash*

crushed; but a revolt had also broken out in Campagna among the legions brought back to Italy after the battle of Pharsalus. Caesar, elected consul for five years, re-established peace, but was obliged at once to sail for Africa where an army loyal to the cause of Pompey had been collected. After a hard-fought campaign, Caesar crushed it at Thapsus in the spring of 46 B.C. He returned to Italy where the senate conferred upon him the office of consul and dictator for ten years. His stay in Rome was then interrupted by a final attempt by the partisans of Pompey, this time in Spain. Caesar arrived in Spain at the end of 46 B.C. and slaughtered his enemies at Munda in 45 B.C.

Caesar's reforms

The periods of tranquillity between the trials and hard-ships of these successive campaigns had been few and brief, yet during them Caesar found time to overhaul the machinery of Roman government completely. The senate had been rejuvenated by an infusion of new members from the provinces and by soldiers with distinguished records. The number of senators was raised to nine hundred, and those drawn from the ancient noble families found themselves outnumbered. As a body the senate's functions were greatly curtailed. The right to declare war or make peace now belonged to the dictator, who also entrusted the treasury to prefects he nominated himself and minted money with his own effigy. The composition of the tribunals was modified to the advantage of the senate, but Caesar himself judged important cases, while on his own authority he issued edicts which relieved him of the duty of consulting the public assembly. The power of the magistrates was weakened and the number of praetors and quaestors doubled. The system of consulship was left unaltered, but in the course of the years consuls were often replaced by substitutes — *suffecti* — and on two occasions consular elections did not take place at all. Instead Caesar nominated prefects. But he went through the motions of submitting his laws to the vote of the popular assemblies and kept the populace happy by providing sumptuous feasts and entertainments. He had no intention, however, of allowing demagogy to revive: public meetings required previous authorisation and the number of people who benefited from the free distribution of corn was reduced. At the same time he attempted to find a solution to the social question which had caused such disturbance in the preceding epoch. Debts were slightly scaled down and debtors in difficulties given a longer time to meet their obligations. What remained of the state-owned lands in Italy was given to families with numerous children, while Caesar, with his share of the war booty, himself purchased land on which to install deserving workers. Numerous colonies were created, and their sites were chosen by Caesar with such discernment that many became cities of commercial importance: Hispalis (Seville), Arles, Cirta (Constantine) and Sinope, among others. The free worker was protected against the unfair competition of slave-labour. Finally great public works in Rome and in Italy gave work to the unemployed. Local government was equally the object of his concern: the *lex Julia municipalis* gave to the communities of Italy a constitution by which they attained a large measure of self-government. The provinces, whose number had been appreciably increased by his own conquests, were freed from the abuses of the tax-farming system by the settlement of a fixed tribute, while peculation by extortionate provincial governors was ruthlessly stamped out.

The Ides of March

These salutary reforms, together with the restoration of public order, earned Caesar universal gratitude which he sought to make use of to maintain and fortify his position of absolute power. For some years he had striven to surround himself with an aura of religious dignity: he claimed divine origin for his family, attributed his victories to supernatural patronage, and in the Roman priesthood held the position of supreme pontiff. After the battle of Munda he allowed statues of himself to be placed in the temples and had himself proclaimed *divus*. He received the right to wear the triumphal toga at all times and to add to his name the title imperator. But beneath the semi-sacred character which these honours bestowed on him lay the real material power conferred by the tribunate. He felt strong enough by the beginning of 44 B.C. to have himself appointed dictator for life with the right to bequeath his powers to his heir, the grand-nephew whom he had just adopted, C. Julius Caesar Octavianus—Octavius or, as he is often called, Octavian. It was his desire to go even farther: at this moment when he was on the point of setting forth on an expedition to destroy the Parthians, he felt that the title of king would be valuable in making a proper impression on the Hellenistic Orient. He had not, perhaps, sufficiently weighed the obstacles. The memory of Rome's defeat at Carrhae was still fresh in the public mind and a war against the Parthians was extremely unpopular. As for the royal title, many Romans remained attached to republican forms and the word king, loathed since the days of the Tarquins, filled them with revulsion. The crowd's behaviour during the festival of Lupercalia — on 15th February 44 B.C. — when they applauded only when Caesar had removed the diadem with which Mark Antony tried to crown him — should have opened his eyes. Nevertheless his self-confidence was such that he resolved to demand from the senate the title of king when away from Rome. This project drew certain uncompromising Republicans to the support of Brutus and Cassius who had determined to bring about Caesar's downfall. On the Ides of March in the year 44 B.C., the very day when the senate met to gratify his wishes, Caesar was assassinated.

Formation of the Second Triumvirate

By murdering Caesar the conspirators had hoped to return to the previous regime and wipe out once and for all everything to do with dictatorship. On the seventeenth of March Cicero, the leading Republican, actually put through a law abolishing the dictatorship for ever and, to restore peace among all parties, he proposed a general

*Colour plate: Top: the Basilica, Pompeii. Barnabys
Bottom: Roman remains at Carthage. A.F.Kersting*

N

amnesty. But among the populace and his veterans Caesar retained faithful partisans. Mark Antony, to whom Caesar had left his private papers, rallied them to his standard by making public the measures, true or supposed, that Caesar had intended to enact for the people's benefit. He roused their fervour by fostering the cult of the dead hero. But the development of the popular movement tended to get beyond his control: he was forced to give pledges of his intentions by passing more liberal agrarian and colonial laws, by granting full Roman citizenship to Sicily, by a democratic reform of the tribunals. In this way Antony succeeded in keeping the urban masses in hand.

Civil war was inevitable between the two parties. It broke out over the distribution of provincial governorships. Antony, who had obtained the province of Macedonia, decided that he preferred that of Cisalpine Gaul which had been given to Brutus. When Brutus refused to exchange provinces the war began. It seemed that Rome had been plunged again into the anarchy which had prevailed before Julius Caesar's time; but an unexpected intervention was to alter the situation. As soon as he had heard of the death of his great-uncle — and father, by adoption — Octavian hurried to Italy to claim his inheritance. Cicero, who under-estimated the qualities of young Octavian, nineteen and timid in appearance, decided to make an alliance with him in order to outwit Antony. Octavian who was popular among the veterans had no difficulty in raising an army among them, while Cicero in a rousing series of orations — known for their

Pompey (106-48 B.C.), a member of the first triumvirate together with Crassus and Julius Caesar. In the Civil War which followed the triumvirate he was defeated by Caesar at Pharsalus.

Demosthenic invective as his Philippics — called for another war. The senate, however, still hesitated before making a definite rupture. The demands of Antony, who was laying siege to Brutus in Modena, caused negotiations at the end of 44 B.C. to break down, and a large coalition was formed against him. The siege was raised and Antony, beaten in April 43 B.C., fled to the region of Narbonne where he found an ally in Lepidus. Meanwhile Octavian, who had received from the senate the proconsular *imperium*, had been joined by Brutus, who had occupied Macedonia, by Cassius, who held Syria, and by the son of Pompey, Sextus, who had gathered a fleet in Spain. The two consuls who led the senatorial forces which defeated Antony at Modena had been killed in the fighting, and Octavian took command. He then asked the senate

to make him consul. The senate refused and Octavian marched on Rome where he forced his election. Thus armed with the *Senatus consultum ultimum* — the supreme sanction in times of internal crisis — the power he held had the authorisation of the law.

But Octavian was by no means in a position to impose his authority throughout the Roman world. In the west Antony was again powerful, thanks to an alliance with the governors of Gaul and Spain, while the east was dominated by partisans of the late Pompey. To deal with this former danger Octavian met Antony and Lepidus at Bologna in 43 B.C. and came to an agreement. From the senate they demanded the creation of a new instrument of government: the constituant triumvirate — namely themselves — which for five years gave them the right to make laws, appoint magistrates and kill their enemies without trial. Immediately new man-hunts were organised in Italy: three hundred senators, of whom one was Cicero, and at least two thousand of the equestrian class, were among these proscribed and slaughtered by Antony's followers. The victims' property was confiscated and the proceeds used by the triumvirate to finance their campaign in the East. There Brutus and Cassius, by extracting funds from the provinces, had raised an army of considerable strength. Their fleet was mistress of the Adriatic and Sextus Pompeius had seized Sicily. Antony and Octavian nonetheless succeeded in crossing over to Macedonia in the summer of 42 B.C. There at Philippi Antony's skill and dash inflicted defeat on the forces of Brutus and Cassius, who both committed suicide.

A coin bearing the head of Julius Caesar, and on the reverse *veni, vidi, vici* (I came, I saw, I conquered) - Caesar's terse message to the Senate on his victory over Pharnaces of Pontus, son of Mithridates the Great, at Zela in 47 B.C. *Archiv für Kunst und Geschichte*

Octavian in the West

The victors then proceeded to share out the provinces and the tasks which still had to be faced. Lepidus, a minor partner in the triumvirate, was returned to Africa, while Antony undertook to pacify the East and raise subsidies there. Octavian returned to Italy, which in theory belonged to the three jointly, in order to distribute land to the veterans and to suppress Sextus Pompeius who had taken Corsica and Sardinia and was endangering the food supply of the capital. These missions were delicate and full of pitfalls, but in accomplishing them Octavian saw the means of making himself master of the West, and in consequence of the entire Empire. To settle the veterans he was first obliged to dispossess many Italian landowners. Their anger was fanned by Antony's partisans, notably his wife Fulvia and his brother Lucius Antonius. On one occasion they forced Octavian to leave Rome but he succeeded in trapping L. Antonius at Perugia, where in 41-40 B.C. he was forced to capitulate. Antony himself appeared before Brundisium in the summer of 40 B.C., but, with his hands full in the east, his object was to reach a working agreement with Octavian. The Pact of Brundisium, negotiated by Maecenas provided for a new division of influence: in exchange for the province of Narbonne, Antony was given a free hand in the Orient.

Octavian had at first to proceed carefully against Sextus Pompeius who commanded the sea. In the Concordat of Misenum in 39 B.C. Octavian recognised Sextus Pompeius' present possessions and promised him Achaia. In the meanwhile Agrippa was working night and day to build up a powerful fleet. When it was ready Octavian took the offensive. Sextus was crushed in 36 B.C. at Naulochus, while Lepidus occupied Sicily. When, however, Lepidus claimed the right to retain Sicily, Octavian turned against him, defeated him brilliantly and in 36 B.C. deprived him not only of Africa but of his title of triumvir. The Empire now had only two masters, but that was still one too many.

Antony in the East

Antony's ambition was also to achieve undivided power, but the methods he pursued were quite different. The situation which he had found in the Orient was difficult. Orodes, king of Parthia, after his victory at Carrhae, had attempted to lay hands on Syria, but in 51 B.C. he was repulsed. The struggle between the triumvirate and the partisans of Pompey had seemed to him a favourable occasion to try again, especially since the latter had solicited his aid. Thus, after the battle of Philippi, two Parthian armies, one of which was commanded by a Roman, seized Antioch, Jerusalem and Phoenicia. In spite of the danger Antony, who was occupied by the affairs of Italy, did not intervene in person; but one of his generals had in 39-38 B.C. succeeded in driving back the Parthians. This allowed Antony to revive the Parthian project which Caesar had planned just before his death, though in a very different spirit. For Antony had met Cleopatra, queen of Egypt, at Tarsus in 41 B.C., and that meeting altered his whole outlook. Falling under her spell, he followed her to Alexandria and from then onwards thought of himself as a Hellenistic sovereign rather than a Roman general. Therefore the object of Antony's Parthian expedition was to strengthen the power of Cleopatra's kingdom rather than avert a possible threat to the Roman Empire. The campaign was, however, not a success. Having advanced into Media Atropatene too late in the season he was unable to take Phraaspa, the capital, and during his withdrawal in 36 B.C. his army was decimated. Henceforth, and in spite of a few half-hearted attempts to save appearances, Antony was interested in nothing but Egypt, which he restored to the territorial extension it had reached in the days of Ptolemy Philadelphus. During the course of a dramatic assembly at Alexandria in 34 B.C., known as the Donations of Alexandria, the children he had had by Cleopatra were proclaimed kings, and presented by Antony with kingdoms and provinces belonging to Rome. Like a new Dionysus united to a new Isis, the Roman soldier gave himself up to the costly and debilitating delights of oriental life.

Julius Caesar (100-44 B.C.). After his defeat of Pompey at the battle of Munda (45 B.C.), statues of Caesar were set up in Roman temples; he wore the triumphal toga and was called 'imperator'. The half-sacred nature of these honours served to conceal his great material power. *Archiv für Kunst und Geschichte*

The triumph of Octavian

The conduct of Octavian in the west was very different. Aided by tried and trusted advisers — Agrippa, Maecenas and his wife Livia — his energy was unceasing and fruitful. In his name Agrippa reinforced the frontier on the Rhine. Octavian himself in 35-34 B.C. conquered Illyria and Dalmatia. In 33 B.C. when Agrippa was aedile, Rome was greatly embellished and its drainage and water supply improved. Thanks to Octavian's wise administration public order was restored and maintained, while the devastation of the civil war was repaired. Finally, Octavian's own modesty, austerity and courage made him appear in the eyes of all as a reincarnation of the ancient spirit of republican Rome. Enemies, however, were not lacking, and his situation became critical at the end of 33 B.C. which was the date at which the triumvirate legally expired. Antony proposed the restoration of the former constitution. In actual fact Octavian occupied no legal position of authority, and he did not hesitate to employ force. He presented himself before the senate with a guard of armed followers and stated his case against Antony whose partisans chose to flee to the Orient. Octavian had himself appointed consul for the following year and made Romans and provincials alike take an oath of allegiance. Then he seized Antony's last will and testament, lodged with the priestesses of Vesta, in which it was seen that Antony bequeathed all his possessions to Cleopatra and her children. The rumour spread that Antony also planned to transfer the capital of the empire to Alexandria. The

195

A stone relief, showing Roman money-lenders. At the time of Actium (31 B.C.), Roman society was devoted to luxury and enslaved to money-lenders. Even before this period, both Caesar and Augustus had had to legislate for the relief of debtors.

subsequent wave of popular indignation compelled the senate to declare war on Cleopatra.

While Octavian occupied the Ionian islands and the western coast of the Peloponnesus, Antony concentrated his army and his fleet around Ambracia, an untenable position which in case of failure and retreat meant that he must sacrifice either the army or the navy. In the engagement between the two fleets in 31 B.C. off the promontory of Actium the issue was for a long time uncertain. The sudden panic and flight of Cleopatra, however, tipped the scales, and Octavian's victory was decisive. Cleopatra took refuge in Egypt where Antony followed her. Octavian did not arrive until the following year. Cleopatra tried to save herself by betraying Antony, who committed suicide. After the celebrated interview in which Octavian kept his eyes cautiously lowered in order not to be seduced, Cleopatra put an end to her life. Egypt was annexed, and Rome's final conquest of the Mediterranean basin was completed.

Roman civilisation

Roman society at the time of the downfall of the Republic was riddled with vice. It was said by a contemporary that the Romans then loved money too much and the profession of arms too little; and, in fact, the thirst for wealth had accustomed all the men of the period to seek at once the satisfaction of their ambition and their taste for luxury. The majority spent money extravagantly and even the richest were crushed by enormous debts. To meet such lavish expenditure they were obliged to have recourse to means which were even more disreputable than participation in tax-farming or plundering provinces. Marriage was thought of as a mere business arrangement and divorce became more and more common.

And yet, culturally, the period was distinguished. When it began Hellenism was in all fields triumphant. All cultivated Romans prided themselves on speaking Greek as well as they spoke Latin. In 81 B.C. envoys from Rhodes could make themselves understood in the senate without the aid of interpreters. The sons of noble families went to Greece — to Athens or to Rhodes — to finish their studies under fashionable rhetoricians and philosophers. Culturally Rome was for the moment simply a Hellenistic province. In religion the old national divinities no longer had their devotees, with the exception of Venus who still represented the life force of the race and whose cult encouraged satisfaction of individual instincts. Filling this vacuum, Pythagoreanism and the mystery cults of Eleusis and Samothrace were at the height of their popularity, while oriental religions brought back by veterans of eastern wars had also begun to spread. Cybele, Mithras and Isis had their followers who with impunity ignored repeated and unenforceable laws passed by the senate to prohibit their worship. On the other hand, certain philosophic doctrines, notably stoicism and epicureanism, liberally interpreted, led to agnosticism and sometimes atheism, while the worst practices of magic and superstition were accompanied by sheer immorality.

In art, eastern influences increased: this can be partly explained by the rich artistic plunder brought back from Asia — by Sulla and Pompey especially — and partly by the fact that numerous eastern artists had immigrated to Italy. The important buildings at Pompeii, for instance — its theatre, its porticoes, its temples — as well as the statues and pictures which adorned them, were all executed by foreign artists or in the Hellenistic manner. Literature also borrowed its forms and its themes from the same source. Roman orators consciously adopted the manner of some school of eloquence which was in vogue in the Greek world. Poetry was confined to strictly imported patterns. But in spite of this slavish adherence to foreign models, or perhaps even because of it, two masterpieces were produced: *De Rerum Natura* by Lucretius, undoubtedly the greatest of didactic poems in which the most abstruse philosophic doctrines are clearly expressed in majestic verse; and the Epithalamiums and Elegies of Catullus, in which flexibility of language and sincerity of passion break from the artificial moulds in which the poems are cast.

Towards the end of the period, however, a true national art began to emerge from the models which until then had held it in bondage. Caesar himself was partly responsible for this development. In the buildings with which he covered Rome, in his own forum especially, and in the painted and sculptured decorations with which he had them embellished, he did not, it is true, break away from Hellenic tradition. Indeed, he often confided the execution of the work to Greek masters: the architecture to an unknown Athenian, the sculpture to such artists as Pasiteles, Stephanos and Arcesilaos. We also know that Caesar's own favourite painter was Timomachus of

Left: a coin commemorating the Ides of March, when Caesar was murdered by Brutus and Cassius (44 BC).
Right: a coin of Octavian (Augustus) with the imperial symbols.

Relief depicting the Archigallus (high priest) of the Magna Mater or Great Mother of the Gods, with symbolic ears of corn, sceptre and tympanum. The Magna Mater personified maternity, and had her counterpart in the Greek Cybele. A temple was built for her on the Palatine hill in 204 B.C. *Anderson*

A relief showing a Roman soldier, with a watch-tower and beacon-tower on the *limes* (frontier) of the Empire. Once they had established a far-flung Empire, the Romans were faced with the enormous problem of guarding it.

The columns of the temple of Castor and Pollux in the Roman Forum. The Forum was a market place and meeting place, surrounded by temples, a prison, a *rostra* or platform for public speakers, the *curia* or senate chamber, and a treasury. *Hoppé*

Mark Antony (83-30 B.C.) who controlled the eastern half of the Empire while Octavian controlled the west after Caesar's death. In Egypt he fell under the influence of Cleopatra and scandalised the Romans by succumbing to the luxurious life of the east. Octavian brought about his downfall at Actium in 31 B.C. *Anderson*

An Egyptian Ptolemaic relief of Cleopatra (69-30 B.C.). The hieroglyphic characters of her name appear on the left. She seduced both Caesar and Antony; when she fled at the battle of Actium, Antony followed, and so lost the battle. *Viollet*

Byzantium. But the artists no longer drew their inspiration from Alexandria, but from classical Athens. And the slightly austere nobility of their manner was far more appropriate than the previous mannerisms to express the dignity and the grandeur which was Caesar's conception of Rome. The new spirit is particularly noticeable

in the portrait bust, of which masterpieces have survived. In the literary field, too, the Roman genius now came into its own. Caesar encouraged the movement by founding the first public library, which he entrusted to the direction of Marcus Terentius Varro, who was known as the 'most learned of the Romans'. Varro not only organised the library but contributed to its enrichment with his own encyclopaedias of vast number and variety. Caesar was himself one of the best exponents of the new school of literature, and the Commentaries which he wrote in his own hand are marvels of clarity and proportion. The historian Sallust wrote in a similar manner. But the greatest author of the period was undoubtedly Cicero. Not only in his orations but in his moral and philosophical works he was the true founder of Graeco-Latin classicism and has influenced literary style ever since.

The most permanent legacy of Rome to Europe and to the European-inspired civilisations which were to grow up beyond the oceans, was in the field of law, and here Cicero's influence was decisive. He combined the old, parochial legal ideas of the Republic with Hellenistic stoic ideals of the brotherhood of all civilised men, who participated, as rational beings, in the order of the universe. These doctrines were later supplemented by the idea of the semi-divine ruler, the saviour who sustained the empire, and harmonised it with the will of the gods.

The original Roman Law was intensely practical, concerned with the affairs of an agricultural people: it was formal and archaic, and sanctioned by ancient ritual which ensured good luck. It was also bound up with the Etruscan cult of omens and divination, and it applied only to the Romans themselves. For the foreigners with whom they had to deal they devised a *ius gentium* or 'law of the peoples' which was more flexible, and it was this kind of law which blended more easily with the original Greek idea of a universal natural law. This idea was now defined in legal terms and related to government, and it gave Roman imperialism a lofty sanction.

The ideal of the statesman, says Cicero, is to make

A fresco from Pompeii showing the celebration of the rites of Isis. The cult of this Egyptian goddess of the earth, fertility and knowledge was introduced in Rome by Sulla in the first century B.C. and survived until about 500 A.D. *Anderson-Mansell*

was assimilated into Christian teaching. When the Western Empire disintegrated, and the invading barbarians brought their own tribal laws with them, the idea of a universal law was kept alive by the Church; and in Byzantium, where the continuity of Roman civilisation long remained unbroken, the Emperors were regarded as the representative of Universal Justice and Universal Mind.

When, in the twelfth century, the study of secular law was revived in Italian universities, it was based mainly on Byzantine Codes, made under Justinian in the sixth century, which transmitted the main Roman Law as something universal and not a mere personal attribute. Justinian's *Codex*, *Digest*, and *Institutes* were the basis of the revival of Roman Law in the medieval West, and the Church law was fundamentally Roman.

Thus the concept of a universal justice and a world embracing Law emerged out of the originally parochial Roman Code after the assimilation of stoic ideals of a cosmic moral law.

The Sacae in India

The invasion of north-west India by the Yueh-chi and the tribes who had come with them put a final end to the Graeco-Indian kingdoms. The most important of the new tribes was the Sacae — or Sakas — whom Mithridates II had submitted to Parthian rule. After the death of Mithridates, however, the Sacae, under the leadership of their prince Manes (c. 80 to 58 B.C.) took Gandhara, western Punjab and Kabul from their Greek rulers. After Manes' death there seems to have been a brief restoration of Greek dominion in Kabul with Amyntas and Hermaios (c. 58 to 30 B.C.). Another kingdom — that which Menander had founded – had been able to survive in the eastern Punjab in the neighbourhood of Sagala — to-day Sialkot. Here several sovereigns with Greek names successively reigned: Straton, Dionysius, Hippostratos and Nicias – the last two towards the year 50 B.C. But a generation later the Sacae, led by Azes, destroyed these last vestiges of Alexander's conquest and extended their own territory to the frontiers of Magadha.

The reign of Siuan Ti in China

Wu Ti had successors, Tchao Ti (86-74 B.C.) and above all Siuan Ti (73-49 B.C.), who were worthy of him. Tchao Ti profited by a war between the Huns and the savage hordes of Jehol and reoccupied Lob-nor where he founded a military colony. Siuan Ti enlarged the Han Empire to an extent it had never before known. Forming an alliance with all the enemies of the Huns he penetrated into Turfan, seized Yarkand, at the gates of India, and installed a governor in the basin of the river Tarim. Civil war broke out among the Huns as a result of these great losses, and one of the claimants to the Hunnish throne asked for the protection of Siuan Ti. Between 49 and 43 B.C. Siuan Ti helped him to become master of Mongolia and, to ensure closer control over him, had him married to a Chinese princess. The rival claimant who had fled to western Turkestan attempted to rebuild his empire. The Chinese thwarted the attempt, vanquished him in 35 B.C., and cut off his head. Finally, during the following reign of Yuan Ti (48-33 B.C.) the Tibetans of the region of Koko-nor were thrown towards the south.

human life nobler and richer by his thought and effort: and the justice which 'gives every man his due' is the expression of a universal moral law, which is 'right reason, congruent with nature'. There is not therefore a confusion of laws applicable to different peoples, but one universal law applicable to all, 'unalterable and eternal'. 'There will not be one Law at Rome', he writes, 'another in Athens: one now, and another later on, but one law for all people at all times; one master and ruler over us all, the inventor, promulgator and enforcing judge.' The authority of Rome was not therefore simply that of conquest, for the arms and laws which imposed the Roman peace were justified by a moral sanction which reflected the order of the cosmos. The aim of the State was not plunder or caprice but to promote the well-being of its subjects and to render equal justice between them. The Romans thus justified public power as an extension of right reason, crystallised in laws which were clear, intelligible, and existing in their own rights. The fluctuating influence of ephemeral politicians could not change them, and if ever they were violated by a tyrant, he would forfeit his moral influence and, sooner or later, be brought down, having no sanction but force and commanding no permanent loyalty.

The conception of an impersonal, clearly formulated universal law which upheld basic human rights, is one of the greatest legacies of the Roman Empire. The brutality of Roman power, the crimes of many Emperors, and the exploitation of subject peoples are familiar; but the ideal had been formulated in a practical way, and the notion of a universal justice reflecting the will of Heaven

199

CHAPTER ELEVEN

PAX ROMANA AND PAX SINICA

31 B.C. – A.D. 192

A slave transhipping oil at Ostia, the busy trading port of Rome. Mosaic. *Viollet*

The victory of Actium left Octavian (soon to become Augustus) master of the Empire. But his authority did not rest on force alone, and to establish a lasting peace and stability he was obliged to organise a new regime, to restore public morale, and at the same time to respect convictions and prejudices which it was not in his power to abolish. He did not at once find adequate answers to these problems; hence the changes and crises in his policy. On certain points his solutions were defective and gravely imperilled the principate, but in the main he hit upon ways and means which met the situation, and for two centuries — two centuries of Pax Romana — the imperial government was based on the system which he had created.

The genius of Augustus

Caesar's heir achieved these results by his own outstanding qualities — and by the happy circumstance that he lived to rule for forty-four years. Though he was never more than a mediocre general, he had a realistic sense of what was possible, and therein lay his true genius. Extravagant ambitions did not tempt him. He knew how to limit his enterprises and when to withdraw from the insurmountable. This quality was served by others: an elevated sense of duty; a methodical and precise mind which enabled him to fill in the gaps in his political education and made him a particularly able administrator; prudence which caused him to leave nothing to chance, to foresee all eventualities, and even to make a written draft in advance of his conversations; and finally a will of iron. In brief, Augustus owed his genius less to mental brilliance than to mental equilibrium.

The establishment of the Principate

At the time of the battle of Actium Octavian was only consul. In the following year, 30 B.C., he increased his authority by obtaining tribunicial powers for life and the right to constitute himself the final court of appeal. When, by 27 B.C., order had been re-established, he made the gesture of resigning these exceptional powers and restoring the constitution. Actually the gesture was simply a means of legalising the new order by an act — presumably free — of the senate. For the senate, as he had foreseen, begged him to accept the government of the provinces where the presence of armies was necessary. This put the military power at his disposal and gave him the diplomatic initiative. At the same time he received the title of *Augustus* which carried with it religious prestige of especial importance. A crisis in 23 B.C., provoked by the discovery of a serious conspiracy by Caepio and Murena, was the occasion of a further strengthening of his position. Though he restored to the senate the right to mint money, he had his former tribunicial powers reconfirmed and was given a proconsular *imperium* — or command — of higher rank than that of all other provincial governors and extending even to Rome itself.

The new regime at about this time began to assume its final shape. Its power relied in the first place on the army. Augustus surrounded himself with a guard of nine praetorian cohorts, while the regular army consisted of twenty-five legions of volunteers who were recruited for long terms of service. The generals were senators, officers were of equestrian or senatorial families, while subalterns and centurions were Roman citizens. The main body of the army was recruited chiefly from the provinces, and foreign soldiers who enlisted were given Roman citizenship on discharge. The total fighting forces numbered around 300,000 men. Augustus also had control over the finances. As well as the *aerarium Saturni*, or public treasury, there was the *fiscus* of Augustus himself, into which were paid the revenues of the provinces, but which met all military expenses and supported the administration. Indirect taxes were still farmed out to companies formed to collect them, but such companies were now strictly supervised. Although Augustus had restored the permanent tribunals of the Republic, justice was actually in his own hands: he could have any case brought before him and, in court of appeal, reverse any sentence. As supreme pontiff he gave juridical opinions which had the force of law. As a magistrate he could define the law and regulate its application. Finally he could at his own discretion have all those he considered undesirables

transported or sent into exile, to safeguard Roman peace.

The traditional organs of the Republican constitution remained in action, but their functions and scope were modified. The machinery of government was still housed in the senate: Augustus gave the force of law to the *senatus consulta*, or decrees, which little by little became the chief source of legislation under the Empire. The senate received the right to hear appeals in certain cases

A section of the Via Appia, the highroad from Rome to Campania built in 312 B.C. by Appius Claudius Caecus. *Allan Cash*

and to try its own members. The senate also continued to govern those provinces which it had not turned over to Augustus in 27 B.C. A direct and fruitful collaboration between the senate and the emperor should, in fact, have been possible; but whether he lacked confidence in the capacity of the senators or whether he preferred to keep the reasons for his decisions to himself, he separated himself from the senate by means of two agencies: first, his own privy council to which he summoned anyone he chose, and secondly a committee of senators, originally drawn by lot but later elected, who with him drafted the decisions of the Assembly. As for the magistrates, their powers were greatly curtailed by the creation of an imperial civil service.

One of the greatest weaknesses of the Republic had been the absence of a body of permanent civil servants. This Augustus remedied, at least in part. For the first time the city of Rome was provided with an administration: an urban police force commanded in the absence of the emperor by a prefect of the city; the *annona* which was responsible for the food supply; a fire brigade of *vigiles*; and various other services like the water board and public works. In the Empire the senatorial provinces continued to be administered by former magistrates, but the imperial provinces were superintended by representatives of the emperor. An imperial legate commanded the troops and dispensed justice, while financial matters were entrusted to procurators — fiscal agents — and the postal system was administered from Rome.

With this growth of public service and the trained ruling classes it created, social category became fixed and indeed, was legally defined. The senatorial class was hereditary, with the proviso that members' property was valued at a minimum of one million sesterces. The equestrian order, on the contrary, was not hereditary, and could be entered only with an imperial commission and a property census of four hundred thousand sesterces. Each of these two classes supplied the administration with functionaries whose relative rank and importance was not at first very precisely determined. Below these privileged orders, the remainder of Roman society was also divided into classes; the body of free citizens had scarcely been enlarged, for Augustus was not generous in granting the rights of Roman citizenship. He no longer added to their number by enfranchising slaves who had been freed. Such ex-slaves formed an inferior social category. A hierarchy was also established among the subject peoples. At the bottom of the ladder were the dediticians — or freedmen not allowed full citizenship because of misconduct during slavery, while at the top the Hellenes received special consideration. The condition of the slaves themselves had deteriorated rather than improved.

One of the finest preserved examples of Roman architecture: the aqueduct at Segovia. Improvements in public works followed the Roman legions wherever they were garrisoned in the Empire or the provinces. *Allan Cash*

This social redistribution was accompanied by religious and moral reforms. After the anarchy of the civil wars Augustus was very conscious of the need for national solidarity. He therefore made every effort to restore the traditional piety of his subjects. The sacerdotal colleges were filled again and the temples rebuilt. As Pontifex Maximus in 12 B.C. he fought charlatanism and viewed oriental religions with disfavour. His work was rounded off by the institution of a new cult — the cult of the Emperor. This cult had first arisen in the east, where as early as 29 B.C. temples dedicated to him had been erected in Pergamum and Nicomedia. But the Emperor only accepted his deification under the epithet of 'Augustus' and then normally in connection with the name of Rome. Nor did he permit himself to be worshipped as a god in Italy where he was content merely to encourage the cult of his *Genius* — or guardian angel — which he associated with the very popular cult of the *lares compitales* — or guardians of the crossroads. This religious revival went hand in hand with legislation aimed at moral regeneration. A *lex Julia* on marriage and another on adultery towards 18 B.C. strengthened the bonds of marriage, consolidated the family, encouraged child-bearing and protected public morals.

The Age of Augustus

The restoration of peace and the return of prosperity won for Augustus the confidence of the vast majority of his subjects, and the echo of their gratitude is repeated in contemporary literature and art. This was Rome's golden age. The co-operation of men of letters was not, to be sure, gained without the prolonged and earnest solicitation of Maecenas, not to mention Augustus himself. But once won round, they became the promoters of ideals dear to the Emperor: the blessings of peace, the defence of agriculture, the grandeur of Rome, and the virtues of its *Princeps* — or first citizen. Though Ovid in his *Fasti* raised his voice a little stridently in an attempt to recall the past glories of his country, like the poets of the preceding epoch, he was more successful in the production of light verse and graceful flattery. Propertius in his *Elegies* evoked the ancient national legends, while Horace drew moral and patriotic lessons from daily occurrences or wittily lampooned the follies of the time. But the noblest voice of the age and the most sincere was that of the poet Virgil whose delicate sensibility and profound patriotism has left an imperishable monument to the glory of Rome and its second founder. Only in the majestic prose of Titus Livius is the epic quality of the *Aeneid* approached. Livy's *History of Rome*, in spite of its modern critics, remains the basic source of our knowledge of Rome's past and still inspires admiration of her accomplishments. In the other arts less successful results were achieved. The freedom of the inventive spirit did not thrive under official inspiration, though recognition must be given to the discreet yet imposing nobility of the *Augustus* of the Prima Porta, the descriptive skill and liveliness of the bas-reliefs of the *Ara Pacis* and the technical perfection of minor arts — such as gem-engraving and metal embossing. All in all, it was in architecture that the spirit of the times — grandiose, slightly cold and aloof — found its most successful expression. The Empire was covered with imposing monuments, such as the Pantheon of Agrippa and the Forum of Augustus, the Maison Carrée at Nîmes, the Pont du Gard, the aqueduct at Segovia. Roads were extended in all directions.

Foreign policy

Although the reign of Augustus gives an impression of being an age of peace, important campaigns were methodically and resolutely carried on which greatly enlarged the extent and security of the Empire. Local rebellions, the aftermath of the civil wars, were pacified by the Emperor himself (north-west Spain in 26-25 B.C.) or by his lieutenants (Thrace, Aquitania and the Alps in 29-25 B.C.). Augustus then set about the task of reinforcing the frontiers. The need for this became apparent in the West in the year 16 B.C. following a defeat which the Sicambri inflicted on the Roman legate of the Gauls, and an invasion by the Rhaeti which threatened northern Italy. In 15 B.C. Tiberius and Drusus, marching one from Gaul

and the other from the Po valley, joined forces on the Bavarian plateau and pushed the frontier forward to the Danube. In the same year Drusus began the conquest of Germany as far as the Elbe. This ambitious plan was abandoned at his death in the year 9 B.C., but Tiberius consolidated his gains to the west of the Weser. Then in A.D. 6 a savage revolt broke out in Illyria which took three years to suppress. In the same year that Tiberius was finally successful in Illyria the army in Germany suffered a disastrous defeat in the forest of Teutoburg, in which Varus perished and three legions were wiped out. Germany had to be evacuated and the frontiers brought back to the Rhine.

In the East the policy of Augustus relied less on arms than on diplomacy. In 25 B.C. he annexed Galatia without striking a blow, and Judea in A.D. 6. He took advantage of the anarchy which reigned among the Parthians during the feeble rule of Phraates IV (37 to 2 B.C.) and of Phraataces (2 B.C. to A.D. 9) to obtain the restitution

A relief showing the legions in combat with the German tribes on the Danube. *Archiv für Kunst und Geschichte*

Above: The Roman amphitheatre at Nimes. In both Republic and Empire the policy of keeping the people happy with bread and circuses was vigorously pursued. The many remaining arenas are sufficient evidence of the important part they played. The first gladiatorial fight took place in 264 B.C. The public quickly acquired a taste for the many brutalised sports that developed from these first spectacles.

Below: The Temple of Castor and Pollux, Rome. First century A.D. *Anderson*

of the Roman Eagles lost by Crassus; and imposed a Roman protectorate on Armenia. He even attempted to provide a king for his Persian enemies by sending back Vonones, a Persian prince who had been a hostage in Rome. In this, however, he was not successful. In 25 B.C. farther to the south, an expedition was sent into the Yemen to open up a trade route to India.

The problem of the succession

Augustus had no son and the question of the imperial succession remained in suspense. At first he designated his faithful minister and son-in-law Agrippa, on whom he had conferred in 18 B.C. the proconsular *imperium* and the power of the tribunate. On Agrippa's death the choice of the Emperor fell on Agrippa's two sons, Caius Caesar and Lucius Caesar, children of Augustus' daughter, who were made consuls and entitled Princes of Youth. But they too died before Augustus. He was then obliged to turn to his step-son, Tiberius, an excellent soldier but a man of moody and suspicious temperament, who had gone into voluntary exile. Tiberius was recalled, adopted by Augustus and in A.D. 4 given tribunicial powers. In the events which followed — the conspiracy of Cinna, the Illyrian revolt, the disaster of Varus in A.D. 9 — Tiberius played an exemplary part and his usefulness to Augustus further strengthened his position. In A.D. 13 he received the full powers of the proconsular *imperium*; the death of Augustus in A.D. 14 left him master of the Empire.

The Julio-Claudian Line

The senate raised no difficulties about confirming Tiberius' powers and relations between them and the new Emperor were at first satisfactory. Tiberius treated the venerable body with deference and respect and hoped, no doubt sincerely, that it would relieve him of some of the responsibility of government. With this end in view he increased its legislative and judiciary powers. Also contributing to the success of the new sovereign was the fact that he had officially adopted his nephew Germanicus, whose popularity was immense. Finally a series of brilliant military operations added glory to the reign: in the years 14 to 16 Germanicus succeeded in again penetrating Germany up to the banks of the Weser. In the East Artabanus III had founded a new dynasty among the Parthians and in 15 conquered Armenia. Two years later Germanicus was sent to the East, where he reconquered Armenia and annexed Cappadocia.

Unfortunately Germanicus died in 19. Uprisings took place in Africa and in Gaul. After the death of one of the wisest of the Emperor's counsellors, Sallustius Crispus, in 20, his influence was replaced by that of Sejanus, the ambitious prefect of the praetorian guards. Tiberius gradually felt the growing hostility of the senate, and his suspicious nature darkened. Mistrustful and over-sensitive to criticism, he gave way to persecution mania and retired to Capri. There, in fear of his life and not daring to leave the island, he got rid of his suspected enemies by means of royal decree or, failing that, assassination. By such means he put to death the children of Germanicus, Asinius Gallus, leader of the senatorial opposition, and in 31 Sejanus himself who had plotted to make

Augustus Caesar (Octavian). A mediocre general by Roman standards, his genius lay in shrewd judgment. Under his direction Rome was for the first time provided with a body of public servants. Octavian had neither the high-flown ambitions nor the divine aspirations of his predecessors. *Anderson*

himself the next emperor. The Empire did not, however, suffer from these executions. An excellent administrator, Tiberius maintained careful control over public funds and kept a close eye on the conduct of provincial governors. Trade continued to thrive — even with the Parthians — and the economic crisis of 33 did not long affect the general prosperity.

In 35 Tiberius designated as his heir and successor a surviving son of Germanicus, Gaius — the future Caligula. Two years later Tiberius died and Gaius, who had inherited the great popularity of his father, was welcomed with enthusiasm. But a serious illness attacked his mind and fits of insanity — some of them murderous — became increasingly frequent. Caligula returned to the despotic policy of Tiberius. He decided that he was a god and ordered the Jews to erect his statue in their synagogues, while his prodigal extravagance exhausted the treasury. His diplomacy was incoherent: he made preparations to conquer Britain, but failed to follow them up when they were completed. He abandoned Armenia and Judea, but annexed Galilee. He had Ptolemy, king of Mauretania killed in order to seize his treasures. At the beginning of 41 he was preparing to sail for Egypt, where serious disturbances had broken out between the Greeks and the Jews of Alexandria, when he was assassinated.

The senate decided it was time to put an end to the imperial regime; but in the palace the praetorian guards discovered a nephew of Tiberius of whose existence Rome had until then scarcely been aware: Claudius. In spite of his obvious terror they saluted Claudius as Emperor. The senate, cowed by the guards, bowed to their decision, and thus created a dangerous precedent. Claudius was inexperienced and dominated by his wives — Messalina, and afterwards Agrippina. Yet at the same time he was cultivated, intelligent and a realist. At heart a Republican, his desire was to renounce the despotic rule of his two predecesssors. His avowed intentions were, however, belied by the innovations which the force of circumstances compelled him to make. The vast increase of administrative duties led inevitably to the formation of a centralised bureaucracy. Before his day the emperors had recruited their assistants from among their own household friends. Claudius continued this tradition, but his nature was pliant and he weakly allowed his own freedmen to rise to the most important positions in the state. He chose them, however, with discernment and made them into skilled ministers. The organisation into bureaus of the imperial chancellery dates from the reign of Claudius. Departmental chiefs, lacking political traditions, without scruples and owing everything to the Emperor, worked constantly for the extension of imperial power, and were detested by the senate. At the same time Claudius made every effort to romanise the Empire: he was extremely liberal in granting Roman citizenship and gave seats in the senate to many provincials. He was reactionary only in religious matters.

His foreign policy was enterprising and greatly enlarged the Empire. His most noteworthy success was the conquest of Britain. Roman traders were already numerous in Britain, but the island was a hotbed of druidical activity which aimed at stirring up trouble in Gaul. The Emperor himself began the campaign in 43. By 47 the Thames valley and the south were subdued without great difficulty, but unconquered bands of Britons took refuge in the mountainous border regions from which they waged guerrilla warfare that delayed completion of the comquest for years. In the east Judea was made a province in 44, and Thrace two years later. In Africa Mauretania lost its independence. Claudius also created colonies, continued to extend the rights of Roman citizenship, and increased the programme of public works.

He had a son, Britannicus, on whom a large party in the senate pinned their hopes. But his wife Agrippina also had a son, Nero, by a previous marriage; and she worked tirelessly for his succession. She persuaded Claudius to adopt him, then for fear that he might change his mind she had Claudius poisoned; and in 54 Nero was acclaimed by the praetorian guards. Nero had been brought up in an atmosphere of intrigue and immorality and he soon gave way to his own criminal instincts. He began by assassinating or exiling everyone who could be of possible danger to him. First he poisoned Britannicus in 55. Then in 59 he had his mother, who had pushed him to the throne only in order to reign in his name, murdered. The death of Burrus, commander of the praetorian guard, in 62, and the disgrace of Seneca, both of whom had attempted to restrain his excesses, left him entirely under the influence of his second wife, Poppaea, and of his favourite, Tigellinus. Thus he could with freedom indulge his taste for histrionics, race chariots in the circus and entertain the public with displays of his musicianship. Since his wild extravagance had emptied the treasury, he issued false money and condemned increasing numbers to death in order to lay hands on their property. Meanwhile, on the frontier in 60-61 a dangerous uprising in Britain, under Boudicca (Boadicea) queen of the Iceni, had to be suppressed. Earlier, in 54-59, Corbulo, an outstanding Roman general, had conquered Armenia. Then, in 62 the Parthians, who had recovered their unity under Vologeses I (51-75), inflicted a disastrous defeat on Corbulo's successor. The situation was beyond the power of the Emperor to deal with and in 63 Nero was obliged to make peace. Then revolts began to break out in the Empire itself. The Jews rose in 66, and in 68 Vindex rebelled in Gaul and Macer in Africa. Vindex, it is true, was successfully dealt with and killed, but Galba, governor of the Spanish province of Tarragona, to whom Vindex had offered the throne, marched on Italy. The praetorian troops abandoned Nero; the senate declared him a public enemy and proclaimed Galba Emperor. Nero was forced to flee from Rome and in 68 committed suicide.

The Crisis of A.D. 68-69

Galba reigned only for a few months. His strict economies alienated both the praetorians and the populace, and in January 69 he was murdered. Otho, who

Tiberius, Roman emperor A.D. 14-37. He was the stepson of Augustus and his succession was the first move towards introducing the dynastic principle in the Empire.

had incited the rabble against Galba, seized power, but simultaneously the legions of Germany revolted and proclaimed one of their own generals, Vitellius, emperor. Vitellius then marched on Italy and at Bedriacum on the fourteenth of April defeated Otho, who committed suicide. The armies of the East, however, refused to recognise Vitellius and hailed as Emperor the chief of the army of Judea, Vespasian. The armies of the Danube rallied to him, marched on Italy, defeated Vitellius at Cremona, and killed him in Rome on the twenty-first of December. The senate then acclaimed Vespasian. Emboldened by these civil conflicts, the tribes of Gaul rose in revolt. Vitellius' march on Italy had weakened the armies on the Rhine and the Batavi took up arms at the call of their prince, Civilis; all the other Gauls at once joined them. Their chieftains proclaimed the independence of Gaul and chose an emperor. But they were incapable of working together, and at a congress which met at Rheims were unable to reach agreement. Their consequent defeat at Trèves towards the end of 70 re-established peace.

The Flavians

Vespasian, the new emperor, was of lowly origin and could reckon on imposing his authority only by good government. By his economies he restored financial solvency and by exploiting the public domains, neglected by previous emperors, he greatly increased the imperial revenue. In Rome the unemployed were occupied on vast public works. The rights of Roman citizenship were even more widely granted and numerous provincials were made senators — which earned the Emperor the hostility of those who were already members of the senate. On several occasions conspiracies, often inspired by philosophical doctrines, stoic and cynic, had to be suppressed, and in 71 Vespasian banished all philosophers and astrologers. Financial considerations limited his foreign enterprises. His son Titus, in 70, ruthlessly stamped out the Jewish revolt by taking Jerusalem by assault, but elsewhere the Emperor strove to maintain peace within the empire. Scarcely more than a few campaigns in Britain and, in north-east Syria, the annexation of Commagene, disturbed the general tranquillity. The provinces were wisely governed and many roads were built which opened regions which had been previously isolated — notably the centre of Asia Minor — to the influences of civilisation. Commerce with foreign countries, India especially, was greatly increased.

Titus, who succeeded him, occupied the throne for the brief period of 79 to 81, and his mild and kindly reign was marred only by the eruption of Vesuvius which buried Pompeii, Herculaneum and Stabiae. Titus was succeeded by his very much younger brother Domitian. Though accustomed to the exercise of power, Domitian had neither his brother's experience nor his prudence. Very satisfied with his undoubtedy considerable abilities, he set himself up as an absolute monarch, insisted on being called *dominus* — or master — and relied on his soldiers whose pay he increased. Since he continued the policy of favouring the provincials and promoted members of the equestrian order to high office, especially that of directors of chancellery departments, he incurred the hatred of the senators. His reply to any senatorial

Nero, son of Agrippina, for whom she poisoned her husband, the Emperor Claudius. Nero's reign was one of intrigue and when finally he was deserted by the praetorian guard in the face of Galba's advance, the Emperor committed suicide. *Mansell*

Nerva and Trajan

The brief reign of Nerva, whom the senate chose from their own number to succeed Domitian, was not free from difficulties. The financial position was weak while the populace and the praetorians, among whom Domitian had been popular, were restive. Neither of these problems was solved and the chief act of an eventless reign was Nerva's adoption of Trajan, who succeeded him at the beginning of 98. The accession of Trajan, who was of Spanish origin, bears witness to the increasingly important part that the provinces now played in the Empire. During Trajan's reign the Italian majority in the senate declined and was in process of disappearing; he recruited senators from as far away as Africa and the Orient. Trajan was not, however, unaware of a decay which had begun to afflict metropolitan Italy and took steps to arrest it. To provide for the care of orphans he developed the *alimenta* that Nerva had founded in 97. In 107 he compelled senators to invest at least a third of their fortune in Italian real estate. He undertook the drainage of the Pontine marshes. The principal seaports of the peninsula were enlarged and provided with greatly improved facilities — which served, however, chiefly to perfect the functioning of the *annona* which continued to supply the populace with requisitioned wheat.

disapproval was ruthless: a number were executed or deported, while others fled abroad in terror. Spies and informers were practically raised to the rank of government officials, while the Emperor's wrath extended to the philosophers who criticised his politics and his private life. They were again expelled from Rome. Domitian was no doubt also exasperated by the difficulties which beset his foreign policy. In 89-90 he succeeded in occupying the strategic border between the upper Rhine and the upper Danube, but on the lower Danube the Dacians invaded Moesia, and in 85 and 86 inflicted a disastrous defeat on the Romans. Though Domitian succeeded in restoring the situation, he was unable to conquer the Dacians. He was obliged to treat with them and even to pay them tribute. Meanwhile in Britain Agricola failed to conquer Scotland. Plots against the Emperor's life continued, and in 96 he was murdered.

The money to pay for these costly enterprises was provided by war booty: the 'gold of the Dacians' solved the financial problem. Thanks to this plunder it was possible to reduce taxes. Reforms also improved municipal administration, but at the cost of increasing State interference. Cities were placed under the guardianship of curators, and the authority of the Emperor continued

A detail from Trajan's column showing the Emperor receiving barbarian envoys. The adopted son of Nerva, Trajan's main claim to fame was his conquest of Dacia. With the spoils of victory he initiated the draining of the Pontine marshes, improved the facilities of the seaports and reduced taxes. *Mansell*

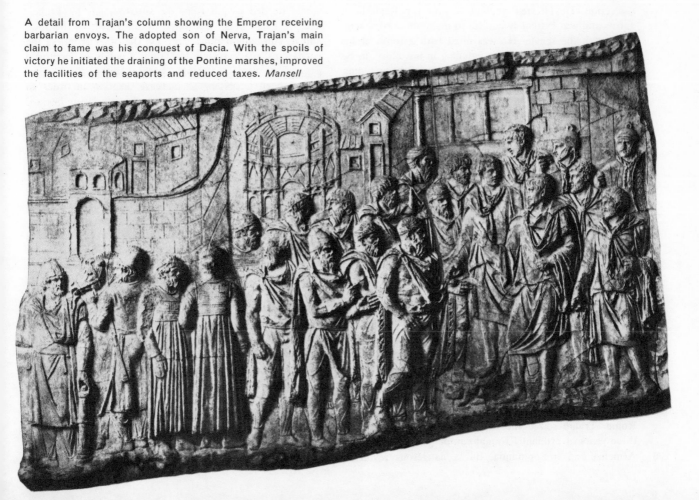

Trajan, Roman emperor A.D. 98-117. He wielded his authority with discretion. To Rome, accustomed to the caprices of absolute despots, his reign was a golden age. *Archiv für Kunst und Geschichte*

to grow. Trajan, however, wielded this authority with discretion. He affected a great respect for Republican forms and was extremely careful to maintain cordial relations with the senate. He was filled with a sense of his great responsibilities and was unfailing in his efforts to be just and humane. After the tyranny of some of the preceding emperors, it was not surprising that to everyone the reign of Trajan seemed like a return to the golden age. When in 114 the senate awarded him the title *Optimus Princeps*—the 'best of princes'—it was in simple recognition of a unanimous sentiment.

Trajan, moreover, needed peace at home in order to pursue an aggressive policy abroad. On the Danube the Dacians were still a constant menace, and he had resolved to subdue them. In 101 at the head of a well trained and ably commanded army he took the offensive. Overcoming the enemy's ferocious resistance he captured Sarmizegethusa, the Dacian capital, and in 102 forced their king Decebalus to become a vassal of Rome. Three years later, however, the war flared up again. In 106 Decebalus was again vanquished and took his own life. The country was annexed, the population deported, and the new province repeopled by an influx of immigrants attracted by its wealth. In the same year the annexation of the kingdom of Arabia Petraea was the first step in the Emperor's eastern designs. Since the time of Nero peace had reigned among the Parthians, though Armenia remained a subject of discord. In 112 the Parthians dethroned the king of Armenia who was a vassal of Rome. Trajan seized the occasion to destroy them. In three years of brilliantly fought campaigns he conquered Armenia and Mesopotamia. But a dangerous revolt of

the Jews, which spread throughout the new provinces, imperilled all the gains Trajan had made.

In spite of savage and merciless repression the Parthians again rose, and Trajan, while maturing his plans to renew the conquest, was obliged to compromise and accept Parthian vassalage. His death in 117 prevented him from carrying out the project.

Hadrian

On Trajan's death the senate recognised as emperor one of his best lieutenants, Hadrian. Hadrian, too, was a Spaniard, and perhaps the most remarkable sovereign of the Antonine line. His contemporaries were struck by the variety of his many gifts, the breadth of his interests and the complexity of his personality. His intellectual qualities were unrivalled, his curiosity omnivorous and his memory astonishing. He was a connoisseur of the arts, and also possessed all the abilities of a great statesman. During the reign of Trajan he had already proved himself a general of great energy and ability and, at the same time, an accomplished diplomatist. But it is above all as an administrator that Hadrian distinguished himself. Profoundly imbued with a sense of the grandeur of Rome, he devoted his great knowledge of state-craft to the service of the Empire, and his grasp of the broad outlines of a situation was equalled by his attention to detail. He was, however, fully conscious of his own power and convinced of the religious nature on which his imperial authority rested. His manner was haughty and abrupt, he tolerated no resistance to his imperious will and, in the end, he was detested.

All the great qualities which Hadrian possessed were sorely needed to put right the situation left by Trajan. The East had been devastated by the revolt of the Jews and its subsequent repression. On the other frontiers the barbarians, made restive by Trajan's policy of territorial expansion, were increasingly hostile. Within the Empire it had been necessary to increase taxation in order to pay for the conquests. Recruits for the army were becoming more difficult to find. Though Hadrian had himself been a distinguished soldier he did not hesitate to reverse his predecessor's policy. The newly won provinces were wisely abandoned, and he returned to the system of setting up buffer states, such as Armenia. Only Dacia and Arabia were retained, because of their strategic and commercial importance. The army was reorganised. Though the framework of the military units remained purely Italian, the actual fighting troops were recruited from all parts of the Empire. Corps of heavy and light cavalry were created. The conditions under which the ordinary soldier lived were improved, but at the same time discipline became stricter and training much more thorough. The army, whose mission was now purely defensive, relied on permanent and continuous fortifications — *limites Romani* — along the frontier. The system was not invented by Hadrian, but he made its application general. It would be an exaggeration to say that Hadrian never made war, but the object of the campaigns he fought was simply to avert dangers which threatened the Empire and not to enlarge its boundaries. The principal military operations which were undertaken during his reign took place within the Empire from 132 to 135 against the Jews who had again revolted.

Statue of Ceres Augusta in the theatre at Leptis Magna, Tripoli.
Shell Photo

The Temple of Hadrian and Marble Street, Ephesus. *Cash*

The Emperor Valerian suppliant at the feet of the Persian Shapur I.
A detail from a rock carving at Naqsh-e-Rustam, near Persepolis.
Roger Wood

Hadrian had called a halt to Trajan's policy of expansion largely from financial necessity, and economic problems occupied much of his reign. In solving them he was led to a reorganisation of the government. The system of collecting taxes was altered: instead of being farmed out to individuals or private companies, taxes were now gathered by government officials. To defend the interests of the Treasury before the courts he created a fiscal advocate, and officers were appointed to superintend municipal finances. He enhanced the value of the imperial domains by further settlement of *coloni* — tenant farmers bound to the soil — and by the exploitation of the mines of Spain. This increased State enterprise called for a strengthened administration. At the head of the administration the Imperial Council, now dominated by jurisconsults, assumed its definitive form. Perhaps the most far-reaching in its consequences of Hadrian's innovations was his systematic appointment of members of the equestrian order to positions of responsibility. In this way a new governing class was created whose importance was to grow at the expense of the senate. Hadrian further weakened the senate by depriving the traditional magistratures of their judiciary powers in Italy, and by dividing Italy into four districts which he entrusted to consular officials. He also conferred the privileges of Roman citizenship on all members of municipal assemblies, and demonstrated his great interest in the provinces by the numerous visits he paid them. In a word, his entire work was to subordinate the senate.

Antoninus Pius

The last years of the reign were overshadowed by the Emperor's illness and family afflictions. He had adopted a Gallic senator, Antoninus, who succeeded him in 138. It was during the reign of Antoninus that the Roman Empire reached the zenith of its power and prosperity, and for this reason, perhaps, his reign appears rather uninteresting and eventless. A few minor campaigns were necessary in Britain and in Mauretania, while in 155 the East was yet again disturbed by a revolt of the Jews. But the Emperor had no need to intervene in person. His relationship with the senate was improved by the revocation of certain of Hadrian's measures, such as the division of Italy into four consular districts. Complete financial stability was restored by the general calm and prosperity, and by the Emperor's economy. Antoninus was especially concerned with humanising the law which Hadrian had, in 131, codified with the publication of the *Edicta perpetua*. His respect for the religious cults of his forefathers and his great wisdom justly earned Antoninus the name Pius.

Marcus Aurelius

In 139 Antoninus had adopted Marcus Aurelius and in 146 made him his heir to the throne. Marcus Aurelius was a philosopher who became emperor in 161. Until then he had never been called upon to assume the responsibilities of power. But the principles which he had derived from his philosophical culture and an elevated sense of his duties as a man and as an emperor gave him the strength, which poor health denied him, to face grave and sudden dangers without flinching. By a tragic paradox

Mithras, a Persian god of Zoroastrian derivation, was often worshipped during the Empire. Engraved dish. *Ashmolean Museum*

A bronze head of Hadrian found in the Thames at London Bridge. A man of letters and an efficient administrator he called a halt to Trajan's policy of expansion. *British Museum*

this Stoic, pacifist and liberal, was throughout his entire reign compelled to be a soldier. It was his destiny to die in arms while reactionary senators, profiting by his absence in their military defence, strengthened their own social positions. His role in internal politics was, in fact, almost non-existent. He revived Hadrian's system of consular officers for Italy, under the name of *juridici*. But unlike Hadrian, he advanced freedmen rather than knights to positions of authority. The senators, however, were able to continue to enlarge their great estates and obtain for themselves a privileged status.

This was because Marcus Aurelius had absolute need of domestic peace in order to carry out his foreign policy. For war with the Parthians had broken out in the Orient again – and again over Armenia. The king of Armenia, an ally of the Romans, having been dethroned, the army of the East attempted to reinstate him but was crushed, while Syria was invaded. Marcus Aurelius gave command of the operations to L. Verus, who had been adopted by Antoninus Pius at the same time as Marcus himself. Verus reconquered Armenia in three years, drove forward into Mesopotamia, and in 166 even invaded Media. But a dangerous situation which had arisen on the Danubian frontier made peace suddenly imperative.

For many years the Germanic world had been perturbed by the migrations of the Goths who from the shores of the Baltic had, in about 120, begun to push southwards towards the Black Sea. Before them they drove the tribes who inhabited the banks of the Danube towards Moesia, the most powerful of these tribes being the Marcomanni of Bohemia, the Quadi of Moravia and the Iazyges of Hungary. The onslaught of these barbarians occurred in 209

O

A section of the Roman Wall at Cuddy's Crag, Northumberland. Guarding the provinces was a heavy drain on the Roman legions.

Systems of walls, watchtowers and beacons were commonly found throughout occupied territory. *Allan Cash*

the middle of 166 at the worst possible moment. The best Roman army was still in the East, the plague which it had contracted there was ravaging the Roman world, and the treasury was empty. In a sudden forward surge the barbarians swarmed across the Alps, descended to the shores of the Adriatic and laid siege to Aquileia. In the meanwhile other barbarians laid waste to Dacia and penetrated Greece and Asia. Panic spread through Italy, but Marcus Aurelius was able to rally the nation's courage and gather the forces necessary to meet the peril. In 167 he raised the siege of Aquileia, and by the following year he had swept the enemy from Roman territory. But he realised that this defensive operation was insufficient; the frontier must, he knew, be pushed further to the north. In 169, therefore, he crossed the Danube and for several years he campaigned in the difficult forest regions of Bohemia and Moravia without succeeding in breaking the resistance of the barbarians. In 175 he was compelled to conclude a hasty truce in order to deal with a usurper, Avidius Cassius. Cassius, to whom he had entrusted an important command in the East, had roused Syria and Egypt to rebellion. He was, however, very quickly slain by his own troops, and the Emperor had little trouble in restoring order. Hardly had he returned to Rome when he had to leave again for the Danube, where the Quadi and the Marcomanni were once more up in arms. In 180 Marcus Aurelius was carried off by the plague before he could accomplish his plans.

Commodus

Three years before his death Marcus Aurelius had named as his successor his son Commodus who was incapable, a drunkard and a profligate. Power at once went to his head, and he demanded recognition and worship as a god. He abandoned the reins of government to his licentious favourites, and renounced the energetic defensive policy of his father. He pillaged the treasury and persecuted the senate without mercy. Not unexpectedly,

plots against his life were numerous; in 192 he was poisoned and, when the poison was slow to work, strangled. In this inglorious manner the Antonine line — which had furnished Rome with so many great emperors — came to an end.

Social conditions in the first and second centuries

Though the social and spiritual evolution of the Mediterranean world in this period took place under the Pax Romana without violence, the changes were nonetheless profound. Since the days of Augustus, society had tended to become more and more rigidly sub-divided into castes. The most striking feature of this process was the emergence of a provincial bourgeoisie: members of the municipal senates, or *curiae*, were drawn from the wealthy classes who, with the approbation of the emperors, ended by monopolising the entire administration. But the growing interference of the state in local affairs eventually left them with little except heavy financial burdens, and from the end of the Antonine era we note among these privileged classes a progressive reluctance to accept office and a distinct weakening of local patriotism. The evolution of the bourgeoisie was accompanied by an ever increasing hostility between the rich and the poor, between the town and the country. The formation of great domains, imperial or private, reduced the peasant to a very precarious situation. Crushed by taxation and debts the countryman could feel little but dislike for the regime. At the first signs of trouble revolts would break out: such, for instance, were the uprising of the Egyptian herdsmen, the *boukoloi*, under Antoninus and Marcus Aurelius, and of Maternus in Spain, and in Gaul under Commodus.

The economic decline of Italy

The economic situation of the Empire, however, remained satisfactory, though prosperity was no longer

The successes of her merchant fleet were vital to Rome. Safe return could be assured only with the favour of the gods. Here Neptune is the central figure, while the figure in the chariot drawn by elephants is probably the Emperor Claudius. *Bruckmann*

to be found in Italy but in the provinces. Indeed, the empire of the Antonines was cosmopolitan, not Italian. In particular Italian industrial activity was dwindling. Since the first century the chief factories of crude ceramics, which flooded the Empire with their cheap products, had been situated in Gaul. The Eastern provinces profited by the displacement of industrial production to an even greater extent. Their wealth was at this time prodigious, and they now monopolised world commerce which in the days of Augustus had still been in the hands of Italians. To a certain extent this arose from the development of trade with the Far East. Egyptian and Syrian merchants went to India in search of spices, and to Turkestan in search of Chinese silks. Envoys between East and West were exchanged: in 99 the Indian king Kanishka sent a delegation to Trajan who in 107 returned the compliment. It is possible that, in 166, Marcus Aurelius sent a representative to China. This commercial activity made the fortune of the 'caravan cities' of Syria, especially of Palmyra which lay astride the trade-routes and served as a distribution centre. But it was not without danger to the economy of Rome, by reason of lack of foreign exchange. All purchases had to be paid for in cash and the drain in gold and silver slowly impoverished the Empire. Italy also suffered from the development of roads along the frontiers: merchants from the East travelled westwards by way of the Danube and the Rhine and thus by-passed the peninsula. The bustle of Italian ports was largely an illusion; for their chief source of activity was unloading grain which had been requisitioned by the *annona*.

Roman culture in the first and second centuries

The position of Italy in the intellectual world was also in decline. Literature, which had flowered in the age of Augustus, now withered. Being the province of aristocrats hostile to the regime, it was regarded with suspicion

by some Emperors. All those forms of literature, such as oratory and history, which could express critical sentiments, declined. Poetry and philosophy alone were still cultivated by, for instance, Lucan and Seneca. There was a minor renaissance under the Flavians and Trajan. During the reign of Vespasian Pliny the Elder wrote an encyclopaedia, the *Historia Naturalis*, while the treatises of Quintilian standardised the pedagogy of the period. Trajan's liberalism enabled Tacitus, the last great classic historian, to write his *Histories* and his *Annals*, in which the opprobrium suffered by the senate is reflected with epigrammatic force, if not always with fairness. After Tacitus there was a decline until the days of the great religious controversialists. Nor was art in a much healthier condition. Little more than formal perfection was aimed at, and sculpture became subservient to the growing demands of architecture. Building programmes, indeed, became more and more ambitious; and the employment of burnt brick covered with a veneer of a more precious material permitted the construction of such grandiose monuments as Trajan's Forum. But this process, though convenient, reduced the quality of the workmanship.

Oriental religions

Under such circumstances the influence of Italian culture on the rest of the Empire could only be limited, especially as the eastern provinces were themselves enjoying a vigorous renaissance at the same time, producing such distinguished writers as Plutarch, who was born in Boeotia, and Lucian, who was born in Syria. But the impact of the East on the Roman world was preeminently in the realm of religion. While the traditional polytheism of Rome decayed and died away, oriental cults had become more and more popular and received the approval of the emperors themselves: Claudius introduced the cult of Athis, while Nero had been initiated into the mysteries of Mithras. In these imported cults

211

what the faithful sought were private guardians, deities who shared their worshippers' burdens, gods who could give comfort and be loved. Hence the popularity of those divinities who had suffered death and resurrection, in whose mythology there was the promise of salvation. Against the fervour of their devotees, the last advocates of philosophical rationalism argued in vain. The new religions gave rise to theological speculation in which the rebirth of Platonism played a major part, and little by little accustomed men's minds to the idea of divine unity, to the reconciliation of conflicting principles, to cosmogonic and mythological conceptions of a universal tendency.

The birth and spread of Christianity

It was in the midst of this religious effervescence that Christianity arose. Its birth, and more especially its diffusion, cannot be explained without reference to the situation of the Jews in the Roman Empire. They were dispersed throughout the Empire and, while they made converts to Judaism, they had also been exposed to the influence of other religions. Those, however, who had remained in Palestine continued with fervent longing to await the coming of the Messiah. It was at this time — probably in the year 28 — that Jesus of Nazareth preached to the multitudes. His passion, crucifixion, resurrection and the imminence of the Last Judgment were the first themes of Christian teaching. Originally limited to the confines of Judea, Christianity, after the persecutions which it suffered in 44 at the hands of the Jews of strict observance, began to win followers in the rest of the East. A leading part in the propagation of the new faith was played by Paul the Apostle, who addressed not only the Hellenes but indigenous populations whose own beliefs had already made them familiar with the concept of a single divine being. Thanks to synagogues of the Jewish dispersion — the *diaspora* — the new doctrine spread rapidly.

Christianity thus emerged out of a Jewish background, but in a context which became increasingly Hellenistic.

The Jewish tradition of a *Messiah*, the Lord's Anointed, originally applied to King David, went back as far as the tenth century B.C.; the Jewish Law and the Prophets went back to Moses and Elijah; while their sacred books — the Pentateuch — were the rallying points of the Jews of the Diaspora, who still looked to the priestly hierarchy at Jerusalem, to whose revenues they contributed. There had been a short phase of Jewish independence after the Maccabean rebellion in the second century B.C., but the Asamonaean priest-kings had been deposed in 63 B.C., when the Romans annexed the country, which they controlled through procurators or client kings. There was thus seething discontent, which gave rise to Messianic fantasies and which was to culminate in a rebellion in the reign of Nero. This was in full flood in A.D. 67, the year in which St Paul was put to death, and, in A.D. 70, Jerusalem was sacked by Titus who plundered the Temple and carried off the Ark of the Covenant and the seven-branched candelabra — sacred emblems of Judaism.

The political background to the teaching of both Jesus and St Paul was therefore tense, and the hope of a Messiah urgent. When Jesus preached of monotheism and righteousness, he was in the main Jewish tradition of the Law and the Prophets, but his doctrine of love and salvation was less militant than the Jewish hierarchy desired. At the same time, when he was acclaimed by the people, the Roman authorities were alarmed. Having settled, as they thought, the fate of a false prophet and of a potentially subversive leader, both Jews and Romans thought the affair closed.

They completely miscalculated. The Crucifixion meant for a handful of Christians that Jesus had proved himself the Incarnate God or Saviour. They therefore organised the nucleus of a separate Church, for they were Jews who had been expelled from their own orthodox community. The earliest Christian organisation goes back to this time, and the followers of Christ (the Greek translation of '*Messiah*') had the Jewish vision of history as a process working towards the redemption of a chosen people. Indeed they expected an apocalypse.

It was St Paul who brought Christianity to the Gentiles, who made it a world influence, and who brought Hellenistic ideas to blend with the original teaching. The essential concern of the various Hellenistic cults, then widespread in the Empire, was with salvation; with escape from the power of demons and malign astrological influences. St Paul taught that this salvation could be won by faith in Christ, and that it could be attained by all Christians, Gentiles as well as Jews. Hence the detestation his teaching aroused among the orthodox Jews, who held that he had blasphemously appropriated their own

Marcus Aurelius addressing his troops; from a bas-relief from the Arch of Constantine. A philosopher with an elevated sense of his imperial duties, he gave Rome fairly sound government and unity in a troubled period. *Mansell*

Right: head of the goddess Roma. Her helmet is decorated with the infant Romulus and Remus, the legendary founders of the city, and the she-wolf who suckled them. *Bruckmann*

rights in their Covenant with God to strangers and swamped the true Jewish teaching in a cosmopolitan, Hellenistic religion. Other Hellenistic influences also affected Christianity. The ritual which was devised to commemorate the Saviour, and which became the sacrament, derives in part from the Hellenistic *agape* or love feast, which was practised in various forms by other salvation cults. And as the Church spread with extraordinary rapidity round the Empire, and in particular in the Eastern provinces, the organisation devised to control it was influenced by the example of other mystery cults, such as the Gnostics and Manichees. Thus Christianity combined its original Jewish element with the cosmopolitan Hellenistic influences, and developed the ritual and the hierarchy which in time enabled it to hold its own with, and finally to supersede other, rival religions. As it captured educated minds, it also produced divines and philosophers who deified its doctrines and emancipated their Gnostic superstitions. It thus became equipped, both by its original inspiration and its hierarchy, to become one of the great religions of world history.

In Rome itself Christians were soon numerous enough to cause the Emperors uneasiness. Christians were at first confused with Jews and in 49 were expelled with the Jews by Claudius. By 64, however, Nero could single them out to blame for the burning of Rome. Under the Flavian Emperors there were Christians even at the Imperial Court, and it was thought necessary to forbid the new religion. The Antonines endeavoured to deal mildly with the faithful: they were punished only in accordance with the gravity of the laws they contravened, and not systematically hunted down. At times, it is true, the hostility of the populace compelled the Emperors to depart from this policy of moderation. The scorn which the Christians displayed for popular beliefs, their refusal, while waiting for the Last Judgment, to participate in political and social life, and their equalitarianism, caused them to be considered dangerous atheists against whom public anger flared up at the slightest pretext. In this way the first persecutions, all local, occurred. But, as the end of the world was slow in coming, it became necessary for the Christians to form a more organised society. Each community chose a bishop to guide it and entered into relationship with other Christian communities. From very early years the primacy of the bishop of Rome seems to have been recognised; he was the successor of the Apostle Peter, and his seat was the capital of the Empire. The intellectual life of the Christian community also developed and the first apologists appeared in the reign of Hadrian. Towards 180 a sort of Christian university was founded in Alexandria. This intellectual activity was not without its dangers, and heresies sprang up in the time of Hadrian and Antoninus. Already controversy was rife between Christian apologists and pagan philosophers.

A section of the richly decorated column in Trajan's forum, Rome. Erected to commemorate his victory over Dacia, the hundred-foot column depicts the events of the Roman campaign in carefully executed detail. *Alinari*

India in the first and second centuries A.D.

The Sacae appear to have reached their maximum power during the reign of Gondophares, from approximately 19 to 45. Their ascendancy was soon disputed by the Kushans, one of the groups related to the Yueh-chi, who had united under their king, Kadphises I (c. 25-30). Kadphises wrenched the district of Kabul from the Sacae, and his successor, Kadphises II (c. 50-78) was an even greater conqueror: in the west he seized the Punjab and in the east he occupied Magadha as far as Benares. After him, Kanishka (c. 78-110) annexed Kashmir and Oudh, and clashed with the Chinese in central Asia. Kanishka became converted to Buddhism and convened a council at Peshawar which failed, however, to restore the unity of Buddhist doctrine.

Earlier Hellenistic cultural traditions, which had not been forgotten during the reigns of his predecessors, now bore fruit in the Graeco-Buddhist art of Gandhara, which was the first school of Indian sculpture which dared to depict the Buddha in human form. It drew its inspiration from Hellenistic models, and the type which was thus created was to spread throughout the Buddhist world as far afield as Japan and the Indian archipelago. Although each region modified the type according to its own conceptions, the manner in which the garments are draped and the characteristic profile of its distant Hellenistic ancestors can be recognised in all its metamorphoses. Under the successors of Kanishka native Indian elements again predominate, not only in the field of art but in that of religion. After 180 we know nothing more of the line of Kanishka which seems to have fallen into decay.

The formation and growth of the Kushan Empire had pushed the Sacae westwards and southwards, where they clashed with the Satavahanas who had founded a non Indo-European kingdom in the centre of the Deccan. Between 50 and 75 they forced the Satavahanas to relinquish Malvan and the region bordering the gulf of Cambay. It was with the Sacae that Roman merchants first had dealings. But the Satavahanas did not admit defeat and a long and bitter struggle between the two peoples ensued for possession of the coast, important because of the growing value of trade with the Roman Empire. At the beginning of the second century the Satavahanas reoccupied the gulf. It was one of their sovereigns, Shri Pouloumayi, whom the geographer Ptolemy mentions under the name of Siri Ptolemaios. Ptolemy also speaks of a prince of the Sacae named Tiastanes (c. 78-110) who had maintained the domination of his people in Malvan. Tiastanes' grandson Roudradaman (c. 120-155) succeeded in reconquering the ports along the gulf of Cambay, and that is all that is known about him on nothing is known about his successors.

The Later Han Dynasty in China

The successors of Siuan Ti in China were ineffectual rulers. The last of them, a child, was poisoned by his chief minister, Wang-Mang, who in A.D. 8 usurped the throne. Wang-Mang undertook important economic and social reforms. He expropriated large private domains for the benefit of the State, instituted a periodic redistribution of land and made loans to needy farmers. But in 18 his work was arrested by a violent peasant revolt which broke out in Shantung, while at the same time supporters of the legitimate royal family revolted. They defeated Wang-Mang in 22, but immediately quarrelled among themselves, which gave the rebellious peasants an opportunity to rape, murder, burn and pillage to their hearts' content. Finally, in 25, one of the Han claimants to the throne was proclaimed Emperor under the name of Kwang Wu Ti, and two years afterwards succeeded in stamping out the peasant revolt. In this fashion the Later Han dynasty which was to endure for two centuries was founded.

During these civil disturbances the foreign possessions of China had also revolted, and Kwang Wu Ti concentrated on the task of rebuilding the empire. His general Ma-Yuan reconquered Tonkin. Then he turned his attention to the Huns, and in 48 reduced Inner Mongolia once more to obedience. At the Emperor's death in 57 the frontiers were re-established and only central Asia remained to be reconquered. This was accomplished during the reigns which followed, thanks not to the Emperors themselves but to a succession of able generals and remarkable governors.

The active and important trade in silk carried across the oases of Chinese Turkestan to the Roman Empire could only prosper under Chinese protection. Command of this vital trade route and of the vast and almost unknown regions it traversed was acquired for the empire by illustrious Pan Tchao. From 73 to 97 he subdued all the native princes along the way and advanced to the frontiers of India, from which in 90 the Kushans, disturbed by his conquests, tried in vain to dislodge him. By his skill and energy, which did not always receive the support and co-operation of the Imperial Court, Pan Tchao emerged with honour from the critical situations into which his adventurous spirit sometimes led him. After a general revolt which followed his retirement from active service his son, Pan Yong, regained his conquests. Farther to the north, Inner Mongolia was also conquered and the Huns who lived there were exterminated in 93 by the Mongol horde of the Sien-Pei. Until the middle of the second century peace reigned in these regions and enabled Buddhism to penetrate China. Towards A.D. 60 the first missionaries had arrived from India, though it was not until a hundred years later that they became numerous.

In order to crush the Huns the Chinese had acted in consort with the Sien-Pei, who proceeded to make themselves undisputed masters of Mongolia and were not long in revealing hostility towards their late allies. In 156 they attacked Leao-tong, and thenceforth their raids over the frontiers became more frequent. What made these incursions especially dangerous was the decadence of China itself, where the Han Dynasty was degenerating. The misery of the people, impoverished by the encroachments of great landed proprietors, led to another ferocious peasant uprising in 184. At the Court rival factions squabbled for ascendancy until in 196 a general, Tsao Tsao, seized power — and the dynasty's downfall became inevitable.

Soldiers of the praetorian guard. In the later Empire, the man
who had the support of the praetorian guard was the most
likely candidate for the imperial title. *Giraudon*

CHAPTER TWELVE

THE DECLINE OF THE ANCIENT WORLD

A.D. 192 to 325

The line of Severus

When Commodus was assassinated in 192 the praetorian troops offered the Empire to Pertinax, prefect of Rome, who strove courageously to restore order to the state. Unfortunately his efforts threatened too many private interests, notably those of the praetorians themselves, who murdered him after he had reigned for three months. They then sold the throne to a rich senator, Didius Julianus, whereupon the armies rose in revolt. In 193 the legions of Illyria proclaimed Septimius Severus emperor, those of Syria chose Pescennius Niger, while in Britain the army declared for Clodius Albinus. Septimius Severus was the first to reach Rome. He then marched on the Orient where in 194 he vanquished and killed Niger. The next two years were spent in re-establishing discipline and annexing Osroene and northern Mesopotamia. He then turned on Albinus who had crossed into Gaul. In 197 Albinus was defeated at Lyons and Severus remained the sole master of the Empire.

Severus was the first Roman emperor who had no ties with Rome. He was of Carthaginian origin and had married Julia Domna, the daughter of a Syrian high priest. He was animated by no sense of Roman patriotism and, first and foremost a soldier, felt little but aversion for the Roman senate, which, in fact, he persecuted for having attempted secretly to aid the cause of Clodius Albinus. The reign of Severus was distinguished by two series of campaigns: from 197 to 202 he remained in the East where he completed the conquest of Mesopotamia; from 208 he made war in Britain against the Caledonians and repaired the celebrated wall from the Solway to the mouth of the Tyne. He died at York in 211. The Empire was inherited by his two sons, Caracalla and Geta. Caracalla, who suffered from persecution mania, assassinated his younger brother and then had all who stood in his way put to death. His reign was little more than a succession of military operations on the Rhine and on the Danube, and finally in the East where he undertook the conquest of the Parthian kingdom. In 217 he was murdered by Macrinus, his praetorian prefect.

Macrinus then seized power, but when he was defeated by the Parthians his army mutinied and in 218 proclaimed another emperor, the grand-nephew of Severus' wife Julia Domna, Avitus — better known as Elagabalus or Heliogabalus. Elagabalus, scarcely more than a boy, was high-priest of the Syro-Phoenician sun-god at Emesa and, interested chiefly in spreading his own bizarre beliefs throughout the Empire, resigned the government to the Syrian princesses of his family. His incredible folly, superstition and vices shocked even the army and in 222 he was murdered by the praetorian guards. He was succeeded by his cousin Severus Alexander, in whose reign a conservative reaction was attempted. The senate was strengthened and heaped with honours. An effort was made to cut down military expenditure by giving soldiers land in place of pay, with disappointing results however. The institutions for distributing food to the poor were revived, and banks were created to lend money to indigent peasants for the purpose of buying land. But these reforms were futile in face of the dangers beyond the frontiers. In 224 the Parthian Arsacid dynasty was overthrown by the Persian Sassanid dynasty, which renewed the struggle with Rome with fresh vigour. In 230 Ardashir, King of Kings since 226, invaded Mesopotamia and Cappadocia, and Severus Alexander two years later liberated Mesopotamia only with the greatest difficulty. Meanwhile on the Rhine and on the Danube the barbarian menace had become graver. In 234 the Alemanni attacked Mainz, and Severus bribed them to withdraw. His soldiers were outraged at the insult to Roman arms and in 235 assassinated him.

Government under Severus and his line

The events which took place during the reigns of Severus and his successors are of less historical interest than the change which occurred in political outlook. The Antonine emperors had shown great interest in the provinces: Severus and his successors were themselves provincials. Their sympathies led them to put the interest of the subjected peoples before that of metropolitan Italy. Thus Caracalla in 212 enacted a decisive measure: his *Constitutio Antoniniana* granted the rights of full Roman citizenship to all inhabitants of the Empire. The consequences of this step were important. The armies were no longer even theoretically officered and organised by Italians. Egypt became an integral part of the Roman world and was given the Roman municipal system. The senate was recruited from all parts of the Empire, especially from the Orient, and provincial senators were now in the majority. The Emperors' entire attention was devoted to the provinces where huge public works were undertaken, road-building receiving especial care. The security of the provinces was assured by the construction of great walls and military camps along the frontiers.

The power of the emperors rested on force alone. Unlike the Antonines, who had tried to maintain at least the appearance of respect for the civil authorities, Severus and his successors did not hesitate to emphasise the character of their power. The army was therefore their chief concern. It was reinforced and on several occasions pay was increased. More opportunities were provided for those who followed a military career: centurions could rise to higher grades, non-commissioned officers were granted the right to form committees to defend their own interests. Command of the legions, once the prerogative of senators, was now given to members of the equestrian order; and, in fact, every soldier, provincial or not, could reach the highest ranks.

The Arch of Septimius Severus, the first Roman Emperor (192-211) of foreign origin. Carthaginian by birth, he was first and foremost a soldier. His reign marks a change in imperial outlook, for his natural sympathies lay towards the subject peoples rather than towards metropolitan Italy.

The new emperors were violently opposed to those privileges which had been established in the days of Augustus. For political reasons the senatorial nobility was decimated. Many other rich men also disappeared and their property was confiscated. Functionaries had to be created simply to make an inventory of such property. Senators were excluded from the highest offices, and their place taken by members of the equestrian class who were themselves increasingly drawn from men with a military background. Members of the bourgeoisie in provincial towns also received scant consideration, and the burdens inflicted on local municipal assemblies were increased. The ten richest men in each city were made responsible for the collection of taxes; and, failing to collect the full amount, they had to make up the deficit themselves. The lower classes were on the other hand well treated: the Roman plebs received free grain and free oil. Workmen were authorised to form themselves into corporations. Much of the legislation was aimed at the protection of the weak, which became one of the basic duties of provincial governors.

The emperors of the line of Severus ruled as absolute sovereigns. The senate had no function other than to approve and register the laws laid down by imperial decree. Even under Severus Alexander, who paid honour to the senate, the essential law-making body remained the Imperial Council, and imperial functionaries had never been more numerous. This ever increasing imperial interference in all departments of government was caused not only by the emperors' conception of power, but also by strict necessity. The growing cost of the armed forces and the inflation which accompanied it compelled the emperors to increase existing taxes and invent new ones: the military *annona,* for instance, was an invention of the period. Faced by the resistance of the tax-payer, coercion became necessary. The property of senators and decurions — or members of municipal senates — was reassessed, and such men were made collectively responsible for the total revenue demanded. A by-product of this system was an increased rigidity in the social order. The classes closed their ranks to newcomers and became hereditary. It was the simplest method of making sure that the taxes were paid. The despotism of the emperors found its legal justification in the works of contemporary jurisconsults: Papinian, Ulpian and Paulus, who were all imbued with the grandeur of the State and argued the superiority of its rights over those of its subjects. Called upon to hold the highest positions, the jurisconsults won acceptance for the theory of absolutism.

A similar tendency can be observed in the contemporary spiritual scene. It was the age of syncretism, and efforts were made to fuse all religions and all forms of belief into a common worship which would be acceptable to all. In his private chapel Severus Alexander, it was said, had images of Orpheus, of Apollonius of Tyana and of Christ. Caracalla, in his edict in 212, expressed his desire to unite all the subjects of the Empire in a single religion; and Elagabalus attempted to impose the universal cult of his Syrian sun-god. Not one of these emperors, however, went so far as to set up a cult of the State. The spirit of the times was, moreover, very susceptible to the message of Christianity, which made great advances. Even though Septimius Severus in 202 had forbidden conversion to the new faith, the Christians were not greatly disturbed. The theological school at Alexandria achieved distinction under Clement, and even more under Origen whose triumph was the adaptation of Platonism — and especially the doctrine of the Logos — to the needs of Christianity. Christians were among the personal friends of Alexander, and during his reign the first provincial synods were convened.

Anarchy and the invasions

The death of Severus Alexander in 235 was to plunge the Empire into anarchy, and anarchy was to open the floodgates to the barbarians. The army proclaimed one of its officers, Maximinus, emperor. Maximinus, himself of barbarian extraction, succeeded in repelling the barbarians on the Rhine and the Danube. He had continued the anti-senatorial policy of Severus and his line, and the senate had countered in 238 by confirming the imperial title of the Gordiani. Gordianus I and Gordianus II however, very quickly vanished from the scene, as did two other imperial claimants, Papienus and Balbinus, whom the senate backed. Maximinus marched against them and had them put to death. As the Danube frontier was no longer secured, the Goths flowed into the Empire and Gordianus III, who had become Emperor in the same year, 238, was forced to pay them tribute. Peace, though temporarily restored in the West, was soon broken in the East by the Sassanid king Sapor — or Shapur — who in 240 seized Nisibis in Mesopotamia and Antioch. Gordianus

A detail from the Arch of Septimius Severus, Rome. It was
the practice of the later Emperors to erect triumphal arches to
commemorate particularly successful campaigns.

III retook Antioch and invaded Mesopotamia; but in 244
he was murdered and replaced by his praetorian prefect,
Philippus, known as Philip the Arabian. Philip purchased
peace from Shapur in order to deal with the Carpi, a
Germanic tribe who had in the meantime invaded Dacia.
He succeeded in driving them out in 247, but internal
strife and attempts to usurp the throne permitted a horde
of barbarians to pour into Thrace. Decius, the general
who defeated them, was then proclaimed emperor by his
troops, and in 249 slew Philippus.

Decius appears to have possessed some statesmanlike
qualities. He grasped the fact that to meet the barbarian
peril the moral unity of the Empire must be restored.
Unfortunately the only means he could see to accomplish
this was to suppress Christianity, and in 250 he launched,
though without success, a cruel and general persecution
of the faithful. The Goths had meanwhile again invaded
Thrace, and to face the danger Decius was obliged to sus-
pend the persecution. He then marched against the Goths,
but in 251 was himself defeated and slain. His successor, 219

Trebonianus Gallus, had even more serious difficulties to confront: an invasion by the Goths of Asia Minor, an offensive by Shapur in Armenia, and finally in 253 a mutiny among his own troops in Moesia which cost him his life. He was briefly succeeded by Aemilianus who met the same fate.

The imperial purple next fell on Valerian, an aged senator who shared the empire with his son Gallienus, to whom he entrusted the East. Both emperors were unlucky in their military operations. Alemanni and Franks poured into Gaul and in 253 penetrated as far as Spain. The strategically important region of the upper Rhine and upper Danube had to be abandoned towards 260. The Goths invaded Greece and Asia Minor, the Berbers of Africa had risen in 253 and Shapur took Nisibis a year later. In 258 there were fresh incursions of Franks and Alemanni into Gaul, and of Goths into Asia. Finally, two years later, the Emperor Valerian himself was taken prisoner by Shapur. In view of the total impotence of imperial power, local authorities took their own defence

Caracalla. During his reign Roman citizenship was given to all inhabitants of the Empire. Under the Antonine emperors the senate's functions were severely reduced and imperial direction became despotic. *Mansell*

in hand. In 258 Postumus in Gaul assumed the title of emperor, while two years later in the East Odenathus, prince of Palmyra, took charge of the war against Shapur with the full approval of Gallienus. The prefect of Egypt attempted, though without success, to imitate these acts of independence in 262. Gallienus in the meanwhile was unable to protect the territories which still remained under his rule. The Goths almost annually pillaged Asia. He did, however, put an end to the persecutions of the Christians, and encouraged the diffusion of neo-platonism. He was a patron of Plotinus, and showed an interest in the artistic renaissance which was then taking place in Greece. His military incapacity led, however, to his downfall. In 267 the Goths inundated the Hellenic peninsula, while in Palmyra Waballath, the son of Odenathus, made himself completely independent. In 268, when he was marching against the Alemanni who had invaded Rhaetia, Gallienus was assassinated and replaced by Claudius II.

The Illyrian emperors

Claudius II was the first of the Illyrian line of sovereigns under whom the Empire regained relative security. Claudius himself repulsed the Alemanni, crushed the Goths at Naissus in Upper Moesia, and re-established imperial authority in Spain. He was, however, unable to prevent Waballath — or rather his mother, Zenobia, the queen regent of Palmyra — from occupying Egypt and invading Asia Minor. On his death in 270 he was succeeded by Aurelian whose reign began badly; for Germanic tribes which had invaded Italy defeated him at Piacenza. In the following year, however, Aurelian drove them out and turned his attention to the East where he defeated Zenobia whom he carried to Rome to grace his triumph. Palmyra was destroyed. Aurelian was equally successful in 273 in bringing Gaul — which was ruled by Tetricus as an independent sovereign — back into the Empire. But he abandoned Dacia permanently and withdrew the boundary of the Empire to the south bank of the Danube with disastrous strategic consequences. And — an admission of the parlous state of the Empire's defences — he surrounded the city of Rome with the massive wall which still stands. Aurelian was assassinated in 275 and succeeded by M. Claudius Tacitus whose brief reign was marked by ferocious invasions of Gaul and Asia. The situation was righted by Probus (276-282) who drove the barbarians from Gaul and made peace with Sassanian Persia. In an effort to repeople the Empire Probus installed numerous barbarian immigrants on land which had been abandoned. At his death, three short reigns occupied the two years which preceded the accession in 284 of the greatest of the Illyrian emperors, Diocletian.

The crisis of the third century

For nearly half a century — since the death of Severus Alexander — the Roman world had been on the verge of chaos, and the consequences were incalculable. The Empire emerged from the period in a state of collapse. Wherever the barbarians had passed they had left behind them waste and ruin, while the peasants whose fields and homes were ravaged, often yearly, had fled. Many of them had been slaughtered and many others had died of starvation. Added to the miseries of war was the scourge of brigandage which had become endemic. Trade had become sluggish, and yet the expenses which the emperors were obliged to meet had become larger and larger. Taxation, though crushing, had proved insufficient, and they had been forced to resort to currency manipulations which inevitably sent prices sky-rocketing and further aggravated the wretchedness of the poorer classes. Profound political and social changes had naturally ensued. Traditional institutions had broken down, in particular the senate, which no longer furnished the military commanders. Governors of provinces, of whom a great number were now drawn from the equestrian order, retained only their civil functions. The covering troops which protected the outposts of the Empire were recruited from among the military *coloni* who were settled on the frontiers. Since their military value was slight, the actual fighting forces were made up of massive formations of armed cavalry in imitation of the Persians. The prosperity of the towns had declined, and they fortified themselves against barbarian incursions with walls. Even Rome was thus protected. The Empire was divided into great military areas, commanding vast territories. The system of voluntary enlistment had given way to obligatory military service and landed proprietors were made responsible for the supply of recruits. The general insecurity lessened the importance of slavery, and during these troubled times many slaves gained their freedom. On the other hand, the lot of the free peasant became more burdensome as control over the great landowners slackened. Many charitable institutions which had been supported by ground rents were ruined, which contributed in no small degree to the decay of traditional religion.

The Illyrian emperors were the first to conceive a general plan to cure these manifold evils. They were of modest birth and, in general, men of little culture; but they were animated by a deep and simple sense of responsibility. Their first duty, they realised, was the forceful expulsion of the barbarians, and this they set about with energy. All else took second place to the essential task, and the will of the State admitted no opposition. They ruled, indeed, as despots. Unlike Severus and his successors, they refrained from terrorising the senate, but they did not even pretend to collaborate with it. They made the weight of their authority felt throughout the Empire by means of an army of imperial bureaucrats. They were well aware of the need to restore the Empire's moral unity, and with this in view they attempted to impose the cult of the Sun as an official state religion. Similar principles had already inspired Aurelian, who proclaimed that he ruled by divine right, created a body of priests of the Sun, divided Italy into provinces and transformed the corporations into public services. It was Diocletian, however, who was most successful in putting such theories into practice.

Diocletian

Diocletian, like his predecessors, was above all preoccupied with military problems and had recourse to the pratice of dividing the Empire into broad military areas. He gave such areas a permanent character and associated their commanders with him in the rule of the Empire. In 286 he shared his title of 'Augustus' with Maximian,

Under Diocletian civil and military functions were separated and provincial governors acted as judges, nothing more. Diocletian also made a determined effort to stabilise the value of money and introduced a new fiscal system. It was under his direction that the Tetrarchy was established. *Anderson*

to whom he had entrusted Gaul. Then, in 293, both Emperors appointed subordinates who were called 'Caesars', Diocletian adopting Galerius, and Maximian, Constantius Chlorus. It was arranged that in the event of the death or abdication of an Augustus, his Caesar would take his place. In this way the Tetrarchy was created, though Diocletian retained his pre-eminence and there was no absolutely rigid division of territory. It meant simply that imperial power could now be represented in all four corners of the Empire. It is also possible that Diocletian hoped that the system would put an end to the ambitions of usurpers. If so, he was disappointed; for from 287 to 296 Britain remained in the hands of rebel generals, and in 296 he was obliged to wage war against Achilleus, who had proclaimed himself emperor in Egypt. The system was, however, successful in that it permitted Diocletian to restore and even to extend the frontiers of the Empire. Maximian re-pacified Gaul, Spain and Africa, while in 295 Galerius subdued the Goths of the Danube. Two years later Diocletian himself imposed the peace of Nisibis on the Persians by which he gained a protectorate over Armenia and, to the north, over Asiatic Iberia.

Diocletian reigned as an absolute monarch and, in imitation of the Sassanid kings of Persia, surrounded himself with the outward splendour and pomp of an oriental sovereign. Throughout the Empire he imposed a uniform system from which neither Egypt nor Italy itself was exempted. As early as 288 he had decided completely to separate civil and military functions, and provincial governors were no longer anything more than judges. In order to facilitate their work, the number of provinces was more than doubled. The provinces were grouped in twelve *dioceses*, ruled by vicars, whose actions were coordinated under the direction of the prefects of the four prefectures which made up the Empire. Local govern-

Chariot-racing and other entertainments continued the bread-and-circuses policy, though the crude displays of earlier days were eschewed by the citizens of culture and here and there voices were raised against organised slaughter as a spectacle.

221

In 70 A.D .Titus had sacked Jerusalem in an attempt to destroy the Jews and had carried off the sacred emblems of the temple for his triumph in Rome. Though persecution of Jews and Christians was a feature of Roman policy for centuries, the monotheistic religions resisted pagan pressure, in the provinces and in Rome itself.

An early Christian sarcophagus, illustrating scenes from the Passion and Christian symbols, the Cross and doves. In style there is no difference between it and contemporary pagan sarcophagi. Both show the change of spirit and artistic outlook that heralded the Middle Ages. *Alinari*

The second-century Roman theatre at Sabratha, one of Tripolitania's three Roman cities; the others were Leptis Magna, originally a Phoenician settlement, and Oea (Modern Tripoli)
Fenwick

Prisoners brought back from successful campaigns, criminals and slaves were the combatants in early gladiatorial fights. Finally the performers were paid professionals.

The Tetrarchy. A late Roman statue. Venice.

An ivory diptych showing the apotheosis of Romulus, son of Maxentius. A.D. 309. British Museum. *Mansell*

ment remained firmly in the hands of municipal assemblies; but their task, in actual practice, consisted primarily in meeting financial contributions demanded of the municipality, and the situation of the decurions, or town councillors, became insupportable. Since their position was hereditary it was impossible to escape the onerous responsibility. The penalty for wealth was thus ruin, and needless to say, the municipal system deteriorated.

The financial and economic state of the Empire was, indeed, in urgent need of attention. Diocletian strove to stabilise the value of money by issuing new currency, while his edict of 301 fixed a ceiling on prices. But in spite of these measures prices continued to rise. He was more successful in reorganising the fiscal system to produce increased revenues, though the details of how this was done are not fully known. It would seem that while the older taxes — capitation and land tax — were retained, the manner in which they were assessed was simplified: for land, the *jugum* — or about five-eighths of an acre — was made equivalent to the *caput* — or poll tax — for persons. This made collection easier and more exact. The tax scale was revised every fifteen years and arbitrarily fixed by imperial proclamation — the *indictio*. Industry and commerce were organised into corporations over which the State maintained strict and planned financial control. To complete his work Diocletian set about the task of restoring the moral unity of the Empire, which at once brought him into conflict with Christianity. There had been no persecution of the Christians since the reign of Gallienus. Christians had become considerably more numerous, and were to be found in all departments of society, including the army. Churches celebrated their rites openly, and did not hesitate to submit their disagreements to the civil authorities. Their intellectual life had become more and more active, and great Christian writers had begun to appear: Tertullian, Arnobius, Lactantius and Saint Cyprian. But the faith was threatened by internal dissensions, and heresies multiplied. The most formidable of these was Manichaeism, which had spread from Persia into the confines of the Empire. Africa was also disturbed by the problem of the *lapsi* — Christians who had, during the persecutions of the third century, denied their faith in order to save their skins. Then, too, pagan philosophers had renewed their struggle with Christianity; Porphyry's *Treatise Against the Christian Religion* was followed by numerous other works attacking it, while at the same time paganism was itself evolving a form of a solar monotheism with its own corpus of doctrine to oppose to Christian theology. This pagan propaganda was not, perhaps, without its influence on Diocletian, but he seems above all to have been aware of the irreducible antinomy between the new faith and the ancient Roman tradition which it was his intention to revive. In 303, therefore, several edicts were published ordering churches to be closed and books sacred to Christian worship to be seized. First the clergy and then the faithful were legally obliged to offer sacrifice in the Roman manner. The struggle which this sparked off was, in the event, to end with the triumph of Christianity.

The breakdown of the Tetrarchy

Diocletian did not reign to see the triumph of the new faith. Stricken with illness, he abdicated in 305, as did

Meleager, the Aetolian hero. From a fourth-century Roman
mosaic. *British Museum*

his co-Augustus, Maximian. Galerius and Constantius became co-emperors, and two new Caesars were designated: Maximinus Daza in the Orient, Flavius Valerius Severus in the West. In the succession, the son of Maximian, Maxentius, and the son of Constantius, Constantine, had been passed over — and again the Empire plunged into civil war. On the death of the Emperor Constantius in 306, his son, Constantine, was proclaimed Emperor by the army in Britain. Maxentius also revolted and in 307 killed Severus, while Constantine assumed the title of Augustus. Diocletian attempted to intervene, but only succeeded in introducing a new rival in the struggle: Licinius. The situation was simplified by the death of Galerius in 311 and by alliances between Maxentius and Maximinus Daza, and between Constantine and Licinius. In 312 Constantine attacked Maxentius, who was master of Italy and Africa and defeated him at Saxa Rubra near Rome. Maxentius perished as he tried to escape over the Milvian Bridge, and Constantine took possession of his domains. A year later Daza, who governed Egypt and Asia, invaded Europe and was killed by Licinius. In the following year a brief conflict flared up between Licinius and Constantine, in which Constantine gained the Balkans. Then, for ten years, peace reigned between the two emperors.

Constantine and Christianity

Peace was also re-established on the religious front. In the beginning of 313 Constantine and Licinius had already met at Milan where they decided to restore the Christians' freedom of worship and to return their confiscated property. From then onwards Constantine showed more and more friendliness towards Christianity, though he may not have become an actual convert. Licinius, on the contrary, continued to persecute the Christians. Constantine's answer to this was the enactment of a series of measures which, especially from 320 onwards,

made the Empire to a considerable extent a Christian state: Sunday was recognised as a day apart; churches were authorised to receive legacies; defendants were accorded the right to be tried by bishop's court instead of by that of the governor. At the same time Constantine himself intervened in ecclesiastical affairs and attempted to pacify quarrelling religious factions. Thus the inevitable and final struggle with Licinius took on the aspect of a religious war. It was brief: Licinius was defeated at Adrianople, again at Chrysopolis, and was put to death. In 324 the Roman Empire once more had a single ruler. The new reign was distinguished by two other acts with far-reaching consequences. After his victory Constantine decided to remove the seat of the Empire to Byzantium which in 330, almost one thousand years after its foundation as a Greek colony, was solemnly dedicated and renamed Constantinople. Five years before this, in 325, he summoned the bishops of all Christendom to convene at Nicaea to resolve the dissension between the heretic Arius, who professed Christ to be of God but less than God, and the orthodox Trinitarians led by Athanasius. The Council issued the Nicene Creed supporting Athanasius. Constantine agreed to enforce it. At this moment the Empire had finally broken with Roman pagan tradition and a new era was about to begin.

Sassanid Persia

The Parthians had been the principal enemies of Rome since the foundation of the Empire. Though they had not been able to preserve the territorial integrity of the Seleucid kingdom which preceded them, the Arsacids had at least retained Persia. But to the mass of their subjects they appeared as foreigners and their feudal monarchy had not succeeded in forging a strong and unified state. They had left local government to local ruling families, and were constantly threatened by acts of secession. The last of these rebellions led to a change

The excitement of chariot-racing was soon to be lost when Rome began to sever her long-established links with paganism and the brutality of a decadent Empire. *Bruckmann*

Colour plate: a hunter. From a mosaic in the Great Palace at Constantinople. Probably executed in the reign of Justin II (565-78). *Josephine Powell*

of dynasties. Towards 212 Ardashir, a princeling of Fars, had revolted against Artabanus V, conquered Kerman, Susiana and Oman, and finally in 224 vanquished and slew Artabanus at Ormizdagan. The new dynasty, known as the Sassanians or Sassanids, traced their descent from the Achaemenidae, contemporaries of Alexander the Great, and laid claim to their original heritage. Presenting themselves as Persian sovereigns, they gave a new impetus to the struggle against Rome. In 236 Ardashir himself succeeded in seizing Nisibis which was the chief Roman military post in Mesopotamia. Shapur I (242-273) was even more successful. Taking advantage of Roman weakness during the troubled reigns of Gordian III and Philippus, he had forced Rome to recognise his authority over Armenia and Mesopotamia. His victory over the Emperor Valerian rendered him master of Osroene. His progress was arrested only by Palmyra. After the death of Odenathus, king of Palmyra, the ambitions of his widow Zenobia provoked a change in the Near Eastern situation however, and Aurelian, as we have seen, re-imposed Roman domination over the deserts of Syria. On the death of Shapur the power of Sassanid Persia suffered an eclipse. The ephemeral kings who followed him were unable to prevent the Romans from reconquering Armenia and Mesopotamia and from penetrating as far as Georgia. Persian expansion was to be resumed under Shapur II, but he was an infant at his accession to the throne in 310.

The Arsacid monarchy had been feudal; the Sassanid kings were despotic and their rule was centralised. The King of Kings, whose power was of divine origin, was surrounded by the ceremonial pomp and dazzling splendour of an oriental court whose traditions went back to the great empire of Darius and Xerxes. He was assisted by ministers who directed the work of a well-staffed chancellery. In the provinces the orders of the government were carried out by royal officials, and to ensure a proper respect for his authority the king relied both on the army and upon religion. The military might of the Sassanids resided chiefly in heavily armed cavalry — the cataphracts—and in light cavalry of mounted bowmen. Mazdaism (orthodox Zoroastrianism in which Ormuzd, a good god, opposed Ahriman, a bad god) became the state religion. The king was himself the head of the cult, though the chief of the Magi very soon played a part of great importance. Priests were numerous and rich and, since they were responsible for public instruction, their influence on the population

was considerable. In order to maintain their predominant position, they displayed great intolerance: Christians were persecuted and heretics, notably Mani the founder of Manichaeism, were ill-treated. This state enjoyed an enviable prosperity. It took over and profited by the trade with China and developed its own industries. Interesting works of art were produced, and in architecture Persia generalised the use of the cupola which spread from there through the West.

During the reign of Valerian both Alemanni and Franks poured into Gaul, and the Goths attacked in Asia. Finally the Emperor was forced to submit to the Persian Shapur I. This humiliation is recorded in a rock carving at Naqsh-e-Rustam.

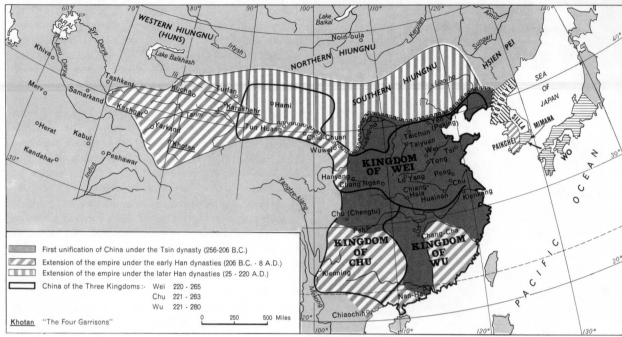

China under the Hans and the Three Kingdoms

India in the third century

In India, the third century is an obscure period. It would seem that the establishment of the Sassanid dynasty in Persia had a detrimental effect on the Kushan Empire. Ardashir may have reoccupied Bactria and brought it under his suzerainty. Graeco-Buddhist art, however, continued to prosper, although Persian motifs appeared and assumed a growing importance. Farther to the south, the successors of Roudradaman continued to maintain their position on the western slopes of the Deccan until the extinction of their line towards the year 304. The dynasty which succeeded them was to endure until the end of the fourth century. Meanwhile the Satavahanas, who had been confined to the lower Deccan, split into two rival states. The event of greatest importance to Indian history at this time occurs when the period under consideration has more or less finished: since the fall of the Maurya empire the region of the Ganges had broken up into petty states of which nothing is known. But at the opening of the fourth century they began to regroup under the leadership of the Guptas, a family from Patna. The first member of the line, Chandragupta I (c. 320-335) imposed his authority on Magadha, to which he added Oudh, the Doab and possibly Bengal — thus foreshadowing the powerful empire his successors were to build.

The Three Kingdoms of China

At this same time China, in contrast, was politically disintegrating. When the general Tsao Tsao assumed power in 196 another general, Souen Kiuan, seceded from the empire to the south of the Yang-tze, while a Man prince, Liu Pei, proclaimed himself emperor at Szechwan. The Three Kingdoms which thus arose — Wei in the north, Wu in the south and Shuh in the west — fought each other for more than half a century, and the

empire which the Hans had built in central Asia crumbled. Finally unity was re-established by the victory of the kingdom of Wei, which was governed in the name of its exhausted royal house by energetic mayors of the palace: the Sze-ma family. The most able of these, Sze-ma Chao (255-265) conquered the kingdom of Shuh, and in 265 his son, Sze-ma Yen, dethroned the royal house of Wei and usurped the imperial throne. In 280 Sze-ma Yen completed the work of his family by occupying Wu.

He then undertook to restore Chinese authority in central Asia, established a military garrison in Lob-nor, and received the homage of the king of Koutcha. The unity of China seemed to have been re-established for the first time in a century.

But towards the year 300 the Emperor of the Yellow River, like the Emperor of Rome, entrusted the defence of his frontiers to the barbarians. The Huns, beginning as confederates, in the end became masters. The era of the great invasions was about to open.

A tiger carved from jade. Chinese.

The formalism of western art was completely absent in the work of eastern artists of this period. This Indian rock carving is in strong contrast with anything produced in the Empire.

THE MIDDLE AGES

During the Middle Ages Western European civilisation suffered a phase of severe decadence. In the Eastern, Byzantine, Empire the continuity was maintained unbroken until the crusaders' sack of Constantinople in 1204, and went on in attenuated form until 1453, when the Turks took over a dilapidated city. In the West, Roman Catholic Christendom took on a new, if uncouth, vitality as the barbarians were converted and settled into the now Romanised lands. Further Christian civilisation gradually extended to peoples in northern and north eastern Europe hitherto outside the Empire.

It took two or three centuries — from the fourth to the seventh — for the decline of the Roman Empire to pass into the creation of medieval Europe, and the latter, when it did come into existence, changed with every century, as new political, economic, intellectual, artistic, and psychological factors replace the old.

A Janus-headed image from a Gallo-Roman vase, found at Beauvay. *Giraudon*

Little by little nations were formed, took shape, and became conscious of themselves. Very soon commerce reappeared, thriving more than ever. With it rose the towns, developing a new social class, the burghers. The spires of medieval cathedrals, like the minarets of Islam, dominated the cities; side by side with theology, philosophic thought groped for its own truths, universities were founded, and the *medrasas*, or trading warehouses, of the Near East.

Medieval technical discoveries opened the way for modern progress, from the rudder to the compass, from the windmill to accountancy, from the stirrup and saddle to the gunpowder which was to bring to an end the age of cavalry.

The Renaissance was already in train during the last centuries of the Middle Ages: in the fourteenth and fifteenth centuries no one can say where one begins or the other ends. It was a period of metamorphosis. 231

THE BARBARIAN INVASIONS

Constantine VI (776-97) with dignitaries of the Church: the Byzantine cross is in the centre, and the figure below probably represents an heretical bishop. Religious controversies divided the Empire at all times, and were particularly disruptive because of the growing political power of the Church. In the eighth century the worship of images was condemned as superstitious by the Iconoclasts ('image breakers'), who were responsible for the destruction of many mosaics and icons. However, Constantine VI and his mother, the Empress Irene, re-introduced image-worship at the Council of Nicaea in 787. In the West, Charlemagne objected to the 'heretical teaching' of the Greeks and compelled the Pope to excommunicate Constantine. The latter's repudiation of the Council is significant of the increasing influence of the Western Empire.

Attila, Khan of the Huns, who in the fifth century swept across the Rhine with his barbarian hordes and descended upon the Empire, threatening to 'water his horse in the rivers of Spain'.

CHAPTER THIRTEEN

THE DESTRUCTION OF THE ROMAN WORLD

THE EMPIRES

A.D. 320-500

On May 1, 305 at Nicomedia, the Emperor Diocletian abdicated his supreme dignity, calling on his successor, Maximian, to succeed him. At the same time, on the other side of the Eurasian continent, China was in the process of reconstructing the earlier vast Han empire. In the middle regions of the Ganges the rise had already begun of the Gupta dynasty which was to unite central India, while in Persia Shapur II, one of the greatest of the Sassanids, was soon to come to the throne.

THE ROMAN WORLD

Of the four civilisations of the known world, that of the Mediterranean was the most brilliant. The energetic measures carried out by Diocletian had brought to an end the economic and political troubles of the third century. Calm had been restored from the frontiers of the Rhine and Danube to the deserts of Africa; and Rome had dealt the Persians a blow that was to banish for fifty years any threat from that quarter. The measures taken by Diocletian to stop the ruinous rise of prices do not seem to have affected the economic expansion, which may have been encouraged by the influx of precious metals from India, Persia, or Ethiopia. In any case the Emperor, by taking stock of all the landed property and increasing taxation, gave the Empire that solid financial basis that had been so sadly lacking during the difficult times of the third century. It was one of the chief reasons for the stability of the fourth, which was achieved only by a relatively debased despotism.

Weakness of the West. Strength of the East

It was the economic scene that showed the contrast between the chief divisions of the Empire. The West had played the dominant role down to the first century, but devastations without and civil wars within had undermined its vigour. The Spanish mines were becoming exhausted; Italy, where malaria was endemic, was handicapped by the immense and sterile estates of the senators; Britain was becoming barbaric; constant brigandage and the raids of Saxon pirates laid waste the whole of Gaul north of the Seine. Only north Africa and southern Gaul retained their place as major sources of supply. Wheat and oil from Egypt and north Africa supported the enormous mass of workless and malcontents that made up Rome. Wines, pottery, arms and cloth still supplied the

trade of Narbonne and Arles, the 'Little Rome of Gaul', but the day had passed when this province could maintain the whole Empire with its wealth. Gradually drained of its substance, preyed on by the separation of its provinces, the Western Empire was in a very vulnerable condition. For the towns, this progressive anaemia meant a threat of famine.

There remained Illyria. Besides the traditional imperial trade route between Narbonne and Alexandria another had been open for a hundred years, an overland route joining Trier to Sirmium, running thence to Byzantium and to the Euphrates, and this alternative route had given the Balkan peninsula an extremely important part to play in the third century. The constant passage of troops and the country's wealth in iron and other ores explain the military superiority of the Illyrians down to the fourth century, but its geography prevented its dominating the Empire.

Three other provinces gradually assumed the leadership of the Empire. First of all, Egypt, which was the granary of the East in spite of inefficient exploitation of the land by the Senate. Egyptian trade was in the hands of the Greeks, as was philosophy. Alexandria, the terminus of the trade route from China and Malaya, was also a literary centre. Secondly there was Syria, enriched by the industry of Tyre and by oriental trade. Caravans carrying gold, incense and the spices of India and China made Syria one of the richest areas of the Empire. And Antioch was the centre of the Christian faith.

It was, however, neither in Egypt, which had remained after all a colony, nor amongst the Levantines that Diocletian considered establishing his capital, but in the province of Asia. The old Ionia had carried on the Greek heritage in its purest form and had assimilated the technical knowledge of Rome; the pagan citizens of Bithynia or Ephesus represented the most stable element in the Graeco-Roman world; while the towns of Asia Minor were exceptionally well placed on the borders of two continents, with the barbarians on one hand, the Persians on the other, in an area from which the trade routes radiated over land sea to Rome, Narbonne, Alexandria, Antioch, Carthage, and Panticapaeum.

It was in this area that Constantine created the New Rome after the disorders of the third century, building it on the site of the ancient Byzantium and calling it, after his own name, Constantinople. The Emperor had chosen the East, giving it a pre-eminence it was to keep for seven hundred years.

The State and Christianity

Diocletian had already attempted to reorganise this Empire whose centre Constantine shifted to the east. Conscious of the superhuman task of the chief of the State, henceforth the object of a deification in which Persian influence was blended with Roman tradition, the Emperor chose a colleague and two lieutenants to function as a tetrarchy. The real power was given to an inner circle, the *comites*, the successors of the Hellenistic *hetairoi*, and the Senate was reduced to an assembly of big landowners, who could discuss the costly honour of providing circuses for the plebs. The administrative work involved was so great, however, that it became necessary to develop a specialised bureaucracy. The Empire thus gravitated towards a caste system whose dangers do not seem to have been appreciated at the beginning of the century.

If the foundation of Constantinople in 330 marks the end of the ascendancy of Rome itself, the official recognition of Christianity by Constantine was no less significant,

that would embrace all sects, were no more than an élite. Constantine may well have thought that the faith he was adopting was just a superior philosophy. In fact he opened the door to all who might care to enter, universal missionaries, converted barbarian chiefs, and before long, with a bishop's blessing, whole hordes of invaders.

The frontiers of the Empire

The Roman Empire was not alone in its prosperity. Mediterranean coins, pottery, and glassware of the period have been discovered in the plains of Hungary, in the Ukraine, and as far away as Pomerania, proving that commerce extended far beyond the walled provincial frontiers, or *limes*. It would therefore be wrong to think of the Empire as a closed fortress, with a surging flood of barbarians without. On the contrary, the gates, though guarded, were wide open to the people of the world beyond, who, all along the Danube, passed to and fro, unaware that they were pioneers. In view of this constant infiltration we can understand how easy an invasion would be if once

The gladiator could choose his weapons; spear, sword and shield, or trident and net. From a fourth-century mosaic. *Mansell*

for the Church was to be the germ of progressive disruption. The Council of Nicaea created a religious organisation parallel to the civil administration. Thus the new faith was woven into the structure of the Empire, the bishop became a political authority, and heresy became an offence against the State. The Empire was Christian long before the decline in the West, and the Church inherited the prestige of Rome. It was also heir to a strong oriental current which had for two centuries been undermining the old pagan patriarchal structure. Christianity favoured Constantinople rather than Rome, and it was merely a concession to the past to have installed St Peter's successor there. At one time it had seemed as though Greek thought might have arrested the progressive leaning towards Syrian, Jewish, and Persian beliefs, but the understanding of the masses was unable to rise to the philosophic syncretism of Plotinus, and at the beginning of the fourth century Iamblichus and his disciples, preaching to the Mediterranean world a universal religion

the guard slackened. The Empire, however, still seemed capable of offering considerable opposition to external pressure: its armies numbered 200,000 men, perhaps even 400,000 — a third on the Euphrates, a third in Moesia, the remainder in Gaul. But what was the army worth? To avoid the risk of pretenders to the imperial throne Roman senators were excluded. So also were slaves. The soldier was thus probably an Illyrian or a Gaul, forcibly recruited by his landlord, and serving without enthusiasm. With him, no doubt, were barbarian mercenaries, who served as shock-troops. But such methods were not without danger, for they played barbarian against barbarian. Moreover, they made it possible for the army to be led by military chiefs who were incapable of speaking either Latin or Greek. The strongest defence lay in the *limes* themselves, often cunningly laid out to exploit rivers considered impassable. Nevertheless these frontiers were not impenetrable; in fact the barbarians had been admitted in compact groups and allowed to settle within them. It was Decius

Detail from the Palestrina mosaic (second century), depicting the exotic life of the Nile. Egypt was a valuable source of wealth for the Roman Empire and a particularly rich granary. *Mansell*

The lid of a fourth-century ivory casket. Brescia, *Anderson*.

who had begun this dangerous practice. In 335 Constantine followed his example by saving 200,000 Sacae beset by the Goths. Constans I, his son, peopled Toxandria with Frankish tribes in 342. All these *foederati* were under covenant to defend their territory against their brothers: the theory was ingenious but its practice dangerous.

Inherent weaknesses

Imperial despotism, the triumph of Christianity, the shift of forces to the East: those were the essential factors of a new order which took more than thirty years to accomplish, and not without causing serious troubles in each of these three domains.

The extraordinary power vested in the Emperor, while making him anxious to conserve it, made others no less anxious to rob him of it. Thus Constantine, on the strength of portents, had his bastard son, Crispus, put to death, believing him to aspire to the diadem, and after the Emperor's death, his eldest son, Constantine II, perished at the hands of the second son, Constans, who in turn was assassinated by a Gallo-Roman officer, Magnentius. Driving Magnentius to suicide, Constantius II, the third son, who had been ruling in the East for the last twenty years, gathered the whole Empire into his hands in 337, and this mean, hard man reigned till 361.

To meet the ever-increasing taxation (the building of Constantinople was particularly ruinous), it was necessary to avoid weakening certain provinces economically. The best means seemed to be to create tenures which bound the farmer and his heirs in perpetuity to the land. In 332 Constantine initiated such a measure, which ushered in a whole series of laws whose effect was to place the ordinary farmer in servile tenure, and to give the big landlords a power which led to their autonomy. In Gaul, Spain and Italy, from 350, the big landowners, less harassed than in the East by the imperial agents, had their own personal guards, and the people they oppressed, unable to cope with the relentless rise in prices, grew restive. There were revolts of journeymen in Africa, risings of peasants in Syria and Sicily, all resulting from this policy. Commerce too suffered from the heavy duties imposed by Constantine. In spite of all the precious metal plundered from pagan temples, the currency was debased until, by 350, it was worth only one fifteenth of its nominal value; for gold continued to flow towards the Danube and further east to pay for iron and mercenaries.

Constantine's attempt, about 327, to arrange a truce between the Arians and the Catholics was speedily frustrated by the narrow bigotry of Athanasius, Bishop of Alexandria. These dogmatic disputes may surprise us, but behind the tenets involved was deep cleavage: between a spiritually minded Church and one sternly wielding temporal power, between the rich and well populated eastern provinces and the weakening western ones, between the mystic and dogmatic East and a West that had remained faithful to pagan morality. It was incumbent on the Emperor to hold the balance, but neither the fiercely orthodox Constans, nor the superstitious Constantius who supported the Arians, was capable of rising above the quarrel. Three times Athanasius was deposed, three times he was recalled. Within sixteen years nine councils had met and had passed conflicting resolutions. So sterile was this persistent controversy that it only strengthened the moral force of paganism.

With all these difficulties, the new Empire could hardly be as vigorous as that of Augustus. Nevertheless, when Diocletian set to work after the economic crisis of the third century, he laid the foundation of an organisation that survived even the downfall of the Roman Empire.

THE ASIATIC WORLD

Persia, half-way to Asia

Constantine's messenger may have been conscious of no great change when he travelled from Syria to Ctesiphon, capital of the Persian Empire. Nevertheless there were local customs long established in Mesopotamia and on the Iranian plateau; and the King of Kings, sacred in person and generally unseen, was the true heir of Babylonian tradition. But behind the imposing façade of absolute monarchy, two great powers gradually came into existence, reaching their peak in the fourth century: the landed aristocracy which also held all the outlying commands, and the Zoroastrian priesthood, richly endowed and the supervisors of education.

The Sassanids were far from cutting pitiable figures beside the Roman Emperors. So redoubtable were their mounted archers that they even prevented Rome overrunning southern Mesopotamia. They regarded Arab nomads and Caucasian marauders as contemptible adversaries. The caravan route joining Ctesiphon to Bactria or Tarim assured commercial prosperity, and Sassanid coins were mixed with Roman in the treasuries of Central Asia.

Persia's intermediate position between the Asiatic world and the Mediterranean was also held by her in the religious field, for Zoroastrianism, vigorous as it was, left room for other modes of thought. It is probable that Christianity, having become the official religion of the Persians' hereditary enemies, the Romans, and enjoying the support of the latter in Mesopotamia, was persecuted, but, on the other hand, the Sassanids were ready to accept all heretics expelled from the West, especially the Nestorians, followers of Nestorius, bishop of Constantinople. Nestorius divided the Godhead into two Persons. God, he said, created Jesus Christ in the flesh, as He had created Adam; but where He withdrew Himself from Adam after breathing a soul into him, He remained in Christ. Thus Adam became a separate being, but Christ was not separate. None the less, said Nestorius, God might have withdrawn Himself from Him also, so that, potentially, Christ was a separate being. This possibility was condemned as heretical, since it opened the way to a denial of the entire and complete divinity of Christ. The Nestorian converts, as they wandered westward, included Turkish tribes and even some Chinese in the deserts of Central Asia. Buddhism, on the other hand, was said by the Chinese monk Fa-hien to have prevailed in Bactria and eastward to Khorassan. Manicheaism was born in Babylonia but flourished above all on the frontiers of Turkestan, whence it drove westward to Rome, Carthage, and Narbonne.

The Hindu golden age

Beyond the mountains of Baluchistan the authority of the King of Kings progressively diminished. This, however, did not favour the Indo-Scythian kingdoms — reduced to the possession of Kabul and the Afghanistan passes and in any case greatly influenced by Graeco-Buddhism — nor the Sacae, deeply divided among themselves. India had gradually absorbed these people, leaving their

Ivory consular diptych. The consul is presiding at the gladiatorial games with the *mappa* raised in his right hand as the signal to begin. *Bruckmann*

236

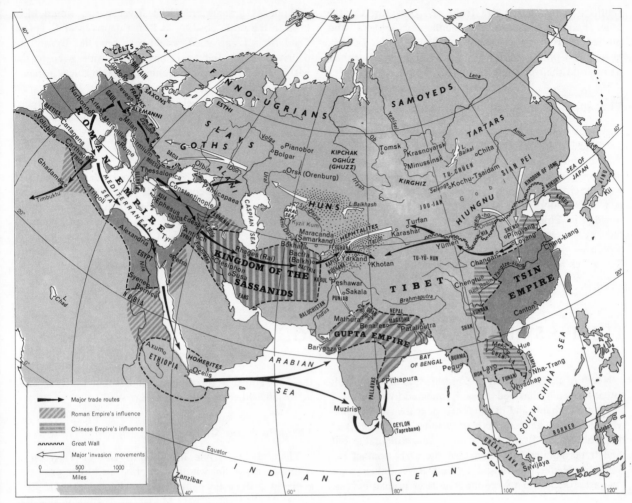

The Ancient World c. A.D. 400

remnants to vegetate in that Indus valley through which had always come invaders and admirers alike. The stable mass of these former conquerors accordingly blocked the passes to the north-west, and India, thus protected from fresh attack, had genuine Hindus ruling once again over the Ganges and the Deccan. For the first time in centuries local dynasties sprang up.

The reunification of Indian territory was the work of the Guptas, the Rajahs of Pataliputra in the province of Magadha, which had formerly witnessed the Maurya unification. Chandragupta I and, still more, his successor Samudragupta (335-85) extended their conquests from the Ganges to Gujrat and to the approaches of Ceylon; only the Deccan evaded them. Coins bearing the inscription of Samudragupta, the great man of the dynasty, abound in the valleys of the Brahmaputra and Indus.

It was during the reign of his successor, Chandragupta II that the monk Fa-hien, crossing the Gupta Empire between 400 and 410 before returning to China, left behind an account of this Hindu golden age. The picture painted by the worthy pilgrim may seem somewhat idealised, with its safe travel, benevolent government and just taxation, but the traces left by the Gupta civilisation both in works of art and philosophy confirm his evidence. Vigour of thought and the peace of the land could only profit from the extreme religious freedom. The religion was Hinduism and the coinage was stamped

with Vishnuist ornamentation, yet the Emperor could show favour to Buddhist monasteries. This fact strikes us the more forcibly when we remember the disasters caused by the unbending dogmatism prevailing in the Roman Empire. Unfortunately this civilisation was eventually undermined by the inadequacy of its administrative organisation and by the attacks of the White Huns from Central Asia. The Gupta Age saw the rise of a remarkable court literature. The poet and dramatist Kalidada (c. 375-455) is the most famous of these writers, and his poems and dramas set new standards in Hindu tradition. The cave paintings at Ajanta reached their greatest brilliance in his time, and gigantic Buddhist *stupas* were built. Graeco-Buddhist and Gupta art were spreading their influence north into central Asia and Tibet and even China, while in Burma and Indonesia Hinâyâna Buddhism was to produce masterpieces of sculpture and architecture. In southern India, also, temples and dagabas reached a fantastic and massive elaboration. Hindu civilisation of the Gupta age was at a climax of vitality, and decisive for great areas beyond India.

Hindu expansion was also carried into south-east Asia, which was roused out of its barbarism. If the evidence of Indianisation is rare in the lower Mekong area of Laos, it is plentiful amongst the Khmers of Fou-nan and lower Burma, which was subject to them, and where Buddhism seems to have been preponderant. The same is true of the

237

southern parts of Sumatra from 420 onwards. On the other hand, the monks, merchants and soldiers who pushed up from lower Annam or Champa as far as Hue, in spite of Chinese resistance, were Brahminists. But their names and their costume remained Hindu.

The apparent strength of China

At this period China, too, presents an impressive appearance. About 280 the Western Tsin Emperor, Sze-ma Yen, captured Nanking and accomplished the first union of China since the Han dynasty. His capital, the old and wealthy city of Lo-yang, became a centre of commerce, and ambassadors were sent there from all parts of the world. But China slept behind her Great Wall, and the security she seemed to enjoy was deceptive. The mountain provinces were already restive and China's grip on the Red River basin and Shansi was uncertain. The Empire

without its granary, the Red River basin, would have been in the same position as Rome deprived of Egypt or Gaul. Shansi, enfeebled, would have been like Byzantium deprived of the Balkan ramparts and wide open to the barbarians. Their grip weakening, the Tsin rulers installed settlers at the foot of the Great Wall from 300 onwards, relying on them to repel their brother Huns or Mongols. But was that reliance justified? Between these two insecure regions, the Red River and Shansi, lay the heart of China, centre of the radiating caravan routes, where silk was exchanged for horses or barbarian slaves. And all this settled wealth lay within a hundred miles of the haunts of nomads. There is considerable similarity between these two empires, the Chinese and the Roman, both maintaining a rich civilisation, but both in the stress of structural changes. But, unlike Rome, China was threatened at its very centre. That is why the disaster was so complete when the barbarian hordes finally fell upon her.

THE FIRST BARBARIAN ONSLAUGHT

North of the mountains of Central Asia lay a difficult route, broken by fortified oases, frequented by Greek and Persian merchants and by Buddhist pilgrims from China, who faced the dangers both of wandering bandits and the Gobi sands. Even to this day, these vulnerable but vital tracts abound in evidence of the early contact between the Mediterranean and the East. Beyond them were the vast stretches that were the haunts of nomad hordes.

The Steppe

To the south lay three desolate areas, the Tarim, the Gobi, the Kizil-Kum; to the north the forests. Here, in perpetual movement across the meagre pastures, lived the barbarians, ever in the saddle, eating, curing their meat, and even sleeping on horseback. For the most part keeping away from settled populations, they wandered sometimes to the extreme limits of the civilised world. Redoubtable archers, they pillaged and destroyed wherever they went. They never attempted to till the soil. When an area fell into their hands, they burnt the towns, blocked the irrigation canals, and destroyed the harvest. Laden with spoils, they then returned to the scorching or glacial steppe. Thus it was that the Scythians of antiquity and the Surmatae of the later Roman Empire had harassed their neighbours. But they learnt from them as well, and the animal paintings of Minusinsk, near Lake Baikal, or of Pianobor on the Middle Volga, show traces of these contacts.

To the south of Lake Baikal wandered Turkish or Mongolian hordes. These were the Huns, short, yellow-skinned men with slit eyes and prominent cheek-bones. Intensely hardy, they were unbridled in their cruelty. Some, crossing the Gobi, tried to establish themselves at the foot of the Great Wall; others reached Lake Balkhash in the first century A.D., probably driving some of the tribes they found there into northern India. Those who had crossed the Gobi were later threatened by the Sien-pi, possibly Mongols from Manchuria, and asked

the Tsin emperor for asylum. And, about the year 250, he installed them within the Great Wall.

The attack on China

This was a terrible mistake. In 304 at Tai-yuen a Hiung-nu chieftain, who had married a Chinese princess, assumed a dynastic name and proclaimed himself Emperor. The arrival of new Mongolian hordes outside the Great Wall precipitated disaster; in 311 the 'Emperor', Liu Yuën, swiftly crossed the Yellow River, captured the Tsin capital and took prisoner the Son of Heaven, whom he forced to wash the dishes at his banquets. Later, in scenes of the utmost horror, the barbarian burnt Chang-an, destroyed the harvest, and in six years drove the Tsin armies to the Yang-tze and ravaged the rich provinces of Honan and Hupeh. Though he had his concubines roasted and brought to table and though he drank from the skull of a fallen Emperor, Liu Yuën, who had a certain veneer of Chinese culture, would probably have established a durable empire but for his death in 318, which plunged north China into complete anarchy. Bands of Turks, Mongols and Tibetans swept across the whole country between Korea and the Kunlun Mountains, founding ephemeral dynasties. A few lasted for a while: thus the Sien-pi Mongols for a time held the country from Shansi to the sea before disappearing, absorbed perhaps by the Tibetans. About 385 the Fukien Empire reached from the Yang-tze to the Great Wall, only to founder after repeated blows from a Turkish tribe, the Tobas.

As for the old Empire, it took refuge in a new capital originally known as Kinling, now Nanking, in the middle of the southern hills, sheltered by the fortified line of the Blue River, where it was to provide an example of the fate reserved for the later Roman Empire. Nevertheless, after 360-365 the wave subsided, for in all this disorder Buddhism influenced the barbarian mind. Thus the continuity of Chinese thought was maintained and the way

set for absorption of the conqueror by the conquered.

Buddha. From the Gupta period, Mathura, India. The clinging drapery is typical of Graeco-Buddhist art. *Government of India*

Seated Buddha. Gandhara. Second to third century A.D. The Greek influence is apparent in the drapery and curled hair; the elongated ears are oriental. *Government of India*

THE GERMANS

The Barbarians on the Baltic

Beyond the Vistula the steppe vanished abruptly. Under moister skies were marshes and tall grasses which brought the nomad horsemen to a halt. Objects showing signs of Buddhist culture have been found as far afield as Denmark, and sometimes carved bone and ivory of Persian origin. Whether such objects are the relics of a trade route across the steppes or of the enterprise of some Greek merchant dealing in oriental goods, we cannot say, but there was certainly another barbarian focus on the Baltic.

It is more difficult to understand the successive waves of northern peoples than those of the Asiatic nomads. Were they due to pressure of population or to advancing Arctic conditions, or to a Finno-Ugric surge from the forests of the north? We cannot tell, but we know that at the beginning of the third century the Goths, having left Sweden, spread from Pomerania to the Carpathians, and then onward to the Black Sea, pushing the tribes they encountered to the westward and thus placing the Western Roman Empire in peril. Then the Germanic world, held by the Illyrians on the one side and by Diocletian on the other, seems to have become more peaceful. The Goths made their home between the Danube and the country beyond the Dniester, while in the West the Saxons settled in North Germany, and the Franks, Alemanni, and Burgundi, forsaking their nomad ways, began to exploit the rich lands between the Harz Mountains and the Danube.

Mid-century attack

Unhappily for the Western Roman Empire, interior difficulties made the defence of the frontiers uncertain.

In the summer of 353 the Alemanni, settled between Alsace and Rhaetia in the lands assigned to them (*decumates*), crossed the Rhine. Perhaps they were called in by Constantius to attack Magnentius, perhaps also the movement of the Goths towards the Iron Gates provoked the Alemanni. In three years the Rhine had been lost from Mainz to Lake Constance and the country had been ravaged for two hundred miles beyond the river. At the other extremity of the Empire, the Sassanids, their power reviving in the person of Shapur II, took Diarbekr and pushed on without difficulty to Edessa, aided by their superior siege-trains. A thorough-going Oriental, Constantius considered the Persian war more important than all else, and prepared his revenge. But, not prepared to abandon Gaul, he instructed his cousin Julian to defend it.

Julian saves the West

Julian is one of the most outstanding figures of the fourth century. Yet this young man of twenty-four had been ill-prepared for his task. An orphan, he had been brought up away from the Court, and he seems to have spent most of his time discussing Homer and Plotinus. Constantius had no other choice, however, and in November 355 he bestowed on Julian the title of Caesar and the hand of his daughter. He also gave him 360 men (including the future St Martin) to repel the Alemanni.

It was therefore a reluctant Julian who arrived at Autun, where he found the Gaulish chiefs so suspicious that he was nearly taken prisoner. By 357 he had gathered 13,000 men, but the Alemanni were 30,000 strong. He met them on the 25 August near Strasbourg. 8,000 Alemanni were left dead on the field and the Rhineland was recovered. This was one of the greatest victories of the fourth century. For four consecutive years Julian was in the field. He took a flotilla up the Rhine, rallied the Franks, and pushed on even to the *decumates*. But it was not till 366, after another slaughter at Châlons, that the Alemanni threat was definitely averted.

Meanwhile Constantius had become jealous of Julian's success and recalled him. Meekly, the young man was preparing to obey, when his friends, in February 360, rose and proclaimed him Emperor. On his way to subdue the rising, Constantius died in November 361, and Julian, whom he had nominated, became his successor.

Cameo of Julian the Apostate (Emperor 361-3). Julian attempted to prevent the drift of the Empire towards Christianity, hence his name ' Apostate '. *Bibliothèque Nationale*

Ambrose of Milan crowning Angilbert. The appointment of Ambrose, a bishop of the western church, marked Valentinian's impartiality in religious matters. *Marburg*

The last days of paganism

The six hundred days of Julian's reign mark the last effort to stem the tide that was sweeping the Empire towards an oriental and Christian structure. A neo-Platonist and a disciple of Iamblicus, he proclaimed liberty of conscience, and reopened the pagan temples. But he allowed Athanasius to re-establish himself in Alexandria and Hilarius in Poitiers. He wanted to see a hierarchy of pagan bishops, paid by the government, balancing the hierarchy of the Church; he tried to formulate a catechism of classical religion; and he wanted to rehabilitate the schools of Athens. But this 'Greek' did not realise the force of the Latin juridical tradition or the power that would have accrued to a Roman senatorial order that had remained pagan. Rome revived might have counterbalanced Constantinople, Athens never.

Julian wanted also to restore the framework of associated towns that had constituted the Empire of the Flavians. He reduced the taxation that was crushing the towns; he tried to stop the rise in prices and the devaluation of the currency; and by stopping the flow of precious metals towards the Danube he was partially successful, for the currency regained the value it had had in 320. But this was only achieved at the cost of an increasingly powerful bureaucracy.

Another task awaited him: to break the Sassanids' hold on the tariffs of the East. To this end he broke with Shapur II in 363. But Julian was not popular, and he marched off to the accompaniment of the sneers of the rich, who accused him of plotting their ruin, and of the poor, who thought he favoured the Jews.

With 65,000 men Julian forced his way down the Euphrates, advancing farther than the legions had done for a century. He reached the Persian capital but daunted by the blazing June heat, could not bring himself to face a siege. Retreating northwards, he was struck down by a Roman or a Persian arrow in front of his tent, and his hopes perished in the sand.

THE GOTHS

Gothic pressure

Before the end of the fourth century a new power, that of the pure Mongols of the Jwen-Jwen, had established itself and disturbed the Huns who had for three hundred years roamed the area between Lake Balkhash and the Aral Sea. Proceeding westwards through the lowlands between the Urals and the Caspian, driving before them the remains of the Wu-sun and Alani tribes (probably of Persian extraction), the Huns were suddenly confronted by the Armenian kings, and turned away towards the Dnieper and the area of the Goths.

So far the Goths had been at peace with the Roman Empire. In Dacia there were Roman colonies, and ecclesiastics, such as Bishop Wulfilas, had undertaken to introduce Christianity (admittedly Arian) to the barbarians, an event of the greatest consequence. Now, however,

Colour plate: a Peruvian warrior figure. Mochica. A.D. 1-900. Mochican ceramics are characterised by their naturalism. Warriors appear to have been given a place of high importance. *British Museum*

spurred by the approaching Huns, the Goths became restive. From 363 they began moving along the Danube.

Circumstances were favourable to them. The Empire, after the brief reign of Julian, was in the hands of two brothers of Pannonian extraction, Valentinian and Valens, and it was weak. Valens, a common despot, was chiefly concerned with defeating Procopius, a follower of Julian who had ruled briefly in Constantinople. While Shapur reoccupied Armenia and all the former conquests of Diocletian, a section of the Goths, under their king Athanaric, made a surprise crossing of the Danube in 367 and began to ravage the right bank of the river. No doubt Valens started strengthening the defences of the lower Danube, but Athanaric received a promise that his people would not be molested.

Valentinian I (364-75). Notorious for his cruelty as a ruler, he is also known to have instituted medical help for the Roman poor. *Bruckmann*

Valentinian

In the West, Valentinian was the last able Emperor. This forty-year-old peasant from Savia, said by his detractors to be callous, cruel, and ignorant, was before all else a soldier. He was a simple man, with few intimates. Carrying on the work of Julian, he wanted to put the whole Empire in a state of siege, treating it as a sort of colossal prison. But in religious matters he showed the impartiality to be expected of an emperor. Whereas in the East Valens, the fanatical Arian, was burning libraries and filling the prisons with recalcitrant bishops, Valentinian in Rome mixed with members of the great pagan families, and allowed the Pope, Damasus, firmly to assert his preeminence. He forbade rival Councils, but concurred in the appointment of St Ambrose to Milan and St Martin to Tours.

Valentinian's military firmness only increased the rigidity of the Empire. The uniting of civil and military authority may have been necessary to the defence of the West, but at the same time it preserved the rigidity of classes, keeping the poor subservient to the rich and thereby further endangering a society that was already condemned to decline. All, rich and poor alike, were taxed despotically.

But Valentinian was too absorbed in the military defence of Rome to care much about social conditions. In Gaul, he vigorously attacked the Bagaudae, who may have resisted military service, and he installed himself at Trier near the Germanic danger. He organised a new system

Colour plate: a Bodhisattva, probably of the Sui Dynasty (589-618), combining Indian mysticism and classical beauty of form. *Victoria and Albert Museum, London*

of defence, which his contemporaries either could not or would not understand, reducing the *limes* to a mere first line of protection, supported in the rear by a series of forts and fortified towns, which could offer shelter against the barbarians.

The Emperor's efforts were not merely defensive. Though defeated in 366, the Alemanni were still to be reckoned with, and from 368 Valentinian crossed the Rhine every other year. In 374 he paid tribute to the enemy. A cowardly surrender, said his adversaries. To Valentinian it was an expedient method for keeping the barbarians in their place, and in the end he was proved right. Apart from an alarm in 378, the Alemanni remained quiet for twenty-five years. Meanwhile, Valentinian's rival, Theodosius, restored Hadrian's Wall, breached by the Scots and then, in 373, went to Africa and subdued the Kabyles who were ravaging the Chéliff valley.

Adrianople

Valentinian's defences were soon to be put to a severe test. In 375 the Huns, led by Balamir, defeated the Heruli and, overrunning the country west of the Volga, encountered the Goths on the Dnieper. The king of the Ostrogoths was killed, and his people fled in panic as far as the Danube. It was with no thought of booty that they came, but to take refuge. Wisely Valentinian refused them his protection. He even advanced towards Sirmium to meet the tribes the Goths had been driving before them. As usual he began with negotiations. In November 375, however, in the course of an interview, he became heated in argument and suddenly collapsed. His death marked a serious reverse for his Empire.

Not knowing what to do, Valens reversed his brother's decision and promised to harbour the Goths. But he soon changed his mind. After sending them hither and thither in Thrace and selling them food at inflated prices during the summer of 376, Valens pushed them back towards the Danube. This treacherous conduct only provoked a counter-blow. The Goths marched on the capital. In August 378, ten miles from Adrianople, they routed the legions in a battle that cost Valens his life. The battle serves as a landmark, for in it the horsemen beat the foot-soldiers, the barbarians overwhelmed the 'Romans'. From now on no troops could stand up to the Gothic squadrons, which advanced freely into the heart of the Roman Empire.

Danger now threatened from all sides. In 378 the Alemanni streamed over the frozen Rhine. Gratian (375-83), now reigning in the West, sent the Frankish king Meroveus to deal with them, then himself marched across the Rhine, but this was to be the last time a Roman army advanced into Germany. In 379 the Goths ravaged Thessaly. The imperial army was now under Theodosius the Great, son of the elder Theodosius, but, suffering an epidemic of the plague, it was unable to offer any resistance.

The pressure was so great that there was now no alternative but to accept the barbarians as *foederati*. Gratian settled the Ostrogoths in Pannonia, and the Scots in northern Britain. He widened the area on the lower Rhine allocated to the Franks. Theodosius gave Moesia to the Visigoths in 382. By these means the Western Empire won a few years of peace but, eaten into by these new 'allies', how was it going to be able to resist another onslaught?

THE VICTORY OF THE BARBARIANS

THE WESTERN EMPIRE WEAKENS

The approach of anarchy

The fourth century, ably opened by Diocletian and continued with dignity by his successors, Constantine, Julian and Valentinian, ended in hopeless anarchy. The dearth of real statesmen and the lust for despotic power in those unfit to wield it steadily undermined authority. Only the great barbarian chiefs could have stepped into the breach, but none dared. In the summer of 383 there were three Emperors in the field: in the East, Theodosius, a pious Spaniard, swift to anger, then to panic; in Milan, Valentinian II, a boy under the tutelage of his mother, Justina; and at Trier, the energetic Maximus, the usurper of Gratian's throne. Round them gravitated barbarian chiefs who no longer deigned to Latinise their names: Merobaud, Bauto and Arbogast, or ambitious prelates like Pope Damasus and Ambrose of Milan. Valentinian II got the better of Maximus, who died in 388, but he subsequently fled to Italy from the masterful Arbogast and committed suicide. The power behind Eugenius, an old scholar, was a barbarian Frank, though only for a short time, for in September 394 Theodosius just managed to win the battle at Aquileia. It looked as if the Roman world might be reconstituted. But it was only a breathing space; Theodosius died in 395.

Internal dissolution

The restoration of imperial authority would in any case have been difficult in face of the ever-increasing incursions of the barbarians, who roamed the north of Britain and the valleys of the Rhine and Danube in marauding bands. Nor could they have been welded into a defensive force, since the army itself was an agglomeration of Franks, Goths, and Alemanni whose only real loyalty was to their own chiefs. Disorder was thus continually growing.

In the East, the people, ground down by taxation and by the oppression of the big landlords, revolted first at Antioch in 387, then at Thessalonica in 390. Putting down this second rising, Theodosius butchered seven thousand people. In the West, the towns that had been the mainspring of Julian's recovery in Gaul and Valentinian's in Africa steadily declined. Those responsible for their defence were merely agents of the big landlords, and the municipal authorities, the *decuriones*, fled, overwhelmed by their difficulties. The only support left to these harassed towns was their bishop, and no fact is more eloquent of the rising power of Christianity in the declining Roman Empire of the West.

To foster commerce, Valentinian had bound both merchants and artisans to their guilds, but nothing availed to stop the flow of money to the Danube and the East or its depreciation, and commercial activity continued to decline. From now on, economic life was centred on the big landed estates. Deprived of their slaves, the big landlords sought to intimidate the local peasants, who gradually became bound to the soil. In the East, after 360,

they were bound by the practice of patronage or *patrocinium*. Before long they came under the landlord's jurisdiction; and the latter acquired the right to have his private guard. The *villa* thus became the living cell of the Empire, and where this institution could not be adopted — in Egyptian Faiyum, Tunisian Sahel, Campanian Baetica — ruin followed. Its evolution explains how the East retained the vitality of the Empire.

The triumph of the Church

As the substance was drained from the old order, it was the Christian Church which filled the vacuum. The Church came to be the new incarnation of Roman unity. In 385 the heads of the great pagan families still cut an imposing figure. But Theodosius, in February 381 and again in 391, denouncing all other faiths, made Christianity a State religion and encouraged the hierarchy to play a part in politics.

Nearly a hundred and twenty new bishoprics were created in Macedonia and Gaul, and the reinforcement of these two essential regions did much to promote the new faith. Now began the conversion of the countryside under the leadership of St Martin, Bishop of Tours from 372. Not for nothing was the peasant called *paganus*: it was necessary to overcome his mistrust, replace the temple with a church, transform a venerated menhir into a cross, and sprinkle with holy water the Druid's sacred mistletoe. At the same time Christian expansion took another form: monasticism.

Obverse and reverse of a coin of Theodosius the Great, Emperor of the East, 378-95. *Archiv für Kunst und Geschichte*

Pope Damasus (366-84).

THE HUNS IN EUROPE

The stricken West

As though deliberately to ruin the Empire, Theodosius named his two sons as his successors, Arcadius in the East, and Honorius, a child, in the West. Both were puppets, one manipulated by a Gaul, Rufinus, the other by a Vandal, Stilicho. A new movement of the Huns who took possession of the Hungarian plains profoundly disturbed the German tribes, putting them in a critical situation. Arcadius massacred a thousand Ostrogoths who had asked asylum, but the remainder he flung back into Illyria. By doing so he disrupted the connections between East and West for a very long time; in fact, to the dawn of modern times, this breach of contact between the Balkans and Italy was a permanent feature of European political geography. Moreover the Visigoths, disturbed in turn

powerless to act. Then, accused of treason, he was assassinated by imperial command, and the West was robbed of its only leader.

Alaric took advantage of the situation to march on Rome. Probably he had no more in mind than assuming the role of Stilicho, but Honorius, after trying repeatedly to buy him off, attempted to starve his troops. Alaric reacted vigorously and in August 410 entered what had been the world's capital and sacked it. For eight hundred years no invader had ever taken Rome, and its fall echoed from end to end of the stricken Empire.

Respite for the West

Alaric then decided to conquer the rich cornfields of Sicily and perhaps North Africa, but at Messina, riding his horse down into the sea, he finally renounced overseas conquests. Then suddenly he died. He was buried under

The Huns swept into western Europe with a ferocity which has made their name symbolic of everything barbaric and cruel. From a painting by the Spanish artist Ulpiano Checa y Sanz (1860-1916). *Mansell*

by their racial cousins, in 396 began pillaging Thessaly and the Peloponnesus, led by Alaric. Five years later they turned to north Italy at the same moment as the Vandals and the Alani, fleeing the Huns, crossed the Danube and overran the Trentino. Stilicho succeeded in arresting this onrush and was preparing to re-establish the *limes* in Pannonia when he learnt that the Empire had received a mortal blow in Gaul.

In December 406 the Vandals and the Suevi, pushed by the Huns, had crossed the frozen Rhine, pouring over in four streams and overrunning the defence posts of the Frankish *foederati*. Mainz, Trier, Tournai, and Amiens went up in flames, and then much of Gaul. At the same time Saxon pirates were active off the coast of Britain. The Italian army refused to follow Stilicho and he was

the river-bed of the Busento, whose waters were temporarily diverted while the grave was dug; since then they have run ceaselessly over the tomb of the conqueror of Rome. More realistic, his brother-in-law, Ataulphus, turned back towards the north. He was concerned less with replacing the Roman Empire than with its restoration by the infusion of new blood and the creation of a 'Gothia'. He married Placidia, sister of Honorius. His son, Theodosius, died suddenly and his successor, Wallia, only succeeded in obtaining the title of *foederatus* and was allowed to settle in Aquitaine.

But one man was able to turn the tide of disaster. This was the Illyrian Constantius III (son of Constantine the Usurper), who with despairing ardour paid court to Placidia. He took the fleet in hand; it was the ultimate weapon of the Emperors against the barbarians, who understood only land warfare. Landing in Spain, he drove the Suevi and the Vandals towards the Cantabrian Mountains. He left the province to be guarded by the Visigoths, but at least he saw to it that they were kept away from the shores of the Mediterranean. Constantius III was at last rewarded by the hand of Placidia, and his father-in-law reluctantly bestowed on him the title of Caesar in 421. It was a short-lived triumph. Eight months later Constantius died, soon to be followed by the unhappy Honorius. He seems, however, to have left the West in a state of calm. Visigoths, Suevi, Franks, and Ostrogoths, all *foederati*, were apparently resigned to live in peace.

The East thrives; the West weakens

Yet it was the East which kept peace at home and proved itself the really healthy part of the Roman Empire. The 'Greeks', as they were already being called, watched unmoved the disaster in the West, and oriental influence now began to assert itself. Beneath the Hellenism could be seen the older foundations, Aramaean, Semitic, or Egyptian, and the dogmatic disputes that raged incessantly were the outward signs of ill-concealed racial conflicts. Rivalling Constantinople was Alexandria, which had fought and conquered Arianism, and Antioch, which called itself 'the new Rome'. In fact neither of them could compete with the splendid position occupied by Constantinople, with the triple ring of fortifications that Theodosius II had built around it. For a thousand years floods of barbarians were to dash themselves to pieces against these walls. At the same time, to maintain the Roman heritage, Theodosius in 427 drew up a code of laws and opened a university.

In the West, the stability left by Constantius III did not last long. In the reign of his son, Valentinian III, still a child, the energetic patrician Aetius, lacking both money and soldiers, made a supreme effort to hold Clodion and his Franks beyond Boulogne, to keep the Visigoths as far as possible from Narbonne, and to repel the Burgundi before eventually settling them in Helvetia.

In Britain, the noble families continued to consider themselves Romans and preserved the memory of their conquerors in their family names. But they were beset by the Scots from Ireland, by the Saxons, the Jutes, and the Angles from Friesland. Repulsed in 440, these enemies slowly gained the upper hand, and twelve years later, were pushing the Britons back into the Welsh hills. About 450, some of the latter crossed to Armorica, giving it their name, Brittany. In Britain, though in the eastern and central parts of the island many of the original inhabitants were exterminated, in the south and west they remained an important element in the population.

On the other side of the Empire the rich lands of Africa were threatened. The Berbers had always been a danger, but this area seemed at least to be safe from the Teutons. In 429, however, Gaiseric, a Vandal, seized a fleet of Spanish ships and, with 80,000 men, sailed through the Straits of Gibraltar and attacked Carthage, which he took in 439. Along his route he caused the most frightful ravages, which have made his name notorious. More sensitive to the loss of Africa than to the loss of Gaul, the Eastern Empire sent a fleet to retake Carthage, but it merely cruised along the coast.

Glass medallion from the Mausoleum of Galla Placidia, sister of Honorius, who became influential enough to be granted the title 'Augusta'. *Mansell*

Attila

This disaster was slight compared to the new danger which threatened the rest of the West. Living in the area between the Volga and the Hungarian plains, the Huns carried out numerous and rewarding raids on the Danube basin from the beginning of the fifth century. Accordingly, about 435-440, the court of their Khan, Attila, showed an unexpected luxury and refinement. The number of prisoners brought in was substantial, and Hellenic influence, superimposed on the art of the steppes, endowed Hun civilisation with a certain style. Both Greek and Latin could be heard in the court, and secretaries of Roman origin kept the Khan informed of foreign events. Attila himself seems to have been remarkable. There is no lack of descriptions of him: yellower than most of his people, frugal, simple, combining the cruelty and violence of his race with a taste for diplomacy, for legal subtleties, and even for formality.

No doubt he would have been content with neighbourly relations, leaving him free to provision himself from the resources of the Empire. It is difficult to believe he could have wanted to destroy the latter. In 440 a treaty was concluded with Constantinople arranging for delivery of cattle, and Attila was given a Roman title. But payment fell so far in arrears that in 448 he was obliged to cross the Danube. He took Philippopolis and was marching on the capital when the Emperor halted him with the promise of an indemnity and pasturing rights in Moesia. During the following year the Greeks went back on these conditions, and it is not impossible that they encouraged Attila to turn towards the West.

Asia conquered in Gaul

In March 451 Attila, followed by 70,000 warriors and their families, crossed the Rhine and drove the terrified Germans before him, for the brutality of Asiatic hordes had not been forgotten in Gaul. Metz fell, and Troyes, Paris and Orleans. Aetius was determined to make a last effort. He had been for a while at Attila's court and understood his methods of warfare. He hurried north, rallying Burgundi, Franks, and Visigoths. During the summer of 451, Attila retired along the Roman road from Orleans towards Troyes. It was on the *Campus Mauriacus*, the Catalaunian plains twelve miles west of Troyes that Aetius gave battle. This famous event was the most important of all the battles during this period of the invasions, and the one whose consequences were the most lasting. To the end of the day the issue was in doubt, but in the night the Huns retreated, protected by their waggons. Their enemies did not dare to follow in pursuit but Gaul was saved.

The following spring Attila made an attempted raid on Italy. His forces were light, as he was merely out to snatch booty. His Huns razed Aquileia, whose inhabitants took refuge on the islands of the Rialto lagoon, the origin of Venice. They were advancing on Rome when they were met by a delegation from Pope Leo I. Negotiations proceeded, but for how long could Attila be halted? He had already sworn to water his horse in the rivers of Spain. Fortune was this time kind to Europe. In the spring of 453, Attila died suddenly. His empire promptly collapsed and his hordes fell back towards the Sea of Azov.

Aetius might now have undertaken the task of reorganising the Western Empire, but in September 454 Valentinian III, accusing him of scheming for the diadem in reward for his services, stabbed the 'last of the Romans' with his own hand. This absurd crime signed Rome's death-warrant. 'You have cut off your right hand with your left,' said a courtesan to whom the Emperor boasted of his deed. Valentinian died soon after. Two months later Gaiseric arrived at Ostia with squadrons of Byzantine ships and pillaged Rome before returning to Carthage in May 455. The Western Roman Empire was now crippled.

SLACKENING OF THE INVASIONS

The Barbarians in Persia

After 450, the surge of the nomads turned towards the passes between the Caspian and the Pamirs; though mountains and deserts provided a natural barrier, both the Sassanid and Gupta Empires were under attack. It was the occupation of the Altai Mountains by the Jwen-Jwen which turned the Mongol barbarians towards Sogdiana. These Mongols, the White Huns, are also called Ephthalites, after Ye Ta or Hephtha, the name of their royal clan. Already in 425 they had been in contact with the Sassanids. The Persians, more accustomed than the Romans to dealing with the peoples of the steppe, had learnt how to adapt their defences to the warlike methods of their adversaries. They employed mounted archers, swift cavalry, and brigades of armoured elephants from which skilful mahouts could lasso their opponents. For fifteen years the great kings, particularly Bahram Gor, enjoying peace on his western wing, kept the Ephthalites out of Khorassan.

The situation changed with the death of Yazdegerd II in 457, when the nobility in north-eastern Persia called in the Ephthalites to support a pretender to the throne.

The Saxon tower of Sompting, with a Rhenish helm-shaped roof, which is unique in Britain. The barbarian invasions spread to the extremities of Europe. *Scheerboom*

THEODERICVS·REX·

Theodoric, King of the Ostrogoths. His rule was peaceful for Italy and during it taxes were lightened, marshes drained, and harbours built.

Later, when the Persians quarrelled with their new allies and tried to get rid of them, the mischief could not be undone, and the new King of Kings, Kavadh, was obliged to cede them the right to occupy Merv and Herat. Towards the end of the century, in the struggles between the popular leader, Mazdak, and the landowners, who in opposition became even more reactionary, Kavadh enlisted Hunnish troops, who thenceforward were in a position to hold the balance in Persian quarrels.

The Barbarians halted in India and China

While one section of the Huns was giving trouble to the Persians, the remainder, at first repulsed (c. 467) on their way down from the Afghan passes, renewed their pressure and in 475 pushed towards Peshawar. At the beginning of the sixth century, while the Gupta Empire was splintering into rival kingdoms (Malwa, Oudh, Bengal) the Huns reached the Indus. Their chief, Mehiragula, 'the Attila of India', ravaged Kashmir. His massacres were appalling, and his passage is marked by the systematic destruction of all evidence of Graeco-Buddhist art. But here, too, the barbarians were halted. After 520 they made no further progress. Nomads from the north, they were probably unable to withstand the tropical climate.

In China, too, the barbarians were stabilised. We have

seen how North China fell into the hands of the Tobas, but to the south of the Yellow River, these Turks found themselves confronted by the old Empire, which at the beginning of the fifth century had been taken in hand by the able general Liu Yu, founder of the first Song dynasty. For a while Liu Yu was even able to rule over the old capitals, Lo-yang and Chan-gan, lost a century earlier (417-418). No doubt the Tobas (later called the Wei) were still very strong in this, the period of their great leader, Emperor Tao (425-446), for against the southern Chinese they disposed of a formidable cavalry and against the Jwen-Jwen of a solid base for supplies. But converted to Buddhism they became progressively more Chinese, the Court and the government being modelled on those of Nanking. Soon their military prowess was on the wane. After a series of efforts from 495 to 507, they gave up all hope of dislodging the Chinese garrisons from the Blue River.

Accordingly, about the year 500 in north China, a little later on the Indus, a little earlier in Persia, the barbarians, contained or absorbed, had ceased to advance. At the same period the waves of invasion into the Roman Empire ended.

The end of the Western Empire

Some efforts were made in the West to save what was left of the Empire. The Emperor Leo I of Byzantium, indignant at Gaiseric's independence and far from resigned to the loss of his African corn, sent a fleet in 466, no doubt of insufficient strength, for Gaiseric burnt it, taking advantage of an armistice. Henceforward the West was left to its fate. The enthusiastic Majorian (457-461) made grandiose but absurd plans to recapture Gaul, and in fact Aegidius, his chief general, succeeded in regaining Arles, Lyons, and the Auvergne. But the patrician Ricimer, an ambitious Suevian, in 461 got rid of both Aegidius and Majorian, and from then on, under cover of puppet emperors, kept the power in his hands till his death in 472.

Gaul was lost to the Empire. If the ruling class of Auvergne held out against Euric, the Visigoth, who was already master of Berry and Provence, it was for the sake of their new-won independence rather than from loyalty to Rome. Further north, Syagrius, son of Aegidius, animated by the same spirit, became a *de facto* 'king' of Gaul between the Somme and the Loire.

Even in Italy, the authority enjoyed by emperors became a mere plaything in the lands of any invader that came along. After one of the last engagements, in 476, Odovacer, chief of the Heruli camping by Ravenna, deposed and imprisoned the young Emperor, Romulus Augustulus, (whom fate had named ironically after the two founders of Rome), and despatched the imperial insignia to Zeno, the Eastern Emperor. Zeno was quite ready to accept the fiction of a re-united Empire, and he made Odovacer a patrician. In fact, in the course of these endless conflicts, the Western Empire had politically ceased to exist.

The last migrations of the fifth century

The barbarians were now firmly settled in the territory of the West. Only the Alemanni and the Ostrogoths were still on the move, the first in Baden and Alsace, the second roaming in Illyria. About 494 the Alemanni attempted to occupy Lorraine and the Palatinate, but they were halted abruptly at Tolbiac, possibly by a coalition of Franks settled along the Rhine. That brought to an end the Germanic invasions of Gaul. As for the Ostrogoths, they approached Constantinople asking to be allotted a territory to settle in. After they had plundered Macedonia, Zeno, to get rid of them and deal with Odovacer at the same time, instructed 'his beloved son' Theodoric to install himself in Italy. Mustering his horde, Theodoric accepted investiture with the purple and set off on what was to be the last barbarian migration in the Empire. His army must have been small when he arrived in the West, for it could all be lodged in the little town of Pavia. Odovacer remained on his guard, but in 492, during a banquet to celebrate their reconciliation, Theodoric had him stabbed.

Theodoric the Great

The patrician Theodoric established himself at Ravenna, as Zeno's representative there, at Milan, and at Rome, and struck coins bearing the imperial inscription. But he added his monogram and in fact was soon laying the foundation of a barbarian kingdom which was to serve as an example for many others, now that the invasions were over, and which could be regarded as a rough draft for that Gothia of which Ataulphus had dreamt. Without mixing his tribes with the Romans, he managed to conserve the best of the imperial administration. He respected the immense estates that made the strength of the ruling class and, Arian though he was, he was ready to listen to the advice of the Church. Theodoric became master of all Italy and Sicily and he occupied Dalmatia, Pannonia, and Noricum. Indeed, it looked as though he were destined to revive the Western Empire. Meanwhile he appointed a senator, Liberius, prefect of the Praetorium of the Gauls, took the sister of the Frankish king Clovis as his wife, and married his own sister to a Vandal and his daughters to a Visigoth and a Burgundian. Thus, after the last of the invasions, the sixth century opened on a comparatively peaceful West and with the Goths apparently masters of the new world.

Consular diptych of Aëtius, the victorious Roman general who for a time saved Rome from the barbarians. Valentinian III, jealous of his power and afraid of his ambition, murdered him in 454. *Giraudon*

Persian filigree bronze. A chimerical animal, showing a high degree of skill in metal working. Fifth century.

CHAPTER FOURTEEN

THE RESTORATION OF STABLE EMPIRES

A.D. 500-630

Clovis, founder of the Frankish kingdom, miraculously cured by St Severinus. Once a minor barbarian king, Clovis became the ' new Constantine ': his conversion in 496 earned him the loyalty of all the Catholics in Gaul, both Visigoths and Franks. This enabled him to establish a Frankish kingdom. *Janet le Caisne*

DIVISION OF THE SPOILS OF ROME

FRANKS OR GOTHS?

Theodoric's glory seemed to augur a restoration of the Western Empire, pacified by the Ostrogoths. His Arianism was an obstacle, but his conversion was not impossible. He would have had also to occupy Gaul, for Italy without Gaul could never constitute an empire. And then there were the fine corn-lands and the towns to the north of the Loire which must have tempted him. Suddenly, however, a dramatic event upset all calculations and threw the whole future of the West into doubt. The Frankish King, Clovis, was baptised by the Archbishop of Rheims, probably in 496. At a single blow the situation had changed: in the eyes of the Church there was now only one barbarian king who counted against any Arian rulers; only one who could claim the support of the bishops, Clovis, the 'new Constantine'.

For two centuries the Franks had been settled on the edge of the great forests which formed the northern limit of the Western Empire. Beyond the road from Boulogne to Bavai there were no Gaulish peasants, no flourishing villas, but low, marshy, uncultivated land, into which no merchant ever ventured. It was there that the Franks had been allowed to settle — a considerable, brutish, pagan people whose chief strength lay in the absence of any indigenous population to oppose them. They were markedly different from the Visigoth or Burgundian warriors, now so completely absorbed into the population of Gaul that little sign of their origin remained. North of Artois the linguistic frontier still marks the ancient domain of the Franks. In their tombs can be found no trace of Roman influence. This strong, violent people, who had remained loyal to their Germanic weapon, the light single-edged *francisca* or missile-axe, was still far from being united. Clovis, a minor king of the Salian Franks of Tournoi, was obliged to resort to killing his rivals before being eliminated himself, and he had to take advantage of every chance he could get. It is wrong to regard him as the undisputed master of a docile people. Almost to the end of his life he had to struggle with rival kings and recalcitrant warriors. A simple man with a somewhat narrow political outlook, he was little more than a brutal, avid chieftain, with a flair for gross treachery.

Northern Gaul falls to the Franks

It was no doubt the lust for booty that had impelled Clovis, as it had impelled so many others, to overrun the last strip of Gaul that was not barbarian. Between the Oise, the Seine, and the Marne was an area of good chalky soil that had long been cultivated and which had perhaps attracted a large number of Gauls. This was the realm of the Gallo-Roman, Syagrius, who showed little interest in perpetuating Roman tradition. In fact, with his handful of armed slaves furnished by a few big landowners, he represented himself alone, and no one doubted for a moment that the seat of Empire was on the Bosphorus. At the first Frankish attack his kingdom collapsed. Soissons was sacked. Syagrius was handed over to Clovis and killed. Clovis then advanced to the Loire. But he had to march hastily eastwards on learning that the Ripuarian Franks were marching on Metz and the Alemanni on Alsace. It took him ten years to defeat them and during that time we hear little about him.

Southern Gaul is taken

In 496 his conversion to Catholicism put Clovis suddenly at the head of the Frankish episcopate. His wife, Clotilda, a Burgundian princess, was already Catholic, and her influence over him was great. Had she and the Church been plotting his conversion? Or had Byzantium a hand in the matter, with a view to an indirect blow against Theodoric? The latter, at any rate, was conscious

Childeric, legendary and historical king of the Salian Franks in the fifth century; father of Clovis. *Hachette*

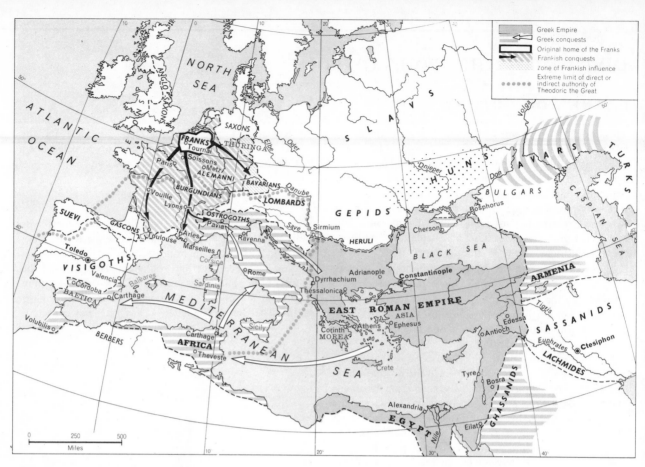

The Empire of Justinian and the Frankish conquest

Clovis. Tradition calls him the first Christian king of France.

of the threat. Throughout the whole of Gaul, Visigoths and Burgundi, citizens and civic dignitaries, and the great Gallo-Roman landowners, all looked forward to the coming of this new defender of the faith and the clergy. Theodoric tried to counter the threat by forming a league of Arian kings, and to thwart his rival he tried to stir up trouble on the Rhine. But once again he was outstripped. Clovis, urged on by the bishops and encouraged by the unpopularity of the Visigoth Alaric II among his own people, crossed the Loire, crushed the Visigoths at Vouillé and, so it is said, killed Alaric with his own hand. With that, all Visigoth resistance vanished. The Gallo-Romans threw open all their towns, even Toulouse, their capital. All Theodoric could do was to fortify Narbonne and Arles, which protected the Mediterranean coast. Clovis's son, Thierry, did not attempt to pursue his father's conquests in this direction.

No doubt Theodoric had been able to keep the most essential route, the Roman road from Italy to Spain. And the defeat of the Visigoths had made it more secure. All the same, the balance of forces had been upset. Clovis, when he received the Emperor's ambassador, Anastasius at St Martin's in Tours and received at his hands the title of 'consul', was probably under no illusions about the Emperor's approval, but Anastasius understood very well he was conferring this distinction on the new master of Gaul. Theodoric accordingly saw the possibility of joining that country to his kingdom vanish. Moreover, Clovis presided at a council which certainly did not flatter the Arian Ostrogoth. He installed himself in Paris, the heart of those rich and well-peopled lands that Julian had earlier chosen as the capital of Gaul. There was nothing

Head of an Ostrogoth king. Sixth century. After establishing themselves in Italy the Ostrogoths preserved Roman institutions, unlike other Teutonic races who remained fiercely independent.

Bowl depicting Chosroes II, King of Persia, who almost brought about the downfall of the Byzantine Empire. The successes of his early campaigns against the Empire were halted by Justinian's general, Heraclius, in a series of defeats culminating in the battle of Nineveh in 628. An indecisive peace followed Chosroes' murder by his son.

Theodoric could do to turn the scales in his favour short of killing his adversary. He was spared this action by Clovis's sudden death in 511.

Uncertainty in the West

Clovis was dead, and the idea of a kingdom was still so foreign to the Frankish warriors that they promptly divided his estate, his four sons receiving shares that were no doubt of roughly equal value. The eldest, the only one of age, received the lands he had won personally from the Visigoths and the whole eastern area to defend as best he might. The other three divided the country between the Loire and the lower Rhine. The Visigothic Aquitaine, too recently conquered, remained undivided and was to enjoy ten centuries of autonomy.

Theodoric might usefully have taken advantage of this situation. He might have strengthened that Arian league which failed to prevent the defeat at Vouillé, he might have come to the aid of the kingdom of Burgundy, vulnerable but still intact. For a wretched bit of territory — probably the Durance valley — he preferred to come to terms with Clovis's sons and take part in the division. It was a grave mistake which left the Franks the whole Rhône valley. With that in their hands, they were soon casting an envious eye on the prosperous port of Marseilles. Apparently Theodoric, still master of Italy and Spain, where coins were struck with his head, was flattered by the idea of playing the arbiter in the quarrels of the Frankish chiefs. He was counting without the eldest son, Thierry, who managed to keep order reasonably well in his sector of Gaul; nor did he consider his own age. He was over seventy, and he died in 526 without achieving his ambitions, leaving the West in a state of uncertainty, with the Visigoths still shaken by their defeat, Gaul divided amongst four brothers, and Italy leaderless. With that, Constantinople came into its own.

THE RETURN OF THE ROMANS

The 'New Rome' had not given up hope of the West, but during the fifth century she had been able to do no more than hold the barbarians at arm's length and, at home, keep the Roman tradition alive. Before adventuring further it had been necessary to revitalise what remained healthy in the stricken Empire. When he suggested the conquest of Italy to Theodoric, Zeno's plan was to have a subject king in the West as well as to rid himself of an awkward neighbour, who was not only pillaging Macedonia but was even threatening the land around Constantinople. Anastasius I, who followed (491-518), understood the situation perfectly. He strengthened Constantinople's defences by the Long Wall shutting off fifty miles of the peninsula. He had eliminated the Isaurian mercenaries, who had been getting out of hand, reorganised the army, and consolidated the forts. And the aged Justin (518-527) had strengthened the capital inwardly by suppressing Monophysitism (the belief that there is only one nature in the person of Christ) and Arianism, whereby his hitherto hostile relations with Pope John I, had been greatly improved. The Bishop of Rome, a possible agent of the Empire in Italy, had been received in Constantinople in the very year when Justin signed with a wavering hand the decree making his nephew Justinian share his throne.

Justinian

The last 'Roman' Emperor was such a towering figure that we are apt to speak of the sixth century as the 'century of Justinian'. In this lively, hard-working Latin of the East, we find on the one hand the absolute Emperor, the despotic authority, the imposing figure delineated in the Ravenna mosaics, produced in his time, and on the other hand, the cruel, passionate despot,

251

Wall mosaic, San Vitale, Ravenna (c. 547). The Emperor Justinian, his courtiers, and Maximian, Bishop of Ravenna, bearing offerings. Justinian devoted his energy to uniting and strengthening the Empire. He recovered much ground lost to the barbarians and social legislation went far towards remedying the evils of a corrupt administration. *Alinari*

susceptible to influence of the East and already tinged with all its colour. Under this dual sway, he devoted all his powers to stemming the tide of events sweeping Constantinople towards oriental monarchy.

If many of his subjects were out of sympathy with his ambition to reconstitute the Empire, they did not include the merchants, eager to get their hands once again on African corn and the riches of Gaul, nor the bishops, anxious to stamp out the Arian kingdoms, nor, lastly, the hungry masses of Constantinople, driven into the city by the oppression of the country landlords. For the people, fresh sources of wheat were imperative, wheat that could be imported without running the gauntlet of Persian or Hun raiders. But if these elements were favourable, the rich of the regime grumbled. In Thrace, in Illyria, in Syria, with their estates grown ever larger by the spoliation of the peasantry and the immense powers they enjoyed, the landlords considered themselves threatened by the barbarians or by the Persians who had advanced in 529 to the approaches to Antioch. In their view it was in another direction that Justinian should exert military force. Living off their own lands, what did they care about African corn? Their opposition for long paralysed the Emperor.

The vital question, however, was whether he could count on the support of the army. Would Belisarius, his faithful general, loaded with honours, turn out to be the conqueror of Rome or a rebellious chieftain lording it over an oriental army? For the answer it was necessary to wait for the general's return from Syria, where he had finally defeated the Sassanid king, Chosroes Anushirvan (the Blessed). This winter of 532-533 was a critical one for Justinian. During what are known as the Nika riots he was howled down by the crowds at the hippodrome, then hemmed in his palace by a mob spurred on by some of the magnates. If Belisarius failed him, his only hope lay in flight; but the Empress Theodora was not prepared to surrender. 'If flight were the only means of safety', she said, as Gibbon puts it, 'yet I should disdain to fly... If you resolve, O Caesar! to fly, you have your treasures: behold the sea, you have your ships; but tremble lest the desire of life should expose you to wretched exile and ignominious death. For my part, I adhere to the maxim of antiquity, that the throne is a glorious sepulchre.' She was proved right. She overcame the hesitations of her husband. Belisarius obeyed. Driven into the hippodrome, 30,000 of the rioters lost their lives. The army had come out on Justinian's side and was ready to march in whatever direction the Emperor cared to choose.

The reconquest

It was in Africa that the Byzantines began. The Vandals were maintaining their position there by ruthless despotism but this did not keep the Berbers in a state of submission. The Vandals' Arianism alienated the Catholics, and it was at the request of the latter that Justinian, having first bought off the Persians, sent Belisarius to Africa. The campaign was not altogether popular, but at any rate the merchants and the bishops were pleased. In two battles in 533, Belisarius defeated the Vandal king, Gelimer and, entering Carthage, ate the feast prepared for his unhappy adversary. Africa was a province once more. Returning to Constantinople, Belisarius drove in triumph through the city with Gelimer at the foot of his chariot. The campaign had been a splendid success, though in the Aures Mountains and on the plateaus the Berbers, invincible guerilla fighters, were still at large.

Encouraged by this first success, Justinian now turned towards Italy. Little more than sixty years had elapsed since Odovacer had sent Zeno the imperial insignia taken from Romulus Augustulus, thereby openly announcing the end of the Western Empire. There were still plenty of senators and landed proprietors who remembered 'Roman' days. In any case Justinian's intervention was legitimised by a request for help from one of Theodoric's heirs, in conflict with the party in power. In 536 a double attack was delivered, through Dalmatia and through Naples. Neither encountered any resistance, and on December 10, Belisarius entered Rome. Ravenna, however, was the capital of the Ostrogoth kingdom and the 9,000 imperial troops were quite inadequate for its capture, since the enemy showed no sign of capitulation. On the contrary, the Ostrogoths won over the Franks by offering Marseilles (not that the Franks did much in return). At the same time the Persians were also drawn in. Breaking the pact made in 532 they pounced on Syria and sacked Antioch. Belisarius had to be recalled, and for six years he wrestled with the enemy in the Armenian mountains. Meanwhile the Huns had reached Thermopylae, and a Goth, Totila, taking advantage of the unpopularity of Byzantine taxation, had entered Rome and advanced as far as Naples. These were critical days for the Eastern Empire. Even from Africa came bad news: a Berber rising and the loss of Carthage. But Justinian stood firm, and on all sides Roman action was successful. Belisarius, who had now fallen out of favour with Theodora, was dismissed and retired to live quietly on his estates, not as one tradition has it to beg in the streets. In a final effort, his successor, Narses, with 15,000 men, held out against successive charges of Gothic cavalry in a battle in which Totila lost his life. The imperial army now reached the Po; it took ten years to mop up all the marauding bands south of the Alps, but Italy had been regained.

Not so Spain, for in order to support Athanagild and the Catholics against an Arian rival, Justinian ceded the ancient province of Baetica, which included Cordova and the fine agricultural country of Valencia. There remained Gaul, which Justinian does not seem to have thought of attacking. Possibly the Church saved the Franks by refusing to bless an expedition against true Christians. Or it may have been that Justinian, after the exhausting Italian campaign, feared the resistance he might encounter. The simplest explanation, however, may be that he was old.

Constantinople, arbiter of the Mediterranean

All the same, Justinian's success had been prodigious. Constantinople had recovered her premier position, lost since Theodosius. Ambassadors poured in from all parts; agents of the Empire travelled to barbarian countries to incite the Lombards of Pannonia against the Gepidae of Bavaria, the Heruli of Dacia against the Hun tribes, the Arab sheiks of Transjordan against the Persians. Meanwhile Justinian had empowered Tribonian to codify the Roman law, and the Codex and the Digests were promulgated, not to honour the past but to provide the foundation of a re-established society. Hellenistic philosophy was no longer fashionable, but Leontius and Pro-

Part of apse mosaic, Sant'Apollinare in Classe, Ravenna. Sixth century. The Triumph of the Cross medallion appears in other Ravenna mosaics. *Mansell*

Theodoric's Palace; a mosaic from Sant'Apollinare Nuovo, Ravenna. The geometrical frieze is a legacy of classical Greece.

copious were in no way inferior to their predecessors of 'Roman' times. The direct heir of classical science, Byzantium jealously collected in her libraries all available works of Greek or oriental learning, the best of which have been preserved in Syriac and Nestorian centres in central Asia. The works of Aristotle were in fact first known to the West by the successive translations from Greek into Syriac and later into Arabic and Latin.

There is no better evidence of this new vigour than the revival of architecture in a style that combined the radial plan of the Syrians and the Persian cupola. Built

253

of brick and decorated with the foliated scrolls and the palmettes of the Sassanids, this was a genuinely new art created for the new Empire. Unlike the West which grotesquely distorted it and Islam which ignored it, Byzantium conserved the art of the human figure; it is there in mosaics, in wooden icons and carved ivories, stiff, hieratic, and draped in antique style, showing an innate feeling for grandeur and a well tried technique. Moreover, by his conquests, Justinian carried Byzantine art to the people of the West: it was to Ravenna that they came for lessons in taste as they admired the mosaics in San Vitale and in Sant'Apollinare in Classe. And at Constantinople when the dome of St Sophia fell, it was replaced by one that rose still higher.

Trade received a new impulse. The war with Chosroes had closed the ports of the Lebanon, termini of the age-old caravan routes to the Persian Gulf and central Asia. Other routes had to be found: a northern one through the Chersonesus in the Crimea and over the Russian steppes, a southern one through Akaba and the Red Sea. The Khan of the Uighur Huns and the sovereigns of Ethiopia were visited by Greek merchants. Cosmos of Alexandria traded in Ceylon and China, while in 554 a couple of monks brought home some silk-worms' eggs concealed in their staffs. These were hatched out in the Peloponnesus, a country of mulberry trees, and silk, so precious a product of the East, was henceforth produced locally.

This success was achieved at great cost. In the West, only the Franks seemed to thrive. Was it only to play into their hands that Justinian had won these fragile conquests? Justinian himself involuntarily encouraged the alienation: the increasing power of the State over the Church could only estrange the Pope and hasten the religious schism between Rome and Constantinople; the rigidity of the civil and the military administration, all-powerful in the reorganised State, fostered the particularism of the various nations firmly incorporated in the Empire.

Only the army could maintain unity, yet the weakness of the army had been revealed by the Italian campaign. By increasing the territory incorporated in the Empire without increasing the internal supply of soldiers, Justinian assigned to the mercenaries a role they might well be tempted to abuse, without at the same time making the frontiers secure against attack. When he died in 565, the Empire looked impressive. Justinian could have had little suspicion of what would happen to it when the first shock came when once again Asia unleashed her barbarians on the West.

NEW INVASIONS

TURKS AND AVARS

In the middle of the sixth century the domination of the Jwen-Jwen over the steppes and the Asiatic plateaus seemed firmly established. The Mongols retained the best country for themselves and kept neighbouring tribes in a state of subjection: the Ephthalites living in the old provinces of Sogdiana and Bactriana at the foot of the Pamirs, and the Tu Kiue (the present-day Turks) established at the foot of the Great Altai, where they worked in metals for the benefit of their masters. Descending from this mountain region traversed by torrents, a Turk called Bu-Min defied and so completely routed the Jwen-Jwen that what was left of them escaped across the desert tracks of the Gobi and took refuge in north China. Bu-Min, now master of the steppes, adopted the title of Khakan, but he had no sooner celebrated his triumph than he died.

One of his sons was drawn towards China, the other towards Persia and India, both, as was usual, seeking richer pastures. As for the first, the chaotic state of northern China, divided between the small Khitai and Toba kingdoms, facilitated his conquests. Within twenty years the authority of the invaders reached to the Great Wall, while their raids even reached Chang-gan, capital of the Wei kingdom. Thus was formed the Turks' oriental empire. The western Turks, on the other hand, were led by Istemi, Bu-Min's brother, who, after the defeat of the Jwen-Jwen, attacked the Ephthalites. The latter, already weakened by repeated Persian attacks, were not able to hold out long, and Istemi's hordes were soon in possession of the oases of Turkmenistan, while the troops of Chosroes, freed by the peace concluded with Justinian, occupied those of Khozasan (568). Settled and nomad marauders were once again at the foot of the Great Wall and at the foot of the Persian plateau (570).

It was in the last quarter of the sixth century that the new barbarian surge gained its full momentum. In China it was not till 590 that the tide was stemmed; this time by a genuine Chinese, Yang Kien, the founder of the Sui dynasty. On the borders of India, the Turks attacked the Persians. No doubt Justin II, the Eastern Emperor, saw in that an opportunity to finish off his hereditary enemies, the Sassanids: Maniakh, the Sogdian caravan-leader who had accepted Istemi's yoke, went to Constantinople by the route across the steppes formerly opened by Justinian; in reply the Greek Zemarchus visited the Khan's camp north of Karachah. Probably less was said of caravans than of alliances, for in 572 Chosroes was attacked by the Turks and the Greeks simultaneously. The King of Kings held out for a while, but in 574 was forced to cede Armenia to the first and Bactriana to the second. Once the Persian danger had been eliminated, it was the turn of Bosphora and the Greek trading stations to suffer.

Byzantine diplomacy no longer had to deal with scattered rival tribes but with an empire; the epic songs engraved on the rock at Kocho Tsaidam sing the praises of the armies of the Khazan, 'the emperor of the seven nations who makes the peoples of the four corners of the world bow the head and bend the knee'. The hereditary chiefs of the Turkish clans reaped so rich a reward that it seemed impossible for their empire to crumble as long as it went on attacking.

254

The Franks' Casket: the side showing Romulus and Remus and the she-wolf. The panel is surrounded by runic inscriptions. c. 700. *British Museum*

Europe threatened again

It was only in south Russia that Europe suffered directly from Turkish expansion. What was left of the Jwen-Jwen and the Ephthalites driven from Sogdiana fled into the Ukraine, absorbing in their passage the residue of Attila's Huns. But these Avars, as they were called, were requested by the Lombards (living between the Dnieper and the Hungarian plains) to help them against the Gepidae. They routed both these tribes, before appearing on the Danube, three years after Justinian's death. The great emperor in his reconquests had pushed his frontiers out too far: how could his successors defend Italy at the same time as Thrace, repel the Sassanids at the same time as the Lombards? So, to defend the eastern front the Emperor Maurice (582-602), the first *basileus*, or joint Emperor, to be born in the Near East, gave up the idea of defending Italy. Alboin and his Lombards were thus able to occupy the North, come down the Alps to the Po, and cross Italy from Milan to Benevento. Admittedly, for want of ships they failed to take Naples or Taranto, and they soon tired of besieging Rome and Ravenna, but the remainder of the peninsula, already ruined by the recently ended Gothic war fell into their hands in 574-575. Byzantium tried to play the Franks off against the Lombards, as they had played off the Turks against the Persians; but the Franks were so destructive, leaving desolation wherever they went, that in the end they had to be bought off.

Even in the East the Greeks found it hard enough to hold their own. The Avars' Khan Baian captured the old town of Sirmium, demanded a heavy indemnity, and when he retired, left the savage Slavonic tribes free to cross the Danube and reach Adrianople, then Thermopylae. These were critical years for the Empire, and they only paved the way to disaster. In 602, a brutish centurian, Phocas, beheaded Maurice and his five sons. Mutinies, risings, refusals to pay taxes, and the defiance of the senate added to the troubles, and the Slavs were able to overrun the Serbian mountains and the Danube valley.

The West spared

Western Europe now seemed ready to recognise the superiority of the Franks. Of course, the Visigoths of Spain were not negligible and their cousins, the descendants of Euric's Visigoths, still centred at Narbonne, would have dearly liked to revenge their defeat at Vouillé; but such a plan was beyond their powers, as their Arianism precluded the support of the Church. The best the Visigoths could do was to dazzle the simple-minded Franks with their wealth and give them their daughters in marriage. In any case they were occupied fighting the Suevi in Galicia and the Gascons whom Rome had not been able to subjugate.

The Merovingian nightmare

It was thus the successors of Clovis who were destined eventually to reconstitute the Empire and maintain a

Coin of Dagobert (obverse and reverse), son of Chlotar II of Gaul and King of the Franks 629-39. *Giraudon*

255

Merovingian bas-relief of a chariot. The figures are somewhat stiff and were later to become more stylised.

certain standard of civilisation in the West, a sorry lot to be called on to play such a part. They were the only barbarians who had no idea of achieving unity, not even by the systematic assassination of rivals. In fact their coarse and turbulent chiefs were known in Gaul only for disorder and cruelty. Wasteful, yet grasping, they wandered in armed bands from villa to villa, living on the produce of one till they moved on to plunder another, returning a little of their own property to the avid, untrustworthy landowners, who complained of the paucity of this largesse. In settling their own family quarrels, they dragged the whole of Gaul into an interminable series of absurd wars and stupid partitions. The country was reduced to barbarism, and lawlessness became the rule, even among the clergy. For every St Gregory of Tours, there was an endless chain of scandalous prelates. On every level the country disintegrated: the estates, which were constantly changing hands, tried to be self sufficient. In each city the harassed count who sat in judgment had to wade through an incredible farrago of barbarian law. Little by little the Roman roads disappeared beneath the weeds; centralised taxation ceased to exist; what trade was left was in the hands of Syrians and Jews, and in the end even they found it too unsafe to travel. Though occupying Marseilles, the barbarians strangled the port by their partition of the Rhône valley. As for the currency, some gold coins bearing the Emperor's head persisted for a while in south-eastern Gaul, but from 580 onwards, north of the Massif Central, barter became increasingly common, payments being made in kind. There was thus a totally closed economy.

For forty years Gaul was rent by an atrocious war, which spread over the area from the Oise and the Seine to Aquitaine in the south and to Austrasia in the east. The cause, or rather the pretext, was the jealousy of two women, the insatiably ambitious Fredegond, a serving-woman who became the wife of the North Frankish king, Chilperic, and Brunhild, a Visigoth princess married to Sigebert, king of the Eastern Franks, who, when over eighty years old, was handed over by her own nobles to Fredegond's implacable son and dragged to death at the heels of wild horses. And what are we to think of Chilperic, the illiterate prince who wanted to invent a new alphabet and, imitating the Eastern Emperor, wanted to be called 'Your Sublimity'? His brother, Gontran, was slightly preferable and, alone of his family, escaped assassination and died peacefully in his bed.

The vigour of the Franks

It is impossible to understand the part played by the Franks in Europe if one concentrates on their atrocious conflicts. In fact, in spite of the civil war, in spite of the attack of the Gascons in the south, the revolt of the Bretons in the west, and the invasion of the Lombards in Provence, the territory remained intact. Indeed, the extraordinary vitality of the Franks made them the masters of Western Europe. At the request of the Emperor Maurice, who paid them a subsidy, they made several expeditions into Italy. Gontran, pushing back the Lombards, occupied Aosta and Susa, controlling the Alpine passes. He even fitted out a fleet, a thing that no barbarian had done since Gaiseric's day, but it sank.

But it was on the Rhine that the Franks played their major part. The raids of Clovis's sons and grandsons drove into Saxony and Thuringia. They contented themselves with a nominal authority over Bavaria and the Alemanni, but the Austrasians moved gradually eastward from Rheims to Metz, pushing back the spearhead of the Avars' thrust (570). Thanks to them, the territory of ancient Germania was taken from Arian hands and attached to the West, a fact of the utmost importance in the history of the continent.

THE VICTORY OF THE SETTLED PEOPLES
The Tang Emperors save China

The growing strength of settled populations advanced more rapidly now than in the fifth century. Here again, China set the example. The usurper Yang Chien, having established the Sui dynasty on the Northern Wei throne, had undertaken to subdue the remainder of the Chen domination around Kiangnan (Nanking) (589): for the first time for three centuries unity had been regained and this important event inaugurated a period of progress for the Middle Kingdom. It was Yang Chien's son, the ostentatious Yang-ti, the 'Chinese Xerxes', to whom it was given to exploit this success. Cleverly making use of the rivalries that divided the eastern and the western Turks, Yang-ti was able to reach the banks of the Tarim and occupy Turfan. He took control of the oases and with them reaped the substantial profits of the trade with India and Persia, but he may have overreached himself in attempting external expansion so soon. Though he was able to advance from Canton to Hué he was defeated in 616 in the Korean mountains where he was attempting to prevent a Turco-Korean combined attack. The Sui dynasty was unable to survive this disaster and the increased taxes that resulted from it.

In 618, Li Shihmin, who had collaborated with the Turks, overthrew the Sui and established the famous Tang dynasty (618-906). First he made his father Emperor, but in 626 he took the throne himself.

Important reforms were at once set in train, aimed at protecting the peasants against the rich landowners, but the Chinese gentry managed to retain their privileges. Taxation was tightened up and administration centred on an elaborate secretariat which controlled the various departments of state. Military organisation was also improved and the authority of civilian government asserted against military magnates.

Head of a monk. Northern Wei dynasty. Sixth century. *Giraudon*

Japanese dance mask. Nara period. Eighth century. *Giraudon*

The Tang dynasty was to witness a great expansion of wealth and culture, decisive not only for China but for Japan and parts of south-eastern Asia; indeed, for the whole periphery of the Empire.

When the Turks attacked Nanking, they were repulsed by the new Emperor. During nearly half a century Li-Yuen and his successor Li Shihmin, who reigned as the Emperor, were able to occupy the Tarim and Yarkand, reach the gates of Dzungaria, exact tribute from the Turks of Turkestan, and, as in the days of the Han dynasty, keep peace in Mongolia and Ordos entrusted to

their allies, the Karluks. Tibet itself, having remained hitherto so isolated, gave the Emperor a wife in 641. Buddhist monks and imperial officials were to be seen everywhere and the peace of China seemed once more to be re-established, with the rule of the empire vastly extended.

The awakening of Japan

Like a pallid reflection of the Tang splendour, an archipelago began to awake from the mists of its legendary history. Drawn, perhaps for ages, along the sea-routes from Indonesia to Japan, the original Ainu had become mixed with Korean, Chinese, Malay and Polynesian stocks. That was the origin of the Japanese. Since before the beginning of the Christian era, an emperor or Temmu seems to have reigned by the Kii Channel, facing many independent 'kingdoms'. Little by little, however, the country was united round Yamato and the Kii Channel, at the expense of the Ainus, who were driven northward. Only these few facts emerge from obscurity. Relations with the continent were practically non-existent, except for the importation of slaves from Kyushu by Chinese merchants. It was during the fifth century that Japan woke up. In 500 the Japanese launched an expedition against Korea which was repulsed. At the same time, Chinese culture began to spread over the islands. A Chinese scribe is known to have been there in 405, and Chinese writings were being read in 461. Then the introduction of Buddhism opened a new period. The triumph of the new religion, made official by an edict of 604, was in reality the triumph of new clans, like the Soga family, over the Mononoga family. It opened the national history of Japan, introducing a firmer moral code, more advanced administrative methods, and a culture of the first order. This Chinese influence, which came chiefly through the Koreans, conflicted with the wandering life of those clans that were still nomadic. The great edict of Kotoku, generally called the Taikwa reforms (645), which appointed officials, instituted a land-tax and abolished slavery, can perhaps be compared in importance with the revolution of the middle of the nineteenth century. By the end of the seventh century universities had been established, and more than fifty monasteries for 15,000 monks.

Indian influence

If Buddhism had been instrumental in awakening Japan, it had also been the instrument of Chinese penetration into south east Asia: Yang-ti had been able to exercise a lasting authority over the Red River basin, and he had even reached Hué. Then small Buddhist communities began to develop in Java, in Borneo, and at Palembang, from which in 644 an ambassador was sent to the Tang court. On the other hand, the reunion of Fou-nan and Tchin-la in the hands of the Khmers arrested the Chinese advance on that side. The emperor Bhavavarman I (598) was Brahminist and it was to the Ganges that he looked for civilisation.

For India, too, had reacted to the blows she had received from the Turks. Established between the Doab and the Punjab, the Vardhana dynasty, after a lengthy struggle with the barbarians of Kabul, was strong enough for

Harsha in 606 to found a powerful kingdom, and, during the forty years of his reign, to extend it till it reached from Bengal to Malva and Assam. In 643 he exchanged ambassadors with the Emperor Tai Tsung. Perhaps a Manichee, in any case extremely tolerant in matters of religion, Harsha was persuaded to support Buddhism, which seems to have spread rapidly. Only the wild mountain people of Maharashtra escaped Harsha's influence. Many Brahminists moved to south-east Asia, where, as we have seen, they spread Indian civilisation. Pulikesin II, the most powerful monarch of the Deccan, seems also to have been in contact with the emperor of the Ganges.

A Buddhist mural from the Ajanta caves. Ajanta painting represents mainly the opulence and brilliance of court life between the fifth and sixth centuries. Not all the subjects depicted can be identified: some are of the life of Buddha, others of everyday life in the court.

The triumph of the Persians

In Persia, Chosroes II (Parvez) had already stopped the Turkish advance towards the south. The danger presented by the alliance of Constantinople with the Turks vanished with the revolt against the Emperor Maurice and the succession of Phocas on the one hand and, on the other, with the Tang Emperor's success in fomenting conflict between the eastern and the western Turks. Thus relieved from pressure, Persian influence once more advanced to the region of the oases, to Khotan, to Turfan, to Kara-shahr, where there are seventh-century frescoes showing the presence of the Sassanids. Right across the Russian steppes, from Perm to the Caucasus, Persian art recovered its traditional sphere of influence. Lastly, controlling the caravan-routes right across Asia, Chosroes II wanted also to secure the trading stations and forts on the south coast of Arabia, the Yemen and the mouth of the Red Sea.

Nevertheless he had still to eliminate the Greeks, and in 613-614 he launched a furious attack. While the Byzantine fleet was struggling with Slav flotillas in the Aegean, and while the Avars besieging Constantinople were within 300 yards of St Sophia, Chosroes took Damascus, advanced to the coast, and took the Holy Cross from Jerusalem and displayed it in triumph at Ctesiphon. Then in 618 he seized Asia Minor from the Greeks, and then Egypt, whose port, Alexandria, was the key to the trade of the East. The days of Darius had returned.

Heraclius saves Byzantium

But the Persians did not allow for the 'luck of the Romans'. Byzantium was not destined to succumb, and in her extremity she found her saviour. The son of the exarch or governor of Africa had the auspicious name of Heraclius. He was greeted on his arrival at Constantinople with the only Latin words the populace knew — and they were corrupt — 'tou bincas, thou shalt conquer'. Born in Asia, this handsome man of imposing stature and keen eye had the makings of a Diocletian. He took in hand the army, which had lost all discipline, while the Patriarch, Sergius, restored the morale of the people. Ready at last in 622, Heraclius acted quickly. Not stopping to take towns, he drove through Armenia and on to Mesopotamia, aided by the Arabs of the Persian littoral. Constantinople was besieged again in 626, but Sergius stood firm. The following year the Emperor recaptured all the lost provinces, camped outside Ctesiphon, and finally returned with the Holy Cross in 629, having concluded a

Sassanid king on horseback. Sixth century. Metal work was highly developed among the Sassanids.

peace with Kavadh II, the son of Chosroes II. The subsequent death of Kavadh and the ensuing anarchy assured the reconquest of the East.

It was a magnificent success, though at the cost of Baetica, which had to be ceded to the Visigoths, since there were no soldiers left in Spain to hold it. In Illyria, Serbian marauders infested the mountains; in Italy the Lombards did not disarm; but, with Africa, Heraclius was assured of his supply of corn and from the Lebanon to Morocco the seas were Greek.

Recarred and Dagobert

Among the barbarians of the West, the Visigoths of Spain were now an established people. Having attained a degree of maturity, these barbarian kings acquired prestige when they acquired possession of Baetica and when they retained Septimania, which the Franks were unable to wrest from them. The monarchy at last found its permanent religious basis: Recarred I was converted and received the blessing of the Church (587). With this, he acquired an authority that was later to be a temptation to Pepin the Short. At his court, Isidore, Archbishop of Seville, compiled his great etymology between 622 and 633. It is at once a book of definitions of the meaning and origins of words, and an encyclopaedia. It was immensely influential far into the Middle Ages, when the fashion was to appeal to authority rather than resort to experiments. The book deals with land and government, with medicine, biology, agriculture, forestry, sport and gladiatorial games. It describes the origins and laws of war, and gives an account of the peoples of Europe, as far as he knew them. It is an extremely elementary but very comprehensive work in two large volumes of the modern text, and an appreciation of it is essential to any deep understanding of the medieval mind. It was at Toledo, at the centre of his territory, that this 'Flavius Reccaredus' lived; and well-conducted councils were held there in whose proceedings the Church's influence on the State can already be seen. In 654 the old 'Breviary of Alaric' was supplanted by the *Liber judiciorum*, a fusion of the codes of two peoples, one of whom was no more than a memory.

In Gaul, Clothaire II, having had the good fortune to survive the massacre of his family, reunited Gaul, and his energetic son, Dagobert I, reigned alone from 629 to 639, during which short period the Merovingians showed ability. Difficulties were not lacking: Septimania and Brittany, which Clothaire coveted, were not to be his; the Gascons were becoming unruly; and beyond the Rhine the Slavs, who had reached Thuringia, were only held in check by a general levy of all Germanic warriors acknowledging the Frankish king. Holding his ground, Dagobert made constant tours of the kingdom to show that he was truly king; he sent missionaries as far as Friesland; he tried to make Paris a second Toledo; and he spoke his mind to Heraclius.

But weaknesses were already appearing. He was obliged to propitiate the big land-owners, and make sacrifices to the separatism always inherent in divided Gaul: Burgundy, Aquitaine, Neustria, Austrasia, the heritage of too many partitions, each part with its own deeply rooted feelings and prejudices. Some looked towards the Saône and the Rhône and south towards the Mediterranean, others were imbued with Visigoth law and little inclined to understand the men of the North; beyond the Loire, the west was vigorous, well peopled, with many estates, the east broader and emptier, with a few great families holding sway.

The work of the Christian Church

But it was in Rome that the revival of the West was most apparent. Refusing to be a relic of the past, a bone of contention between Eastern emperors and barbarian chiefs, the city, freed by the invading Lombards from Greek tutelage, found a new prestige in sheltering the spiritual adviser of the kingdoms of the West, Pope Gregory the Great, who in 590 had accepted the guardianship of the sacred city, and had twice repelled Agilulf, the Lombard king. Gregory first made himself a duke, then the heir of ancient Rome, elected by the popular tribunes. His work was not confined to Italy. If the Lombards were slow in turning towards Catholicism, the Visigoths, like the Franks, had already taken the step. Gregory looked even further afield: his agents went as pilgrims to Carthage, then to the misty lands of Britain, and to Ireland, where a sometimes unorthodox monasticism had been maintaining the faith brought there in the fifth century. In 597 St Augustine arrived at the court of Ethelbert, the Saxon king of Kent, and laid the foundations of the

Archipiscopal coffin, seventh century. The Byzantine emblem in the centre is the Shining Cross of Constantine's dream before his battle with Maxentius in 312. *Mansell*

Church at Canterbury. After him, Theodore increased the number of bishoprics and reformed the Irish monasteries, and the Church established itself in the Western Isles.

Between 630 and 650 the settled world seemed to have regained its equilibrium, with the Tang dynasty in China, Harsha in India, and Heraclius at Constantinople having triumphed over the barbarian nomads. The other invaders — the peoples led by Dagobert, Agilulf, and Recarred — had already been gradually absorbed into the Roman orbit. The two great universal religions, Christianity and Buddhism, were moving outwards in conquest of new territories, to Britain, Japan, and Java. The other great religions, Zoroastrianism and Brahminism, seem to have been less vigorous, as were their followers, the rajahs of India and Shahanshahs of Persia, who now played secondary parts in the political world. Was it this area between China and the Mediterranean which gave rise to new beliefs? Certainly there was room for a new universal and also a new political domination. Heraclius, victor of the Persians, was celebrating his triumph at Constantinople, when the Arabs surged out of the desert.

CHAPTER FIFTEEN

THE ARABS

A.D. 630-770

Bourgin

THE ARAB CONQUESTS

The men of the desert

The sudden raids carried out by Arab horsemen and camelry came as no surprise to the Greek or Sassanid soldiers stationed on the borders of the desert, for they had long been dealing with these semi-nomadic tribes scattered along the Syrian *limes* or occupying the ruins of Chaldean cities, alternately repelling them and tolerating them, and finally enrolling them in their own forces. The Greeks and Persians had learned how to exploit the rivalries of these proud, warlike people. The Lakhmids camped near Kufah were vassals of the King of Kings, and from 602 undertook to patrol the coast on behalf of their suzerain. The Ghassanids, on the other hand, were ruled by a sheik who called himself a 'Patrician' and visited Basrah from time to time to report to Greek officers and keep them informed of the situation in the desert. Both tribes had some semblance of an organisation; so what could be feared from the wild nomad tribes that wandered in the vast empty spaces beyond? The only places which showed any real activity were Yathrib (later Medina), occupied by Jewish settlers who traded with Egypt, and Mecca, a centre of caravan routes. The Yemen, in the south-east, aroused a certain envy, but this ancient kingdom of Saba, which had successively attracted the Romans and the Abyssinians, was now subject to the Sassanids. Driving long caravans of camels, the Yemen merchants travelled to the banks of the Euphrates and the Jordan, and returned laden with their famous perfumes.

The physical stamina of the Arab nomads was bred of exposure to extreme privations and long journeys in a landscape devoid of all human life. The discipline of a life of alarms and ambushes had forged in them a spirit of fierce resistance and fanatical obedience. They were a race of thinkers and fighters who had not yet discovered an ideal capable of developing their full potential. So far Christian charity, the hope of the Jewish Messiah, or the

Manichaeism of the Persians had made little appeal to them, rarely enough to draw them away from their ancestral idols, the spirits of the desert or the 'Black Stone' of Mecca.

Islam

The only people to profit from the old religion were the settled merchant families, such as the Khuraishites of Mecca, who made money out of the Ka'aba, the goal of endless pilgrims. Thus, when one of the Khuraishites, Mahomet — quite an unimportant member of the tribe — claimed to have received divine visitations and demanded the destruction of all idols on pain of hell fire, his prophecies caused first laughter then hatred amongst his relations. But Mahomet had won over his wife, Khadija, who promptly placed herself and her wealth at the service of the new creed, according to which the Archangel Gabriel had appeared to Mahomet during a retreat in the desert and had revealed to him the submission — *islam* — to a single God, *al Ilah*. His stay in Mecca becoming impossible, Mahomet fled with his disciples in 622.

This flight, the Hegira, led him to Yathrib, a place more favourable to monotheism. There, Jews and Arabs listened to this newcomer who wanted to rename their town Medinat-an-Nabi, 'City of the Prophet'. After three years of preaching, reading, and meditation, Mahomet's work had taken shape in his mind. Mixing Jewish or Christian belief with the aspirations of the desert, his creed had a persuasive force which had been lacking in the religions of settled peoples. Though often resembling other oriental religions both in practice and dogma, it suited the warlike tendencies of nomad tribes; and, constantly preying on the caravans of his Meccan relations, Mahomet, now a confirmed raider, inaugurated a religious war.

Islam means 'submission' — the context is the attempted sacrifice of Isaac by Abraham — and implies 'brotherhood' among all Moslems, since human distinctions are of no significance against the omnipotence of Allah. This revelation is enshrined in the Koran, with its uncompromising command 'Set not up with Allah any other gods.' The appeal of the religion was reinforced by the vision of Paradise, the reward of all those who died in battle against the infidel, and by the fear of a scalding and scorching hell. The desert Arabs were united in a holy war against the infidel just when over-population and, possibly, a drought in the interior of Arabia were provoking them to attack on the settled lands. This holy war thus combined an ideal with economic motives. Its success was in part the result of the demoralisation of the Byzantine territories of North Africa and Palestine under excessive taxation.

The Arabs on the march

By 625 Mahomet was ready to fight Jews and Christians as well as the heathen and idolatrous Khuraishites. In the war that followed — so far no more than a tribal war — Mahomet was successful and five years later he re-entered Mecca, the uncontested leader of a new faith. One of his first acts was to legitimise the 'Black Stone', which now became sacred. He next had to convert neigh-

Mounted archer of the Umayyad period. Detail of fresco from Palmyra. *Larousse*

bouring nomads. This was easy enough with the tribes of the Hejaz, who had for long been under the influence of the Khuraishites; not so easy in the south-east and in the Yemen, where the merchants, familiar with the Gospels or the Torah, looked askance at the Koran. On the other hand, if Heraclius and the successors of Chosroes gave a good reception to Mahomet's ambassadors, the Arabs more or less subject to those rulers did not hesitate to repulse the Prophet's horsemen. Before he could surmount this obstacle, Mahomet died in June 632. He died, it seems, without having 'considered his succession', and his father-in-law, Abu Bekr, the first of his disciples, stepped into the breach. Adopting the title of Caliph (successor), he took over the direction of the movement. No doubt prompted by the love of war much more than by loyalty to the leader, the Moslems stood by Abu Bekr and helped him finish the Prophet's work. Even the southern tribes, from the Yemen and the Hadramut, so far recalcitrant, lent support. On the northern frontier, the Lakhmids were thrown back to the Euphrates, the Ghassanids to the Dead Sea. Chaos in Persia and the absence of Heraclius explain the rapid conquest of the desert. When Abu Bekr died in 634, one of the most extraordinary and sudden conquests of all time had been made.

The conquest of Persia

Called on to succeed Abu Bekr, Omar proclaimed a *jihad* or holy war, an outlet for Moslem heroism and the desire for expansion. In principle the *jihad* was endless, since its object was to convert the whole world. Peace was thus regarded as a mere pause in the campaign. The belief that all who were killed in it went straight to paradise ensured unflagging zeal.

The Sassanid Empire was the first to succumb. In 635 the Arabs crossed the Euphrates, though not without difficulty, and at Kadisiya, near Kufah, engaged the army of Yazdegerd III. The Persians were completely routed, and the victors captured the standards of Chosroes, which had once flown over the Bosphorus. Retreating farther and farther towards the East, Yazdegerd, now a king without a kingdom, at last found refuge beyond the desert plateaus of his country, at the foot of the Hindu Kush, where he lived quietly and died in solitude sixteen years after his defeat.

Other conquests

In 635 the Greek Empire also trembled. Khalid, one of the greatest of the Arab generals, having already taken Damascus, encountered Theodore the Sacellarian's disorganised army on the banks of the Yarmuk. Helped by the local unpopularity of the Greeks, Khalid had no difficulty in defeating them, and he then proceeded to take Aleppo and Antioch (capital of Syria), and Jerusalem. Another army, led by Mu'awiyah, reached the foot of the Taurus mountains in Armenia, there to learn that Heraclius had died.

Before his death he had already learnt of the invasion of Egypt, the richest province of the Empire, in 639. There, too, the Arabs found a climate unfavourable to the Greeks. As in Syria Monophysitism — the belief that there is only one nature in the person of Christ — had made rapid progress in these regions, and religious quarrels had soon led to political confusion. It was perhaps thanks to the patriarch Cyrus's grudge against Constantinople that the Moslems were able to take Alexandria in 642. Then, when Cyrene and Tripoli had been captured, Amru, driving across the desert, suddenly appeared in 647 on the frontiers of Tunisia. Within ten years an Empire had been carved out which stretched from the Gulf of Sidra to the Pamirs, and from the Caucasus to the Yemen. This capital event has had consequences of far-reaching importance down to our day, interrupting the normal relations between Europe and Asia.

The Arabs and the settled peoples

This empire of nomads who had lived by pillaging the lands they took suddenly revealed a new capacity for change, and we see them anxious to break new ground, building towns in the lands they conquered: Kufah, Bassora, Baghdad and Fostat (later to become Cairo). We see tribal warriors, whose caliph, like the leader of any band, had habitually taken one-fifth of the spoils, settling down to bureaucratic occupations.

Desert nomads became landowners, looked after their property and paid a tax, sometimes even to infidels. For these proselytes of a new faith did not attempt to force conversion by the sword. Occupation was in the first place purely military, the laws, customs, and religion of the natives being respected. But their treatment of all Moslems, Arabs and converts with absolute equality was a powerful influence in the hands of the Caliphate and did much to establish its dominion, a dominion based on the intelligent self-interest of a subject people treated with respect. The Arabs' danger lay in being absorbed by their subjects. And when, in 644, Omar was assassinated by a malcontent and was succeeded by his cousin, the easy-going Othman, the Arab element began to disappear among the multitude of Levantine governors, Persian scribes, Egyptian tax-collectors, and Greek architects. Soon a pro-Arab reaction began to prevail. A dissident group supported Ali, the Prophet's son-in-law, and assassinated Othman in 655. But in the end the victor in this internal struggle was the governor of Damascus, Mu'awiyah who succeeded in 661 and founded the Umayyad dynasty.

Having lived among Greeks, whose language he spoke,

The Arab conquests

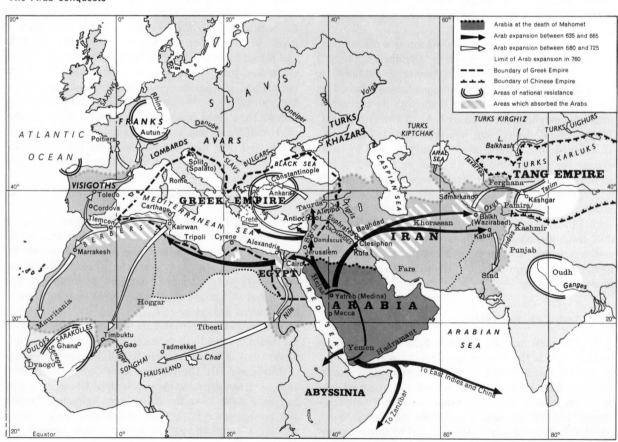

this new caliph set about moulding his empire into the traditional image of eastern imperialism. He took care to name his son as his successor, thus breaking with the elective principle of the Arab nomads, and he coined money like any heir to Byzantinism. Successful soldiers, whose gains had been at the cost of the blood of the Prophet's family, Mu'awiyah and his son, Yazid, though proclaiming themselves leaders of the Arabs, were careful not to delegate power to the wild nomads of the desert. By employing Greek and Syrian officials, some of whom were Christian, they broke still further with the ideals with which the great conquests had started. We must not be taken in by the efforts of the third Umayyad, Abd-al-Malik (685-705), to replace the administration in Arab hands. His acts were designed simply to keep up appearances.

Nothing could possibly stop the drift, and the caliphs from now on must be regarded as the successors of the Sassanids or of the Eastern Roman Emperors. This was a source of grievance to the Khuraishites, hostile to the principle of Umayyad heredity, to the Shiites, attached to the descendants of the Prophet, and lastly to the bulk of the Arabs, hostile to the Syrian entourage. But military successes, though achieved under able governors rather than able caliphs, sustained the dynasty, and provided spoils with which to pay the native officials. From now on, the Umayyads could safely establish themselves at Syrian Damascus.

The Arabs in Central Asia

Expansion, halted for a time by internal struggles for power, started again in 680. Beginning with more raids, it was soon transformed by lack of opposition into conquest.

In Central Asia the splendid Tang period seemed to be on the wane. Kao-tsung died in 683 and his concubine, once the legitimate successor was eliminated, retained her power by despotism. The reign of Chung-tsung, resumed after the empress's death, collapsed in a series of palace plots and adulteries. Externally, the situation was threatening. So far the Chinese had known how to turn the rivalries of Turkish tribes to their own advantage, but now the Tibetans were occupying Kashgar, while the eastern Turks, under the energetic Kutluk Khan, had come down to within reach of Peking. With Kutluk's death, the danger seemed to be averted, but his brother Kapagan, who succeeded him, gradually gathered round him all the nomad tribes and pushed on as far as Nanking, where he married a Chinese princess. It seemed that he was destined to emulate the exploits of Bu-Min; and the steppe was again to be the reservoir of invaders. But the situation had changed. During the second half of the seventh century, the Turks had themselves been hard pressed by the Moslems, who, in 652, were able to advance to the Oxus, to Balkh, and, ten years later, beyond the Afghan mountains to Kabul. As elsewhere, the Arab advance was halted briefly at the close of the century by internal conflicts, but in 706 it started again, when Kotaiba ibn Moslim, governor of Khorassan, secured Samarkand and the approaches to the Aral Sea. Then, in 712, he invaded Ferghana and the following year entered China. Helped by fresh Turkish and Tibetan attacks on the Chinese, he may even, in 714, have reached Kashgar, the most important of the oases in Turkestan, which had been so painfully recaptured by the Tang campaign. Arabs and Chinese had now come face to face.

The Arabs in India

From Kabul, which they captured in 661, the Arabs turned their eyes towards India, where they knew there was no coherent force to stop them. In 647 the great Harsha had died, and the empire he built had been unable to survive him, Since then, all that had faced the Arabs had been the rival kingdoms of Kabul, Kashmir and the Punjab, all tempting objectives. Moreover the protection the Tang dynasty afforded to the Turks of Kapica was shown to be merely nominal the moment Kabul was captured by the Moslems. In 711 Mohammed

Mecca: the Ka'aba, the sanctuary of Islam. It contains the Black Stone, supposedly given by Gabriel to Abraham, and even before Mahomet it was a shrine. It is covered yearly with a new black brocade *kiswa*.

263

Kasim led his Arab troops across the vast and desolate mountains of Baluchistan, reached the lower Indus and the province of Sind, then turned up towards the Punjab. The conquest of this region was eventually to prove lasting and profitable.

North Africa taken

The Arabs had more difficulty in pushing on to Tunisia. Not that the Greeks put up much resistance. Military organisation was poor and morale was lowered by Africa's religious hostility to Constantinople, now in schism. Besides, the Empire had another enemy in the Berber population. But the Libyan desert separated the western regions of Africa from the rest of the Arab territories, making all operations precarious. Still, a fresh effort was made in 660, by Ukba, who founded Kairwan, a town whose defences showed clearly the Moslems' intention of permanent conquest. This town soon became one of the holy cities and one of the intellectual centres of the Maghrib. In a bold dash, Ukba reached Tlemcen, perhaps even the Atlantic, where, like Alaric, he may have ridden down into the water calling the heavens to witness that he could march no farther. His conquests were indeed at an end, for on his return he was slain in the Aures mountains by the Berbers, who were far from submission. The Greeks, with their control of the sea, repulsed several advances on Carthage. Two attacks were made in 695, but not till 699 was the town taken.

The Arabs in Spain

In 711 Musa ibn Nosair authorised his client Tarik to carry out a raid on the Spanish coast. With 7,000 men, the audacious Berber rounded the Rock to which he gave his name, Jebel Tarik (Mount Tarik) or Gibraltar, and landed at Algeciras. It was in the Visigoth kingdom, and looked solid and prosperous. By the River Barbate, Tarik found the army of the king, Roderic, and one hour's fighting was enough to dispose of it and the Visigoth kingdom, which disintegrated. What became of Roderic, no one knows. Tarik drove on to Cordova and occupied Toledo. Hastening to Spain with 10,000 troops, Musa took the whole country in two years. It was an astounding success, and altogether stupefying to Europe of that time. Ignoring a few pockets of resistance in the northwest, the Arabs crossed the Pyrenees, took Narbonne, then forked out to the Garonne on the one side and the Rhône on the other. In daring raids they took Arles and Toulouse in 725 and even Autun. Eudo (Odo) the Duke of Aquitaine, thoroughly shaken, was driven back in disorder to the north of Bordeaux.

After the Persians, after the Greek garrisons in Asia Minor and Africa, after the Turkish tribes and the Visigoths, was it now to be the turn of Gaul, the richest area in the West, to be conquered by the Arabs and become a satellite of Islam?

The duel with Constantinople

As though to grasp the Mediterranean in a pincer movement, the Arab forces had meanwhile attacked the Eastern Empire, apparently an easy prey, for the power was now in the hands of a boy, Constans II, grandson of Heraclius. To the south of the Danube, the Slavs were terrorising the population; but this threat was negligible compared to that of the Bulgarians, who had been driven from the Sea of Azov into the Dobrudja, and had by 642 reached the confines of the Byzantine Empire. The Arabs were accordingly launching their attack under ideal conditions. Armenia was occupied and the slopes of the Taurus. Then, with a fleet of ships from Syria, Mu'awiyah occupied Cyprus, and then, in 654, Rhodes. In 655 he drove off a Greek squadron. This time it was supremacy on the seas that was at stake and the opening of Constantinople to naval attack.

The internal struggles of the Umayyad caliphate postponed the danger for several years. But in 674 an Arab fleet attacked the walls of Constantinople. It looked as though this was the end of the new Rome. The Emperor, Constans II, after trying to restore order in Africa had then moved his court to Syracuse, with a view to establishing a base for attacks on the Arabs at Kairwan. But this energetic ruler was assassinated and Constantine IV Pogonatus succeeded him. The latter was able to hold the Moslems at bay, but not to induce them to discontinue their attacks. Between 674 and 677 their squadrons reappeared each spring, and there was renewed talk of moving the seat of the Empire to Rome. But again internal struggles among the Arabs intervened. Moreover the Greek fleet was put in order by Constantine, and a new weapon, Greek fire (a mixture containing naphtha), did great damage to enemy ships. This time Byzantium was saved.

Urged on by their entourage — Syrian, Egyptian, or Greek — the Umayyads were still determined to take Constantinople, and the confusion which reigned under

An old print of Mahomet, ready for battle. Islam achieved conversion by the sword rather than by persuasion.

the unstable Justinian II seemed to offer an opportunity. While the Bulgars were threatening on the north, 1,800 Arab vessels arrived in August 717, and blockaded the town. The siege lasted a year, but meanwhile the imperial throne had been seized by Leo III, the first of the Isaurian Emperors. He took vigorous action. The arrival of the Bulgarian troops he had brought over, the defection of Egyptian crews, and again the effects of Greek fire, all helped to persuade the Arabs once more to give up the attempt. A storm is said to have scattered their already demoralised fleet, and the Arabs were so disgusted that for long they foreswore all naval ventures. But the Greek triumph was short. If the Arabs had lost afloat, they were invincible on land. In 737 Leo III suffered several raids from Asia Minor, and two years later, 150,000 Moslems, stripping the country bare in their passage, advanced as far as Nicaea, and the standard of the Caliph floated once again over the Bosphorus.

Thus the Arabs, less than a hundred years after the death of the Prophet, held the Mediterranean from the Bosphorus to Egypt, from Egypt to Spain. Their wealth became enormous. By the trade routes from the East, by the caravan routes of the Sahara and Turkestan, came corn and gold, ivory, and silk. The settled populations cowered under repeated attack — in the Straits, in Turkestan, in Aquitaine. But already in 718 Islam was checked under the walls of Constantinople; one after the other and employing very different tactics, the Franks, the Chinese and the Greeks stopped its advance, in 732 at Poitiers, in 736 at Kashgar, and in 738 at Akroinos.

THE CONQUEST HALTS

IN CENTRAL ASIA

The halting of the great Moslem invasions was due in the first place to the exaggerated spread of the empire and the initiative delegated to local chiefs. It was also due to the stiffening of resistance, each opponent making war according to the genius of its people: on the one hand the massed foot-soldiers of the Chinese, on the other the swift ships and Greek fire of the Byzantines and the heavy cavalry of the Franks.

The Tang dynasty, as already described, had established an efficient centralised government, ruling over vast and prosperous territories. It saw a great age of Chinese literature. The famous poet Li-Po (701-62) sought but failed to find promotion at the Tang court of the Emperor Hsuän-tsung. His contemporary, Meng Hao-jan, and the poet-painter Wang-Wei also won fame at this time.

But the Tang period is most celebrated for its sculpture and painting. Human and animal figures of superb design were placed in the tombs of the wealthy, and brush calligraphy, already highly developed under the Han, attained new virtuosity. Painting on silk already showed a romantic sensibility to landscape. All this high civilisation developed against a background of far flung prosperity.

But the nomad menace remained. The formidable Hsuän-tsung reverted to the traditional policy of dividing the nomads. His ruthless taxation enabled him to send a powerful army to Turkestan, which in 736 drove the Arabs from Kashgar and regained control of the oases of Tibet. An acute economic depression marked the last years of the emperor's reign — he being then absorbed by senile love affairs — and lasted for ten years after his death. The despotism of the viceroy Kao Sien Che now prompted the surprising coalition of the heathen Karluk Turks and the Arabs of Transoxiana. The Chinese were driven back to Kashgar and their defeat was the signal for a more or less general revolt by the Khitan nomads of north China, the tribes of Korea and Yunnan, and the Tibetans. The Emperor abdicated in the midst of these disasters, and the vassal kingdoms of the Pamirs and Kabul threw off Tang influence. The Chinese were saved, however by the loyalty of the Uighur Turks, who helped them to retake Lo-yang and to pacify the whole region. In reward for this they were given control of the oases and it was now the Uighurs who stopped further progress of the Arabs.

Tang pedlar figurine, eighth century - the most famous period of Chinese painting and sculpture. *Victoria and Albert Museum*

THE REALIGNMENT
OF THE EASTERN EMPIRE

Byzantium turns East

In Constantinople we see a similar stiffening. The period which elapsed between the triumph of Heraclius over the Sassanids and the new drive shown by the Isaurian dynasty in the middle of the eighth century was marked by the final desertion of western politics and the adoption of an oriental outlook. After Justinian had swung the Eastern Empire back into the Roman orbit, Constantinople had hesitated for a while, but the invasions of Slavs, Avars, and Persians in the first half of the seventh century, followed by Bulgarian attacks and Arab conquests, determined the future of Constantinople. Constantinople could only be saved at the cost of Rome and Carthage; this realignment of the Empire between 630 and 760 set the pattern of the Byzantine world during the remainder of the Middle Ages.

A page of the Syrian Gospel; eighth century. Byzantium had now recovered from the austerity of iconoclasm, as this representation of the Mother of God shows. *Brogi*

The decisive change was not effected in a day. The first Arab pressure in Asia Minor had threatened the position of Constantinople, and Constans II was also concerned with restoring the situation in Italy. Between 663 and 668 he strengthened the garrisons in Sicily, as well as those of Rome and Ravenna, which he was determined to hold against the Lombards. This was the last effort to save the West. But after Constans was assassinated, his successor abandoned the attempt.

Slavs in the Balkans

Relations with the western Mediterranean had already become difficult. Now that the Arabs held Carthage, the seas were unsafe. The overland route through Syria was no safer, for Serbs and Croats were installed as *foederati* in the Bosnian mountains, from which they had driven out the inhabitants; those of Salona, for example, took refuge round Diocletian's palace, the future Spoleto. Other tribes, coming south down the Vardar, entered Macedonia and advanced to the outskirts of Salonica and even into Greece. The Bulgars in 679 were settled south of the Danube, facing the Balkans. No doubt Constans II and his successors kept them in hand by occasional police operations or the awarding of honours; thus the Bulgar Kaghan Terbelis was able to assume the title of Caesar; but the whole political aspect of the country south of the Save and the Danube was permanently changed.

The efforts of the Isaurians

The savage reprisals carried out by Justinian II led to a rising in the first year of Leo III's reign, during the siege of Constantinople in 717. A strategist from Anatolia, Leo the Isaurian, who may have been a Syrian and was certainly an oriental, eventually won the struggle:

we have already seen how this able despot and clear-headed organiser disposed of the besieging fleet in 718, thereby inaugurating the Christian offensive against Islam. His son, Constantine V, followed his example, surprised the army of the Caliph Hisham, which had advanced as far as Nicaea, and defeated it soundly in 739 at Akroinos in Phrygia. After that, the Arabs were pushed back in Cilicia, and in 746 the army of Constantine V occupied Cyprus. Helped by an Armenian revolt, the Greeks reached the Euphrates, and the Moslems resigned themselves to a thirty-year truce, a period during which the relations between the two rival empires greatly improved. Leo III learnt Arabic, while the Caliph Yazid II is said to have agreed, at the request of the Emperor, to repatriate monks who fled into his territory.

For a long period the Bulgarian threat was serious. In 755 an advance of the Bulgars brought them to the gates of Constantinople. Under these circumstances Constantine V attempted to strengthen the Empire by the same transfer of populations as Heraclius had successfully accomplished. The conversion of the Bulgar Khan in 777 and the posting of Greek garrisons amongst his people meant that they were now integrated in the Empire.

Iconoclasm

If the external situation had improved since the military and financial chaos which Leo III had inherited in 717, the Empire was nevertheless torn by religious conflicts. The growing part played by religion, and even superstition, in medieval Byzantium is plain. It is hardly possible to conceive the importance of a dispute like that of the images. More was involved, of course, than approval or disapproval of the superstitious reverence accorded to images and saints. The monks who fostered this exaggerated popular cult were a growing economic danger, particularly in Asia Minor, for their properties were extensive and exempt of all taxation. It was therefore through political considerations as well as oriental religious austerity that the Isaurians reacted against a superficial and mercenary cult. The moderate Leo III confined himself to the proscription of images in 726, but Constantine V was ruthless, conducting a campaign of repression that was often marked by excesses. The destruction of mosaics and other works of art, the dispersal or compulsory marriage of monks, the humiliation and even the execution of dignitaries, created intense opposition in the Cyclades, in Greece, and in Sicily, and when the Emperor died in 775 the issue was far from settled.

The Byzantines driven from Italy

And now an external setback occurred. Ever since Justinian's time, relations between the Pope and Constantinople had been increasingly embittered. Already the weakness of the Greeks had forced Rome to look to the West for support against the Lombards, but she was still more alienated by the Greeks' religious independence. In 653 Constans II had seen fit to withdraw Ravenna from the sphere of Papal authority. He had made her bishop autonomous and had thrown the Pope, Martin I, into prison. An Oecumenical Council in 680-681 had approved the triumph of Rome over the Monophysite heresy and now Leo III began to legislate in religious matters, persuading an obedient council to confirm his proscription of images. After 725 the Lombards showed increasing vigour. Repelling them needed far more money and soldiers than the Isaurians possessed. Nothing, then, stopped Liutprand from taking Ravenna nor, when he had withdrawn, his successor Aistulf from retaking it. The Greeks' failure to help led the Pope to refuse the taxes owed to the *basileus*, and next to repudiate the iconoclastic edicts. In 738 Gregory III, in a moment of alarm, had vainly turned for help against Liutprand to the Franks, who were strong, near at hand, and orthodox Christians. But in 753 at Pavia, after meeting Constantine's ambassadors and Aistulf (who had decided to march on Rome), Pope Stephen II suddenly made up his mind. Without realising the gravity of his decision, he determined not to accept help from the Greeks, and promptly left for the Alps to seek asylum with the Frankish king, Pepin the Short. The decision opened a new period in the history of Europe. Italy had opted for the West, and on her side of the Adriatic the Greeks were now to be outsiders. Moreover, the success of the Franks had been officially consecrated. The coronation of Charlemagne in 800 and the whole story of medieval Christianity were implicit in the decision of Stephen II.

THE TRIUMPH OF THE FRANKS

The difficulties experienced by the Eastern Empire between 500 and 700 had never produced the least danger of dissolution. The Empire's economic strength was such that even the Umayyads were forced to imitate its currency in order to enter the field of Mediterranean trade. The Frankish kingdoms, on the other hand, though spared invasion, showed early signs of a disintegration unknown since before the time of the Romans. And the Carolingian revival, at the time of the Isaurians, issued from a chaos of opposing factions, whose only strength lay in their prosperous landed estates. The one point in common now between the East and the West was the ascendancy of religion.

Triumph of the landed nobility

The reign of Dagobert in Gaul covered the last ten years of the Merovingian control. The year 637 marks the decline of Frankish external expansion and internal economic activity.

Endless squabbles ensued on Dagobert's death. Two facts alone stand out in this obscure period. Firstly, there was no prince capable of keeping the region united: new principalities were formed, generally following the lines of old divisions, and within them local characters were consolidated. From 670 no prince of the north held authority south of the Loire: a 'Duke' Lupus reigned in complete independence in Aquitaine, and he was followed by a 'Prince' Odo or Eudo; and the Councils themselves were purely local. South of the Garonne, the Vascons had no contact with the rest of Gaul; dukes or independent bishops ruled in Burgundy. As for the new elements, the Alemanni and the Frisians, who had joined in by becoming Christians, they merely added to the general disorder.

Secondly, each of the various units had its great landowner whose estates were run by a steward. If he had several estates they were run by a *major-domus*. The King's estate itself was run by a 'mayor of the palace', a position that was to lead to supreme power. But the Merovingians themselves let their royal estates decay and deprived their family of their only means of remaining strong; an aristocracy gorged with landed wealth had nothing more to hope from them. It was north of the Loire, north even of the Seine, that this struggle was strongest, for the southerners had so far produced more missionaries and bishops. Almost to the end, the Neustrians, who may have been the more numerous and had at any rate richer estates, held the advantage. But by eliminating each other the rich families made their country all the weaker. It was to one of these families that Ebroïn belonged, the ruthless and cunning mayor of the palace who has been credited with political designs because he annihilated the Neustrian nobility before falling himself under the axe of one of its survivors (681).

The north-east, in particular, was a land of immense estates. Here it was the Arnulf family, originally from the Moselle, that rose to power by winning the office of mayor of the palace. Their designs were frustrated for a while by the premature action of Grimoald, who tried to make his son king, but, with the German support they were long to enjoy, they soon recovered their position, and in 687 Grimoald's grandson, Pepin of Heristal, won control of Neustria. It nevertheless took his illegitimate son, Charles Martel, seven years to secure this heritage for himself.

Poitiers

A proud and brutal warrior, a successful tribal chieftain rather than a statesman, Charles Martel recalls Leo

Carolingian horseman, from St Gall Psalter; ninth century. The armour is still quite light, and the only weapons are lances and round shields. *Mansell*

the Isaurian. He entrusted his missionary work to northerners, Irishmen and Anglo-Saxons, rather than to the southerners who had hitherto been doing it, emphasising the Nordic, almost German, character of his rule. Moreover, the *regnum* expanded eastward towards Bavaria and Swabia, now once more under Frankish authority. These warlike countries were ripe for the missionaries, such as St Boniface (Charles's adviser), Willibrord, and Sturm, who took the Gospels beyond the Rhine. But the favour Charles showed to the Church in no way deterred him from seizing huge monastic estates. He distributed land thus appropriated amongst his adherents; this policy went so far to consolidate his power that he did not bother to set up a Merovingian king. The pastures taken from the monks no doubt helped him to form the powerful Frankish cavalry. With that, Charles possessed a striking force that the Visigoths had lacked, and one that greatly assisted him in repulsing the Arabs, whose raids were reaching Bordeaux and Autun.

In 732 Eudo of Aquitaine was flying before the advance of Abd-ar-Rahman, the governor of Spain. The defence of the faith and the reconquest of Aquitaine drew Charles into the field. Abd-ar-Rahman, whose raid may well have reached Tours, was surprised on his return journey near Poitiers in October 732, and he himself was left dead on the field. Gaul was saved. Though the Arabs remained pugnacious, they could no longer carry out widespread raids with impunity. Charles still had many difficulties to overcome in occupying the north of Aquitaine, then the valleys of the Saône and Rhône. Meanwhile his brother Childebrand was busy from 736 to 738 clearing the Rhône delta of Moslem marauders. Help even had to be obtained from Liutprand's Lombards to throw the enemy back across the Pyrenees. Finally, however, the capture of Narbonne in 759 deprived the Arabs of their foothold in Gaul.

Pepin the Short, son of Charles Martel, who appealed to the Pope to decide who was king of the Franks, he who held power or he who wore the crown. The Pope chose the former, and Pepin was anointed in 781.

The Carolingians inherit the West

On his deathbed in 741 Charles Martel, like any barbarian king, divided his realm between his two sons; but the two parts were soon reunited in the hands of the eldest, Pepin the Short. All he needed now was the title of king. But was it possible to disinherit the last descendant of Clovis? Probably there were no truly royal lands left, or royal revenue, except in the Aisne valley; but a reverence for the royal shadow lingered among the people. Pepin still lacked the blessing of the Church which had made the Visigoths sacred. Sounded on the question, the Pope, St Zacharias, agreed to send St Boniface to crown Pepin king of the Franks, and at the same time he arranged for the last of the Merovingians, Childeric III, to retire into a monastery.

The Papacy had thus been won over, and the only obstacle — the Lombard alliance — was no longer of any significance now that the Arab peril was averted. In 753 Pope Stephen II fled to Gaul. Pepin met him, held the bridle of his horse, and the Pope solemnly blessed the now legitimate king. In return, Pepin promised the pontiff protection in the name of the whole of Gaul. The ruling powers of Austrasia repudiated this new orientation, but finally became resigned to it. Beaten in 755 and again in 756, Aistulf, king of the Lombards, gave up the struggle. The *basileus* had thought for a moment that Pepin would work for the Greeks; he now refused — to no avail — to confirm the title of patrician taken by the Frankish king. But when the latter died in 768 the game

Charles Martel, 'the hammer', so called because of his great victory over the Arabs at Poitiers (732). *Hachette*

was lost for the Byzantines and for the Lombards. Masters of the Christian West, allies of the Papacy, victors against the Arabs, the Franks had won the long struggle begun three and a half centuries earlier among the ruins of the western Roman Empire.

THE STABILISATION OF THE MOSLEMS

The Abbasids

Defeated at Poitiers and in Asia Minor, and halted at the foot of the Pamirs, the Moslems were no longer in a position to resume their conquests. The Umayyads were handicapped because, unable to make the civil administration Arab, they had not had the courage to put it entirely into the hands of the subjected peoples: for the Arab clients of the sovereign, the *mawalis*, were opposed to any break with their nomad traditions, and even the indolent Yazid II was forced to live in the desert with wild, unruly tribes. But the settled populations grew tired of obeying masters who appeared from time to time out of the desert just to collect taxes. This lack of discipline explains the series of military set-backs, and these, because of the resulting dearth of spoils, involved renewed taxation, even on those who had been converted. Already overstretched, the Arab Empire was, from now on, the victim of rekindled local patriotism which, though loyal to the new faith, sought to escape taxation and recover political independence. The revolts of the Persian garrisons at Khorassan and the spread in 735, first among the Berbers, then in Spain, of the Kharijites' teachings of purity and equality, are characteristic of these strains.

It was in accordance with this tendency that Abu'l Abbas, exploiting a vague relationship with the Prophet, gathered all sorts of malcontents round him in the East: Persian soldiers from Merv and Kufah, heavily taxed Iranian landowners and sincere believers who reproached the Umayyads with spilling the blood of the Faithful. The old Caliph Marwan II fell near Mosul in 751, and Abu'l Abbas began his reign with the massacre of the Umayyad family.

The new Islam

The victory of the Abbasids, however, was not a victory of the Arabs, for the Persian element had played a preponderant part in their success. Nor was it any sort of Persian revenge, for the Persians already embraced Islam. The significance of the Abbasids' seizure of power was the triumph of the settled populations converted to Islam over the nomad conquerors. There was another factor, however, which helped to give the Arab world a new aspect. Syrian forces sent among the Berbers and to Spain to crush Kharijism discovered an Umayyad who had miraculously escaped the slaughter of 750, and welcomed him as a saviour. From Kairwan this Abd-ar-Rahman I crossed the Strait of Gibraltar, accompanied by his freed slave Badr, entered Cordova in 756 and proclaimed the restoration of his family.

Surging in the middle of the seventh century into a peaceful, sedentary world that had been debased by the barbarians, the new conquerors upset the established order in the Mediterranean, as they had in India. It had taken a hundred years for the initial impetus to slacken and the conquests to stop. By then, the Franks were firmly established as the leaders of the West; Constantinople, under Slav influence, entered its medieval period; China had recovered its equilibrium. Even the invaders, victims of their own conquests, had undergone a transformation, both in Baghdad and in Cordova, and had become a settled people. From now on these new partners, heirs of the Visigoths and the Sassanids, were to play much the same part in the Mediterranean scene as their forebears had of old. Save for piracy in the Mediterranean, the Arab wave had subsided and the conquerors had settled down.

Arab children at a Koran School in the desert. Their way of life has hardly changed since the early days of Islam.

CHAPTER SIXTEEN

THE END OF INVASIONS

A.D. 770-925

The front of the 'Dalmatica of Charlemagne' from St Peter's, Rome, showing Christ as Judge of the World (Byzantine silk, thought to be twelfth century). The dalmatica was a loose tunic with wide sleeves which became fashionable in Rome in the second century. *Mansell*

A more or less stable half-century elapsed between the wave of Arab invasions and the attacks of the northern barbarians of the ninth century. During the second half of the eighth century, at a time when Moslem civilisation was at its zenith, the Abbasids were able to establish a lasting domination. With Spain and most of North Africa hived off, their Empire had gained in solidity what it had lost in extent. Internal troubles were negligible. The Abbasids, relying on a supposed descent from the Prophet, vigorously put down the revolt of the Alids, which broke out mainly in the Hejaz, particularly in Medina (762) and Mecca (186). The absolute obedience

the Abbasids demanded was not of the sort given to a military chief: it was as pontiffs that the caliphs wished to be respected. On the other hand, the wars waged against the Christians became wars of prestige. Apart from the raids of Mahdi or Harun, which reached the Bosphorus, military activity was confined to fortifying Tarsus, Adana, and Mitylene, the lower slopes of the Taurus, and the upper Euphrates. Under the truce, a tribute had to be paid by the *basileus*, and delays in payment explain the punitive raids.

Nevertheless, to maintain their position, the Abbasids were obliged to rely on the great Persian families who had put them in power, to grant them land and confer honours upon them. The cessation of conquests having dried up the spoils, the Abbasids had to concern themselves with economic matters to maintain the ever more complex services of the State; hence the interest they took in the factories of the State (*tiran*). Accordingly those links between Asia and the Mediterranean which had been the chief objective of the Sassanids were re-forged. Merchants and other travellers took once more to the caravan routes and the seas. Samarkand was linked with Canton, Kabul with the Ganges, Pelusium and Baghdad with India and the Comoro Islands. The silk bought from the Greeks or the Chinese could be found everywhere from the Pamirs to Kairwan and even among the Christians of the West.

The role of the Persians

It is by the luxury of the Court that the increase in wealth may be judged. The Abbasid caliph was no longer an emir camping in the field opposite his enemies. He was the *imam* of the Faithful. Soon he would be calling himself King of Kings, and indeed his surroundings are Sassanid in style and splendour: an unseen sovereign loaded with riches, the object of a ritual adoration in a palace of a thousand pillars. He was surrounded by officials and scribes, his council had become the 'divan'; his ministers are 'vizirs', and the imperial post had its stages at the very places where the envoys of Darius or Chosroes I changed their horses. Social castes were divided much as in former times, and, by keeping religious sects intact, the caliphs conserved the traditional groupings of the Middle East: Egyptian Christians, Syrian Jews, Zoroastrians, and the strange Sabaeans who worshipped Orpheus as a god.

Persian noble families were in charge of the posts and the treasury and were keepers of the great seal. Thus the Barmecide family occupied the Vizirate from 786 to 803. After the family's notorious disgrace, others stepped in, deciding whether Mansur or his uncle should succeed to the caliphate on the death of Abu'l Abbas in 754, or Al-Hadi or Harun ar-Rashid on the death of Al-Mahdi. Harun finally succeeded (786-809). A contemporary of Charlemagne, he was one of the few Caliphs whose name was known outside Islam. It still is, for, according to tradition, it was for him that the Scheherazade, drawing on Persian folklore, related the stories that were to while away the thousand and one nights. The Arab poetry that the nomads were once able to impose on their subjects was a thing of the past. With its capacity for neologism, the language of the Koran had seduced the élite of the conquered peoples, but from the eighth century in Baghdad (somewhat later in Kufah and Basrah) Persian thought was reborn. The metaphor and the imagery are still Arab, and the metaphysical inspiration is often Greek, but Persian national genius had reawakened, and Firdousi was shortly to write in sixty thousand verses the *Book of Kings*, a complete history of Persia. The legend of Sinbad the Sailor was Persian, and the travel tales of Kotaiba and Masudi in the tenth century; Persian too was the poetry — sometimes bitter and cynical, often sensual and erotic, but always humorous — of writers such as Akhtal in the eighth century and Abu Nuwas in the ninth.

The Moslems also rekindled the flame of classical science. Indefatigable travellers, Arabs and Syrians reached Zanzibar and the Guinea coast, Cape Verde and Java, Canton and Japan. Their ships may already have been steered across the Indian Ocean. Certainly the learned men of Baghdad already knew the world was round, measured a degree of longitude, and revived the astronomy of the Chaldeans. Jewish alchemists and men of medicine translated Galen into Arabic. To write his *Annals of the Prophets and Kings*, Tabari delved for fifteen years in Greek and Persian libraries. Architects and mathematicians from Constantinople and Samarra came to the East's centres of learning.

The same spirit of intelligent imitation was at work in the field of art. As in the time of Darius, the Persians surrounded themselves with Greek artists, and, for their mosques, followed the plans of Syrian basilicas and the ornamentation of the Sassanid palaces: rectangular plans, classical columns, minarets whose form was derived from the lighthouse, buttresses and portals worthy of Chosroes, cupolas in the tradition of the Middle East. The same tendency prevailed at Samarra and Fostat, and a little later at Kairwan, at Marrakesh, and in Sicily.

The character of the Maghrib

Almost isolated from the Caliphate, the Maghrib and Spain pursued an evolution in which oriental traits were combined with local traditions. By the middle of the eighth century the Arabs in the Maghrib comprised no more than a number of compact groups living in the towns — factious groups, often very harsh with the Berbers, whom they failed to understand. It seems to have been to keep them in check that the Abbasids in 800 granted autonomy to Aghlab, governor of Ifrikia (now Tunisia); in return they asked only the payment of tribute. Aghlab duly formed an emirate at Kairwan, which soon became hereditary. At Tahert the Persian Abd-ar-Rahman ibn Rostem, a Kharijite no doubt, had succeeded by 761 in reviving that great market, to which came the caravans from the desert and pedlars, sometimes from as far as Basrah.

In the west, on the other hand, Idris ibn Abdallah, calling himself an Alid, stirred up a rising of the Awraba tribe. Harun had him poisoned, but in vain, for his son Idris II (791-828) won control of the central plateau and founded Fez, giving Morocco its capital and first dynasty.

Detail of wooden panel. Umayyad period; eighth century. The stylised leaves and geometrical patterns indicate the triumph of Islamic iconoclasm. *Cairo Museum*

Byzantine tapestry, thought to be eighth century. The repeated pattern of the lion medallion is of Persian derivation, and an example of the oriental influence predominant in the Empire at the time. *Mansell*

The zenith of Moslem Spain

On the other side of the Strait of Gibraltar, the ninth century represents the peak of the Moslem regime in Spain. It had taken several decades for the restored Umayyad and his successors to be accepted by the chiefs of Arab or Syrian marauders. Since Poitiers there had been little discipline in Spain, particularly in the north, where the Pyrenees offered impregnable retreats. To local governors, or *vali*, it seemed preferable to turn for help to the Franks rather than bend before the stern authority of the Emir. To reassert himself, the latter was obliged to side with the Berbers: Syrians and Arabs were gathered into the towns under surveillance; the revolt around Cordova in 796, savagely crushed by Hakam, is an episode in the rivalry between the conquerors. However, lacking reinforcements, the Africans, too, allowed themselves to be submerged by the natives, some of them not converted, or even by foreigners (*sakaliba*, 'Slavs') to whom the office of kaïd of the market, a local authority, often passed.

Cordova was a dominant centre of Moslem culture. The various phases of construction of its extraordinary mosque reflect the stages of that culture between 785 and 980; here Roman methods, still active, brought interesting new forms to oriental ideas: superimposed tiers of many-coloured arches and ribbed cupolas. This continuity with pre-Moslem tradition no doubt explains the prosperity of this province, famous for its weapons, leather goods, and silks — a province moreover that had never suffered seriously from raids by the Franks or by those Christians who had taken refuge in the north-west of Spain.

Islam and the Negroes

Islam had also stirred Africa out of its lethargy. The repulse of the people from the Atlas and the Sahel had no doubt already been accomplished in Roman times, and the Berbers were already masters of the Sahara when the Arabs arrived. In any case, the presence in the Haggar and Tibesti Mountains of non-Negro groups whose beliefs were tinged with Christianity is evidence of contact with Coptic Ethiopia or with Tunisia, which had at one time been Christian. The faith of Islam was a vigorous spur to the Berbers, who, about 800, drove the Tukulors and the Wolofs as far as Senegal. Moreover, in the ninth century almost all the black dynasties seem to have been replaced by others of white origin, Berbers perhaps. Such were the Dya-Ogo of Diara, south of Senegal; circa 850 they spread from the Gambia to Aoudaghost; or the Songhoi of Dahomey who, circa 890, occupied Gao, and a hundred years later made it their capital; or again the Hausa of the lower Niger, whose king circa 890 was a certain Abu Yazid. The only kingdom which escaped white domination was the empire of Ghana, whose creation seems to have dated from the fourth century, when the Sarakulle settled at Khumbi between the Niger and Senegal. At the beginning of the ninth century this empire of the Sahel stretched from Timbuktu to Kayes and from the upper Niger to Hodh. At the end of the tenth, the Sarakulle occupied Mauretania, where Moslems were numerous, and it was perhaps the excesses of the former which provoked the Almoravid rising.

Islam was not introduced into these regions before the eleventh century. On the other hand, white traders were active, and Arab civilisation had penetrated deeply. Caravans escorted by Berbers maintained commercial links and cultural contact between black Africa and the Mediterranean. The introduction of the camel greatly assisted her between the seventh and tenth centuries, and we can trace the spread of customs in clothing, food, textiles, and building right down to lower Senegal.

The Sahara traffic, directed towards Egypt or Tunisia, used the regular tracks whose termini were Khumbi, Timbuktu, and Gao, in the south, and in the north, Tripoli, Tahert, and Marrakesh. The salt of the Sahara, the gold of the upper Niger, the copper of Agades, and the slaves of Guinea were traded for dates, coral, and textiles.

STRENGTH OF THE BYZANTINE EMPIRE

Soundness of structure

The abandonment of Italy led the Isaurians to intensify the oriental character of their Empire. They increased the number of provinces (*themes*) in Asia Minor and the Balkans. Spiritual power gained progressively on temporal power: in 787 a Council rehabilitated the veneration of images. Orientalisation was to some extent checked, however, by the flow of Slavs into the Empire. Unlike the Abbasids, the Isaurians, in their rural code, limited the size of estates and encouraged a free peasantry, perhaps on behalf of the Slavs. It matters little whether this was a fiscal measure (all these freemen being taxed) or a political measure taken under Slav pressure; the point is that

Colour plate: a detail from the Codex Zouche-Nuttall showing the ceremony of making new fire. Mexico. c. 900. *British Museum*

A battle outside the walls of a town. A wall painting from Fostat.
Egypt. Twelfth century. *British Museum*

it prevented the growth of estates to a size which would make them avid for autonomy.

Unfortunately, after the death of Constantine V in 775 and that of his son Leo IV (Kazan) soon after, military disturbances and Arab attacks marked the years of Constantine VI's minority. Thereupon the Empress Irene, widow of Leo IV, reappeared; this beautiful woman was passionate and religious, a fervent image-worshipper, and intensely ambitious. She dominated young Constantine completely, beating him, choosing a wife for him, and forcing him to marry. When he came of age, Constantine forebore to push his mother aside, a restraint for which he paid dearly. Unimpeded by any maternal feelings, she treacherously undermined his authority. At last in 797 she deposed him and had his eyes put out. Having thus possessed herself of full powers, she adopted the title and vestments of *basileus*. Few sovereigns have had such detractors and admirers, both enthusiastic. The official historians of the day were kind to her, but then she was lavish in her gifts to them. Her reign was not, however, devoid of merit. If she was obliged to pay tribute to Harun ar-Rashid and allow Charlemagne to install himself as Emperor in Rome, she promoted art and letters and, by reducing taxes, encouraged trade.

But the army was discontented, and the patricians worried; a revolt broke out in October 802 which brought

Empress Irene (752-803). Her restoration of image-worship earned her the place of a saint in the Orthodox Church. *Historisches Bildarchiv Handke*

the minister of finance, Nicephorus, into power. Irene was sent to die in Lesbos. With his financial ability, and enjoying the support of the army, Nicephorus set about increasing the revenue. He taxed estates heavily and, for greater security, abolished the fiscal immunity of the Church. This won him the hatred of the monks of the reformist Studion monastery, whom he was obliged to disperse.

External dangers averted

Suddenly there was acute danger. Cramped on their Danubian pastures, the Bulgars wanted the land at the foot of the Balkans. Their terrible Khan, Krum, advanced into Macedonia. Nicephorus, who attempted to stop him, was killed in July 811, and his skull is said to have been made into a goblet for his enemy. In the disarray caused by this sudden reverse, Krum reached Versinicia and the Bosphorus seemed to lie open before him. But, as in 717, the Empire, on the verge of disaster, found its saviour. The Anatolian strategos, Leo the Armenian, seized power and, in the autumn of 813, threw the Bulgars out of Thrace. Unable to strike back, Krum died six months later, and his son Omurtag concluded a thirty-year peace. Moreover, solid fortifications closed the Adrianople road to the Bulgars, and Omurtag, an admirer of Byzantine luxury, remained at Preslav, his capital, and threw his country open to Greek influence.

Thirty years of peace with the Bulgars and a twenty-year truce with Baghdad saved Constantinople. In the West she still had the islands off the south of Italy and the chazars of the Don or the Armenians were far from wars, for the dispute over the images had cropped up again. The final downfall of the iconoclasts, after various vicissitudes, one of which cost Leo the Armenian his life (820), allowed the Emperor to assert his dominion against the Church. The strength of the army, said to have been 70,000, made it possible in 821 to crush the revolt of the Slavs of Macedonia.

As of old, Constantinople exploited the rivalries of potential aggressors, Slav or Asiatic. Gifts and envoys came streaming to the imperial palace, and the gifts from the Khazars of the Don or the Armenians were far from being mere tokens. The Emperor Theophilus (829-842) exchanged not only politenesses with the Caliph Mamun, but men of learning.

THE CAROLINGIAN WEST

Charlemagne

In the middle of the eighth century, both Charles Martel and Pepin the Short, advancing into Aquitaine and Italy, had reaffirmed the traditional expansion of the Franks. But in their enterprise there were essential differences between them and the administrative, lay, and military Isaurians. For one thing, the Franks received support only from the landowning nobility and the bishops. Even so, in spite of the land granted them, the vassals remained unreliable owing to the lack of royal agents to supervise them. Union with the Church, on the other hand, appreciable since St Boniface, accentuated by the alliance with Rome, and finally secured by the efforts of Charlemagne, gave the Franks both councillors and also

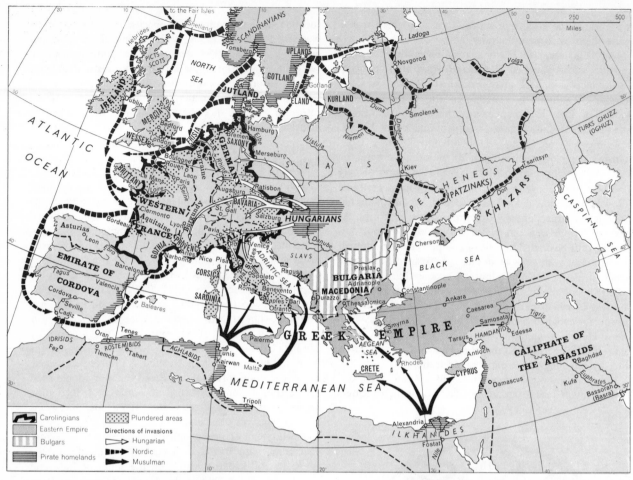

The last invasions

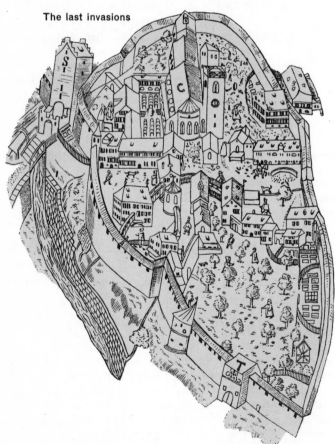

A plan of the monastery founded by St Gall on Lake Constance. The earliest university foundations were monastery and cathedral schools. *Historisches Bildarchiv Handke*

Charlemagne's crown of gold set with emeralds and sapphires and his monogram: the letters signify 'Karolus'. *Mansell and Giraudon*

administrators able to read and write. This, in itself an advantage, gave the Franks a stimulus towards religious expansion, which was another advantage.

Charlemagne was under thirty when he became king in October 768. His appearance at that time had nothing in common with the bearded, pensive old man depicted by the poets of the twelfth century. Tall, soon to become portly, with a prominent nose, a thin voice, a moustache, and no beard, he was a keen hunter and a man of iron constitution. He had eight wives and fourteen children. In religion, he was a militant believer; he was a barbarian chief, despotic and unhindered by bureaucracy. Compared to the Italians, the Franks seemed to have newly

Bronze statuette, supposedly of Charlemagne, from the Cathedral Treasury of Metz. A son of Pepin, Charlemagne waged religious war throughout Europe, converting whole nations by the sword in an attempt to break the last strongholds of paganism. From these beginnings he conceived the idea of establishing a Holy Roman empire.

emerged from an intellectual void. Charlemagne could read — he could even read Latin — and, though he was never able to write, he showed a great advance on the men of the seventh century.

Towards unity in the West

In forty-six years of unceasing campaigns, he established the authority of the Franks. In Aquitaine concessions had to be made to separatist sentiment, and the king made his son prince of that country. Land was distributed to the magnates, who called themselves 'Goths', just as in the time of the Goths they had called themselves 'Romans'. Friesland and Brittany were dealt with; Bavaria lost its liberty in 788, and its duke, Tassilo III, was forced to retire to a monastery. The new authority that was established in each territory preserved local customs in its legislation, and this authority was further strengthened by an ecclesiastical reorganisation. On the borders of Carinthia, government was in the hands of Arno, Archbishop of Salzburg.

In Italy Charlemagne could not leave the Pope to face the danger of a return of the Byzantines nor exposed to Lombard blackmail. For a while restrained by his wife Ermengarda, daughter of the Lombard king Desiderius, he took action in 773, at the request of the Pope, Adrian I. Having taken the Po valley and banished Desiderius to a monastery, Charlemagne still had eight years of struggle before subjecting the Lombard dukes and creating an Italian kingdom for his son Pippin, and even then Spoleto and Beneventum held out against him. This incomplete

solution of the problem gave Italy a political aspect that it was to retain till the nineteenth century, and whose effects are still visible on the economic plane: the north and Tuscany being linked to the Continent, the south to the Mediterranean. This was to some extent a relic of the work of Justinian.

The birth of Germany

In northern Germany, the pillage of the Saxons became intolerable when they threatened the monasteries of Thuringia and the villas of the great Austrasian landowners. The Franks held only the zone of mountainous forests in which Varus had perished. In 772 Charlemagne decided to get this area under control. After five years of campaigning, with raids as far as the lower Weser, and the installation of a bishop at Paderborn, he considered the area secure; but in fact security was not to be attained until the Franks occupied the unknown misty plains on which the Saxons were settled. In 778 the Saxons, under Widukind, had slaughtered some missionaries and soldiers, and Charlemagne decided on a conquest that was both religious and territorial. The campaigns lasted seven years, during which his armies pushed as far as the Weser, then on to the Elbe. The campaigns were exhausting, and so tried were the Franks that they were provoked into an atrocious massacre of 5,000 hostages. Finally Widukind surrendered and was baptised.

For three days pardons were showered right and left, and Charlemagne could well believe himself the victor. But his despotic legislation could be to no effect unless the Franks occupied Saxon territory. In 792, fighting broke out again, and the country had to be occupied during the winter. For five years Charlemagne marched to and fro in Saxony and as far as the Elbe, seizing hostages and founding bishoprics. Fighting broke out again in 801, and lasted two years, with large-scale deportations and the planting of colonies. In 805 there were still more revolts, and finally, thirty-three years after the first campaign, a lasting peace was established. But out of this long struggle between the Saxons, the Franks, Thuringians, and south Bavarians, the Germany of the ninth century was born.

A set-back in Spain

In contrast to this lasting accomplishment, the results of the struggle with the infidels in Spain were meagre. The difficulties of the Umayyad regime in Cordova were an encouragement to the *valis* in the north, and it was at the behest of one of them that Charlemagne crossed the Pyrenees in 778 and advanced on Saragossa. The spoils were rich, and on the return journey the Basques were tempted to despoil the spoilers. In 778 a section of the Frankish army was ambushed at Roncesvalles and destroyed, amongst them Roland, prefect of the Breton March. Following on the heels of the Franks, the emir took the offensive and even reached Narbonne, where he was stopped. A counter-offensive followed in 795 under the command of 'Goths', but it accomplished no more than the occupation of the southern slopes of the Pyrenees from Barcelona to Huesca. This was a poor reward, though the Christian king of the Asturias could now be regarded as a subject of Charlemagne.

Louis the Pious at Aix-la-Chapelle, receiving the ambassadors of Leo V, Emperor of the East, after Charlemagne's death in 814. The Greeks had brought Leo's recognition of Charlemagne as *basileus*, the formal acknowledgement of the Empire of the West.

Charlemagne becomes emperor

By intervening in Italy, Charlemagne had acted on behalf of the Pope, and had even extended the territory granted him by Pepin the Short. But Adrian considered himself entitled to dominion over all the West. And Charlemagne was soon thinking of disengaging himself, beset as he was with difficulties with Byzantium in Istria and elsewhere, and anxious to conciliate the Lombards, whose numbers could not be ignored. So relations between Charlemagne and Adrian deteriorated. The Pope, annoyed by the intrusion of Austrasian counts and by the projected agreement between Charlemagne and Byzantium, struck out on his own, minted money, and recruited soldiers. But at his death in 795, his successor, Leo III (unpopular in Rome and soon the victim of assassination attempts) had no help for it but to turn to Charlemagne, and in 799 he put his honour and the fate of the Church in the latter's hands. In December 800 Charlemagne was received deferentially in Rome, and on Christmas Day the Pope blessed him, crowned him, proclaimed him emperor and *augustus*, and did him reverence. Much has been said about this event. If Charles was displeased, it could only have been at the initiative taken by the Pope, for, according to Byzantine procedure, it was popular acclamation that made an emperor. But much thought must have been given to the restoration of a Western Empire; the clergy saw in Charlemagne a pillar of the Church, a champion of the faith, the only man worthy of the supreme title. That there was anything incongruous in a barbarian succeeding the Roman Emperors does not seem to have occurred to any of the Anglo-Saxon or Franco-Germanic clergy.

The restoration of 800 was the final step in the evolution that had started with the victory of Clovis. The breach between East and West had been well and truly established, and the old historians were not altogether mistaken when they made the Middle Ages begin with Charlemagne.

If the evolution of the previous hundred years could have foretold this end, there was still a political and legal problem to be resolved. Byzantium could only regard Charlemagne as a usurper. But it happened that a woman was reigning in the East: might it have been possible to marry the Empress Irene with the barbarian conqueror? We cannot say. Irene was dethroned in 802, and Nicephorus broke off negotiations. To force the latter to recognise him, Charlemagne attacked Venice and other Greek commercial ports on the Adriatic. But he could do little against his rival's command of the seas. It was the Bulgars, by killing Nicephorus, who turned the scales, though the reluctant recognition of the Greeks did not reach Aix till 815. As for the Persians, they regarded the coronation as a blow to the Byzantines, and courteous ambassadors were exchanged between Charlemagne and Harun ar-Rashid. After all, they shared the same enemies at Cordova and Constantinople.

Unfortunately Charlemagne does not seem to have regarded his title as anything more than a personal dignity. He even made the mistake in 806 of deciding to divide his empire amongst his sons in true Frankish manner. Fate defeated this aim, for, when he died in 814 at the age of seventy-five, only one of his sons survived him.

The new Empire

Louis the Pious, who now became Emperor, was a strange figure, mixing the warlike qualities of the Franks with the influence of the Church triumphant. He was forty years old, educated, gentle, and susceptible to influence; he was sensual but a keen churchman, impulsive but a muddler. He arrived from Aquitaine with Benedict, Abbot of Aniane, who was the incarnation of the resentment of the southerners against the northerners. Wala and Adalard, two of Charlemagne's councillors, were promptly dismissed. Under the thumb of the Church, the monarchy began to turn into a theocracy. Stephen IV came to crown the new Emperor with his own hands, and he returned convinced that he would enjoy complete independence at Rome. Louis, who had been leading an itinerant life from villa to villa, now settled at Aix-la-Chapelle. In 817 he announced that his eldest son, Lothar, was to be co-emperor and was to have authority over his brothers, thereby jettisoning the barbarian principle of division. His decision reminds us of Diocletian's proposed tetrarchy. But parallel with this theocratic conception of power, another was elaborated by Lothar's partisans, also composed of clergy. According to this the Church was to remain subject to the State. At Benedict's death, it was this principle which gained the day, and in 824 the Pope was once more placed in tutelage.

These were really no more than palace intrigues, with little effect on the Empire. But they show how the position had changed since the days of Ebroin. Would anyone then have predicted these subtle discussions? With them came a literary revival. During the barbarian upheavals, Latin culture, cut off from the Eastern Empire, had gradually dwindled. If the classical heritage had been conserved by Isidore, Bishop of Seville, or in England by

Bede, what good was it to brutal men who could barely stammer in halting Latin the miracles or lives of the saints? But a sudden revival was effected when Charlemagne attracted Italians to his court after his campaign in Italy and also invited Anglo-Saxons like Alcuin, amongst whom classical Latin had been maintained. Paul Diaconus was his Mediterranean equivalent. There were long discussions, syntax was purified, plans were made for the advance of education. With Louis the Pious, writers produced florid pedantic poems, imitating the classics. Byzantine disputation took place, such as those between John the Scot, better known as Erigena, and Gottschalk the Austrian. Most of this work had no serious value, but running through this budding European literature, we find traces of the epic genius of the Germans and the Gallic flair for synthesis.

Art, too, struggled to emerge from the no-man's-land in which little had been produced but poor imitations of Roman sanctuaries and a primitive technique, drawing inspiration indiscriminately from various sources — the animal drawings of the steppes, coarse Germanic beads, or grotesque human figures entwined with acanthus leaves borrowed from some ancient ruin. In this field the Mediterranean art, encountered in Italy and Spain, was a revelation. At Aix and at Germigny, the Carolingians imitated it on a small scale, with success. Mosaics and ivories are Byzantine, cupolas Asiatic, but already the dawn of a local genius is seen. The first vaults of bonded stone date from the end of this period.

The stability of the Mediterranean area at the beginning of the ninth century allowed commercial dealings to be reopened between the four powers who shared the coasts. The Arab invasions must have dealt a severe blow to the maritime traditions of classical days, but it is improbable that sea-borne trade ever stopped completely. The prosperity of Arab trade with Asia and the maintenance of relations between Constantinople and Italy and the Middle East prove the persistence of economic activity. But the Christian West had suffered far more in the four centuries of administrative chaos that had led to the decay of its towns. The rudimentary local government introduced by the Carolingians was powerless to stop that decay, particularly in southern Gaul. All the same, there had never been a completely closed economy, and at the opening of the ninth century exchanges did exist. Only a few special items, however, such as arms and slaves, were traded at any distance. Such trade linked two important areas: the North Sea and Channel area with its ports open to Frisian and Saxon trade; and the Po valley with its ports trading with the East. And while the Carolingian silver denarius was stabilised, and Arabian and Sicilian money was in circulation in the West, gold coins were current in Gothland, in central Italy, and in Britain, now under Saxon kings.

Originality of the Anglo-Saxons

In Britain, whose history is from the start different from that of the Continent, an original civilisation came into being. While Ireland was still in a state of confusion, the Picts overcame the Scots on the moors of Scotland. In the eighth century Angus MacFergus was paramount in the Highlands. After a last rally, when Cadwallon defeated Edwin at Hatfield Chase, the Britons were soon

driven into Wales and held in check there by the forts along the Severn and the Mersey. At the same time they were abandoned by the Church, no longer prepared to tolerate archaic ritual and schisms. Then followed a long struggle between the various Anglo-Saxon kings. The Jutes were uppermost in Kent at the beginning of the seventh century, the Angles during the eighth century in Mercia and York, the religious capital of the north. Offa, King of Mercia (757-96) issued gold coins with Arabic inscriptions, a sign of the commercial relations between the Mediterranean and Britain, which had always enjoyed a monopoly of tin.

We must not be misled by Offa's apparent weakness. In Mercia the occupation of the land was further advanced than on the Continent; the rural communities were very strong and the king more certain in the obedience of his *earls* than Charlemagne in the support of his counts. But it was in the south, in Wessex, that the main political and cultural centre of Anglo-Saxon England was to emerge. The Laws of king Ine of Wessex, written down in the last decade of the seventh century, show a strengthening of the king's power and of the power of the Church. They insist that anyone who breaks the Church's or the King's peace has committed a public offence, to be expiated by a fine, and they substitute fines for blood feud. Further, they encourage good farming and the peaceful settlement of questions of land right and trespass: they mark a transition from tribal to territorialised Law. The Anglo-Saxons systematically tried

Gold coin (obverse and reverse) of Offa, King of Mercia (757-96), with Arabic inscription. It is the earliest coin ascribed to an English king; the inscription is unique in English coinage.

to fix the responsibility for a man's conduct: 'Every man', they asserted, 'must have a lord'; or he should belong to some guild or brotherhood, which would be responsible for him.

Thus, out of the original tribal laws of the pagan invaders, the idea of a central authority sanctified by the Church and collaborating with responsible elements in society grew up, an authority which would protect property and enforce a public law.

The original tribal moots and assemblies were also adapted for more peaceful times, and formed a nucleus of local government. Further, the Scandinavian rules of procedure, their custom of electing a Law Speaker, and putting aside weapons and drink when attending their assemblies, were to contribute to the development of ordered and responsible government. All this took place in an area which was small enough to be governed from Winchester and London.

Beyond the Elbe

Beyond the Elbe was the country of barbarians of whose movements we can form only a dim picture. The

Slavs were in contact with the Byzantines from 600 onwards, and with the Saxons and Thuringians from the end of the eighth century. In punitive expeditions against them, Charlemagne crossed the Elbe and the Riesengebirge twice between 789 and 812, and Louis the Pious again between 820 and 824. On the other hand, the Franks took advantage of the anarchy into which the Avars had fallen after losing contact with Asia to clear them out of Bavaria, opening the Danube trade route and also seizing the riches stored in their camp or *ring*. After eight years of war, the defeated people were parked in a reserve, but the Franks did not occupy the plain, unwisely leaving a vacuum likely to attract other nomads. Krum's Bulgars and the Slavs of Croatia were encouraged to raid it. Already Greek missionaries and Italian merchants were penetrating into the upper regions of Poland, the former to convert the Slavs, the latter with an eye to the trade that might follow.

The revival of the West at the end of the eighth century was caused by the combination of the only three forces that had retained any vitality: the Frankish landowners, the educated Anglo-Saxon clergy, and the Roman papacy. But the appearance on the scene of the unruly Slavs threw doubt on this precarious equilibrium, for behind them were the Hungarian hordes, spread over the Don basin. And now, to this perennial danger from the steppes was added another coming from the sea, the danger of the Arab corsairs and the Norsemen.

THE LAST INVASIONS

The Hungarians

The Turko-Mongol tribe of Uighur, spread from Manchuria to the Irtysh, had in the middle of the eighth century saved the Tang Empire in China from threatened destruction at the hands of the western Turks. This nomad empire had considerably outstripped the other inhabitants of the steppe, thanks to its writing, based on Syriac. But about 840 the Uighurs were defeated and driven towards the Tarim oases by another nomad tribe, the Kirghiz of the Yenisei, who had remained uncivilised and do not even seem to have been numerous. Down to the fourteenth century what civilisation they had was borrowed from the Uighurs.

At the same period the peaceful rule of the Chazars weakened. These Turks, possibly a residue of Attila's Huns, were settled at the beginning of the eighth century round the Terek and the Don and were in contact with the Byzantines; the daughter of one of their Khans was the mother of Leo IV, hence nicknamed the Chazar. Greek engineers had helped in the building of a capital at an elbow of the Don. Arab, Byzantine, and Jewish merchants went there for furs, and the rumour spread to Constantinople that the Khan practised Judaism. Between 850 and 890 the Pechenegs, a wild Turkish people, overran their country from the Don to the Sea of Azov. In so doing they disturbed the Hungarians, regarded as vassals of the Chazars.

The origin of the Hungarians is doubtful. Their language is Finno-Ugric, but a Turkish ruling class seems to have dominated them and furnished their royal family. Obliged to flee south-west, the Magyars tried to cross the

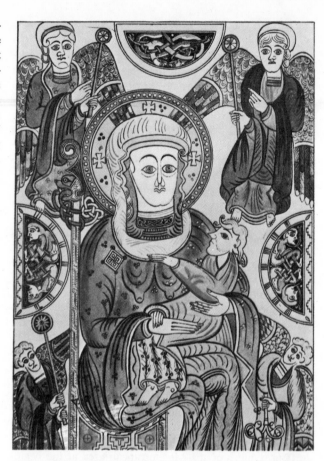

Madonna and Child, from the Book of Kells, a copy of the Gospels. Celtic; eighth century. Unlike later Anglo-Saxon work the technique is stylised rather than naturalistic; it is the earliest Christian art of its kind.

Danube in 880, as the Goths had before them. Repulsed by the Bulgars, they moved into Transylvania and from there, in 890, on to what is now called the Hungarian plain. The savagery of their raids once again brought Asiatic danger, forgotten for a century, to Christian lands.

The Vikings

After the emigration of the Goths, the populations of Jutland and the Baltic islands maintained their links with the tribes living in Central Europe. The influence of the art of the steppes can be seen in the bronzes and chased silver of the sixth century found at Nydam in Denmark and Götaland in Sweden. Runic characters are mixed with Greek ones in the old Gothic writing. Nevertheless the Nordic tribes were still primitive in the eighth century, and human sacrifices were frequent.

At the end of the eighth century Schleswig and the island of Gotland were trading with Gaul and various eastern countries. Swedish iron and furs were paid for in Arab or Greek money, hoards of which have been found. It was at this time that the Nordic people started on their conquests. This expansion has been explained as being due, first to over-population and the lack of new lands to bring under cultivation, estates passing to the eldest son, leaving the younger ones to fend for themselves; second, to banishment of nobles to strengthen royal power; and lastly to the simple lust for pillage. There are definite signs of movement, from 780 onwards, from Upland, Westfjörd, and Jutland. Under

their *jarls*, the Swedes sailed to Courland and Ladoga, the Norwegians to the Shetlands and Faroes. Vikings
(a word of doubtful origin) are known to have landed in
the Hebrides, on the north coast of Ireland, and on the
southern shore of the Thames estuary (787-95).

Having come to trade and been badly received, the
Vikings turned to pillage. The Irish give credit to the
clan Hy Neill for the victory at Killarney. Gaul was the
next victim, a raid being carried out at Dorestad in
809. Charlemagne had to take steps to guard Boulogne
and the Scheldt estuary. In the east the water-road south
from the Baltic was dotted with Swedish fortified trading
stations: Novgorod, Smolensk, Kiev; and the Varangians, as the population was called, having mixed with
Slavs, came finally to be called Russians.

Between 813 and 820 the Norsemen attacked Friesland, the lower Rhine, the lower Seine, Ireland, and Northumbria. In 838 a mixed body of Varangians and Russians
— this is the first time the latter appear in history —
came as far as the walls of Constantinople.

Thus started the long series of raids executed by the
Norsemen. Each spring Viking crews of thirty or forty
embarked in their long, swift high-prowed ships. Ascend-
ing rivers, they would stop opposite town or abbey.
Grounding their ships the warriors would then seek to
surprise the place. If the raiders were successful, the inhabitants were slaughtered and the spoils brought aboard.
Before long the Vikings, seizing horses, rode inland, ravaging the countryside. They were fierce pagans, from
a prehistoric background of countries untamed by Rome.

The Arab Corsairs

In Ifrikia the Aghlabid emirate, which ruled with
Berber support, had difficulty in holding the Arabs of
the towns in check from 805 onwards, and it may well
have been to keep them otherwise occupied that the emirs
encouraged raids on the neighbouring coasts. Their squadrons were half Spanish, half African, and they raided the
Balearic Islands, Corsica, Calabria, and even Nice. Charlemagne was obliged to fit out flotillas at Genoa and Lucca
to deal with these corsairs, whose raids were in many
respects like those of the Norsemen — open galleys, precise objectives, pirates turning into mounted marauders
on land. But there was one great difference: the Norsemen attacked churches in preference to villages, as they
were after sacred treasure rather than civic wealth. The
corsairs' fury was largely religious and their procedure
less savage; for, as they preferred to take prisoners and
exact ransom, the slaughter was less.

THE WEST DEVASTATED

The Carolingians and the landowners

Varying views on the part to be played by the Church
may have fomented bitter disputes among the clergy, but
they do not seem to have shaken the stability of the Empire. There was however, one serious threat. The Carolingians had triumphed only with the assistance of the
landed nobility from which they themselves had sprung.
The prosperity of the towns might be based on Lombard

Bronze Age Viking helmet and shield. Horns were a symbol
of power for the pagan Vikings, who sailed their un-decked ships
as far west as Labrador. *Danish National Museum*

and Frisian trade, and beyond the Rhine smallholders
might be numerous, but it was the large estates which
formed the basis of the Empire's economy. Such estates
had in many cases come down intact from the later
Roman Empire. It was thus the interests of the landowners that counted, and each noble was a focus of reviving separatism, a tendency that crystallised round Lothar,
eldest son of Louis the Pious.

At Worms, in 829, when a division of the Empire was
being planned, this prince, jealous of the share allotted
to his half-brother Charles, took the lead in a revolt of
the nobility, the prelude to innumerable civil wars.

Between 830 and 840 the Emperor's sons revolted
against him six times. Twice he was disarmed and deposed. Ultimately, despite the opposition of the Church,
a division was agreed on. Pepin took Aquitaine in the
sixth century, Louis the German took the conquests beyond the Rhine, Charles the Bald took Neustria, and
Lothar took Austrasia, Provence and Italy. In fact, in
each of these regions only the counts had any real power.
In Thuringia, Bavaria, Aquitaine and the Meuse, the local
rulers behaved at home as though they were absolute
masters. In external affairs, it was often their abrupt
change of front which determined the success or downfall of a prince. Within the limits of these new divisions,
ancient nationalities asserted themselves. The death of
Louis the Pious in 840 settled nothing. Pepin had died
in 838 and, of the three princes left, Charles and Louis
the German united against Lothar. Their agreement, the
'Strasbourg Oaths', is remarkable in that each prince
pledged himself in his own vernacular, the first documents in 'French' and 'German'. In 843 a lasting agreement was finally signed at Verdun, an agreement that
fixed for centuries the frontiers behind which France
and Germany were gradually to be constituted, France
west of the Meuse and Germany east of the Rhine. Between these two areas stretched a long corridor, essential
when one considers that it included Rome and Aix-la-
Chapelle and thus the great trade route joining Friesland

Lothar, eldest son of Louis the Pious. *Hachette*

Friesland to the Gironde, destroying Dorestad, Etaples, Nantes, Rouen and Bordeaux. The monks fled, taking their relics with them, and the nobility fled too. Only the peasantry was left to be massacred. Each year the princes paid the invaders handsomely to go away. Only Lothar saw the remedy; he offered the *jarl* Roric territory in which to settle. After 855 the Norsemen advanced up the Elbe, the Seine and the Loire. Seizing horses, they rode into the Auvergne; Amiens, Paris, and Orleans were put to flames. Others attacked Spain and Morocco, and, passing into the Mediterranean, burnt Pisa in 859. In Britain after 834 the Norsemen sacked London and then advanced to Bedford and York. Only the Irish put up a stiff resistance.

The Mediterranean coasts were the prey of the Arab corsairs. After 827, the Aghlabites stormed Greek towns in Sicily and Calabria, and in 841 captured Bari and Tarentum. They surprised Ragusa and Durazzo; based on Corsica and Sardinia, they laid waste to Campania and Tuscany; they attacked Marseilles and Arles. And in August 846 they raided Rome, ravaging the outskirts and desecrating St Peters'.

Western France at its nadir

The raids of the Norsemen had brought large areas of France to a state of confusion. They now wintered inland; from 879 to 889 they devastated the countryside between the Loire and the Rhine, held up only by a few sieges. When there was a pitched battle the invaders were heavily defeated — by Louis III, for instance, in 881, and by Odo in 888. To eliminate the danger, Charles the Simple decided on a great sacrifice; in 911 the *jarl* Rollo was given permission to settle his bands in the Caux area. But such fierce warriors were not easily converted to the peaceful pursuits of agriculture: the raids continued — in Artois, in Brittany, in the Bessin. Soon Rollo claimed the Orne, then the Cotentin. Was all Gaul to be gradually swallowed by the Normans, as they may now be called?

Who was to summon the force to stop them? When in 888 Charles the Fat was deposed, the western Franks had chosen Odo, the defender of Paris. 'Duke of the Franks', he ruled the territory between the Seine and the Loire. This was too much for his jealous rivals, who crowned the Carolingian, Charles the Simple. Bitter rivalry ensued: Charles upheld the Austrasian and even the Lorraine tradition; Odo supported the Neustrian. In 898 Charles won supremacy for a while, then Robert, Odo's brother, and finally, in 923, Robert's son-in-law, Rodolph of Burgundy.

And for what ridiculous strips of territory was all this fighting about? For the villas of the Oise and the Aisne, handed down from the days of the Merovingians, admittedly a solid, well populated nucleus of what would later be called 'France'. To the north of the Seine, a powerful fief, the Vermandois, came into prominence towards 940, and for a while its unscrupulous count, Herbert II, held Charles the Simple in his hands. In Flanders the counts maintained their independence. Brittany gained freedom between 844 and 846; her chiefs repulsed Charles the Bald, advancing as far as Mans. South of the Loire the situation was still worse. Charles the Bald exhausted himself trying to hold Aquitaine, whose separatism infected even the princes he sent to rule it. The 'Goth' territories

to the Po valley. This was the future Lotharingia. Under these conditions only the Church could give any unity to the Empire; though even that seems far from assured when we consider the struggles of Pope Nicholas I, who sought to discipline the princes, and Hincmar, Archbishop of Rheims, champion of the Church of Gaul. Certainly from 855 imperial authority was merely a word. Louis II, Lothar's son, never set foot outside Italy. The only question that was in doubt was whether a buffer state would persist between the future France and Germany. In the event no stone was unturned on either side to appropriate this legacy from Lothar. In 858 the first 'Franco-German war' took place. Against all expectations, it was the westerners who won and in the course of his harassed life, Charles the Bald acquired both Lotharingia and Italy. At Christmas 875 he was consecrated with the imperial crown he had wrenched from the moribund Louis the German. This final chance for a stable Empire faded two years later when in 877 Charles died.

In vain Pope John VIII offered the crown to a Carolingian. Neither Louis the Stammerer in the West nor Louis the Young in the East wanted so perilous a title. For a while the idea of offering it to Basil I was current, a supreme confession of impotence. And if Charles the Fat, youngest son of Louis the German, accepted the crown in 881, thereby reuniting the Carolingian inheritance, he was not to enjoy it for long. Ill and betrayed by the German counts, he was deposed late in the year 887. Thenceforward the title of Emperor had no meaning, though in Italy, Guy, Duke of Spoleto, and Arnulf, illegitimate son of Carloman, king of Germany, masqueraded as such and engaged in bitter wars against each other.

The looting of the West

The prolonged insecurity under the raids of the corsairs and the Norsemen could only precipitate ruin.

After 834 the Danes yearly devastated the coast from

of the south-east and Gascony in the south-west were no longer under any external control after 840. Forty years later wars were being fought in Aquitaine between marquesses and counts, with the king a mere onlooker.

At the same time the route which joined the rich Austrasian estates with the Mediterranean was broken. Already in 855 this region had been divided into Lotharingia (or Lorraine) and the old Burgundy, which stretched down to the sea. With the complicity of the local bishops, the Lorrainer Boso succeeded in 879 in detaching a 'Kingdom of Provence' in the south. Similarly, the Austrasian Rodolph in 888 detached the middle part centred on Besançon. By making his illegitimate son, Zwentibold, 'King of Lorraine' in the north, the Carolingian Arnulf formally accepted this division of the Rhône-Rhine trade route into three sections.

Disruption of Germania

Although less divided, Germania suffered too. In spite of Arnulf's courage — his reign as 'king' began in 888 — everything fell into ruin around him. He had the consolation of being crowned in Rome, but he died in 899. And when his son, Louis the Child, the last of the German Carolingians, died in 911 at the age of seventeen, the choice of a successor from among the counts was unfortunate, since it fell on Conrad, Duke of Franconia, who enjoyed so little prestige that he was barely able to hold his own.

And then, despite the influence of the Church, national divergencies reappeared: Lorraine in the old lands of Austrasia; Bavaria and Saxony each with their own ethnic characters; Franconia and Swabia. Moravians and Czechs infiltrated in small groups, reaching the Main, and for a while their chief, Svatopluk, was master of a vast overlordship stretching from Swabia to the Carpathians. It was because it was a blow to the Slavs that in 890 Arnulf welcomed the arrival of the Hungarians on the Danubian plain, which had been deserted for a century.

The Hungarian terror

The havoc wrought by the Hungarians can only be compared with that wrought earlier by the Huns. Harvests were burnt, cattle slaughtered, houses and churches left in cinders. All the men were killed, the children mutilated, the women tied to what was left of the cattle, which was then driven off to the raiders' camp. From the year 900 Hungarian raids were pressed to the borders of Italy, then into Saxony and Bavaria. From 912 they advanced farther still to Swabia, Thuringia, Lorraine, and even Burgundy. In the end the greatest attraction was Italy, a country in which petty princelings waged absurd, ferocious internecine wars. The Popes, quickly succeeding one another and often debauched, joined in the conflicts. The body of one was disinterred, tried in public and thrown into the Tiber. Accordingly the Hungarians had little difficulty in crossing the Alps, and from 921 to 926 they were ravaging North Italy and Tuscany. A few ventured as far as Nîmes and even Narbonne. In these regions their bands were as daring as the corsairs. The latter were unremitting in their activity. From their mountain posts north of St Tropez, they even on one occasion appeared in mid-winter at St Gall in Switzerland.

Anglo-Saxon tenacity

The small Anglo-Saxon kingdoms were the only ones to hold their own. The energetic Alfred the Great, king of Wessex, clinging to a few loyal footholds, finally saved England in May 878 at Edington in Wiltshire. The Danish *jarl* Guthrum consented to be baptised, and was left with the north-east of England. Until his death in 899, Alfred had to pursue the struggle, which was then continued by his son, Edward the Elder. But in Mercia and East Anglia forts were already being built which testify to the reconquest.

The reign of Alfred was, indeed, a turning point in the history of England. He was a great war leader, and the first of the English kings to organise a navy, striking at the Norsemen in their own element. He was also highly civilised for a layman: as a boy he had twice made pilgrimage to Rome, and he was interested in books and geography. He brought continental men of learning and artists to his Court, and commissioned translations of classical works into Anglo-Saxon. He encouraged his nobles to become literate and he codified and combined the laws of Wessex, Mercia and Kent. His rule not only consolidated and helped to civilise Wessex, it provided a

A scene from the Franks' Casket.

base from which the Danish-dominated parts of the kingdom could be subdued by his successors, though the Anglo-Saxons were never to destroy the Danish influence and it was an Anglo-Danish kingdom which was to be invaded by the Normans in 1066.

In the north, the Scots under Kenneth Macalpin held out, but in Ireland the clans were overpowered by the Norwegians and Danes, who by 915 had reduced the country to a state of chaos.

It was in these dark years, when the West seemed to be perishing, that the dominant traits of medieval Europe were in fact being drawn. To stop invaders, kings had been forced to purchase loyalty by giving away their property. But it was in vain.

It was necessary to exact the performance of obligation, and the attachment of duties to the tenure of land grafted on the movement of patronage and fidelity, whose origin goes back to the later Roman Empire and to the fifth century. The confusion between the duty and its reward, between the *honor* and the *beneficium* gave rise in the middle of the ninth century to the notion of feudality whereby the holder of a fief promised to provide a contingent for the feudal host — the striking force of the realm. Hereditary succession to fiefs had often come to be accepted by 800. In spite of the panic of monks and the shame of Rome, the Church remained strong, winning over even the pirates; for the Latins brought the gospels to Scandinavia, the Greeks to the Slavs (870-880). It was indeed the Christian spirit which was the only sign of unity, the only hope of union.

PERSISTENCE OF THE GREEKS

Why the Byzantines lasted

Apart from the crisis it went through in the ninth century, Constantinople thanks to its long history, showed greater strength than the West. Besides, for the first time, a stable dynasty came into power, bringing to an end the incessant usurpations. Using as a pretext the replacement of the patriarch of Constantinople, Ignatius, by the layman Photius, a patrician, Basil had the weak Michael III assassinated in 867, and his uncle Bardas in the previous year, in order to assume the imperial crown himself.

Basil I, founder of the Macedonian dynasty, was an illiterate peasant of fifty-six, but clear-headed and methodical. After some hesitation, he accepted Photius as patriarch and therewith the schism with Rome (879). The nineteen years of his reign were a prelude to the triumphant one (from 886 to 912) of his son, Leo VI, a devout churchman imbued with a sense of imperial greatness. His authority over the Church was reaffirmed; his officials were trained in loyalty to the regime and his control of the bureaucracy enabled him to make his power hereditary.

Serious territorial losses

Nevertheless the military situation on the frontiers was a permanent cause of uneasiness. Relations with Islam had become strained during the reign of Theophilus. In 838 the Caliph Mutasim advanced as far as Ancyra, taking 6,000 prisoners and forcing Basil I to send small garrisons to Tarsus, Samosata, and Caesarea, to keep that neighbourhood reasonably safe. Constantinople suffered, like the West, from the corsairs. In 824 Crete and Cyprus were lost, while the Moslems had obtained a foothold in Sicily. The Aegean was infested with these pirates from Tunisia and Egypt. But a maritime counter-attack, impossible for the Carolingians, was still within the capacity of the Greeks. In 842 the Aegean was cleared of raiders; and in 853 Michael III burnt Damietta, on the Nile delta. It was, however, under Basil I that the most daring operation was carried out. Whether it was with Carolingian assistance or not, the Greeks reoccupied Venice, then Bari (871), then Tarento (882). They had to give up hope of recapturing Sicily; and in 904 corsairs based on Crete succeeded in raiding Thessalonica and carrying off 20,000 Christians; but the Empire was able to withstand these reverses.

Like the Carolingian Empire, the Eastern Empire had to withstand simultaneous attacks from south and north.

Constantinople bore the extreme forefront of the Scandinavian thrust; the 12,000 Russians who attacked in 860 did not persist; on the Bulgarian front the thirty years' peace concluded with Omurtag and renewed by Boris I had been reinforced by the progress of conversion among the Bulgars. But Boris retired to a monastery and in 894 his son Simeon reopened hostilities, indignant at the heavy taxes imposed on her merchants. In 904 he won Albania and Macedonia, pushing the Greeks coastwards. His campaign of 923 gave him Adrianople and Thrace and took him to the walls of Constantinople. Simeon nevertheless agreed to return to his own territories after being awarded the title of Caesar and *tsar*, while the head of the Bulgarian Church was awarded that of Patriarch of Preslav.

Peace was maintained for fifty years. But only a hundred miles from the capital, the Bulgars held most of the roads down to Adrianople and the Aegean. In this way a 'Greater Bulgaria' had evolved, Christian and Slav, and by the beginning of the tenth century an 'eastern question' was looming over the Empire.

THE RETURN OF PRE-ISLAMIC TRADITIONS

The end of the Abbasids

The decline of Islam was not caused by attacks from without nor by the scramble for land by disinherited princes, but by the revival of earlier traditions of ruling subject territories through non-Arab administration. This practice had been encouraged by the Umayyads and by the Abbasids. The victors had always been greatly outnumbered by those called on to advise them, by the Greeks and Syrians in the seventh century, and the Persians in the eighth. These came to dominate the State. Later it was the Turks who took control of the Empire, and since they had no particular aptitude for the task, progressive decline began. The submission of the Abbasids to their Turkish praetorians from the reign of Mutasim (833-42) onwards completely undermined the prestige of the caliphs, who moved in 836 to Samarra, where they stayed till 892. The Turks even dared to assassinate one of them. On every side separatist claims were being made. In Egypt. Ahmad ibn Tulun became the first of a Tulunid dynasty. In Persia, the nobility, which had always held the power in the eastern provinces, started a Mazdaist movement in 838. The decline of the caliphate was in fact hastened by various sectarian and social movements. After the revolt of the Negro slaves in Basrah in 880, the agitation of the Carmathians (expropriated Syrian peasants) spread between 890 and 905 to Mesopotamia, to the coastal area of the southern end of the Persian Gulf, and even to the Yemen. Their bands, comprising all sorts of malcontents and marauders, led by Abu Tahir, burnt Kufah and Basrah, and had the audacity to force their way into Mecca and take possession of the Black Stone.

The moment seemed to have come for the Persians to take over government again, and in 945 one of them, Ahmad, of a largely Turkish descent, was already established in Fars and Jebel; he now entered Baghdad and took the title of emir, which his successor quietly dropped in favour of the traditional Shahanshah.

In the north-east, the Samanid Nasr I, of pure Persian stock, claiming descent from the Sassanids, established a kingdom between the Syr Daria and Khorassan (874). Face to face with the Turko-Mongols, he seemed in every way the successor of Chosroes.

Unsettled state of the West

In the western areas of the Moslem world local autonomy became general. After the Tulunids, the Ikshidids established their rule in Egypt and in southern Syria; in the Maghrib, the Berber tribes, falling into anarchy, let the Tahert emirate decay (906) and then that of the Aghlabites in Kairwan (909); in Morocco, lastly, marauders from the Rif sacked Fez in 922.

The stability of the Umayyads in Spain is, in contrast, surprising. Abd-ar-Rahman III (912-61) put down several urban revolts, and in 929 adopted the title of Caliph. Christian resistance still persisted in the north-east, Alfonso III (866-910) pushing his raids as far as Toledo; but after him the Asturias was divided into three: Leon in the east, Castile in the centre, and Navarre (soon to be occupied by the Muslims) in the west.

AMERICA AND ASIA

Early American civilisation

Apart from the arrival of the Scandinavians in Labrador about 1000, and the possible arrival of some Chinese Buddhists 500 years earlier on the Pacific coast, the American continent had no contacts with the outer world during the Middle Ages, except perhaps with Polynesia.

There do not seem to have been any arrivals from northern Asia across the Bering Strait for a thousand years or more before Christ. In any case, the principal centres of civilisation were fixed by the first centuries of our era. This halt of immigration was certainly one of the causes of the deserted condition of the western continent, whose population did not exceed one per square kilometre between the latitudes 30° North to 30° South at the time America was 'discovered'. Since the fourth century, two distinct centres of civilisation existed, appreciably different in spite of certain common features. One was in Mexico, the other in the Andes. Both flourished on high plateaus within the tropics, that is, under conditions rarely found in the Old World outside Java. In both centres, life was maintained by a semi-nomadic agriculture comparable to the slash-and-burn methods of primitive tribes of Africa and south-east Asia, leaving the soil to produce a wild cereal, maize and sweet potato. In both centres gold, silver and copper were produced between the fourth century and the sixth, but neither had knowledge of iron. The only animals bred were sheep for wool, dogs and guinea pigs for food and, in the Andes, llamas for transport. The Mexicans had turkeys. A degree of technical achievement was reached in weaving, ceramics, metalworking, and sculpture — this last justly famous — but neither knew the use of money, the lathe, or the potter's wheel. The differences are so striking that it would be pointless to look for mutual influence, except perhaps within the sphere of art. In the fifth century, the spread of the Maya civilisation in the north was based on the

A Peruvian vase in the form of a blind beggar. Mochica period. American civilisations were developing independently of European and Asian civilisations; the three were to meet in the sixteenth century. *Giraudon*

activities of temple cities; while in the south the life of the clans — at the most we can call them tribes — forbids the use of the word 'empire' to describe even the Inca territory.

Mayan culture

About the first century of the Christian era, an extraordinary culture grew up in Central America. Between the fourth and the ninth centuries, the cities built by the Mayas — Palenque, Copan, Uaxactun, and Yaxchilan — disputed the control of Guatemala, Yucatan, and the Tehuantepec isthmus. The influence of their culture reached down to the equator, and the Zapotecs and the Mixtecs of south-west Mexico may be regarded as their pupils. By the seventh century, the Mayas had acquired a great knowledge of arithmetic. Society was based on property, in individual or family ownership, a phenomenon practically unique in America then. In spite of the conflicts between the ceremonial cities, Maya civilisation seems on the whole to have been peaceful. Its highly stylised sculpture is never of warlike scenes, and the rites of the dualistic religion do not seem to have included human sacrifice, customary as this was among the other tribes.

The contemporary civilisation in the area of Teotihuacan, further north, which may have been of Olmec origin, cannot claim the same rank. It is worthy of mention, however, as being the first to call attention to the remarkable position of the valley of Mexico.

The Andes

Until the arrival of the Europeans, the Arawaks and the Caribs of the West Indies seem to have been in the Stone Age, as were the peoples of Guiana, the Pampas, and the Amazon basin: but in the Magdalena valley in   283

Lintel from House 'G' at Yaxchilan, Guatemala, c. 709. A
penitent, kneeling before a priest, mutilates his tongue with a
rope of thorns. *British Museum*

present-day Colombia. Chibchas and Quimbayas seem to have grown relatively wealthy by exchanging gold and salt with neighbouring tribes. On the Peruvian coast, between the Gulf of Guayaquil and Arica, various tribes wielded power before the sixth century, including the Mochicas, a tribe of sailors and fishermen, who seem to have faithfully obeyed a leader, the *chimu*, and who have won considerable prestige with their art, which is surprising in its realism.

On the high plateaus inland, the nomadic Quechuas wandered between the upper valley of the Marañon and the northern shore of Lake Poopo, their herds of llamas providing transport from the mountains to the coast. Some tribes settled at an early date at Tiahuanaco near Lake Titicaca, where they exerted a military and theocratic domination which foreshadowed that of the Incas and formed the basis of an Indian population which has persisted until today.

China in disorder

Saved by the Uighur Turks from disaster, the Tang rulers had, by 760, lost authority over Tibet and the Yunnan. In Central Asia they were supplanted by their protectors, who sought to counter Islam by a revival of Manichaeism. These doctrines, contaminated by the old Nestorian heresy taking refuge there, had reached China, where a Nestorian metropolitan figures in the year 800. But when the Uighurs were overcome by the Kirghiz, the Tang regime could no longer hold out. Peasant risings began in 875; roads were unsafe, and merchants either fled or revolted; in the southern ports and in Shantung hungry crowds turned on Arab traders and lynched them; Canton rose. Death spread over the country. The Tang government appealed both to the Tibetans and the Kansu Turks, but these 'allies' merely appropriated Shansi and the Ordos. From 903 the revolt became general. In the end nine kingdoms were at each other's throats. In 939 Tongking seceded from China.

In Japan, Buddhism and Chinese influence became so strong that the war against the Ainus became a holy war. During the Nara epoch (710-784), there were 80,000 monks, one in sixty of the population. The imperial court had made itself the champion of the new ideas, so that Buddhism and monarchy went hand in hand. In 767, Dengyo, a monk, after long meditation, formulated the creed adapted to Japan's national genius. But if the emperors showed exemplary piety, their absorption in prayer did not favour good government. The road was thus wide open to conflict between the great families: Taira, Minamoto, Tokugawa and, above all, Fujiwara. This last family rose rapidly in the new capital, Kyoto. From 780 they provided tutors for the imperial children; from 790 they intermarried with the royal family; from 806 they provided the prime minister; and, in the middle of that century, regents. In them we see the equivalent of the mayors of the palace, and the social structure that followed has been regarded as feudal. In fact the redistribution of the land in the end favoured officials and nobles, though a persisting class system had superimposed the hierarchy of persons. The struggle against the Ainus maintained a military structure, and the decline of public order allowed mounted bandits to hold peasants up to ransom, and Manchu pirates to infest the coasts.

Tang demon. Under the Tang, China was once more unified and the arts flourished in this long period of peace. *Victoria and Albert Museum*

Disorder in the Hindu world

The Hindu world, as though exhausted by the eastward dissemination of its civilisation, now began to disrupt. Brahminism took the upper hand with the Pratiharas on the middle Ganges (the heirs of Harsha) and the princes of Kashmir in arms against the Moslems of Sind and Kabul (780-810). It was south-east India which now became the fortress of Hinduism: the belligerent Rashtrakutas of the Deccan and the Cholas of the Carnatic began in 800-825 to extend their dominions northward.

South-east Asia developed slowly. On the Annam hills, in Champa, and in Laos, Buddhism progressed. The empire of Sri-Vishaya in Sumatra was the centre of a Malay domination which stretched from western Java to the northern part of the Kra Isthmus. On the borders of Cambodia, a new Khmer empire was formed by Javanese princes, and all, or nearly all of it was Hindu, as is shown by the names of the kings, the rites which deified them, and the temples of Angkor, the capital in 900.

Thus southern Indian influence, predominantly Hindu, spread into the Indo-Chinese peninsula and far into Indonesia.

285

THE RISE OF EUROPE

The four states of Europe, Slavonia, Germany, France and Rome offering homage to Otto III, Holy Roman Emperor from 983 to 1002. Otto III's Gospel, c. 1000. Bamberg. Munich Staatsbibliothek. *Marburg*

SCLAUINIA   GIRMANIA   GALLIA   ROMA

CHAPTER SEVENTEEN

THE AWAKENING

A.D. 925-1050

EUROPE SAVED FROM INVASIONS

THE TRIUMPH OF GERMANY

Otto the Great

When Conrad of Franconia died in 918, the German dukes who chose the Saxon king, Henry the Fowler, to succeed him nominated a born leader. Yet Saxony had been hitherto a source of disorder in Germany, and Henry, chiefly preoccupied in holding off the Danes and the Slavs and reoccupying Lorraine, was considered by the south Germans to be ignoring the more urgent Hungarian threat. But Henry, though paying tribute to the Hungarians, was merely biding his time and reorganising his army. Then, in 933, he swooped confidently down from the north and for the first time crushed the annual Hungarian raid on Thuringia. This victory assured his family's succession, and in 936 his son Otto succeeded him.

It took Otto three years to subdue the feudal chiefs of middle Germany. As soon as he was crowned he set out to re-establish a quasi-'Carolingian' authority. When a dukedom fell vacant, he promptly eliminated the heir. By 940, with Saxony and Franconia in his hands, Bavaria in his brother's, Swabia in his son's, Lorraine in his son-in-law's, and Mainz and Cologne in his nominees', he felt he could aim even higher, particularly as he had made sure that the Church was well disposed.

Otto was now twenty-eight, a big, red-haired, impetuous soldier, no man of letters but a religious man of moderation and good sense. He was confident of himself as the soldier of the Church and the heir of Charlemagne — a difficult example to live up to, but within his capacities. He had to hold sway, not only over Germany, but also over France and Italy; he had to repel Hungarians, Saracens, and Slavs; he had in a word to reconstruct the Empire. It took him barely thirty years.

Unsettled state of France

Distraught by the difficult times she had been through in the ninth century, France had not yet recovered. On the return of Louis IV (d'Outremer) from England, where he had been brought up by his mother's family, he was involved in a struggle with Hugh the Great (the son of Robert I of France) who ruled the area between the Seine and the Loire. Their conflict opened the way for Otto, and he intervened in 939, 940 and 942, and gave his two sisters in marriage to the two combatants. He favoured the Carolingian Louis, however. Louis, though tenacious, was less troublesome than the intriguing Hugh, who before long had made himself a new mayor of the palace, interposed between King Louis and his counts.

Louis was forced to surrender Laon and the suzerainty of Normandy. Taking refuge in Aix, he asked for Otto's help, and the latter intervened again; but Louis died in 954. Hugh then occupied Burgundy and attacked Aquitaine. But no power was formed in the West to rival Otto's. In June 956 the ambitious Hugh died, and the opportunity offered to his house seemed to have passed by, leaving Otto unopposed. The latter's nephew Lothar, son of Louis IV, was advised and commanded by another uncle, Bruno, Archbishop of Cologne, and in 964 the young Carolingian was only too glad to marry Otto's step-daughter and to pay his respects to the King of Germany.

German expansion

Arab corsairs had been less active off the coasts of Italy since the fall of the Aghlabites, and Otto was able to capture their mountain post at La Garde-Freinet. But after the death of Hugh of Arles, for a while master of Lombardy, Italy was in confusion. What respect could

Miniature showing Ezra writing. Copy from the Codex Amiatinus (late seventh century) made by English Benedictine monks at the Durham monastery of Jarrow, famous for its association with the Venerable Bede. The numerous Benedictine abbeys of Northumbria were at once a bastion against the Irish mission at the time they were founded in the seventh century and a repository of learning preserved despite the destruction of the buildings by the Danes in the eleventh. *Laurentian Library, Florence*

Colour plate: detail from a twelfth-century Viking tapestry. A typical horseman of the feudal period: heavy chain mail, helmet with nose piece, long, pointed shield and short lance. Face, hands, feet and horse go unprotected. *Presses Artistiques*

Otto the Great, first of the great German Holy Roman Emperors, who, by having his family consecrated at the time of his own coronation in Rome (962), re-established the imperial concept and introduced into it the notion of heredity. *Historisches Bildarchiv Handke*

Otto the Great receiving Berengar II of Lombardy (952). On this occasion Berengar and Adalbert became formally Otto's vassals and this assured Otto of the eastern gateway to Italy. But Berengar remained rebellious, and was not finally crushed until 962, a prelude to Otto's coronation in Rome.

the Theophylact Popes enjoy when their womenfolk, mistresses or mothers, laid down the law? It was thus towards Italy that in 951 Otto turned his warlike zeal. At Pavia he was made 'king'.

If under his leadership the Germans reached Rome, their influence was also spreading east of the Elbe at the expense of the Slavs. Starting in the ninth century, missionaries had made many converts among the Czechs, though not without setbacks, as when Wenceslas, Duke of Bohemia, paid for his faith with his life in 936. Under the impulse of Hermann of Swabia and Gero, margrave of the area between the Elbe and the Oder, various new bishoprics were created.

The last of the Hungarians and the Vikings

For seventeen years Otto I had been obliged to ignore the Hungarians, and the latter had taken advantage of it. In 937 they had begun ravaging middle Germany, Lorraine, Burgundy, and Italy as far south as Monte Cassino. In 954, becoming reckless, they rode to the Rhine, crossed it and raided Metz, Cambrai, Rheims and Châlons. In the spring of 955, 100,000 horsemen are said to have besieged Augsburg. Something had to be done. Fully aware of the danger, Otto mustered a strong force and eight columns converged on the River Lech. The battle lasted ten hours and the issue was in doubt to the end. Finally Otto won the day; the Hungarians fled in disorder and were pursued beyond Vienna and hacked to pieces. At a single encounter, the danger had

been removed: there were to be no more Hungarian horsemen in Germany. In 970 their chief Geza and 5,000 of his warriors were baptised, and a little later his son Wajk was to become St Stephen.

Otto played a smaller part in arresting the piracy of the Scandinavians, who were still operating in 930 in Gaul, in 950 in England, and in 970 in Ireland. From those dates resistance strengthened and their visits became fewer. In Ireland King Brian Boru gained a great victory over the Danes at Clontarf in 1014, though he lost his life in the battle. In England the fortified boroughs of Edward the Elder and Aethelstan protected the country south of the Humber, and, with the help of King Malcolm of Scotland, Guthfrith the Danish king of York was defeated. In Gaul the Normans were becoming more civilised, though they went through a brief revival of paganism, which involved the assassination of William 'Long Sword', son of Rollo (942). In any case, maritime adventurers were now tempted by longer expeditions. At the beginning of the tenth century, they touched on Greenland and possibly reached Labrador. At the same time royal power was consolidated at the end of the ninth century with Harald Haarfager as King of Norway, and about 930 with Gorm as King of Denmark.

The new empire of the West

Master of Italy and Gaul, sovereign at home, missionary to the peoples on the eastern frontier, Otto had saved Christianity at the battle of the Lechfeld and had

The Bayeux tapestry was executed towards the end of the eleventh century. It records the events of William the Conqueror's invasion and defeat of England. *Top*: William's fleet lands at Pevensey. *Centre*: Edward the Confessor sends his envoy, Harold, to Duke William. *Bottom*: a lively detail from the battle which ended in French victory. *French National Tourist Office*

saved Germany two months later on the Recknitz, where he beat the Slavs. The imperial concept, long nourished by the Church, once more came into its own. The time had come to restore a dignity that no shoulders had been broad enough to carry since those of Charles the Bald.

Quietly marching into Italy, Otto the Great was crowned and proclaimed Emperor in February 962. At the same time his family were consecrated — a new idea, and a clever one. But the 'restored' empire, was not really comparable to Charlemagne's. Though the Papacy under Leo III had already accepted lay tutelage, now, under John XII, this tutelage went further and was more lasting. Missionary activity was taken out of the Pope's hands, as was the reform of a clergy corrupted by simony and the commercial exploitation of shrines and relics. The voices which now spoke in the name of the Church announcing the Christian revival were those of the abbots of Cluny — Odo, Maiolus (Maieul), Odilo and Hugh — the true moral leaders of the West, whose influence lasted (between the four of them) 180 years. Thus the new Emperor dominated the Church much more completely than did his predecessors.

In 800 the Church was able to pride itself on having resuscitated the ancient Roman Empire, but such an idea could hardly be entertained a century and a half later, when the authority of the prince, bereft of all administration, was based only on his own personal domain or the good will of his vassals. In Germany Otto could regard himself as the heir of the Carolingians, and he had robbed the national dukes of their autonomy; but in Gaul and Italy there was no authority that could be taken from the princes except that over their personal estates. It was the superiority of the German social structure which gave Otto's empire its true character. Like Charlemagne, Otto created a 'Holy Roman Empire', but this time it was a German one.

The Germans cut off from the Mediterranean

The new structure reflects, also, the attraction of the Mediterranean for the Germans. This feeling was inherited from the early barbarians, who had felt themselves barred from that centre of civilisation. But there was also a serious calculation that, in order to be master of the West, it was more necessary for the new Saxon empire to dominate Italy than it had been for the Gallo-Frankish one. And in Italy, besides Rome which the emperor visited in 962, 963 and 966, there was Naples in the hands of the Greeks and Sicily in the hand of the Arabs.

The Byzantines were alarmed, though without envisaging a long war; and by marrying the ravishing Theophano, daughter of Romanus II, to Otto's son they were able to hold on to their Italian possessions. Otto installed a trusted soldier, Pandulph Iron-head, in Capua and Benevento; but if the Emperor was intending any further moves, he left them to his son, for he died in 973.

Otto II was not yet twenty. He was attractive, light-hearted, and cultivated, but lacking in good sense. He plunged into an Italian adventure regardless of the danger threatening from the Danes and the Slavs. Acting without the Greeks, who warily held back, he equipped a fleet in Campania for an assault on Sicily. In vain did German counts request his return to the Elbe, in vain did the Bavarians warn him of the Czech danger: his fleet sailed

Otto III, a capricious yet able ruler who wished to revive the Empire in its classical grandeur, but died at only twenty-two. From Otto III's Gospel. *Historisches Bildarchiv Handke*

Coin depicting Aethelstan, King of England (925-939), brother-in-law of Otto the Great. *British Museum*

and was duly sunk by the Moslems off Cape Calonna on July 13, 982. Otto did not live much longer: he died in 983 at the age of twenty-seven. With that, southern Italy was closed to the Empire for two centuries.

Otto III

Otto's Greek widow, Theophano, was left with a child of three, and she governed on his behalf in a manner worthy of Otto the Great. Bavaria and Bohemia were contained. In this completely German sphere she was helped by Willigis, Archbishop of Mainz, but not in the thoroughly Greek education she gave her son. Otto III is an example of what might have come of the fusion of the two Empires dreamt of by the clergy. He was a Greek in his culture, in his capriciousness and ambition, in his taste for luxury and grandiloquence. He was a Roman and pupil of Gerbert, Abbot of Bobbio, in his thorough knowledge of jurisprudence and dreams of a Roman type of hierarchy. But, as St Adalbert discovered, there was yet another side to his character, barbaric, naive, and passionate; he was a man who only laid down his arms to walk barefoot as a pilgrim.

The pursuit of a will o' the wisp dominated his life, from the time he succeeded his father at the age of sixteen: it was to reconstitute the Empire of Constantine. Repelling Danes and Slavs was a pastime. He preferred to be in Italy, and he went to Rome yearly. There, in Greek fashion, he nominated *protovestiaires* (masters of the wardrobe). In 999 he had his mentor made Pope, and Gerbert took the name of Silvester II, after the Silvester of Constantine's day. In the year 1000, Otto III had Charlemagne's body exhumed in great pomp. The following year he returned to Rome and there he died suddenly on January 23 1002, at the age of twenty-two. His strange, ineffectual reign did not advance the cause of the Empire, and within a quarter of a century of his death the work of Otto the Great was in jeopardy.

THE GREAT DAYS OF BYZANTIUM

At Constantinople two events ushered in the tenth century: the conflict between Basil I and the Caliph, and that between the admiral Romanus I (Lecapenus) and Simeon, Tsar of the Bulgars. These were of the utmost consequence to the century, for they led to the recovery of Syria and the elimination of the Bulgars. For sixty-five years the emperors made way for their lieutenants, contenting themselves with a divided rule. Constantine VII (Porphyrogenitus) only came into real power after the age of forty, and then only to occupy himself with philosophy, etiquette, or gastronomy. His daughter-in-law Theophano, regent for twelve years, put power into the hands of her lovers, astutely chosen amongst the most able generals. It was these favoured soldiers, Bardas Phocas, Nicephorus Phocas and John Tzimisces, who were the real rulers.

It was a glorious period for the Greek armies, whose men regarded themselves more and more as Christian crusaders, or as the authentic heirs of the Roman legions, though in fact fused into their ranks were Slav and Spanish troops, Russians and Chazars. The spoils made recruiting easy. In 960 the army was said to comprise 140,000 men, about three times as many as Otto the Great could muster.

The defeat of Islam

From 927 a series of campaigns succeeded in clearing the foothills of the Taurus Mountains. The disintegration of the caliphate had already allowed Diarbekr, then Aleppo and Mosul, to fall into the hands of the Hamdanids, one of whom Ali, the 'Sword of the Empire', held his own. The Greek offensive was fully operative under Nicephorus Phocas, a keen tactician and the idol of his men. By marrying Theophano he became Emperor from 963 to 969. To be able to conduct combined operations, Nicephorus wanted to regain command of the seas, lost for 150 years. Three thousand vessels were used against Crete for six months before it fell in March 961. The occupation of the island led to a series of successes. Tarsus and Cilicia were taken, then Cyprus; in 962 Aleppo was captured, but only temporarily; in 986 Emesa

(Homs) fell: and in the following year, after an absence of three centuries, the Greeks entered Antioch. Finally, in 969 or early 970, they recaptured Aleppo.

Nicephorus lost his life, killed by John Tzimisces, who had succeeded him as Theophano's favourite. He succeeded him as a military leader too. Another campaign started in 973, and the Greeks advanced triumphantly to the Tigris, to Baalbek, to Damascus; in 975 the Emperor's horsemen reached Jerusalem. His death a few months later brought an end to the Greek advance, but their success was nevertheless startling.

The Bulgarian danger

That was enough to give prestige to the Macedonian dynasty, though its security was always threatened by the Bulgars, who, since Simeon, had been installed within a hundred miles of the capital. When the truce was broken in 967 an attempt had been made to make use of the Slavs of Kiev against the Bulgarian tsar, Boris. Then in 970 Tzimisces organised a combined attack on Silistria, and the Greeks took the Bulgarian capital, Preslav.

After the death of Tzimisces, another tsar, Samuel, reoccupied Rumelia, defeated the Greeks near Sophia, and occupied Thessaly and Thermopylae. He does not seem to have been eager to attack Constantinople, however, preferring to make sure of a Balkan empire. In 987 he seized the Adriatic ports, and in 995 Thessalonica on the Aegean; his horsemen even reached Athens and Corinth. A new threat seemed to be hanging over the Byzantines' heads: their country was in danger of becoming an Asiatic bridgehead in Europe.

Basil II

Basil II was under twenty when he assumed power. A robust, jovial, blue-eyed horseman, of scant education, he is the only *basileus* to be depicted in armour. We see him as a short, thick-set, bearded man. He had neither friends nor mistresses. A hard task-master, pursuing his aims tenaciously, he stands on the same level as Justinian or Heraclius.

In 996 he attacked Samuel and drove him out of Greece; then he cleaned up the coast of Epirus. Therewith began a duel reminiscent of Charlemagne's with the Saxons. Every year from 1001 onwards Basil attacked, driving Samuel back village by village, and at the same time warding off counter offensives. One fortress after another was taken: Berrhoea, Vodena, Ochrida, Serdica. Samuel still held out, but finally in 1014 he was surprised and routed in the Struma valley. After the battle Basil returned 15,000 prisoners to him, blinded and with their hands cut off, guided by a dozen one-armed, one-eyed men. At the sight of them Samuel was so overcome that he fell ill and died. There were nevertheless four more years of fighting, before the Bulgars were forced back to the ruins of Sirmium. Victory now established, the country was annexed and fortified, and the Bulgars were enrolled into the Greek army. Their costumes, clergy, and dignities were, however, preserved.

To strike at the source of the nomad danger, Basil II wanted, like Justinian, to dominate the steppes. Not caring to undertake the conquest of the region, he was tempted by the idea of undermining the power of the

Nicephorus Phocas surrounded by his officers. Miniature of the eleventh century. *Larousse*

The raising of Lazarus. Illustration from Otto III's Gospel. *State Library of Munich*

Turko-Mongols by pitting against them the Russians, whom he considered easier to handle. In this tactic he followed Charlemagne, who broke the power of the Avars, but thereby left a vacuum that attracted other nomads. In the course of his victorious campaigns, Basil had already had contact with Serb and Croat tribes, disorganised and docile. Relations with the princes of Kiev had been good since conversions began in 960. In 988 St Vladimir was baptised and at the same time was given the hand of Basil's sister, Anne. In exchange he offered 6,000 mercenaries. It was this alliance which made it possible to destroy the Chazars on the middle Volga and to subject the Pechenegs in Moldavia.

The power of Byzantium

The empire of Basil II had recovered, except for Egypt, its extent in the fifth century. His authority beyond the frontiers was as great as Justinian's had been. The decadence of the caliphate in Baghdad, on the other hand, seemed irremediable. The Buyid prince, Adod Addaula (977), had incompetent successors. The Syrian emirates had practically ceased to exist, for the Hamdanids had been destroyed by Nicephorus Phocas,, the Ikhshidids by the Fatimids, now in control of Egypt. The Fatimids, now the only Moslem rulers of any stature, made an alliance with Basil in 1001, and Syria was divided. Thus the Greek garrisons from Tripoli to the Tigris occupied the positions in which the Romans and the Sassanids had once been face to face; the princes of Armenia were

Coin of John Tzimisces, who succeeded Nicephorus as Theophano's lover and as Emperor in 969. Under him the Greek advance into the Middle East progressed rapidly. *British Museum*

291

The Buyid prince Adod Addaula. Gold medal from Fars, Persia. Abbasid period. *Private Collection, Teheran*

vassals of Basil, as their forefathers had been of Trajan and Diocletian.

In the west, admittedly, the Sicilian outposts were lost (969), but Basil reorganised the Italian *themes*. In 1018 a Katapan took in hand the administration of the strongholds in Apulia, Calabria, and Campania, with a view to denying the German Caesars access to Gaeta, Troja, and Naples. The West, as we have seen, was at this time under the rule of an empress of Greek blood.

Internal strains

The prestige of the Macedonian dynasty, sanctified, hereditary monarchs fortunate in war, was based, in the eyes of the dazzled barbarians, on the unparalleled splendour of their court, their religious rites, their pomp and their Greek fire. A military despotism after the manner of the later Roman Empire had been fashioned to cope with the growing burdens of administration. The emperor appointed the hierarchy of dignitaries and bureaucrats; the nobility gravitated towards the palace rather than the army, victorious though the latter was. The progressive divorce between the routine activities of the towns and the rough life of the camp soon became a dilemma: were matters ultimately to be settled by the *coups d'état* of soldiers supported by a people oppressed by officials or by the despotism of invisible mandarins supported by the clergy? To put the alternatives briefly: was it to be hippodrome or cabal?

It is significant that the vitality of the medieval Eastern Empire was largely derived from the Ionian coast and the Anatolian plateau, regions that were henceforth decisive. Thus the power of the capital, indeed its function, was thrown in question by the landed nobility of Asia Minor, who disposed of both troops and money, and thus formed a sort of Greek feudal order. The *coups* of Bardas, Nicephorus, Ducas, and Cantacuzene between 976 and 995 introduced a new element. Basil II understood the danger, and in 996 he forbade nepotism and the illegal seizure of land. In so doing he tried to save the moribund smallholder, the backbone of the army, but his effort was in vain.

The recovery of Crete and the market towns on the Euphrates, the Russian alliance and the discomfiture of the Chazars, were followed by a revival of trade in 980-1000 (earlier than in the West). Agreements made with Venice and Amalfi gave the Byzantines access to Italy and central Europe, and their monks could travel along the Danube. Traffic seems to have been even heavier to

Four arhats (disciples of the Buddha) and two attendants witnessing the ascension of the arhat Darbha Mali-Puta, c. 1178. Buddhist philosphers of the late twelfth century were putting forward doctrines of reconciliation far in advance of those current at the same time in the West. *Museum of Fine Arts, Boston*

the steppes and to the East. Through Cherson and the lower Danube came fish and salt, flax and corn, Baltic amber, tin and copper; through Edessa and Tripoli, came silk, spices, and honey. Constantinople was once again the warehouse of the Mediterranean.

THE LAST ARAB MIGRATIONS

While north of the Mediterranean Europe was beginning to revive, south of it the Arabs were giving ground to the people they had conquered. Already in the East the Persians had taken the lead, while in Spain power had passed from the Umayyads to the Berbers. For a time at the end of the tenth century, the Caliphs of Cordova were surrounded once more in glory in the person of Ibn Abi-Amir (Almanzor), who inflicted severe defeats on the Christians of Leon and Castile and recovered Barcelona in 985; but his raids and those of his son Muzaffar were not serious enough to ruffle Europe.

The Fatimids

The last of the dynasties based on Arab supremacy had disturbed the Maghrib for a century. In 894 a missionary had announced the coming of an *imam*, a descendant of Ali and Fatimah, the Prophet's daughter, and had roused the Kabyles and expelled the Aghlabids of Tunisia (909). The heralded *imam*, ubaid-Allah al-Mohdi, founded a despotic dynasty, the Fatimids, at Kairwan, so oppressive a rule that in 943 a Berber revolt broke out in the Aures mountains, under the leadership of Abu Yazid.

The Fatimids proclaimed themselves Caliphs. Breaking down Berber resistance, they occupied the high plateaus of Biskra and Tlemcen and, for a while, Morocco, thus reunifying almost the whole of the Maghrib. What they had wanted from the first was to install themselves closer to the sacred places. In 913, 918, and 936 they advanced on Egypt, but succeeded in taking only a few fortified positions. But a final determined effort by the Caliph Moizz resulted in the fall of the Ikhshidids both in Egypt and southern Syria: in 969 he won a victory at Giza, then at Ramleh and Damascus. When he had entered Fostat he renamed it al-Kahvia (the Victorious).

The establishment of this new dynasty in Egypt was of the greatest importance. There was now a third caliph in existence, between the Umayyad caliph in Cordova and the Abbassid caliph in Baghdad, under the thumb of the Persians. The Fatimids were Shiites by persuasion, masters of Egypt, southern Syria and the Red Sea, and holding such towns as Alexandria, Tyre and Damascus, and seemed to promise the Moslem world new vigour and prosperity. The third, Hakim — unstable, now lavish, now mean — won the goodwill of the *basileus*, though still barring his way to Jerusalem.

The Maghrib isolated

The departure of the Fatimids threw the Maghrib back into anarchy. The Caliphs' clients, the Berber emirs of the Zenaga tribe, could hold their own only to the east of Tenes, the west passing into the hands of the Zenata, a tribe aided by Cordova, who in 973 conquered Morocco. After the year 1000 the Zenaga gave way to the Zeirids at Kairwan and to the Hammadites in Algeria. In 1017 Cairo seemed to be abandoning the Maghrib, and the Umayyads did the same.

Thus, at the beginning of the eleventh century, an ethnic rupture seems to have been accomplished, for there was no longer Arab rule beyond the Syrtes. There was also political rupture, since the Maghrib was no longer under the same rule as the East. This part of Islam, isolated by the desert, was now handed over to the West, an event that stamped its subsequent history.

MEDIEVAL EUROPE IN WORLD CONTEXT

Civilisation under the Sung dynasty

North of the Yellow River the fierce Khitan Tatars seemed on the verge of absorbing the nine or ten kingdoms which emerged from the disintegration of the Tang empire, when in 960 an able general, Tai-tsu, set himself the task of reuniting China. As a matter of fact, it was his successors who accomplished the task and founded the Sung dynasty which saw one of the greatest phases of Chinese civilisation. Tai-tsung (976-997) and Chentsung (997-1022) had little difficulty in occupying southern China, but Yunnan and Assam resisted reconquest. In the north the Tibetans and the Tangutans of Hia refused to allow the reopening of the north-western caravan routes. Sometimes the Khitan Tatars attacked, sometimes they were attacked, and then, as neither side conquered, a peace was signed in 1004 establishing a frontier to the southward of Peking. The Sung emperors were as wise as they were original, and the frontier was not violated for a hundred years.

To repair the ruin caused by two centuries of warfare a period of calm was needed, during which old traditions and the arts of living could be revived. The emperor Hwei-tsung, himself a poet and painter, keen on excavation and numismatics, encouraged printing, ceramics, and intellectual pursuits. In this peaceful atmosphere, Chinese philosophy worked towards the concilation which eight centuries of barbarian pillage and the military despotism of the Tang dynasty had stifled. The philosopher Chu-hi, at the end of the twelfth century, sought peace of the soul in a combination of Buddhism and Confucianism. The Sung dynasty witnessed also the teaching of Wang Ngan-chi, a socialist before his time, who in 1073 wanted to establish maximum prices, a fixed scale of wages, and a ministry to supervise farming and give agricultural subsidies. The Chinese of this era were far ahead of feudal Europe in their thought.

Japan and Indochina

A brilliant period was now to start in Japan, with the Fujiwara as mayors of the palace. One of them was Fujiwara Mashinaga (966-1027), who had two sisters and four daughters married into the emperor's family. The latter's court — given over to banquets, poetry readings, and travelling — was a sensitive, elegant world, whose feminine charm might have been somewhat superficial, yet was endowed with a certain austerity imposed by its Buddhist principles. Outside the palace insecurity and the absence of imperial authority played into the hands of the nobles, who recruited armies of peasants on their estates. These armies belonged to their 'feudal' lord, the Minamotos or the Tairas, rather than to the State. These two families, great landowners of the Tokyo plains or the reclaimed territories of the north, rivalled the Fujiwara family in the middle of the eleventh century. Then gradually central authority declined and the country drifted towards a state of feudal anarchy.

With the fall of the Tang dynasty, Indochina began to live a life of its own. In 939 Tongking escaped from Chinese tutelage and formed the empire of Dai Co Viet under a succession of families. Advancing towards the mouth of the Mekong, the new state attacked the coastal kingdom of Champa. Four times in the course of the eleventh century the capital, Cham, was taken; in 1070 the gateway to Annam was firmly in the hands of the Dai Co Viet, amongst whom Buddhism predominated.

The power of the Khmer Empire

Established since 900 on the shores of Lake Tonle-Sap, the Khmers, under Suryavarman I, extended their rule between 1002 and 1049 to the frontiers of their ally Champa and to the valley of the Menam, and the northern part of the Malay peninsula was subjected also. The architecture of Angkor shows the spread of Sivaism, Buddhism being confined to the élite.

Lastly the Burmese kingdom of Pagan included, under Anuradha (1044-77), the valley of the Irrawaddy as far as Pegu and the upper Salwen, and this military and Buddhist domination provided a security hitherto unknown; by introducing a vast irrigation scheme King Kyanzittha

Knut and his queen, Aelfgyfin, placing the great gold cross on the altar of Newminster Abbey, East Anglia. Knut made an exceptional effort to win the loyalty of his English subjects and not to appear to them as a conqueror. Eleventh-century miniature.

(1086-1112) was able to make Burma a granary of rice from the eleventh century onwards.

The maritime empires

A feature of the eleventh century was the rise of rival maritime powers in south-east Asia. Since the beginning of the eighth century the domination of Sri-Vishaya had encountered no rival in the Malay archipelago: nevertheless the centre and east of Java, inclined towards Brahminism, gradually emancipated themselves from this tutelage from 925 onwards. In 1024 Airlanga proclaimed Java's independence. Meanwhile, there was a strong maritime power in southern India. In 985 ardent Sivaists, the Cholas, formed an empire under Rajaraja the Great, who in the space of thirty years overpowered the kingdoms of Madura and Cochin, and the coast of Orissa south of the Mangalore-Yanaon line, at a time when south-west India was flourishing. Rajaraja then added Ceylon to his gains, and there showed the utmost tolerance towards Buddhism. His son Rajendra I (1014-42) transformed the empire by sailing his squadrons deep into the Gulf of Bengal, to the mouths of the Irrawaddy and then on to the Malay archipelago, where he destroyed the kingdom of Sri-Vishaya.

This fifty-year triumph of the Cholas gave renewed vigour to Hinduism and Hindu commerce, and it explains how the Deccan was able to resist Arab penetration. The seas were so completely under their control that even the Khmers and the Sung dynasty thought it best to humour them. With that, the sea-routes were much safer than the caravan routes across Mongolia, thereby giving south-east Asia a commercial position of first rank.

THE AWAKENING OF THE BALTIC AND NORTH SEA STATES

The rise of Denmark

The principalities established in Gotland, Jutland, and its neighbouring fjord, did not develop until after the death of Otto I. The Dane, Harold Bluetooth, seemingly a Christian, subdued Norway, leaving the north to his client Haakon. His son, Sweyn Forkbeard was a pirate who renewed the raids on England during the strife between Constantine, king of the Scots, and the Saxon descendants of Aethelstan, Edward and Aethelred II. These ultimately became annual, being aimed at Kent and around London, the most prosperous and populated part of the country. In 991, with the Norwegian Olaf Tryggvason, he crushed Aethelred the Redeless in Essex and exacted tribute.

These activities were interrupted by the internecine warfare between the Scandinavian marauders. Olaf, a Christian with Slav support, encountered the pagan Sweyn, assisted by the Swedes. The battle took place near Helsingborg in the year 1000. Olaf was killed at sea, and Sweyn occupied the Straits and the estuaries of the Vistula and the Duna. Eric, Haakon's son, held Norway on his behalf. Meanwhile Aethelred gave orders for all Danes in England to be slaughtered on St Brice's day. Among them was Sweyn's sister.

Sweyn attacked in 1003, but was unsuccessful. After

1007 he advanced step by step from York towards London. In 1010 he took Canterbury. London, outflanked, was taken in January 1014. Sweyn was triumphant, but when he died in February, the position of the Danes seemed insecure. Sweyn had left a son, Knut, who, though only twenty, was a worthy heir. In 1015 he received the submission of Wessex, and then recaptured London. Edmund Ironside's gallant resistance could not hold him and by November 1016 Knut was in command of all land north of the Thames. His success was timely, for Olaf the Saint had rebelled in Norway and Anund Jacob in Sweden. Knut returned to Norway and was kept fighting till 1030, when he at last defeated Olaf near Trondheim.

Knut in command of the seas

Settled at Winchester, Knut governed England. His sons, Sweyn and Harthaknut, ruled Norway, Denmark, the coasts of the Baltic states and Poland. Sweden was loyal, as were Iceland and the Orkneys. Making a pilgrimage to Rome, Knut received the blessing of the Pope. His empire was united by the seas, and his ambassadors at Kiev and in Poland kept an eye on Scandinavian merchants.

Under Knut, the Baltic became economically and culturally the Mediterranean of the North. From Iceland to Greenland, and from there to Vinland (Labrador) sailed Scandinavian missionaries; from Gotland to Hamburg, Kive and Novgorod, the coinage in circulation testified to Scandinavian trade. The opening of Flanders to trade was the natural consequence of this new development. Baldwin V, who became Count of Flanders at the time of Knut's death, received his widow and his commercial inheritance; his policy towards England and his work of reclamation marks the awakening of the Low Countries.

After Knut's death in 1035 his empire was split, Norway going to Harald, grandson of Olaf the Saint, Denmark to Sweyn Estrithson, but the Scandinavian countries were henceforward part of Europe.

BIRTH OF THE SLAVONIC STATES

The effect of Scandinavian commerce on the one hand and peace in Asia on the other was to stimulate the Slavs, an event comparable in importance to the awakening of the Scandinavians.

The birth of Poland

The Polish tribes beyond the Elbe, united in the time of Otto I by a Christian 'duke', Mesco, came under German influence at a period when the conversion of the Hungarians made them feel more secure. Independent bishoprics sprang up at Cracow, Kolberg, and Breslau. Even so, St Adalbert of Prague, known as the apostle of the Prussians, was struck down by a pagan hand. Boleslav the Great took over a Poland which extended no further than Mazovia, Silesia, and the middle region of the Vistula.

From now on the Germans beyond the Elbe found themselves flanked by a Slav nation. Between 992 and

1013, Meissen, Lusatia, Bohemia, and Moravia were raided by the Poles. Henry II, heir of Otto III, counterattacked in vain, and in 1018 he was forced to cede the 'Slavonic Marches' between Elstev and the Oder. Boleslav negotiated with Knut, welcomed Danish merchants, and died with the title of king in 1025. His son, Mesco II, was to lose the lands beyond the Elbe, but he occupied Pomerania, and Poland was henceforth a Baltic power.

Constantine IX Monomachus, one of the Emperors whose ineffective rule foreshadowed the end of the Macedonian dynasty.

Russia

The Czechs, converted since the death of St Wenceslas, struggled in vain against Conrad II, the successor of Henry II, obtaining only the independence of the bishopric of Prague. But the Hungarians were more successful. In 1030 Stephen, their king, halted Conrad on the Leitha, and three times between 1051 and 1054 King Andrew repulsed Henry III. They lost Moravia, but retained the Hungarian part of the Danubian plain. The Germans, on this front, were forced to wait.

Spurred into commercial activity by the Varangians, or Russians, the Slavs of Novgorod and Smolensk were led by chiefs of predominantly Scandinavian origin: Roric, Oleg, Igor. There was a moment when Igor's widow, Olga, seemed ready to receive the Christian faith from St Adalbert of Prague and the Germans. His fall was a blow to the Germans, and Olga turned towards the Greeks. Sviatoslav offered to help the Byzantines against the Bulgars, supplying 6,000 troops, and then his son Vladimir married Anne, sister of Basil II. The destruction of the Chazar empire about 970-90, desired equally by Byzantium and Novgorod, was the first step in Russia's development.

At one time Boleslav I of Poland was pressing towards the Dnieper. To ward off the danger, Yaroslav the Great moved to Kiev, the religious capital. It was from there that he sent his daughter Anne to marry Henry I of France. Kiev was a commercial town on the route from

ПРОТИВЦПЕУЕNБГЪ

A meeting of the Council of Vladimir the Great, 980–1015, son of Sviatoslav and married to Anne, sister of Basil II. Old Russian painting, from Poland. *Historisches Bildarchiv Handke*

the Baltic to Constantinople; it was also a fortress against the Pechenegs (Patzinaks) whose hordes were driven to the Bug and then across the Danube and into Thrace and Macedonia. From there they were pushed northward by the Byzantines between 1059 and 1065, till they were once again attacked by the Grand Dukes of Kiev. Thus a power was established on one of the major continental trade routes which was capable of fostering the revival of commerce.

UNREST IN WESTERN CHRISTENDOM

The approach of the year 1000 may have kindled superstitious fires among the peoples of the West, haunted by their belief in the devil. The terror was probably much less than has been thought, but the date was still symbolic, and in the feudal decentralisation in which Europe was born a spark began to glow. Europe 'put on a white surplice', the bishops, returning to an earlier role, urged peace on the feudal lords, propounding the idea of a truce of God; in Burgundy and at Le Puy, the clergy in 990 were demanding the cessation of senseless marauding,

and the movement soon spread to Picardy and north Italy. All these were still faint signs of the stirring of the Christian conscience. For all that, there was a long way to go; for the chroniclers tell us resignedly of wars, calamities and disorders between 970 and 1040.

The disorder in France

The West was still in a state of disorder. Lothar, the Carolingian, was a shrewd prince, but too ambitious, so that his reign was passed in bickering with the Emperor, in a succession of fruitless forays on Aix, Laon, Verdun, and Paris. Thanks largely to Adalbert, Archbishop of Rheims, and Gerbert, the future Pope Silvester II, Hugh Capet was elected king, on the sudden death of Louis V in May 987. Thus, by a stroke of fortune which Hugh Capet took advantage of, the last descendants of Pepin of Heristal disappeared, victims not so much of the growing feudalism as of their lack of heirs.

Hugh had few assets: astuteness, twenty bishops appointed by himself, and a few fortified positions, such as Orleans and Laon. A ridiculous power, judged by its dispersion and the insecurity of the roads even around Paris; but he had a hold on a number of good trade routes through some of the richest and most highly populated land in Europe. Establishing his son, Robert the Pious, as his heir was in itself an accomplishment (996) when election was the normal rule. Robert had Burgundy for a while, but was unable to hold it, his suzerainty becoming a mere form. For a while the French kingdom vegetated ingloriously. But amid the storms of the obscure reign of Henry I, the latter did at least make some lasting alliances, so that, at the coronation of his son Philip I in 1059, the Dukes of Aquitaine and Burgundy, and the Counts of Flanders and Anjou did homage — a good omen. A more doubtful omen was the absence of the Duke of Normandy.

It was a happy period for the rapacious barons who plundered the countryside before undertaking a showy and exaggerated penance. If he had not been such a bungler, Odo II of Blois might have changed the course of history. Holding Chartres and Blois, then Beauvais, Meaux, and Troyes he hemmed in the Capet's domains. At the same time he tried to capture Burgundy, then Lorraine, where he died in 1037.

Germany in difficulties

It might have been supposed that Otto I had saved Germany from the fragmentation caused by feudalism, but is seems doubtful that he had done so when we take stock of the situation on the death of Otto III. Henry II was patient, jovial, peacefully inclined, and more preoccupied with councils than the Polish war. Boleslav the Great drove him back to the Elbe and the position of the Saxon seemed compromised, as it was in the West when the Count of Flanders seized the mouths of the Scheldt. Only the death of Odo II of Blois saved Lorraine for the Empire. Another setback was suffered in the kingdom of Arles, where Henry could not make the unruly barons submit to him.

The power of the Emperor had no territorial basis. Superior to the dukes, he was not one of them, and heredity infiltrated again into the fiefs, which began to break up. Conrad II was a brutal, ignorant soldier, but he had

Bas-relief showing the Christian symbols of the fish and a cross. *Archives Photographiques, Paris*

sense enough to see the danger. In 1024 he began to undermine the power of the bishops and the feudal lords, and to look after the smaller vassals, whom he encouraged to deal directly with him. But with that, Germany began to lose the advantage of a firm social structure.

Mediterranean unrest

The Christian countries of the Mediterranean were also beginning to show a promising spirit. In Spain it took the form of a military counter-offensive. Reacting to the Moslem provincial kings, Sancho III of Navarre (994-1035) enlarged his country by the addition of Aragon and Castile. After him, the country was divided again between Ramiro of Aragon and Ferdinand of Castile and Leon, but the important factor is that in 1027 the Gascon Sancho William and the Aquitanian William V lent troops to the Spaniards, the first move in what was to be the Christian reconquest.

In Italy a double movement was active. The people fretted under the German occupation, often becoming violent and assaulting the soldiers. Only brutal reprisals prevented general revolt. Yet the idea of a kingdom of Italy was revived. The towns in particular were roused: Cremona, Pavia, Brescia, Venice, towns which Conrad favoured by opposing the bishops. The burghers grew bolder: in 1017 one of them, at Bari, enlisted Norman marauders and defied the Greeks.

When Conrad died in 1039 his successor, Henry III, managed with difficulty to assert his authority. He deposed three Popes and appointed a fourth, a German, who crowned him in 1046. But Italy was dissatisfied and already bands of Normans were in Campania.

The end of the Macedonian dynasty

In the East a zone of weakness developed. On Basil II's death there was an immediate rift between the army and the civilian authorities. The Church kept closely in touch with the palace; and in July 1054, the patriarch Michael Cerularius burnt papal bulls and sent away the Pope's envoys. Thenceforth there were two Christian Churches. On their side, the Emperors reinforced their civil power, and administrators were trained in a school of law. Successful generals were kept in their place. But there was no power to quell a rising of the army, and a succession of feeble emperors was an encouragement. Constantine VIII, a drinker and an eccentric, did not last long; he was followed by his daughter Zoë, or rather by her lovers, Michael V, an epileptic whom she had strangled, and the amiable Constantine IX (Monomachus), a handsome cavalier. Naturally there were constant military plots made by discontented generals. In 1056 one of them, Isaac Comnenus, stirred up the people and had himself proclaimed Emperor. The army had now turned on Constantinople the forces which for the last century the Macedonians had been so careful to keep directed towards the frontiers.

With Christendom thus weakened in the East, the West had to help when a graver danger threatened. Slav and Baltic trade was advancing, new forces were rising in Spain and Italy, French and German feudalism was ready to reconquer the Mediterranean, which had been virtually lost for several centuries.

CHAPTER EIGHTEEN

THE BEGINNING OF EUROPE'S EXPANSION

A.D. 1050-1200

Detail of two kings from the tympanum showing the Apocalypse,
at Moissac, a twelfth-century example of Romanesque art.

CHRISTENDOM

THE RE-AWAKENING OF ROME

The revival of faith

Ever since 950 Europe had been gradually awakening. Little by little the Church reassumed its mission. At Le Puy in 990 the bishops suggested the idea of a 'Truce of God'. Moved by faith or self-interest, kings and feudal lords in France and north Italy rallied to it, and those of Germany followed later. With that started the long struggle for reform pursued and revived at each episcopal vacancy. Only when Rome passed into the hands of the Lorrainers in 1049, however, could much headway be made. In 1073 Hildebrand became Pope Gregory VII and henceforth reform was imposed by Rome.

Hitherto it had gone little further than the inculcation of purity. The monks groped for some new expression of their need for physical activity and the mortification of the flesh. There resulted St Bruno and his Carthusians (1084), St Robert and his Cistercians (1098), opening sanctuaries in which the sons of kings and labourers could meet in peace. From Clairvaux St Bernard appeared, lecturing Christendom, of which he was often the inspiration, and offering the assuaging cult of the Virgin Mary.

New churches were built everywhere and there was an expansion of building begun in Carolingian days: barrel vaults, towered porches and Lombard decoration had their origin at Germigny, Aix, Ravenna, and even Cordova. But the revival of faith among the monks turned architectural activity towards the monasteries themselves. The result was collective, anonymous, and pious. Architecture became the art medium of the Middle Ages, as painting was the medium of the Italian Renaissance. All along the pilgrim roads, from the Rhine to Santiago de Compostela, from Burgundy to Monte Gargano, the churches imitated one another. The first examples, those built about 1000, showed Moslem and Byzantine influence. But in the course of the next century the style of the West, Romanesque, asserted itself. The heavy, dark, eleventh-century churches no longer sufficed to house growing congregations. They needed side-aisles, ambulatories, and chapels for their relics. Naves became higher, lighter, flanked by buttresses, pierced by larger and larger bays. If the general lines were the same, each province added original features: the many-coloured volcanic stone of the Auvergne, the round tiles of Burgundy and Poitiers, the curiously Byzantine cupolas of the Perigord, the triumphal façades of Provence, the arcades and colonnettes of Tuscany, and the Carolingian tradition of the Rhineland. The human figure appeared everywhere, on the capitals and in the stained-glass windows of the nave, on the spandrels of the doors and colonnades. Still stiff and awkward, the innumerable figures of bishops, knights, and peasants mark the birth of Romanesque.

The awakening of the countryside

The slackening of feudal wars and the reorganisation of the fiefs are probably among the chief causes of two centuries of social change. For the new men, new land and new villages were required. Reclamation, drainage

Figures of the damned from the tympanum showing the Last Judgment at Autun cathedral. In the twelfth century human figures began to appear in church architecture and were a characteristic of the newly born Romanesque style. *Marburg*

and deforestation began early in the eleventh century in Normandy, Burgundy, and Lombardy, and dykes were built in Flanders. Soon new technical advances were to be seen: more efficient harness, metal ploughshares, and the shoeing of horses, all necessary to further the work on the rough new soil. The horizon of the village broadened with the conquest of the land and famine became more infrequent as the dark edge of the forest receded.

The peasants benefited from the decline of the predatory barons. Communities hitherto isolated could meet and help each other. No influence was more powerful than this in the forging of Christian unity; no movement was more widespread in Europe during all the centuries between the Neolithic and the machine ages.

The awakening of commerce

It is difficult to say whether commercial development was the cause or the consequence of the increased prosperity of the country. The Baltic and the Mediterranean were the two poles for trade.

From the island of Gotland, merchants journeyed to Novgorod and Kiev; they shipped wood and fish to London and Bruges, then at Rouen loaded another cargo of corn and cloth. In the south, Venice had since 992 maintained relations with Alexandria, Palermo, Kairwan, and Damascus, thereby supplanting Amalfi and Gaeta. Outward bound with German metals or Italian fustian, her ships returned with silk and cotton, sugar and spices. Between 1015 and 1030 Pisa, Lucca, and Genoa began trading, and then Barcelona, Marseilles, and Narbonne. Whether they borrowed capital or pooled their savings, the merchants banded together in guilds or brotherhoods. The early merchants had been adventurers: now they had be-

Troubadours, such as those which entertained the courts of Aquitaine. Miniatures of the eleventh century. *Larousse*

As from the twelfth century, entertainment in feudal courts became more refined and troubadours took the place of common minstrels. In northern France and Germany *trouvères*, lyric poets of the *langue d'oil*, carried on the tradition. Thirteenth-century Heidelberg manuscript. *Larousse*

Romanesque Europe

◎	Italian trading cities
●	Italian counting houses
▶	Italian trading routes
▣	Northern trading centres
■	Northern counting houses
▪▪▪▶	Northern trading routes
† Cluny	Main pilgrimages
	Zones of greatest activity
	Greek Empire in 950
	Greek domination in 1030
	Danish Empire in 1030
	Danish domination in 1030
	Western Empire in 1030

come carriers, dealers, shipowners. So great were the profits made on eastern trade, particularly in Italy, that soon bankers and money-changers were jostling with drapers and goldsmiths. This growing class of burghers brought back to Christian lands the power that had been so long neglected, the power of money.

The awakening of the towns

The country folk needed local markets, and the merchants needed safe stopping-places on their journeys: hence the development of the towns. Along the rivers and the pilgrims' roads, a string of towns grew up, where inns accommodated travelling merchants, and fairs were held. Such were Ghent, Lille, Ypres, Bar-sur-Aube, Provins, Verdun and Ratisbon. Within their walls lived freed slaves and ruined nobles. Here was born the power of the bourgeoisie.

The feudal world was worried. To defend themselves the burghers proclaimed their freedom and bound themselves by oath to defend it. The same thing was happening everywhere: in Venice in 1032, Milan in 1067, Lucca in 1068; then the Lombard towns and Genoa; a little later Marseilles (1128) and Aquitaine. In the north it was Le Mans in 1069, Cambrai in 1077, St Quentin, and all the area between the Seine and the Meuse. Thuringia, Saxony and Bavaria followed somewhat later at the end of the twelfth century.

A slow displacement of forces took place: where the revival of commerce and the rise of the towns occurred, and where the new agriculture was able to feed a larger population, the pulse of Christendom quickened. This was often at the expense of the older, inland regions, for the first importance now passed to the coasts, Lombard or Ligurian, the plains of Aquitaine and the Elbe, the shores of the Channel and the banks of the Rhine.

THE VITAL CENTRES

Groping for Italian unity

Though they had already appeared in the Mediterranean, the Normans had never attempted to settle there. After the death of Knut, however, they were driven to expand, and by 1009 there were bands of Normans in Italy acting as mercenaries. In 1030, their leader was garrisoned in the fortress of Aversa. From there he surprised and took Gaeta, and by 1042 another chief had occupied Apulia. In 1053 Robert Guiscard, an adventurer, co-ordinated these sporadic efforts. He defeated the Greeks, took Calabria, then Brindisi and Taranto; in 1071 he took Bari and in five years eliminated Greek rule from southern Italy. Not content with that, his son Bohemond attacked Epirus and even reached Thessaly, only the lack of money forcing him to withdraw.

The Papacy, in conflict with the German Emperor, decided it might be useful to employ the new and unexpected power that had risen in the Mediterranean. In 1059 Nicholas II ceased to think of Robert as a brigand and began calling him his 'vassal'. Before long, the next Pope, Gregory VII, had engaged his services.

The idea of uniting Italy seems to have escaped the Papacy, but it continued to haunt the minds of some Italians. Like the reform of the Church, it was in Lorraine

that the idea of reconstituting the dominions of Lothar I originated. Godfrey the Bearded, Duke of Upper Lorraine and leader of the Rhineland's opposition to the Emperor, acquired for himself and his children a strange double principality by his marriage in 1054 to the widow of the margrave of Tuscany. It might have been the nucleus of an Italian power, but he was dispossessed of his heritage by the Emperor on the death of his daughter-in-law, Mathilda, in 1115.

The development of the towns, too, was adverse to the cause of unity. The Lombard towns joined in a federation in 1092, under the leadership of Milan, but that was only to fend off a threat from Germany. Italy was to remain the battlefield of Popes and Emperors, the coveted land of the French and the Germans, and was destined to be divided. As she was in the ninth century, so she was to remain for a thousand years.

Venice, Genoa and Pisa

It was the division of Italy that allowed the rise of the commercial republics. The feeble part played by Venice, Genoa, and Pisa in the internal rivalries of Italy is striking. They were like neutral zones, and their neutrality was the basis of their strength, their wealth and their influence.

It was they who made Italy an essential part of eleventh and twelfth century Europe. Merchants from all over the continent came to them for the products of the East. The privileges they obtained from the Holy Land from 1100, and from Constantinople between 1126 and 1142, put the Mediterranean in their hands. Greek ships no longer dominated it. In 1122 and 1148 Venice acquired bases in Corfu and the Cyclades to enable her to enforce her rights.

The troubadours of Aquitaine

Between Nîmes and Leon, between Poitiers and Barcelona, a new world was being born, of native genius, long stifled by Rome and the barbarians. Early in the twelfth century, the rise of the towns had already begun. Marseilles, St Gilles, Montpellier, and Narbonne turned towards the East, Bordeaux and Bayonne towards England. In the valleys were a host of landless seigneurs dreaming of adventures and expeditions overseas. But the Aquitaine of Poitiers and Toulouse was above all a land of luxurious, refined courts, in constant festivity, full of *joie de vivre*, courts where religion was discussed and where lyric poetry had made a place for woman denied her elsewhere. The melodious accents of the *langue d'oc*, the passion of the south — playful or violent, lyrical or erotic — animated the troubadours' poems celebrating war, love, or nature. In these courts, lyric poetry shone above all else. One of the first troubadours was the Duke of Aquitaine, William IX, himself. The Truce of God, born in these regions, brought a peace unknown in the north; for Aquitaine was divided from the French kingdom till the dawn of the thirteenth century.

The awakening of Spain

Pulses were also throbbing beyond the Pyrenees. Spain was awakening. Moslem culture might still be dominant

in art and thought, but from the time the Cluniacs and other pilgrims had reached Santiago the death-knell of Mohammedan Spain had sounded, and the reconquest of the lost territory was regarded as a crusade, a national crusade, inspired by religion and patriotism.

And this was the opportunity the seigneurs of Aquitaine had been waiting for. Some even came from Provence and Burgundy. In 1031 the last caliph had disappeared in general anarchy. Those Moslems of any vigour that were left withdrew to Seville, still preoccupied with their trade with the Maghrib. Thus the road was open for the Christians, who were being urged on by the enlightened Papacy. In 1073 Guy Godfrey, Duke of Aquitaine, took the field himself. Later it was the Duke of Burgundy. Then Alfonso VI of Castile crossed the Douro and the Tagus and in 1085 entered Toledo, the old capital. Spain's history as a nation had begun.

The heritage of Knut

The Flanders of Baldwin V, fully occupied with drainage operations and urban development, was in a position to inherit only one part, an important economic part, of Knut's legacy. From 1060 Bruges was the focal point of northern trade; at the same time Ypres became a market and Lille began to flourish.

In England Knut was succeeded by two barbarous and incompetent sons, and the power behind the throne became the Danish earl, Godwin, who had Alfred, the elder son of the Anglo-Saxon King Aethelred by his second marriage to Emma of Normandy, blinded and sent to a monastery, where he died. But Edward, his brother, now the representative of the House of Cerdic, survived to rule under the influence sometimes of Godwin, sometimes of the Normans. On Edward's death in 1066 Harold

The cupola of the twelfth-century Romanesque cathedral at Zamora, Castile. Zamora was of great strategic importance in the early years of the Reconquest and was the subject of numerous disputes. *Yan*

Part of the Alcazar, Seville's chief monument of Arab civilisation. This palace was begun under the Almohades in 1181 and contains fine work comparable with that of the Alhambra at Granada. Spanish medieval architecture bears strong Moorish influence even when it was not in fact the work of Arabs; in particular the churches were often rebuilt under successive rulers and faiths and have something of all their styles.

302

Godwinsson proclaimed himself king, a usurpation that seemed justified by his crushing victory over the Danish king, Harald Hardrada, an emulator of Knut, who was killed in the battle. Harold had scotched Scandinavian hopes in England. The country was free — for nineteen days.

William the Conqueror

At a time when the Normans in the south were active in the Mediterranean, those in France were equally vigorous. Their rich soil had great economic potentialities, and since 911 the power of the Dukes of Normandy had grown continually. The fighting qualities of the Normans could not be worked off against their own chiefs, nor were they threatened by their neighbours, sheltered as they were behind the wooded hills of Maine and the rivers of the Vexin. The Church was kind to the Dukes and even generous. Across the Channel, compact groups of Normans were to be found in the English court and among the clergy. One of these groups was at Canterbury; moreover, Edward the Confessor was a cousin of Robert the Devil and had lived for some time at Rouen. Among the Normans it was considered possible that their duke might inherit England.

Robert's natural son, William, Duke of Normandy, was tough and irascible, religious, and moral in his private life to a degree rare in that age. He was at the same time energetic and thoughtful. He was one of the most remarkable rulers of the Middle Ages. He had, moreover, induced Harold Godwinsson to renounce any claim to the English throne, and rendered his oath the more sacred by a trick, for he had concealed beneath the altar on which Harold had taken the oath a relic said to have been the bones of St Edmund. Further, Harold had become, in feudal parlance, his 'man'.

William thus had some moral claim to the English throne: the Church supported him, as did Flanders; King Philip I of France was still a boy; and William, with pious pretexts and blessed by the Pope, landed at Hastings in 1066 and defeated Harold. He was crowned in London on Christmas day.

England had been drifting into regional independence and gravitating towards the Baltic; William turned her towards Flanders and France, an act of cardinal importance in European history. In distributing land, he established his barons and, with them, Continental customs and laws throughout the country. He stopped short of allowing big fiefs that could became powerful; the holding of land was registered in the Domesday Book. He kept the Church in hand. From his son, Henry I, dates the establishment of the Royal Exchequer, which put England in advance of other European countries.

All this was not without a struggle. Till 1072 Saxon resistance in the north, and after that rapacious barons jeopardised William's achievements. He was followed by his sons, William Rufus and Henry I (1106-1135), who managed to retain their heritage. It seemed that this new power across the Channel might one day master France.

The house of Capet

Nominally France was the suzerain, but William the Conqueror had no intention of being a vassal. The portly

Seal depicting Edward the Confessor.

St Thomas Becket, successively Chancellor and Archbishop of Canterbury under Henry II, who was assassinated in his own cathedral in 1170.

303

William the Conqueror at Hastings receiving a messenger from Harold. Part of the Bayeux tapestry, which shows the sequence of events in the conquest of England in 1066. *Mansell*

Henricus quartus henrici imperatoris filius admodū puer patri succedens Lxxxvij gusto & annis. L. regnare cępit loco ab au regnauit

Henry IV, German Emperor (1056-1106). *Historisches Bildarchiv Handke*

Thomas Becket, with Henry II of England and Louis VII of France. Becket spent the years of his exile (1164-70) at Pontigny and Sens under the protection of Louis and the Pope (at that time himself exiled in northern France).

Philip I was a narrow-minded man, with the cunning of a peasant anxious to add a little to his land. Helped by Anjou, he occupied the French Vexin (1077). The two kingdoms were now contiguous, but William died in 1087 before trouble had broken out. Philip occupied a few forts, bought various estates, and still put a little money by. When he died in 1108 the royal domains reached to Bourges.

Louis VI, the Fat, had only to follow suit. Against Henry I he played his usual cards — the Counts of Anjou and Flanders, and various tractable bishops. In 1125 there was an alarm: Henry had appealed to his son-in-law the Emperor. When Louis VI raised the urban militias the Emperor withdrew. But the French king's most important work was to set his own domain in order, so as to be master in his own house. His reign ended with what seemed a happy alliance: his son, Louis VII, married Eleanor, heir to Aquitaine. Southern France seemed to be opening its doors to the house of Capet.

Henry Plantagenet

On the death of Henry I, England fell into political confusion. Louis VII had only to leave his ally, the Count of Anjou, to conquer Normandy. Then Louis left for the Holy Land, leaving his kingdom in the hands of the ecclesiastic Suger (1147). Suddenly there was a dramatic development. Henry Plantagenet, heir to Anjou and Normandy (1151), acquired Aquitaine by marrying Eleanor, Louis's wife, divorced by him in 1152. Henry's mother, Matilda, had vainly claimed the throne of England throughout Stephen's reign (1135-54). But on Stephen's death in 1154 Henry ascended the throne of England.

At twenty-five, Henry Plantagenet, now Henry II, was an athletic, indefatigable young man, given to uncontrollable fits of rage, despite a warm heart. He was not primarily a man of war, but an administrator, even a jurist. An Angevin who wished to end his days on the banks of the Loire, and who governed exclusively through men of continental outlook, he was unaware of the commercial or maritime role that England could have played. With his absolute authority and the ritual of his court, he could only be compared to the Pope, and in this he inevitably offended the Church. He thought it a shrewd move to make his friend Thomas Becket Archbishop of Canterbury, and he did so in 1162; but Becket later became a fanatical opponent. There followed rupture, an exile, a pardon, and in 1170 Becket's assassination in his cathedral.

Master of Ireland, for a time of Wales, of Toulouse, and of Brittany, Henry intervened in the Mediterranean, concluding alliances with Castile, Savoy, and Sicily. He dealt with the Emperor as with an equal, and his prestige was such that he was able to procure the election of the only Englishman ever to be made Pope, Nicholas Breakspear (Hadrian IV). Henry was, above all, a great realist and administrator. He extended the traditional Anglo-Saxon principle of the 'King's Peace' to cover the whole land, not merely the immediate presence or property of the king. He extended also the rights of the royal law-courts to have jurisdiction over appeals from baronial courts and over questions of land tenure in dispute. Although he did not compel men to appeal to a novel royal authority, he offered them better justice. Further, he used

The aftermath of Canossa (1077): this contemporary miniature shows it to have been far from the final triumph of Gregory VII (Hildebrand) over the German Emperor Henry IV. Henry expelled Gregory, replacing him by Guibert, Archbishop of Ravenna, who became the anti-pope Clement III. Gregory died in exile in 1085; the dispute continued until the Concordat of Worms (1122).

juries to help in deciding cases brought before the royal courts, a process which began to supersede the ancient custom of trial by battle or ordeal, and appointed professional judges, whose functions were later differentiated in the King's Bench and the Court of Common Pleas. He extended the royal authority by the use of writs. Thus Henry II's reign saw the foundation of the great structure of English Common Law which was to be decisive for the future of the English-speaking peoples. It was this achievement, and the breadth of Henry II's political outlook that made him outstanding in north-west Europe.

But behind all the rivalries of kings and kingdoms there was an underlying thread of unity. If Romanesque was the art of Christendom, the legendary epics were the expression of north-western Europe. From all directions ancient stories were handed down: those of the Vikings related in the Icelandic sagas, those of the Saxons in stirring poems like the ninth-century *Beowulf*, those of the Bavarians in the *Nibelungenlied*, of the Rhinelanders in *Gudrun*, epics which kept alive the exploits of the barbarians of former days. There were the *chansons de geste*. Troubadours wandered from castle to castle, miming and declaiming their lays to assembled nobles, who might often recognise themselves in the tales. That the lays often made fun of kings — even Charlemagne — is a testimony to the growing strength of feudalism.

THE STRUGGLE FOR PRIMACY

German difficulties

By the middle of the eleventh century, Germany had lost the cohesion that had made it superior. The Emperor had held his position only by dismembering the fiefs and so fragmenting royal power; with his authority gradually undermined, he let power fall into the hands of the strongest. At the end of each reign, hereditary succession was imperilled. On the death of Henry III the succession fell to a minor, on the death of Henry IV there was civil war (1106), and on that of Henry V (1125) a series of usurpations.

Regional hostilities, too, revived. Henry IV was embroiled in a bitter struggle with the Saxons. This was a real civil war (with the southern nobility ranged against the peasantry of the north) aggravated by the rivalry between the Welfs of Bavaria and the Hohenstaufens of Swabia (1072-1075). The Rhineland resisted imperial authority; one of the Godfreys of Lorraine hacked a way for himself across Italy; Robert of Flanders advanced beyond the Scheldt; forts sprang up blocking passage along the Rhine; all Henry V's forces were deployed against them, then Frederick I's. If this rich and populous region succeeded in breaking away from Germany, the trade reviving along the Rhine would be lost to the Empire, passing to Flanders, Friesland, or England.

Frederick Barbarossa between his two eldest sons: the future emperor Henry VI, and Frederick, Duke of Swabia. After ending his struggle against the Papacy by the Peace of Venice (1177) and restoring order in his domains, he set off on the Third Crusade in 1189 but was accidentally drowned in Cilicia. *Larousse*

A twelfth-century fresco at Salzburg. *Boudot-Lamotte*

Popes and Emperors

The reviving faith called for a reviving Papacy. In 1059 Nicholas II made the first move for reform by announcing the freedom of pontifical elections. The German clergy was hesitant: were they to go on obeying their Emperor, Henry IV, excommunicated by the fierce Hildebrand, who in 1073 had been swept into papal office by the crowd of Rome? He was an ardent and domineering mystic, this Gregory VII, completely devoted to the ideal of reform. He was insistent that the temporal should be ruled by the spiritual, and there was soon a rupture between him and the Emperor, who claimed the right of investiture. Each deposed the other; consciences were disturbed, loyalties divided. In the end, feeling was against Henry; abandoned, he could only sue for peace. For three days in 1077 he stood penitent and barefoot before the castle of Canossa until the Pope relented and pardoned him absolutely.

It was a mistake to do so, for Henry soon renewed the conflict. Excommunicated again, he had an anti-pope elected, marched on Rome, and entered it in 1083. Gregory fled to Salerno, now in the hands of his allies, the Normans. He died there in May 1085. But it was impossible to halt the advance of the revitalised Church. In 1088 Urban II became Pope, a man of action and breadth of outlook who rallied the Normans, armed the Lombard towns, and spoke of an Italian kingdom. At Piacenza he reaffirmed the primacy of the Church. At Rome he pursued its reform. At Clermont in 1095 he preached the First Crusade. Christendom was united in taking up the

cry, and Henry IV, fleeing before his rebel son, died in August 1106. Henry V was as sound a ruler as his father, but a certain lassitude set in. Finally at Worms in 1122 French clergy proposed a compromise on the vexed question of investiture: the Emperor was to preserve feudal suzerainty over benefices but was not to confer the ring and crozier. The Church was now free of secular tutelage.

Frederick Barbarossa

But the struggle for primacy was not finally settled. Neither the Papacy nor Frederick Hohenstaufen, King of Germany in 1152, had any intention of yielding. Mature for his years, Frederick Barbarossa was a red-bearded man, a graceful speaker, a determined fighter, dominating, ambitious, a good leader of men. Among monarchs, he regarded only Henry Plantagenet as his equal. Naturally he reopened the quarrel, dashed to Rome, and forced the Pope to crown him (1155). Then, town by town, he occupied Lombardy. Resistant Milan was razed (1162); when Alexander III protested, Frederick I appointed a new Pope. Nothing daunted him. Though the King of France gave asylum to the fleeing Pope, Henry Plantagenet was conciliatory. But Italy, driven to despair, revolted. Frederick, who was in Rome with an army riddled with the plague, withdrew northwards. At Legnano, in 1176, he was crushed by the Lombard militia and obliged to fly the Tyrol. To avoid the worst, he went to Venice and held the Pope's stirrup (1177): this humiliation, exactly a century after Canossa, is a presage of the authority of the Pope over Christian Europe.

Moslem knights. Like their Christian adversaries, they were bent on supporting their faith by the sword. Christian miniature of the eleventh century and Arab miniature of the thirteenth century.

THE DUEL BETWEEN CHRISTENDOM AND ISLAM

THE MOSLEM ATTACK

Lethargy of Islam

Since the year 1000 the influence of Moslem culture had contributed to the development of Romanesque, and now, in the eleventh century, it seemed in a position to teach the Christians philosophy too. The Persians, in translating Greek works and commenting on them, had gradually cleared a ground on which their faith and their reason could meet. Avicenna (980-1036), and his contemporary, Biruni, opened the field for the commentators on Aristotle. In Spain Averroes (1126-98) exerted a lasting influence on Christian dialectic.

But, though reaching these intellectual heights, Islam seemed unable to muster material strength. Egypt was one day to rule Mesopotamia and the Holy Places, but for the moment the Fatimids were beset with sedition and economic difficulties. Since Basil II, Hellenic influence had reached Cairo, where the vizir Badr al-jamali used Greek engineers and sailors in peaceful employments. Left to itself, the Maghrib was in a state of anarchy. The Fatimids, unable to hold out there any longer, left these western districts to savage Nubian tribes who ruthlessly destroyed all settled life in Tunisia, driving the Berbers back into the mountains. This catastrophe permanently broke the links between the two parts of Islam, and for a long time made Africa a land of confusion. The Christians profited, advancing everywhere: in Sardinia (1022), Corsica (1090), Toledo (1085), and especially in Sicily, where Robert Guiscard and his Normans took Messina in 1061 and Palermo in 1072.

The rise of the Turks

The Turkish tribes to the north of Lake Balkhash at the time of the Kirghiz migrations had remained pagan. Searching for new territory, some of them, the Kipchaks (also called Kumanians or Polovtzi) moved towards the Ukraine in 1035. Their vanguard crossed the Danube in 1065, but was thrown back northward.

On the other hand, between the Caspian and the Pamirs, the Persian Samanids, occupying Bokhara since the end of the ninth century, gradually allowed Turks converted to Islam to hold positions of power. The infiltration was assisted by the emirs of Kashgar, who were also Turks. About 970, a Turkish slave raised a rebellion at Ghaznah, in central Afghanistan. In 999 his son Mahmud brought the Samanid dynasty to an end, founding the Ghaznawid one that succeeded it. He advanced to within 130 miles of Baghdad; then, with his flank guarded by the mountains, he turned south-east, making for the

307

St George and the dragon. Fresco from Goreme, Turkey, a relic of the passing Crusaders. *A. Cash*

Kabul passes and India. It seems probable that he had already come to an understanding with the Chinese before embarking on the venture. Since the time of Harun, Islam had made no move beyond the Indus; the advance of the Ghaznawids was therefore an event of the utmost importance. Two centuries of peace in India promised a tempting booty. Descending the Hindu Kush, the Turks took Peshawar, crossed the Indus (1005), took Lahore (1010), and reached the Ganges. Though soon debilitated by their conquest, they imposed their faith permanently.

The Turkish advance

The Turks of the Seljuk tribe had, like others, served the Samanids, and they now served the Ghaznawids. Their chief Tughril Beg lay in ambush by Nishapur, and, surprising the Ghaznawid Masud, crushed him and took possession of the whole Persian plateau (1038-40). Then, rallying all the Turks eager for pillage, Tughril marched west, showing no mercy. The Persian world was at this time so decadent that it saw in him a restorer of order. For his part, Tughril Beg was delighted with Ispahan and stayed; he took over the Persian administrative framework. In 1055 he entered Baghdad. Given the title of Sultan and King of Kings by the Caliph, Tughril, an orthodox Sunnite by faith, seemed the legitimate heir of the Arabs. Thus a new warlike people arose, animated by the faith they had adopted to take the place of decadent states, like Persia, or states that were being Hellenised, like Egypt.

Since the tenth century, Constantinople had kept a firm hold on the Syrian coast and Anatolia. Neither Isaac

Comnenus nor Constantine Ducas were weaklings, but they were peacefully inclined and ready to economise on defences. Tughril Beg ravaged Armenia and reduced some Greek fortified positions, but the *basileus* did not take action. Tughril's successor, Alp Arslan (1063-72), turned eastward, but raids on the Byzantine Empire became more frequent than ever. In the end the Emperor, Romanus Diogenes, marched into Armenia, only to be heavily defeated near Manzikert in 1071.

Though Alp Arslan was killed soon after, this Byzantine disaster was of crucial importance. The garrisons in Syria were disheartened, and the Turks took Antioch, Damascus, and Jerusalem. The Fatimids hastily fortified the Nile delta. Seljuk *fedaïs* ran wild over Asia Minor and even in Nicaea; pirates from Smyrna operated in the Dardanelles. At the same time the Pechenegs advanced to Adrianople. With the old Asian possessions lost, the Danube forced, and Greece ravaged by the Normans, Alexis Comnenus was beaten on all sides, and the Greeks had only one direction in which to turn for help — the West.

The Moorish advance

But the West was under attack too. In southern Senegal, fanatical elements from south Morocco had by 1030 laid the foundation of a new empire, that of the Almoravides or Murabtis (hermits). They first turned southward, spreading Islam among the Negroes. With Berber help they overthrew the Ghana empire, the Berbers having always had an envious eye on the salt-mines of Ankar. In 1054 Aoudaghost was taken; from 1061 to 1076 Yusef occupied the Sahel, which he converted to Islam. Although, after the eleventh century, the Almoravides allowed various states to re-establish themselves on the ruins of the Soninké empire, their religion spread widely: about 1070 to the princes of the Mandingo on the upper Niger, about 1080 to the Songhoi at Gao, about 1086 to the Kanem north of Lake Chad. The Negro Hausas seem to have been the only people to resist the new faith.

Between 1059 and 1082 Yusef conquered Morocco, Oran, and Algiers. On hearing of the fall of Toledo, he sailed for Algeciras, and in 1086, forced the Christians to fall back at Zallaka. The Castile forces asked for help, and troops came quickly but in vain from Limousin and Provence. The Christians tried to support the local 'kings', and Rodrigo Diaz was for five years master of Valencia. Then Ali, Yusef's successor, occupied Seville, Valencia, Saragossa (1102-11), and advanced as far as Barcelona.

After an interval of two centuries, the Christians had begun to think themselves delivered of the Moslem threat. And now Turks and Moors were suddenly threatening both the Bosphorus and Aquitaine, as in the eighth century.

THE CHRISTIANS HIT BACK

The First Crusade

Arab fanaticism had been inspiring thoughts of revenge among the Christians ever since Carolingian times. The Saracens, on the other hand, thought of the Levantine markets. But if the Byzantines could maintain armies

Pope Urban II presiding over the Council of Clermont (1095) where he roused the enthusiasm of all western Europe for the First Crusade. Urban's decisive leadership rallied to his cause knights and peasants alike. *Mansell*

within easy reach, how could the West send troops so far afield, even if the expansion of the population was already pushing in that direction? Until the year 1090, the Papacy had merely encouraged private ventures. The Flemish fighters of the Danube, the Norman adventurers in southern Syria, and the warriors in Spain, all blessed by the Pope, went on what might be called pre-crusades.

Tension increased, pilgrimages to the Holy Places were forbidden by the Turks, and all returning from the East spoke of delivering the Holy Sepulchre. There were moreover many knights fallen on evil days ready to welcome any opportunity of going off to fight for a noble cause. Many, in fact, had already 'rehearsed' their crusade in Spain. All that was needed was leadership to co-ordinate these factors. It came from Urban II.

At Clermont in 1095, the Pope's eloquence aroused religious enthusiasm, and rallied all hesitant spirits. Following it up, he toured Aquitaine and Provence with the Bishop of Le Puy and the Count of Toulouse, a veteran of Spain. A first-class organiser, Urban II had already informed himself of the situation in the East and had made contact with the Greeks. His decisiveness united European effort in a way that was quite unprecedented.

The cross sewn on the crusader's clothes was a fine recruiting emblem, and it served better than any oath to bind into some sort of unity the enormous armies which were mustered.

In the Rhineland simple priests calling on the people to serve the will of God, enrolled enormous, ill-organised bands of soldiers and peasants who were ready to resort to pillage. Even in the regions Urban did not visit, the barons raised large contingents. Between the Seine and the Meuse a considerable force was raised under the Duke of Normandy and the Count of Flanders, another

between the Meuse and the Rhine under the Duke of Upper Lorraine, Godfrey de Bouillon. Another group of Normans under Bohemond, son of Robert Guiscard, joined the 'official' army under Raymond of Toulouse. The kings, more cautious, stayed at home.

The West marches East

Either by luck or calculation, the moment was favourable. After twenty years of reverses, Greek fortune, under Alexius Comnenus, was improving. The *basileus* was educated, diplomatic, cautious in his approach, judicious, and for that reason judged by the Latins to be dissimulating and lacking in conviction. In 1091 he had the Pechenegs cornered by the Maritza, and wiped them out completely. Moreover, the Seljuk danger seemed to have diminished, for the sultans were unable to handle their own unruly bands. Malik Shah, for instance, spent his whole reign trying to curb them. With his death, disintegration was accelerated: local emirs or atabegs set up independent rules in Armenia, Syria, and Anatolia; round them the Turks massed, and in parts of Asia Minor they turned the old Greek agricultural estates into Asiatic pastures. Taking advantage of Turkish enfeeblement, the Fatimids had by 1098 taken Jerusalem and southern Syria. By 1096 the Byzantines had recovered the territory in the neighbourhood of the Bosphorus. In this situation, the arrival of the Crusaders was no longer such a godsend to the Greeks and their unexpected arrival was coldly met by Alexius. Apart from the wars of Charlemagne, this was the first time since Justinian that the two Christian worlds had come into contact. It was also the first time the barons of the West had visited the East. Disillusionment was general among the crusaders.

309

Manuel I Comnenus (1143-1180) who wished his reign to be brilliant and succeeded only in diminishing the strength of Byzantium. Though claiming to dominate all, he left Byzantium grappling with hostile Westerners and strengthened Turks.

Proud of their civilisation, the Byzantines looked down on the haughty but vulgar barons, and they laughed at their religions and their customs. Noisy, avid, unstable — were these not the Goths, the Varangians come back to life? In return the Europeans were only too ready to accuse the Greeks of cupidity, heresy, and even of treason. The penniless, ill-equipped bands of peasants would not listen to the Emperor's advice, and he allowed them to be massacred. Then in July 1096 he sought to enrol the barons as his vassals, hoping that they would recover for him the lands that had been lost in Asia. They duly did him homage, in June 1097, though the Normans resolved to break their oaths whenever it was convenient to do so. Misunderstandings thus became jealousies and duplicities.

The Victory of the Cross

The march of the crusaders encountered great hardship. Alexius soon revealed his objective — chiefly Anatolia. This apostasy was the more galling after the disillusionments suffered during the year's siege of Antioch. Indeed, but for the inertia of the Seljuks, the crusade would have been disbanded in the spring of 1099.

In July, Italian reinforcements enabled the crusaders to move down the coast and reach Jerusalem. In the religious excitement, all parties were united. In July — the month in which Urban II died — the Holy City was taken. It was necessary to occupy the town with forces that had been much reduced. Fortunately the loss of Syria put the Fatimids in a critical position and they were repulsed. The Seljuks tried a few raids, to no avail, and efforts to obtain help from Aleppo or Damascus came to nothing, because of Moslem disunity. The *basileus* was not interested, busy as he was hounding his own enemies in Asia Minor till his death in 1118. There was thus nothing to stop the 'Franks' taking possession of the littoral. This

was the task of Baldwin, who became 'king' of Jerusalem (1100-18). The support of Genoa, Venice, and Pisa were recompensed with great commercial privileges.

The recovery of Antioch, and the return of the Byzantines to Cilicia and Smyrna, returned the initiative in the East to the Christians. Similarly, the reoccupation of Sicily by the Normans (1096) and the rout of the Almoravides from Saragossa to Granada gave them the initiative in the West. Thus, within thirty years, the Christians had reoccupied positions in Spain, Sicily, and Syria that had been lost for three or four hundred years. The taking of Jerusalem cast a religious glow over the rise of Europe, a symbol of its reborn faith; Frankish settlement overseas was a tribute to its vital expansion; and the recovery of its oriental trade was the reward of economic energy.

THE RECONQUEST OF THE MEDITERRANEAN

Once again the Eastern Empire had raised its head. But during the glorious fifty years following the death of Alexius I there were unmistakable signs of decadence. Moreover, Ionia, the region that had been essential to the Empire since the ninth century, had never been completely reconquered and repopulated. Alexius tried to raise mercenaries, to redistribute land to compensate landowners driven out of Asia; but all his schemes failed for lack of money.

Between 1096 and 1204, the two Christian worlds were in permanent commercial and diplomatic contact; but, facing the West, Constantinople seemed for the first time to be losing her footing: the facilities granted to Italian merchants robbed Greek currency of its old-established supremacy as well as the Empire of her trading profits. Henceforth Constantinople tended to serve as a warehouse, and the day was not far off when the Venetians would come to conduct their business there. No doubt the luxury and splendour of the town, said to have a population of 600,000, was still glorious to Western eyes, but it also provoked envy. Moreover, on all sides the tortuous politics of the Greeks offended the West.

Manuel Comnenus

Becoming Emperor in 1143, Manuel I was a vigorous man, a good soldier but a mediocre general. In a stormy life he had mixed new Latin ideas with Greek traditions. He flaunted his mistresses, he studied medicine, started the fashion for tournaments, and in general behaved as a modern. But his disorganised, importunate actions gave an impression of aggressiveness. He spoke of restoring his authority in Syria, in Hungary, even in Italy. His fleet was seen at Taranto in 1149, at Ancona in 1151, and at Bari in 1155. He embarked on subtle negotiations with the Pope for recovering Rome, and sought to enlist the Lombards, Henry Plantagenet and, finally, the Guelfs, against Frederick I. His constant changes of front in his dealings with Venice led to a reverse, and in 1158 he abandoned Bari. In 1156 he broke with Rome; in 1171 Venice ravaged Euboea and Corfu as a reprisal for her own molested merchants. By these steps, which offended everybody, Manuel made the Latins hate Constantinople

The Krak des Chevaliers, most famous example of the strongholds of the Franks in the East. It was built to the north of the kingdom of Jerusalem in the early twelfth century by the knights of St John of Jerusalem. Crusades came and went in the East leaving few Westerners behind; but the religious orders such as the Templars and Hospitallers redressed this tendency somewhat, holding out with great tenacity. The Krak yielded to Saladin in 1188 only after a long struggle.

and increased the Greeks' contempt for them as well.

As though to flaunt before the eyes of the West what was left of its superiority, Byzantium made a final effort. Her decorative art was still unrivalled. Her sumptuous mosaics were imitated at Monte Cassino, Venice and Kiev. And the intellectual effort did not slacken: at the University, at the school of law, at the *studium generale*, scholars were at work copying, compiling, commenting on the classics. They considered themselves the direct heirs of Athens and Rome, and by that very fact perhaps renounced all further development, in contrast to the West, where minds were vigorous and enterprising, anxious to reconcile faith with reason. At Constantinople there was no search for the new. The Greek genius concealed within its radiant culture a mental sclerosis as dangerous as the petrification of the Empire.

A setback for the West in Syria

The Frankish state in Syria formed little more than a coastal fringe. In spite of the mountain forts that were built, they were exposed to constant raids from the Saracens, who still occupied many of the neighbouring heights. Moreover, apart from the kingdom of Jerusalem, none of these states was self-sufficing. Their supply of food was at the mercy of the merchant cities of Italy, which, in the last resort, had the final word in deciding on the survival or extinction of their customers. Again, the Frankish population of these states was dangerously small. Colonists more than crusaders, their princes advocated intermarriage between Europeans and the Syrians or the Armenians of Cilicia. Their policy was to keep the balance, even when this involved making an alliance with Damascus against Zangi, the atabeg of Mosul and Aleppo.

On the other hand, the Byzantines increased their hold on northern Syria. John Comnenus, son of Alexius I, reminded the Western princes of their promises: the Armenians had recognised his suzerainty in 1137, and Raymond of Antioch had pledged himself when John's death occurred. Thus weakened, the Franks let Zangi take Edessa and his son Nur-ad-Din reach the walls of Antioch (1144-46). The fiery speeches of St Bernard sent great numbers of knights to the East in the spring of 1147, among them Louis VII of France and the Emperor Conrad III. Manuel Comnenus saw them arrive with displeasure, and showed it. He even warned Nur-ad-Din of their coming. After heavy losses, the crusaders, throwing good sense to the winds, flung their armies against the allied amirate of Damascus.

And they did not even persevere. The siege of Damascus was abandoned after four days. The Second Crusade was at an end, and the two monarchs returned to Europe in 1148. When Nur-ad-Din killed Raymond of Antioch in 1149 and captured Damascus in 1154, Moslem Syria was reunited.

The success of the Greeks

At that point the Franks could do nothing but renew their alliances with the Greeks. Manuel, offering one of his nieces to the King of Jerusalem, made his entry into Antioch in 1158 and re-established the patriarchate. Lost in a crowd of Greek princes, Baldwin III of Jerusalem limped in the rear. The Emperor did not stay with him long, preferring to dispute Egypt with Nur-ad-Din. King Amaury of Jerusalem (Baldwin's brother) was won over to this audacious project, thinking it would strengthen the Frankish state. And the Fatimid regime seemed thoroughly degenerate: Armenians and Kurds scrambled for the vizirate; twice (in 1164 and 1167) the Franks occupied Cairo and exacted tribute; and a Greek fleet was stationed at Ascalon, then at Damietta. So far, the crusades had served only to advance the traditional interests of the Greeks.

The Normans in the Maghrib

At the moment when the Byzantines were regaining their authority over Egypt, the Normans established a foothold in the Maghrib. Roger II of Sicily, blessed by the Pope in 1130, and (after prolonged fighting) accepted as king by the rest of Europe, had created a strange oriental government in the midst of a mixed half-Moslem world. A rival of Manuel Comnenus, he disputed the possession of Corfu and Euboea, and even planned an abortive attack on Constantinople itself. Making use of his strategic and commercial position, he embarked on numerous overseas adventures: in 1135 his men occupied the island of Gerba, in 1145, Tenes, then Tripoli, Gabes, Sfax and, in 1154, Bone. He opened up Tunisia to the merchants of Genoa and Pisa, his allies.

Thus the Christians, having conquered the banks of the Tagus and those of the Nile, and now threatening Kairwan and Cairo, seemed about to grasp the whole of the Mediterranean.

THE END OF THE ROMAN WORLD

Folly of the Sung dynasty

Meanwhile, in Far Eastern Asia, the southern Sung dynasty had won peace and prosperity in the eleventh century at the cost of abandoning the northern territories to the Khitan Tatars and the western territories to the Uighurs and the Tibetans, and the Chinese flattered themselves that they were keeping these barbarian tribes closely in check and at the same time gradually subjecting them to their influence. Indeed, by 1100, the Tatars were so weakened that the reconquest of their territory seemed easy. Suddenly deciding to recover Peking, the emperor Hwei-tsung invited a completely uncivilised tribe, the Nüchih Tatars, to attack the Khitan. These strange allies duly crushed the Khitan between 1114 and 1122, driving the latter westward, but they then picked a quarrel with the Chinese and in 1125 advanced southward.

Chinese resistance collapsed under this shock attack. In scenes of incredible panic, the invaders crossed the Hwang-ho, then the Yang-tze, capturing the emperor and advancing their raids to within 120 miles of Canton. The

Movements of Christians and Moslems in the twelfth century

Roger II of Sicily receiving his crown from Christ. Roger II had a long struggle to gain universal recognition of his sovereignty.

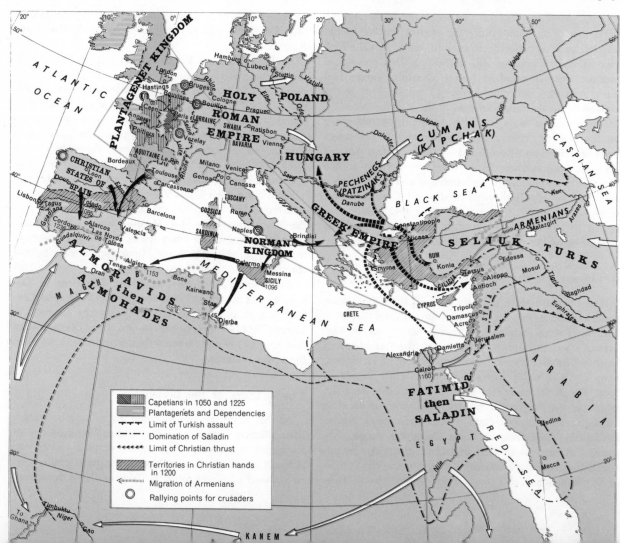

312

ΡΟΓΕΡΙΟC ΡΗΞ   ΙC   Χ

Crusaders in combat. Miniature from a late twelfth-century German manuscript. *Archiv für Kunst und Geschichte*

Saladin, sultan at Cairo, who preached the doctrine of a Moslem holy war and whose expansionist ambitions and success provoked the Third Crusade in 1189. *Historia Photo*

Nüchih, however, who now called themselves Kin, agreed in 1138 to relinquish all land south of the Hwai-ho. The peace was broken in 1161 and 1206, but the Kin dynasty absorbed Chinese civilisation very quickly. Moreover they were themselves harassed incessantly from 1135 onwards by Mongol tribes operating in the Khingan Mountains. In 1161 the Kin had to make a great effort to crush the khan, Kutula. As for the Sung dynasty, they were happy to have got off so lightly. They increased the defences on the Yang-tze, which had been crossed for the first time for centuries; then they went back to their ceramics and neo-Confucian discussions, to be caught completely unawares when the Mongol tempest finally broke, but ruling over a civilisation so massive and wealthy as to be largely impervious to political change.

Moslem conquests in India

Driven westward by the Kin, the Khitan Tatars (or Kara Khitai) overpowered the Uighurs of the Tarim in 1125, and then subdued, one after another, all the Turkish tribes north-west of the Oxus (1140-1144). The Khitai were Buddhists, so Moslem territory was reduced to its ninth-century proportions. The Turks thrown southward across the Oxus submerged the Persian elements found there, and agricultural Bactria became pastoral 'Turkestan'. With this, the Turks provoked renewed Moslem expansion towards India and towards the Mediterranean. Stimulated by these new pressures, the Afghan mountaineers of Ghor, east of Herat, continued the Moslem conquests of India.

The capture of Richard Coeur-de-Lion. The Third Crusade (1190) was little more successful than the second. Having failed to deliver Jerusalem and made terms with Saladin in 1192, Richard fell victim to intrigue on his return journey. He was held prisoner for over a year by Leopold, Duke of Austria. *Bibl. de l'Univ. de Berne*

The Greek disaster

Since the death of Malik Shah in 1192, the Seljuks had been worn down by their fighting against the Persian Shiites as well as against other Turkish tribes anxious to step into their shoes. From 1102 to 1157 the sultan Sinjar tried desperately to cling to the fringe of the settled world, but was unable to withstand the irruption of the Khitai. Thenceforward Turkish tribes drove on into Persia, including the future Ottomans. Between 1194 and 1214 the Persian plateau gradually passed into the hands of the shah of Khwarazm, who had neither the time nor the capacity to organise his domain before Jenghiz Khan attacked.

In Armenia and Anatolia the Turks of Sivas and Konia enlisted the support of these wandering tribes, and when Manuel Comnenus finally attacked in 1176, he was surrounded and crushed at Myriokephalum. The victor does not seem to have done much more than to reoccupy the Aegean coast, but the victory was nevertheless decisive. Manuel's disaster put an end to Greek plans for Asia; that was the end of her prestige, which was already badly compromised in the West.

It was not long before the Frankish positions in Syria were to find themselves weak and isolated before a new danger coming from Egypt.

Saladin

Concerned about the Franco-Greek intervention, Nur-ad-Din appointed the Kurd Saladin vizir at Cairo in 1169. Saladin abolished the Fatimid caliphs in 1171 and proclaimed himself sultan. A good-looking man of thirty, he was a careful and tenacious soldier; he was a magnificent leader, chivalrous and courteous, intervening in the middle of the battle to provide his enemies with ices and fresh horses, to enable them to continue the fight. He did much to improve relations between the two worlds, but seemed devoured by ambition. Rapidly he overcame the Yemen, the Holy Cities, Damascus, Aleppo and Mosul. His raids struck at Anatolia and Libya, perhaps even Gao.

Saladin's hold on Africa seems to have been firmer than on the Levant. Relations with the Moslem rulers of Bornu and Gao brought the reopening of the caravan routes from Egypt to the Chad and the Niger, and his communications with Ethiopia and Zanzibar through the Red Sea or the Nile explain how the flow of gold and slaves consolidated the commercial supremacy of Egypt at the expense of the Persians, and favoured his own political ambitions. It was as much to appropriate the markets of Syria as to serve Islam that Saladin decided to crush the crusaders.

The Franks, at loggerheads with one another, put up no more than a modest resistance. Baldwin IV alone showed fight and even forced Saladin to withdraw. But after Baldwin's death prudence and patience were all Saladin needed to win. Foolishly adventuring, the Frankish barons were overwhelmed and captured near Tiberias in July 1187. Within five months Saladin had reduced practically all the Christian strongholds, only a few barons holding out at Tyre and Antioch.

The fall of Jerusalem roused Europe to renewed zeal — and renewed rivalries. A new and stronger crusade was spoken of. Frederick Barbarossa, Philip Augustus of France, and Richard Plantagenet started east between March and September 1190 preceded by the Italian barons. Saladin feared Frederick, but the latter was drowned in Cilicia in June 1190, and the German contingent dispersed. Philip and Richard arrived at Acre in the spring of 1191. His feats of arms earned Richard the name of Coeur-de-Lion; the Christians won the littoral from Armenia to Ascalon, but not the Holy City. This, the Third Crusade, was a partial success, and it gained Cyprus as a strategic base for the West.

The Almohades

As in the days of the Seljuks, Islam was militant in both East and West. In Spain, Alfonso I of Aragon had ventured as far as Granada in 1120, and Alfonso VII of Castile had reached Cordova in 1147, the year the Portuguese took Lisbon. Meanwhile things had changed on the Almoravid front. About 1122 a south Moroccan hermit started preaching a return to the unity of the faith; his followers, Unitarians or Muwahhadis (our Almohades), were soon masters of the Atlas, of Marrakesh, then of Morocco. Attacking the Almoravides, they advanced into Tunisia. In 1146, they crossed to Spain and occupied Seville. The conquest was slow but Yusef II finally subjected all Moslem Spain, and Yakub defeated the army of Castile near Alarcos.

Thus Islam still seemed capable of great vigour. Yet the successes were limited and temporary. For the Christian world was flourishing, and if some peoples, like the Greeks, were in decline, it was a feature of the age that there were plenty of others to take their place.

THE NEW EUROPE

German influence in Central Europe

The Slavonic peoples, redoubtable a century earlier, weakened in the twelfth century, and the Scandinavians, though still trading, were in a state of political conflict and unable to exert influence on their neighbours. In any case, with Mediterranean trade again in full swing, the continental routes had diminished in importance. The Church, moreover, was exerting an influence in Central Europe, opening it to Western civilisation.

So long as they were preoccupied with Italy, the policy of the Emperors (Henry IV and Henry V) was to preserve the nominal alliance with the Czech and Polish dukes, occasionally calling them to order. After 1130 the expansion of the German population led to systematic occupation of land beyond the Elbe. Both Germans and Flemings were involved, and a long struggle dominated the policy of the local princes. At Lübeck in 1158, at Rostock in 1165, and at Stettin in 1180, the Germans imposed the Christian faith and filched Scandinavian trade.

Slowly the Western Slavonic States — Bohemia, Moravia and Poland — became little more than extensions of the Empire. Meanwhile the Russians of Kiev, harassed by the Kipchaks, were driven northwards to Vladimir between 1169 and 1203.

Taking advantage of the Greeks' preoccupation with the East and the Germans' with Italy, King Koloman

Stone carving of a crusader, Magdeburg Cathedral. The introduction of such carvings in the interior of churches is indicative of the importance of the military in Christianity during the twelfth century. *Marburg*

of Hungary had attacked Prague in 1107 and in 1112 had overcome the Croat princes and reached the Adriatic. Between 1129 an 1131 John Comnenus re-established his authority over the Serbs and forced Hungary to become a protectorate. This traditional policy of the Greeks irritated Frederick I, but the series of defeats suffered by the Byzantines under Manuel's successors obliged him to abandon Dalmatia — in any case fallen under Western influence — to Bela III of Hungary.

Eclipse of the Empire

By 1180 Frederick I was the accepted sovereign of German burgraves, Slav kings, and rebellious vassals like Henry the Lion. His masterstroke was the marriage he arranged between his heir, Henry VI, and Constance, daughter of Roger I of Sicily.

Henry, a diplomat with an eye to the main chance, came to the throne in 1190. His marriage brought him the Norman kingdom, but not without four years of warfare. The Empire was now firmly installed in the middle of the Mediterranean. In 1194 the Ottonian dream was realised at last. But Henry aimed still higher: master of the West, suzerain of Cyprus, brother-in-law of the heiress to the Eastern Empire, he took up the crusade in 1195. Was it to be Constantinople or Jerusalem?

In 1197 he died of a fever leaving a two-year-old heir. So much hatred against Swabian and Teutonic despotism had accumulated that region after region rebelled: the Rhineland, Westphalia, Tuscany, and even Sicily broke away. Henry's brother, Philip Hohenstaufen, claiming the imperial crown, found himself opposed by Otto Welf, son of Henry the Lion. The war that resulted lasted for ten years.

In 1198, at the moment of German eclipse, Innocent III became Pope at the age of thirty-eight. With a clear, practical mind, he was a shrewd lawyer and able politician. When he pronounced in favour of Otto IV, he emphasised the humiliation of the Empire.

Philip Augustus

In the West, economic development and the pressure of growing populations played into the hands of the house of Capet, providing both money and military strength. As for the Angevins, they found it difficult to choose between their island kingdom, England, and their fief, Aquitaine, richer but less secure. When he became king of France in 1180 Philip II was young, but ripe for his years. He firmly decided to break out of his narrow boundaries.

Philip Augustus aided Richard in his revolts against his father, Henry II of England. Henry, abandoned by all, took refuge in Anjou and died there in 1189. But the boisterous Richard, disdaining England (where he spent only five months in the course of ten years), promptly broke with Philip. The first to return from the Third Crusade, Philip wantonly plotted Richard's imprisonment in a castle on the Danube. Henry VI was only too ready to side against the brother-in-law of Henry the Lion. When freed, Richard sought vengeance on Philip, who was forced to give ground. In the midst of his success Richard was killed in March 1199.

Bouvines

On Richard's death, there was only his brother, John Lackland, for Philip to deal with. The need for allies experienced by the two enemies, as well as by the two pretenders to the imperial throne, marks the dawn of European politics on the grand scale. The French allied themselves to Philip Hohenstaufen of Swabia, and John allied himself to Otto IV. The subtle Philip Augustus laid claim to the Plantagenet estate and in 1204 took Rouen, Caen, Angers, and Poitiers. In a single campaign, he seemed to have won the day.

But it was not to be. In Germany Philip of Swabia was assassinated and fortune began to favour the other side. A coalition was formed against France. Otto IV, John, and the Count of Flanders joined forces, and the Pope took England under his protection. In 1214 John attacked Philip at Poitiers and the Emperor attacked him in the north. In July of that year Philip's 10,000 men routed Otto's 15,000. Otto retreated and the Count of Flanders was taken prisoner. This 'national' victory at Bouvines was a triumph for the French, ruined the prestige of the Germans, and broke up the coalition. In 1215 Otto was in retreat again, this time from Frederick II and the French. From now on, these were the two powers that were to dominate Europe.

France gropes for unity

A new France rose up, heir to the world of *Romanitas*. If she had access to the Mediterranean, she would be mistress of Europe. The moment came: the North threw itself upon the South, which had become plagued with Catharist heresy. The *perfecti* led a life of stern austerity, leaving the remainder, the *credentes*, to enjoy life. Raymond VI of Toulouse supported the Albigenses. In vain St Dominic had raised his voice against the heretics; in the end Innocent III in 1208 offered the fiefs of Toulouse to any who would take them.

To win indulgences and at the same time to annex rich lands simply by marching down the Rhône valley was a sufficiently tempting offer to bring the barons pouring southward. Simon de Montfort's brilliant victory against Peter II of Aragon completed the rupture between

Aquitaine and Spain, when he entered Toulouse in 1215 and made himself Count of Toulouse. A sudden reverse cost Simon his capital and his life (1218), but the king had only to exercise his habitual diplomatic cunning and the affair was concluded, opening the Mediterranean to the kings of France and the riches of the south to their subjects.

France, so successful in arms, now snatched from the south the beginnings of Gothic art, bringing it home to the Ile-de-France, to Picardy, where the Romanesque had never flourished. No doubt the basic ideas had come from elsewhere: the Gothic transept, a simple vault of reinforced ribs, is frequent in the Moorish cupolas of the eleventh century, and was used at Durham and in Burgundy at the beginning of the twelfth. But the abundance of towns north of the Seine attracted workmen, architects, and money. Immediately the Gothic became an urban art, destined for the Church. It was necessary to build on a large scale with plenty of windows, and the Gothic arch made the tall nave with wide bays possible. Almost immediately work was started on the great cathedrals: St Denis 1132, Sens 1140, Paris 1194. Meanwhile, the clerical élite flocked to the new schools.

Withdrawn from the world behind monastery walls all through the tenth century, thought, like architecture, took advantage of the changes of the eleventh. Thinkers, emerging from the monasteries, installed themselves in the schools set up in the towns, where merchants and pilgrims brought news of intellectual progress in other countries. The first branch of learning to benefit from this development was philosophy, hitherto an intellectual pastime, which now turned to consider the problems of God and Truth. St Anselm might go on affirming that faith preceded all reasoning (*credo ut intelligam* not *intelligo ut credam*), but he and the celebrated school of Chartres now found themselves confronted by dialecticians like Berengarius of Tours. The intellectual world was waking up. The rationalist Abelard duelled with the mystic St Bernard. Out of this was born balanced humanism in the twelfth century, and, by the end of that century, Europe was to reach a degree of maturity that made possible the great intellectual rebirth that followed the discovery of the writings of Aristotle, who was to dominate all thirteenth-century thought.

ISOLATED WORLDS

South-east Asia

The Turkish conquest of northern India split the Hindu world. The Deccan was in chaos: the Maharashtra empire was destroyed; that of the Cholas disintegrated after 1150; King Parakrama Bahou's Cingalese failed to supplant it. In Burma, Buddhism, hitherto uncontested, now had its critics and opponents; after 1170 this country, essential for the food-supply of Asia, was weakened by schism. King Narakatisitu did not succeed in putting the country in order again until the end of the twelfth century.

In contrast, the Khmer empire flourished; its great kings and builders, Suryavarman (1112-52) and Jayavarman VII (late twelfth century) maintained Cambodia's

independence and conquered the Champa. People flocked to their capital, whose prestige rested on its wealth and the splendour of such monuments as the vast temples of Angkor-Wat and Bayou.

Japan

With the decline of the Fujiwara family, Japan fell into a state of feudal anarchy. Between 1156 and 1185 the three families, Fujiwara, Minamoto, and Taira, were engaged in civil war. In 1185 Yoritomo Minamoto destroyed the fleets of his rivals and in 1192 assumed the title of shogun, or general-in-chief. With that, a military dictatorship was born that put an end to the incessant vendettas. The emperor unseen in his palace, the feudal lords free on their estates — that for the next six centuries was the political pattern of Japan.

Africa

All we know of the African forests at this time are the warlike expeditions of the kings of Gambaga in the Mossi district of the middle Volta, although an empire was certainly formed in the twelfth century between the lower Congo and the Kwango. In Rhodesia, the Bantus of the Monomotapa — whose ruined cities suggest that they may have ruled over a powerful kingdom — traded in gold with the Arab merchants of Zanzibar.

Change in America

In America, profound changes took place between the tenth century and the thirteenth. We can only guess the causes: possibly the expansion of populations in areas no longer sufficient to support them, and the desire to take prisoners for sacrifice.

The little we know of the tribes of the American prairie may explain the movement of peoples from the north. Still in a primitive state even in the tenth century, these peoples seem then to have traded amongst themselves by exchanging mica, furs, shells, copper and crystal. In many cases the objects traded may have been valued for their ritualistic significance, but valued highly enough, nevertheless, to cause the movement of a tribe. Thus the

The burning of the Palace of Sanko, an incident of the struggle for power between the Fujiwara, Minamoto and Taira families which plunged Japan into anarchy from 1156 to 1185. *Museum of Fine Arts, Boston*

Hokoham of Arizona served as intermediaries between the Anasazi fishermen of the Pacific coast and the Mohaves of Ohio, who seem to have extended their raids from Lake Superior to Florida. Between the sites of Yuma at the mouth of the Colorado River and Pecos in south Texas, the people called Pueblos, apparently settled, no doubt suffered from the raids of their neighbours, to which perhaps must be attributed the southward displacement of tribes till then encamped north of the Tropic: the Toltecs in the tenth century, the Chichimecs in the eleventh, and the Aztecs in the twelfth.

The Toltecs, who are believed to have been a still uncivilised Olmec tribe, had a legendary chief, Mixcoatl (cloud snake) who raided Teotihuacan before settling at Tula, further north, c. 920-940. If they adopted Olmec civilisation, the enterprising Toltec warriors extended their rule into the Maya world under chiefs who incarnated their god Quetzalcoatl. The Toltecs proved good agriculturalists, cultivating maize, cotton and beans. They had armour of quilted cotton and obsidian-tipped clubs. But their greatest skill was in building. Engaged as mercenaries by Maya towns, they helped to keep their quarrels alive. Built about 1050, the cities of Yucatan — Uxmal, Chichen-Itza, and Mayapan — succeeded in preserving their civilisation till the end of the twelfth century. Then, between 1150 and 1194, disorder spread over the whole area, with the destruction of Chichen-Itza, raids by pilfering Chichimecs and by the Aztec bands who appeared in 1168 on the shores of the Texcoco.

In South America a movement of people seems to

have occurred in the west, not so much on the coast as inland up the valleys, though there is no evidence of its having come from the other side of the Andes. The Chibchas of Colombia were united by a chief, the *Zipa*, who seems to have been of Bogotan origin. His rule was absolute, both as pontiff and military leader, for he was the incarnation of the sun, a prototype of the Incas. The same phenomenon appeared on the high Peruvian plateaus. The rule of the Quechuas of Tiahuanaco seems to have weakened towards the end of the tenth century. In the beginning of the thirteenth, one of the nomad mountain tribes of the Urubamba River, that of the Incas, had a legendary chief or *capac* called Mano and their capital was Cuzco; moving down into the plateau they subjected the tribes there. During the reign of the third *capac*, Lloqui Yupanqui, the whole Callao plateau had been subjected — a prelude to the extraordinary conquest of the following century.

Meanwhile, on the North Atlantic side of the Old World, the growing energy of Europe at the dawn of the eleventh century enabled it to withstand blows that would once have crushed it; in Spain, as in Syria and amongst the Slavs, Christianity triumphed. At the same time its centres of activity moved outward. After prolonged conflict, the political units that had hitherto been in the first rank, the Normans, the Angevins, the Germans, the Byzantines, receded before the two that were to dominate the thirteenth century, the great century of medieval France and a French-dominated Papacy.

In Asia, Islam was definitively shaken, except in India. Elsewhere, Persia, Syria, Ukraine, and Turkestan had weakened and were disintegrating. They would find themselves without any defence when, in a sudden uprising from the steppes, the redoubtable hordes of Jenghiz Khan, a heterogeneous band of warriors united for plunder, swept westward and eastward in their headlong rush.

Minamoto ne Tametomo, the famous archer, one of the Minamoto family which, after years of anarchy, in 1192 established a peace that lasted six centuries. Early Japanese print.

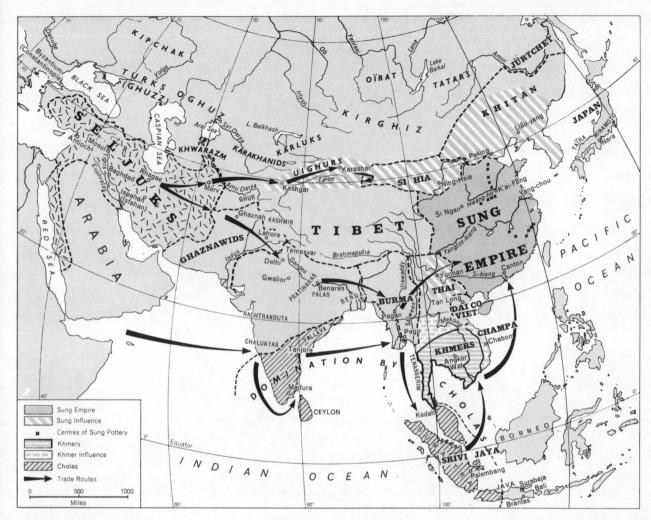

Asia towards the year 1030

Bas-relief of a puma. Decoration at the foot of the pyramid dedicated to Quetzalcoatl at Tula, Mexico. Toltec. *De la Rüe*

St Francis of Assisi (1182-1226), portrait painted fifty years after his death by Cimabue. Giotto, Cimabue's disciple, may have conveyed better the joy of the Franciscan life, but this fresco strikes the imagination and expresses more the calm energy of the 'poor man of Assisi', with his features lined by penance. *Anderson*

CHAPTER NINETEEN

WESTERN EUROPE IN THE THIRTEENTH CENTURY

The history of the thirteenth century seems to revolve round the concept of a universal empire. The ideal of a world ruled by a single authority is perennial, but it has never been so near realisation in Europe and the Far East as it was in the thirteenth century. On the one hand, in the West, was the great edifice of pontifical theocracy, on the other, in Asia, was an empire which, in the course of twenty years, had become the largest that had ever existed, that of the Mongols. But the universal empire was not to be. The Christian empire could never spread beyond the borders of Europe, and within those borders geographical, ethnic and political division proved ineradicable. The Mongol empire was to find its impetus checked when it came into contact with the old world.

THE PAPACY AND THE EMPIRE

Above: Frederick II (1212-50), consecrated Emperor by Innocent III, who failed to realise that Frederick was the one man who could stand in the way of his own plans. *Larousse*

Left: Innocent III, possibly the greatest pope of the Middle Ages (1198-1215), who came near to establishing pontifical theocracy.

PONTIFICAL THEOCRACY

The theocratic conception

The theories of Innocent III, who occupied the papal throne from 1198 to 1216, were to some extent based on those of Gregory VII and Alexander III. Like his predecessors, he based his teaching on the Scriptures, and justified his *plenitudo potestatis* by the fact of his being the Vicar of Christ. His rule over the world was of a twofold nature: spiritual, because the Pope was the head of the universal Church, no particular church being able to escape from the primacy of Rome; temporal, because he was invested with the government of the world, asserting his supreme authority through the intermediary of princes. The Pope did not actually exert a direct temporal power, and had no right to intervene in feudal matters; but as Pope and kings had to collaborate to establish the reign of Christ, any political act was liable to be considered a sin; and, as it was incumbent on the Vicar of Christ to see that divine law was observed, he was justified in taking up any matter, however political, that the kingdoms were concerned with. This was the logical consequence of the theories already advanced in the eleventh and twelfth centuries according to which the superiority of the Papacy over any and every monarchy was indisputable, firstly because kings receive unction from the hands of priests, and because he who gives is greater than he to whom it is given; secondly because 'royal power borrows from pontifical authority the splendour of its dignity, as the moon receives its light from the sun and is therefore inferior to it'.

It was Innocent III's personal contribution in this matter to analyse precisely the distinction between the religious and the political interventions of the Papacy, an analysis which none of his predecessors had made so clearly. Confronted by opposition from highly organised monarchies, he could not rely on formulas as general and vague as those of Gregory VII. But, as Brémond says, 'by this very precision, which in some respects is a limitation, the pontifical doctrine acquired a force it

had so far lacked', and by being defined it was the more firmly asserted.

Moreover the doctrine of pontifical theocracy, which was only groping its way in the eleventh and twelfth centuries, was now co-ordinated. By establishing a Roman Christianity under the supreme authority of an omnipotent Vicar of Christ, an authority under which everyone would have his place laid down by divine order, Innocent III planned the perfect symmetry for the great ideological syntheses of the thirteenth century, in which the teaching of St Thomas Aquinas reached the ultimate in universality.

The means

Innocent III had more suitable and more forcible means of putting universal rule into practice than any possessed by Gregory VII. Since the twelfth century the habit had grown of appointing papal legates to the Church of a particular country. These representatives of the Holy See were now fairly general, and, under Innocent III, the appointments were permanent. They were a powerful means of centralisation, enabling the Pope to keep a constant eye on everything. To this institution inherited from his predecessors, he added two other means which were promptly to prove their effectiveness. These were the utilisation of the mendicant orders then being formed, and the multiplication of the bonds of vassalage between the national States and Rome.

At the end of the twelfth century the wealth of the Church had provoked reaction which, in its more extreme developments, bordered on heresy, and had on all sides called attention to evangelical poverty. It seemed that the time had come to make a new appeal to the bewildered masses by showing examples of that poverty. For this the monks had to emerge from their retreats, walk the roads, and preach the gospel to those who had forgotten it or turned away from it. Their preaching was above all necessary in the towns; for the urban development of the twelfth century had undermined the old ecclesiastical organisation which had been created for a purely rural society. Two men had been profoundly alive to these needs: the two great founders of monastic orders, St Dominic, the Castilian noble, and St Francis. Enthusiasm had already begun to rise in the wake of these preaching friars and Minorites, when Innocent III decided to exploit the movement, directing it wherever its need was felt; and the Church did indeed find the mendicant orders splendid auxiliaries both for combating heresies and for giving a lead to sovereigns.

As for the exploitation of vassalage, it was all the more efficacious for lying within the feudal framework, that still being the chief basis of public law. The vassal prince who did homage to the Pope and paid him annual tribute became an intermediary between the Holy See and its subjects, and the Pope by virtue of his suzerainty had the right to exercise permanent control over his vassal. Innocent III, who already had Aragon, Portugal and Sicily as his vassals, was soon to have England. For John, unnerved by his deposition by the Pope in 1211, and under the threat of invasion by Philip Augustus, in 1213 declared himself vassal of the Holy See in respect of England and Ireland, with an annual tribute of a thousand pounds. Innocent did not fail to underline the full consequences of this act, saying: 'The sovereignty in your hands is now stronger and more august than before, for your kingdom has become sacerdotal and the sacerdocy has acquired a regal character.'

The results

Was this attempt by Innocent III to establish the Papacy's *dominium mundi* a success? On the religious side, certainly, success was complete. Christianity consolidated its positions and spread to fresh regions, with emphasis laid on expansion in the Baltic and Spain. The new military Order of Swordbearers, created by Innocent in 1200 and reinforced in 1224 by the Teutonic Order (for the Third Crusade), converted the Prussians to Christianity and then proceeded to bring the Gospels to the Finns, Esthonians and Lithuanians. And while the crusade gathered force in the Baltic, the Christian reconquest of Spain began again after the setbacks of the twelfth century at the hands of the Almoravides and the Almohades. The great victory of Las Navas de Tolosa in July 1212 rang the death-knell of the Moslem domination of Spain. In some fields Innocent's actions were decisive. The Fourth Lateran Council held in 1215 constitutes the highest point in his reign. All Christendom came to hear the Pope proclaim the primacy of Rome and in the name of this principle draw up a valid legislation for the universal Church. Two patriarchs were present, those of Constantinople and Jerusalem; two others, those of Antioch and Alexandria, sent representatives. With them were 71 archbishops, 412 bishops, 800 abbots and countless representatives of princes and towns. Before all Christendom assembled in Rome, Innocent III sought to legislate as a universal sovereign; in the launching of a new crusade, in the measures to be taken against heretics and Jews, in the reform of the clergy, and in the declaration of the duties of States towards the Papacy.

The church of St Francis of Assisi, decorated by Giotto with scenes from the life of the saint. St Francis, son of a merchant family, founded the great mendicant order and himself gave the lead in renunciation of worldly goods. By exploiting the movement, Innocent III was able to deflect some of the popular unrest over the disproportionate wealth of the Church. *Lala Aufsberg*

No one questioned the primacy of Rome, at any rate in the spiritual field.

In the political field Innocent III was less successful. Several of the Council's enactments, aiming at the complete independence of the Church from the State, were never put into practice. Some princes had at once raised objections, first and foremost the King of France, Philip Augustus, so tenacious, yet at times so devious. No doubt the king had no intention of breaking his long-standing alliance with the Holy See, but he was apt to be contemptuous of Roman thunder. 'It is not for the Roman Church', he had said to Clement III in 1189, 'to take sanctions against the kingdom of France on the pretext that the king, careful of the honour of his crown and anxious to avenge his wrongs, has taken stern action against disloyal vassals.' With Innocent III the king went still further, defying him for twenty years over his matrimonial conflict with Ingeborg, flouting his interdict, and only bowing in 1213 when he needed the Pope's support at a time when he was toying with the idea of invading England.

But the great obstacle to the theocratic principle was the other power which claimed universality, the Empire, whose rivalry with Rome had lasted for centuries.

IMPERIAL RESISTANCE

Frederick II

Grandson of Frederick Barbarossa through his father Henry VI, and of Roger II of Sicily through his mother Constance, Frederick II was one of the strangest men of the thirteenth century, so unlike other men of his time that none understood him. *Stupor mundi*, the abbot of St Gall called him. Born and bred in Sicily, he was before all else a Sicilian.

His childhood was spent in the streets of Palermo with the boys of the many nationalities that rubbed shoulders at this focal point of the Mediterranean. He spoke Italian, French, Greek and Arabic, as well as Latin and, on occasion, German. More intelligent and more cultured than most of his contemporaries, his curiosity led him into many fields: science, astrology, venery, art, and poetry. He collected rare animals and was proud of his menagerie; he was on the best of terms with Moslem princes, and in 1236 the Sultan of Egypt made him the present of a giraffe, the first to be seen in Europe. In 1232, the Sultan of Damascus, Al Ashaf, sent him a planetarium thought to be worth 20,000 silver marks.

Brought up in such close contact with oriental potentates, it is not altogether surprising that, when travelling, he was followed by a harem, or that he took a bath every Sunday, which scandalised the Abbot of Winterthur, Jean le Sage. A sceptic, completely emancipated from the views current in his age, but a realistic sceptic, Frederick was one of the first proponents of experimentalism. To prove that the soul died with the body, he had a man shut up in a barrel and left to die there (obviously the soul would be unable to escape); to discover the relative effects of sleep and exercise on the digestion, he made one man sleep while another took violent exercise, then had them both disembowelled to study the intestines. He himself wrote a treatise on falconry, based on very accurate observations of the habits of birds and even on attempts at artificial incubation. He came to the conclusion that 'one is bound to believe what is proved by the force and logic of nature'.

Frederick II stands out from his century, the century of cathedrals, of chivalry, of St Louis, of theocracy. Bewildering to thirteenth-century minds he may well be compared to Roger II, but many historians see in him a forerunner of the princes of the Italian Renaissance,

open as he was to a variety of intellectual influences, independent and critical in mind. More loosely, he may be compared to the enlightened despots of the eighteenth century, whose preoccupations and behaviour he shared. He was in many ways a man of his age, and he died a Christian. But he was always a 'disturbing Christian' who shocked his contemporaries.

Frederick began by reorganising his Sicilian kingdom, for he wanted to make use of his power to further his great political ambitions. He had inherited the perfect bureaucratic organisation of Roger II. He amplified it, and the Constitutions of Amalfi went far beyond the Assizes of Ariano in centralising the country's administration. This was a triumph of Roman Law and the notion of the State, and the general spirit is rationalist, authoritative, and so contemptuous of custom that Gregory IX called Frederick the destroyer of public liberty; the clergy were subject in first judgment to the secular courts and temporal power was independent of spiritual power. At the height of the quarrel, Frederick never ceased reiterating that as the heir of Constantine he exercised a universal sovereignty. That affirmation of principle opened the great struggle into which he was to drag Sicily, the struggle with the Papacy for what was nothing less than the European hegemony.

The conflict down to the Treaty of San Germano

From the start the Papacy was forced to realise the magnitude of the political mistake committed by Innocent III in 1211; Frederick II showed himself a skilful tactician. Taking advantage of the weakness of the new Pope, Honorius III, elected in 1216, he promptly scored a point in 1220 by getting his son Henry, who had been King of Sicily since 1212, elected King of the Romans. This was before he himself had been crowned Emperor; moreover it completely ignored the undertaking made to Innocent III never to attempt to unite the two crowns of Sicily and Germany. And within seven months Frederick was crowned Emperor by Honorius III.

On the strength of this success, Frederick showed his hand, revealing his intention of asserting his authority over Lombardy. He summoned a diet to Cremona at Easter 1226 and at the same time rounded up his Sicilian vassals, calling on them to join in an expedition to northern Italy. This made it quite clear that he intended to make Sicily a close partner of the Empire. Going still further he sought to re-establish between Sicily and North Italy the territorial connection that had been broken by the cession to the Holy See of the duchy of Spoleto and the march of Ancona, and he claimed the right to enrol contingents in those two territories. This time Honorius III became alarmed and protested. At the same time he prevented the rupture between the Emperor and the Lombard League by insisting on arbitrating between them in January 1227.

The Pope's meekness towards Frederick II was astonishing. It is explained perhaps by the Pope's preoccupation with the crusade he was planning, for which he needed the Emperor's help. But what a part Frederick played! He took the Cross in 1215; he promised to go in 1216, 1217, and 1218, but still he did not go. Finally in 1219 he seemed to have made up his mind; indeed his departure was fixed for June. But it was postponed

Seal of Bishop Conrad of Scharfenberg c. 1220

until September, then again to March 1220, to May, to the autumn, to March 1221, each time with letters making plausible excuses. The point was to secure the imperial crown before going; and in the end the Pope crowned him. Even then he hung back. After the death of Honorius III in March 1227, Frederick went on playing the same game. But not for long, for Gregory IX was a man of a different stamp from his predecessor.

Gregory IX had a strong personality. He was ascetic, he was a *grand seigneur*, an eminent jurist, and a consummate theologian; he was clear-headed and intractable, and, with his entry on the scene, the struggle became passionate, violent, and unforgiving. Frederick tried once more to evade the issue: he embarked in September 1227, but turned back, on the pretext of sickness amongst the crew. Then Gregory acted. On September 29 he pronounced the sentence of greater excommunication and extended the interdict to the kingdom of Sicily. Frederick adopted a wounded air, and in inflammatory letters publicly accused the Pope of bad faith. All the same he embarked again in June 1228, and sailed for Acre. This, the Sixth Crusade, was an extraordinary enterprise. It was led by an excommunicant who promptly entered into negotiations with the sultan of Egypt for the cession of Jerusalem and the other Holy Cities ... for ten years.

This constantly postponed crusade had been little more than a pretext for a breach between the Pope and the Emperor. With his usual clear-sightedness Gregory IX had realised that the contest had to be played out in another field. For what was really at issue was the hegemony of Italy. The Pope could not allow Frederick, by getting hold of Spoleto and Ancona, which seemed his obvious intention, to encircle the Papal State.

Taking advantage of the Emperor's absence, Gregory passed to the attack in Italy and in Germany. Against Sicily he organised a veritable crusade, and on the mainland his mercenaries conquered half of Frederick's Italian possessions. In Germany he set up an anti-king, but on this side the results were poor, except in Bavaria. In any case, the unexpected return of Frederick, who landed at Brindisi in June 1229, rapidly reversed the situation. Gregory IX realised what a difficult task he had undertaken, and agreed to negotiate. Long and painful discussions led to the preliminary agreement of San Germano, transformed into a final treaty at Ceperano in August 1230. Frederick obtained absolution from the Pope, but at quite a high price: the relinquishment of most of the royal privileges over the Church of Sicily. Beyond that none of the grave questions that were at the root of the conflict were settled.

The success of Frederick II

Taking advantage of the truce between Rome and the Empire to consolidate his position in Sicily, Frederick II also turned to Germany, where his son Henry had started a rebellion and was now in possession of the government. At the same time the principalities were being fortified, making them a threat to royal authority. Frederick soon got the better of Henry, who submitted in 1235 and died in semi-captivity in 1242. He was not very successful in subordinating the princes, but he did appreciably increase the royal domain in Germany.

Frederick's chief preoccupation was elsewhere. In Italy, he now openly attempted to join Sicily to Germany, by incorporating in his empire all central and northern Italy. Against him stood the Lombard League, supported by Gregory IX in the background. After his great victory over the League at Cortenuova in November 1237, Frederick was uncompromising: he announced his intention of subjecting the Italian communes to his own absolute authority and of making Rome the capital of the Empire. Then Gregory acted, and quickly. He threw himself wholeheartedly into the Lombard cause, signed a treaty with the towns of the League, and at the same time reconciled Venice and Genoa. Then, in March 1239, he pronounced the sentence of excommunication on Frederick for the second time. He gave as his reason the Emperor's religious policy in Sicily. The real reason was of another order: his refusal to allow his Lombard allies to be subdued.

The death struggle (1239-50)

The conflict at once acquired a dramatic character and brought violent reaction throughout Christendom, which was seized with a sort of 'sacred horror'. This was particularly the case in Italy, swayed as it was by the great devotional movement inspired by the popular preachers — above all the disciples of St Francis. Rarely had the tone been so violent: in the strongest, most apocalyptic language, Frederick II was presented as the Anti-Christ, belonging to the cursed race of vipers. On the other side, propaganda made a legend of Frederick Barbarossa and depicted his grandson as a saintly man charged with the duty of chastising a corrupt Church. Each side accused the other of heresy. Further, somewhere between the two extremes a rumour circulated that Frederick was an evil beast sent by God to punish the Pope. Never had Christendom been so disturbed. In the midst of this storm events moved rapidly.

Gregory IX convoked a general council to meet in Rome at Easter, 1241. Frederick decided he must at all costs prevent its assembly, knowing it would confirm the Pope's sentence. He got the Pisans to scatter the Genoese fleet that was bringing the English and French prelates to Rome. Then, neglecting the eastern frontiers of Germany which were at that time being attacked by Ogdai's Mongols, he marched on Rome just at the moment — August 1241 — when Gregory IX died. The latter's successor, Innocent IV, was to show the same energy and perspicacity as his predecessor, and in addition a diplomatic talent the other may well have lacked. Negotiations started, but in spite of the desire for peace felt throughout Christendom, and in spite of the increasingly alarming situation in the East, where the sultan of Egypt had recovered Jerusalem, they broke down.

Taking refuge in Lyons, a town within the Empire, but near to the kingdom of France, Innocent IV summoned a council, which in July 1245 deposed Frederick and released his subjects from their oath of fealty. A few months later, the Emperor's sons, descendants and followers were put under sentence of excommunication. By these means, the Pope succeeded in shaking Frederick's authority, without, however, being able to impose in all areas the two successive anti-kings he had elected, Henry Raspe and William II of Holland. But in Italy the Pope's successes were decisive. Frederick failed to take Rome,

Wolfram of Eschenbach departing for the crusades. Living at the end of the twelfth and beginning of thirteenth centuries, he himself considered his military prowess to be his claim to fame; but he is known to posterity as a Minnesänger and author of ' Parzifal '. *Larousse*

Pope Gregory X (1171-6) delivered to the bishops the Constitutions of the Council of Lyons (1272), which was intended to end the Great Schism. *Larousse*

suffered a serious defeat outside Parma, and lost Ravenna, which under the influence of the Franciscan preachers turned towards Innocent IV. While treason spread all round him, his natural son, Enzio, fell into the hands of the Bolognese and was thrown into prison, where he died twenty-three years later. Indomitable, Frederick still stood up to his enemies, but died in December 1250.

Victory of the Papacy. The Great Interregnum

Frederick's death did not put an end to the struggle. His son Conrad IV, king of Germany, was a serious threat to Innocent IV, but having subdued southern Italy, he died prematurely in May 1254. Then the Pope occupied southern Italy and took Naples, but he too died, in December 1254.

A new adversary of the Papacy came forward in the person of Manfred, another natural son of Frederick. Taking advantage of the weakness of the new Pope, Alexander IV, he occupied Sicily, flouting excommunication, and then revived his father's claim to northern and central Italy. But this was little more than bluff, for Manfred's position in the very chaotic Italy of the time was anything but secure. It was not even secure in Sicily, and with the accession of Pope Urban IV, an energetic and determined Frenchman, the final act of this colossal struggle began, an act in which the Emperor's claims were to be dashed completely and Sicily and the German Empire were to be permanently separated.

On all sides the Guelfs raised their heads — in Florence, Siena and Lucca. Manfred's party was wiped out of Lombardy, Tuscany and Rome. More serious still, the Pope at last discovered someone of sufficient stature to

be pitted against the Hohenstaufen, and he offered the crown of Sicily to Charles of Anjou, brother of Louis IX of France (St Louis). Charles agreed to renounce the imperial throne and all claims to central and northern Italy and accepted the Pope's suzerainty over Sicily. At the call of the latter, a campaign was launched against Manfred, who died outside Benevento in February 1266. Urban IV never knew of the Angevin's victory, as he himself had died in October 1264.

His successor, Clement IV, another Frenchman, delivered the final thrusts in the long duel. The last Ghibellines had gathered round the son of Conrad IV, Conradin, a boy of sixteen, who made a supreme effort. He entered Rome in July 1268, landed in Sicily, but in August was finally defeated by Charles of Anjou in the battle of Tagliacozzo. Hunted from town to town, this unfortunate descendant of Frederick II was caught, tried for treason, and beheaded in October 1268.

From the great struggle begun in the eleventh century the Papacy had emerged victorious, but with diminished prestige. Descending into the political rough and tumble, it had in the end smirched its authority and blunted the spiritual weapons it had put to material ends. For her part, Germany fell into the confusion of what is called the Great Interregnum, that period of German history between the disappearance of the Hohenstaufen and the election of Rudolph of Habsburg in 1273. It is not a strictly correct term, since the imperial throne was never actually vacant: there were pretenders enough — William of Holland, Richard of Cornwall, Alfonso X of Castile — but none was powerful enough to impose authority on the Electors, divided as these were in their choice, nor on the feudal world which was in a state of anarchy. No doubt Rome still possessed great power over the Church, but the dominant role in Europe from the end of the thirteenth century was no longer to be played by the Papacy, which had been morally and spiritually exhausted in the long struggle it had engaged in.

327

WESTERN EUROPE

The leadership of Western Europe now assumed by the house of Capet is to be explained by the fact that France at this moment achieved a balanced synthesis of all the forces of the period. Politically she had reached the stature of a great power. Her monarchical government was growing constantly stronger, modernising and perfecting its administrative methods, while conserving the traditional feudal base. The feudal monarchy itself may be said to have ended with St Louis, so that the accession of Philip the Fair heralded a new age.

Social and economic factors contributed to the stability of France. In the thirteenth century agriculture, the basis of feudal economy, had enjoyed great prosperity; France, favoured by the fertility of her soil and the extent of her territory — greater than that of any other European state — was in a position to prove her economic superiority on the land. The development of agriculture did not preclude that of the towns which had risen with the revival of trade in the twelfth century, and which still flourished in the thirteenth. This development increased the role of the bourgeoisie; but it did not yet involve the formation of an urban proletariat like that whose unrest disturbed the economy of the towns in the fourteenth century, for trades were still closely organised in guilds. It was indeed in a spirit of peace and good sense that St Louis had the *Livre des Métiers de Paris* issued by the Provost of Paris. These statutes of the commercial and industrial guilds served as a model for other towns. As for the nobles, they too were enjoying a stable economy, for they were not yet threatened by that shrinking of their revenue which in the fourteenth century tended to lower their status.

There was stability, too, in the intellectual sphere, and this made for great syntheses of thought and great artistic creations. This fame radiated far beyond the national frontiers, and men were attracted from all over the Western world to study the culture and civilisation of the France of St Louis.

ACHIEVEMENT OF FRANCE UNDER THE CAPETS

The move towards the Mediterranean

The death of Simon de Montfort raised once again the question of who should occupy the Albigensian region of Aquitaine, for Simon's son Amaury was no successor to his father, and the general feeling in the Languedoc supported Raymond VI. Amaury appealed to Philip Augustus, who sent his son and heir, Louis, to the south; but though he kept the situation under review, Philip Augustus did not wish to get too deeply involved.

Becoming king on the death of his father, Louis VIII decided once and for all to establish royal authority in the south. The problem was now changed, for since Amaury had ceded his legal rights to Louis emphasis was no

Rudolf of Habsburg, whose ascension to the imperial throne, aided by Pope Gregory X, made the fortune of the Habsburg family and brought to an end the so-called 'Interregnum'. *Lala Aufsberg Foto*

Expansion of the royal domain from St Louis to Philip the Fair

longer placed on the necessity of combating heresy, but simply on the conquest of the Languedoc.

Urged on by the new papal legate, Cardinal of Sant'Angelo, who acquired a great influence over Louis VIII, the expedition started. Raymond VII, who had succeeded his father, came in vain to Bourges suing for absolution. He was solemnly excommunicated by the legate in January 1226. The expedition thereupon turned into a military parade, and the whole of the Languedoc came under the King's rule without further difficulty. But Louis VIII died on his journey home in October 1226. His reign had been a decisive step in the southward advance of the Capets. Admittedly Raymond VII tried to take advantage of the revolt against Blanche of Castile to recover his lost territories, but he had to give in in the end, and the Treaty of Paris signed in April 1229 legalised the French acquisitions. The senechalsies of Beaucaire and Carcassonne were transferred definitively to the Crown, while the ground was prepared for the subsequent incorporation by the kingdom of the western part of the Languedoc, the Toulouse district.

Originally confined to an area round the Seine, the kingdom of France now for the first time reached to the shores of the Mediterranean and was absorbing regions different in culture and civilisation. The fusion of these territories with France was accomplished only after several decades. But this extension to the Mediterranean coast was to provide the kingdom with new means of action and open up new horizons, leading it within the space of fifty years to the grand perspective of a full-scale Mediterranean policy.

The regency of Blanche of Castile

After the conquest associated with the name of Philip Augustus, after the extension of the kingdom southward associated with that of his son Louis VIII, the problem remained how to fuse the newly acquired territory into the national identity. This was a delicate task, demanding an altogether exceptional, indeed an irreproachable sovereign, whose stature and moral prestige were such as to be capable of uniting what his predecessors had merely assembled. France had such a king in St Louis.

The submission of the great feudal lords to royal authority had been accomplished by the end of Philip Augustus's reign, but the structure of the monarchy was still fragile. Furthermore when Louis VIII died prematurely he left a son of twelve to take the throne. The age of the king made a regency necessary, despite the risks attendant upon that institution. Trouble began at once. The barons, quick to raise the standard of revolt, sought to dominate the formidable regent, Blanche of Castile, the king's mother. Indeed the barons actually tried to seize the young king, but were foiled by the intervention of the people of Paris, who escorted him from Montlhéry to Paris; this attempt was unprecedented in the history of the house of Capet, on no member of which a vassal had ever laid his hands. To fear that France might now lose the benefits that her kings had won for her in the last two centuries would have been to misjudge the outstanding qualities of the regent. The barons imagined they would have a weak woman to deal with, but they found themselves facing one whose coolness and will-power were exemplary. Backed by the Council and by the population

of the towns she got the better of the barons, sometimes by diplomacy, sometimes by force of arms. Feudal disturbances continued intermittently, however, and in 1236 St Louis had to put down a revolt of the barons of Poitiers; but the existence of the monarchy was never again to be in peril. In 1248 St Louis was able to go on a crusade and be absent for five years without the least danger to his regime. When Blanche of Castile handed the government of the country over to her son the French monarchy had finally surmounted all dangers, and the revolt of 1226, being the last of them, has a decisive place in French history.

The education and character of St Louis

The boy who was to preside over the destinies of France and leave an imperishable memory was given a serious education, but one which differed considerably from that of other princes of his time. Under the stern eye of his mother, the young Louis had led an almost monastic life. He was a sensible, friendly boy, and remarkably quiet. All his life he radiated a charm which his contemporaries found irresistible. All who came near him were struck by his 'angel face' and the clearness of his blue eyes. Direct and loyal, he abhorred all hypocrisy. Yet his delicacy of

Cloisters at Gloucester Cathedral, the first example of fan vaulting (1351-77). Dedicated in 1100, like many another cathedral built in the twelfth and thirteenth centuries it was based on an original abbey foundation, in this case of the seventh century.

mind and kindness precluded neither energy nor justice. All his inborn virtues were developed to the full by his education, making him a model of Christian virtue. His profound religious feeling was frank and sincere, as far removed from ostentation as from bigotry. An absolute and unquestioning faith was accompanied by a charity which knew no limits, prompting him to take an interest in the hardships of others, distribute alms lavishly, and tend even lepers with his own hands; for he was, as he himself said, 'transfixed by pity for the unfortunate'. This exemplary Christian was also a brave and chivalrous knight, one of those who fought in the rearguard of the retreat from the ill fated crusade in Egypt. Ill at the time, he would throw himself into the thick of the fray and accomplish prodigies of valour. At a time when chivalry was on the wane, St Louis was still the ideal suzerain '*franc de coeur et joli de corps, débonnaire, doux et humble, peu parleur*'.

With St Louis's conception of his duties as a man and as a Christian, it was inevitable he should be a great king. He attained a wide European prestige.

Above: St Louis. *Right:* Simon de Montfort, who took the Cross to follow Louis on his 1248 Crusade but ultimately remained behind to quell disturbances in Gascony.

The government of St Louis

With such a sovereign it was obvious that the house of Capet would go from strength to strength. St Louis had no intention of destroying the feudal structure in order to enhance the power of the king. He continued to gather his vassals in council when a major decision had to be taken. In other words, he abolished no institution for the sake of his own power. Thus under him the monarchy, though superior to any feudal authority, was still deeply enmeshed in feudalism. Nevertheless, under St Louis royal authority ceased to be a vain word; it was universally respected. What Philip Augustus had sought to achieve by force or diplomacy, what Philip the Fair

was to accomplish with his gifts as an administrator and jurist, St Louis obtained easily by virtue of his precise and scrupulous sense of justice, his prestige, and his shining morality. Though the French monarchy was still a feudal monarchy in the thirteenth century, under him the royal power encountered no obstacle; in fact it spread further and grew stronger.

It had most often to assert itself in the judicial sphere. For the king was, above all, the chief administrator of justice. Soon the judgments of St Louis acquired such a reputation that every one wanted to come to him for justice, not only those who lived in the royal domain, but even the people on the estates of the barons. As in the England of Henry Plantagenet, the royal jurisdiction began to extend, taking over some of the functions of the seignorial courts through the increasing frequency of 'royal cases', a sort of privilege accorded to certain burghers in towns outside the royal domain whereby they were heard by the King in person. Though it had for long been possible to appeal to the King against the judgment of a seignorial court, in practice delays and difficulties generally made it impossible. A growing number of royal agents scattered over the country made the right of appeal far more accessible. It was principally by the concentration of justice in the hands of St Louis, whose judgments were generally acknowledged to be fair, that royal power spread far beyond the extent of his domain.

This extension of the King's exercise of justice was possible only if he possessed a competent central administration and sufficient agents capable of hearing cases on his behalf. Since the early Capets, provosts had existed in the various territorial areas to represent the king, but, as they bought their appointments and lived on the revenue of their office, they became practically irremovable and increasingly beyond royal supervision. It was therefore necessary to appoint new agents, nominated by

the king, paid by him, and removable at his behest: in a word, officials appointed to serve the kingdom. These were the magistrates and seneschals, who became numerous under the reign of St Louis. They dispensed justice in the name of the king, were paid from the national exchequer, saw that royal ordinances were observed, and watched for abuses in the provost's court. While local administration remained unchanged, central administration multiplied its ramifications, and its various branches gradually became differentiated. The extension of the royal domain and the increasing complication of administrative tasks led to a specialisation of the members of the Curia charged with government. Moreover, the extensions of the field of royal justice gradually led the specialists in legal problems into the habit of meeting in a judicial section of the Court, which later became the nucleus of Parliament. No doubt this double evolution was no more than embryonic in the time of St Louis: its full importance was to become obvious only in the next century. But now, in a feudal setting, it was already a promise of what was eventually to come — the modern state with a firm judicial, administrative and financial framework.

This universally recognised and respected authority was employed by St Louis to maintain the order and peace of the kingdom. Without disturbance, without violence, he introduced a number of profound internal reforms. The interdiction known as the *quarantaine le roi*, forbidding the family of a murdered man to take vengeance on the murderer for a period of forty days after the crime, did much to suppress feuds. St Louis abolished many deplorable customs; in the royal courts litigants were no longer allowed to appeal to the 'judgment of God' (judicial duel), for as he said fighting is not the way of the law. Gradually a modicum of justice and gentleness was introduced in a period that knew them only too little.

Settlement of the first Anglo-French conflict

The old quarrel between the houses of Capet and Plantagenet continued half-heartedly. Henry III did what he could to recover the lands confiscated from his father in 1202. In face of this, St Louis might well have relied on feudal law and seized the last fiefs held by the Plantagenets in France; his grandfather, Philip Augustus, would have jumped at the opportunity. But Louis IX acted otherwise. After crushing Henry, he restored to him, under the Treaty of Paris of 1259, not only part of Guienne, which he had just occupied, but the suzerainties over the viscounts of Limoges and Perigueux formerly held by Philip Augustus. St Louis felt that they had been held illegitimately — a magnificent example of a scrupulous opinion beyond the understanding of the rough barons of the thirteenth century. It is not surprising that the king's own advisers protested vigorously at what they regarded as weakness and folly. He made an act of faith in feudal law at a moment feudalism was beginning to decline. St Louis acted as a lover of peace, so that his children and those of the King of England should love one another, and considered he had acted for the best interests of France in settling the conflict between the suzerain and his Plantagenet vassal, for he obtained from the latter admission of his vassalage. As St Louis said: *'Il n'était*

St Louis. Statue from the church at Mainneville (Eure), one of the masterpieces of thirteenth-century French sculpture. The work expressed the nobility and calm strength which are popularly associated with St Louis. *Viollet*

pas mon homme et il entre en mon hommage'. Thus the conflict between England and France that had started in 1152, a conflict which has sometimes been called the first Hundred Years' War, was ended in 1259. St Louis had set his heart on the peace that now began, and he expected it to last. The future was to decide otherwise, but the good king had done all he could to make it permanent.

The prestige of St Louis

Straight dealing won for St Louis a prestige hitherto unknown that spread far beyond his frontiers. From the four corners of Europe came requests for his arbitration. Dukes and even kings asked him to settle quarrels, between the Dukes of Lorraine and Burgundy, between the Kings of Hungary and Poland, between the King of England and his barons. Almost always the disputants bowed to his judgment. Never in the West had a king enjoyed such a reputation, and even from Central Asia envoys conveyed the greetings of the Khan of the Mongols to the king whose fame had reached him.

The great ascendancy gained over his contemporaries, reflected in the name he has left to history, could only strengthen the institution of monarchy, and his fame redounded to the credit of the house of Capet. The King in France was regarded not as a distant and traditional authority, but as a benevolent, venerable, almost saintly one. Lastly, the prestige of St Louis enhanced the reputation of France, whose position both materially and spiritually was without equal in the thirteenth century. Indeed the age of the great cathedrals was an age of great brilliance for France.

Philip the Fair and his légistes

The personality of Philip the Fair, St Louis's grandson, who became king on the death of his father Philip III in 1285, is difficult to assess. Was he a cold and realistic statesman, infatuated with his own authority with no scruples in his use of it; or was he, as others believe, a weak and hesitant king, led by dishonest advisers? For us Philip the Fair remains what he was to his contemporaries, who vaunted his fine presence and handsome face: an enigma. However that may be, the thirty years of his reign were of capital importance to the French monarchy.

It marks indeed a decisive step in the transformation of royal power. Influenced by the diffusion of Roman law, and the virtual disappearance of imperial power during the Great Interregnum, the position of the French kings grew stronger, both nationally and internationally. He might indeed have been called the *de facto* Emperor of the West. In the event it was enough for him to be 'emperor in his own kingdom'. That affirmation had important consequences — the principle that the king does homage to no one; repeated attempts to make him the only source of law; the perfecting of the judicial and financial institutions as they slowly drifted away from

The conflict with Rome

The personality of Pope Boniface VIII goes far to explain how the conflict between the spiritual and temporal powers flared up again. Proud, sharp-tongued, quick-tempered, and scornful of men, Boniface took up the theories of his predecessors, but amplified them and carried them to an extreme. He was, moreover, an expert canonist, skilled in building up arguments for a theocratic system which flattered his vanity. The conflict started in November 1295 over the problem of clerical contributions to the expenses of the State. Instantly the Pope, going far beyond the immediate question, issued his bull *Clericis laicos* in February 1296. Adopting a violent, polemical tone, he accused Philip of wanting to reduce the clergy to servitude, and he forbade the French clergy to agree to any contribution to taxes. Philip countered by prohibiting all export of gold or silver without his consent, thus depriving the Pope of his revenue from

St Louis departing for the Seventh Crusade in 1248. While the Pope and Emperor Frederick II battled for political power, St Louis gathered forces for the Crusade, thus in some measure transferring the spiritual leadership of Europe into his own hands. From *Le Chronique de St Denis*.

the Curia Regis, to become in the middle of the fourteenth century two separate bodies, Parliament and the Chambre des Comptes.

A slow and tentative development, no doubt, which left the traditional character of royal power more or less intact under Philip the Fair, and effected no sharp change in institutions. But a new spirit was apparent in the councillors of the king. The great barons and some of the lesser nobility of the old domain still had their places in the *Conseil*; but since the annexation of the southern regions councillors of a new type appeared, well versed in Roman law and generally referred to as the *légistes*. They served the kings — or rather the monarchy — with passionate zeal, and introduced a conception of the State unknown in the feudal world. For them the king was not a suzerain bound by custom, but an absolute monarch whose will was law. The *légistes* were responsible for the progressive disengagement of royal power from its feudal background. Thanks to them the monarchy moved towards an authoritative and more national standing. Various favourable circumstances contributed to this development, one of the most important of which was the quarrel with the Holy See, the quarrel between spiritual and temporal.

Woodcut showing St Louis and his two brothers Alphonse and Charles taken prisoner by the Saracens in 1250. They were released only in exchange for a large ransom and the surrender of Damietta. *Archiv für Kunst und Geschichte*

Peter's Pence. This decision made Boniface retreat, for the reopened struggle against Sicily demanded all the money he could raise. In a second bull issued in July 1297, he suspended the application of *Clericis laicos* whenever the money was raised for the defence of the realm. But now another, still more serious conflict arose, over the royal prosecution of Bernard Saisset, Bishop of Pamiers.

Boniface took the argument to extraordinary lengths, formulating in his bull *Ausculta fili* of December 1301 the most extreme theocratic doctrines, placing the Pope, as head of the Church, above all kings and kingdoms. Philip then sought to rally public opinion to his side, calling an assembly of the three orders in Paris in April 1302. This assembly is regarded as being the first form of the States General, and it was here that Pierre Flote made an incendiary speech against the Roman claims. But he could not prevent the assembly of the Roman Council of November 1302, following which Boniface issued his celebrated bull *Unam Sanctam* which declared that the sword spiritual belonged to the Pope alone, who delegated the sword temporal to the Emperor and, through him, to princes, but only to be used for the benefit of the Church and according to the will of the Pope. That amounted to claiming that the Pope had the power to control sovereigns in all their acts of government. Never had Innocent III gone so far. But this time Philip retracted, for he was now deprived of the services of Pierre Flote, killed at Courtrai. In his *Responsiones* of February 1303, he ceded to the Pope, with a few minor reservations.

Intoxicated by his triumph, Boniface VIII demanded total submission. But the situation had changed: Nogaret had joined Philip's Council. Scorning to enter into the papal arguments, he switched the discussion to the realm of fact and even attacked Boniface in person. He demonstrated that the latter was not legally Pope, since the abdication of his predecessor, Celestine V, had been irregular, and moreover that he was guilty of heresy and simony. Those were the charges brought by Nogaret before the assembly of barons and prelates held in the Louvre in June 1303. A few weeks previously, Nogaret had visited Italy, where he had schemed with the Colonna family, implacable enemies of Boniface. Informed of the meeting at the Louvre, the Pope prepared a bull of excommunication, which was to be published on September 8. Nogaret, learning the date, acted quickly. At dawn on September 7, his men, accompanied by a small force commanded by Sciarra Colonna, attacked the papal palace of Anagni. Boniface, abandoned by all and insulted by Colonna's men, was arrested by Nogaret 'for the defence of the faith and in the interest of the Church'. The following day Boniface was released by the people of Anagni and escorted to Rome; but, shaken by his experience, the old Pope died a month later.

The Anagni episode made a great impression by reason of its tragic grandeur. People were still more impressed when they vaguely grasped the true significance of the event. For this unprecedented blow at the moral dignity of the Pope was an irreparable defeat for the theory of pontifical theocracy. It was moreover the beginning of a series of capitulations, first with Benedict XI releasing Philip from his sentence of excommunication, then with Clement V, who fell completely under the King's orders. Thus, at the dawn of the fourteenth century, the edifice constructed by the Popes of the thirteenth collapsed:

theocracy was dead in fact and theory. The *légistes* had put forward a conception of royal power which absolutely precluded the papal claims; for it declared the dissociation of the two powers (spiritual and temporal) and the strict subordination of the Church to the royal power. The *légistes* had even affirmed the king's temporal independence of the Emperor. The struggle with the Pope had allowed the monarchy to take stock of itself. Accordingly the two axes of the medieval world — the supremacy of Rome and the supremacy of the Empire — were irremediably shaken, and therewith a wide political horizon was opened to the French.

THE PROBLEMS OF THE MEDITERRANEAN

Birth of French imperialism

As a result of the collapse of the traditional powers of the Empire and Papacy, new perspectives were opened up before the emergent medieval realms. Could they, jointly or singly, take over universal dominion and thus relieve the Empire and the Papacy of their responsibilities? For England, only slowly to become conscious of herself, such a theory was out of the question. Besides, at that moment her king was struggling with his barons and paralysed by a revolt of the Scots. But France?

During the last quarter of the thirteenth century the Kingdom of France was easily the greatest power in Western Europe. Pierre Dubois, a disciple of St Thomas Aquinas writing at the time of Philip the Fair, laid it

Scenes from the poem 'Parzifal' by Wolfram of Eschenbach depicted in a thirteenth-century manuscript. This is one of the earliest examples of German secular literature and of its illustration. *Archiv für Kunst und Geschichte*

down as a self-evident principle that the 'universe' should be governed by the King of France. First of all, with the agreement of the Pope, he should assume sovereignty over the Papal States, with which would accrue the homage of Sicily, England and Aragon, all vassals of the Holy See. Lombardy would easily fall into his hands. After that it would be the turn of the Eastern Empire, Castile and Hungary. Germany could easily be brought under French suzerainty, since Philip's sister, Blanche, had just married the son of Albert I. Thus, under the aegis of France, perpetual peace could be established throughout Christendom. These were not the visions of a monomaniac, for many of his contemporaries shared his illusions.

This dream of universal dominion was from the start out of step with the realities of the age, and it faded in a series of efforts at expansion. In a moderate form, however, it was to be effective, firstly to the east, in those intermediate regions that had been the cause of disputes between the French and Germans ever since the division of the Carolingian empire by the Treaty of Verdun and which were now only loosely attached to a harassed empire. In 1293 Philip the Fair established his suzerainty over the Ostrevent from Douai to Valenciennes; in June 1301, in accordance with the Treaty of Bruges, the Count of Bar did homage to the King in respect of his lands lying west of the Meuse; in 1312 Lyons was attached to the royal bailliage of Macon; lastly the convention of Vincennes of February 1295 had already recognised the *de facto* occupation of the county of Burgundy between the Saône and the Jura.

Further north, the successes were less obvious. The Count of Flanders was a vassal of the King of France only in respect of the western part of his lands. Flanders, an important trading centre, was the theatre of perpetual conflict between the urban patricians and the Count, and between the latter and his barons, so that circumstances were favourable to the infiltration of royal power, which could also exploit the constant appeals of the Flemings. Finally, Philip the Fair decided to take the whole county into his own hands. The reaction was violent: in May 1302 the French were slaughtered in the massacre of Bruges, and in July the royal army was routed by the Courtrai militia. In spite of the vengeance wreaked at Mons-en-Pévèle in August 1304 and the Treaty of Athis-sur-Orge made in June 1305 by which the Count capitulated, the question of Flanders was not really settled, and it paralysed French politics during the last years of Philip's reign.

In the Mediterranean French influence was to enjoy more freedom, as in this area there seemed to be no power able to offer serious opposition.

Italy's political disintegration

Italy was a tempting prey, for politically she was hopelessly fragmented. A few feudal states still existed in the north-west: the county of Savoy, the marquisate of Saluzzo, and the marquisate of Montferrat. But these curious survivals from former regimes were limited in their wealth and their capacity to act. The Lombard League, which had stood up so bravely against Emperors in the past, disintegrated conclusively after 1252. The two great sea-powers, Venice and Genoa, were more or

Burgos Cathedral, Castile, founded in 1221 and built by a French architect, who modelled it on the Gothic cathedral of Bourges. The surge of cathedral building throughout Europe at this time and the predominance of French architectural influence testifies to the growing stature of France.

The Angevin empire at its greatest strength, in 1280.

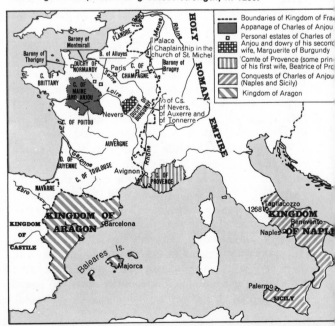

less always at each other's throats; Venice, absorbed in her oriental enterprises, was moreover inclined to neglect her continental territory, of which she had a considerable amount in the lower valley of the Po. In the Papal States the authority of the Rector, the Pope's representative, was constantly disputed by the towns and by the secular nobility. But the ideal field for intervention was southern Italy, where the authority of Manfred, the son of Frederick II, had been thoroughly undermined by the opposition and the intrigues of the Papacy.

The communal movement, which reached its height in the twelfth century, had tended everywhere to produce this proliferation of sovereignties. The towns formed small urban states, spreading out to the borders of the county of which they had formerly been the county towns. They were the forerunners of the principalities of the fifteenth century; but now, at the end of the thirteenth, the process of agglomeration was far from being completed. Northern and central Italy was a mosaic of little states, centred on a town, jealous of one another and all equally powerless.

To make a complex situation still more complex, in each city were two opposing sides, the Guelf and the Ghibelline. From Tuscany, where it had started, this internecine struggle spread to every Italian town. The Ghibellines, who happened to be involved in the fortunes of the Hohenstaufen, shared a moment of triumph with Manfred, and came to be regarded as representing imperial resistance to the Pope's claims to temporal power. The Guelfs, on the other hand, were regarded as the defenders of the Church and the Papacy. That being the case, it might be thought that the influence of the two families would tend to simplify the political currents involved. In reality it was quite impossible for anyone striving to establish a lasting authority in Italy to count on either of these two factions, as their positions were always fluctuating, being at the mercy of local influences, and success obtained with their help invariably led nowhere.

The Spanish kingdoms

In contrast to the anarchy in Italy, the Spanish kingdoms seemed to be already following a definite route, and Spain now figures for the first time in Europe's political scene.

The thirteenth century had been the period of reconquest. It had opened with the crushing victory of Las Navas de Tolosa in 1212, in which the armies of the Christian kings of Spain — Alfonso VIII of Castile, Peter II of Aragon, and Sancho VII of Navarre — had together wiped out the forces of the Caliph al Nasir. From this moment the *Reconquista* accelerated; a parallel drive was made from Castile, united with Leon during the reign of Ferdinand III (1230-52), and from Aragon, particularly under James I (1213-76). The Castilian thrust penetrated Estramadura and northern Andalusia, Alfonso VIII taking Caceres and Merida, while Ferdinand III took Badajoz, Cordova and Seville. Ferdinand's son, Alfonso X, forced the Moors to cede all these places in 1282. The kingdom of Aragon, united with Catalonia since the twelfth century, now wrested from the Moslems a strip of the Mediterranean coast. James I took Majorca between 1229 and 1235, then Valencia and the surrounding area between 1238 and 1253,

and lastly the Moorish kingdom of Murcia in 1265-6. Thus by the end of the thirteenth century the Moslems had no more than a small part of southern Portugal, Algarve, and the territories which comprised the kingdom of Granada.

But after these brilliant successes the reconquest slowed down. Combined Castilian and Aragonese forces took Gibraltar in 1296, but that was the last contribution by Aragon to the common enterprise, for her ambitions turned elsewhere when she discovered a new vocation in the Mediterranean. As for Castile, torn asunder by dynastic squabbles under the reign of Alfonso X and weakened by the troubles during the minority of Ferdinand IV, she sank for a while into obscurity. It was with Aragon that France was to come into conflict over her Mediterranean ambitions.

The struggle between France and Aragon

The Pope's appeal to Charles of Anjou, brother of St Louis, to assume the leadership of the Guelf faction against Manfred is a testimony to the prestige of France. Though St Louis refused to support his brother, the latter, having defeated Conradin at Tagliacozzo in August 1268, lost no time in consolidating his hold on the mainland and in Sicily. Very soon, despite the terms of the treaty signed in 1264 with Urban IV confining him strictly to his kingdom of Sicily, Charles embarked on a vast policy of expansion. Circumstances were favourable to him, for the Holy See was vacant for three years after the death of Clement IV. Not only did he dream of establishing his rule in central Italy but, reviving the oriental designs of Roger II and Frederick II, he nursed the hope of destroying the Byzantine Empire, which was now on its feet again, and of leading a crusade against the Moslems. The second part of Charles's programme never came within his reach, for he had no sooner made his plans for attacking Constantinople than he was ordered by St Louis to join his crusade. Even so, Charles hoped to make use of his brother's enterprise for his own ends, and it is probable that he did play a part in drawing St Louis away from Egypt towards Tunis, where the Caliph Mostansir had given asylum to certain Ghibelline refugees and failed to pay the tribute due to the Hohenstaufen. The expedition, which was tragic to St Louis, turned out very well for Charles. He made the Caliph sign a treaty in which he promised to pay the arrears of the tribute and henceforth to double the yearly sum. Charles intended the money for his designs against Constantinople, but during the voyage home the treasure was lost, so his plans had to be put aside.

But when the throne of France was ascended by the weak and easily influenced Philip III, Charles's prospects brightened again. After the downfall in 1278 of Pierre de la Brosse, who had been adviser to St Louis, Charles was the most influential person at court, and he saw to it that France underwrote his own ambitions, which were antagonistic to those of Aragon.

Hatred between Charles and Peter III of Aragon, who came to the throne in 1276, was of long standing. Charles had married Beatrice of Provence, formerly promised to Peter, and thus had snatched the Provençal heritage from his hands. He had prevented James I coming to Sicily, and had supported the Catalonian barons in their rising against Peter in 1276-7. Peter III, on the other hand, had in 1262 married Constance, daughter of Manfred, whom Charles had driven out of south Italy. More important than all else, Charles had installed himself at Naples, which the great burghers of Barcelona regarded as being within their commercial zone.

Playing on the discontent of the Sicilians, who resented the rough treatment they received under Charles of Anjou, Peter III spurred on the movement of revolt, which came to a climax in the Sicilian Vespers, the massacre of the French in 1282. Charles sent a fleet to the rescue, but it was sunk off Trapani by the Calabrian admiral Reggiero di Lauria. Charles then had to leave Sicily to the Aragonese and fall back on his mainland possessions. He hoped, however, to obtain the use of French forces to overcome his Spanish enemies. The new Pope, Martin IV, favoured the Angevins and excommunicated Peter III, declaring him deprived of his kingdom of Aragon. He entrusted the execution of the sentence to Philip III. As suzerain of Aragon, he then offered the crown to a son of the King of France. Since by the treaty of Corbeil in 1258 St Louis had renounced all suzerainty over the ancient Spanish March, it seemed that France had turned away from all adventure beyond the Pyrenees. Would the King now let himself be inveigled into an undertaking what might well be a *guerre de magnificence*? At length an 'Aragon crusade' was decided on in January 1284. An army of considerable strength marched under Philip III himself, and occupied the Roussillon, drove into Catalonia and took Gerona. It then withdrew under the strain of an epidemic. The King died on the way home in October 1285. Peter III died twenty-five days later; and Charles of Anjou had already died in January of the same year.

This first war of conquest beyond her frontiers thus ended in a setback for France. The fact that she undertook it was nevertheless a sign of growing power. It was also a sign of a new age, and the end of that reign of 'equity' to which St Louis had accustomed his people.

The ramparts of Avila, a town of great strategic importance in medieval Castile.

FRENCH CULTURE IN THE THIRTEENTH CENTURY

Language and literature

French culture radiated over all Europe. The essential vehicle of it was the language, that *francien* dialect of the Ile-de-France which had rid itself of its more strident qualities and appealed to an ever-increasing number of people.

This diffusion is explained by the expansion of the royal domain itself and by the fact that in the thirteenth century the Kingdom of France was by far the most densely populated area of western Europe. The essential role played by lines of communication must also be taken into account, for along them ideas, customs and influences could find their way. The importance of the Fairs of Champagne — that great international meeting place — cannot be exaggerated. In fact French became the language of big business in the thirteenth century. Nor must we forget France's military influence through the steady flow of French knights to England, south Italy, and the Middle East, as well as to Spain during the crusades of the *Reconquista*. The political as well as the commercial contacts helped to extend the diffusion of French culture.

Thus the French language, the language of chivalry — that institution that knew no frontiers — became the language of the élite all over Europe. Every cultivated man visited France, and he sent his sons to study there. All over Europe French tutors could be found. Everywhere the work of Vincent de Beauvais, Adam de la Halle, Rutebeuf and Jean de Meung was being imitated; they were imitated in Catalonia, in Portugal, in Germany, in Italy, and it was in French that the Florentine Brunetto Latini wrote his masterpiece *Le Trésor*, justifying himself thus: 'And if some would ask why this book is written in Romance, in the language of the French... it is because their speech is more delectable and more common to all'.

Fourteenth-century chapterhouse vaulting at Wells Cathedral, Somerset. England withstood the influence of French Gothic styles more firmly than continental Europe. Early English and

Decorated styles predominate at Wells Cathedral, built in the late twelfth and early thirteenth centuries. Wells then retained some of the importance it enjoyed in Saxon times. *Scheerboom*

The University of Paris

A sign of France's cultural leadership was the extraordinary reputation of the University of Paris during the thirteenth century. Most of the universities founded during that century, whether German, English, Italian or Spanish, modelled their organisation on that of Paris. The greatest thinkers of the age had to establish their reputation in Paris. The German Dominican, Albertus Magnus, taught there from 1245 to 1248; the Franciscan, St Bonaventura of Tuscany, from 1250 to 1256; and the greatest metaphysical genius of the age, St Thomas Aquinas, from 1252-9 and from 1269-72. Students flowed in from all parts of Europe. Matthew of Paris tells us there were three thousand in the colleges there in 1214. As a seat of learning Paris was unrivalled.

Diffusion of Gothic art

The overriding influence of French culture was still more complete in the field of artistic creation. The thirteenth century was the golden age of Gothic art, which fully deserves the name *opus francigenum* given it by contemporary commentators.

Right from its birth Gothic art was closely linked with the primacy of French civilisation and the authority of the French kings. Created and developed within the royal domain — within that Ile-de-France which was the very heart of the kingdom — Gothic art reflected in its diffusion throughout the kingdom the progress of the monarchy. It went on spreading beyond the Ile-de-France until it became the art of the West.

In Germany the cathedrals of Bamberg and Naumburg were inspired directly by the first Gothic buildings in France, Laon and Soissons. The cathedrals of Strasbourg and Cologne, whose choirs, probably of French origin, were constructed by Master Gerhardt, were both inspired by Rheims and Amiens. In Spain the cathedrals of Toledo, Burgos and Leon derive directly from Bourges. And the influence of the French masters went much further afield: to the Near East with the fortresses of the crusades; to the cathedrals of Famagusta and Nicosia; to Antwerp, Malines, Utrecht and Breda in the Low Countries; to the cathedral of Uppsala built under the direction of Etienne Bonneuil; to Poland where St Stanislas of Cracow had an exact copy made of Amiens; to Hungary where Villard de Honnecourt and Jean de Saint-Dié built the cathedral of Alba Julia, finished in 1287. The fact that thirteenth-century religious architecture all over Christendom was derived from that of France was not due entirely to the favourable historic conditions which enabled France to export her artists and her ideas. It was due also to the intrinsic value of Gothic architecture, whose formula is unique, with its three basic features — ogive ribs, the broken arch, the flying buttress — where Romanesque style had been made up of several

337

Henry III of England and Queen Eleanore (sister-in-law of St Louis) returning from Gascony, possibly after the signing in 1260 of the treaty that ended the First Hundred Years' War. He returned to unruly barons in England, and it took him seven years to suppress them. *Giraudon*

distinct formulas. The overall result is that regional variety is much less marked in the Gothic.

Naturally, in the course of spreading to other countries Gothic architecture underwent a certain amount of adaptation. In Germany it tended to become more emphatic, more exaggerated, more dramatic in its sculptural expression. In Scandinavia the use of wood introduced certain modifications; while in Italy, where Romanesque tradition was more vigorous, the bays were fewer and smaller. As for England, she showed herself more resistant to French influence, though many cathedrals, Salisbury and Lincoln for example, strongly reflect it.

Nevertheless Gothic architecture in its purest form remains, by virtue of its unity, the perfect expression of that cultural upsurge of the thirteenth century which reached out for universality. It expresses also the harmonious balance aimed at by the men of that time, a balance that was short-lived, like the French ascendancy in the golden age of St Louis.

TEMPORARY ECLIPSE OF ENGLAND

The implacable conflict between the two great traditional powers, the Papacy and the Empire, had enabled one of the chief national monarchies to extend its cultural and political influence, and to play a leading part in western Europe. That part might be snatched from her by the other national monarchy that had developed at her side, Plantagenet England. But in England the thirteenth century was one of internal difficulties surrounding the monarchy. For if the monarchy of France developed slowly towards a more and more authoritative, almost absolute rule, that of England was modified by the development of parliamentary institutions, one of the outstanding features of her history.

Magna Carta

The origins of the difficulties surrounding the English monarchy were multiple. The Plantagenets, more continental than insular, had only too often sacrificed England to their interests across the Channel. It has already been remarked that Richard Coeur de Lion, in a reign of ten years, spent only five months in England. This Continental policy of the Plantagenets had, moreover, brought disillusionment. After the sorry end of Henry II, the fame won by Richard was ephemeral; then came the humiliating defeat of John at the hands of Philip Augustus, which certainly undermined the prestige of the dynasty. The conduct of John at home, and the assassination of Arthur I of Brittany, still further discredited the monarchy. Bereft of chivalrous qualities, all-important in those days, John also suffered from a nervous disorder which made him oscillate between buoyancy and acute depression. Able but unlucky, he cut a poor figure as a sovereign compared to the cool and astute Philip Augustus, to say nothing of St Louis, and it is not surprising that with him started a succession of royal capitulations that may be divided into three stages.

Firstly, Magna Carta. Feudal opposition, already powerful under Henry II, became still more assertive under John. There was no lack of grievances: the crushing taxation to finance the war against Philip Augustus, the humiliations suffered by the king on the Continent, the scandals of his private life, the conflict with the Church over the See of Canterbury and John's consequent excommunication. The revolt, which had been incubating for some time, broke out violently after the disasters of Bouvines and La Roche aux Moines. In May 1215 the rebellious barons occupied London. John, taking refuge at Windsor, at first refused to make any concessions, but in the end, aware that all were against him, he accepted Magna Carta, the charter William Pitt was to describe as the 'Bible of the Constitution'. It simply gave effect to the clauses of the petition which the barons had previously presented and which the King had agreed to. It confined itself to re-establishing those feudal rights which, since Henry II, the kings had been wont to ignore. Naturally it did not establish a parliament, nor any sort of permanent control of the government by an elected assembly; it did not even give the barons the right to nominate the king's officers; lastly, it did not formulate the principle of taxation by consent. It nevertheless struck a decisive blow at the tendency of royal power to become absolute, and to that extent it took a first step in the evolution of England's constitutional monarchy. And, as it joined the burghers of the towns to the other two parties, the Church and the feudal lords, we can say that it was the politically conscious elements in the English nation which imposed precise limits to the prerogatives of the Crown.

The principles of Magna Carta, once laid down, invited further development. And they were developed all the more readily because John's son, Henry III (1207-72), was a feeble sovereign destitute of political acumen. Married to the daughter of the Count of Provence, he offended the English by surrounding himself with Frenchmen, whom he loaded with favours, and also by his complete subservience to the Pope. Accordingly, little by little, Parliament emerged from the Great Council and became more conscious of itself as opposition to the king grew. In 1258 Henry was forced to underwrite the Provisions of Oxford, which were followed the next year by the Provisions of Westminster, establishing a permanent control of the royal exercise of power by a baronial council, while four knights in each county were to enquire into the wrongs done by local sheriffs. Little came, however, of the plan drawn up in 1265 after another revolt of the barons. Their leader was Simon de Montfort, whose father of the same name had fought in the crusade against the Albigenses. This Simon de Montfort was brother-in-law to Henry III by his marriage to Eleanore Plantagenet. At Evesham in 1265 Henry III revenged himself on Simon de Montfort for his earlier defeat at Lewes, but he was not able to stem the current which was running against absolute monarchy.

His successor, Edward I (1272-1307), although enjoying much more prestige than his predecessors, had also to accept this evolution. Pressed by the need for money to continue his wars with the Scots and the Welsh, he conceded some of the demands of his barons. The centre of power in England was now no longer the royal household, but the King — in Parliament. The Commons, made up of knights and burgesses, were not yet formally an integral part of Parliament, but they were used for consultation. From this precedent vital developments were to follow.

The growth of English power

Though her internal political struggles helped to turn England away from the larger affairs of Europe, they did not hinder her from acquiring a firm administrative framework as well as increased organisation of her national resources, which later allowed her to meet France as an equal, though the latter was bigger, richer, and more populated. The administration of justice in England was firmly established by the end of the thirteenth century. Exact procedure was laid down by the second Statute of Westminster of 1285, and trial by jury became general. The counties were administered by sheriffs, and these officers definitely deserve the name of officials from the beginning of the fourteenth century. Henry III and Edward I were legislating kings and in this capacity they were assisted by genuine jurists versed in Roman law, like Franciscus Accursii, the most remarkable among them.

The vicissitudes of British history did not stop the progress towards unification. The custom of making the king's brother Duke of Cornwall dated from the middle of the thirteenth century. Wales resisted English hegemony longer, but the Welsh King Llywelyn had to accept the suzerainty of Henry III under the Peace of Montgomery in 1267, and his independence was further modified in the Peace of Conway in 1277. Success was slower in Scotland. Though Robert Bruce's alliance with France did not save him from submission in 1297, the spirit of resistance was asserted by William Wallace, and after the defeat of the English at Bannockburn in 1314 the Scots kingdom remained independent. As to Ireland, it had been at least nominally subjected by Henry II. With these reservations, it may be said that the thirteenth century was an important stage in the unification of the British Isles.

Keeping out of major engagements, England was biding her time. Meanwhile her progress had been considerable. To quote Pirenne: 'The nation and the sovereign were associated in the government of the country. If limits had been fixed to the king's power, if, alone amongst his peers, he had to forswear purely dynastic wars and confine himself to those campaigns approved and subsidised by his people, he was the stronger from this cohesion. From the end of the thirteenth century, the policy pursued by England was a national policy in the full acceptance of the term. Therein lies the contrast she showed through the centuries: agitation and internecine struggles at home, coinciding with continuity of foreign policy and a persistance and tenacity in execution never seen elsewhere.'

Edward I's Parliament of 1295. Edward summoned this assembly, consisting of representatives of the Church, lay magnates and two citizens, or burgesses, from each city or borough, because he felt the kingdom was threatened from various directions, and that ' what touches all should be approved by all '. This assembly was the model for all future English Parliaments.

CHAPTER TWENTY

FRINGE EUROPE AND ISLAM
IN THE THIRTEENTH CENTURY

THE FRINGES OF EUROPE

EASTERN EUROPE

The Latin empire of the East

It was really Venice that gave birth to the Latin Empire of Roumania in that she was largely instrumental in diverting the Fourth Crusade, which had been launched by Innocent III for the recovery of Jerusalem from the infidels, into whose hands it had fallen in 1187. The doge Enrico Dandolo had agreed to transport the crusaders for 85,000 silver marks, and he led the fleet himself, for Venice wanted to divert the operation to its own ends. Unable to pay the sum bargained for, the crusaders were obliged to stop on the way and recover Zara,

just captured from Venice by the King of Hungary. It was then that a wonderful opportunity was presented to the Venetians by the request for help made by Isaac Angelus and his son Alexius IV, joint Emperors of Byzantium, who had been dethroned by Alexius III. In spite of the protests of Innocent III and the reluctance of the crusaders, Dandolo successfully carried out the attack on Byzantium in July 1203. Isaac and his son were restored to the throne. But in February 1204 they were again dethroned in an anti-Latin rising led by Alexius

Murtzuphlus, son-in-law of Alexius III. That left the Latins with no choice but to take Byzantium a second time, and the Venetians were only too keen. In April 1204 the town was taken and sacked during three days, Alexius V having taken to flight.

When the booty had been shared, it was the turn of the Empire itself to be divided. In May Baldwin IX, Count of Flanders, was crowned at St Sophia, and he received as his personal domain the European coast of the Sea of Marmara and, in the western part of Asia Minor, Bithynia, Mysia, and the islands of Samothrace, Lesbos, Chios, Samos and Cos. But he got only five-eighths of Constantinople. The remainder, which included St Sophia, went to the Venetians. In fact, they got the lion's share: Epirus, the Ionian Islands, Acarnania, Aetolia, the Peloponnesus, Gallipoli, Heraclea, Adrianople, and the islands of Naxos, Andros, Euboea and Crete. The doge had a dispensation from doing homage to the new Emperor; lastly, the newly appointed Latin patriarch was Thomas Morosini, a Venetian. The weakness of the Emperor was further increased when he was obliged to grant numerous fiefs to the chief crusaders. Thus William of Champlitte and Geoffrey de Villehardouin, the chronicler's nephew, founded the principality of Achaea, and Otho de la Roche the duchy of Athens. In the end Innocent III accepted the *fait accompli*, hoping it would lead to the union of the two Churches.

The Greek Church was not completely destroyed. Based on Nicaea in Asia Minor, it managed to survive. But this was a blow from which it was never to recover. The events of 1204 were a distant preparation for the fall of Constantinople in 1453.

Fall of the Empire of Roumania

Baldwin's reign as Emperor was fully occupied in taking possession of his territories. After successful engagements in Anatolia, enabling him to occupy Mysia, he was forced to return post haste to Europe to face Johannitsa, Tsar of the Bulgars, with whom he had become involved in a pointless quarrel. He was defeated near Adrianople in 1205 and taken prisoner, and the first Latin Emperor of Roumania died in captivity.

By now, a year after its creation, this Empire was practically reduced to the town of Constantinople. Fortunately his successor, Henry of Flanders, was a remarkable soldier and an able administrator. In 1208, at Philippopolis, he defeated the Bulgars decisively and delivered Thrace from their menace. Turning to Asia, he was

The Sultan's messengers discussing terms of ransom with Christian prisoners. After a thirteenth-century manuscript.

The minaret of a mosque, from which the muezzin (priest) gives the call to prayer at the appointed hours.

even able to occupy the whole Bithynian coast and almost all Mysia. Furthermore, by some astute moves in favour of the Greek clergy, he was able to win over the civil population. But he died prematurely in June 1216 and his death gave the signal for disintegration. The incapable Peter de Courtenay, who succeeded him and reigned from 1221 to 1228, lost the whole of Macedonia, the Asiatic territories, and most of the islands. A last flicker of spirit glowed under the rule of the octogenarian John of Brienne, ex-king of Jerusalem, who governed the empire during the minority of the young Baldwin II. With a hundred and sixty knights and some foot soldiers, he put up a magnificent defence of Constantinople for eleven months, when it was besieged by John Vatatzes of Nicaea and Asen, Tsar of Bulgaria. The town was finally saved by the arrival of a Venetian squadron in 1236. But on the old man's death decline rapidly and inexorably set in again. Baldwin II went from one court to another in the West begging for help; to buy the help he needed, he sold the relics of his churches. All in vain: no one would listen to him, and the Latin Empire was irrevocably lost. Reduced to no more than the capital, it lingered on till at last in July 1261 Michael Palaeologus took the town by surprise and drove Baldwin out.

Thus, fifty-seven years after its creation, the Latin Empire of Roumania collapsed; it was an extraordinary and fragile political creation, threatened from its birth (as had been the Greek Empire) by its Balkan neighbours, and threatened too by all the Greek despots of Asia Minor and Epirus who had never been completely brought to heel. Its foundations were too unstable to withstand the hostility of the local population and the rivalries among the conquerors themselves. It is surprising that it lasted half a century; it certainly would not have done so without the powerful support of the Venetians, anxious to make the most of this foothold in the East — a support which, even after the fall of Constantinople, enabled the Latins to stay on for a time in Morea.

Survival of Latin states in Greece

In 1205 William of Champlitte, assisted by Geoffrey de Villehardouin, undertook the conquest of the Peloponnesus, and completed it without difficulty in 1207. Wisely, Champlitte left the ports of Corone and Modon at the foot of the peninsula to the Venetians, for their alliance was useful. After Champlitte's return to France, Villehardouin completed the occupation of the Peloponnesus and founded the principality of Morea. The establishment of the Franks here was less precarious than in the Empire of Roumania, for Villehardouin pursued an intelligent policy towards the Greeks. He allowed the big landowners to retain most of their property, weaving them into his own feudal organisation. Moreover his son, Geoffrey II, who reigned from 1218 to 1245, increased Frank colonisation by attracting a number of knights

John Alexander, Tsar of Bulgaria, his wife Theodora, and his sons John Asen and John Shishmanich. *British Museum*

from Champagne, Burgundy and the Franche-Comté. Thus he avoided the great weakness in the Empire of Roumania and the Frankish states of the Near East — the small number of Westerners compared to the native population. Lastly, a strong line of fortresses was constructed to hold back the Greek mountain people of Laconia, who had never been thoroughly subjected. This achievement was compromised, however, by the megalomania of William, brother of Geoffrey II, who, wishing to extend his suzerainty to Euboea and the Archipelago, offended the Venetians and spurred the barons of central Greece to form a coalition against him. Defeating William at Kastoria, the Greeks forced him to relinquish the four principal fortresses of Morea: Mistra, Geraki, Monemvasia, and Maina. William took his revenge at Prinitsa (1264), but he was never in a position to reoccupy Mistra. As a last resort he appealed to Charles of Anjou, whom he acknowledged as his suzerain. He also married his daughter to one of Charles's sons. Accordingly, at his death in 1278 without male heir, Morea became a simple dependency of the Italo-Angevin kingdom, and remained so for over a century.

The other Frankish principality in Greece was the Duchy of Athens. Under the La Roche dynasty it served Morea as a bastion against any Byzantine interference, particularly during the reign of John, duke from 1263 to 1280. After the absorption of Morea by the Angevins of Naples, it became the most brilliant Latin state in Greece. The splendour of the court at Thebes, the favourite residence of Guy II (duke from 1287 to 1308) was celebrated throughout Christendom. But his successor, Walter V of Brienne, avid for conquest, engaged some Catalan mercenaries with whom he was soon in dispute. Trying to get rid of them, he was defeated at Orchomenus in 1311, and he and all the French knights in Greece were slain in the field. The jubilant Catalonians set up a sort of military republic under the suzerainty of the Aragon King of Sicily. It lasted till 1387.

This battle marks the abrupt end of the French regime in the eastern Mediterranean.

Bulgaria under the Asen dynasty

The part played in the Balkans by the Slav states grouped north and north-west of the Byzantine Empire must not be underestimated; in particular the part played by the second Bulgarian Empire, whose interventions were continual during the brief existence of the Latin Empire of Roumania.

The founder of the second Bulgarian Empire was Ivan Asen I, the famous Johannitsa. Bulgaria had been virtually independent since the 1186 rising, and in 1201 the Emperor, Alexius III, was forced to acknowledge the fact. A great territorial expansion then began, reaching to Nis and Belgrade, which was taken from the Serbs, and also into Hungary and Macedonia. A rapprochement with the Church led in November 1204 to Johannitsa's coronation as King of Bulgaria by the legate of Innocent III.

Henceforth the Bulgarian kings, firmly supported by savage Kumanian horsemen, their redoubtable allies of the southern steppes of the Ukraine, occupied a position in which they were able to hold the balance between the Latins and the Greek despots of Nicaea and Thessaly.

At first Johannitsa wanted to be on good terms with the Latins, but he was rebuffed. So, turning against the despot of Thessaly, he adopted the role of the defender of Orthodoxy, hoping to revive the Greek Empire to his own advantage. In April 1205, he inflicted a disastrous defeat on Baldwin I at Adrianople. The Graeco-Bulgarian understanding did not last long, however, and Johannitsa was soon fighting the Greeks of Thrace and Macedonia. During the campaign he was assassinated while besieging Thessalonica (1207). After the ineffectual Boris, who reigned from 1207 to 1218, and who renewed attempts to make friends with the Latins, Ivan Asen II began what was to be the most successful reign of the Bulgarian Second Empire. A remarkable administrator, an excellent leader in war, a great builder, he turned his capital Trnovo into a large and beautiful city which sought to rival Constantinople. He revived the title of tsar. So great was his renown that, on the death of Robert de Courtenay, the Latins seriously considered inviting him to be tutor to the young Baldwin II; but the idea fell through on account of clerical opposition — an unfortunate turn of events, for the hostility of the powerful tsar was dangerous. He had recently crushed the despot of Epirus, Theodore Comnenus, at Klokonitza (March

found permanent refuge in Constantinople in 1280 after a revolt of the boyars had substituted George, the first of the Terterovski dynasty. By this time the great days of medieval Bulgaria were over.

Serbia under the Nemanyich dynasty

Further removed from Byzantium, Serbia's contacts were with the Adriatic and the Morava-Vardar trade route; accordingly her policy, in contrast to Bulgaria's, was constantly turned westward.

The great founder of the Serbian nation was Stephen Nemanya, who retired to a monastery in 1196. His second son — also Stephen — succeeded him in 1200. It was he who won for Serbia her complete independence from Constantinople by assuming the title of king in place of that of Grand Zhupan (governor). To assume the royal crown, consecration by the West was necessary, and he was crowned by a legate of Honorius III in 1217. This was the second time the Papacy had intervened in the coronation of a Balkan king. The king's subjects had remained rigorously Orthodox, however, and he succeeded in obtaining from Constantinople the recognition of Serbia's religious autonomy. He was then crowned a second

For both Bulgars and Serbs, the goal of every effort was the destruction of Constantinople, from Kalojan to Stephen Dusan. Orthodox Christianity remained the religious and cultural link between the Balkan peoples. *Larousse*

1230). Disgusted by the attitude of the Latins, Ivan Asen II took the lead in an anti-Latin league which besieged Constantinople. The latter was defended by the heroic John of Brienne, and we have seen how the siege came to be raised. After another rapprochement with the Latins and the Pope, he broke with them again in 1239. Two years later he died.

The death throes of the Second Bulgarian Empire lasted seventeen years. The last tsars of the Asen dynasty had to cede tract after tract of their territories to Epirus or Hungary. One of them, Constantine Asen, tsar from 1258 to 1277, began the practice of calling in the Mongols of the Volga. From then on, internal disorder increased, encouraging the intervention of more powerful neighbours. The dynasty came to an end with Ivan Asen III, who

time by his brother, St Sava, and the Pope approved of this second coronation, although it was done according to Orthodox rites. It was during his reign that Serbia first became conscious of political identity. His reign was also notable for remarkable economic development and for the establishment of commercial relations with Venice.

The death of Stephen I in 1228 was followed by two undistinguished reigns (those of Radoslav and Vladislav), during which Serbia fell under Bulgarian influence and was even overrun in 1241 by the Mongols of the Golden Horde. Serbian fortunes revived, however, under Uros I (1243-76) whose reign compares chronologically and politically with that of St Louis. With peace at home and abroad, trade revived and the position of the monarchy was consolidated.

Three knights in chain-mail from the west door of the Cathedral of Trogir, Yugoslavia, by the Croatian sculptor Radovan. *Groevic*

After the short reign of Stephen Dragutin (1276-82), who improved relations with the Pope, Stephen Uros II Milutin entered on one of the most remarkable periods in the history of medieval Serbia. Reigning from 1282 to 1321 (at the same time as Philip the Fair) he was, like his French counterpart, a realist and an opportunist, and under his rule the country expanded considerably towards the Adriatic. Cleverly playing his cards, sometimes using the West, sometimes the East, he began the occupation of Macedonia by taking Skoplje in 1282. Michael Palaeologus was too occupied elsewhere to be able to retaliate, and his successor Andronicus II had no other resort than to offer his daughter Simone to Milutin. The king was tempted by the idea of joining Serbia to the Byzantine Empire under his authority, but his policy, considered too favourable to Byzantium, provoked nationalist reaction, which he succeeded in putting down but which nevertheless prompted him to approach the Pope — Clement V, the first of the Avignon Popes — with an offer to bring his country into the Roman Church. Nothing came of the suggestion, however, and the Serbian Council remained separate. When he died in October 1321, Milutin left a considerably enlarged Serbia, stretching from the Adriatic to the Danube, a country at peace and prosperous. This 'holy king' prepared the way for his grandson, Stephen Dusan, who in the fourteenth century was to be the creator of Greater Serbia.

CENTRAL AND NORTHERN EUROPE

German vigour in a chaotic Empire

The dominant event of central and northern Europe in the thirteenth century is the renewal of German expansion, and the revival of the old antagonism between the Germans and the Slavs. This phenomenon is the more strange in that it occurred during the Great Interregnum, when the Holy Roman Empire seemed to be drifting towards its ruin. The imperial crown was being claimed by three pretenders, William of Holland, Richard of Cornwall, and Alfonso X of Castile, each supported by a group of electors, backed in turn by some king or Pope. Now that there was no vigorous Hohenstaufen hand to rule them, the German nobles were coming into their own again, with their burgraves and their marauding knights (Raubritten), against whom the only protection lay in the urban confederations, such as the Swabian League, the Hanseatic League, or the Confederation of the Rhine. The renewed expansion was thus in no way the work of the Emperors, who had neither power nor prestige. It was due rather to the powerful feudal lords of the east, and in particular to the margraves of Brandenburg and the dukes of Saxony.

This expansion had the character not so much of a

conquest as of a genuine colonisation, for it accompanied a sharp rise in the German population, which overflowed into those regions abandoned by Germans of the fourth century, when they had been unable to resist Slav pressure. The expansion was effected by compact groups, generally from towns, who settled among the Slav peasantry, with whom they did not mix at all. In this way they created outposts of Germanism far to the east and north. They were powerfully supported by the missionary work of the German military orders along the Baltic, whose efforts were directed at exterminating the pagans rather than converting them. This holy war did much to consolidate Germanism in the Baltic countries, and in doing so it raised a barrier between the Slavs and the sea, Russia and Poland being driven inland.

GERMAN COLONISATION

In Hungary and Bohemia

The kingdom of St Stephen had risen to temporary greatness during the reign of Bela III, who freed the country from Byzantine domination and put its Government on a solid basis. But Bela III died in 1196 before he could deal with the danger threatened by the big landowners, who aimed at getting the royal power under their tutelage. The quarrels between the two sons of Bela III over the succession only made matters easier for the landowners, and in 1222 Andrew II was obliged to promulgate the so-called Golden Bull, in which he undertook to assemble yearly a diet of the nobles, and promised not to impose any taxes without their prior consent. Lastly this 'Magna Carta' of Hungary recognised the right of the landowners to revolt should the king fail to honour his engagements. This capitulation of royal authority led Hungary into a state of latent anarchy which greatly facilitated the infiltration of German colonists, who were called in by Bela IV to recolonise the land devastated by the Mongols. It was the Germans who founded Buda.

German infiltration into Bohemia was still more overt. It was facilitated by the fact that the country had for long been in close contact with Germany: it had been part of the Carolingian Empire and then part of the Holy Roman Empire. In 1203 Ottokar I was raised to the dignity of king by Philip of Swabia; in 1207 when Ottokar went over to the support of Philip's adversary, Otto of Brunswick, the title was confirmed by the Pope. Ottokar was obliged to accept imperial suzerainty, and till his death in 1230 he was dominated by the Empire. With the high offices of state filled by Germans, the latter took up permanent residence in Bohemia, and progressively ousted the Slavs. From 1253 there was a national revolt.

Taking advantage of the difficulties besetting the Empire on the death of Frederick II, Ottokar II, the third of the Premyslide dynasty, brilliantly established the authority of the monarchy. Already in possession of the archduchies of Austria, he acquired Styria and took Carinthia. He even disputed the title of King of the Romans with Rudolph of Habsburg, whose entry on the scene brought to an end the Great Interregnum. Ottokar's authority now reached from the Bohemian Diamond to the Adriatic. He would never have acquired such status had he not relied on the German burghers in the towns, the only element capable of furnishing the resources necessary for his great ambitions. The end came with his defeat and death in 1278 in the battle of Durnkrut. The victor, Rudolph of Habsburg, put Bohemia back under imperial tutelage and the last kings of the Premyslide line, Wenceslas II (1278 to 1305), and Wenceslas III (assassinated in 1306) were simply the representatives of a reinvigorated Empire. In 1310, however, John of Luxemburg came to the throne, and French influence succeeded German influence in Bohemia.

In Poland

Anarchy and confusion in Poland facilitated German expansion. The death of Casimir II in 1194 and the scramble for the throne had led to acute disorder in the country. Various dukes in turn — those of Mazovia, Sandomir, and Great Poland — appropriated the grandducal title. Henry the Bearded, Duke of Silesia, dreamt of making his son, Henry the Pious, King of Poland. It came to nothing, for the younger Henry fell heroically at Liegnitz in 1241 halting the Mongol hordes. For half a century the horizon of these dukes was no wider than their own region, and they showed themselves quite incapable of stopping the expansion of their redoubtable neighbour Brandenburg, whose surplus population was constantly infiltrating along the borders of Great Poland and Western Pomerania, and advancing towards Eastern Pomerania, which they slowly nibbled away.

The Baltic crusade

Since the end of the twelfth century, the German ports of Bremen and Lübeck had multiplied their commercial links with the pagan population of Livonia. At the same time missionary work had been launched by the archbishops of the Great German See of Bremen and Hamburg. A bishop of Livonia had been appointed, but conversion was slow. In 1199 Innocent III invited the Christians of northern Germany to go on a crusade to Livonia; little was achieved, however, as the crusaders merely stayed the number of months needed to fulfil their vows. Then, in 1202, Albert, Bishop of Riga, had the idea of founding a military order, a permanent army on the model of the Hospitalers, but independent of Rome, taking orders only from him. These were the Knights of the Sword. Once again the effort failed in its avowed object, and there were many pagan reprisals which ended only after the Knights of the Sword had in 1237 fused with the Teutonic Knights, the two orders being brought strictly under the Papacy. The decisive step was the colonisation of the whole of Prussia, which was followed by the conversion of all the Baltic peoples from the Vistula to the Niemen.

The imprudent appeal made in 1226 by Conrad, Duke of Mazovia, to the Teutonic Knights opened a huge field of action to German colonisation. For, as the Knights advanced, they built strongholds along the rivers which were to become centres of German colonisation and finally the first towns of Prussia: Kulm, founded in 1232, Thorn, founded in 1231, and Elbing, founded in 1237. This German penetration naturally encountered some violent national resistance, and for forty years the struggle was merciless. It ended in 1283 with complete German possession, by which time a large part of the original population had been exterminated. The appeal of a Pole had resulted in the establishment of a new German state, cutting Poland off from the Baltic.

Russia turns her back on Europe

German expansion eastward prevented the expansion of Russia towards central Europe. Split into fragments by quarrels over succession, under the loose primacy of Kiev, Russia was in a state of anarchy at the beginning of the thirteenth century. Moreover, shut off from the Baltic by the Germans and hemmed in by the Poles, she was also constantly threatened by the Polovtzi or Kumanians inhabiting the southern steppes. The great trade routes which had once made Kiev an active commercial centre were now closed. At the time the Byzantine-Kievan civilisation was sinking, a great movement was taking place in the region of the middle Volga, amounting to an eastward swing of the Russian population. In fact, Russia seemed to be turning her back on Europe and settling down to a purely rural civilisation. But the dynastic conflicts were to be just as bitter in the new principality of Vladimir as they had been in Kiev. Fragmented and enfeebled, she could not resist Mongol attack.

THE BALTIC WORLD

Danish resistance to German expansion

Danish power had spread considerably under the reign of Knut VI (1182-1202), who had occupied parts of Pomerania and Mecklenburg and imposed his tutelage on Lübeck and Hamburg. His successor, Waldemar II, who reigned from 1202 to 1241, obliged Norway to pay tribute. Inevitably Danish expansion, which in 1219 reached the borders of Esthonia, came into conflict with German imperialism. After his initial successes, Waldemar II was taken prisoner by the Count of Schwerin in 1223, and Danish expansion was halted. Waldemar II made a final effort in 1227, but his defeat at Bornhöved in the same year definitively put an end to Danish ambitions, leaving the Baltic to the Germans.

The Swedes spread into Finland

There was one area of the Baltic in which German expansion was always to be rebuffed: in Finland, which had been open to Swedish infiltration since the twelfth century. As Swedish colonisation developed, conversion had spread far along the southern coast by the end of the century, particularly round the town of Turku, since called Abo. The Swedes encountered less opposition to their expansion from the native Finns than from the Slavs, particularly those of Novgorod, who supported the pagan population of Karelia.

From the middle of the thirteenth century, the Swedes made a great effort under Earl Birger. The Hame area of the lake district was conquered, and the town of Tavastehus founded. Earl Birger's grandson led a victorious expedition into Karelia to put an end to the Slav menace. In 1293 Viborg was founded, and the Swedes, pushing the Russians before them, reached the shores of Lake Ladoga. The Russians counter-attacked along the southern coast of Finland, and in 1318 burnt Turku. Finally the Baltic merchant towns, finding the war harmful to their trade, intervened and imposed a settlement. The peace of Nöteborg was signed in August 1323; this fixed the eastern frontier of Finland, and gave the Swedes trading rights in Novgorod. Furthermore the two parties undertook not to construct any new fortifications in the part of Karelia they occupied. Finland was now definitely controlled by Sweden and the Roman Church.

THE MONGOL ADVANCE AND THE RECESSION OF ISLAM

Europe, fragmented and torn asunder by the great duel between Pope and Emperor, seemed quite unfit in spite of the French ambitions already described to undertake the leadership of a universal Empire. Now, out of the wastes of Central Asia, a new and formidable power emerged: the Mongols. Under their young chieftain Jenghiz Khan, they launched their assault upon the world.

THE MONGOL EMPIRE

Jenghiz Khan the Conqueror

The warrior who in the space of twenty years was to make himself master of Asia was born about 1154 or 1155 in one of the Oirat tribes that had been driven by the Turks to the west of Lake Baikal. These tribes, perpetually at war with one another, led a rough, wretched life, wandering over the Siberian steppes. Mongol tradition has it that the future Jenghiz Khan was born holding in his right hand a clot of blood like a red stone. As a young man, he was distinguished by his height, his broad forehead and his long beard, as well as by his curious grey-green eyes. Soon becoming chief of his tribe, Temujin, as he was called, was elected Khan by his fellow tribal chieftains. 'We have decided to make thee Khan,' they said. 'We shall ride in the forefront of the battle. When we take women or girls we shall give them to thee. We shall go in the forefront of the hunt, and what we kill we shall hand to thee. If in the course of the battle we disobey thy orders or if in peace we encumber thee, then leave us in solitude.'

The new Khan now abandoned the name of Temujin (blacksmith) and assumed that of Jenghiz, which no doubt indicated the universality of his power. His election induced the tribes to gather together under a single authority. Endowed with a remarkable sense of organisation and discipline, he carefully assigned duties to each member of his *ordu* (a word meaning 'tent' and from which the word 'horde' comes). Above all he instituted a formidable military organisation. Everybody between fifteen and seventy was enrolled in the army, which was under the orders of highly organised officers. A new tactical procedure was adopted: attack by large bodies of horsemen, unencumbered by infantry and co-ordinated by an elaborate system of signalling by pennants. The extraordinary mobility and discipline of these Mongol formations left the heavy Moslem and European armies powerless. For in one day Jenghiz Khan's horsemen could devastate land in a radius of sixty miles and then be ready to do the same again the next day. It was because they were thus able to appear first here then there that their opponents were inclined to exaggerate their numbers.

The proclamation of the Mongol Empire

Responding to the appeal of the Kin dynasty in China, who wanted to throw off the yoke of the Tatars, and with the assistance of another tribe, the Keraits, Jenghiz Khan destroyed Tatar power; the date of this is uncertain, but probably lies between 1194 and 1200. A new campaign launched in 1202 practically exterminated them altogether. 'Let us take advantage of our victory,' said the chieftain. 'Let us kill all the males that are taller than the axles of our wagons. The rest we will divide among us as slaves.' This success over the Tatars gave Jenghiz Khan absolute control over eastern Mongolia. Two years later he exterminated his former allies, the Keraits, which gave him central Mongolia; and a few months later still he exterminated the Naimans, which gave him western Mongolia.

Mongol warriors, from a thirteenth-century Japanese scroll. Jenghiz Khan's empire at this time stretched from Hungary to Korea. *Japanese Imperial Collection*

A Tatar leading a camel laden with all his possessions. The Tatars were a nomadic tribe whose power was destroyed by Jenghiz Khan. Chinese scroll painting; thirteenth century.

Master now of all Mongolia, he wanted his Khanate confirmed by all the tribes subjected, and in 1206 their assembly sanctioned the title of Khan which the conqueror had assumed ten years before. The Mongol Empire was now founded in law as well as in fact. There was still the universal empire to build.

The conquest of Peking

It was south-eastward, towards China, that Jenghiz Khan struck first. Three neighbouring states provided the target: firstly north China under the Kin or Golden dynasty, which was occupied by the Nüchih Tatars, a tribe related to the Manchus; secondly south China, where the Sung dynasty ruled over the Chinese national empire; thirdly, to the west near the Tibetan border, the Tangut kingdom, which had been founded two centuries earlier by a people of Tibetan race but Chinese culture. The latter had enjoyed a favoured position between the Far East and Persia, and had been the starting point of the famous 'silk route'.

Jenghiz Khan was unable to make a frontal attack on North China, protected as it was by the Great Wall, so he decided to outflank it by striking first at the Tangutans. But in this attack against a sedentary people, Mongol strategy, perfect for the steppes, was unsuccessful. Successful invasions of the Tangut kingdom took place in 1208 and these were a preliminary to a large scale attack on north China. As a pretext he was out to avenge the indignities long inflicted on the Mongol tributaries of the Kin dynasty. After two unsuccessful campaigns, Jenghiz Khan was able in 1213 to breach the Great Wall in two places, and to invade China with three armies. He blockaded Peking, which he would probably never have been able to take but for a revolt of the garrison, who opened the gates to him in 1214. There were still six more years of fighting before Jenghiz Khan's general, Mukuli, was able to wrench Chihli from the Nüchihs. Even then he had not captured their last stronghold, Honan, which fell in 1233, six years after the Khan's death.

The Western drive

The relative slowness of the occupation of China is largely explained by the fact that Jenghiz Khan could devote only part of his forces to that operation, absorbed as he was from 1218 onwards by the Mongol offensive against eastern Turkestan. For more than a century this area had been occupied by the Kara-Khitan Tatars, but the body of the population had long since become Moslems. The kings of the Kara-Khitans, or Gur Khans, had shown great religious tolerance; but in 1211 a Naiman chief, Kushluk, taking refuge in the country from Jenghiz Khan, had overthrown the king and taken his place. Then, under the influence of his Buddhist wife, he unwisely persecuted the Moslems, and moreover had the audacity to provoke Jenghiz Khan by attacking various Turkish tribes that were his vassals. A single campaign in 1218 disposed of Kushluk, giving the Khan possession of the old-established Kara-Khitan empire. The Mongol empire was now in direct and constant contact with the Moslem world.

A new, unknown, and mysterious world, consisting of the Sultanate of Khwarazm (west of Turkestan), eastern Iran and Afghanistan, now lay before Jenghiz Khan, and he hesitated to attack it. The Shahs, who were of Turkish origin, had become Islamised. Despite the instability of this empire, Jenghiz Khan was greatly impressed by its extent and thought only of establishing commercial relations with it. But when in 1218 his envoy was killed, he decided after much hesitation to attack. Three armies attacked the Sultanate in 1219, with himself at the head of the centre one. One by one the towns fell: Bokhara in February 1220, Samarkand in March, Kurkanj, the capital, in April 1221. Everywhere the slaughter was complete. The fleeing Shah, Muhammad, died of exhaustion.

It only remained to deal with the Khwarazmian dependencies, eastern Persia and Afghanistan. Eastern Persia, that is, Khorassan, was rapidly overrun, Merv taken in February 1221 and the inhabitants slaughtered, Nishapur taken in April and razed to the ground. The conquest of Afghanistan, defended by Muhammad's son, Jalal-ad-Din was much more difficult. Jenghiz Khan had to lead his armies in person to avenge reverses inflicted on his subordinates, and finally in November 1221 he won a decisive but dearly bought victory on the banks of the Indus. The conquest of these settled regions had lasting consequences on Mongol history. The conquest of the Khwarazmian empire can hardly have been much less brutal than the others, with the same massacres, the same pillage, the same destruction, but it was none the less a turning point of the Mongol advance in that the invaders seem to have become conscious of the advantages of urban life. By its victories the heir of old civilisations, the 'Empire of the steppes' was in the end to carry on their traditions.

It is remarkable that after the victory of 1221 Jenghiz Khan did not venture farther and attack the sultanate of Delhi, where Iltutmish, the greatest of the 'slave kings', had reigned since 1210. The Khan may have been impressed by the power of the Sultan — master of northern India from the Indus to the Gulf of Bengal — whose position had just been confirmed by the Caliph of Baghdad, the highest authority in the Moslem world. A simpler explanation, however, is that the Mongols were daunted by the heat, overcome by a climate they could not bear. However that may be, they were never able seriously to tackle India, in spite of several attempts by Jenghiz Khan's successors, and in spite of the decline of the sultanate of Delhi after the death of Iltutmish.

The raids in Persia and Russia

Pursuing Sultan Muhammad, Jenghiz Khan's two generals, Chépé and Sabutai, reached the Caspian, and they decided to probe further, not with a view to immediate conquest, but rather to reconnoitre and prepare for future expeditions. This raid took them across western Persia, plundering as they went, then on to the Caucasus, where in February 1221 they crushed a Georgian army near Tiflis. From there they went down towards the steppe of southern Russia. After decimating nomad Turkish tribes on the Black Sea coast, in May 1224 they encountered the Russian armies of Kiev, Galich and Smolensk. The battle, on the banks of the Kalka near Mariopol, ended with the utter defeat of the Russians. But Chépé and Sabutai had no intention of settling in Europe. They crossed the Urals and returned to Mongolia.

The end of Jenghiz Khan

After a final campaign to deal with the Tangutans, which despite failing health he had insisted on leading himself, Jenghiz Khan died in August 1227.

He had conquered an empire so vast that, in his own words, it was a year's journey from the centre to either end. He had had no time to organise it: that task he left to his successor, Ogdai. Nevertheless, before his death Jenghiz Khan had sketched out the main lines of organisation. Taking the advice of a Khitai general Yeh-lu Ts'u-ts'ai, who had come over to the Mongols, he disregarded the suggestion of his other generals that the conquered countries should be entirely destroyed and their populations massacred. Convinced of the advantages to be gained by 'a moderate tax on land, duties on merchandise, and taxes on salt and iron, all estimated to bring in 500,000 ounces of silver a year, 80,000 lengths of silk, and 400,000 sacks of corn', he was thinking at the end of his life of giving his empire the administrative framework without which exploitation of its resources was impossible. This was the origin of the Mongol exchequer and the institution of *darughas*, imperial bailiffs charged with tax collecting, recruiting auxiliary troops, and organising postal stages for the imperial service. This bare outline was to be filled in by Ogdai, Jenghiz Khan's third son.

Ogdai the Organiser (1227-41)

The son whom Jenghiz Khan chose to succeed him seems to have been more pacifically minded than his brothers or his father. Accordingly, the influence of Yeh-lu Ts'u-ts'ai, already strong during the last years of Jenghiz Khan's reign, was predominant during Ogdai's. And it was probably his influence which introduced Chinese

Ogdai receiving his portion on the death of his father, Jenghiz Khan. From *Le Livre des diversités et merveilles du monde*. Larousse

administrative customs into the Mongol empire. As Yeh-lu Ts'u-ts'ai liked to say: 'The empire was won on horseback, but you cannot govern on horseback.' Ogdai therefore decided to build a capital at Karakorum, in the very middle of Mongolia. A new scale of taxes demanded one head of cattle out of every hundred from nomad tribes, while settled populations were to pay a tithe of the harvest. Pastures were strictly allocated among the various tribes, and a general system of postal relays was enforced throughout the empire, a feature which excited the great admiration of the Venetian explorer Marco Polo. Wells were dug at intervals along all the roads of the great desert of Central Asia. In other words, the Mongol sovereign humbly sat down to learn from the settled peoples his father had subjugated. But the conquering spirit of the Mongols was not yet extinguished. Westward and eastward Ogdai carried on the unfinished conquests that were his legacy.

Seal of Bela IV of Hungary (1235-70).

Jenghiz Khan, the 'perfect warrior' (1162-1227), who conquered an empire so vast that it took two years to cross its breadth.

A battle between the followers of Islam and the fire-worshippers. Fire-worship was part of the Zoroastrian religion, whose de- votees were persecuted during the Moslem invasions of Persia. *Victoria and Albert Museum*

Ogdai's conquests

The last bastion of the Kin rulers, Honan, was attacked in 1232 by by Ogdai and his younger brother Tulé, assisted by the veteran Sabutai. In May 1233 the capital was taken and the last of the Kin dynasty committed suicide; the Kin were finally swept out of existence in 1234. The Mongols were now neighbours of southern China, still under the Sungs. The latter attempted to dispute the Mongols' right to Honan, and this led to invasion in 1235; but it was no more than a marauding raid, for the Mongols promptly evacuated the regions they invaded. The conquest of south China was postponed, as was that of Korea, whose capital was only temporarily occupied in 1231.

In 1225 Afghanistan had fallen back into the hands of its heroic defender Jalal-ad-Din, who after his defeat on the Indus had succeeded in crossing the river under a rain of arrows. During the winter of 1230-31 a powerful Mongol army occupied the country. Jalal-ad-Din fled and disappeared. Western Persia was kept under military occupation and 'governed on horseback' for ten years before any civil administration was introduced. From there the Mongols entered Anatolia, whose Seljuk sultan became a vassal of the Khanate.

At the same time a formidable army was concentrated between the Aral Sea and the Urals, under the command of Batu, with the veteran Sabutai once again assisting. At the end of the summer of 1237 the Urals were crossed, and within a month all the peoples between the Urals, the Caspian and the Volga were subjugated: the Kip-

chaks, the Kumanians, the Volga Bulgars and the Alani. Then, in an astonishing winter campaign, Sabutai attacked the Russian principalities west of the Volga. Before the thaw of 1238 had transformed the ground into a quagmire, the principalities of Ryazan, Vladimir and Moscow no longer existed.

Now very firmly encamped in the southern steppes, Sabutai next proceeded to regroup his army and in November 1240 flung it against Kiev, the great centre of the Ukraine, which fell on December 6. In March 1241 a Mongol force struck at Poland and within a month Cracow was in flames. Reinforced by Templars and Teutonic Knights, the army of Henry II, Duke of Silesia, tried to stop the Mongols at Liegnitz but was annihilated on April 9. Another Mongol force under Batu and Sabutai had entered Hungary. King Béla's fine army was totally exterminated on Mohi Heath on April 11, and the whole of Hungary occupied. In a month's campaign all the land between the Baltic and the Danube had fallen into the hands of the Mongols. Kadan, sent in pursuit of Béla IV, followed him through Croatia to the Dalmatian coast and was still following him from island to island when suddenly, to the astonishment of the western world, the Mongols started homeward, evacuating Hungary, Silesia, Poland, Transylvania, Moldavia and Bukovina. Ogdai had died, and all the princes, all the army leaders, went back to Mongolia, where a council was summoned for the election of a new Khan. Of all the conquered regions west of the Urals, only the south Russian steppe as far as the Danube was occupied, though Russia proper remained a vassal state for centuries.

Kublai Khan (1260-94)

Ogdai's death brought a temporary halt to Mongol conquest. The short reign of his son, Kuyuk, was preceded by a four years' regency. On Kuyuk's death in 1248 a new regency was established to fill the gap before another election, held in 1251; this gave the Khanate to Mangu, son of Tulé, who was the youngest of Jenghiz Khan's sons. This period was one of corrupt governments, quarrels and fratricidal wars, and any large-scale military operations were inopportune. Military strength was kept at a high level, however, as is shown by the efficiency of the punitive expedition under Hulagu, Mangu Khan's brother, which was sent to Central Asia from 1256 to 1260. Baghdad fell in 1258 and the last Abbasid caliph, Mustasim, was taken prisoner and trampled to death by horses. For a short time Syria was taken from the last of the Ayyubid sultans; but it was soon lost again, after Kitabuka's defeat by the Mamelukes of Egypt at Ain Jalut near Lake Tiberias in September 1260. Indeed it seemed that orders from imperial headquarters in Karakorum had little effect upon the dependent kingdoms of the West, which were administered by the descendants of Jagatai in Turkestan and by Batu's descendants further west. The empire ceased to be centred in Mongolia, in fact, with Mangu Khan. Kublai, who was living in Peking, was led to direct his conquering efforts towards the southeast, that is to say, towards the China of the Sung dynasty, Japan and Indochina, and even Indonesia.

The conquest of Sung China

The attack on south China had begun under Mangu, who had put in charge of operations his brother, Kublai. Seeing that it was hopeless to launch a frontal attack against a country defended by a vast system of forts and covered by the high mountains of the Kunlun, Kublai set out to outflank the defensive system from the southwest. Going through Tibet, he came down the upper valley of the Yang-tze into Yunnan, which was subjugated by the end of 1253. It was there that Kublai took up residence. From there the Mongols drove onwards, reaching the Tongking delta in 1257. In the same year south China was attacked by Mangu and his lieutenants on four sides: from Suchuan, from the middle Yang-tze, from the lower Yang-tze, and from Tongking and through Kwangtung. In 1259 Mangu's death halted operations, and for eight years Kublai was paralysed by the revolt of one of his brothers. The final assault was delivered in 1267 by Bayan, a general in Kublai's service and a man of great ability. In 1276 Lingan, the capital, fell. Canton held out for a while longer, but the defeat of the last Chinese squadron at Ichang in April 1279 led to the final surrender of the town. Kublai Khan was then the recognised ruler of all China and the first of the Yuen dynasty.

Disintegration begins

This conquest of the oldest and most brilliant of all Asian civilisations marks the culminating point of the empire founded by Jenghiz Khan. Kublai was now lord of all the world between the Danube and the East China Sea, though he was far from exercising within that world

the authority of his predecessors. Firstly, the dubious way in which he came into possession of the Khanate raised doubts about the legitimacy of his power, and they persisted throughout his reign. Besides, he seemed more and more to lose sight of the fact that he was a descendant of Jenghiz Khan. If no longer a nomad, for he lived in magnificent palaces, at least he was, like his ancestors, a passionate hunter. But his tent, though made of leopard-skin, was lined with ermine and sable, and so beautifully quilted that no puff of air, no drop of rain, could find a passage. He was a Mongol, but a Mongol sufficiently impregnated with Chinese influence to fall naturally into place as the founder of a Chinese dynasty. Reaction against him was inevitable and, making due allowance for personal ambitions and jealousies, we must see in the revolt of Kaidu and of Kublai's brother, Arikbuka, the instinctive protest of the true nomad against a Khan who had departed from the family tradition. Significantly, it was Mongolia, the cradle and heart of the empire, which was the centre of resistance to the Khan.

Thus by the time Kublai died, in 1294, the Mongol empire was already crumbling, at all events as a universal empire. It was perishing as a result of its excessive size, which had made some sort of fragmentation necessary for administrative purposes, and the fragments had tended to become absorbed by the older civilisations which existed there before. At the end of the thirteenth century the empire was still formally intact, but when, in 1301, Kublai's heir received homage from the other Khans, the Mongol followers of Jagatai had become Turks, those

Marco Polo, the Venetian merchant who travelled across Asia to Cathay. An observant traveller, his accounts of his journeys revealed to an incredulous Empire the riches of Cathay.

Niccolo, Maffeo and Marco Polo at the court of Kublai Khan. Merchants in search of wares, they first visited China in 1260. When they made a return visit, the Khan appointed them his envoys to the Pope, seeking a ' hundred men of learning ' to teach the Mongols the ways of the West. *Mansell*

from Persia Persians, and those from China Chinese. Paradoxically, the empire had been killed by a victory that had been too complete. For the Chinese, the Mongol conquest meant that their whole country was now under alien domination, a fate which it was again to suffer after the intervening period of the native Ming empire (1368-1644), when the Manchus conquered China.

The Mongols, true to their original far-flung ambitions, were not content even with the conquest of all China. In 1281 Kublai Khan launched an expedition against Japan. In the next year his armies attacked Burma, and in 1284 they overran Cambodia and Annam. In 1292 Kublai even sent an expedition to Java, which failed. Tropical rain forest in Indonesia, like the northern forest of Muscovy at the other end of the Empire, stopped the advance. Internally, the Mongol period was to be important. The Mongols made their capital at Peking, which became the centre of a vast administration, and a city of enormous palaces. The Chinese gentry, who had come to terms with the conquerors, enjoyed a continuing prosperity, but the peasants suffered terrible exactions and, surprisingly, the Mongols, unlike the sceptical Confucian Chinese élite, took kindly to Buddhism and Taoism, and endowed monasteries on a great scale. They also greatly encouraged cosmopolitan trade, even favouring foreign merchants at the expense of the Chinese; but this commerce tended to drain the empire of its currency and depreciate its value. In consequence, not only was their

empire to prove relatively ephemeral; its internal effect on China was in time to provoke formidable popular discontent.

Diplomatic contacts with the West

The Mongol flood had beaten against the walls of Western Europe without being able to break them. But the effect of the disturbance in Asia caused by the Mongol onslaught was keenly felt throughout the old western continent. The Mongols had made the West conscious of the existence of Asia, and by opening the lines of communication closed under Islam, had enlarged the horizon of feudal Europe. Never before had Asia been seen in all her grandeur and wealth. Never had she come so close.

The 'Mongol peace' had been purchased by torrents of blood, but it had none the less imposed law and order in Asia and had made the trade routes safe. From the West missionaries and merchants ventured along them. In 1245 Pope Innocent IV sent the Franciscan monk John of Pian di Carpine, accompanied by Benedict the

Colour plate: Gloucester Cathedral. Fan vaulting in the monks' washing quarters. *A. F. Kersting*

The Condottiere Guidoriccio da Fogliana. Fresco by Simone
Martini. Siena. 1328. *Josephine Powell*

Pole, to invite Ogdai's son Kuyuk to become a Christian. In 1248 two envoys of the Mongol governor of western Asia, himself a Nestorian Christian, were sent to St Louis to propose an alliance against Islam. St Louis, much impressed, sent an envoy to Mangu, who was elected Khan in 1251; this was André de Longjumeau, one of the most reputed oriental missionaries, who took with him a tent of precious material fitted as a chapel, for Louis was persuaded that the Khan was ready for conversion. Mangu sent him home with presents, including a sheet of asbestos, whose incombustible properties were much admired in Europe; but he showed no desire to become a Christian. Not disheartened, St Louis next sent William of Rubruquis, this time not as an ambassador, but frankly as a missionary. Again he had no success. Nevertheless, while proclaiming his intention of conquering the world, Mangu added a little wistfully: 'But if, by the power of your eternal God, the world is to be united in peace and joy from East to West, we shall then see what we must do.'

The great beneficiaries of the Mongols were the merchants. Two of them, Niccolo and Maffeo Polo of Venice, had already been to China in 1260, and they returned in 1271, this time with Niccolo's son, Marco, who stayed there till 1295. It was at Marco's dictation that a Pisan writer, Rusticiano, wrote the famous *Livre des diversités et merveilles du monde*, revealing to dazzled Europe the riches of China, which they called Cathay. The marvels were true enough of the China of Kublai Khan, with its 200,000 vessels laden with pepper and spices that plied yearly on the rivers, with its paper money in currency everywhere, with its combustible mineral, coal, its printing presses, 'tissues that are thrown into the fire to clean them, wine that flows from the trees, and horses with black and yellow stripes'. Europe listened open-mouthed, then despatched its merchants and its missionaries. Fifty years after Marco Polo, the Genoese had flourishing trading stations in China, a Catholic archbishop was resident in Peking and another at Tsi-nan-chu. As early as 1274 a Mongol bishop sat at the Council of Lyons, and in 1287 the Nestorian monk, Rabban Bar Sauma, born near Peking, visited Philip the Fair in Paris and received communion from Nicholas IV in Rome.

The limits of the Mongol Empire

By unifying Asia, the Mongols had facilitated contact between East and West. In the flush of their success they had come near to realising a universal empire. The symbol of their empire and the sign of their unity was the Great Khan himself, their political as well as their religious chief, so that the universality of the empire could go no further than the personal cult. Like the Christian empire, it therefore had its limits, though these were doubtless greater in extent. The conquests of the Khan may have expressed the will of Tengri, the Lord God of the Heavens, but the effective instrument of his will was the huge army of horsemen, who galloped from end to end of Asia, and even into Europe. Asia, being less subdivided than Europe, naturally allowed a much more rapid conquest. Eventually the Mongols found themselves facing big empires which had only to be struck down at a blow for the invaders to gain dominion. The first victims were the huge settled empires — China, the Russia centred on Kiev, and Persia. Stunned by the Mongol

shock, these great states seemed for long to be paralysed. But apart from the fact that it was limited to Asia, the Mongol empire could only be ephemeral, for it was structurally weak and quickly built in an unnaturally fast expansion by conquerors of a lower cultural level than the conquered. Its expansionist impetus died away on the threshold of Europe. Jenghiz Khan and his successors had imposed Mongol domination at the point of the sword over almost a whole continent; but they had still not founded the universal empire. On the other hand, with permanent relations re-established between the East and the West, the moment seemed to have arrived for Europe and Mongol Asia to strengthen their links, so that together they could crush their hated neighbours, the upholders of Islam.

THE RECESSION OF ISLAM

The great Moslem drive of the twelfth century waned almost as rapidly as it had risen; the beginning of the thirteenth century saw the decline of the Almohades, who for a short time had forged the political unity of the Mohammedan West from Tunis to Cordova and had given the Maghrib its period of power. This brief phase was followed by a period of decline and anarchy which lasted through the fourteenth and fifteenth centuries and witnessed the launching of the Christian offensive against the Moroccan coast.

The decline of the Almohades

The last Caliph of the Almohades, Nasir, succeeded in re-establishing his authority over Ifrikia (now Tunisia) lost by his predecessor, Mansur; but he suffered an irremediable disaster in Spain. When Alfonso VII of Castile undertook to avenge his defeat at Alarcos, Nasir went out in person to meet the Christians. As already observed, the complete defeat of his army in the plain of Las Navas de Tolosa in 1212 had serious repercussions on the whole Western world. If they had not been stricken by the plague, the Christians would have marched triumphantly into the south; even so, the disintegration of the Moslem states in Spain had already begun by the time of Alfonso's death in 1214. In the same year Nasir, morally overwhelmed by his defeat, abdicated in favour of his son, Mostansir. With that the empire of the Almohades began to collapse.

The reign of Mostansir (1214-24) was entirely spent in painful struggles in Morocco against the agitations of the Beni Marin (Marinides) and in Ifrikia against the recalcitrant Almoravid Arabs, who were being reformed by Yahya. After 1224 dynastic difficulties were added to these troubles. Seeing his opportunity, Ferdinand III of Castile backed one of the pretenders, Mamun, Mostansir's brother. With the support of twelve thousand horsemen provided by Ferdinand, Mamun gained the day in 1230; but he rejected Shiite doctrine (that of the Almohades) in favour of the orthodox Sunnite doctrines. Going still further, he authorised the foundation of the Church of Our Lady at Marrakesh. And while the Caliph and his son Rashid wore themselves out in combating the multiple rifts which tore the Maghrib asunder, the Almohade state fell to pieces in Spain. A mass of little

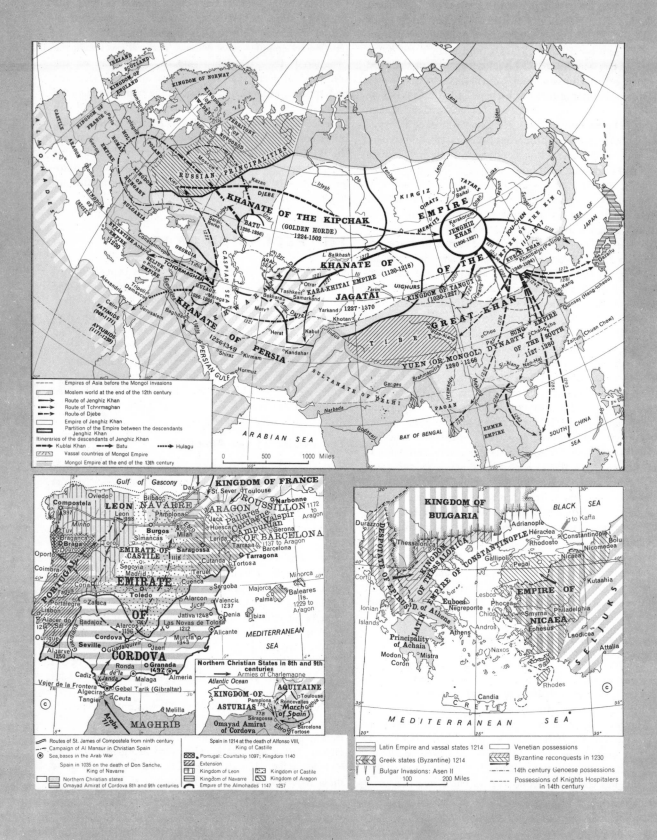

Above: The Mongol Empire in the thirteenth century
Left: Spain under the Arabs and during the Christian Reconquest
Right: The Latin Empire of Constantinople

kingdoms rose on the ruins of the empire and bound themselves as vassals of Ferdinand III. Then, after the fall of Seville in 1248, all Spain except Granada was reconquered. Ferdinand III died in 1252 as he was preparing to invade Morocco.

The end was now approaching. The Emir of Tlemcen, Abu Yahia Yarmorasen, proclaimed his independence in 1236. The Hafsite governor of Ifrikia, Abu Zakariya, assumed the title of emir in 1237 and made Tunis his capital.

Lastly, the Marinides occupied the kingdom of Fez while waiting for their opportunity to chase the Almohades out of Marrakesh. They accomplished this in 1269, thus putting an end to the Almohade dynasty.

Tunis and Tlemcen

Four dynasties emerged from the disintegration of the empire of the Almohades: the Nasrides of Granada, the Marinides of Fez, the Abd-el-Wahides of Tlemcen, and the Hafsites of Tunis. Torn by palace revolutions, weakened by internecine conflicts, these feeble kingdoms were powerless to stop the progress of the nomad tribes of the Hilalian Arabs towards independence, and they drifted further and further into disruption and anarchy.

The Hafsite caliphs of Tunis claimed to have inherited the traditions of the former caliphate of the Almohades. Abu Zakariya (1229-49), supported by the nomads of the central and eastern Maghrib, occupied Constantine, Bougie and Algiers; in 1242 he took Tlemcen from Yarmorasen; finally he imposed his authority on the Marinides of Fez. Although bearing only the modest title of imam, he won sufficient prestige outside the Maghrib for Frederick II to sign a commercial treaty with him. With his successor Mostansir (1249-77) the dynasty reached its highest point. Mostansir had to ward off attacks by St Louis and deal with family rivalries; his position in Ifrikia was often precarious, but he nevertheless enjoyed considerable prestige, thanks largely to the support of the nomad tribes; his relations with the Marinides were amicable; his court at Tunis was a great centre of culture. In 1259, at an investiture in Mecca, he was designated heir to the Abbasid caliphate, and he thereupon assumed the title of caliph. After Mostansir, however, the dynasty drifted aimlessly from one crisis to another until the beginning of the sixteenth century, when it was finally liquidated by the Turks.

According to the chronicler Ibn Kaldun, the founder of the Abd-el-Wahid dynasty, Abu Yahia Yarmorasen, had made Tlemcen, the capital of the central Maghrib, 'the protective metropolis of the Zenata tribes'. A pleasant residential town, its commercial position was excellent, for it stood at the junction of the trade routes leading to Oran and Tafilalt. But its political position was unfavourable, wedged as it was between the Marinides of Fez and the nomad Hilalians. Indeed the kingdom of Tlemcen always led a precarious existence, and was never able to create a firmly established empire.

Nevertheless, Abu Yahia Yarmorasen reigned from 1239 to 1283 without encountering dynastic opposition and, with the support of the Beni-Zorba and other nomad Berber tribes, was able during that period to keep his adversaries at bay. But the Marinides began their offensive as soon as his son, Abu Said Othman, started to reign and before long they imposed their suzerainty.

The rise of the Marinide dynasty of Fez

At Fez, too, it was the revenge of the Zenata nomads which brought the Almohade regime to an end. This time, however, the change was not made abruptly, but in the course of a long and bitter struggle. Unlike the Abd-el-Wahides, the Zenata tribe of the Beni Marin refused to accept the sovereignty of the Almohades, and taking advantage of the weakness of the latter after the death of El-Said captured Mequines, and the last Almohade caliph disappeared. Now that Marrakesh was taken, Abu Ysuf determined to pacify the whole of Tafilat and Sus, which had become provinces of the Abd-el-Wahid kingdom; but he was not able to wipe out all centres of resistance. At the same time, taking advantage of the fact that Alfonso X of Castile seemed to be hesitating, he vigorously resumed the offensive in Spain. After his victory at Ecija in 1275, he forced Sancho IV to return the works of art taken by the Christians at Cordova and Seville, and he annexed Tarifa, Algeciras and Cadiz.

Difficulties began, however, under his successor, Abu Yakub (1286-1307). Harassed by subversion in Sus and by his unending conflict with Tlemcen, he lost Tarifa and Algeciras and was forced to cede Ceuta to the Emir of Granada. He was then assassinated by a eunuch. Things were no better under his successors, until in 1331 Abul Hasan came to the throne and began to reconstitute the Maghrib empire. He brought the Marinide dynasty to its highest point, ruling from the Atlantic to Gabes in Tunisia.

Nevertheless, by and large Islam was in recession. The Caliphate of Baghdad collapsed in 1258, struck down by the Mongol Hulagu. Only one bastion stood firm, the Egypt of the Mamelukes, who not only repulsed the Mongols but drove them out of Syria. Nevertheless, at the end of the thirteenth century, the Moslem world was living through difficult times. Under pressure from the Christians in the West and threatened by the vast Mongol power in the East, its very existence was in jeopardy.

The thirteenth century came to an end without having realised a universal empire. Naturally the attempt had failed, even if the Mongol empire, driving forward with unparalleled brutality, had for a time come within sight of occupying much of the ancient world. If it had failed to swallow Western Europe or India, it had for the first time established real international, even intercontinental relations.

The Mongols at least established better communications across the heart of Asia and made contact with the West; from these contacts came some positive results: the reforging of economic links, the better understanding of the geography of Asia, and the enlargement of cultural interests — yet, when all is said and done, no solid political achievements came of their struggles.

THE FOURTEENTH AND FIFTEENTH CENTURIES

Venice in the fourteenth century. Though distorted, this view from a book by Marco Polo is not entirely imaginary: one can distinguish the horses of the St Mark's façade, the old palace of the Doges, the columns of the Piazzetta. The city was at the height of its power in the fourteenth and fifteenth centuries.
University-Press

CHAPTER TWENTY-ONE

RELIGIOUS AND POLITICAL CHANGE IN WESTERN EUROPE

The fourteenth century saw the failure of the grandiose conceptions of world empire and a reversion to more limited objectives. The degree of order — political, religious, and cultural — realised for a brief moment in the thirteenth century was soon overthrown and by the middle of the fourteenth century that long series of disturbances had already begun which were not to cease until well into the middle of the fifteenth.

THE TRIALS OF THE CHURCH

The Papacy in Avignon (1305-78)

The seventy-three years during which the Papacy was removed from Rome — generally called the 'Babylonian captivity' — has generally been regarded as one of the critical periods of the Church. Though the Holy See no longer enjoyed the prestige it had won in the thirteenth century, though the days of theocracy had passed, we must not exaggerate the extent of this fall. The Popes continued to play an important part in international affairs, for example by intervening between France and England and postponing the outbreak of the conflict, and again by keeping alive the fading idea of a crusade. Moreover it was during the Avignon period that the chief departments of papal administration — the exchequer, for instance — were given their final shape. This was a major achievement, resulting in the creation of a well established bureaucracy. It is nevertheless true that the seizure of Pope Boniface VIII at Anagni had dealt a serious blow to the Papacy's moral and political prestige. Moreover the Popes had been so absorbed in the ramifications of Italian politics that they had neglected their duties as arbiters and guides of Christendom.

The election of Clement V and the Council of Vienne

The Avignon Papacy was in fact heavily mortgaged, thanks largely to the conditions under which Clement V was elected. After the short term of Benedict XI (1303-04), the conclave met in July 1304. It was entirely preoccupied with Philip the Fair's intention to hold a posthumous trial of Boniface VIII, and with the attitude to be taken towards the perpetrators of the outrage of Anagni. Endless negotiations and official manoeuvres explain the long duration of the conclave. Did Philip the Fair exert pressure? Certainly envoys from France were present in Perugia, where the conclave was still sitting in the middle of April 1305, and were far from being inactive. Certainly the man eventually proclaimed Pope on June 5, 1305

was Bertrand de Gouth, Archbishop of Bordeaux, whose close relations with the King of France were well known. There seems, however, to have been no prior understanding, at least not a precise one, between them. But the king had very soon realised Clement's acute lack of will-power, probably due to his bad health. And indeed Clement never opposed Philip's injunctions with anything more serious than delays; in the end he always did exactly as he was bid.

From the start, Clement V took a decision that was to have grave consequences for the Papacy: he installed himself, with his Curia, at Avignon. There were many reasons for not going to Rome: the situation there was very disturbed; for the sake of the proposed crusade, France and England had to be reconciled, and the Pope could do more to that end if he were on the spot; above all, Clement wanted to prevent the trial of Boniface VIII, and for that reason he felt he must be in close contact with Philip's court. Clement wanted also to be close to Vienne, where Philip had summoned the Council that was to try Boniface.

The other question Philip wished the Council to deal with was the dissolution of the Templars. The two questions were really settled before the Council opened in October 1311. By February the accusers had withdrawn their charges against Boniface; by June the Templars had been condemned. In April 1312 the Council did no more than solemnly ratify the suppression of the Order of the Temple ordered by the bull *Vox in caelo*, barely touching on the other points on its agenda. It brought nothing new to the question of the reform of the Church, nor did it decide anything about the crusade. There were, however, some innovations in its way of going to work, which were to reappear in later councils; these were the referring of questions to commissions, instead of dealing with everything in plenary session, and the allocation of places on those commissions to men of various nationalities, so that national points of view were properly represented.

A new idea was mooted by Raimon Lull, who suggested that the heathen should be converted by preaching rather than by force of arms.

The idea of the crusade had indeed had its day. From the middle of the century its place was taken by that of the conquest of souls by missionary workers.

The Popes at Avignon and pontifical finance

The question that dominated the next conclave, after the death of Clement V in April 1314, was whether or not the Papacy should return to Rome. Protracted discussions were held with the quickly succeeding kings of France, Philip the Fair, Louis X, and Philip V; finally, after the transfer of the conclave to Lyons, on the doorstep of France, and after twenty-eight months of argument, Jacques Duèse, a French prelate from Cahors, was elected. He took the name of John XXII.

Energetic, indefatigable indeed, despite his advanced age, he tackled problems of all sorts. But his major preoccupation was Italy, and he launched a crusade against the head of the Ghibelline party, Matteo Visconti. Considering that a return to Rome should be preceded by complete political control of Italy, he claimed for himself the Italian throne, for there was at that moment no Emperor. Failing in this objective, he decided to fix the seat of the Papacy at Avignon. It was in any case more central, farther from the ever-fluctuating frontiers of Christendom, and thus a quieter place for the curia, which was constantly being increased by the great work of centralising the administrative framework of the Church. For this purpose, John XXII had the papal palace considerably enlarged.

That work was to be carried on by his successors, Benedict XII (1334-42) and Clement VI (1342-52). Benedict, an austere monk intent on peace, set out to endow the Papacy with his own moral prestige, and he abandoned the political manoeuvres of his predecessor in Italy. Clement VI, on the contrary, a great and ostentatious nobleman, was in some respects a forerunner to the Renaissance popes. Neither of them showed any intention of going back to Rome, and it was Benedict XII who in 1335 undertook the vast building operations, which in ten years were to double the size of the great papal palace. Clement VI went further; having bought the sovereignty of Avignon from Joanna I of Naples for 80,000 golden florins, he made Avignon one of the most splendid courts in Europe. The expenditure involved in all this building, as well as in the political campaigning in Italy, made necessary a great development in the organisation of finance and taxation by the Church. The income that had hitherto sufficed was now no longer enough, and taxes were put on the granting of ecclesiastical benefices. The general principle was laid down that the Pope, having an overall right over all Church property, was at liberty to intervene in the presentation of benefices. This in turn led to the enlargement of the curia and a centralisation of administration, which transformed the Papacy into an efficient government.

Towards a return to Rome

The monastic tradition that had inspired Benedict XII returned with Innocent VI (1352-1362). He was sensitive

Jerusalem besieged. The town is surrounded by a vast encampment of tents. The besieging crusaders are shown outsize, towering above the ramparts. Fifteenth-century manuscript. British Museum. *Mansell*

to Italian criticism, particularly Petrarch's, against overcentralisation, excessive taxation, and the worldly splendour of the Papacy. Protests against abuses were heard on all sides, and some of the loudest were against absentee bishops. Was not the Bishop of Rome precisely that, so long as he stayed at Avignon? On the other hand, during the absence of the popes there had been disquieting movements in Rome, the most spectacular of which had been the democratic agitation of Cola di Rienzo in 1347.

The political situation in Rome was not yet sufficiently favourable, however, for Innocent VI to undertake the transfer back to Rome; but his successor, Urban V (1362-70), the only Avignon pope since to have been beatified, did restore the Papacy to Rome for a time. In spite of the objections of the cardinals and the protests of Charles V, now King of France, he made his entry in October 1367. Three years later he was back at Avignon. At Rome he had felt himself to be at the mercy of the least uprising, and the Papal States were threatened both by the revolt at Perugia and the troop movements of Bernabo Visconti. A few days after his return to Avignon, in December 1370, he died, as had been predicted by St Bridget of Sweden.

It was left to Innocent's successor, Gregory XI, elected December 30, 1370, to bring the Papacy back to Rome finally. Even now the return was put off several times, as the Pope wanted first to have transformed into a peace treaty the truce concluded at Bruges between Edward III and Charles V. When Gregory finally arrived at Rome in January 1377, he found a very disturbed situation, and like his predecessor he might have gone back to Avignon,

Above: medieval Avignon. Contemporary drawing showing the Papal palace enlarged by John XXII and Benedict XII (1334-42) thus underlining their intention of remaining at Avignon.

Bishop Wolfhard von Roth. Early fourteenth century. Augsburg Cathedral. The dispute between Empire and Papacy was confused and sharpened in many instances by local ecclesiastical disputes, and the bishops of Augsburg opposed the Pope.

had he not died prematurely in March 1378. The Romans made no secret of their intention of electing another pope in schism if the Papacy withdrew again.

The Great Schism of the West

Never did the Church go through such a crisis as that of the fourteenth century. Not only were two, and very soon three, popes in existence (the Church had known antipopes in the past) but deep questions of conscience underlay the schism, and, more serious still, these questions were backed by rival national interests. This was a characteristic feature of the fourteenth century, when national consciousness was on the rise and the medieval belief in a universal order was fading.

The double election of 1378

In April 1378 the conclave elected as Pope Bartolommeo Prignano, Archbishop of Bari, who took the name of Urban VI. The election was unanimous, save for one vote; but the voting was influenced by the menacing discontent of the Roman mob.

In spite of this, there can be no doubt that the cardinals considered the election valid. It was not till some months later that some of them, in particular the French ones, ruffled by the violent, headstrong, clumsy manners of the new Pope, began to claim a scrupulous concern about the conditions under which the election had been held. Having taken refuge at Fondi, they declared they had voted under constraint and proceeded to elect another Pope in September 1378. This was Robert of Geneva,

John Wyclif, the fourteenth-century reformer whose teaching had a similar effect in England to that of St Francis in Italy, though it was never widely accepted in England. He was dissatisfied with the political activities of the Church and, on the theological side, with the Church's lack of concern with everyday life. Wyclif's opposition to the Holy See was accentuated by the schism in the Papacy. *Historia Photo*

John Hus, being led to the stake, condemned for his work *De ecclesia*. A disciple of Wyclif, he carried his doctrines to Bohemia, where they became the national religion. Luther was later to be influenced by Hus and thus indirectly by Wyclif. *Bibliothèque Nationale*

who became Clement VII, and who installed himself in Avignon in June 1379.

The schism at once took on a political aspect, for Charles V of France recognised Clement VII. So did France's allies, Scotland, Naples, and the Spanish kingdoms. England, north Italy, Hungary and Poland supported Urban, as well as most of Germany, only the parts under French influence — Lorraine, the County of Bar, the Duchy of Luxemburg and the bishoprics of Metz, Tours and Verdun — deciding for Clement.

The Schism becomes threefold

There were three possible courses to end the schism: for the claims of the rival popes to be submitted to arbitration; for both to resign, followed by a fresh election; or for a general council to be summoned. From the first, however, all such solutions were blocked by the obstinacy of the two contestants and by the determined support each received from his principal backer, France or England. For a moment the death of Urban VI in October 1389 offered a hope, but it proved fugitive, for the Roman cardinals promptly elected a successor in the person of Boniface IX.

The University of Paris, the highest intellectual authority of the age, now suggested the second solution, abdication by both parties; this seemed a hopeful course, as before electing a successor to Clement VII (died September 1394) the Avignon cardinals had promised to work for union after the election. But Pedro de Luna of Aragon, on becoming Pope Benedict XIII, repudiated his undertakings and suggested the calling of a Council to examine the claims of each party.

The Church of France withdrew its promise of obedience to Benedict XIII in July 1398 but, in view of the bad faith of the 'Urbanists', restored it to him in May 1403.

A meeting was planned at Savona between Benedict XIII and Gregory XII (who had succeeded Boniface IX), but it never took place and at last a Council was summoned. The cardinals of the two sides having withdrawn their obedience, the council met at Pisa and proceeded to elect a third pope, Alexander V, who was soon followed by John XXIII. With matters thus more confused than ever, yet another Council became necessary. The Council of Constance took the precaution of first laying down the principle that it derived its authority directly from Christ and was thus above the Pope — a vitally important principle to assert. John XXIII and Benedict XIII were deposed and Gregory XII abdicated. Martin V was elected and almost universally recognised.

The disarray of Christendom

The schism had come to an end, and the unity of the Roman Church was never again to be threatened. But Christendom emerged from the dissension badly shaken. The fifteenth century was not profoundly religious, but much had been destroyed during those years of trouble. The religious crisis was accompanied by the breakdown of many fundamental political, economic and social structures; all this was a preparation for the building of a new world.

Intellectual ferment in the universities even affected

questions of doctrine. Religious minds were bewildered. Among the more cultured, many turned towards feeling, the impulses of the heart; theology ceased to be speculative and became mystical; the Rhineland Dominicans, Johann Tauler and Heinrich Suso take the place of St Thomas Aquinas. The popular preachers had immense success with the people. They too appealed to the feelings, and sometimes, by methods very near to charlatanry, incited extreme unrest. Groups of flagellants sprang up, superstitions were widespread, and these excessive and theatrical practices became a real perversion of religious feeling. Lastly, in this general ferment of ideas, heresies were revived, almost all of which were hostile to the priesthood and called for a return to the scriptures. Exponents of such ideas in England were Wyclif and his disciples and the Lollards. In Bohemia, John Hus inspired a movement that was both anti-Roman and anti-German. Though burnt at stake, he started a Czech national movement which survived him.

Thus, by its failings, the Papacy, more intent on political manoeuvring than spiritual guidance, and thus unable to satisfy the growing mystic longings of the faithful, was to a great extent responsible for the rupture in the sixteenth century, the Reformation.

THE FIRST MAJOR NATIONAL CONFLICT: THE HUNDRED YEARS' WAR

The dream of union ends

From the wreck of the ancient world, was there, at the beginning of the fourteenth century, any hope of unity? The intellectual and artistic activity of France, her material prosperity, and the power of her kings were still impressive. But the exceptional expansion of French agriculture in the thirteenth century made the economic stagnation that spread through all the rural districts of the West early in the fourteenth more keenly felt. The economy of the future, the new mercantile and industrial economy, developed in the Low Countries and England, in the Rhineland and north Italy. Keen intellectual rivalry now came from other centres, from Oxford and Salamanca. To crown matters, France was to exhaust her energies in the Hundred Years' War.

Reasons for the Anglo-French conflict

The war waged by the two chief monarchies of Western Europe for a hundred and sixteen years (1337-1453) started for purely feudal reasons. The Treaty of Paris signed in 1259 had left the kings of England in an impossible position: the vassal of Aquitaine, a king himself, being obliged to do homage to another king. Moreover the vassal saw his continental possessions being steadily nibbled away by his suzerain, until by 1328 they had been reduced to a narrow coastal strip, Guienne, between the Charente and the Adour. The new king of England, Edward III, decided to end this humiliating expropriation and with it the conditions of the Treaty of Paris. But the argument over Guienne was soon overshadowed by another problem: whether or not the vassal was to do homage to his suzerain. Several interviews between Edward III and the new French king, Philip VI, failed to decide the point.

The Hundred Years' War is sometimes explained as a dynastic quarrel, but whether Edward II, a grandson of Philip the Fair through his mother Isabella, had a legal claim to the French throne is still far from clear. Either the right of succession passes to or through daughters — in which case Jeanne de France, daughter of Louis X, would have passed the title to her son, Charles the Bad, King of Navarre — or the female line is excluded, in which case Philip VI was the rightful heir. Edward III was quite aware of this, and if he laid official claim to the throne, he did so for the sake of having another card to play in the struggle for his continental possessions, a card which would rally subjects whose loyalties were undecided. Never did he think seriously of pressing his claim.

Miniature from the Luttrell Psalter. Sir Geoffrey Luttrell, setting out for France from his home in Somerset and receiving his helmet from his wife. Manuscript of the first years of the Hundred Years' War; 1340. *British Museum*

As for the economic causes of the Hundred Years' War, they have often been exaggerated. The question revolved around Flanders: sheep-breeding England had for long been economically complementary to manufacturing Flanders. But this link tended to weaken rapidly under Edward III, during whose reign England was developing a wool industry of her own, and was anxious to free herself economically from Flanders, though in the next century the connection was restored. In 1337 Edward forbade imports of foreign cloth or exports of raw wool.

That did not prevent a certain political understanding between England and Flanders. The latter could be a valuable base for operations against France, and it was also a country that appeared to have an inexhaustible supply of fighting men. Lastly, the Count of Flanders and Edward III (as Duke of Guienne) were both restive vassals of France, both resentful of the latter's encroachments. So, though Flanders was involved in the quarrel between Edward III and Philip VI, it was not particularly for economic reasons. When all allowance is made for other factors, to the end of the fourteenth century Anglo-French conflict was essentially feudal in character. The English nobility, standing solidly behind their king, saw in the war nothing more than a lucrative sport. The two kings were French in blood and culture; the two peoples did not know each other. If national sentiment was awakened during the struggle, it was (for the English) because of the 'bad faith' shown by the French, and (for the French) because of the length of the war, and the misery caused among the people by the ravages of the enemy.

Preliminary moves

But what, at the beginning of this long national conflict, was the strength of the two parties? At first glance, French superiority would seem overwhelming. The population of France was some fifteen million against England's three or four; the King of France had his domain well under control, thanks to a constantly improved administration; his vassals were, on the whole, loyal and his frontiers undisturbed. The King of England, on the other hand, with his power restricted by Parliament, had constantly to defer important decisions for the advice of his barons; moreover, he had uncomfortable neighbours in both the Scots and the Welsh. The balance seemed strongly tilted against England. Yet it was England who had the upper hand in the first years of the war. This unexpected reversal of form was due, in the first place, to the personalities of the two kings. Philip, irresolute and unimaginative, followed the simple and easy policy of his forebears which had succeeded so well through six reigns: the policy of slowly and systematically appropriating snippets of his vassal's territory. This time, however, the King of France was matched against an adversary his predecessors had not known, a King of England who brushed aside legal arguments and was ready to take up arms against his suzerain. For his part, Edward III cleverly masked his intentions. The only way for him to succeed against France's disproportionate strength was to raise the dynastic question, to induce Philip to relinquish the suzerainty of Guienne. It was a risky game, for when he declared himself King of France he had no money and his allies were unreliable. But since Philip took no advantage of his opportunities this mattered little. Again

and again, if he had taken the offensive, Edward would have been crushed and stripped of his last remaining continental possessions. But Philip never learned how to harry his enemy remorselessly. Always he gave him time to regroup his forces after each campaign.

This explains why the military operations of the early years of the war were on such a small scale, apart from the naval battle of Sluys fought in 1340. Diplomatic exchanges, on the other hand, were of capital importance, particularly in Avignon, where the Popes made every effort to prevent a breach between England and France, for peace in Europe was the first prerequisite for the launching of another crusade. They were in a weak position to mediate, however, suspected as they were of being dominated by the King of France. On the whole the suspicion was unjust, for, except in the case of the first Avignon Pope, they pursued an independent policy. Under Benedict XII, papal policy was hostile to French interests. Benedict was clear-headed and tenacious, but proud, and much too preoccupied with playing the part of arbiter in European problems for carrying out the practical task of keeping Europe at peace and organising a crusade. Often he paralysed Philip's timid initiatives, the latter being completely under his influence. He prevented Philip from acting as mediator between England and Scotland, delayed the alliance of France with the Empire, obliged Philip to revoke confiscation of Guienne from the English, and stopped him each time he planned an aggressive move, whether in Flanders, Guienne, or Brabant. This pressure would have been justified, with a view to keeping peace in Europe, if similar pressure had been exerted against Edward III. But Edward simply deceived the Pope, and the many truces arranged by Benedict XII evaded the real problems at issue, showing the complete hollowness of the Papacy's claim to special skill in arbitration.

From Crécy to Poitiers

On October 7, 1337, Edward III took the initiative: he assumed the title of King of France and instructed the Bishop of Lincoln to call on Philip VI to surrender his throne. That was nothing short of a declaration of war. Military engagements began at once. They followed a pattern that was to be maintained throughout the interminable struggle. The King of England, with his limited resources, sought for a quick decision in open country, for he was ill-equipped for a long struggle. This meant that if the French held off, refused battle, and cut off their enemy's supplies, they would soon be the victors. Charles V and Du Guesclin understood that perfectly. But each time the French chivalry came trooping into the field against the well-trained English army they were defeated by the terrific fire-power of its archers.

In the first stages of the war, the English were outplayed. In the campaign in 1339, Philip VI entrenched himself solidly at Buironfosse, and the English, soon running short of provisions, had no choice but to retire to Brabant. But the war started again in 1345 over the succession of Brittany, and when the English were withdrawing north of the Somme, Philip was unwise enough to attack them, near the village of Crécy on August 26, 1346. The result was a complete disaster for the French, who lost 10,000 knights on the battlefield. The King of

An episode from the battle of Crécy (1346) as depicted in Frois-sart's ' Chronicle '. A Fleming, Froissart gathered material in France and England and gave an unbiased contemporary ac-count of the Hundred Years' War. At Crécy, the agile English archers won the day over the French, with their cumbrous heavy armour. *Larousse*

France fled. He had ample resources to fall back on, and though the victory won great renown for the English, it gained them little advantage except that they were left in peace to besiege Calais, which fell in 1347.

A nine-year truce followed before the war started afresh in 1355. This time the principal English effort was in the south. Edward's son, the Black Prince, advanced from Bordeaux towards Tours. Faced by the French army, now under John the Good, they held back; the encounter came in September 1356, five miles south of Poitiers. Weak though his forces were, John the Good threw his three clumsy battalions one after the other against the English fortified positions. The battle was decided by Jean de Grailly, who encircled and destroyed the last French battalion. The battle cost both sides dearly: 2,500 Frenchmen and a quarter of the English army lost their lives. Poitiers was not an irreparable defeat for the French — it was perhaps less grave than Crécy — but among the prisoners taken by the English was the King himself.

Murmurs of revolution in Paris

The effects of the French defeat were largely political. With John the Good a prisoner, the throne of France was vacant, though the King was still alive. The situation was unprecedented. France was bewildered. Charles the Bad, King of Navarre and son of Jeanne de France, was in prison (for inciting Normandy against John), and the Dauphin, Charles, was a boy of eighteen, either unknown or little respected. The country seemed to be drifting help-lessly.

The States General of northern France which had been summoned the year before by John the Good, opened in a stormy mood in Paris on October 17, 1356. Discontent had long been rising against the government and against the feudal lords, who seemed too ready to resign them-selves to defeat, and it now came into the open.

Everyone demanded reforms, everyone proposed re-forms, even Charles the Bad from behind his prison bars. Robert le Coq, the spokesman of the dissenting faction, 363

Above: men, women and children, peasants from the North who had taken part in the Jacquerie rebellion, being taken prisoner by the troops of Charles the Bad, king of Navarre; 20,000 peasants were massacred. *Bibliothèque Nationale*

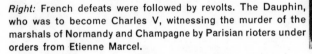

Right: French defeats were followed by revolts. The Dauphin, who was to become Charles V, witnessing the murder of the marshals of Normandy and Champagne by Parisian rioters under orders from Etienne Marcel.

demanded the elimination of several of the king's counsellors, holding them responsible for the ills into which the kingdom had fallen. He suggested the formation of a new council of twenty-eight members, chosen by the Dauphin from the members of the States General, to meet regularly twice a year. What was aimed at, it seems, was the institution of a kind of constitutional monarchy. But the States General were to find in the Dauphin a doughty adversary, possessed of a calmness and shrewd tenacity that none had suspected. He raised objections on the vital issue of the replacement of counsellors, which was the pivot of the new system. And in November 1356, using as a pretext a visit to his uncle, the Emperor Charles IV, at Metz, he adjourned the States General till the following year. He knew well that the opposition was effective only in Paris, where it had the support of the municipal magistrates. In any case, though there were two meetings in 1357, the discussions were of little value.

The escape of the King of Navarre in November 1357 brought new developments. It seems that, behind the desire for reform, Robert le Coq was planning a *coup d'état* to replace the Valois line with the line of Navarre. Etienne Marcel, another reformer, was playing a more subtle game. He dreamt perhaps of a constitutional monarchy firmly founded on a communal basis, as in Flanders or Catalonia. France was to be a federation of communes,

united under monarchical authority, with the dominant part played by the commune of Paris. But Marcel could see no hope of persuading the Dauphin to accept a constitutional role without the temporary support of the King of Navarre. It was a dangerous game, for Charles the Bad was in league with the English, and Marcel knew it. But the States General had obviously failed and commanded no confidence.

As the States General weakened the revolutionary period began. In February 1358 3,000 rioters, led by Etienne Marcel, forced the gates of the Louvre, and in the Dauphin's chamber, and in his presence, hacked down Robert of Artois, Marshal of Normandy, and Jean de Conflans, Marshal of Champagne, the two counsellors who were regarded as most hostile to reform. After that Marcel put on Charles's head the blue and red hood of Paris, clearly showing his intention of exploiting the monarchy. But in so doing he had abandoned conciliatory manoeuvres for revolution.

Marcel promptly exploited the Dauphin's position. He forced him to take four burghers designated by him into the royal council, and to accept for himself the title of regent, so that he could no longer block reform by sheltering behind his father's authority. But just when he thought he had won, Marcel found that he had underestimated the Dauphin, believing that he had been a tool in the hands of his advisers, and that he, Marcel, had only to take their place to take similar advantage of a compliant nature. Charles, however, acted quickly and with guile. On the pretext of presiding over an assembly of nobles at Senlis in March, he escaped from Paris, where he had been virtually a prisoner. He then summoned the States General to meet at Champagne on May 4. He knew he could count on the nobles, the clergy, the provincial assembly, and even the States General if not convened in Paris; the choice of Champagne was an extremely shrewd one, as that province had not forgiven the murder of its marshal.

The Regent now moved on Paris, occupying Montereau and the market town of Meaux, cutting off the town's food supply. It was at this moment that another revolution broke out, the Jacquerie, the peasant rising of the Ile de France and Picardy, a movement born of misery but without clearly defined aims. Charles of Navarre intervened and quelled the rising in three weeks. Etienne Marcel toyed for a while with the idea of exploiting the Jacquerie for his own ends, but he was too cautious to become involved, and in the end the rising was put down without having had any political influence at all.

During this time the Dauphin's troops still encircled Paris. On June 14, 1358 Charles of Navarre entered the town with Etienne Marcel's approval and assumed the title of *Capitaine de la Ville*. In a last desperate gamble, Marcel offered the throne of France to Charles of Navarre and was proposing to open the gates of Paris to the Anglo-Navarrese troops. He had no time to put his offer into execution: on July 31 at midnight he was cut down by Maillard, head of the Valois party in Paris. On August 2 the Dauphin entered Paris, acclaimed by the people. At the Hotel de Ville he spoke of reconciliation and proclaimed a general pardon. He even promised a pension to Etienne Marcel's widow. Nothing remained of the movement started in 1355.

The Treaty of Brétigny and Calais

While the foundations of the French monarchy were crumbling, the military situation was deteriorating daily. Nominally the truce signed at Bordeaux by the prisoner king in March 1357 was still in force, but bands of English and Navarrese troops went on plundering and burning the countryside. The only defence was what was organised on the spot, local bands of partisans under *condottieri*, the most celebrated of whom was Bertrand Du Guesclin. The peasants sought protection in abandoned manor houses and monasteries. Some of the men who rose to be their leaders were remarkably able. In this way an effective resistance was organised, the expression of an early but vague form of patriotism, which none the less transformed the course and the significance of the war.

It was under these conditions that Edward III decided that he must conclude a definite peace, while he could still take advantage of John the Good's weakness and levity. The Treaty of London, which Edward persuaded his prisoner to sign in March 1359, was tantamount to capitulation, with John handing over the sovereignty of more than half his kingdom. Edward's great mistake, however, was that he negotiated with the wrong party. The affairs of France were now more and more firmly in the grasp of the Regent. Cleverly, he united all opinions behind him, just as Philip the Fair had done during his conflict with the Pope. The States General, which he summoned in May 1359, repudiated the Treaty of London, and Charles took advantage of the occasion to persuade them to vote him a subsidy and to restore to him the twenty-two court officials who had been removed at their instigation. He was certainly regaining his ground.

At that, Edward decided to strike decisively. A new campaign took him in mid-winter to Rheims, which he was unable to enter. Charles's strategy was perfect: to avoid pitched battles, to close all towns that could be defended, and to create a vacuum round the English army. It was a costly strategy, for the country was ravaged, but it was effective. Edward's army found it increasingly difficult to keep going, and it arrived at the walls of Paris exhausted and starving on March 31, 1360. There, a storm destroyed Edward's supply train and he was ready to sue for peace. Negotiations opened at Brétigny, near Chartres, where a draft was drawn up; the treaty was ratified at Calais on October 24. Edward III renounced all claim to the French throne; the King's ransom was reduced from four million to three million crowns; Edward was given Aquitaine, but the French kept Touraine, Anjou, Maine and Normandy, that is, the territory that John the Good had surrendered in London. Two-thirds of the provinces ceded to Edward he already held as fiefs. The only difference was that he would now hold them in full sovereignty without any feudal obligations. The Treaty of Brétigny was in this respect much more modern than those that preceded it.

For France the terms were harsh, but they were not crushing, particularly as, with supreme cunning, the French negotiators had introduced two articles into the final draft signed at Calais without Edward's noticing, whereby full ratification of the Treaty was delayed.

Thus, as the English historian Stout writes: 'The Treaty of Calais was somewhat less definite in reality than in appearance.' It was in fact, unlike the previous truces, an armistice with no time-limit, but one that contained the threat of revenge.

Charles V and the revival of France

John the Good was liberated after the signing of the treaty, leaving his second son, the Duke of Anjou as a hostage pending the payment of his ransom. But, when the hostage escaped, the King felt obliged to return to captivity, in which he died in April 1364. He left a heavy legacy to his son, but Charles had ripened young in years of adversity. He was well able to handle the problems he inherited.

Of delicate build and complexion, Charles was a studious man, familiar with legal procedures and able to make good use of them. He was an able diplomat, and a good speaker; he was patient and circumspect, believing in moderation in all things and mistrusting haste. His was a rare combination of balanced qualities. For his methodical mind, governing according to principles, politics was an applied science, for he knew how to make use of his hard-won experience. Not that he can be depicted as a liberal ruler: he was an absolute monarch, unwilling to share his authority with anyone, but he valued and invariably sought advice before making a decision. His government was thus both expert and authoritarian.

The court of Charles V. All the nobles of the land were present, including the royal children (the Dauphin is at Charles's left). Below the king stands the Constable of France, Du Guesclin; in the lower right corner, the admiral Jean de Vienne. These seem to be true portraits of historical characters drawn without flattery. Fourteenth-century miniature. *Larousse*

Devoted to the interests of France, he considered himself responsible only to God and his conscience. His was thus a royal power which disciplined itself for the good of all, a precursor of the 'enlightened despotism' of the eighteenth century. In any case the general discipline which the King imposed on all the country, combined with his solicitude for the public welfare, resulted in the rapid recovery of France.

The new King was faced by three urgent tasks: to put an end to the agitation fomented by the King of Navarre, to stop the marauding of the 'Grandes Compagnies' (the armed bands at loose in the country since the Treaty of Brétigny had deprived the military forces of their occupation), and to prepare for an attack on Calais, and rid the kingdom of the English.

Charles of Navarre was soon dealt with. Bands of

Navarrese troops under the command of the Captal of Buch were marching on Rheims to prevent Charles V's coronation, fixed for May 19, 1364. As they were crossing the Eure at Cocherel they were fallen upon by Du Guesclin and his mercenaries and cut to pieces. All the Navarre leaders were killed except the Captal, who was taken prisoner. Charles the Bad then gave up the struggle. At the Treaty of Avignon, he surrendered his fiefs of Vexin, Mantes, and Meulan, which had been so threatening to Paris. He soon started intriguing again, but Navarre had ceased to be dangerous.

The liquidation of the Grandes Compagnies was a bigger problem. Ever since Brétigny these bands had been scouring the country and terrorising the inhabitants, adding still further to the hardships caused by the war. Their dissolution was sought in three ways. Destruction by force was attempted in 1362, and failed. The next attempt was to employ them outside the country. Hungary was a possible destination, but in the end Charles V decided to send them to Castile under Du Guesclin, to help Henry of Trastamara against his half-brother Peter the Cruel, King of Castile. The first campaign ended in a victory for Henry, who ascended the throne as Henry II; but when he had sent back to France most of his mercenaries, Peter attacked again, supported by English troops sent by the Black Prince. Henry's army was crushed and Du Guesclin taken prisoner (1367). The following year more contingents arrived from France, allowing Henry once more to reverse the situation. Du Guesclin, who had been ransomed, inflicted a decisive defeat on Peter at Montiel (1369). Peter was killed the following day during an interview with his brother.

This was a blow to the English, who had been backing Peter. Though the Compagnies came out of the affair considerably weakened, they were still not disposed of. A last solution offered itself to Charles: to enrol them as permanent troops in the royal army and subject them to discipline. A statute of January 1374 forbade the raising of any Compagnie without royal licence, and organised the Compagnies into *routes*, each of 100 men, commanded by a captain responsible to the King, paid by him, and entitled to give orders in his name. Thus a new sort of army was created, altogether different from the loose feudal bands known hitherto, an army which was to prove itself invaluable when the war against England started again.

The war begins again

By the appointed date, November 1361, many of the renunciations had yet to be completed, in particular in respect of Limousin, Périgord, Quercy and Rouergue. From then on, the strict terms of the Treaty of Calais concerning new renunciations had been violated, but the English seem to have failed to notice the fact or to have overlooked it. Charles V was careful to say nothing of these irregularities. Wanting to gain time, he acted as though all were in order, but he was actively preparing. Having persuaded his uncle, Emperor Charles IV, to adopt an attitude of benevolent neutrality, he made a formal alliance with Henry II of Castile which procured him the active support of the Castilian fleet. Then he successfully wooed Flanders by marrying his young brother, Philip the Bold, with Margaret, daughter and sole heir of Louis of Male, Count of Flanders. This was a great diplomatic success, full of danger for the future perhaps, but depriving England of her most strategic foothold on the Continent. And now the occasion Charles had waited for presented itself: the Count of Armagnac, John I, refused to levy the taxes decreed by the Black Prince, governor of Guienne. On being threatened, John appealed to Edward III, who made the mistake of refusing to hear him. John then appealed to the King of France, who was still his suzerain. Charles V supported the appeal, and in June 1369, Edward retaliated by once more proclaiming himself King of France. War followed.

Avoiding pitched battles, whose risk had been only too well established, the French reconquered the whole of the south-west piecemeal between 1369 and 1371. In October 1370 Charles made Du Guesclin Constable of France, thus putting even royal princes under his command. Du Guesclin immediately set about breaking Poitou and Saintonge, the chief centres of English resistance. By the end of March 1373, these two provinces and also Aunis and Angoumois had been recovered. That left Brittany, whose duke, John IV, was sympathetic to England. Du Guesclin's brilliant campaign of 1373 obliged him to fly. Except for Brest, which was retained by the English, the duchy was cleared; Guienne was recovered and only Bordeaux remained in English hands.

Edward III died in June 1377. The Black Prince had already lost his life in 1376, so the throne passed to Edward's grandson, Richard II. At the beginning of 1378, Charles V could look confidently to the future, but he died on September 16. Prospects then looked far

Du Guesclin, made Constable of France by Charles V in 1370. Though under Du Guesclin's command Charles's armies suffered a series of major defeats, his personal courage, his tenacity and policy of avoiding pitched battle gradually redressed the balance and kept up morale through a series of minor victories. *Hachette*

from hopeful. Brittany was already restive, for its annexation to the kingdom had been carried out too harshly, without regard to local susceptibilities; the schism between Rome and Avignon was as acute as ever; and the invaluable Du Guesclin lost his life in Auvergne while trying to subdue one of the last of the leaders of the Grandes Compagnies. The reign of Charles V was a fine one: the English now held only Calais, Cherbourg, Bordeaux and Bayonne. But the effort of twenty troubled years had strained France to breaking point. The provinces were restive. Charles V died leaving his work unfinished and a child of twelve to follow him on the throne as Charles VI.

The two regencies

The almost simultaneous death of Edward III and Charles V ushered in a new period in the conflict. The similarity in the situations in England and France is striking. On both sides of the Channel the king was under age, with uncles acting as regents; in both countries there were disturbances in the towns, symptoms of widespread popular discontent. One cannot but remark the closeness in time of the revolt of the *Compi*, the wool carders of Florence in 1382, the revolt of the Ghenters, led by Philip van Artevelde in 1382, the rising of the *Maillotins* in Paris in March 1382, and even the more rural movement in England led by Wat Tyler and the Lollard preacher, John Ball. These social disturbances were all directed against the ruling powers, and there can be no doubt that the defeat of the Ghenters by Charles VI at Roosebeke was an event of decisive importance, for in the disturbed state of France at that moment, the defeat of the King would have meant the end of the Valois.

Under these conditions, neither England nor France was in a position to break the tacit truce that had been established between the two countries on the death of Charles V. When Charles VI assumed the reins of power in France in November 1388 and Richard II in England the following May, a reconciliation took place. In 1396 Richard married by proxy Charles VI's eldest daughter, Isabella, then seven years old, and the truce was to be prolonged until 1423. Richard also promised full support for French policy in Italy and in the papal schism. But this was unpopular in England, and growing discontent and family vendettas led eventually to the fall of this intelligent but neurotic king, overthrown in 1399 by his cousin, Henry Bolingbroke. To support his somewhat questionable title to the throne, as Henry IV, Bolingbroke had to exploit anti-French feeling. His ambitious, energetic son, Henry V, who reigned from 1413 to 1422, had even grander ideas than his forebears, wanting to recover the whole of Aquitaine as laid down by the Treaty of Brétigny, and also to claim the throne of France into the bargain. Not even Edward III had hoped for so much. Thus, under the Lancastrians, the conflict became more nationalistic and less feudal than it had been before. At the same time England's cause was greatly favoured by the civil war which broke out in France, with each side in turn requesting English intervention.

Charles VI and the civil war in France

For eight years the government of France had been in the hands of the King's four uncles, Louis, Duke of Anjou, John, Duke of Berry, Philip the Bold, Duke of Normandy, and Louis II, Duke of Bourbon. For eight years the French acquiesced and found money for princely politics pursued for private ends with no concern for the general welfare. Suddenly, in November 1388, Charles VI, now twenty, announced his intention of governing himself. This *coup d'état* was engineered, not by the King, but by his younger brother, Louis of Orleans, with the backing of the former advisers of Charles V whom the princes had removed from office.

For four years the country was governed by this odd team: the slapdash and ambitious young Louis and the representatives of the remarkable administration of his

The Black Prince. Effigy from his tomb in Canterbury Cathedral.

predecessor. Then, in August 1392, the King lost his reason, and both he and his kingdom entered a long-drawn agony of thirty years. Forty-three times the light of reason returned, forty-three times it was extinguished. In the periods of remission Charles was lucid but ready to agree to anything proposed to him. The fact that the King could perform the acts of his office and appear in public, even if only half conscious of events, weakened the regency. Round the feeble-minded King, conflicting ambitions and influences were active. One of the first consequences of his madness was the elimination of the former advisers of Charles V and the return of the dukes.

The two factions

During the life of Philip the Bold, the situation was not too bad, for Louis of Orleans had some respect for Philip's age and experience, and a precarious balance was maintained around the King. On Philip's death in 1404, however, the situation deteriorated. The rivalry between the new Duke of Burgundy, John the Fearless, and the Duke of Orleans sharpened. Exploiting the latter's unpopularity with the burghers and people of Paris for his extravagance and dissipation, John had him assassinated in 1407, and then claimed it to be a patriotic action. This was the signal for the civil war which was to rend the kingdom for twenty-five years. For support, Charles of Orleans, Louis's young son, relied chiefly on the great barons of Berry, Burgundy, Brittany and Alençon, and, after his marriage with the daughter of Bernard VII, Count of Armagnac, the seigneurs of the south-west. As a result the Orleans

Colour plate: the marriage of Richard II and Isabella, daughter of Charles VI of France. Chromolith from the *Chronique de Froissart*.

Mariage du Roi d'Angleterre et d'Isabelle de France

Above: the capture of Richard II (disguised as a Friar Minor) by Henry Bolingbroke (1399). Humiliated, he was brought to London where he formally renounced the throne. He died the following year after a winter's imprisonment in Pontefract Castle. Early fifteenth-century manuscript. *British Museum*

Parliament confirming the deposition of Richard II in favour of Henry Bolingbroke (Henry IV). Henry's moral claim to his cousin's throne was weak; he had acquired it by force and relied on Parliament to give his accession legal validity. He roused popular support by exploiting anti-French feeling. *Mansell*

A battle between Bahram Chubinah and Khusran Parwik. A Persian miniature from the manuscript of the Shahnama. c. 1490. *British Museum*

party came to be called the Armagnacs. The Burgundy party had to rely principally on the complex personality of John the Fearless, a subtle, twisted, unscrupulous political manoeuvrer, though it also had the more or less constant support of the population of Paris, still smarting from the repression of the revolt of the *Maillotins* in 1382. But in thirty years Paris had changed. Etienne Marcel had gone, and it was now the more turbulent of the corporations (the butchers and skinners) who excited the discontented masses and were ready for any *coup de force*. John the Fearless saw in them a tool.

Throughout 1412 and 1413 Paris was in a state of constant unrest. At the instigation of the Duke, the King promulgated the famous ordinance of May 1413, the *ordinance cabochienne*, which instituted certain reforms. But this was no more than window-dressing, as the malcontents realised at once. No one was disarmed, and the regime of the abattoirs went on as before, strengthened by the execution of the leading Armagnacs. The rising came to an end, however, when Bernard VII forced his way into Paris in July 1413 and John the Fearless fled to Flanders. With that, Armagnac terror was substituted for the Burgundian one. Inevitably, the war with England flared up again.

Agincourt and the Treaty of Troyes

In England, Henry V realised that this was the moment for revenge, particularly as two sides in France had simultaneously solicited his help. He amused himself for a while by entering into discussions with them, then suddenly in 1415 declared his intention of enforcing his own

369

claims by arms. The campaign of 1415 was an exact repetition of that of 1346. Henry V took Harfleur, on the estuary of the Seine, but his disease-ridden army was forced to make a slow retreat northwards. The French army raised by the Armagnacs engaged the English at Agincourt, north of Amiens, on October 25, 1415. The lessons of Crécy and Poitiers had taught them nothing, and in thick mud and under driving rain the French army was utterly defeated. Seven thousand Frenchmen were left on the battlefield, and they included the flower of French chivalry. Among the prisoners were Charles of Orleans, the Duke of Bourbon, and Jean Boucicault, Marshal of France. Henry V embarked next day at Calais.

John the Fearless was now able to regain some of his lost authority, the discredited and leaderless Armagnacs having lost all cohesion. Henry V had landed in Normandy in 1417, and John, troubled by this development, sought a rapprochement with the Dauphin, who, since 1417, had been Lieutenant-General of the King and was the last hope of the Armagnacs. John's plan was to be reconciled with the Dauphin, then to eliminate his advisers and rule in his name. At the same time, as a line of retreat, he took care not to upset the Queen, Isabella of Bavaria, who, exiled from Paris by her son, had set up a rival government at Troyes. John the Fearless of Burgundy met the Dauphin, Charles, three times. At the third meeting, on the bridge of Montereau, there was a scuffle in which the Duke was felled with an axe by one of the Dauphin's followers.

The murder of Montereau was decisive. France was split into two factions. The new Duke of Burgundy, Philip the Good, after adding Flanders and lower Belgium to the inheritance of the house of Hainaut, became one of the most powerful sovereigns of Europe. His policy remained that of his fathers: to dominate France. He hesitated to seek favours of Henry V, but his advisers were urging him to avenge his father, and he knew he could not do so without English help. Isabella, moreover, unable to forgive her son's sentence of exile, supported Philip. Out of all this came the Treaty of Troyes, which sought to put an end to the dynastic struggle opened in 1328 by making Henry V heir to the throne of France. The so-called Dauphin was ruled out of the succession on the grounds of bastardy, on the confession of his own mother. Catherine, the last unmarried daughter of Charles VI, was given to Henry V, who thereby became the 'real son' and who, while the mad king remained alive, would act as regent with the apanage of Normandy. Such were the humiliating terms to which France agreed.

So Henry V had achieved his object, the dual monarchy; and Philip the Good had missed his, for Henry had made up his mind to govern Burgundian France himself, without any intermediary. But the Treaty of Troyes suffered from one defect, both in form and substance. For three centuries the throne of France had passed from father to son, and to depart from the custom seemed to the medieval mind a supreme wrong. Even if his son was spiritless, a tool of the Constable of France, and unconvinced of his own rights, the French people were by no means certain that Charles VI had the right to disinherit

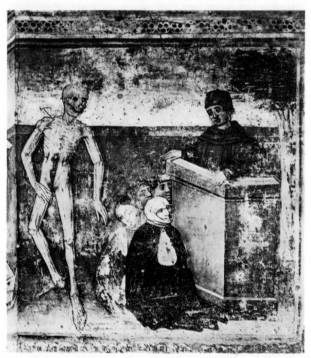

Allegorical fresco depicting the Black Death. This plague swept across Europe from the Crimea (1346) to Sicily, Genoa, Provence and England (1348), and had spread to Scandinavia and Germany by 1350. It recurred about every ten years and reduced the population of medieval Europe by a third. For about a century population ceased to rise, the formerly developing economy stagnated and the scourge shook the foundations of religious belief. *Lala Aufsberg Foto*

Territory ruled by Charles the Bold, Duke of Burgundy, 1433-77.

his natural heir in favour of his son-in-law. But no-one knew what course of action to take until the right person came forward to become the centre of a counter-attack. That person was Joan of Arc.

Joan of Arc and the liberation of France

Until Joan of Arc appeared, the Dauphin's cause seemed hopeless. Henry V had died in 1422 and his father-in-law, Charles VI, lived only two months after him. The Duke of Bedford, regent for the young king, Henry VI, kept order with energy and wisdom, but his resources may have been considerably less than those of Charles VII in his 'kingdom of Bourges'. However, the latter's military position grew weaker as each month passed. Against Bedford's small but coherent and well disciplined forces, Charles had only wild and unruly Armagnac bands to rely on, under such leaders as La Hire, Poton de Saintrailles, and the Count of Dunois, the Bastard of Orleans. The only good force Charles managed to assemble was defeated at Verneuil in 1424. Everywhere the English offensive gained strength, and, in October 1428, Orleans, the strategic centre of France, was besieged. Charles VII, discouraged and surrounded by plots and intrigues, thought of taking refuge in Castile or Scotland. The fall of Orleans was expected at any moment, bringing with it the triumph of the house of Lancaster.

Then Joan of Arc changed the course of events. This is not the place to relate her adventure in detail, but rather to place it in its historical setting. Joan came from Domrémy, one of the Dauphin's last fiefs north of the Loire, and according to her it was there that she was entrusted with her mission. It is impossible to establish her divine inspiration as a fact, but none can dispute the individual and collective mystic sense of the age, or the important part it played in history. France was overcome by physical and moral sufferings and had nothing left to believe in but miracles. Prophets and visionaries sprang up everywhere, even in the Dauphin's entourage. Certainly at the time everyone believed Joan's powers to be supernatural, and the only point to decide was whether they were derived from God or the devil. Joan's mission was intimately linked with the question whether the King was or was not the legitimate son of his father, a question which was troubling the minds of the people, a question no available evidence could settle. So divine evidence—the evidence Joan was to bring to the Dauphin at Chinon—was necessary. It had even been besought: for in his extremity, on All Saints' Day 1428, in the silence of his own chamber, the Dauphin had asked God to deliver him of his doubt. And two days after his arrival at Chinon in February 1429, in the course of a private interview, Joan had given him the answer, telling him he was the King's son and the heir to France. With that, a paralysing doubt faded away. In those days there was no distinction between loyalty to the king and patriotism. Once the king was consecrated there were no longer two kings of France to choose between; the whole edifice of the Treaty of Troyes came tumbling down. Henry's dual monarchy was a thing of the past.

Joan's extraordinary intervention had saved the country, for, short as it was, limited in its sphere of action, it was decisive; the King was saved, France was saved. Joan's career was indeed short. On May 8, 1429 Talbot raised the siege of Orleans; on June 18 he was routed at Patay. On July 17 the Dauphin was crowned at Rheims, and from that moment no Christian could doubt that he was the legitimate sovereign. So incredible were the events leading up to his coronation that it all seemed miraculous. The disgrace of the Treaty of Troyes was effaced by the sacrament; the Armagnacs became loyal subjects of the King instead of lawless partisans of the Dauphin; the Burgundians could no longer take their orders from Bedford without committing open treason. After the coronation, Joan considered her mission at an end. But enthusiasm was roused and she was persuaded to remain in the King's service. But the hesitations and intrigues of the Court, and the emptiness of the exchequer forbade all action of an ambitious nature. Joan was wounded in an unsuccessful attempt to capture Paris. Six months later, defending Compiègne, she was taken prisoner when leading a sortie against the Burgundians in May 1430. That brought the career of the inspired shepherdess to an end. The Duke of Burgundy handed her over to the English, and with the eager concurrence of the Bishop of Beauvais and other French divines she suffered a long trial at Rouen and then was condemned to be burnt at the stake in May 1431. That did not undo her work: on the contrary, it consecrated it, for to preach one's faith and die for it was the supreme proof of Christian virtue. That being so, the trial at Rouen, far from proving the falsity of her mission, as her detractors hoped—for they thought her a witch—merely seemed to establish its authenticity.

Richard Beauchamp, Earl of Warwick (1382-1439), being received as Captain of Calais, a post which he held under Henry V at the time of Agincourt. Warwick was later to be charged with the education of the young Henry VI and in 1430 superintended the trial of Joan of Arc. Late fifteenth-century manuscript.

Scenes from the life of Joan of Arc, taken from *Vigiles de Charles VII* written only a few years after the events. *Top left:* Joan succeeds in obtaining an audience of the Dauphin and is led before him. He gives her command of his forces and Orleans is captured. She goes on to recapture other strongholds along the Loire (*top right*). Five weeks later she has Charles crowned at Rheims (*below*). But she fails to take Paris and is wounded there. Joan of Arc, while attempting to raise the siege of Compiègne, is captured by John of Luxemburg and sold to the English. *Larousse, Giraudon, B.N.*

In the eyes of the French, she was to become a saint and her visions prophecies.

The impulse had been given and doubts assuaged. It nevertheless took another twenty years to recover the last of the provinces. For this there were sufficient reasons. France was exhausted, a prey of the Skinners (a new form of the Grandes Compagnies), and generally weighed down by epidemics, crushing poverty, a heavy mortality, and the apathy of Charles VII. Pathetic appeals were made to the King by people at the end of their resources. Nothing much could be done, however, until France and Burgundy were reunited in September 1435 by the Peace of Arras. By ceding the towns of the Somme (St Quentin, Amiens, Corbie, and St Riquier) which formed a line of fortresses protecting Artois and threatening Paris, and by promising to make *amende honorable* for the murder at Montereau, Charles VII re-established the suzerainty of the house of Valois over the Dukes of Burgundy. The Peace of Arras spelt the final ruin of the Armagnac party, who had supported Charles in his younger days. Charles now abandoned party leadership to become the king of all Frenchmen. The evolution begun at the coronation of Rheims came to its conclusion. The final reconquest was fought on two fronts, Normandy and Guienne. In Normandy a methodical campaign was carried out by a new type of army consisting of artillery with a small but well disciplined body of foot-soldiers. This campaign gradually grew in momentum, to end with French victory at Formigny in April 1450. The recovery of Guienne was harder, for here the inhabitants, unlike the Normans, were not well disposed towards the French. They had close commercial links with England and had enjoyed the relative autonomy the English had allowed them. Nevertheless a single campaign under Gaston IV of Foix and the Sieur d'Albret, helped by Dunois, ended with the occupation of the whole province. A final offensive launched by the English ended in the disaster of Castillon

in July 1453. Only Calais and the County of Guines remained in English hands. The latter were now, to all intents and purposes, driven out of France. That had been Joan of Arc's aim and it only remained to rehabilitate her fame. After difficult negotiations with Pope Calixtus III —for there was no court of appeal against the Inquisition—he revoked her sentence in 1456.

Thus ended, without any treaty, the war that had lasted 116 years.

Joan of Arc, while attempting to raise the siege of Compiègne, is captured by John of Luxembourg and sold to the English. A scene from *Vigiles de Charles VII*, written a few years after the event. *Larousse, Giraudon, B.N.*

WESTERN EUROPE AT THE END OF THE FIFTEENTH CENTURY

LOUIS XI

When Charles VII died in July 1461, many problems still remained to be solved, concerned either with the new unity of the country and its government, with the remains of the great feudal system, or with international affairs in a Europe that was beginning to assume a definitive shape. All these problems Louis XI was to tackle with consummate adroitness. A man who dealt craftily with everybody, even with God, he had a fertile, subtle, perceptive mind, which enabled him to reap advantage even from the mistakes which his feverish and impulsive activity led him only too often to commit. He had a sort of eclipsed genius, for his reign was blessed by no grand political achievements. Yet, by its length and its stability, it was of great importance for the French monarchy.

The power of Burgundy

Amongst the great feudal families whose power was still, in 1461, a threat to the monarchy and an obstacle to its government, the Dukes of Burgundy were the most redoubtable. One might almost hesitate to include them among the families of France. For their territory, extending from Holland to the Jura and the Saône, overlapped both France and the Empire, and the Duke of Burgundy was regarded as a great duke of western Europe as much as a French prince. Philip the Good (1396-1467), who founded the famous Order of the Golden Fleece in Bruges in 1430, dazzled Europe with the splendour of his court. Some of its banquets have become historic, like the *banquet du faisan* of 1454, so called because Philip and his guests took oath upon a gilded and bejewelled pheasant to embark on a crusade against the Turks, who had just taken Constantinople. Like his fathers, Philip was a patron of the arts. In the days when Hubert and Jan van Eyck perfected the technique of oil painting and were producing the best of their work, Philip the Bold had invited Claus Sluter, the sculptor, to his court at Dijon, to decorate the Chartreuse de Champmol.

A monk copying a manuscript. In the later Middle Ages the monasteries were still the repositories of learning, religious and secular, a function which the development of printing and the growth of the universities were gradually to take from them.

Philip the Good might well be tempted to change his ducal coronet for a crown. Louis XI understood perfectly the danger such a power would be, flanking his kingdom on the east and north.

The monarchy triumphs over feudalism. Peace with England

In combating the last great feudal magnates, the King no doubt considered that he was following the age-old policy of his predecessors, but at the back of his mind the thought must have been present that his first objective, 'Greater Burgundy', was a reincarnation of the ancient Lotharingia. Even before the death of Philip the Good, Louis XI, fully conscious of the inevitable conflict ahead, had in 1463 bought back the towns on the Somme.

Almost at once war broke out with the League of Public Weal, a league of the great nobles. Philip was not among them, but they had the support of his son, the future Charles the Bold. The League's idea was to curb Louis's power by making his younger brother, Charles, Duke of Berry, regent. The aim of 'public weal' was proclaimed in order to win the support of the masses. Louis XI, supported by the towns, manoeuvred to break up the League, and after the indecisive battle of Montlhéry in July 1465 he succeeded in disarming his adversaries at the price of various concessions and pensions and the restitution of his recently bought Somme towns to Burgundy, and the gift of Normandy as an apanage to his brother, Charles. But Normandy joined two of the principal duchies, those of Brittany and Burgundy (with Flanders), and effected a direct entente with Edward IV of England.

Louis had the cession of Normandy annulled, pronouncing it inalienable, and offered his brother Roussillon instead.

That was the signal for the formation of another League, made all the easier by the death of Philip the Good in 1467. He was followed by his much more aggressive son, Charles the Bold, who in 1468 married the sister of Edward IV. Trusting to his persuasiveness, Louis XI dashed to Peronne, where the Duke of Burgundy was staying. It was a risky move, but by flattery and reasonableness Louis was well on the way to succeeding when the news arrived of the revolt of Liège against the Duke, to the cry of *vive le roi*. The movement by Louis's agents had broken out prematurely, and Louis himself was caught. He was promptly imprisoned, and freed only at the price of various concessions. Charles, the King's brother, was to be given Champagne and Brie, instead of Normandy, and the King—this was the humiliating stroke — was to accompany the Duke on his reprisal expedition to Liège.

In the last of the feudal risings, in 1472, Charles the Bold's thrust was broken by the resistance of Beauvais. With that the period of the great feudal coalitions approached its end. Louis XI prepared for the decisive struggle. By skilful negotiations with the English, who at Charles the Bold's request had landed in force at Calais, he paved the way for the Treaty of Picquigny, signed in August 1475, which brought to an end the conflict between England and France. The treaty was mercantile in spirit, the English being bought off with seventy-five thousand crowns. The last adherents of chivalry might reproach the two sovereigns for having forsaken honour for trade, but both Louis and Edward IV were thoroughly pleased with the deal.

Having signed the treaty with England, Louis now bent all his talents to the problem of Burgundy. Anyone else would have thought the moment had come to crush his rival by force of arms: not so Louis, who preferred the subtler weapon of diplomacy. And instead of dictating to the Duke at Soleure, he offered him a nine-year truce and even encouraged him in his dream of a royal crown, a dream in which he was later to become ensnared. Events moved rapidly. Louis persuaded the confederated Swiss cantons to become reconciled with Sigismund, Archduke of Austria, and he promoted the alliance between the free towns of Alsace, Sigismund, and the Swiss. He signed a pact of mutual assistance with the Emperor Frederick III and a formal treaty of alliance with René II, Duke of Lorraine, who felt himself threatened by Charles the Bold. Charles certainly had an eye on the duchy, which, in his hands, would have united the two parts of Greater Burgundy. Becoming more and more entangled, and not knowing where to turn, Charles decided first of all to take his revenge on René II, whom he drove out of Nancy; then he turned on the Swiss, who routed him at Granson, and then, in 1476, at Morat. Meanwhile René had returned to Nancy, and Charles attacked him. The battle was fought outside the town in January 1477, and once again the Burgundians were defeated. Two days after the battle the body of their Duke was found in the frozen snow.

The great state of Burgundy had virtually ceased to exist. Without putting a single soldier in the field, without openly breaking the Truce of Soleure, Louis XI had triumphed. He took most of the spoils: Picardy, Artois, Boulonnais, Burgundy, and Franche-Comté, but not Flanders. And he was unable to prevent the marriage of Charles's daughter, Marie, to Maximilian, son of the Emperor Frederick III. The introduction of the house of Habsburg in the Low Countries, was to raise a new peril for the French monarchy.

French diplomacy expands

The revival of French power had been so rapid and so complete that, from the reign of Louis XI onwards, the political pattern of western Europe was centred on France. For the first time since Philip the Fair, the King was able to intervene actively in European affairs beyond his own frontiers. At the same time international affairs became more complicated and more closely knit.

Charles VII entering Toulouse. Timorous and badly advised at the start of his reign Charles ended by re-establishing sovereignty over the Dukes of Burgundy and driving the English out of France. The consequent strengthening of French power was not the least of Joan of Arc's 'miracles'. Archives of Toulouse. *Larousse*

The time had passed when small political units could exist, and European realms became conscious of increasing interdependence.

Louis XI was on the watch for any renewal of danger from England, and he was haunted by the prospect of another Anglo-Burgundian alliance. To prepare for it, he sought alliances in the east, particularly with Frederick III, who was busily enlarging his patrimony by marriages. In Savoy, French influence was strong. For Louis XI had married Charlotte of Savoy, and his sister, Yolande, had married the Prince of Piedmont, who was to become Amadeus IX of Savoy. There can be no doubt that it was Louis's dream to annex the country, for his thoughts were turning towards Italy now that he had become the ally of Francesco Sforza, Duke of Milan. On Francesco's death, the French successfully supported one of his sons, Lodovico the Moor, against another, Galeazzo. At Florence, Louis saved the Medicis (also his allies), when they were threatened by the conspiracy

375

of the Pazzi family, who were supported by the Pope and the King of Naples. Louis's policy in Italy followed a consistent plan: constant intervention, readiness to arbitrate, but never to undertake military action. It was a wise policy which his successors soon forgot.

Louis's Spanish policy was, on the contrary, a perilous one of conquests and annexations, which dangerously diverted French energy. He understood the need to maintain the traditional alliance with Castile in face of the increasingly close collaboration of England and Portugal. He seems to have obtained some substantial advantages, such as the conquest of Roussillon, and the marriage of John of Albret with Catherine of Navarre, but these were outweighed by the danger of the unification of the peninsula after the marriage of Isabella of Castile with Ferdinand of Aragon in October 1469. That marriage, which Louis was unable to stop, added to that of Maximilian with Marie of Burgundy, was to have important consequences.

France under Anne of Beaujeu

Louis XI had made France the first power in western Europe. His work was temporarily endangered after his death—for his son Charles VIII (1483-98) was weak and incapable—but it was saved by the regency of Charles's sister, Anne, and her husband Pierre de Beaujeu. The States General of 1484 granted Pierre all the subsidies he asked for, without seeking any major political concessions in return. He was thus able to get the upper hand in the *Guerre folle*, the last feudal insurrection, which ended pitifully. He also succeeded in getting the marriage of Anne of Brittany and Maximilian annulled, after which he forced her to marry Charles VIII. This young king was subsequently to risk his kingdom in an absurd adventure in Italy which cost him Artois, Franche-Comté and Roussillon.

Despite all these losses, if we take stock of Europe at the end of the fifteenth century, we find no country whose wealth and power compared to that of France.

The Wars of the Roses

England, finally defeated in her great struggle with the Valois kings and, save for her hold on Calais, expelled from the Continent, fell at once into the bitter civil war between the houses of York and Lancaster, a war which went a long way to annihilating the old noble families of England. With the Battle of Hexham in 1464, the white rose triumphed and Edward IV of York set aside the intermittently imbecile Henry VI who had inherited the madness of his Valois grandfather.

Edward IV's reign saw an economic and social revival after the setbacks of the early fifteenth century. The monolithic peasant society which had been the basis of the old medieval order had broken up, releasing the new yeoman vigour which was to be the basis of a much more healthy society. The foundations of many a later Tudor noble house were laid at this time, when administration was no longer solely in the hands of the clerics. The Wars of the Roses had been an affair of the nobility, not of the masses, and the prosperity of London, Bristol and Norwich was little affected by these 'King's games'. Moreover, the latent powers of the crown, which were

The building of a ship, about 1480. Such vessels were to form the basis of English maritime expansion. Contemporary woodcut. *Mansell*

to foster Tudor order and expansion, were revived with the Yorkist monarchy. Edward himself was a good man of business who participated in the prosperous wool trade with Flanders, as well as a first-rate soldier. Like his grandson, Henry VIII, he was large and handsome, with the attributes of a Renaissance prince. The conception of government was becoming more businesslike, as witness Fortescue's *Governaunce of England*, the first treatise on politics in the English tongue. In spite, also, of nascent anti-clericalism of the new urban middle class, the fifteenth century in England saw great achievements in architecture and stained glass—as in the superb chapel at King's College, Cambridge. It was in this century that Eton was founded, All Souls' and Magdalen Colleges at Oxford, and many other foundations.

The life of the towns was full of vigour and the Court learnt from the Burgundians a new splendour of ceremonial and dress. While there were undercurrents of change which were to destroy many late medieval institutions, the late fifteenth century in England laid the foundations of Tudor society, itself destined to be a springboard to the beginnings of an oceanic expansion.

The Yorkist regime collapsed mainly through the workings of dynastic chance. Edward IV died at the height of his career at forty, and his brother Richard III seized the throne at the expense of his nephew, Edward V, who, with the young Duke of York, was probably murdered at his uncle's orders. But the event would not have destroyed the Yorkist house had Richard III's own son, the Prince of Wales, not died in 1484.

The way was thus left open for Henry Tudor, Earl of Richmond, a descendant through his mother from John of Gaunt, and through his grandmother from Catherine, widow of Henry V, who had secretly married a Welsh adventurer, Owen Tudor.

Henry Tudor landed in Wales, and with the help of Welsh forces and through the treachery of the Stanley family to the king, defeated and killed Richard III at Bosworth in 1485. The new king, Henry VII, made peace between the houses of Lancaster and York by marrying Elizabeth of York, daughter of Edward IV, and with a precise skill laid the foundation of the powerful Tudor monarchy.

The seven German Electors who for four centuries from 1356 controlled the election of Holy Roman Emperor. The Pope no longer had a voice in this election, but the Emperor lost his former authority. Miniature from the *Codex Balduinus. Historisches Bildarchiv Handke*

Left: Alfonso V King of Aragon and Sicily. Relatively free of internal disputes he conquered Naples where he reigned as Alfonso I. Fifteenth-century manuscript. *British Museum*

Germany and the decline of the imperialist idea

Since the fall of the Hohenstaufens, Germany had ceased to be a great power. It was merely a collection of countries, principalities, and smaller fiefs of inextricable complexity. 'Emperor' became an honorary title with no authority behind it. In any case the character of the Empire had changed. The Golden Bull of 1356 remained for four centuries the fundamental law of the Empire. It put the election in the hands of a college of seven German Electors, and thenceforward the Papacy had no voice in the choice of an Emperor. The Holy Roman Empire had become secular. After the death of Charles IV in 1378, the House of Luxemburg-Bohemia held the throne (with Wenceslas and Sigismund) till 1437. Then the Electors called back the Habsburgs, who had already enjoyed two periods of imperial office, with Rudolph I (1273-91) and Albert I (1298-1308). But if they now chose Albert II, it was because they knew him to be weak.

Similarly in 1439, they passed over the young Elector of Brandenburg whose power seemed too dangerously ambitious and elected Frederick of Styria, of a junior Habsburg line, again on the grounds of incapacity. It would appear that they deliberately maintained a grandiose façade with nothing behind it. The weakness of the Empire and the powerlessness of its component states explain the formation on its frontiers during the fourteenth and fifteenth centuries of independent groups, such as the permanent confederation in 1291 of the cantons of Schwyz, Uri, and Unterwalden, which broke away from Habsburg domination in 1315. This weakness also underlies the decline of German influence in eastern

Europe over the same period. It would have been difficult at that time to select any prince capable of bringing order to the chaotic state of Germany.

Nevertheless the Habsburg Frederick III (1440-93), who did nothing to revive the prestige of the Empire—though he was the last to be crowned in Rome (1452)—succeeded in having his son Maximilian recognised as his heir, and therewith established the hereditary principal, *de facto* though not *de jure*, in favour of his House. It was an able move, and with the marriage of Maximilian to Marie of Burgundy, the way was prepared for the rise of the Habsburgs to European domination—not that anyone foresaw it at the end of the fifteenth century.

Condottieri and tyrants in Italy

The fragmentation of Italy was less pronounced than that of Germany. Instead of numerous tiny units, Italy had half a dozen regional states. Even so, they were small, perpetually at war with one another, and living in a tangle of shifting diplomatic combinations. If one looked like becoming powerful, a combination was promptly formed against it. As Cavaignac has said, 'the balance of Italy gave a foretaste of what the balance of Europe was to be'. These wars were strictly professional, conducted by the *condottieri*, who knew neither feudal loyalty nor national sentiment. On the other hand, the intense rivalry which rent both towns and feudatories throughout the twelfth and thirteenth centuries had brought tyrants into existence almost everywhere, and whether or not they exerted their power benevolently—and they sometimes did—it was based on no valid title. Aeneas Silvius, 377 later Pope Pius II, writes sadly: 'In our Italy, so fond of change, where nothing lasts and where no old-established families exist, valets may easily aspire to become kings.' Milan, Ferrara and Padua were all ruled by tyrants. This was a common pattern. There were few exceptions: Naples and Sicily were still in the hands of the old Aragonese dynasty; Florence had been ruled since 1434 by a family of bankers, the Medicis, who tried to win all Tuscany; Venice was still under her old patrician republic, turning her back on Italy, though ready to intervene in the quarrels of her smaller neighbours. Lastly, there was Rome, where the Popes, as temporal rulers, all too often forgot that they were also the spiritual sovereigns of Christendom.

This breach with the past was due chiefly to the absence of political unity—that being the age-old weakness of Italy. But, just as Greece of the fourth century B.C., fragmented and torn by internecine strife, was the initiator of Rome, and the great leader in thought, so did the Italy of the Quattrocento constitute a school for the rest of Europe. In the thirteenth century France had been without artistic or intellectual rival, but now Italy had taken over. It was the country of Petrarch and Giotto which now offered the world the Florentine masterpieces of architecture, sculpture, and painting, the works of Brunellesco, Donatello, Ghiberti, Fra Angelico and Botticelli. Throughout Italy centres of culture were formed, whose light was to radiate all over fifteenth and sixteenth century Europe. The Duke of Moscow came to Italy, looking for architects to embellish the Kremlin; it was from Italy that the sovereigns of western Europe (Louis XI, for instance, and Ferdinand of Aragon) drew their political ideas. Francesco Sforza was a mentor to Louis XI. It was from Italy, the home of political subtlety and diplomacy, that the sovereigns of the fifteenth century learnt the art of exploiting 'reasons of State'. But Italy,

A condottiere. Typical of fifteenth-century Italy he was halfway between the medieval knight and the Renaissance prince. Though cultured he was often a brutal soldier, frequently a mercenary; sometimes a church-builder, he was just as often excommunicated.

intellectual guide though she might be, would never become the dominant political power on the Continent.

Spain and Portugal

The two countries of the Peninsula, which the sixteenth century was to see in the forefront of international affairs, were in the fourteenth and fifteenth centuries still on the fringe of Europe. Down to the middle of the fourteenth, both were engaged against the Moors, and after that they entered a period of internal struggles, dynastic squabbles and conflicts between sovereigns and nobles, particularly in Castile. After the unification of Spain by the marriage of Ferdinand of Aragon and Isabella of Castile in 1469, the Reconquest was finally completed by the taking of Granada in 1492, while Portugal was advancing the Christian thrust towards Morocco. The end of the century marked the starting point for the great maritime adventures of these two countries, decisive for the history of the world.

The victory of Alfonso XI of Castile (1312-49) on the River Salado in 1340 marks the end of the attempts of the Moors of Africa to regain a foothold in Europe. Only the little kingdom of Granada was left as evidence of former Arab domination in Spain. The Castilians now engaged in civil war under the reign of Peter the Cruel (1350-62) and then under his half-brother and murderer, Henry of Trastamara (1362-79). There were constant wars against Portugal, Navarre, Aragon, the kingdom of Granada, and the partisans of Peter the Cruel's sons. After the short reign of John I, Henry's son, there was a disturbed period during the minority of Henry III, followed by his troubled reign in which all operations against the Moors were unsuccessful. Lastly came the feudal struggles during the reigns of John II (1406-54) and Henry IV (1454-74), who was almost dethroned by his nobles.

During this time Aragon, suffering much less from internal troubles, employed her energies in Mediterranean expansion and secured a foothold in Sicily and southern Italy. As for Portugal, her energies under Afonso V were drained by the conflict with Castile, which she lost at the Battle of Toro in 1475. During the truce that followed Portugal increased her pressure on the Moslems of North Africa. Ceuta was taken in August 1415, in the reign of John I (1385-1433), and, in spite of the disaster at Tangier in 1437, Afonso V (1438-81) continued to advance. Ksar-es-Srir was taken in 1454, Anfa (Casablanca) in 1463, Arzila and Tangier in 1471. Henry the Navigator, a younger son of John I, became one of the most remarkable figures of the fifteenth century, passionately devoted to religion and science. From his palace-observatory of Sagres, perched on the craggy cliffs of Cape St Vincent, he despatched expedition after expedition to the Gulf of Guinea. Portugal was now beginning to discover her maritime future. Her mariners, intent on sailing to Asia round Africa, explored far down the West African coast, until they came to the tropical forest kingdoms of Guinea; and they discovered Santos and Madeira. All this was preparatory to a much wider expansion round the Cape to India and Indonesia, which was to give Portugal a great maritime commercial empire and was to be the first decisive assertion of western European sea power against the great land powers of Asia.

A fresh impulse was given to Spain by their Catholic

majesties Ferdinand and Isabella. Together with Henry the Navigator they instigated that outward surge which was to end in Europe's domination over the world, the surge towards North Africa, towards the Indian Ocean, and, lastly, towards the New World that was suddenly to be revealed—America.

In the still groping Europe of the late fifteenth century everything pointed towards French supremacy. For no one, at that moment, could have foreseen the coming union of the Spanish and imperial forces by the marriage of Maximilian's son, Philip the Handsome, heir to the empire and to the Duchy of Burgundy, with Joanna the Mad, the heiress of a united Spain that was reaching out to all corners of the world.

Francesco Foscari, Doge of Venice 1423-57. Though Venice was at the height of its power Foscari was personally unlucky and died a broken man. *Historisches Bildarchiv Handke*

An English ship at Lisbon being received by John of Portugal in 1385. Fourteenth-century manuscript. From the *Chroniques d'Angleterre* of Jean de Wavrin.

The fleet and tents of the Crusaders outside Constantinople. During the Fourth Crusade, the centre of Christendom had been looted and sacked by Christians who had set out to free the Holy Cities from the Saracens. Ships were comparatively small at this period; with the invention of gunpowder in the fourteenth century they became larger, with several masts instead of one.

CHAPTER TWENTY-TWO

ON THE FRINGE OF EUROPE

EASTERN EUROPE

The Byzantine Empire and the Palaeologi

The Fourth Crusade had dealt a mortal blow to the Byzantine Empire. Even after its revival under the Palaeologian dynasty (from 1265) the great days of the Comnenians were over. Not that the Palaeologi did not produce great emperors—Michael VIII and Manuel II were of considerable ability—but the Empire was incurably stricken. Confined since the middle of the fourteenth century to Constantinople and its neighbourhood, part of the Peloponnesus, and four towns on the Black Sea, it was completely undermined by palace revolutions, social disturbances, religious disputes, the depredations of mercenary bands, and permanent financial difficulties. To these must be added the many external dangers: Bulgarian and Serb encroachments, Venetian and Genoese rapacity, and constant pressure from the Ottoman Turks. All things considered, it is surprising that the Byzantine Empire lasted another two hundred years.

The man who restored the Empire, Michael Palaeologus, was remarkable. He succeeded in keeping a rein on the ambitions of Venice and Genoa, and also called a halt to the designs of Charles of Anjou by instigating the massacre known as the Sicilian Vespers. But his successor, the cultured and affable Andronicus II, had no military ability. Moreover, reversing his father's policy, he obstinately thwarted all attempts to reunite the Eastern and Western churches. His support of the Genoese against the Venetians led to nothing but disappointment. He was moreover quite incapable of standing up to the Ottomans, who robbed him, piece by piece, of Asia Minor. Thinking with their help to hold back the Turks, he engaged Catalan mercenaries (the Almogavares), but he soon found them unmanageable and had to get rid of them. He ended his life in a monastery, deposed by his grandson, Andronicus III, in 1328.

The new Emperor was a better general, but he was a spendthrift, a lover of luxury, and with little liking for governmental duties, which he left to his friend and confidant, John Cantacuzene. On his death, his son, John V, was not of age and civil war immediately broke out. John Cantacuzene was victor, and made himself Emperor, as John VI. But the Empire, too gravely undermined by these disturbances, declined. Social and religious disputes and foreign intervention robbed her of her remaining energies. John VI abdicated in 1355, after yet another civil war, handing the throne back to the Palaeologi in the person of John V, the rightful heir. The latter, however, had little ability. Three times dethroned, three times reinstated, his long reign, from 1355 to 1391, was simply a record of further decline. How far it had sunk is shown by the story of its last days, the saddest and most tragic of its long history. The Sultan Bayazid, at the gates of Constantinople, obliged Manuel, second son of John V,

Plan of Constantinople. Dominating the Sea of Marmara on the south and the Golden Horn on the north, and surrounded by great sea walls, it withstood siege after siege. *Mansell*

to help the Turks take the last Greek town in Asia Minor, Philadelphia. Then he helped John VII, the son of Andronicus IV, himself the eldest son of John V, to dethrone his grandfather in April 1390 (John V's third dethronement). Soon Manuel replaced his father on the throne. John V then made haste to reinforce the defences of the town, fearing a return of the Turks. Bayazid ordered him to proceed no further and to demolish the work already executed, which he obediently did before dying of discouragement.

The last struggle for survival

When Manuel II, the second son of John V, came to the throne, the situation in the Empire was critical. Demetrios Cydones, the writer, in a letter to Theodore Palaeologus, Manuel's brother and despot of Morea, shrewdly analyses the causes of decline. 'This ancient evil', he says, 'which is the cause of the general ruin is still at work. I mean the quarrels between emperors for their shadow of power. To defend that shadow they have been forced into the service of the barbarian and they have no other means of remaining alive. Everyone knows that the one to whom the barbarian gives his support will be future master. The emperors thus necessarily become themselves the slaves of the barbarians.' There was no longer any question of a revival of the Empire. All Manuel II could do, with his strong personality and remarkable diplomatic talents, was to postpone for a while the day of reckoning. 381

Bayazid made steady progress. He overran Bulgaria in 1393 and Thessaly and Morea in 1395. Manuel appealed to the West, and the West responded. A new crusade was organised, one of the last united efforts of Western Europe. Grouped round Sigismund, King of Hungary, were the Teutonic Knights, the Knights of St John of Jerusalem, the Wallachian foot-soldiers under the Voivode Mircea, and 10,000 knights sent by Charles VI of France under the orders of Marshal Boucicaut and the Count of Nevers, the future John the Fearless. The expedition ended in the Battle of Nicopolis in September 1396, a resounding defeat of the Christians, due partly to their lack of discipline and the foolish bravado of the French barons. Thereupon Manuel started on a journey

son Mahomet II, an intelligent and ambitious leader. At once he completed the encirclement of Constantinople, and closed the Bosphorus with the fortress of Rumili Hissar on the Asiatic coast. The final siege began in early April 1453. Mahomet had a force of 250,000 men and formidable artillery strength. The town was defended by 9,000 —and its impregnable walls. On April 18 the first assault failed, as did four further attacks. Mahomet's advisers advised him to withdraw but he determined to try again, on May 29. Constantine, hearing of this plan, ordered processions on the day before, and in the evening at St Sophia what Diehl has called 'a veritable requiem mass for the dying Empire' was celebrated. At one o'clock on the next morning the assault was launched. Twice it was

A view of Constantinople, from the Luttrell Psalter. The inhabitants used to beat off assailants by pouring 'Greek Fire' (a combination of pitch-blende and sulphur) from the battlements. *Mansell*

to Western Europe to solicit further help in person. He was splendidly received, particularly in Paris, where he stayed four months, but, except for a few subsidies from Henry IV of England and the promise of 1,200 men by Charles VI, the imperial pilgrim returned empty-handed after an absence of over three years. The fall of Constantinople, closely blockaded by Bayazid's forces, seemed imminent and inevitable, when astonished Europe heard that Bayazid had been defeated and captured at Ancyra. The Emperor sent presents to Tamerlane in gratitude for this providential victory.

The collapse (1453)

The twenty-three years of the reign of John VIII, Manuel's eldest son, were the last years of respite. The difficulties of Murad II in Asia Minor, and the revolt of the Albanians gave the Byzantines an opportunity of reasserting their authority in Morea. In 1440 a crusade was launched by Pope Eugenius IV. Taking part were Ladislas, King of Hungary, Alfonso V, King of Aragon, Vladislav, King of Poland, the Voivode of Transylvania, and the heroic Janos Hunyadi. Together, they succeeded in defeating Murad II at Nis in 1443. But Murad avenged this reverse at Varna in 1444, and again in the second battle of Kossovo in 1448. A few days later John VIII died. When the last Emperor Constantine XI (Dragases) came to the throne in 1449 his Empire consisted of Constantinople and its suburbs, which, for thirty years, had been almost constantly besieged.

Two years later, in 1451, Murad II was replaced by his

repulsed. Mahomet then threw in his last reserve, his 12,000 janissaries, and they failed too. But at dawn, on the 'sinister' Tuesday, May 29, treachery revealed to the Turks a small unguarded postern, through which they surged to take the defenders from the rear. Constantine XI died fighting. His body, recognised by its purple buskins, was later found on a pile of dead. In a scene of apocalyptic grandeur the Byzantine Empire which had lasted for a thousand years crumbled, and, by a curious irony, its last defender bore the name of the founder of the city so long the glory of the East.

The Serbia of Stephen Dusan

The moribund Byzantine Empire had certainly had no chance of resisting Ottoman pressure into the Balkans. Might the young Slav states have done better? In the short reign of Stephen Uros III (1322-31), the Serbs had disposed of their Bulgarian rivals. The Bulgarian Tsar Michael, who had invaded Serbia, was left on the battlefield of Velbuzd in 1330, in a defeat that crushed Bulgarian power for ever. The way was then open for Stephen Uros's son, Stephen Dusan, to take the leading place on the Balkan peninsula.

A remarkable leader in war and a shrewd diplomatist, Stephen Dusan at once seized the chance offered by the Bulgarian defeat, the hopeless decadence of the Byzantines, and the fact that the Turks were not yet on the scene. In a few years he had taken Thessaly, Epirus and almost all of Macedonia from the Empire, and, by turning Bulgaria into a vassal state, he dominated almost the whole of the Balkans. At the same time he raised the primate of Serbia to the dignity of patriarch, thereby emancipating him from Byzantine control. On Easter Day 1346 at Skoplje, he was crowned 'Emperor of the Serbs and the Greeks'. To round off his work, he established the administration firmly, published his *Zakonnik*, or code of laws, and actively developed the country's economy by making the roads safe, resuming trade with the Venetians, and exploiting the mines.

It only remained for him to take Constantinople. With that, the Balkans would have been able to present a solid front against the Turkish encroachments, the dangers of which Dusan saw only to clearly. He possibly thought himself more worthy of the title of 'Captain of the Christian Church' than of Byzantine Emperor, powerless and degenerate. In 1355 he advanced to the

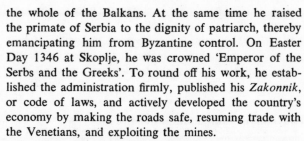

Andronicus III (1328-41). With John Cantacuzene he managed for a time to halt the inevitable decline of the Empire. *Larousse*

Stephen Dusan, who dreamed of capturing Constantinople but died within reach of his goal.

assault. He took Adrianople and was approaching Constantinople when, on December 20, he died of a fever. It may well be that his premature death was a decisive turning point in the history of the Balkans, even in the history of Europe. Had he been able to introduce new blood into the tottering Greek Empire, the Turks might never have invaded Europe. At the time of his death, the Sanjak of Brusa, Sulaiman, crossed the Dardanelles, took the fortress of Gallipoli and established the bridgehead from which later conquests would be launched. Thus the Turks established their first foothold in Europe at the very moment when the one man who could have repulsed them died.

Kossovo

Dusan's successor, Stephen Uros V, was a man of smaller stature, and the burden he inherited was too heavy for his shoulders. Greater Serbia began to disintegrate, and the Hungarians took Belgrade. After a period of anarchy the Serbs made a desperate effort to recover, rallying round their new Tsar, Lazar, who marched against Murad I, who had just taken Nis. The two armies met in the plain of Kossovo near Skoplje in June 1389. Lazar was taken prisoner and beheaded, and Serbia became a vassal of the Ottomans.

That situation lasted for seventy years, with Serbia providing troops for the Sultan, and paying a heavy yearly tribute. The disaster had not completely crushed Serbian vitality, but she was in no position to renew the

John Cantacuzene made himself Emperor as John VI in 1341, but was so unpopular that he was forced to abdicate and retire to a monastery in 1354. *Larousse*

struggle, or even to oppose a fresh Turkish advance, after the fall of Constantinople.

Within the next three years almost the whole of the country was swallowed up by the Ottoman empire, providing a valuable base for later advances towards the Danube.

The end of Bulgarian independence

George Terteri, who became Tsar in 1280, after the fall of Ivan Asen III, survived on subsidies, sometimes from Charles of Anjou, sometimes from the Emperor, and sometimes from the Golden Horde, to whom he was supposed to pay tribute. During the long reign of Svetslav (1295-1322) a national reaction grew up against the domination of the Tatars, but it was only a brief—and final—revival in the long history of Bulgarian decline.

After Svetslav's death, everything fell to ruin. The southern cities surrendered to Constantinople; an independent principality was formed round Sliven, and a small kingdom round Vidin, in the west. Finally Michael Shishmanich I, the 'little King of Vidin', was elected Tsar by the northern Bulgarians on the death of George Terteri in 1323. Allied to Andronicus III, Michael thought himself strong enough to put aside his wife, Anne, daughter of Stephen Uros II, and to break with Serbia. Misfortune followed, for the defeat of Köstendil cost Michael his life and ushered in a period of Bulgarian vassalage which lasted thirty years. Bulgaria, undermined by internal separatism and the dissensions of the boyars, weakened by the religious struggles between the Bogomiles and the Adamites (who did not hesitate to go over to Islam after the Turkish victory), was not even able to take up the Slav cause after the death of Stephen Dusan. She stumbled on in a state of chaos until, three years after Kossovo, Bayazid struck the final blow at her independence. In July 1393 he entered Trnovo, and for the next five centuries Bulgaria was a Turkish province.

Decline of German influence in Eastern Europe

German influence, which had been strong in central and eastern Europe in the thirteenth century, suffered a reverse at the beginning of the fourteenth. Everywhere it was curtailed, and anti-German national feeling began to assert itself in Bohemia, Hungary, and Poland, and even among the Russians, who disputed German influence in the Baltic.

In Bohemia, the turning point was reached with the rise of the Luxemburg dynasty, which began with John the Blind, married to Elizabeth, younger daughter of Wenceslas II. John's son, Charles IV, surrounded himself with Walloon advisers and administrators, and was himself French in culture and language. Adopted by his Czech subjects as a national prince, he systematically resisted German influence. In 1348 he founded the university of Prague, modelled on that of Paris. He endeavoured to favour trade and brought into existence a national middle class in opposition to the German burghers. He thus paved the way for the anti-German explosion under Charles's son, Wenceslas III, which was to take a religious form under the influence of John Hus. On the death of Wenceslas in 1419, his brother Sigismund came to the throne, but when he died without issue in

1437, the crown passed to his son-in-law Albert of Austria, who was also King of Hungary. But Bohemia was not to be absorbed into the Habsburg empire. Anti-German feeling was so strong that a section of the Bohemians who had formed round the Taborites (followers of Hus) preferred to give the crown to Casimir of Poland. In any case, Albert II of Austria died in 1439, leaving his throne to his posthumous son, Ladislas V. Ladislas, like his father, was recognised only by the Catholic nobles. Nationalist revolt was inevitable, and it broke out on Ladislas' death in 1457, bringing to the throne a Czech noble, George of Podebrady. But Bohemia was not to be independent for long. In 1471, on George's death, Vladyslav Jagiello, son of Casimir, King of Poland, succeeded. This meant that German influence was still being submerged, and this remained the pattern until the seventeenth century.

In Hungary the reign of Bela IV (1235-70) marked the zenith of German colonisation, and in 1273 the kingdom gave its support to Rudolph of Habsburg to stop Czech expansion. At that time the country was completely under German influence, but reaction soon set in. The Hungarian nobles, brushing aside Albert of Habsburg, whom Rudolph had wanted to put on the throne, turned to Andrew III, and, on his death, to the grandson of Charles II of Naples. In adopting Frenchmen from Naples, representatives of the House of Anjou, the Hungarians were clearly out to frustrate the designs of the Habsburgs. Of these Angevin kings, the first, Charles Robert (1308-42) was not particularly remarkable, but the reign of his son, Lewis I (1342-82) marked the climax of the dynasty. During it Moldavia and Croatia were annexed, and the whole Dalmatian coast taken from the Venetians. Lewis intervened in Italy, and in Poland, where he became king. His reign did much to promote French influence and to restrict German influence. Afterwards, confusion prevailed in the country. Charles of Durazzo's reign was very short and the long reign of Sigismund of Luxemburg (1387-1437) was overshadowed by the Turkish peril. The reign of his son-in-law, Albert of Austria (1438-9) was not long enough for Habsburg rule to be established in the country. From now on Hungary, a European outpost, was to serve as a rampart against Islam.

In Poland, German penetration reached its peak after the retreat of the Mongols in 1241. German colonists took over the reconstruction of Silesia while the Teutonic knights pushed forward towards Mazovia, Polish Pomerania, and pagan Lithuania. Moreover, to hold its own against the episcopate on the one hand, and the Czechs on the other, the dynasty was obliged to lean on the towns, that is, on the German element. When Casimir the Great (1333-70) undertook to establish a centralised monarchy after the pattern of the Bohemian one of Charles IV, he had again to rely on urban support against the independence of the nobles. But a reconciliation with the latter, when Lewis of Hungary came to the throne in 1382, gave the regime a much more national character, and German influence declined. It declined still further under the next king, Vladyslav Jagiello of Lithuania, who married Lewis's daughter Jadwiga. The principality of Lithuania, though independent, fell within the Polish orbit. It had emerged from paganism in 1251 when Prince Mindovg had been converted to Catholicism. And Vladyslav II brought with him into Poland the Lithuanian's long hatred of the Germans, and in particular of the Teutonic Knights who for so long had been waging what was in effect a war of extermination. The hour of revenge had come. The combined Polish and Lithuanian armies had been defeated by the Tatars in 1399, but they got their revenge on the Germans in July 1410, when the Polish-Lithuanian army crushed the Knights at Tannenburg, a battle in which German power received a decisive blow, though it lingered on for another fifty years. In the Peace of Thorn in 1466 Casimir IV deprived the Teutonic Knights of Pomerania and Danzig, and the towns of Marienburg, Kulm, and Elbing on the right bank of the Vistula. The Teutonic Order kept East Prussia, but only as vassals of the King of Poland, to whom the masters of the Order had to swear their fidelity in person within six months of election. Poland now had an outlet to the sea and German penetration of Slav countries was halted for many years.

Thus throughout central and eastern Europe there were murmurs of national feeling by the middle of the fourteenth century. But the Turkish peril was too acute for Hungary, Bohemia and Poland to exert much influence on the West, for which they served as buffer states.

The coalescence of Russian territories

Further eastwards, Russia, or Muscovy as it was to be known, was beginning to coalesce. To the north of the territory held by the Tatar Khans of the Golden Horde, various independent principalities had subsisted. The republic of Novgorod continued to serve as an in-

termediary between this further Russia and Lithuania. The Grand Duchy of Kiev had lost its former splendour. Transylvanian Russia, whose capital was Vladimir, was, in the fourteenth century, split into a large number of little duchies perpetually fighting one another. One of them, however, the principality of Moscow, was soon to rise above the rest. The able and energetic Dmitri Donskoi may be regarded as the first architect of the foundation of Russia. He succeeded in imposing his suzerainty on the principalities of Tver, Rostov, and Ryazan. He even subdued Novogorod for a while. More important, he was the first Russian prince to shake off submission to the Golden Horde, now in full decline. His victory at Kulikova in 1380 over Khan Mamai was the first great Russian triumph. The advantage gained by Dmitri Donskoi, the first ruler of all Russia, was compromised for a while by the mediocrity of his two successors, but under his great-grandson, Ivan III (1462-1505), the country advanced again, with the occupation of Novgorod and Tver and the Khanate of Kazan. Muscovite influence reached Crimea, and Ivan was soon in a position to call himself ruler of 'all the Russias'. He further improved his position by marrying Zoe, daughter of Thomas Palaeologus, Prince of Achaia. This marriage marked the entry of Russia into the European dynastic community, and enabled future Tsars of Russia to consider themselves heirs of Byzantium. Already western influences began to seep into Moscow. Artists and artisans went in large numbers to Moscow, where they made important contributions to the building of the ducal palace in the Kremlin.

A page from a Viennese illuminated manuscript showing Lewis I the Great (1342-82) of Hungary. The reign of this Angevin king was brilliant for Hungary; Moldavia and Croatia were annexed, and the Dalmatian coast seized. *Archiv für Kunst und Geschichte*

The fall of Constantinople, by a Czech artist. The Empire had lingered on in Constantinople as a 'monstrous head without a body'; in 1453, after a bitter siege, the city fell by treachery to Mahomet II and was sacked by the Turks. Valuable manuscripts and works of art were luckily saved: the Italian Renaissance owed much to these remnants of a great civilisation. *Alinari*

NORTHERN EUROPE

The decline of the Hanseatic League. The Union of Kalmar

German influence, receding in central and eastern Europe, found itself threatened even in its Baltic fief. Nevertheless the Hanseatic League had succeeded in establishing solid political and commercial holds on both sides of the Baltic, despite stubborn opposition from Waldemar IV, King of Denmark (1340-75). In the end, the latter had to yield. The Peace of Stralsund in 1370 was a triumph for the Hansa towns, who won exemption from all customs duties, the establishment of trading stations in Denmark, and the right to be consulted whenever the Danish throne became vacant. Thenceforward the whole coast from the Gulf of Finland to Flanders was controlled by the Hansa. Another German success was the overthrow of Magnus, King of Sweden, in 1363 by Albert of Mecklenburg, leader of the German party. Then the energetic daughter of Waldemar III, Margaret, married to King Haakon VI of Norway, became regent of the country on the death of her husband. Victorious over Albert of Mecklenburg and Sweden in 1389, she had a firm grip of the country, save Stockholm. She even succeeded in persuading the nobles of the three Scandinavian countries to accept her successor designate, Eric of Pomerania, as ruler of Sweden, Norway and Denmark, under one crown by the 'Union of Kalmar' in 1397,

Russian icon depicting St Nicholas. Novgorod School, thirteenth century. Even after 1453, Byzantine art flourished in other parts of Eastern Europe, particularly in Russia.

though each country was to keep its own laws and customs. But the Union was soon to run into difficulties.

The difficulties of the Union

The centre of the Union was Denmark, whose kings of the Oldenburg line were weak and tactless. The best of them, Christian I, was too busy dealing with Schleswig and Holstein to deal with separatist tendencies within the Union. Norway was weak and did not count for much, but Sweden was so hostile to the Germano-Danish monarchy and to the Hansa that German influence was gradually eliminated there till finally the Union itself was broken by Gustavus Eriksson Vasa in 1523, who was to reign until 1560, and who was one of the great personalities of Swedish history.

Poland as a Baltic power

The decline of the Hanseatic League and the vicissitudes of the Union of Kalmar left Poland free to develop in the Baltic. For the Poles, cut off from the Black Sea by the Turks, were anxious for outlets in the north. After the defeat of Christian I of Denmark in 1471 by Swedish insurgents under Sten Sture, Poland threw herself into the struggle for the Baltic. Danzig became a model port, and Poland started to build up an export trade. Here, in the north, the Germans were pushed back once again by the Slavs.

The recoil of Europe

Europe may thus be said to have shrunk in the fourteenth century and to have withdrawn westward, shifting the centre of gravity of Christendom. Society was pro-

foundly disturbed. The Great Schism and the proliferation of heresies were paralleled in the erosion of the dependence and reliance of man on man, of country on country. They were reflected in the economic sphere by those urban disturbances which set the proletariat against the mercantile oligarchy; in the shift of populations, aggravated by the scourge of the Black Death between 1348 and 1350; and lastly, in the political sphere, by the mutual hostility of national realms and, within them, the hostility of various elements towards the monarchy. Such is the balance-sheet of Europe in this difficult and uncertain period, out of which so much initiative was to come.

The political history of the continent, here fully described, marked, indeed, a great upsurge of vitality, already long apparent in the two greatest centres of prosperity, the Italian and Flemish cities. The Italian Renaissance had its origin far back in the thirteenth century, and it was based on the vigorous life of city-states, a form of polity alien to the rural peasant society of the Middle Ages and to the world of the feudal warriors who had dominated Europe since Carolingian times.

One factor which brought about the expansion of Europe in the late fifteenth and early sixteenth centuries was the need to go out and get luxuries (which were becoming more difficult to come by as the position in the Levant and the Middle East deteriorated). A further factor in expansion was the designing of better ships—at first by the Portuguese under Moslem influence. The use of the compass and better maps were also decisive.

The macabre aspects of the later Middle Ages, so heavily stressed by Huizinga, should not obscure the outstanding vitality of the age, to which the Italian Renaissance, now being assimilated in the North, had long contributed. Its spirit of enterprise accounted for many achievements of early modern times.

387

Soldiers of the Khanate of Persia.

CHAPTER TWENTY-THREE

THE MONGOL DECLINE AND ISLAM'S REVENGE

Islam, having staggered under the Mongol blows, began to revive in the fourteenth century. Her advance in central and northern Asia cut the Mongol empire off from Europe, and forbade any expansion to the west.

But the Mongol force was not extinguished all at once. Though weakened, it was still considerable during the last third of the thirteenth century, and the penetration of south-east Asia continued.

MONGOL REVERSES

Ephemeral Sino-Mongolian progress

After three unsuccessful expeditions against Burma, the Sino-Mongolian prince Ye-Su Timur, one of Kublai Khan's sons, took the capital, Pagan, and the country became a tributary of China. At the same time it was divided into principalities governed by Thai chieftains. For the most important result of the collapse of Burmese power under Mongol blows was the infiltration of the Thais of Yunnan into Indochina and Burma. This was not a military invasion: for a long time the peoples of the north had been edging southwards down the valleys. But the Mongol invasion, which struck down the Burmese royal house and weakened the Khmer kingdom of Cambodia, accelerated this movement. In fact the Thai hegemony might be said to have been established under the aegis of Jenghiz Khan. Take one example among many: at the end of the century, the Thais of the middle Menam (the Syams) extended their power over the whole Mekong valley and Cambodia and the Malay Peninsula. Their king, the great conqueror Rama Kamheng, imposed on his subjects a social and political structure borrowed from the Mongols. In a Siamese inscription dated 1293 the style and content of Jenghiz Khan's oath to his electors can be detected. It runs: 'During my father's life, I served my father... When I caught game or fish, I brought it to my father, if I had any fruit, whether sweet or sour, I brought it to my father. If I attacked a village or a town and returned with elephants, boys, girls, silver, or gold, I gave them to my father. My father died, leaving me with my elder brother. I went on serving him as I had served my father. Now, with my brother dead, the whole kingdom falls into my hands.'

The fall of the old Hindu influences of south-east Asia was thus an after-effect of the Mongol conquests; an indirect effect for, in the end, the Sino-Mongolian armies had only temporary successes in the Indochinese peninsula.

The Yuen Mongols repulsed by Japan

As already described, twice Kublai Khan attacked Japan. The Japanese put up a fierce resistance, but many of the Khan's difficulties were explained by the storms encountered by his unskilled seamen. Since the decline of royal power, beginning during the twelfth century, Japan had fallen into a feudal government under the shoguns, the 'mayors of the palace', who kept the emperors in humiliating subservience until the nineteenth century. In short, Japan resisted Mongol pressure by isolating herself completely for many centuries, thus preserving her archaic institutions until the beginning of the twentieth century.

Failure of the Java expedition

The Javanese kingdom of Shinghasari—a highly cultured man according to some, a wretched drunkard according to others—had been considerably enlarged during the reign of Kritanagara (1268-92). The King had overthrown the Sumatran empire of the Maharajah and had brought the island and its dependencies on the Malay peninsula under his rule. He considered himself strong enough to reject envoys sent by Kublai Khan to receive homage in 1280, 1281 and 1289. In 1292 the great Khan decided to send an expedition. Meanwhile Kritanagara had been dethroned. But his son-in-law, Vijaya, succeeded in employing the Sino-Mongolian forces to depose the usurper to the throne, after which he drove the Khan's forces into the sea. All that the latter had achieved was the restoration of the legitimate rulers of Java.

The dynasty, reigning at Majapahit, reached its zenith under Rajasanagara (1350-88). At that time Javanese seafarers had spread over almost all the East Indies, and they formed the greatest sea power of Asia, though their empire was not truly Asiatic. Deeply imbued with Islamism, it had no truly continental elements. After the Mongol reverses the Asiatic continent turned away from the sea, with serious consequences; among these were the destruction of what had been the economic unit of south-east Asia, the decline of the Khmer empire and southern India, and the weakening of Mongol China.

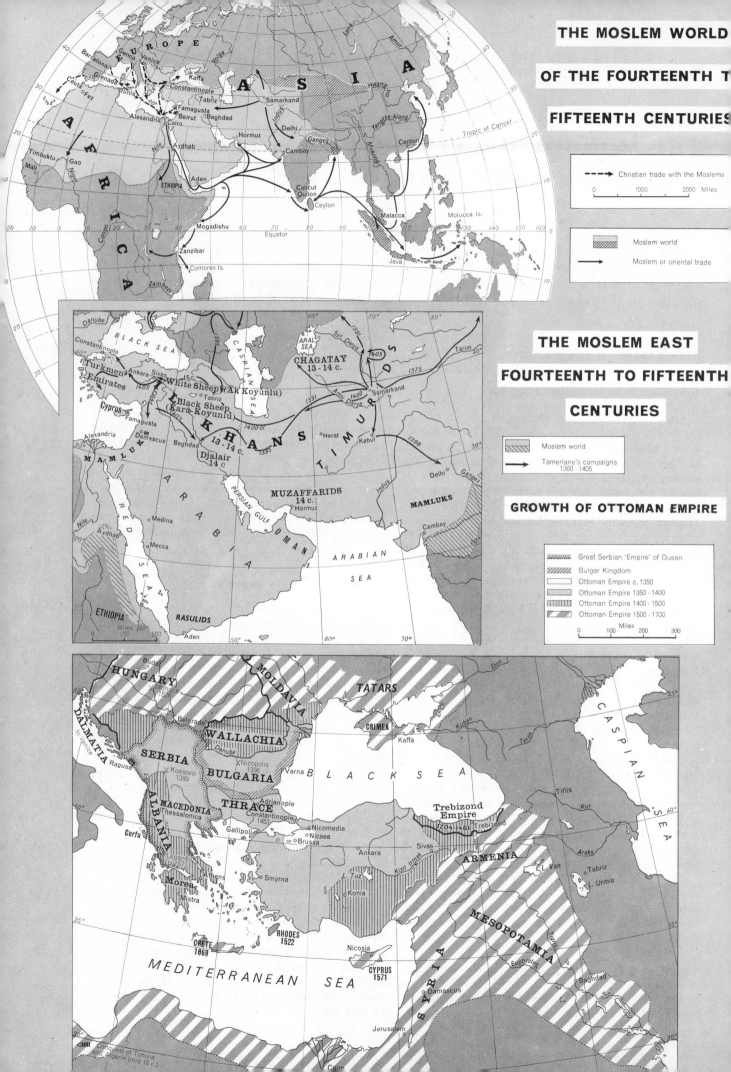

THE MOSLEM WORLD
OF THE FOURTEENTH T[O]
FIFTEENTH CENTURIES

----➤ Christian trade with the Moslems

0   1000   2000   Miles

▨ Moslem world

➤ Moslem or oriental trade

THE MOSLEM EAST
FOURTEENTH TO FIFTEENTH
CENTURIES

▨ Moslem world

➤ Tamerlane's campaigns 1360 - 1405

GROWTH OF OTTOMAN EMPIRE

Great Serbian 'Empire' of Dusan
Bulgar Kingdom
Ottoman Empire c. 1350
Ottoman Empire 1350 - 1400
Ottoman Empire 1400 - 1500
Ottoman Empire 1500 - 1700

0   100   200   300   Miles

The recovery of Siam

The Mongol invasion had led indirectly to the decline of the Khmer empire. Driven out of the middle Mekong by the Thais, they were then driven out of the Menam valley by the Siamese. Soon they were confronted by a still greater danger. A Thai chieftain, ruler of the city of U Tong, fleeing from cholera, had in 1347 built a new capital, Ayuthia, on the lower Menam. This was the centre of the first historic Siamese kingdom. From 1349, the Khmers came under the Siamese yoke, but the conquerors very soon assimilated the political organisation and the material civilisation of the conquered, while the capital was shifted from Angkor to Pnom-Penh in 1450. The substitution of a young and vigorous kingdom for an enfeebled one was to raise a permanent barrier against further Mongol advances towards the southern part of the Indochinese peninsula. Even the kingdom of Champa (much reduced by the beginning of the fourteenth century) was able to defy the Mongols. In 1292 King Juyu Simhavarman III forbade Kublai Khan's fleet, bound for Java, to put in at Champa.

The Chinese revolt

The weakness of Kublai Khan's successors encouraged the hopes of those who had never willingly accepted the Mongol regime in China, particularly amongst the southern Chinese, who had been the last to offer resistance. For three years the insurgents had little success, hampered by rivalry between the leaders of the various bands. Then one Chu Yuen-chang, son of a poor peasant of the lower Yang-tze, succeeded in imposing himself as leader of the national revolt. In 1356 he captured Nanking and set up a regular government. Gradually eliminating his rivals, he became master of Canton in 1367, after which he marched on Peking, which was only half-heartedly defended by the emperor Yuen Toghan Temur, an unworthy descendant of Jenghiz Khan. Peking fell in September 1368. The victorious army proclaimed Chu Yuen-chang emperor and the native Chinese Ming dynasty was founded. The new emperor took the name of Hung-Wu. In the course of his long reign, which lasted till 1398, he set out to restore the ancient aristocratic and Confucian China that the Mongol rule had never wholly destroyed.

By a curious reversal of destiny, the second emperor after Hung-Wu, Yung-Lo (1403-24), revived the conquering tradition of the Mongols, this time on behalf of the Chinese nation. He undertook the conquest of Mongolia and, to be nearer the scene of his campaign, transferred his capital from Nanking to Peking, which he completely transformed, building the 'Forbidden City' inside the 'Imperial City'. He also built the Temple of Heaven and the Altar of Agriculture. From Peking he launched his campaign against the Mongols, supporting a rival tribe, the Oirads, against the Khan's forces. Nor was the new China's lust for conquest confined to the north: in 1407 Annam and the Red River delta were occupied, though only temporarily. Yung-Lo dreamt of establishing a great maritime power which would extend from Champa to the Sunda Isles, from Malacca to Aden, a power which, had it been realised, the Portuguese seafarers would have encountered towards the end of

Tamerlane. His ambition was to restore Jenghiz Khan's empire. *Lala Aufsberg Foto*

The dome of Tamerlane's mausoleum, Gur-Amir, Samarkand.

Yoritomo, leader of the Minamoto clan in Japan (1185), hunting at the foot of Mt Fuji. *Museum of Fine Arts, Boston*

the century. But the Chinese had no leaning towards maritime empire. The educated people were hostile to foreign conquests, as costly as they were useless, and the global outlook of Yung-Lo did not last. Ming China renounced further adventures in south-east Asia.

The Mongols repulsed in India

The Khanate of Jagatai, created by Jenghiz Khan's youngest son, lay on the north-west frontier of India. This was potentially dangerous for the sultans of Delhi, for the Khan of Jagatai—closed in on the west by the Khanate of Persia—had no outlet except through India. These Mongols were not very strong, however, and Delhi was able to put up strong defences on the Indus, with the result that, in the second half of the thirteenth century, incursions were reduced to raids, destructive but of no lasting effect. On the first of these raids, in 1241, the Mongols plundered Lahore, but with no political results; on the second, invading Sind, they had to abandon the siege of Uch before the determined resistance of Balban, the minister of Nasir-ud-din Mahmud; on the third, the Mongols again entered Sind but retired immediately on Balban's approach. The disorders which broke out on Balban's death in 1285 (he had become sultan in 1266) and which brought to the throne a new dynasty of Khilji Turks, encouraged the Jagataids of Afghanistan to try their luck again. Two attacks, one in 1296, the other in 1298, failed. The new sultan Ala-ad-din was indeed a leader of the first rank. Another attempt, in 1304, was a complete disaster. With that, India was for many years to be safe from the Mongols, in fact until the appearance of Tamerlane.

Repulse by the Mamelukes

The Khans of the Hulagu line in Persia had long been pushing towards the Aegean Sea. The Seljuk emirs be-

came their vassals, and it was inevitable that the Mongols should come into conflict with the Mamelukes of Egypt. Abagha, who was *Il-khan* (the Khan) from 1265 to 1282, was anxious to work with the Christians, but when they were unresponsive, he decided to attack Egyptian Syria alone in 1281, though he was unable to make much headway. His successor, Arghun, followed the same policy and encountered the same lack of co-operation from the Christians. His attack, too, failed in 1291, and another attempt in 1299. Mongol power was definitely petering out, and before long the Persian Khanate was to fall asunder. At the death of Abu Said in 1335, there was rapid decline and a turmoil of religious quarrels. The Turkish emirates in Asia Minor won their independence, following the lead of Osman, who declared the independence of his tribe and himself 'Emir of the Turks' in 1299.

The Mongols in Russia

The Khanate founded by Jenghiz Khan's eldest son, Juji, was more durable, the Mongols holding the south Russian steppes. But its unity and cohesion were not to withstand the onslaught of Tamerlane, and at the opening of the fifteenth century the Golden Horde was no more than a memory. By this time, these Mongols had been Moslem for a century and a half, that is, since the death of Batu, a younger son of Juji. Batu's brother and successor, Bereke, was the first convert. For a long time the Mongol chiefs resisted Islam, but what could the four or five thousand pure-blooded Mongols who had followed Batu do among the masses that had quickly succumbed to Islam?

The centre of the Khanate was Sarai, in the valley of the lower Volga, but the apanages of the Batu family spread far to each side. The western apanage was that of Nogai on the Black Sea, the eastern one that of Orda, Batu's eldest brother, the land of the White Horde stretching between the Urals and the River Obi.

The Mongols descended from Juji were first given as their mission the conquest of Europe. They were never able to undertake it, being too fully occupied with the affairs of their neighbouring Khanates, particularly the Persian. Weakening in the process, they were soon too enfeebled to exact their tribute from the Russian princes who were their vassals. The reign of Uzbeg Khan (1312-40) can still be called a fine one, though the earlier impetus had gone, and during the reign of his successor, Janibeg Khan, the Uzbegs began to decline. They were unable to drive the Genoese out of Kaffa in 1345 or to take Azerbaijan from the weak Il-khans of Persia. In the anarchy which followed Janibeg's death Mamai forced his way to the throne, only to suffer the humiliating defeat of Kulikova in 1380 at the hands of Dmitri Donskoi, Duke of Moscow. Then, after the storm let loose by Tamerlane, the Golden Horde collapsed. The Khanate of Crimea broke away in 1420, that of Kazan in 1438. In 1475 Crimea had come under the yoke of Ottoman Constantinople. Kazan became a vassal of Moscow, as did Astrakhan in 1466. With that the Golden Horde had completely disintegrated.

The conquests of Tamerlane

Tamerlane's first steps, like those of his illustrious forbear, Jenghiz Khan, were slow and difficult. His childhood and adolescence were also similar in being full of portents announcing his future greatness. His father, Teragai, head of the tribe of the Berlas, had a dream, in which a young warrior of great beauty handed him a sword. As soon as he touched it, lightning flashed from the blade, illuminating all around. A sheik explained the exact meaning of the dream: 'Thou shalt have a son who will conquer the world at the point of his sword, and who will convert all men to Islam and clear the world of the darkness arising from the new and the false.'

Tamerlane's native land was Transoxiana, the only green land between the Amu-Darya (Oxus) and the Syr-Darya (Jaxartes) and at that period in a state of anarchy, each tribal chief trying to gain power over the rest. Tamerlane (the 'lame Timur', so named after an accident in youth) succeeded, partly by persuasion, partly by trickery, in playing the other chiefs off against each other until he became one of the three most powerful men in Transoxiana.

Togluk Timur, Khan of the Jagatai Mongols, now invaded the country, but Tamerlane had his own plans. Making his submission, he allowed the invaders to crush his rivals. 'A political arrow fired at the right moment invariably finds its target in the heart of the enemy.' He was counting on becoming governor of Transoxiana in the name of the Khan, but the latter appointed his own son. Tamerlane fled from Samarkand and bided his time, taking refuge in Afghanistan, where he gradually gathered round him all the malcontents who were fretting under the invader's rule. At last, in 1363, he succeeded in driving Togluk Timur out of his country, assisted by his brother-in-law, Hosain, whom he assassinated and in 1369 he became sole master. Reviving the Kuriltai, or assembly of chiefs, he had himself elected emir.

With Togluk's death in 1364, Tamerlane's ambitions grew and he invaded Turkestan. It took five campaigns spread over ten years to subdue it. In 1376, in his capital,

Mongol horsemen crossing a frozen river. Under Tamerlane, the Mongols even reached Moscow. From a French manuscript at Edinburgh University.

Samarkand, he had himself proclaimed Khan of all the Jagatai and Jenghiz Khan Mongols. Then turning westward to Khwarazm in the lower Oxus he annexed it in 1378 after four campaigns.

The lust for conquest

Tamerlane was not yet master of a vast empire. His centre was Transoxiana and the neighbouring territories of Khorassan, Afghanistan, and eastern Turkestan. Even the nucleus of his future empire seemed hastily built, and somewhat shaky. The conquered territories had not yet been assimilated, in fact they were all ready to break away at the first opportunity. Was Tamerlane really planning to reconstruct the great empire of Jenghiz Khan? His hold, even on the Khanate of the Jagatai Mongols, was none too secure. He was a sick man, fifty-six years old. Yet, possessed by an elementary lust for conquest for conquest's sake, he was to fling himself into a wild, unremitting struggle, pursued almost blindly without any pre-arranged plan. Unlike Jenghiz Khan, he was able to justify his conquests on religious grounds. He was called upon to chasten the degenerate or erring Moslems of Persia, Mesopotamia, Asia Minor, or India. But he was unable to rise, like Jenghiz, to the stature of a great ruler.

Little was left of the former splendour of the Mongol Il-khans. After the extinction of Jenghiz Khan's line, the Khanate of Persia had disintegrated. Accordingly Tamerlane had little difficulty in mopping up the little emirates that shared the ruins. In 1374 he took Herat, but it soon broke away again. He came back in 1381, razed the town, and buried 2,000 men alive as an example. In 1383 a rapid thrust took him to the shores of the Caspian, where he took Astarabad. In 1386 and 1387 he directed a powerful drive against the province of Fars in southern Persia, that being the heart of the old Khanate. Taking advantage of the death of the old shah, Khoja, Tamerlane took Ispahan and Shiraz. Then, when the people of Ispahan slaughtered the garrison he had left, he returned and had 70,000 heads piled in heaps all round the ramparts. But the southern part of the country was still restive and, under the leadership of Mansur, the princelings of Khuzistan revolted again in 1393. A fresh campaign of Tamerlane's ended with Mansur's death. The princes made their

Tamerlane, from a German print. *Larousse*

power. The latter hit back in 1391, though without much result; but in the spring of 1396 he crossed the Caucasus, caught the enemy on the Terek, and in a hard-fought battle, which he nearly lost, crushed Tuqtamish and then pursued him to the Volga, the Dnieper, and the Don, the tribes in all these areas being either annihilated or scattered. The Ukraine was ravaged, but Moscow was disdained, for, having been burnt by Tuqtamish in 1382, it was of no further interest. But Tana on the Sea of Azov was utterly destroyed, as was Astrakhan, and the Horde's capital, Sarai. The Golden Horde was never again to raise its head.

Towards a universal empire?

Tamerlane's empire had now reached a considerable size. Its centre was still Transoxiana and eastern Turkestan. In addition, he controlled all Persia and was suzerain of the Golden Horde. At the age of sixty it seemed he might now give up conquests and undertake the work of internal reorganisation. But his desire for conquest was an obsession. In the midst of the festivities to celebrate the victory over the Golden Horde, he informed his generals of plans for another campaign, this time against India.

The Indian campaign

Was Tamerlane attracted by the almost fabulous wealth of India, or by the idea of emulating Alexander the Great, with whom he liked to compare himself? More likely it was simply the power-mania to which conquerors fall victim.

Taking advantage of the anarchy that was rampant between the Indus and the Ganges, the governors employed by the Turko-Afghan sultans of Delhi had been making themselves independent. In 1393 Malik Sarwar Khwaja had broken away to form the small kingdom of Jaunpur, north of Benares; in 1394 the governor of Malwa followed suit; then the governor of Gujrat in 1396. Such small units could only be an easy prey to Tamerlane. Despite the murmurings of his generals, he attacked in 1398. On December 17 Delhi was taken and pillaged. Tamerlane took the throne of the sultans of India and received homage from all the surrounding governors and emirs. He had no intention of annexing the country; he merely chose the rajah of Multan from those who had made submission and appointed him governor. Then, after pushing on to the Ganges and slaughtering people by the thousand, he returned to Samarkand leaving a land of ruins behind him.

Ancyra (1402)

Even now, there was no respite in the feverish urge to conquer. No sooner had he finished with India than western Asia invited his attention. Ahmad, the sultan who had been chased out of Baghdad in 1393, had recovered his capital, with help from the Mamelukes of Egypt, and had even invaded Azerbaijan. Still more provocative, the new Ottoman sultan, Bayazid, the conqueror of the western crusade, had just conquered Sivas, an emirate that was Tamerlane's vassal. In 1399 Tamerlane recovered both Azerbaijan and Sivas. Then, ignoring Anatolia, he

submission, but were all executed. With that, the whole of Persia was annexed to Tamerlane's empire.

In 1393 Tamerlane marched against Baghdad, then under the sultan Ahmad. The army moved too slowly for him, so he put himself at the head of a detachment, 400 strong, and by forced marches arrived unexpectedly, and entered the capital unopposed. Ahmad had just time to escape to Egypt, where he was given asylum by the Mameluke sultan, Barkuk. Tamerlane then moved towards the Syrian frontier, but he refrained from crossing it, wanting first to secure control over the last areas remaining free between the Euphrates and the Caucasus. He finished off the conquest of Armenia and Kurdistan, begun the previous year. Then, just as all Syria and Asia Minor was trembling at the prospect of an imminent invasion, Tamerlane turned back. He had just received alarming news of the activities of the Golden Horde.

The expedition against the Golden Horde

When Tamerlane first became an emir, Tuqtamish, a prince of the White Horde, had succeeded with Tamerlane's support in raising himself to the rank of Khan, and, though himself a follower of the Jenghiz Khan line, he had accepted the suzerainty of the emir of Transoxiana. Then, attacking the Golden Horde, Tuqtamish had beaten Mamai, who had in any case lost his prestige by his defeat at Kulikova. Thus Tuqtamish now commanded all the territories west of the Urals controlled by the Golden Horde. And, showing great ingratitude to Tamerlane, to whom he owed his success, he refused any longer to do him homage, accusing him of having usurped the inheritance of Jenghiz Khan. In 1385 he crossed the Caucasus, and fought a successful action with some of Tamerlane's lieutenants in Armenia. But he suffered a severe reverse at the hands of Tamerlane's third son Miran Shah. In 1388 Tuqtamish pressed on again, this time attacking Transoxiana, the cradle of Tamerlane's

drove into Syria, to punish the Mamelukes. All the Syrian towns, including Damascus, were wiped out. Now, turning back towards Mesopotamia, he regained Baghdad in a vicious attack. There remained only Bayazid's account to settle. The decisive battle was fought near Ancyra (Angora) in 1402. Despite the heroism of the janissaries, the Ottomans were completely routed. Amid the fearful carnage Bayazid was taken prisoner and died a few weeks later. In five months the whole of Anatolia had been taken.

The end of Tamerlane's empire

Back in Samarkand, Tamerlane decided to continue the campaign that was to crown his work. To be master of the world, he must still strike down the Ming dynasty in China, as the Sung dynasty had been struck down by Kublai Khan. Tamerlane had once recognised the suzerainty of the Ming emperors, as heirs to the Yuen dynasty, and he could no longer bear to be anybody's vassal. In failing health, he knew he had to act quickly. Shivering with fever, but indomitable, he set off in December 1404. He managed to reach Otrar, on the Syr-Daria, where he died on January 19, 1405. Within the space of fifteen years his empire had vanished. A 'Timurid' domination lingered in just one place until the end

of the fifteenth century. In the sixteenth century one of Tamerlane's descendants, Babar, was to found the empire of the Great Moguls in India.

Tamerlane's extraordinary career has deceived many. To his contemporaries, particularly, he was another Jenghiz Khan. But the age of Jenghiz Khan had passed, and Tamerlane was a prodigious anachronism. For, if Tamerlane's invasions were inspired by the same motive as the Khan's, that is, the expansion of the nomads of the steppes, if this fresh surge had the same sudden and violent force, and if the two empires were similarly ephemeral, Tamerlane's had nevertheless a different historical significance. It had a new context: the Islamisation of the Turks with all its evil consequences for the rapprochement of the different sections of the Old World. This time it was Moslem fanaticism which inspired the movement of the nomads, a fanaticism which forbade all assimilation and unification. If the new conquests were Mongol in their nature, their spirit was not. The victory of Ancyra echoed all over Christendom, sounding an illusory note of hope. It was in no sense a victory over Islam, now in full advance. It simply marked a momentary halt in the expansion of a particular Moslem state, that of the Ottomans. Tamerlane's place is somewhere between Jenghiz Khan and Mahomet II or Sulaiman the Magnificent.

EXPANSION OF ISLAM

It was Islam—whose pressure had brought the disintegration of Jenghiz Khan's empire — which now caused the fall of Tamerlane's. For Islam's new expansion was to be the work of conquering Turks, who brought with them the landed feudalism which was profoundly hostile to the centralised State, and was a cause of political decomposition. Everywhere, Mongol unity was replaced by independent principalities, which themselves tended to split up still further. If Islamised Persia rejected the suzerainty of the Khans of Karakorum, their new-won independence was accompanied by dissolution into a plethora of small emirates, united under Tamerlane but soon reverting to their individualism. It was in India, however, that the progress of Islam had the worst political consequences.

The sultanate of Delhi

Freedom from the Mongol peril had enabled the sultans of Delhi to complete the conquest of the area between the Indus and Ganges, begun in the thirteenth century but neglected in the defence of the Himalayan frontier. At that time, too, expansion into Malwa and the Deccan had to be postponed.

The sultans of the Khilju dynasty were able to take Malwa in 1300, and Ala-ad-din overpowered the little Hindu kingdoms of the Deccan one by one—Daulatabad in 1309, Telingana in 1311, Pandya, in the extreme south, in 1312. But their loyalty was uncertain, and another dynasty had to come into power before it was possible to speak of the unification of India under the sultanate of Delhi. This was the Tughlak dynasty,

which started its career in 1320, and whose most outstanding member was Muhammad Tughlak, who reigned from 1325 to 1351. He divided India into 23 governments: 10 on the Indus, 6 on the Ganges, 1 each in Malwa and Gujrat, and beyond them 5 in the Deccan. The only parts to escape his authority were Kashmir, Nepal, and Ceylon. The authority was, of course, often no more than nominal, and Muhammad Tughlak had to put down a dozen rebellions, sometimes of the people, sometimes of the Moslem governors themselves. At his death, not only was revolt smouldering everywhere, even to the gates of the capital, but the whole of the south of the Deccan, except the Sultanate of Madura, had become

A Persian bowl, thirteenth or fourteenth century.

completely independent. If the long reign of his cousin and successor, Feroz Shah Tughlak, was more peaceful, it was because he had resigned himself to a more restricted area, confined to northern India.

Effects of the Turkish occupation of India

The way of life brought by the Turks was, as has been said, entirely feudal and land-owning. It was in the hands of an all-powerful military aristocracy, and it involved political splintering and a purely rural economy. Moreover, each time the Turks occupied an area, agriculture tended to decline, and the land often reverted to steppes, at any rate to pastures, these being necessary for horsemen descended from nomads.

In southern India also, the occupation by the Turks had adverse results. The age-old Dravidian zest for seafaring, which had made the people of the Deccan the foremost mariners of south-east Asia, was often discouraged, and with it, the influence of Hindu civilisation. The mastery of the sea was now going to pass to the Majapahit kingdom in Java, and then to that of Malacca, both soon to be Islamised.

Mahomet assisting at a siege, guarded by the angel Gabriel. From the *Jami ut Tavarikh*, by Rashid-ad-Din, 1314-15.

Islam in Java and Malacca

The long reign of Rajasanagara marks the point at which the Javanese kingdom of Majapahit reached its maximum size and prosperity. It was then that Java took over from the Deccan the command of the seas. Then, on the death of King Vikramavardhana, a war of succession broke out in 1401, between his nephew and heir and his brother-in-law, Virabhumi, which drained the strength of the country. In the course of these troubles a certain Paramesrava, banished from Java, took refuge at Tumasik (now Singapore). From there he was driven out by the King of Siam, and he then founded Malacca (1402). He won the support of China against Siam, receiving from the Ming emperor the title of King of Malacca. In little time he had established his kingdom as a rich commercial centre, which before long had taken Java's place as the chief maritime power of south-east Asia. Above all, Malacca became an active centre for the spread of Moslem teaching, for its founder had been converted.

This was the story on all sides, from the end of the fourteenth century, with the spread of Islam in the wake of the Arabs, who captured the spice trade in the Indian

Ocean. By 1413 the religion of the Prophet had gained a firm foothold in northern Sumatra, where it had been gradually spreading since the end of the thirteenth century. Malik Ibrahim, the preacher who died in 1419, had helped to introduce Islam into Java, where, by the end of the century, it had gone far to supplant Hinduism. This religion had a refuge in the island of Bali, however, where it remains to this day, playing in the East Indies, according to Coedès, 'a similar role, in preserving Hinduism, to that played by Tibet in preserving Indian Buddhism'.

The People of the Pacific

Meanwhile in the vast spaces of the Pacific a Neolithic culture had long been spreading eastwards of the Moluccas and the Philippines. In New Guinea, the Solomon Islands, and Fiji and its dependencies, a people of Papuan and Negroid racial affinities had spread over a large area. Beyond, in the even wider area of Polynesia, peoples of superior physique and culture, probably with a Caucasian strain, had colonised Hawaii and, even in the twelfth century, New Zealand. By the later Middle Ages they had reached Easter Island, and may have had contact with the South American coast. Originating in Indonesia, they were superb navigators, covering in their canoes distances never before attempted by man. It was not until the European explorers of the sixteenth century circumnavigated the globe that comparable maritime enterprise took place.

The Mamelukes of Egypt

In 1260, the Mongol Kitabuka, Hulagu's general, had learnt to his cost the strength of the Mamelukes. The sultan Kotuz had beaten him by Lake Tiberias. The Mamelukes were but newly established, after the *coup d'état* which had unseated the Ayyubid dynasty. The latter had been weakened by the crusade of St Louis, and the captain of the Turkish guard, Aibak, assumed the reins of power without first eliminating his master. It was his successor, Kotuz, who, wanting to regain control of Syria, came into conflict with the Mongols, whom he was the first to repulse. With that a long struggle began, during which the Mongols and the Mamelukes wrenched Syria from each other's hands; finally the Mamelukes emerged the victors. When Tamerlane came along, they felt strong enough to offer asylum to the dethroned Sultan of Baghdad and provide him with the means of reconquering Syria and then Mesopotamia. Later, when Tamerlane's empire was disintegrating, they acquired a solid foothold on the shores of the Red Sea, their power reaching as far as Aden, which they used as a commercial link with the trade of the Indian Ocean. But it was the Ottomans who were the final instrument of Islamic expansion in the West, and at one time it looked as though they might overrun the whole of Europe.

The Ottoman Turks

The rise of the Ottomans was one of the effects of the Mongol invasions. After it had swept over them, the Seljuks of Asia Minor were unable to recover. Even the sultanate of Rum, the most prosperous in the twelfth century, remained prostrate. Among the many ruined emirates of Moslem Anatolia, a Turkoman tribe that had left Khorassan during the Mongol conquest entered the service of the Sultan of Rum. This was in the first quarter of the thirteenth century, and during the remainder of that century it was stationed to the north-west of Phrygia, near the old Dorylaeum.

It was under Osman, son of Ertughril, that the conquests started. During his reign, from 1299 to 1326, he gradually appropriated neighbouring Byzantine territory. In 1299 he took several places between Brusa and Nicaea; in 1301 he beat the Byzantines at Nicomedia (Izmid); from 1308 onwards he took, one after the other, the fortresses protecting the frontier of the Nicaean empire; his decisive success was the occupation of Brusa in 1326.

His son, Orkhan (1326-59), proved even keener for conquest, and simultaneously fought the Byzantines and the Seljuks. The first he beat in 1329 at Maltepe, and in the same year he took Nicaea; Nicomedia he took in 1337, leaving only Scutari. From the Seljuks he took Pergamus and the whole of Mysia. Assisted by his brother, Al-ad-Din, he reorganised the army. So far it had consisted of feudal horsemen, called on when needed, and

A tomb mosque in Cairo, one of the Tombs of the Mamelukes built in the fifteenth century.

Caravans of camels and horses had made their way to Cathay since the time of Marco Polo. These tentative trade links established by the West with China and the East were severed by the exploits of Tamerlane. *Larousse*

a militia of foot-soldiers, who also served on a temporary basis. There was no regular army. Later, the new troops —known to us as janissaries—formed a regular professional army. They were recruited among the subject peoples, including Christian youths, all systematically taken from their families after careful selection; they were deeply attached to their sultans, and formed the body of the Ottoman army; completed by four corps of horsemen, or Spahis, they were a fine military force. But they were all the Sultan's slaves. It was in Orkhan's reign that the Turks first obtained a permanent foothold in Europe, at Gallipoli.

In the reign of his successor, Murad I (1359-89), The Turks pushed into the Balkans. In 1357 they had taken Adrianople, in 1361 they took Demotika. The vice was already closing on Constantinople. The alarm was raised in the West and a crusade launched in 1363. But it had no success. Disheartened, the Emperor decided to recognise the suzerainty of Murad, after which he occupied the lower valley of the Vardar, advanced his outposts to the Adriatic, and took Monastir in 1380. Then, attacking the Bulgars, he took Sofia in 1385. Lastly he established himself firmly in Salonica, in 1387. Murad I fell at last in 1389, murdered on the battlefield of Kossovo apparently by a renegade Serb. Here the Serbs made a last hopeless stand against the Ottomans.

Murad's death did not weaken the impetus. His son, Bayazid I, called *Yilderim* or 'Thunderbolt', subdued various Serbian and Bulgarian princes, then turned towards Greece, where he took Thessaly in 1391. The whole of the Balkans was now subject to the sultan. It seemed that Constantinople was doomed, for yet another crusade had come to a tragic end in 1396 at Nicopolis. The miracle happened all the same, with the sudden advance of Tamerlane's horsemen, who in 1402 captured Bayazid

on the battlefield of Ancyra. The defeat shook the young Ottoman Empire severely, for it was not yet secure. For ten years it was to be further shaken by dynastic quarrels, cleverly exploited by Manuel II Palaeologus. By setting Bayazid's sons at each other's throats, he was able to recover Salonica and some of the coast of the Sea of Marmara, thus relieving Constantinople of a little pressure. And on their side, the Serbs too were able to recover some of their lost territory.

After the death of Mahomet I in 1421, his policy of rapprochement with Greece was reversed. The new sultan, Murad II (1421-51) set about systematic conquest of the Balkans. He came up against a strong opponent in Janos Hunyadi, voivode of Transylvania, who inflicted on him many defeats, the most serious of which were at Nis and Krusevac in November and December 1443. Murad was so discouraged that he abdicated, after arranging a ten-year truce with the crusaders. The truce was broken, however, by Ladislas of Hungary, and Murad, who had resumed power, crushed him at Varna in 1444. He followed up this victory by completing the conquest of the Balkans and occupying Greece. It was left to his successor, Mahomet II, to crown these years of effort by taking Constantinople in 1453. He then proceeded to subdue the principalities of Wallachia and Moldavia, the Aegean Islands, Albania and, lastly, the Crimea in 1479.

At the head of an empire which included the whole of Anatolia and the whole of the Balkans to the frontier of Hungary, the Ottoman sultan was now the greatest power of the eastern Mediterranean. Supreme chief of the Moslems, he could claim supremacy over all the princes of Islam in Africa and Asia. Successor to the Byzantine Emperors, he was, in theory at least, head of the Greeks as well as the Slavs in the Balkans and on the Danube. The presence of the Ottoman Empire astride the Bosphorus, ready to march at any moment, this time towards the middle Danube and central Europe, completely transformed the problems of the Mediterranean, and even those of the rest of Europe. Asia now had eastern Europe in her grasp.

The Moslems of the Maghrib

In the Maghrib, Islam was on the defensive. It was there that the Moslem world came in contact with what was now the most vital part of Christendom, the countries of the Iberian Peninsula. On the whole, though confusion followed the disintegration of the empire of the Almohades, the Moslems put up hard resistance to Spanish and Portuguese offensives, and their positions were still more or less intact when, in the following century, the Turks forced the Maghrib to accept the authority of the Sultan of Constantinople.

The Marinid dynasty of Fez was at its zenith under Abu'l Hasan (1331-51), who succeeded in reconstituting the Maghrib empire from the Atlantic to Gabes. He was even strong enough to pursue an aggressive policy abroad, and he dreamed of a reconquest of Spain. But a crushing defeat at Salado put an end to his hopes. After his reign, anarchy followed. On the death of Abu'l Abbas in 1393, confusion was such that Henry III of Castile was able to land troops in Africa for the first time. In 1399 he besieged and took Tetuan, but a nation-wide counter-offensive soon drove him out. A little later, in 1415, the royal princes of Portugal, Henry and Ferdinand, landed at Ceuta and took it.

Salvation came with the Beni-Wattas, a younger branch of the Marinids, who at Abu Said Othman's death in 1428 imposed themselves as 'mayors of the palace'. For thirty years, from 1428 to 1458, it was they who governed, though in the name of the weak Marinid ruler. They met the Christian peril with vigorous action, and fostered national and religious revival. The first of them, Abu Zakariya, forced a Portuguese army to capitulate when it tried to take Tangiers in 1437, and he forced the Portuguese to give up Ceuta. At the same time religious fervour was rising and taking the form of Sufi mysticism, a reaction against worldly Islamism with strong appeal to the masses. It was also in 1437, the year of the victory over the Portuguese, that the tomb of Mulay Idris was discovered in Fez. This gave fresh impetus to the Idris cult, which Abu Zakariya exploited to the full.

New disorders started in 1458 and again danger threatened from the Christians. Afonso V of Portugal took Tangier in 1465. In 1471 the Beni-Wattas finally supplanted the Marinids and the Wattasi dynasty began.

But in 1497 they were unable to prevent Tangier being taken a second time by the Portuguese, nor the loss of Melilla to the Spaniards in the same year.

The Negro Moslems

Under the impulse of Almoravid expansion, Islam had made great progress in Negro Africa in the eleventh and twelfth centuries. In the Sudan the three great empires were all Mohammedan. The empire of Mellé issued from the disintegration of that of Ghana. Spread on either side of the upper Senegal and the upper Niger, it was ruled by some remarkable sovereigns. Mansa Ulé (the

Red King), who reigned from 1255 to 1270, went on a pilgrimage to Mecca; Mansa Kunkur Musa (1307-32) called in the architect Es-Saheli, the creator of Sudanese architecture in cobwork and fired brick, whose form is influenced by the style of the Maghrib. He also brought jurists from Egypt and Morocco and a large number of merchants; during his reign, 'the greatest of the medieval Sudan', the Mellistine empire stretched from Senegal to the south Algerian oases and to the great bend of the Niger. His brother, Mans Suleiman (1336-59), maintained the empire, but it declined after his death, weakened by the attacks of the Songhoi. The Songhoi empire, centred on Gao on the middle Niger, was at one time a vassal of the Mellé empire, into whose shoes it stepped. This was the great period of Timbuktu, a flourishing intellectual centre from which the preaching of Islam spread southwards. This empire reached its highest point at the end of the fifteenth century, under Sunni Ali (1465-92), a brilliant, cruel, and capricious ruler.

At the same time several Hausa states had come into existence in the central Sudan, between the Niger and Lake Chad, the most important of them being the one centred on Kano. One of its rulers, Yeji (1349-85) was visited by Moslems from Mellé and converted to Islam.

Murad I, sultan of the Turks. A courageous soldier and a clever diplomat, he laid the foundations of the Ottoman Empire.

At the beginning of the fifteenth century Queen Amina was reigning. She fortified her towns strongly and extended her kingdom to Benue, from where she exacted tribute. But soon this kingdom was swept aside by another, that of Bornu on the shores of Lake Chad.

Islam thus penetrated to the heart of Africa, so far in fact that Maghrib scholars of the fifteenth century—of no small reputation themselves—did not hesitate to go to Timbuktu to follow the African scholars. It must be added, however, that only the sovereigns and upper social levels adhered to Islam, the masses remaining loyal to the beliefs of their ancestors.

A Mexican Maya divinity. From the Le Corner collection. *Joyce and Larousse*

CHAPTER TWENTY-FOUR

PRE-COLUMBIAN AMERICA

The Aztec invasions of the twelfth century set in motion the history of the great empire in which the peoples of Central America were to be absorbed. At the same time, in another centre of native civilisation, the Peruvian, the Inca empire flourished and spread.

It would be impossible to attempt to establish the precise synchronisation of these two centres or to seek a causal connection between them. Suffice to say that the two great empires conquered by the Spaniards came into being at roughly the same time.

THE AZTEC EMPIRE

About 1168 a tribe from the north settled on the central lagoon of the Mexican plateau. From there they spread out rapidly, occupying Tlaxcala and other towns, slaughtering many of the Toltecs and making slaves of the rest. Little by little, these two peoples intermarried and effected a complete fusion of the Aztecs and the Toltecs; the latter were much more advanced in civilisation, and were destined to influence their less numerous conquerors, much as the Gallo-Romans influenced the invading barbarian hordes of the fifth century. At the end of the thirteenth century, this feudal, military society was rent by clan struggles for the possession of the land, but it gradually formed itself into a confederation of tribes. It was at the end of this feudal phase that the Aztec empire was born. The Tenochas, the most efficient of the Aztec tribes, who lived on islands in the Lake of Texcoco, founded Tenochtitlan in the early fourteenth century. They extended the area of their agriculture by creating artificial islands in the lake made of vegetable fibre and mud, then built causeways between the islands. In this setting, comparable perhaps to that of the earliest settlements of Mesopotamia, they created a city which was not unlike Venice. As their military prowess advanced, they were able to subdue the tribes of the lake shore, and to extend their commerce. Their city became rich, with enormous temples and palaces, and their government was centralised. At its head was a chief, originally elected from amongst the warriors, the *tlatoani*, or councillors, who represented the different clans. In 1376 an exceptionally strong leader, Acamapichtli, imposed his son as his successor, and he can be regarded as the founder of the dynasty which lasted until the arrival of the Spaniards.

By 1409, the authority and prestige of the chief were such that, on his death, the nobles chose his brother to succeed him and continue the dynastic principle. His authority was, however, fairly local, for there were some towns round the lagoon which at the beginning of the fifteenth century did not recognise it. The third ruler of the line was killed by the inhabitants of a neighbouring town, without the people of Tenochtitlan taking vengeance. With the accession of the fourth, Itzcoatl, in 1428, the empire bgean to expand rapidly. He seems to have

An Aztec stone mask representing a flayed god, Xipetotec. Fourteenth century. Mexico. The Aztec civilisation was destroyed by Cortes in the sixteenth century. *British Museum*

been a remarkable leader in war, and he was above all a skilful diplomat. He succeeded in forming a federation of the three principal cities of the lagoon, Tenochtitlan (Mexico), Texcoco, and Tlacopan. This union, which first subdued the remaining independent towns on the lagoon, made possible the Aztec empire. Itzcoatl's son, Motenczoma I, had been designated by his father but never elected. After overcoming the Mistecas in the region of Puebla, he extended the empire to the Gulf of Mexico, and south to the Pacific. At the same time he overcame the Otomis, a mountain tribe to the north of the lagoon. His successor extended the occupation of the Pacific coast to the north-west and the south-east. But this expansion was too rapid, and many of the conquered peoples were permanently on the verge of insurrection. Some of them, later on, were only too glad to support the Spaniards. But the empire never spread to the peninsula of Yucatan, where the Mayas and the Itzas maintained their independence.

The Aztec regime can hardly, in fact, be called an empire in the European or Asian sense, since it was

A mosaic pectoral ornament in the form of a two-headed serpent, perhaps Mixtec, of the fourteenth or fifteenth centuries.

based mainly on the desire to obtain captives for sacrifice. The Aztecs were obsessed with the conviction that the whole cosmic process would come to an end if human sacrifices were not provided. Their elaborate military Orders, the Jaguars and Eagles, were therefore constantly directed to war, in order to obtain the necessary captives, and even in the intervals of peace they would get their prisoners through ritual games. The victims regarded—or were supposed to regard—their short sufferings as a privilege, since they would immediately attain heaven. The Aztec priests sacrificed at the top of great flights of steps, from which their victims were then cast down.

Yet against this background of ritual horror, the people maintained an elaborate and prosperous civilisation which produced notable sculpture and textiles. They had a pictographic script ,and devised elaborate ritual dances; their pottery was outstanding, and although they were ignorant of the potter's wheel, they achieved an extraordinary variety of shapes and colours, decorated with floral and animal designs. They smoked tobacco—a habit then unknown anywhere else—used rubber, and made *pulque* —a drink—from the agave; they had tomatoes, beans and various gourds and squashes unknown to Europe.

When the Spaniards reached Mexico, the famous Montezuma, Motenczoma II, had been reigning since 1503.

He was a fine soldier, luxury-loving and artistic, though at times given to asceticism. He proved to be an astute diplomat in his dealings with the European conquerors. On the eve of the empire's collapse, Montezuma was overcoming the last pockets of resistance in the centre of the plateau, those of the Zapotecs and the Tarascos. The seventh ruler had been assassinated by the nobles in an attempt to curb royal domination, but that had been the last flicker of resistance. Since then the monarchy had been supreme, the power of the last two kings never being questioned. Montezuma had transformed the nobles into performers at the splendid ceremonies centred round the monarch. There were levees attended by 500 nobles, barefoot and in wretched clothes, solemn dinners at which the King ate alone under a canopy of feathers, the councillors remaining at a respectful distance, while dozens of nobles did the waiting. A punctilious etiquette surrounded every detail of the sovereign's life. Thus the Aztec empire, carved out by the sword in four or five generations, was a curious mixture of advanced civil and military organisation and customs that were still primitive. At the beginning of the sixteenth century it was about to enter a more stable phase in which its civilisation would have been able to flourish more completely; but the Spanish conquest diverted the main lines of its evolution.

THE INCA EMPIRE

The rise of the Incas is strikingly similar to that of the Aztecs. Their tribe went through the same phases as the Aztecs, but two centuries earlier. At the end of this period, with the rise of the fifth *capac*, Yupanqui, in 1197, the Quechuas began to expand, moving out of their native valley, the Urubamba, an affluent of the Amazon lying to the north of Lake Titicaca. Yupanqui overpowered all the Aymara tribes round the lake and then extended his empire to the coast, which he reached for the first time in the neighbourhood of the Arequipa. For a moment his impetus was arrested by a surge of barbaric tribes coming from the south-east. These were semi-nomad people consisting of the Diaguites joined with another tribe, the Antiguaylas, both coming from the prairies of the valley of the Salado, a tributary of the Parana. But, as soon as Yupanqui had dealt with these people, the onward march was resumed, the regime being made all the stronger by revising the dynastic principle so as to reduce·

A Peruvian Inca vase in the form of a seated and bound prisoner. As the Aztecs fell to Cortes, so the Incas fell to his compatriot Pizarro in the sixteenth century. *Giraudon*

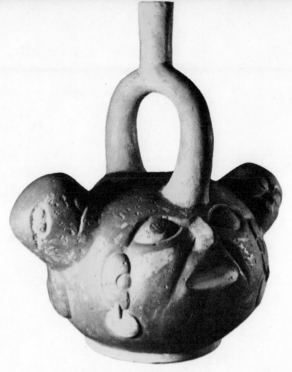

An Inca stirrup-vase in the shape of a human head. *Giraudon*

the power of the nobles. Henceforth the election of the *capac* was to be a mere formality performed by his brothers. In the middle of the thirteenth century, the conquest advanced resolutely southwards, following the line of the Andes. The seventh *capac*, Yaccar Huaccac (1289-1340), tried to extend the empire northwards, attacking the Chimu, or Yuncas, in what is now Ecuador. But the great conqueror was Pachacuti (c. 1438) with whom the final phase of Inca expansion began. His son, Topa Inca Yupanqui (1471-93) further extended his conquests, so that the empire was at its height in the second half of the fifteenth century. Quito, the main city in Ecuador, was taken, and the country round Lake Titicaca subdued, while the Chimu peoples on the Peruvian coast were forced to surrender. The Inca armies were able to operate both in mountainous country at over 10,000 feet, and in the tropical forests and valleys of the coast. Topa Inca Yupanqui built the mighty fortress of Sacsahuaman, which guarded Cuzco, the Inca capital, where gigantic walls survive. The Empire now extended from Quito to what is now Santiago, though barred from expansion into the eastern tropical forests by the barrier of the Andes. As in Mexico, the conquered tribes were far from being assimilated and were constantly in revolt. Accordingly Huayna Capac, the next ruler (1493-1523), thought fit to divide the enormous empire between his two sons, so that they could keep a closer eye on their subjects. The elder, Huascar, had the south, with the old capital, Cuzco; his brother the north, with Quito. It was not long before the brothers fell out—much to the advantage of the Spaniards.

Despite these weaknesses, the foundations of the 'empire of the Sun' were firmer than those of Mexico. For one thing, the civilisation of the conquerors was further advanced on that of the conquered than was the case in the north, and, though the Incas' realms were vaster—stretching well over two thousand miles from north to south—they were more closely knit. A trained administration, complicated but effective, controlled the daily life of every subject, laying down his hours of work,

his leisure, and even his clothing. On the arrival of the Spaniards, the system of roads was without doubt the best in the world. It consisted of two great arterial roads, running north and south, one serving the plateau, the other the coastal strip, joined by a large number of cross-roads, and completed by side-roads leading to isolated points in the *cordillera* or to the virgin forests of the east. These roads were straight, broad, and well paved; streams were bridged by lianas; and, at many places in the mountains, broad steps were cut in the rock. Inns were posted along the roads to serve both travellers and the official runners who carried messages by relays. Such was the efficiency of this relay system that a message from Cuzco could reach a point 1,200 miles away in five days. Nothing is left of this prodigious network, soon torn to shreds by the invaders' heavy wagons and the horses' hoofs, for which they were not designed. Naturally they greatly helped the Spanish conquests; but till then they had been invaluable in providing the central government with an overall system of communications which greatly assisted the work of the officials. These were never of the tribe they governed. In the space of some hundred years, this Inca empire built up an advanced system of state socialism. The civilisation which it controlled was based upon the ancient cultures of the coastal peoples—in particular the Chimu—whose way of life the Inca mountaineers assimilated. The potato, which originated in the Bolivian highlands, was one of its economic contributions to the world, and the Incas had herds of llamas and alpacas. The government was sanctified by elaborate ceremonial, which centred on the sacred Inca (Sapa Inca) himself, and it was ruled by a vigorous dynasty, whose cult was the worship of the Sun. They took captives, but they made them work instead of devoting them to sacrifice, and although they were illiterate, they calculated tribute on a kind of *abacus*. They had magnificent pottery and cotton and wool textiles superbly coloured with dyes. Their civilisation was in general certainly the most politically advanced in the Americas.

403

MEDIEVAL RETROSPECT

The history of the last two centuries of the Middle Ages tells the story of the winding up of a long period. During it, all the traditional values that had formed the basis of Western civilisation were challenged: the unity of religion under the direction of Rome, the ideals of chivalry, the feudal organisation of society. They completed the transformation of the old civilisation of Asia, first at the hands of the Mongols, then at the hands of the Moslems. China, having undergone a national revolution and thrown off the Mongol yoke, entered one of its more prosperous and culturally brilliant phases, which was to be followed, after the fall of the Ming dynasty before the alien Manchus in 1644, by a phase of foreign domination but of the maximum territorial expansion. Vulnerable as this pre-industrial civilisation was to prove before European enterprise and superior technology, and stagnant as its conservative and bureaucratic culture appeared to the West, it was to remain the dominant cultural and economic power in the Far East.

In Japan the aristocratic feudal government which had long taken over power from the monarch, was to be superseded by a peasant soldier of fortune who created a unified state, and attempted to attack China, but died in 1598. His family was ousted by the Tokugawa Shoguns who were to retain power until the mid-nineteenth century. During the sixteenth century the Portuguese, the English and the Dutch opened up trade with Japan, and Jesuit missionaries made many converts, though the principal trade was in armaments from Europe. But the Tokugawa were to inaugurate a policy of isolation which shut out almost all foreign influence on Japan for over two centuries, though during that time Japanese culture was to flourish.

In India the Mogul conquest begun by Tamerlane and consolidated by Akbar was to create a new blend of civilisation which to some extent combined Hindu and Moslem in the administration; but the basic incompatibility of the two ways of life remained, and in the eastern basin of the Indian Ocean the Moslem influence also clashed with and often triumphed over the original Hindu civilisation, so that there came to be a contrast between Java and Siam.

At the other end of the Eurasian continent, the Ottoman advance had destroyed Byzantium and planted an Islamic power in the Balkans and on the lower Danube; while the North African territories bordering the Mediterranean were to resist European efforts to reconquer an area which had been an integral part of the Roman Empire. Most of Negro Africa still remained mysterious, though the Portuguese had much contact with the west ern coasts; and the Americas were still unknown.

Against this world wide prospect the later Middle Ages in Europe show a civilisation which had suffered a considerable setback in the Levant and on the Danube, and in which the old medieval institutions of Empire and Papacy have gone into decline. But the great initiatives of the sixteenth century, which were to give Europeans the mastery of the world, and revolutionise science and technology, have their roots in the fifteenth, when under medieval conditions the influence of Renaissance Italy was transforming the mentality of northern Europe and combining medieval institutions, ideas and art with a new outlook. This change was based in part on an economic revival, on new methods of banking and administration, and upon an alliance between the rising monarchies, modelled a good deal upon Italian practice in operating on a greater scale, with the new urban mercantile interests whose mentality was to shape the future.

INDEX

405

406

407